I0763123

MODERN MAJESTY

THE BRITISH ROYAL FAMILY IN A NEW ERA

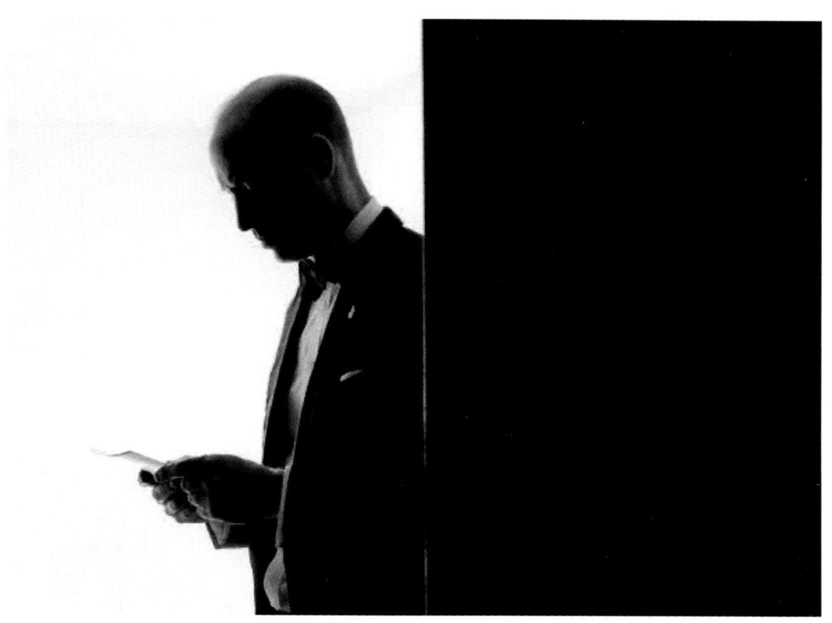

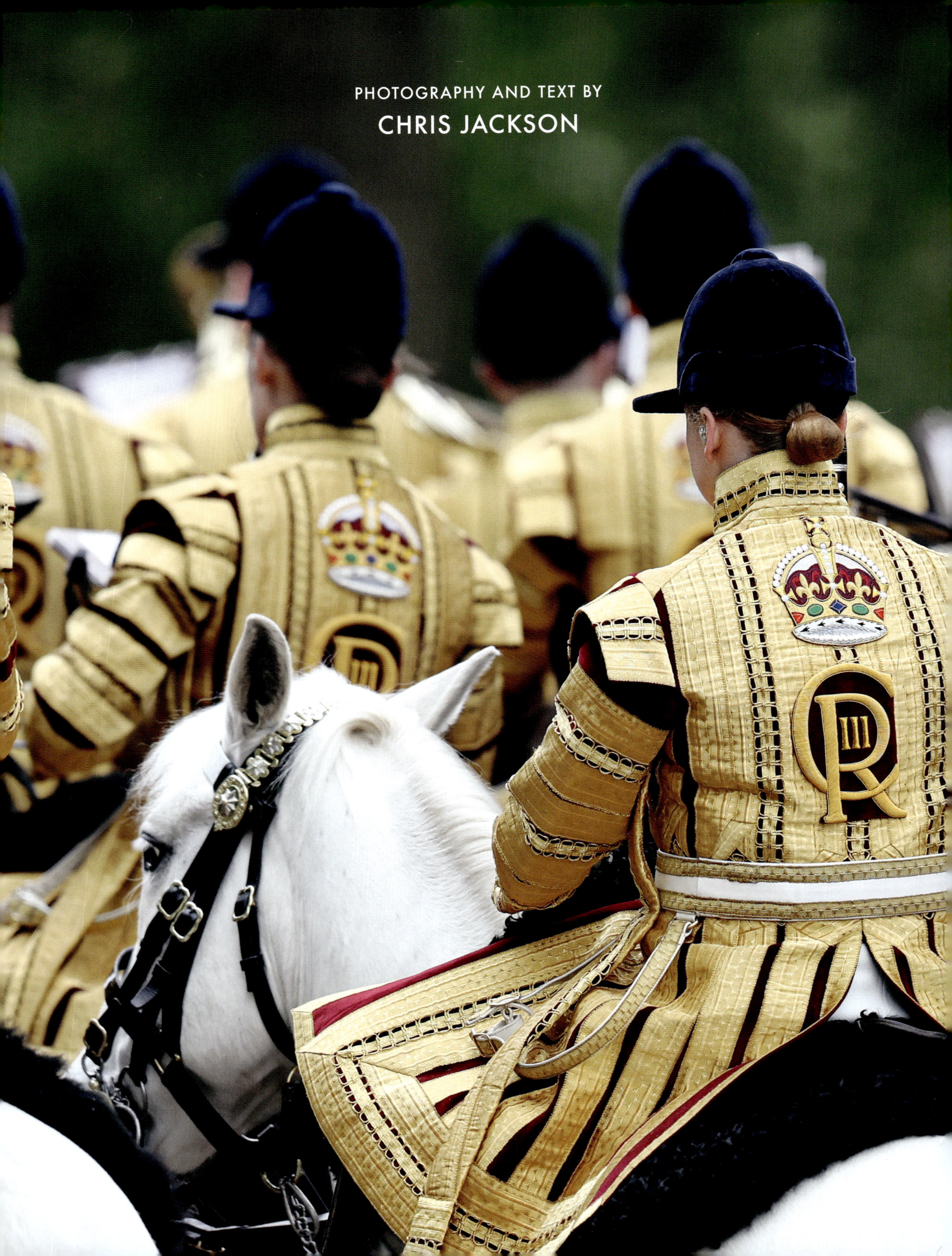

PHOTOGRAPHY AND TEXT BY

CHRIS JACKSON

MODERN MAJESTY

THE BRITISH ROYAL FAMILY IN A NEW ERA

RIZZOLI
NEW YORK
New York Paris London Milan

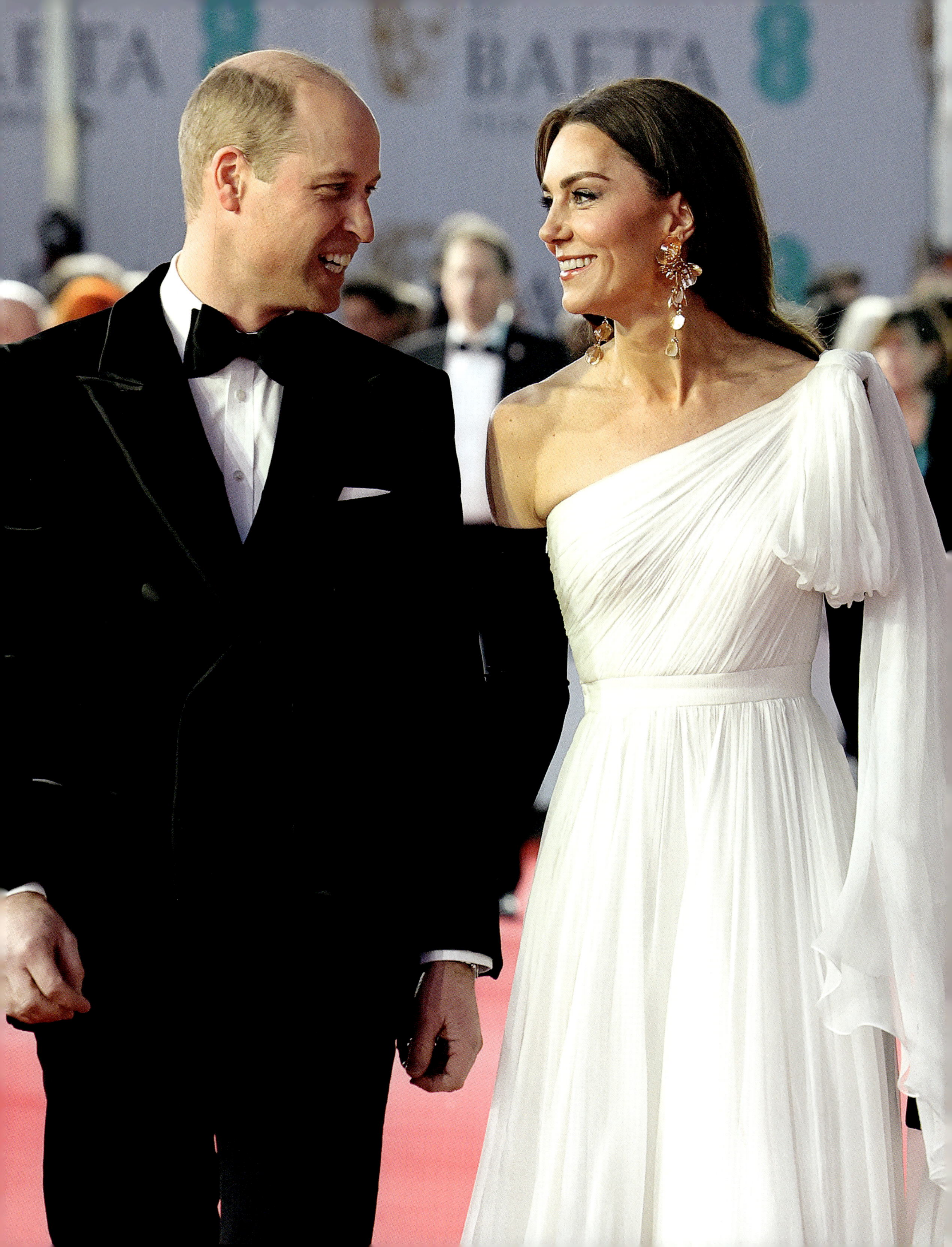
BAFTA

CONTENTS

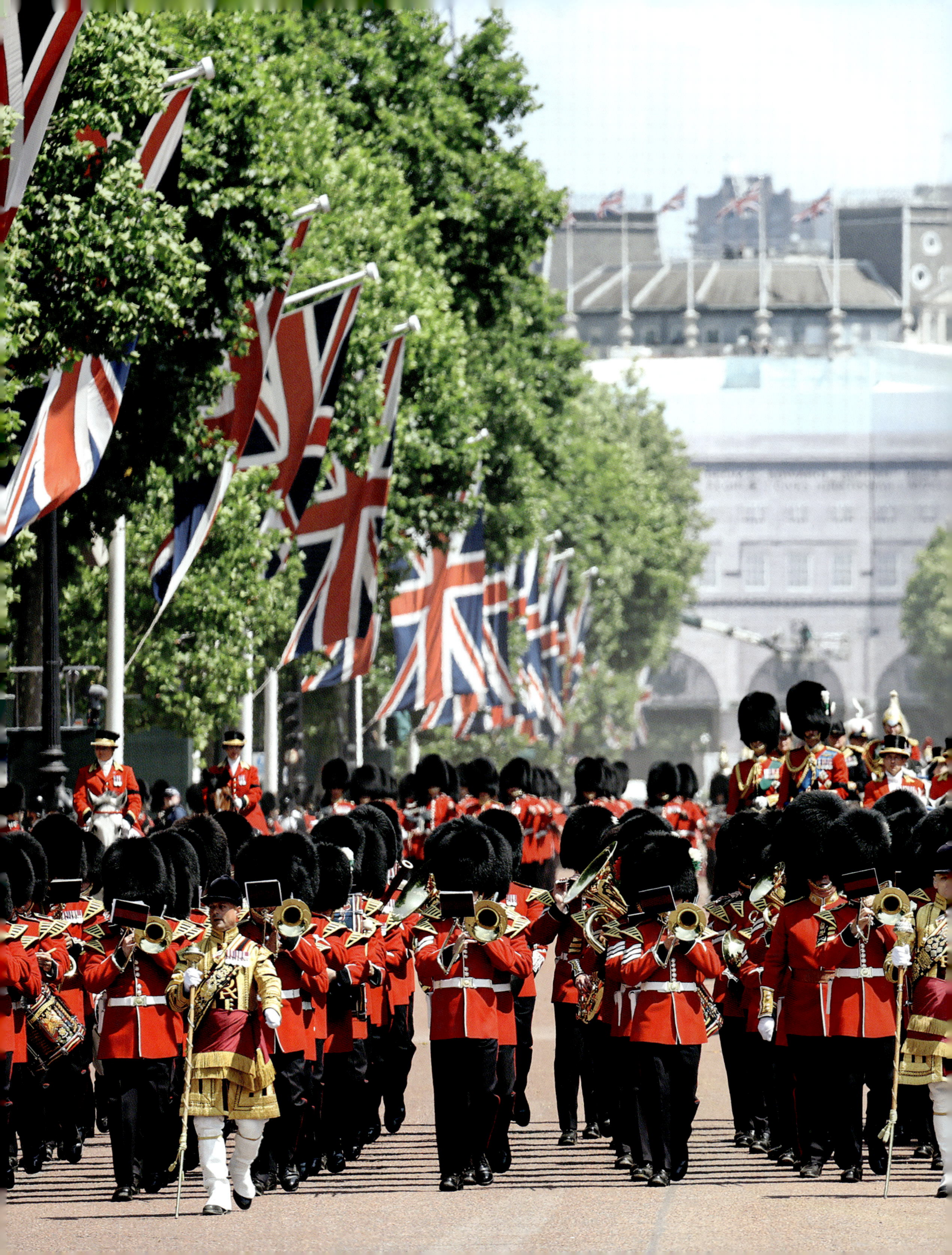

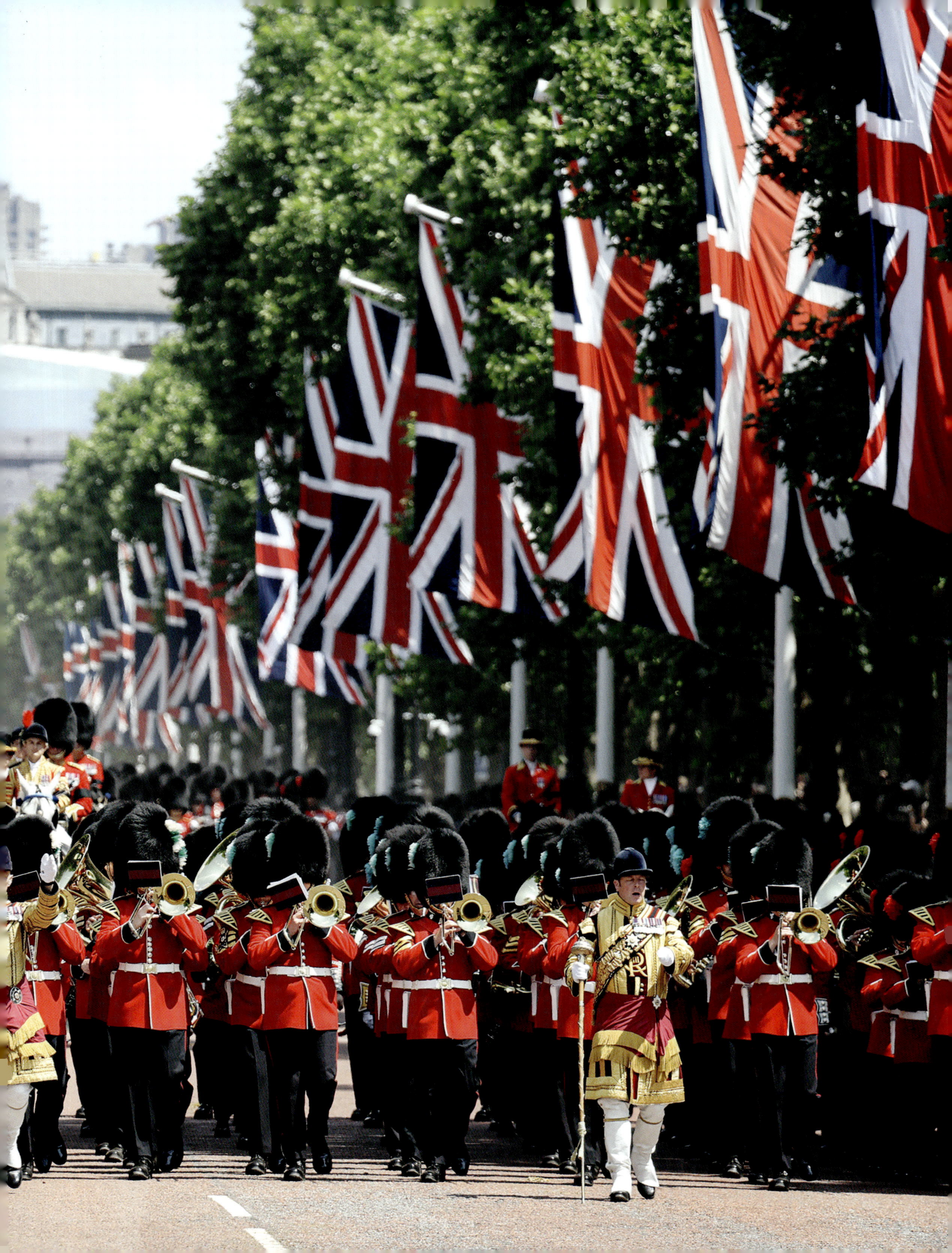

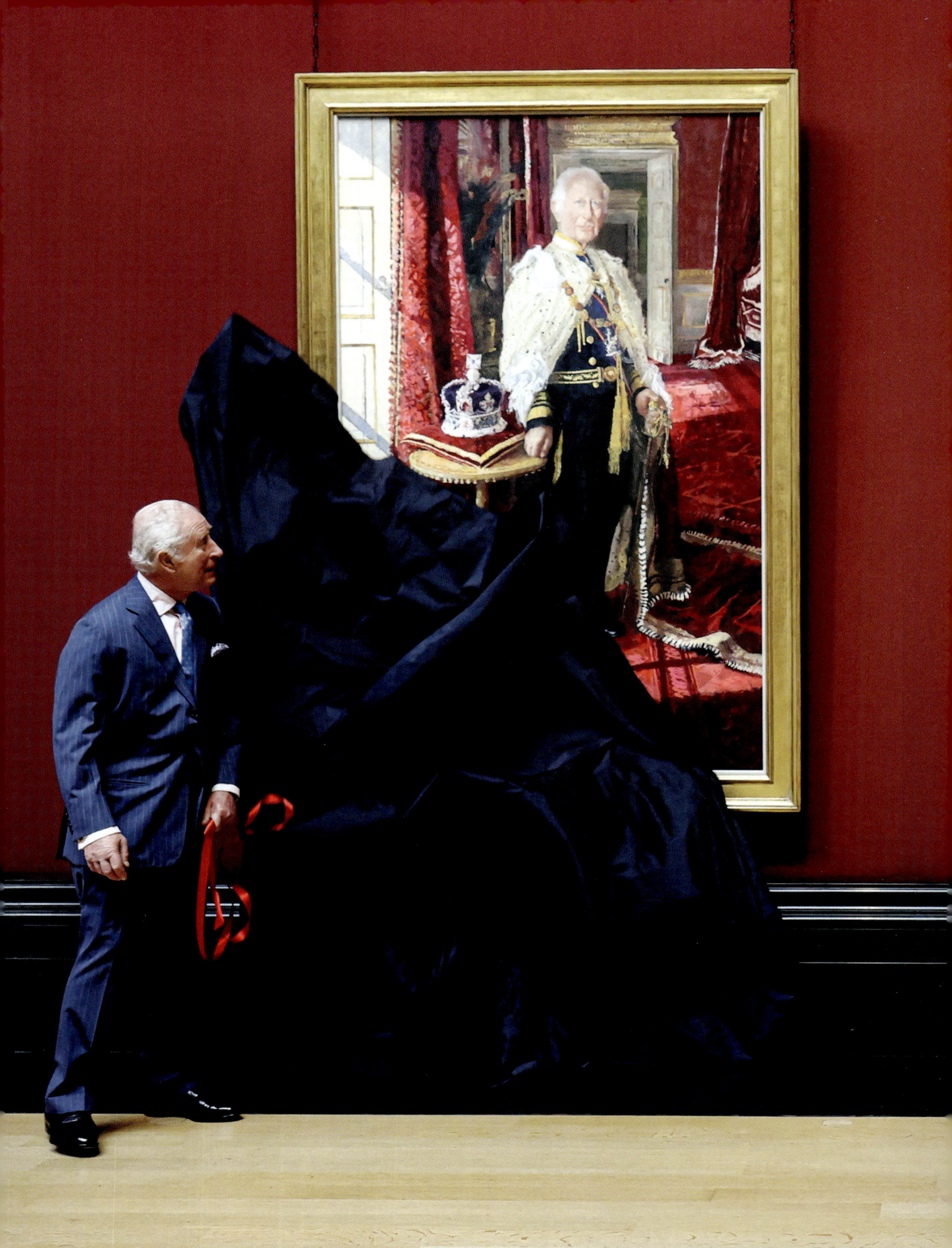

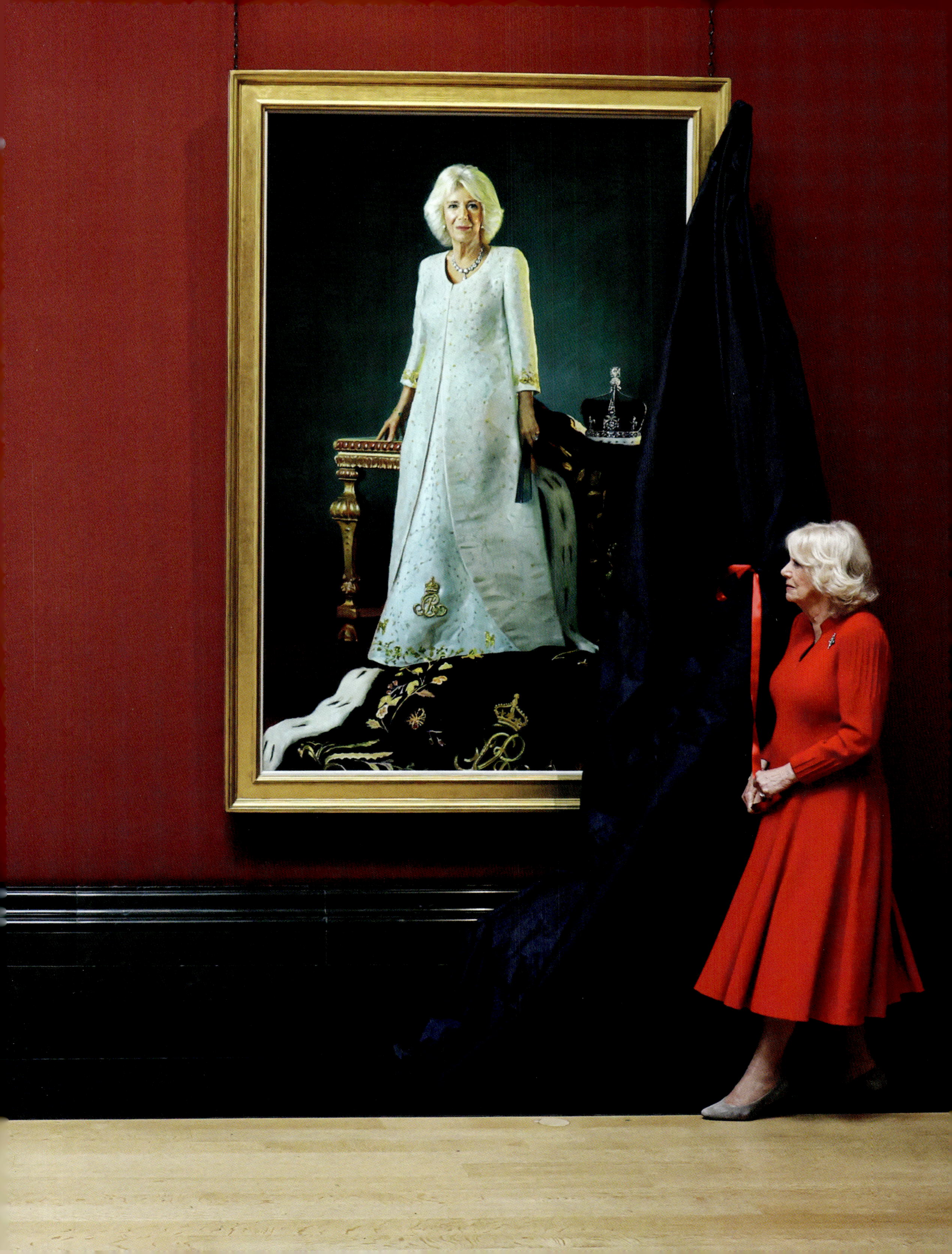

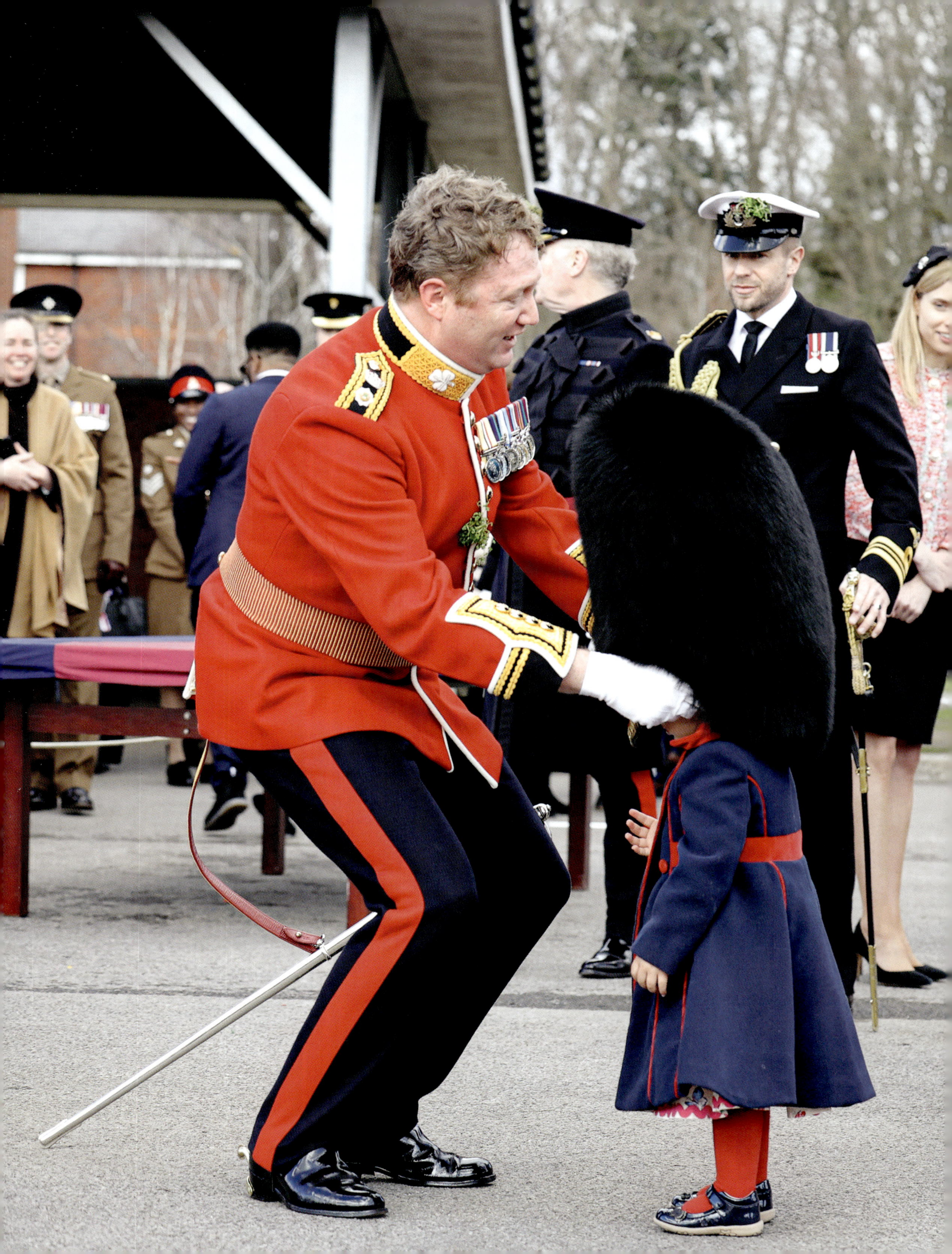

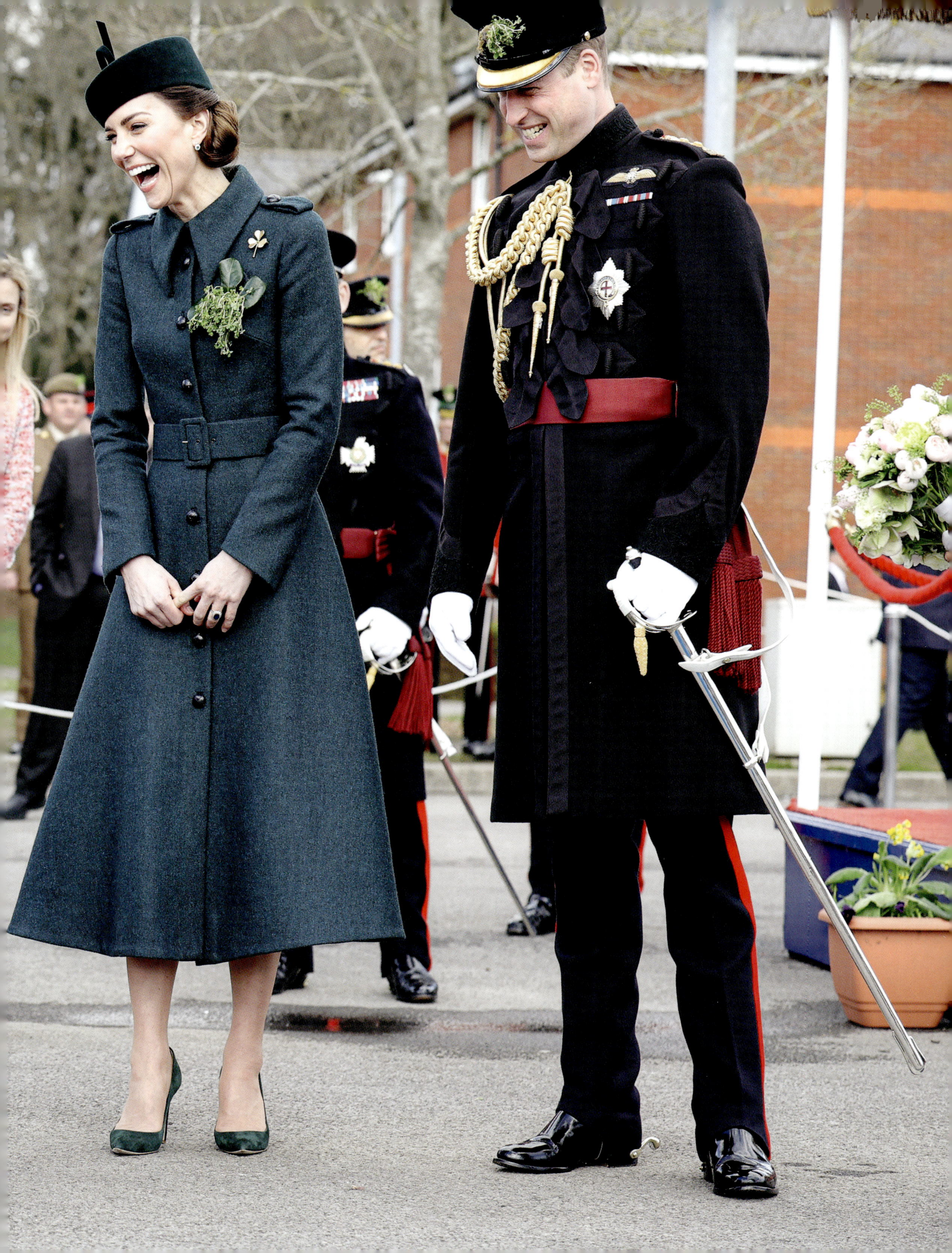

INTRODUCTION
BEHIND THE CROWN

I heard the roar of the crowd before I saw it. Crouching behind the newly crowned King Charles III and Queen Camilla, I was within touching distance of the ermine fur on their ceremonial gowns. My goal to record this moment from such a unique perspective, never seen nor allowed before, was a mildly terrifying prospect, but I had a task to focus on and steadied my nerves by concentrating on the angles I needed to realize this historic picture. As the royal couple stepped out onto the balcony, the scene of so many unforgettable moments, I knew I only had seconds to capture the shot of them waving to their adoring public. The wave, the crowds, the crowns – the composition had every ingredient of a winning photograph, but I was very aware of *my* visibility as millions watched around the world and my colleagues on the Queen Victoria Memorial trained their long 600mm lenses on the figures above the red velvet draped over the front of the balcony. The last thing they needed was me appearing in their iconic photographs that would be whizzing their way around the globe in minutes. Tilting the screen on the back of my camera, I popped up for a matter of seconds, raising my arm aloft to achieve the elevated angle I needed to get the crowns and the crowd at the correct perspective. Moments later I heard a roar graduate down the Mall as the Red Arrows flew overhead and knew another opportunity was presenting itself. A low angle was required for this shot, safely out of the view of the world's media, as I captured one of my favourite images from the day.

As a royal photographer you have a front-row seat to many historic occasions, and the Coronation was certainly one of the highlights of my career. I have travelled around the world for twenty years with both King Charles and Queen Camilla, and I felt an overwhelming sense of gratitude to be with them at this moment – it felt like I had come full circle. Little did I know of the trials that lay ahead for the couple and the wider royal family in the coming months. As I write now, we have entered a new phase of "normality" for the monarchy, with King Charles and Queen Camilla working harder than ever.

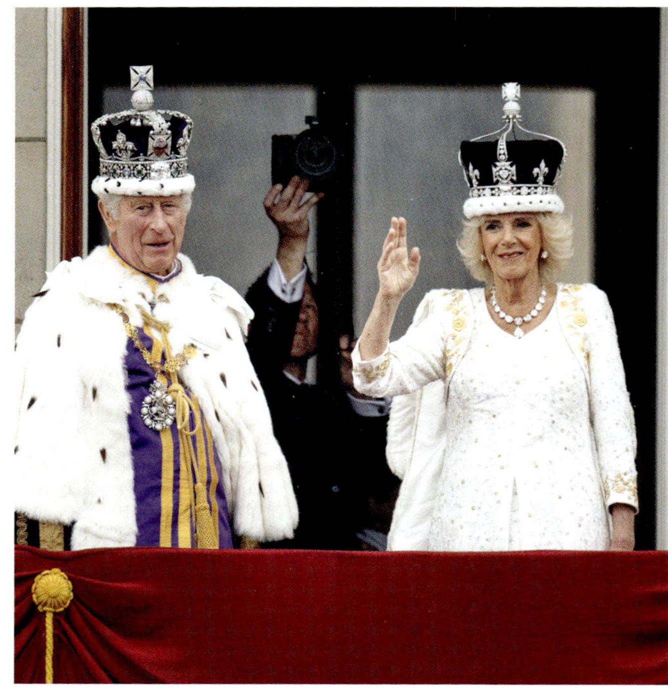

Finally in the role he has coveted his whole life, King Charles III is a man on a mission, a mission only more focused by his health issues. You only need look at his gruelling workload to appreciate his commitment to the future of the crown. He has been greatly helped and bolstered by his dedicated family, who have firmly stood by his side during these demanding times. The Princess of Wales has, of course, faced her own health struggles with admirable resilience and fortitude. Her recuperation has clearly involved an almost spiritual bond with nature and the environment, while the love and support of her children and family has formed the cornerstone of her recovery.

Challenges aside, the royal family has entered a new and exciting era, and the institution shows no sign of slowing down. Looking back at my first book, *Modern Monarchy*, it feels as if we are now in a very different time for the British royal family, with a distinct set of engagements for the

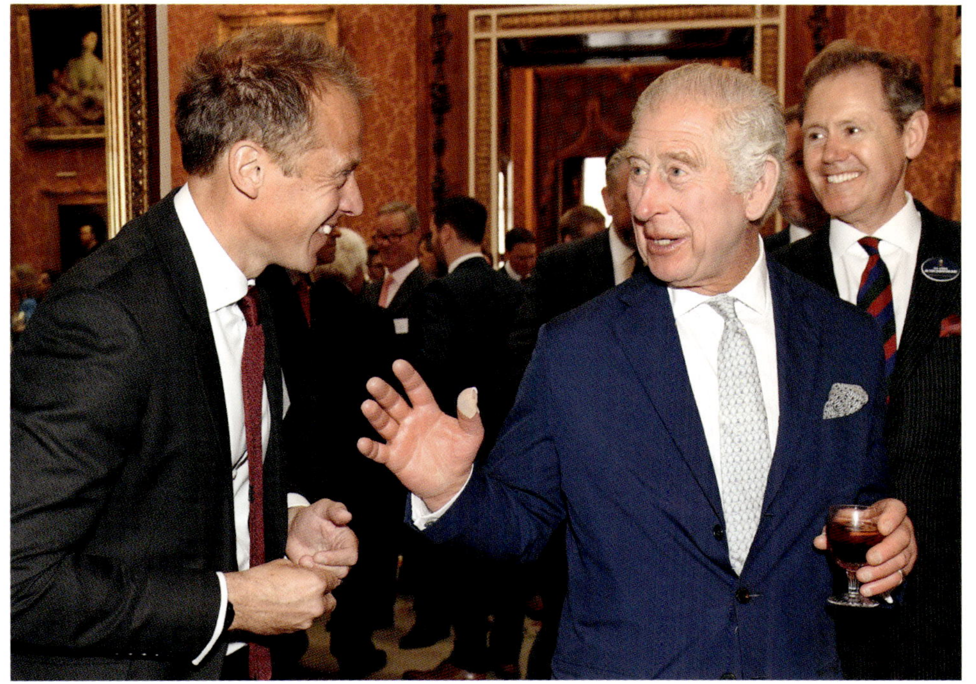

Opposite
Getty Images photographer Chris Jackson photographs King Charles III and Queen Camilla on the Buckingham Palace balcony during the Coronation celebrations, 6 May 2023.
Photo: Chris Furlong/Getty Images

Left
Chris Jackson shares a joke with King Charles at a reception at Buckingham Palace, October 2023.
Photo: Nicky J Sims/Getty Images

working members. Life for me as a royal photographer could not be busier as I bounce between various members of the family. Their multifaceted roles, not only as figureheads and advocates for various charities but also as ceremonial figures and statespeople, award them a unique position and influence that they employ around the world to uphold tradition while simultaneously moving with the times. The following pages present some of the most well-known royal photographs of our age alongside equally powerful images that capture unexpected and fleeting moments, providing an unrivalled insight into the characters and personalities that make up the royal family. The more intimate, yet very honest, photographs show a side of the royal family that is rarely seen by the public, while those capturing their majestic appearance at historic occasions delight the millions of people watching around the world who relish these glittering formal events. Above all, I hope they reveal the individuals – their sense of duty and their commitment to their people – that form this historic institution.

Page 1
Prince William reads his notes backstage at the 2023 Earthshot Prize Awards in Singapore, 7 November 2023.

Pages 2–3
Members of the Household Cavalry Mounted Regiment make their way down the Mall on the 80th anniversary of VE Day, 5 May 2025.

Page 4
William and Catherine walk down the red carpet at the EE BAFTA Film Awards 2023 at the Royal Festival Hall, 19 February 2023.

Pages 6–7
Musicians from the Massed Bands of the Household Division parade down the Mall during Trooping the Colour, 14 June 2025.

Pages 8–9
King Charles III and Queen Camilla unveil their official Coronation State Portraits, painted by Peter Kuhfeld and Paul S. Benney respectively, during a visit to the National Gallery on the second anniversary of their Coronation 6 May 2025. The portraits are now part of the Royal Collection.

Pages 10–11
The Prince and Princess of Wales laugh as Lieutenant Colonel Robert Money puts a bearskin hat on his daughter Gaia's head as they attend the 1st Battalion Irish Guards' St. Patrick's Day Parade at Mons Barracks, Aldershot, 17 March 2022.

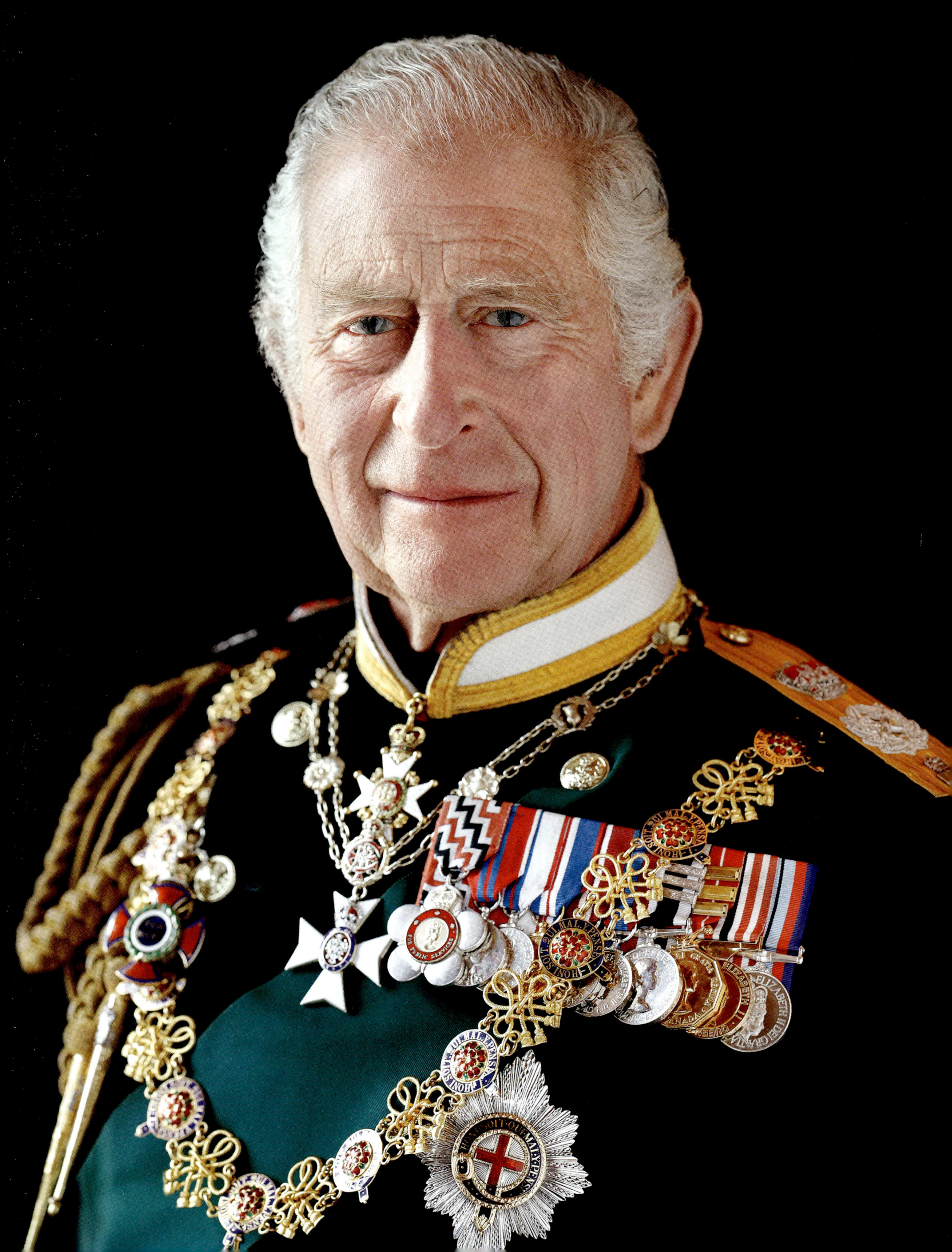

1

KING CHARLES III

PORTRAIT OF A KING

In the role he has spent his life preparing for, and as the longest-serving Prince of Wales in British history, King Charles III came to the throne at ease with his position at the head of the royal family. Then, faced with unexpected health challenges, he was frustratedly forced to take a step back to undergo treatment. Yet, in 2024, King Charles returned with renewed passion and vigour, determined to make up for lost time, so much so, in fact, that it has been a struggle to keep up with his packed diary of royal engagements!

With an unshakeable energy and clearly committed to the ceremonial role of king as well as his other offices – Head of State, Head of the Commonwealth, Head of the Armed Forces and Head of the Church of England – Charles is the epitome of a modern king. He is approachable and accessible to the people he meets across the country on a weekly basis, but also maintains a sense of mystique that served Queen Elizabeth II so well through her life.

Charles has an incredible ability to connect with people in a genuine manner in a very short space of time, partly due to his innate curiosity and interest in the lives of others. He is a man for whom passions run deep, and it is his country, his home in Highgrove, Scotland, and his family that constitute the four most important parts of his life, as reflected in the coming pages.

THE CORONATION

Having the privilege of shooting "behind the scenes" at the rehearsals and on the day of the Coronation of King Charles III and Queen Camilla on 6 May 2023 gave me an intimate viewpoint of the most historically significant event I have been lucky enough to photograph. The stories behind the jewels, crowns, carriages, fur, and the ceremony itself stretch back hundreds of years, and records of these proceedings form the fabric of British history. Rehearsals were an important part of this documentation, and I was able to capture much of the preparation. Rather unfortunately I had managed to put my back out in the weeks running up to the assignment, so spent much of my time focusing on getting from one side of the room to the other without grimacing in pain. I certainly was not moving gracefully, much to the amusement and sympathy of the Queen!

Opposite, top
The Prince of Wales shares a joke with King Charles as they attend rehearsals for the Coronation at Westminster Abbey.

Opposite, below
Queen Camilla sits in the Gold State Coach, next to the Sovereign's Orb, as she takes part in rehearsals for the Coronation in the Royal Mews at Buckingham Palace.

Pages 18–19
(top left) The intricately crafted Anointing Screen during rehearsals at Buckingham Palace. The specially created screen of fine embroidery by the Royal School of Needlework is held by poles hewn from an ancient windblown Windsor oak and mounted with eagles cast in bronze and gilded in gold leaf.

(bottom left) Queen Camilla waves to pageboys as she departs Buckingham Palace in the Diamond Jubilee State Coach for the Coronation at Westminster Abbey.

(right) At the base of the Coronation gown, designed by Bruce Oldfield, there is a tribute to Queen Camilla's rescue dogs: representations of the Jack Russell terriers, Bluebell and Beth, were embroidered in gold-hued thread by the Royal School of Needlework, of which Queen Camilla has been a patron since 2017.

Pages 20–21
The "Robe of Estate," made in purple velvet by Ede & Ravenscroft, was hand embroidered by the Royal School of Needlework using goldwork, a technique that dates back more than a thousand years. The design was themed around nature and the environment, including the floral emblems of the United Kingdom and featuring such insects as bees, butterflies, a beetle, and a caterpillar.

Pages 22–23
From the balcony of Buckingham Palace, the newly crowned King and Queen wave to members of the public gathered around the Queen Victoria Memorial and down the Mall.

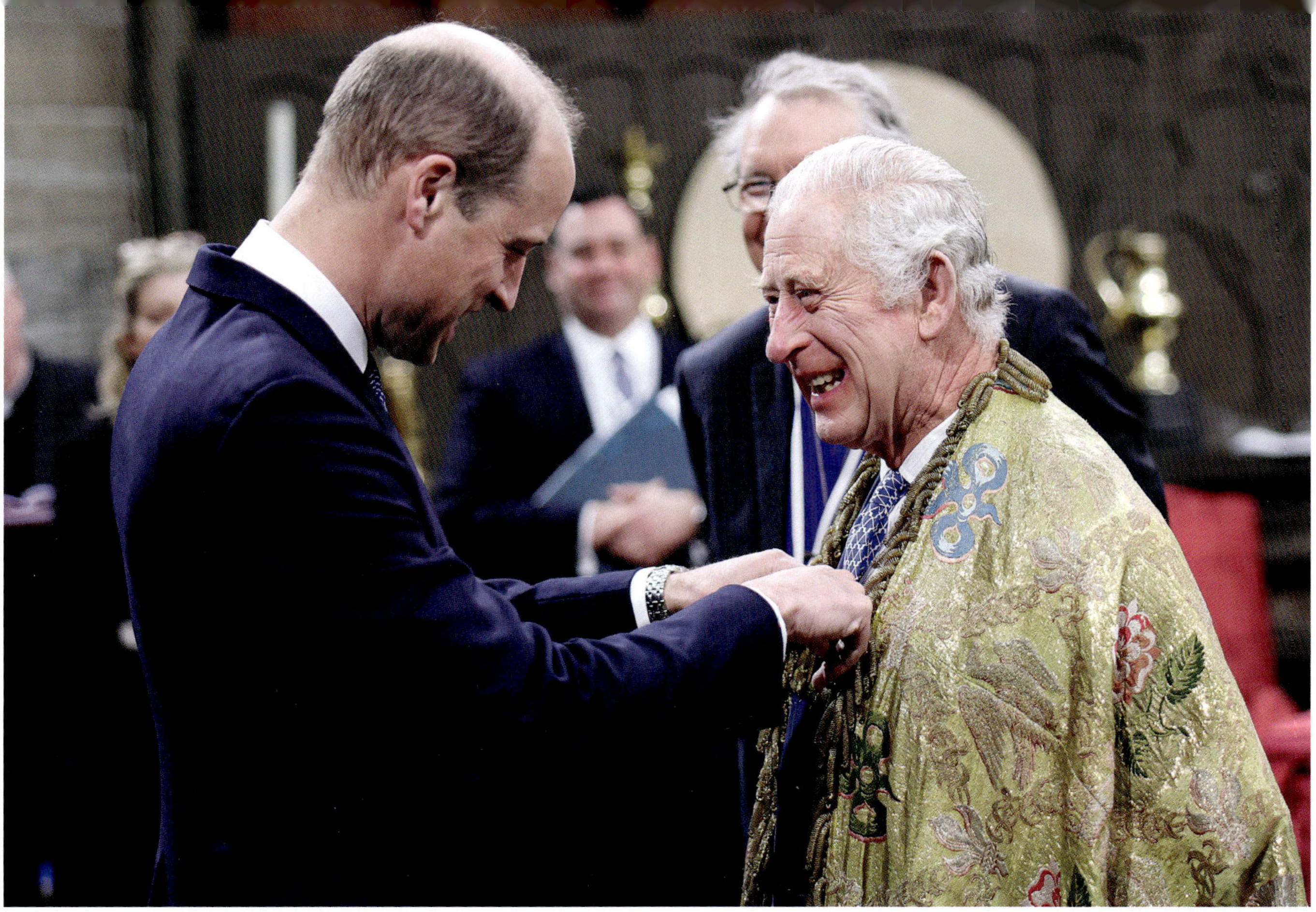

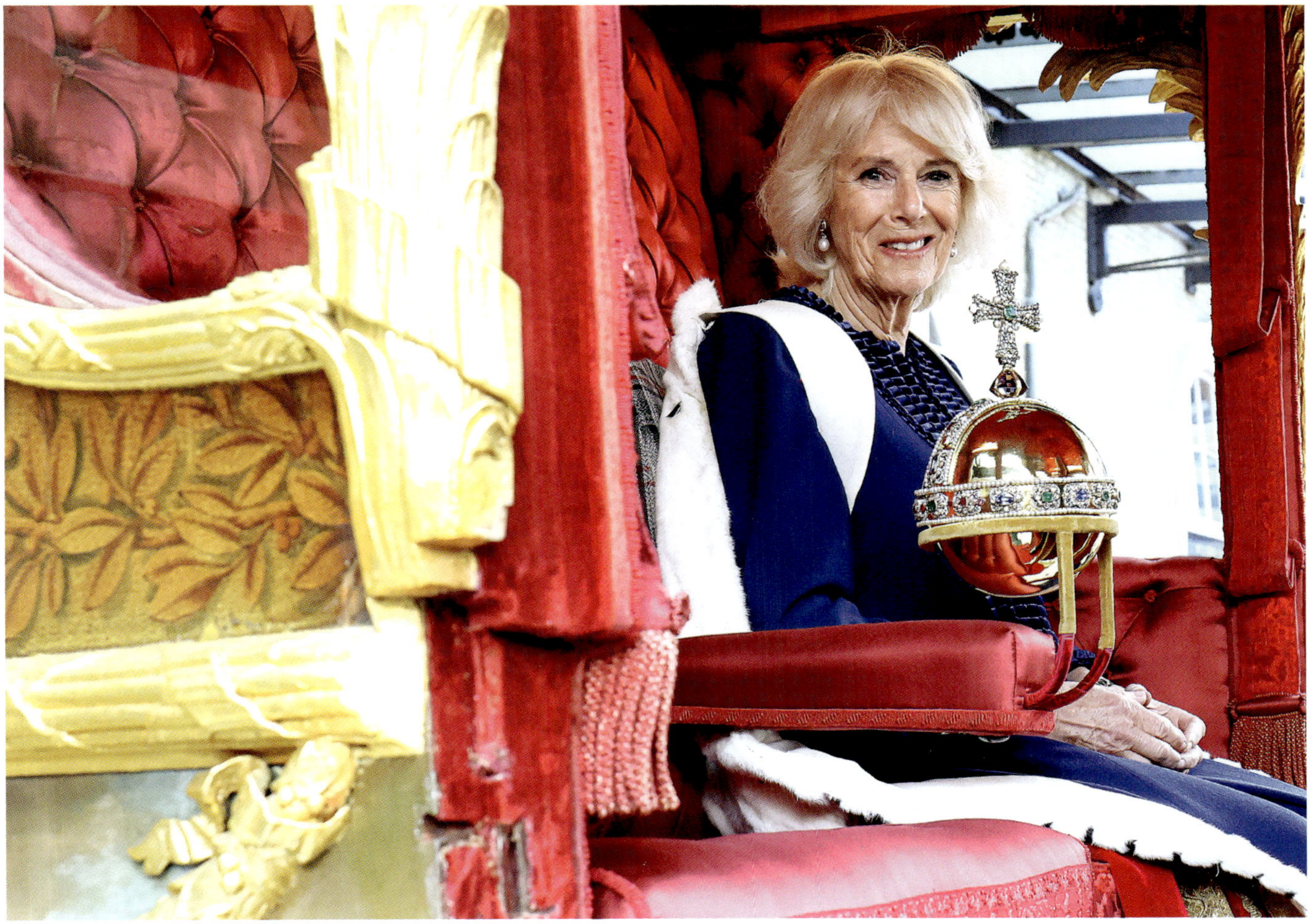

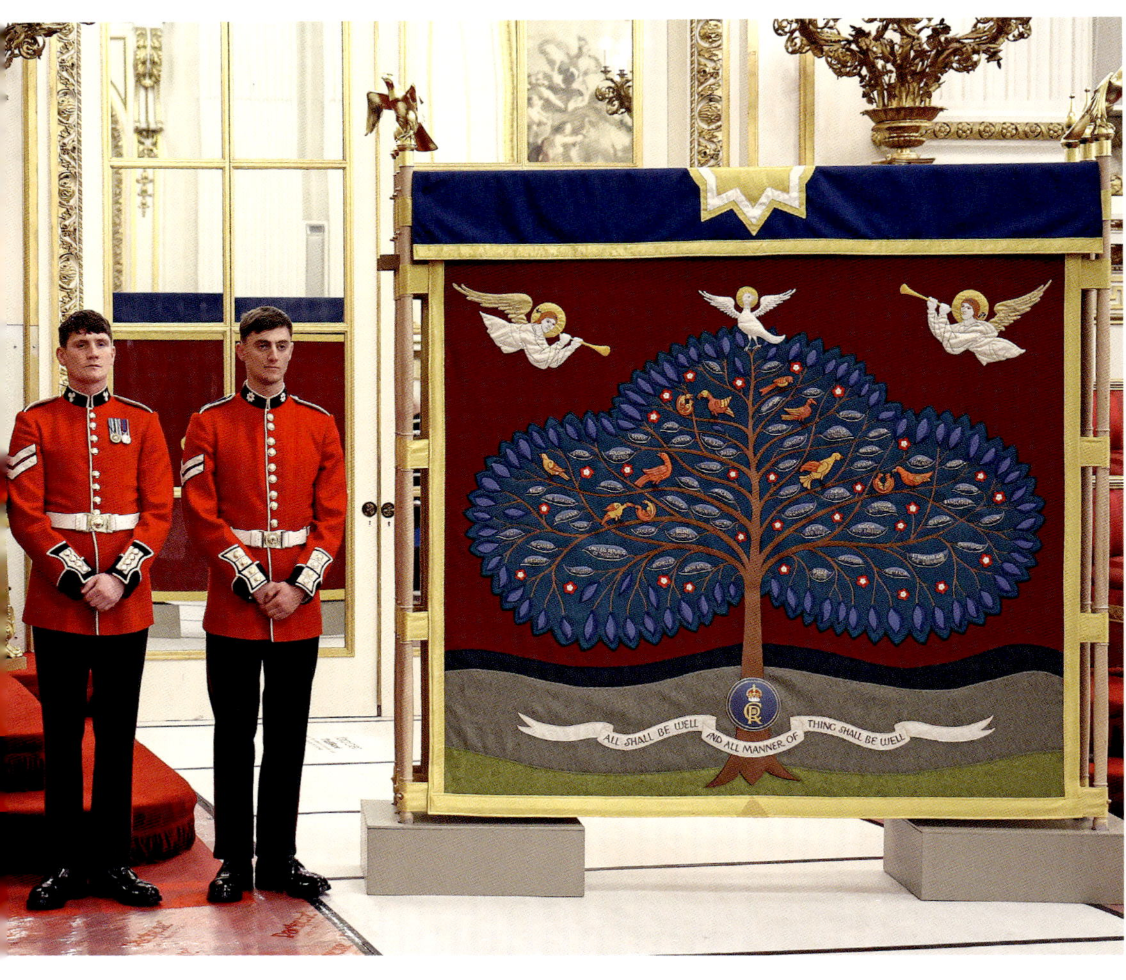
ALL SHALL BE WELL AND ALL MANNER OF THING SHALL BE WELL

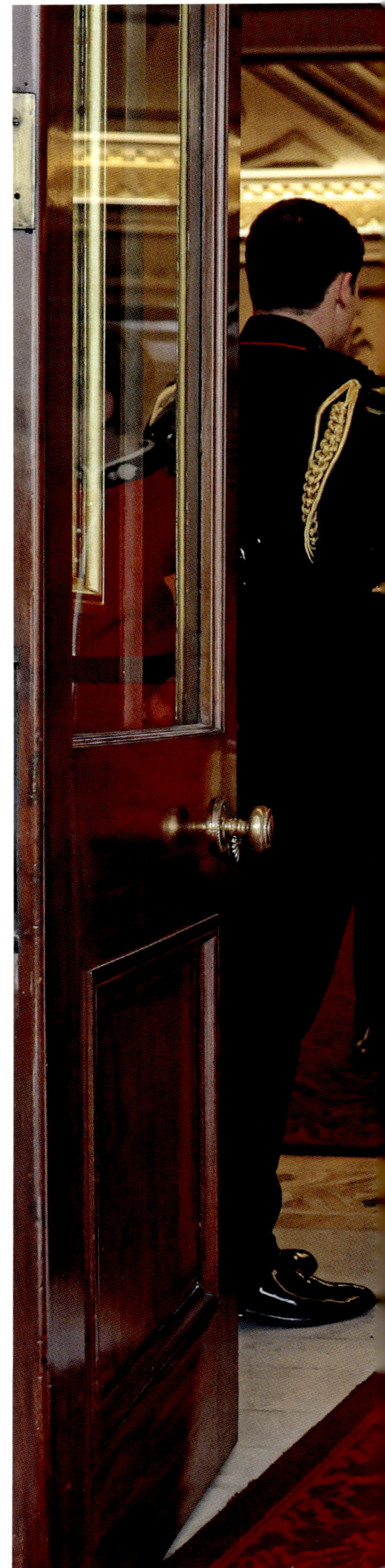

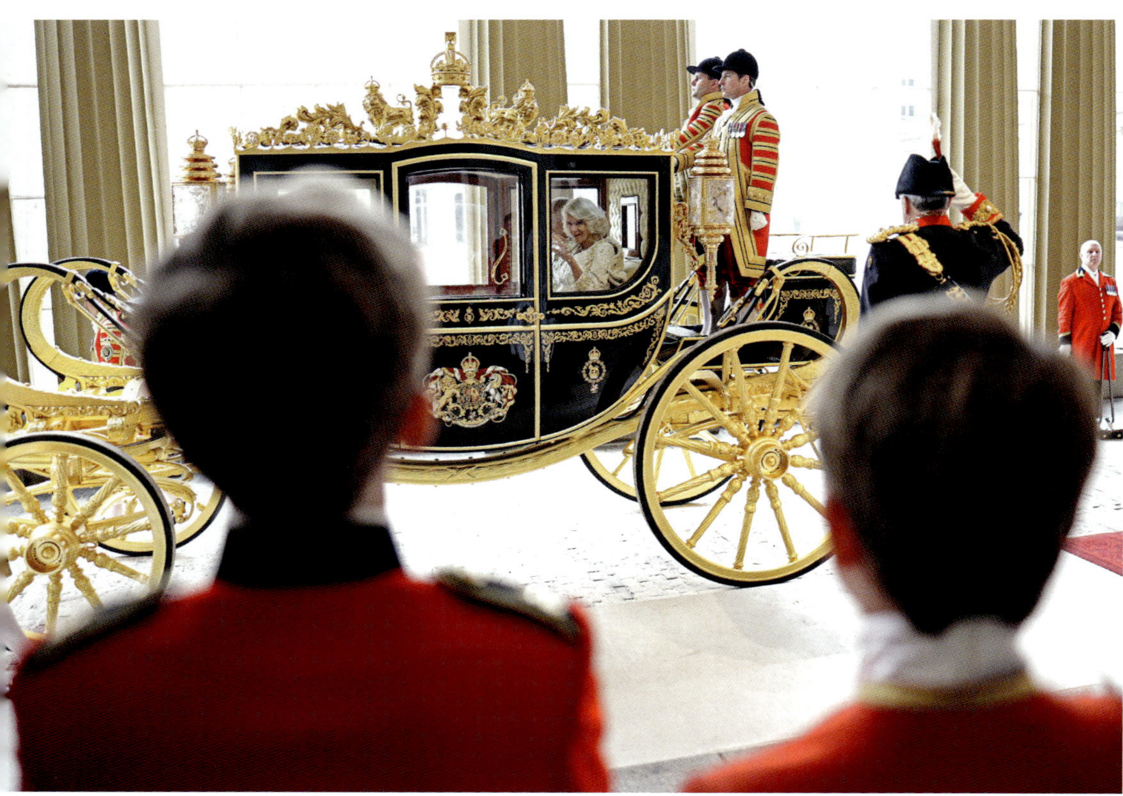

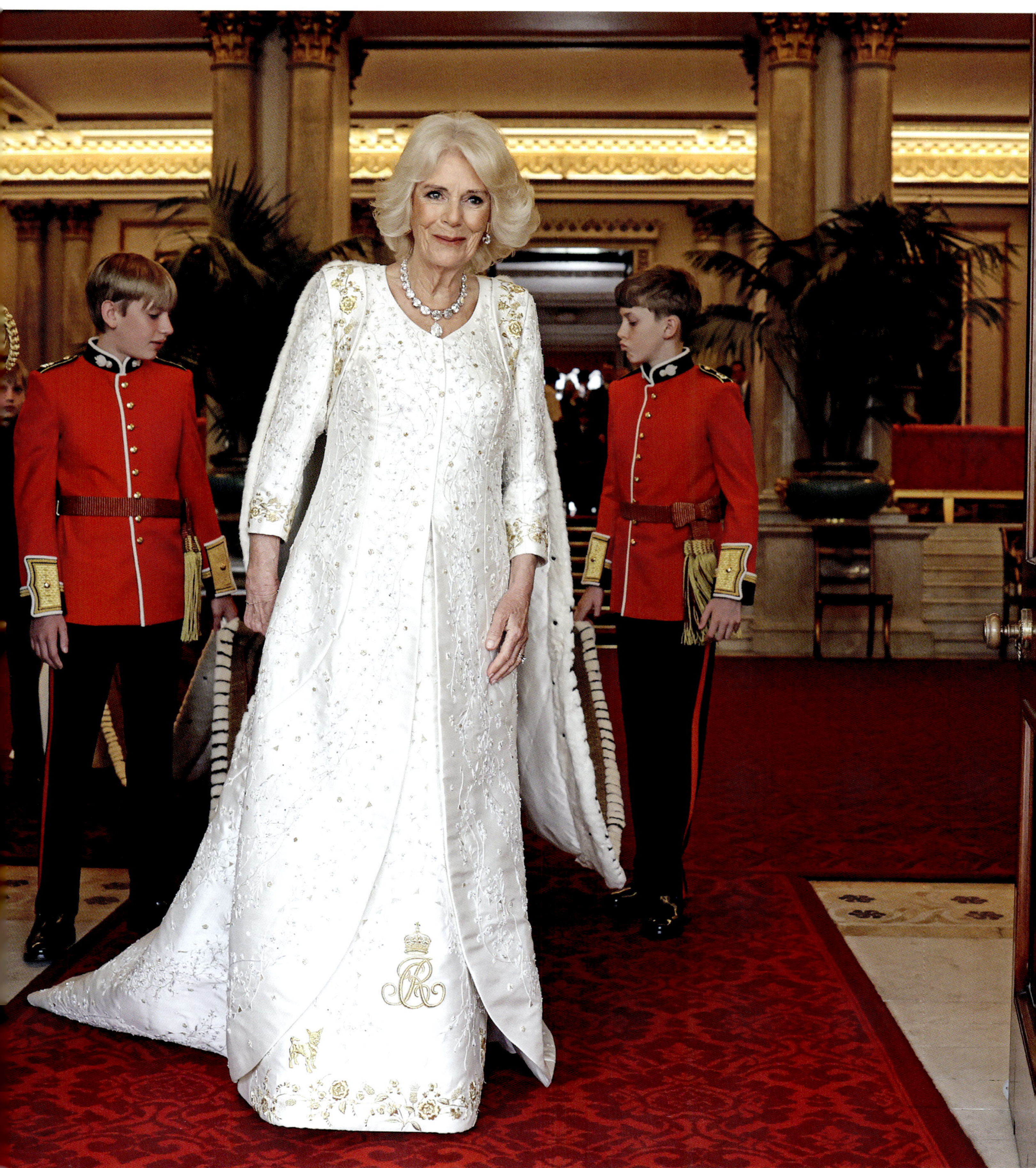

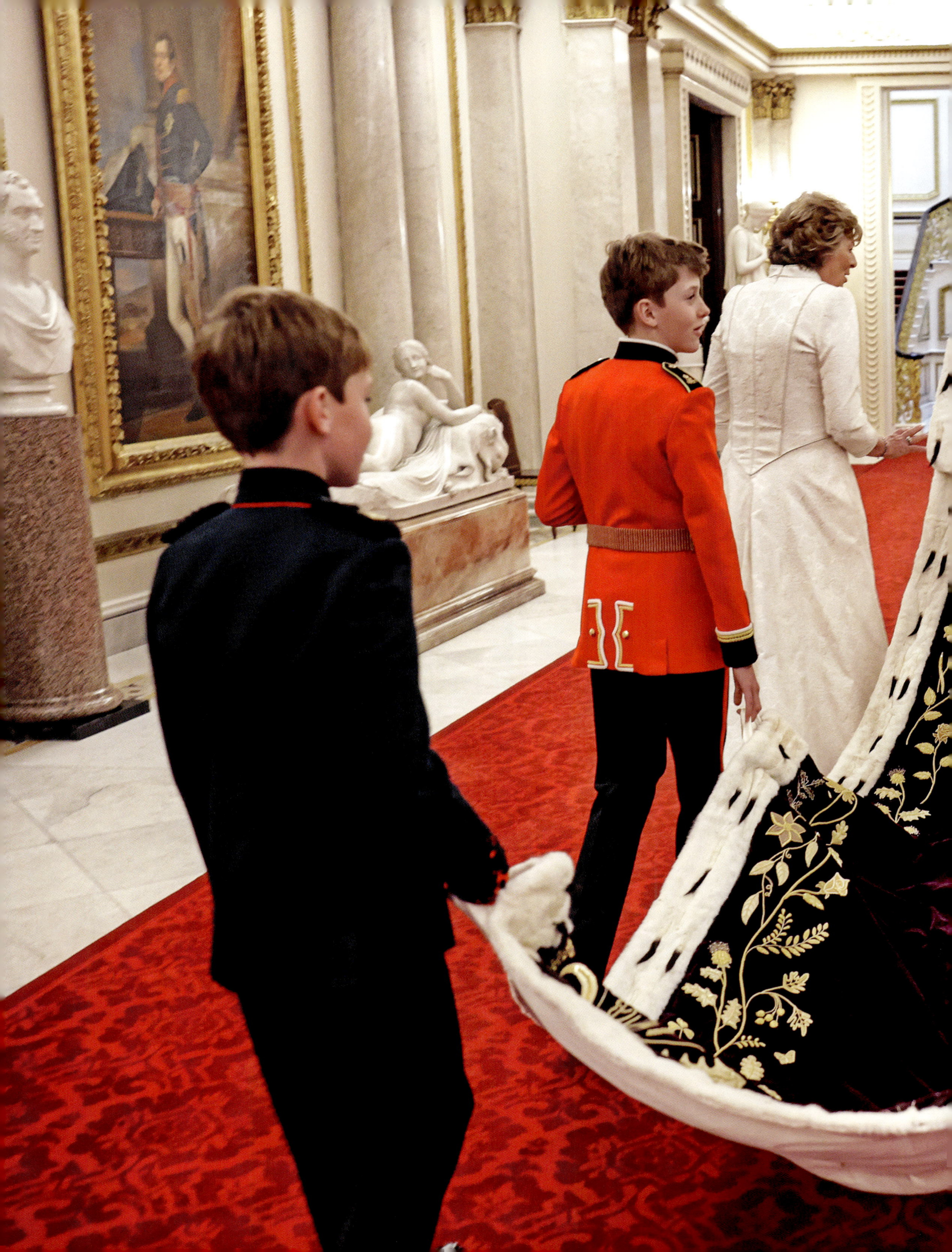

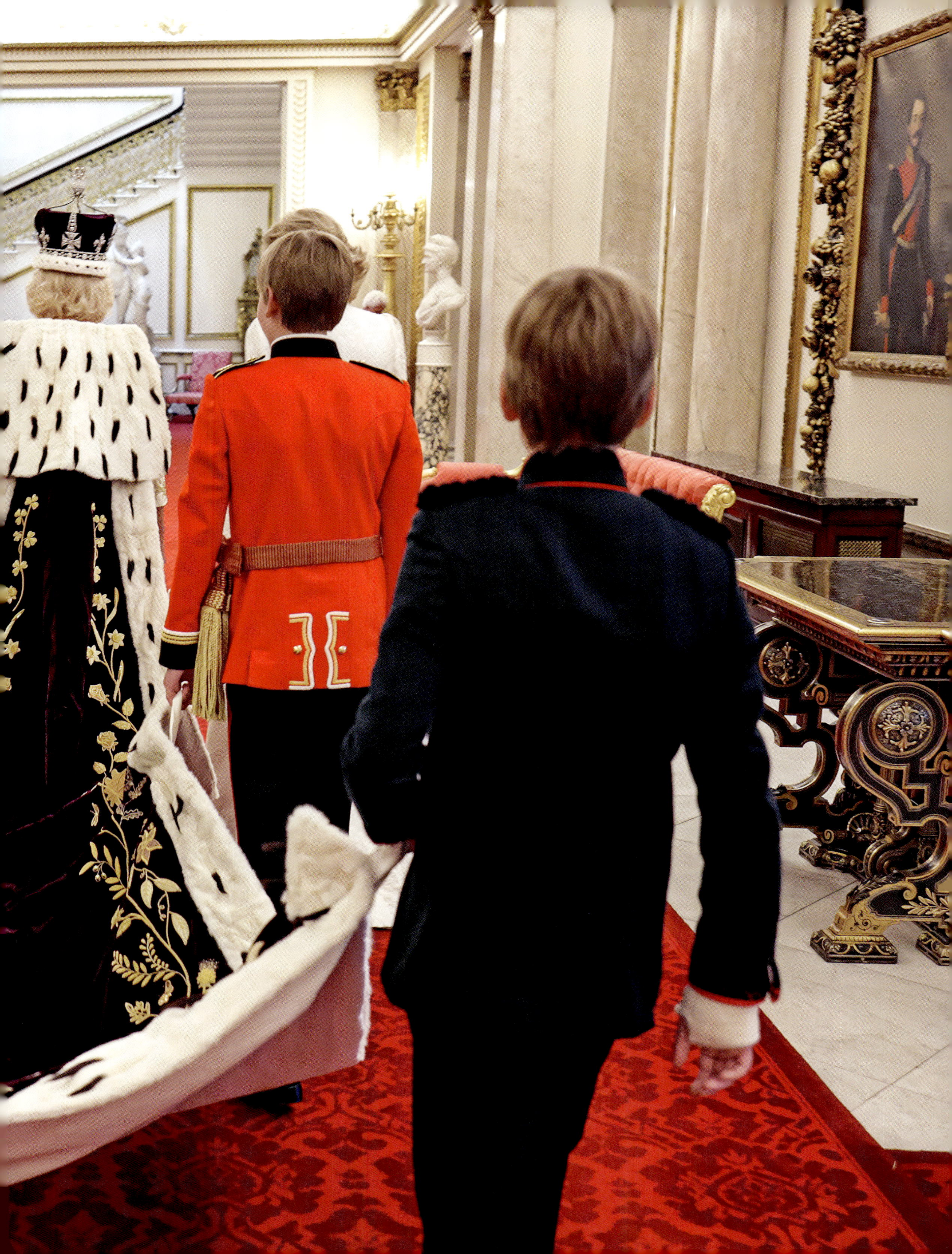

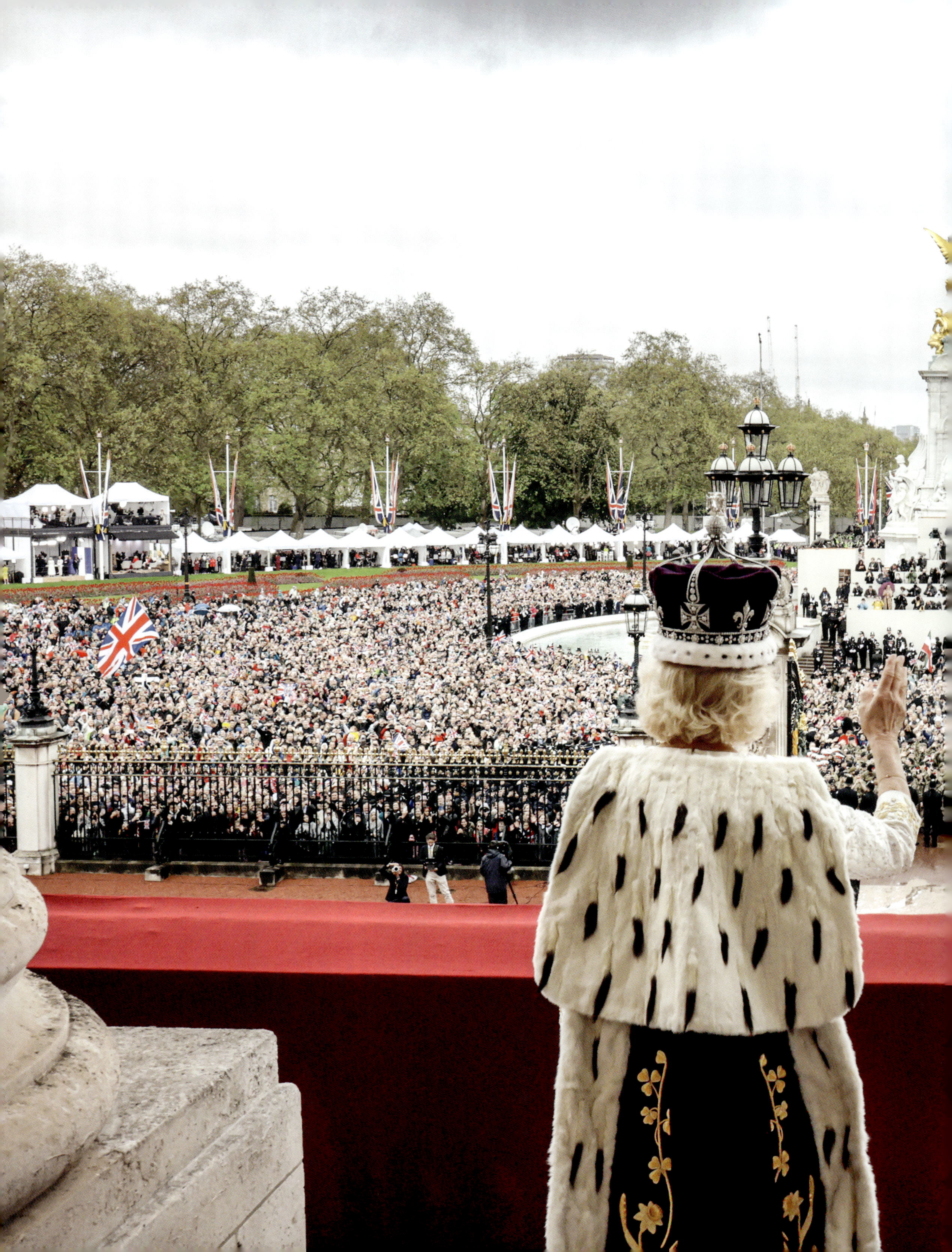

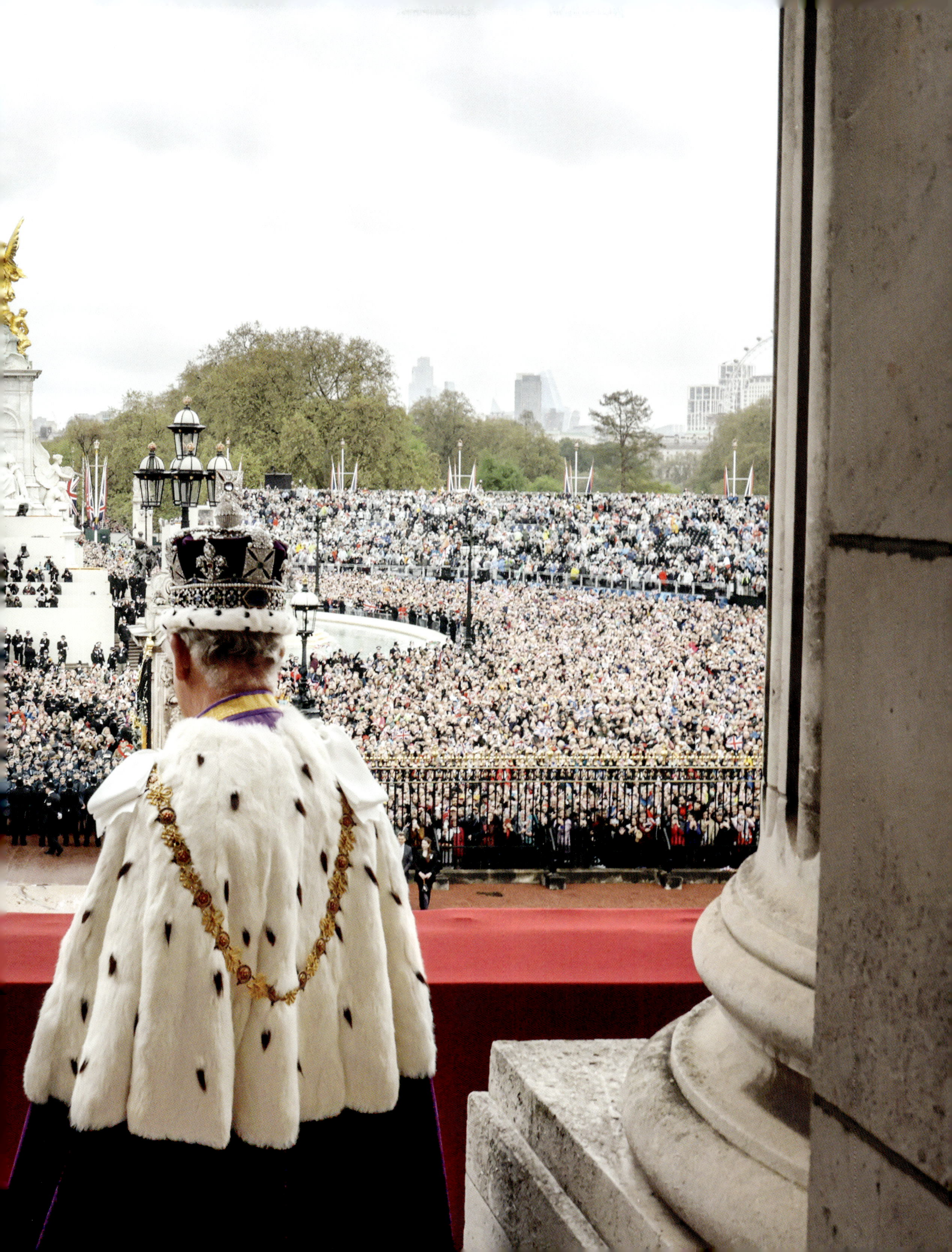

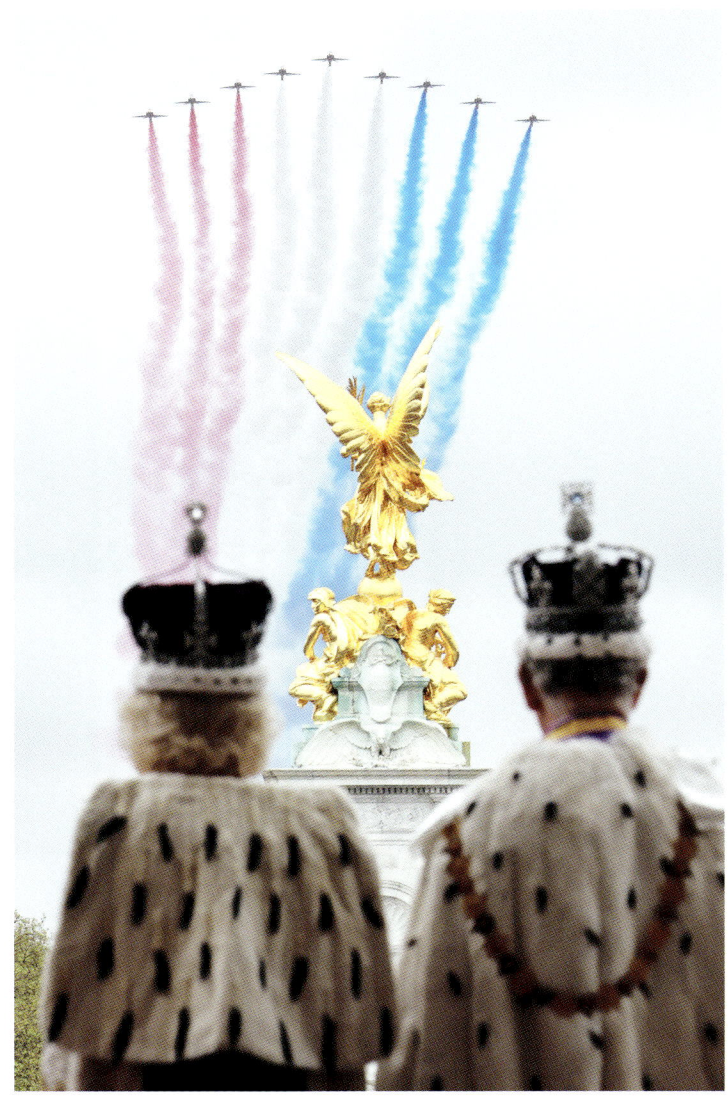

The Royal Air Force (RAF) Red Arrows fly down the Mall and over Buckingham Palace in celebration of the Coronation.

Opposite
Queen Camilla smiles before walking onto the balcony at Buckingham Palace to cheers from the public. Now known as Queen Camilla's Crown, this crown had been made for the Coronation of Queen Mary in June 1911 and was selected for re-use at the Coronation in 2023.

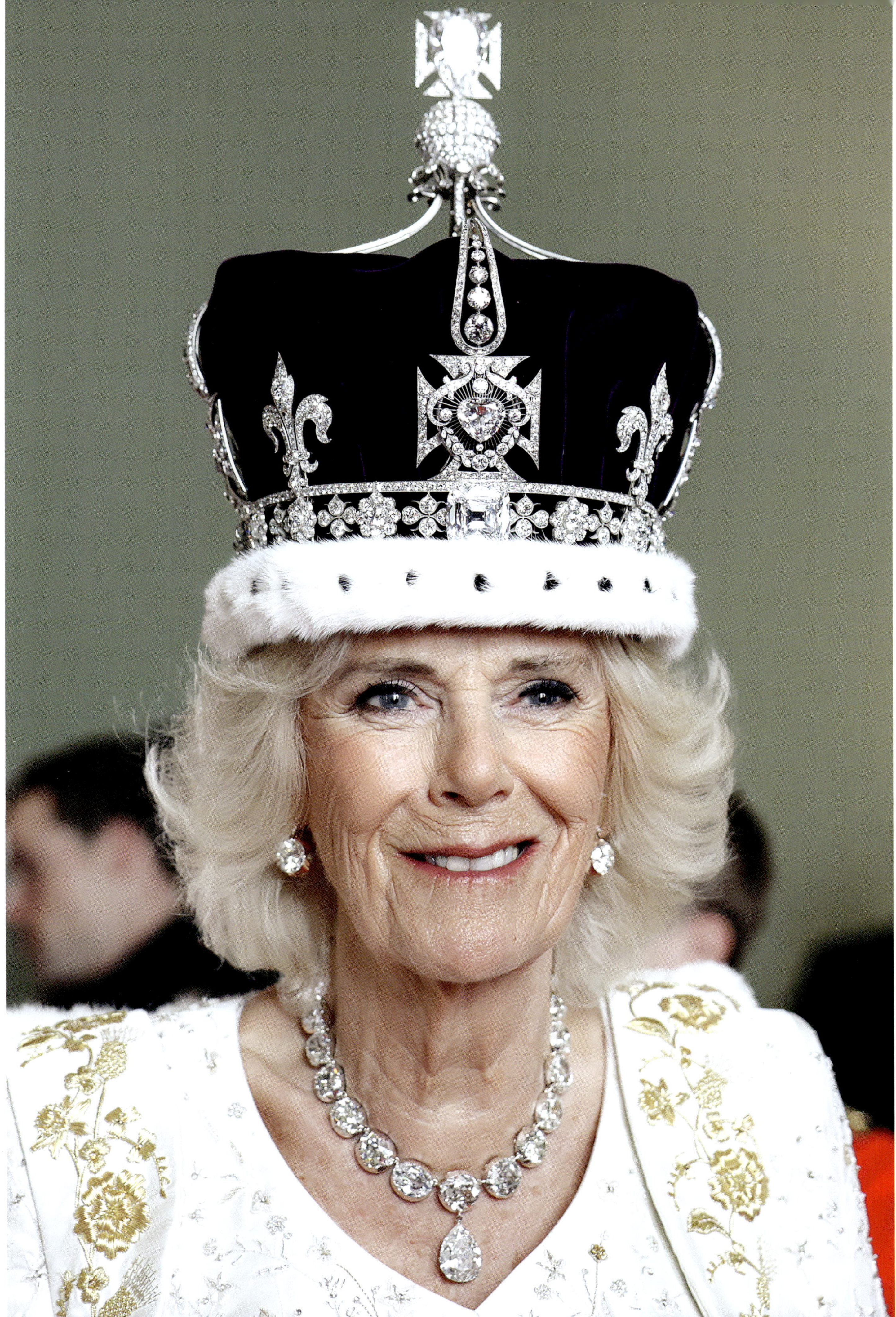

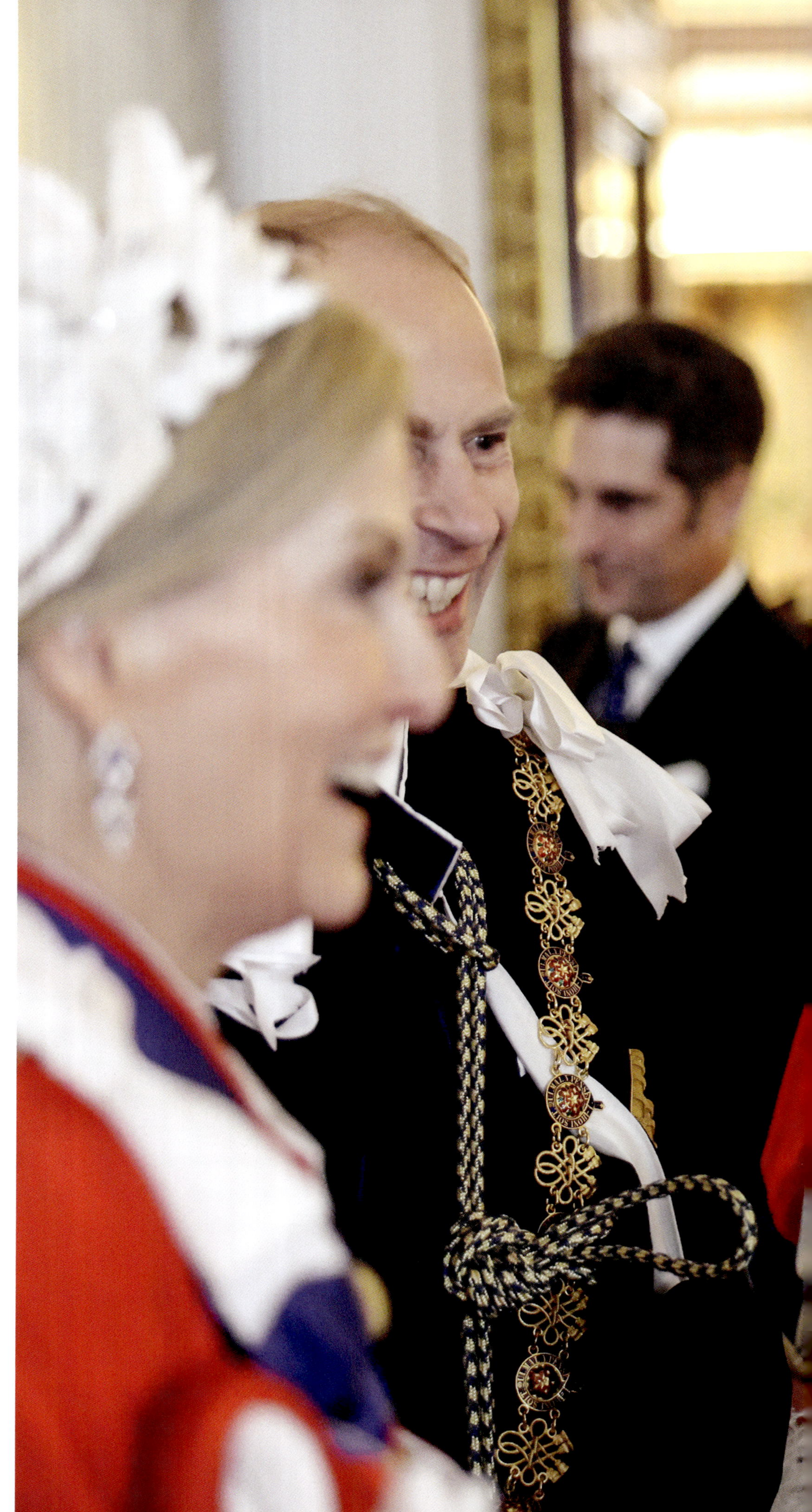

Catherine, Princess of Wales, smiles as she shares a joke with King Charles III and the Duke and Duchess of Edinburgh after the Coronation. The Princess wears a stunning headpiece designed by British milliner Jess Collett in collaboration with Sarah Burton, formerly of Alexander McQueen.

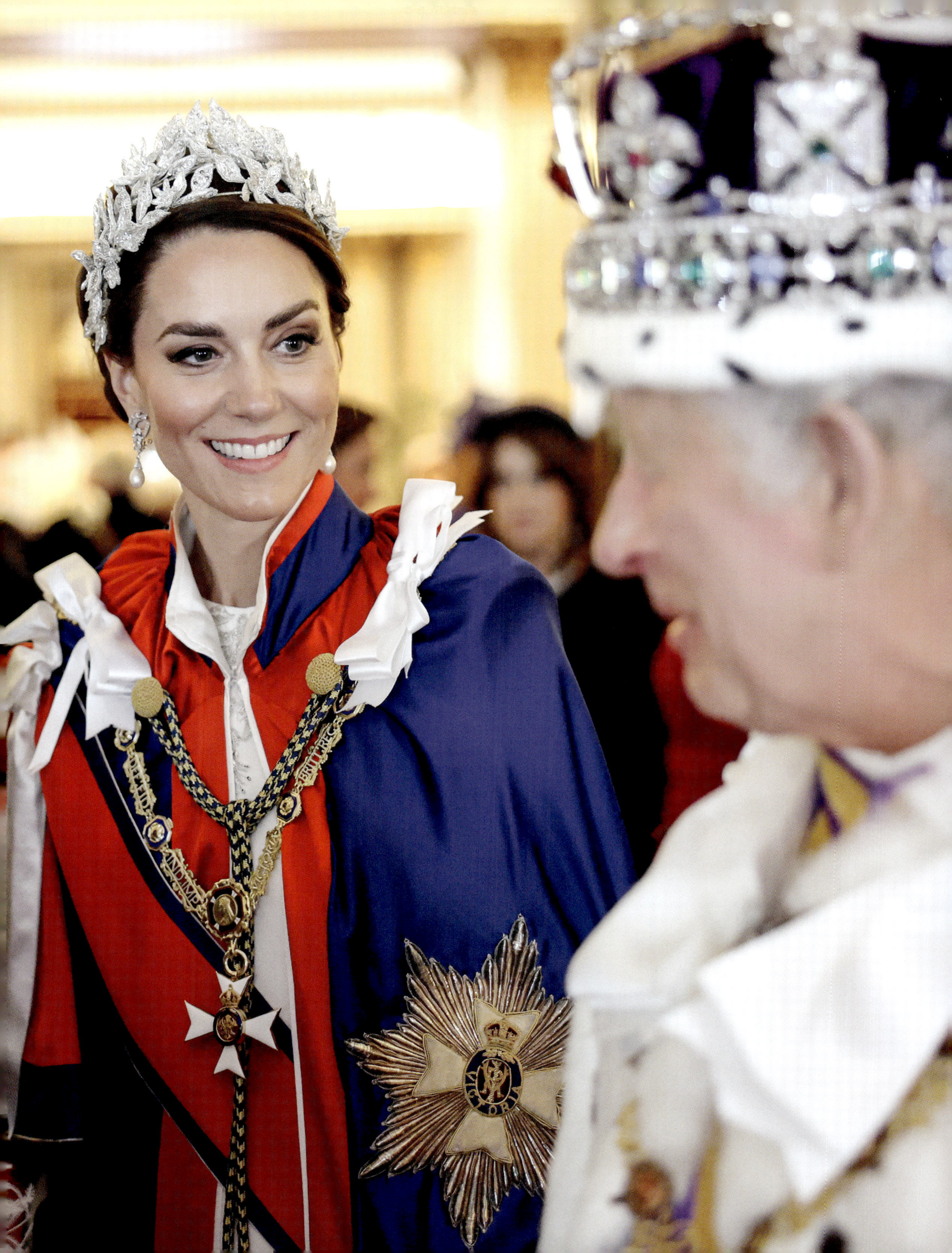

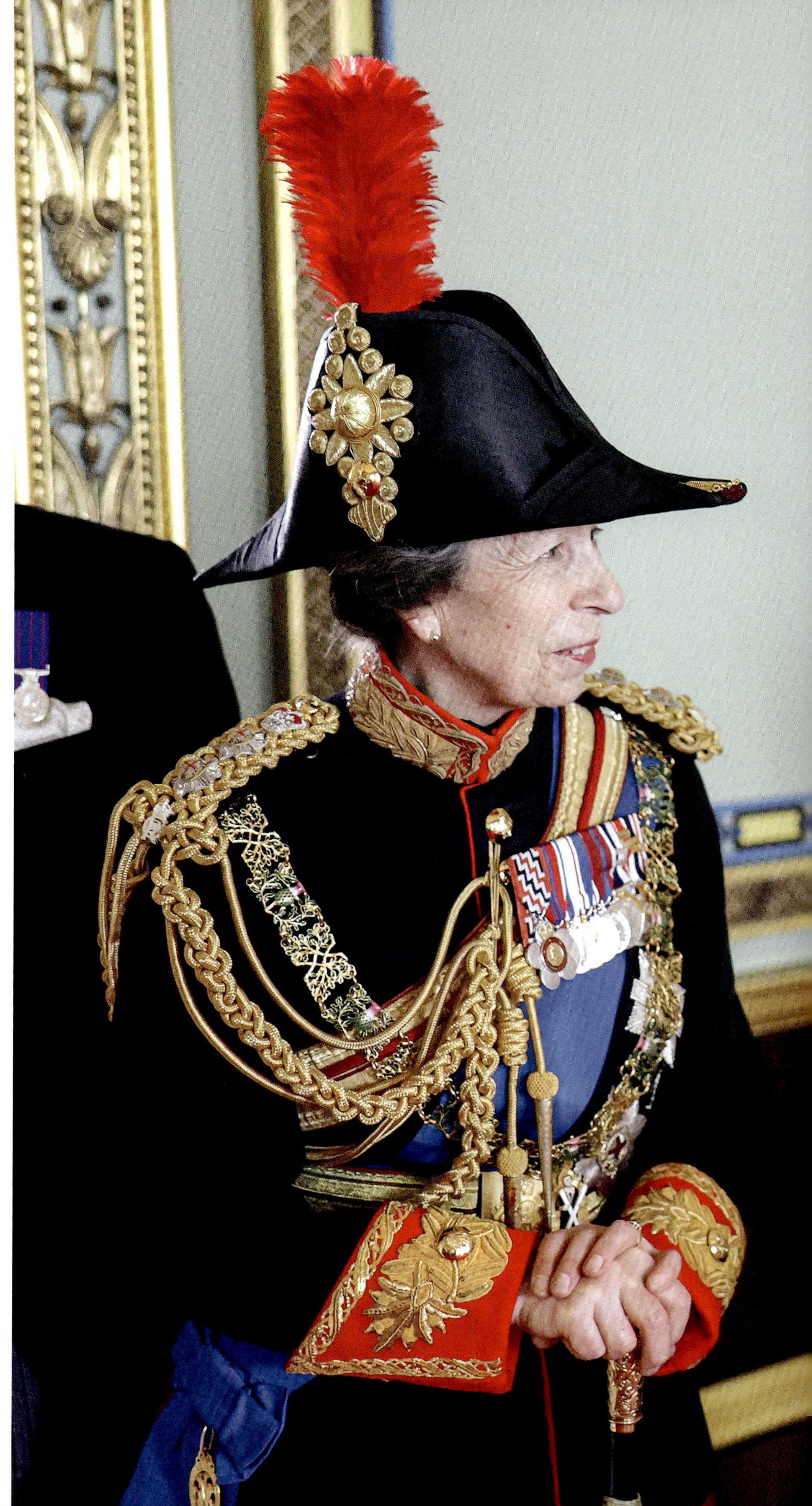

King Charles III speaks to his sister Anne, Princess Royal, in the Centre Room behind the iconic balcony at Buckingham Palace after the Coronation.

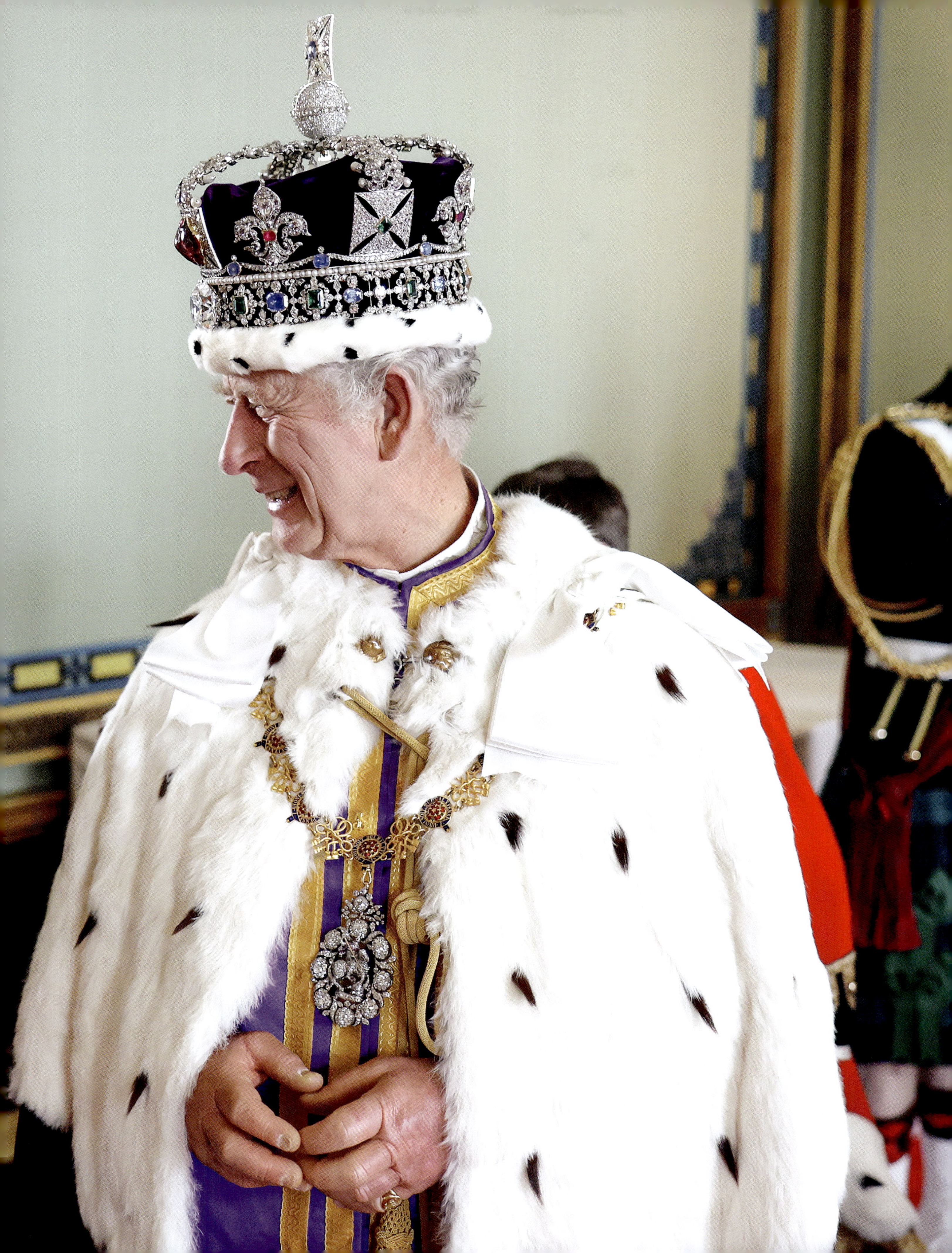

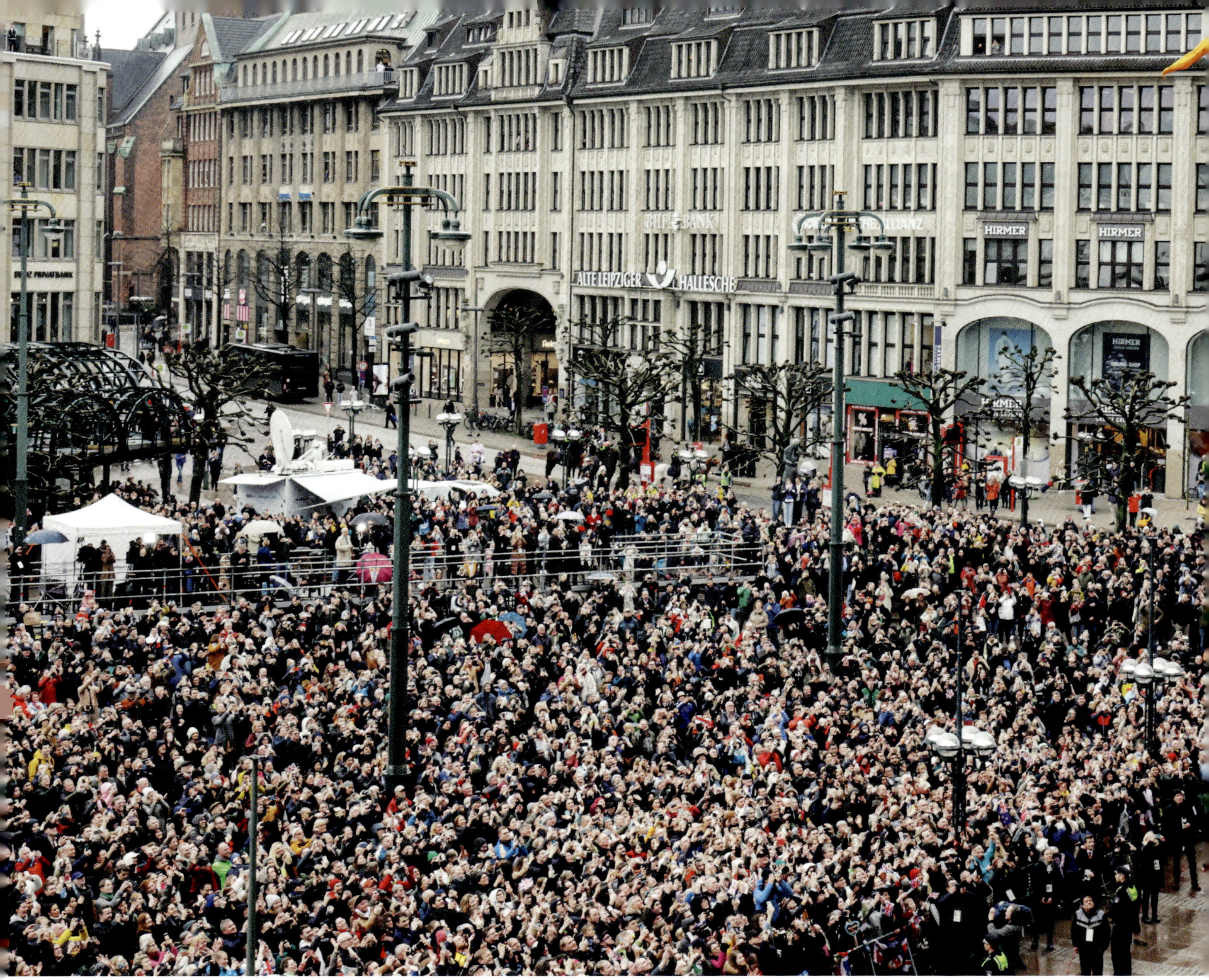

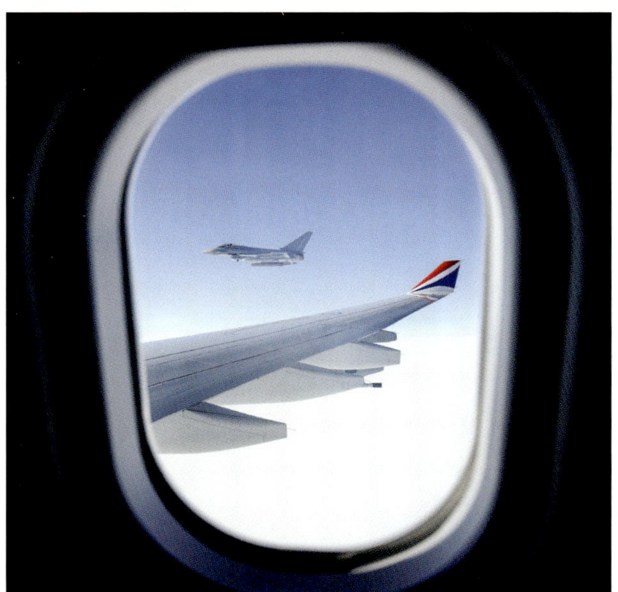

THE FIRST STATE VISIT

As I tucked into my very British meal of beef and potatoes on the Royal Air Force (RAF) Voyager en route to Germany for the King and Queen's first foreign State Visit in March 2024, I was surprised to see that our plane was being accompanied by a German Eurofighter Typhoon jet. It was at this point I realized that everything had changed – we were in a new era and things were being done differently. The crowds that gathered outside the Town Hall in Hamburg, eager to catch a glimpse of the new King and Queen, were exuberant and vast despite the damp March weather. The royal couple spent a good while greeting members of the public and had many gifts thrust into their hands, including a giant cookie!

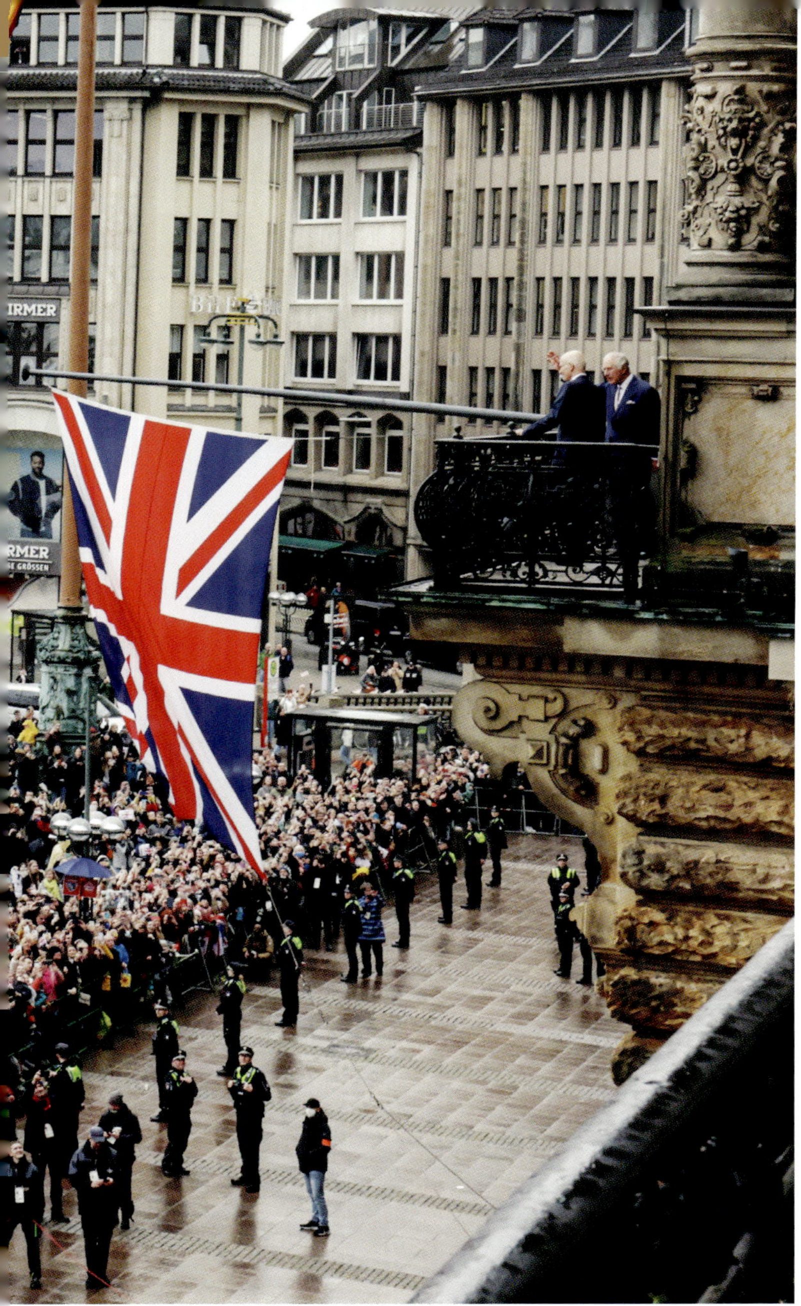

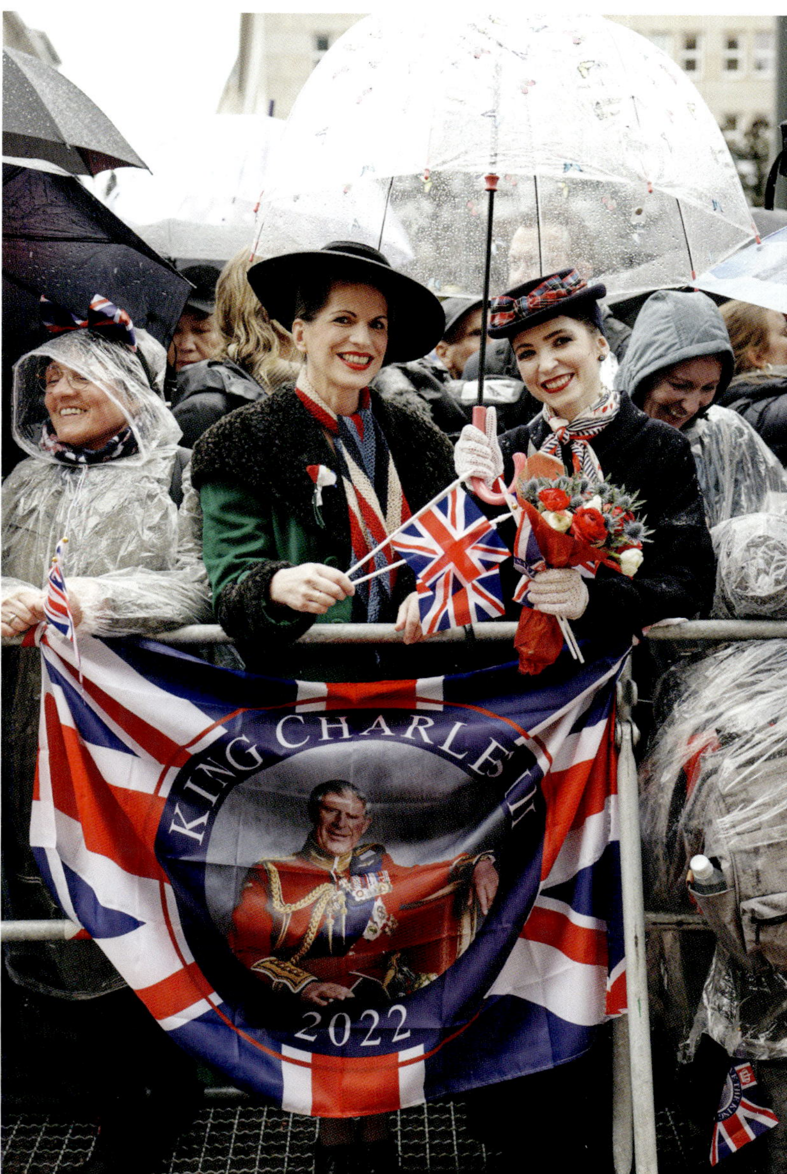
2022

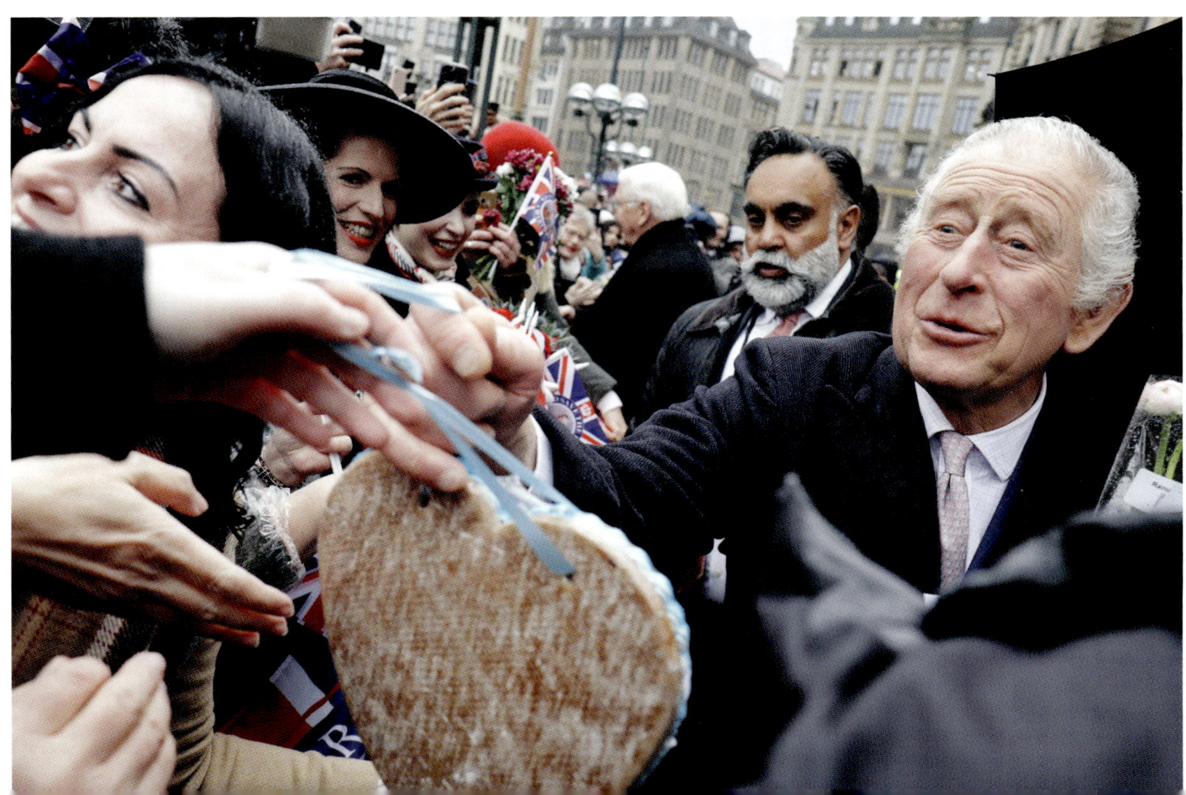

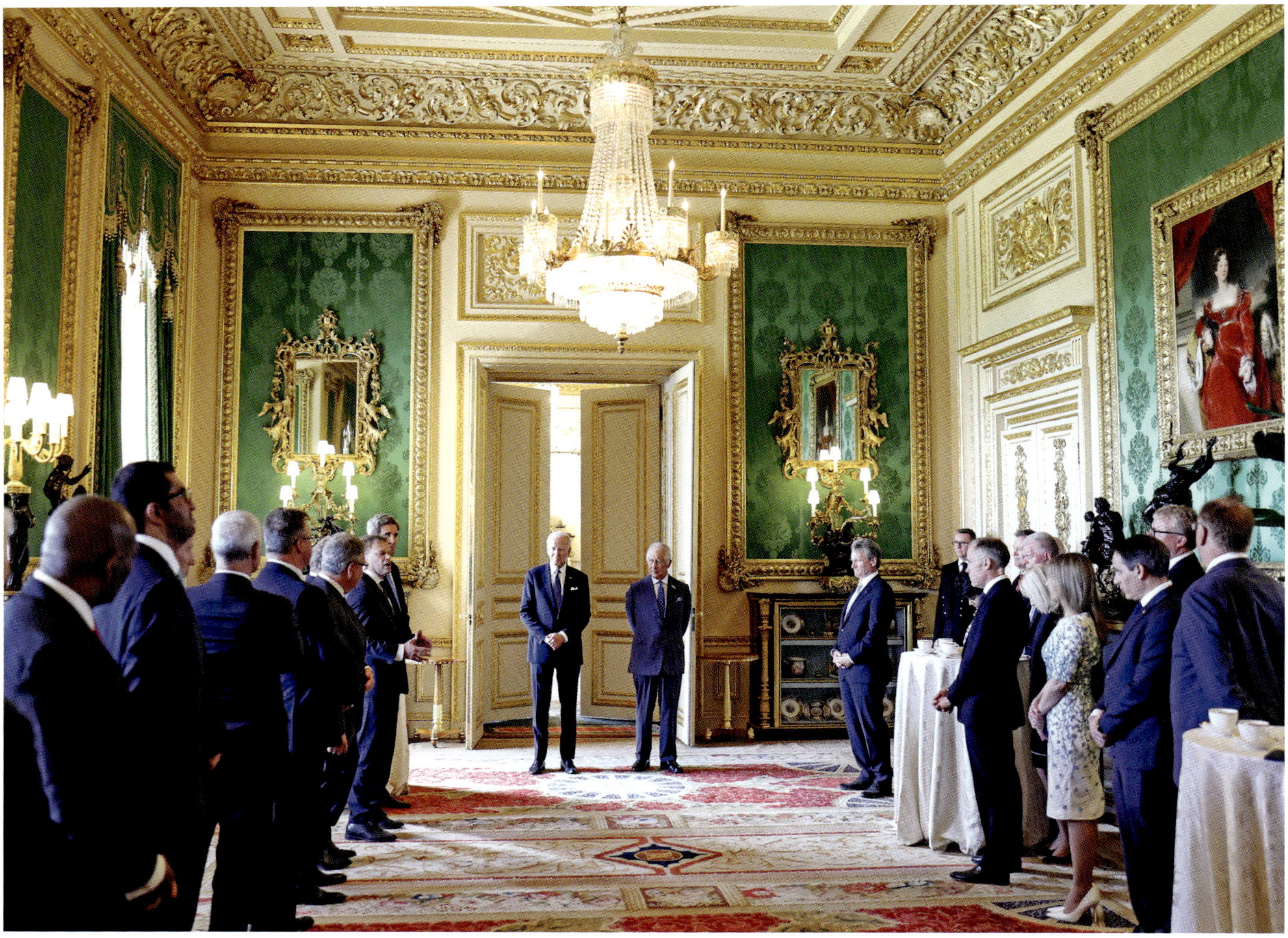

CHARLES AS STATESMAN

King Charles III is in the unique position of being able to exert influence at the highest level of international relations in order to enact positive change. This, of course, involves meeting and greeting not only politicians from around the world but also global royalty. His charm and warmth are respected and appreciated by royals and heads of state worldwide.

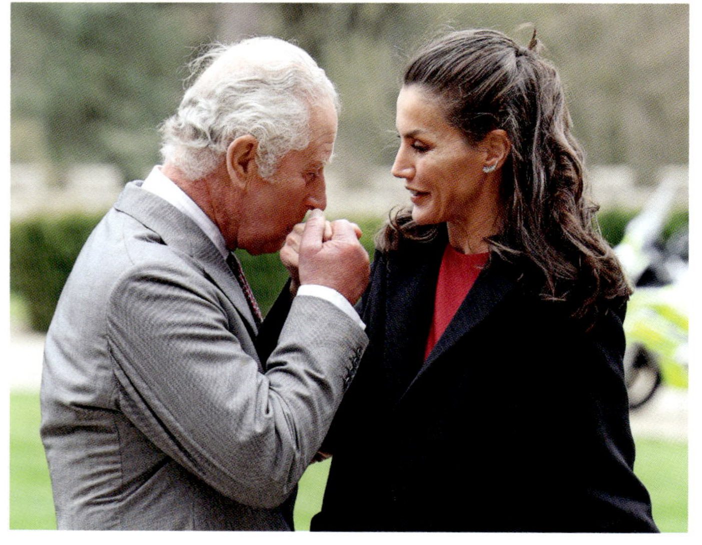

King Charles and President of the United States Joe Biden attend a Climate Finance Mobilisation forum at Windsor Castle, 10 July 2023.

Left
Queen Letizia of Spain is greeted by Charles at Auckland Castle in Bishop Auckland, 5 April 2022.

Opposite and overleaf
The State Banquet at Windsor Castle in honour of French President Emmanuel Macron and Brigitte Macron, who visited the UK on a State Visit, 8 July 2025.

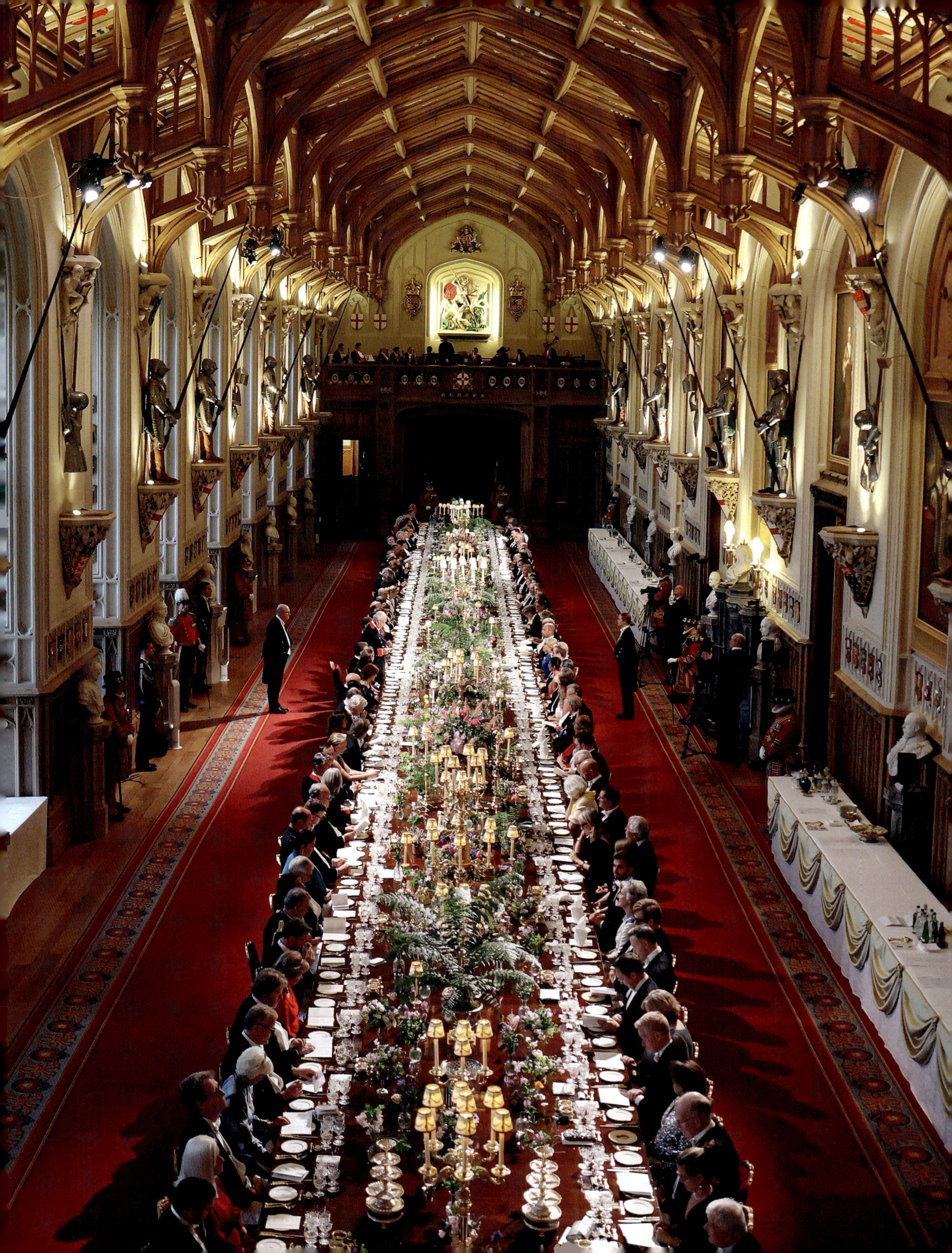

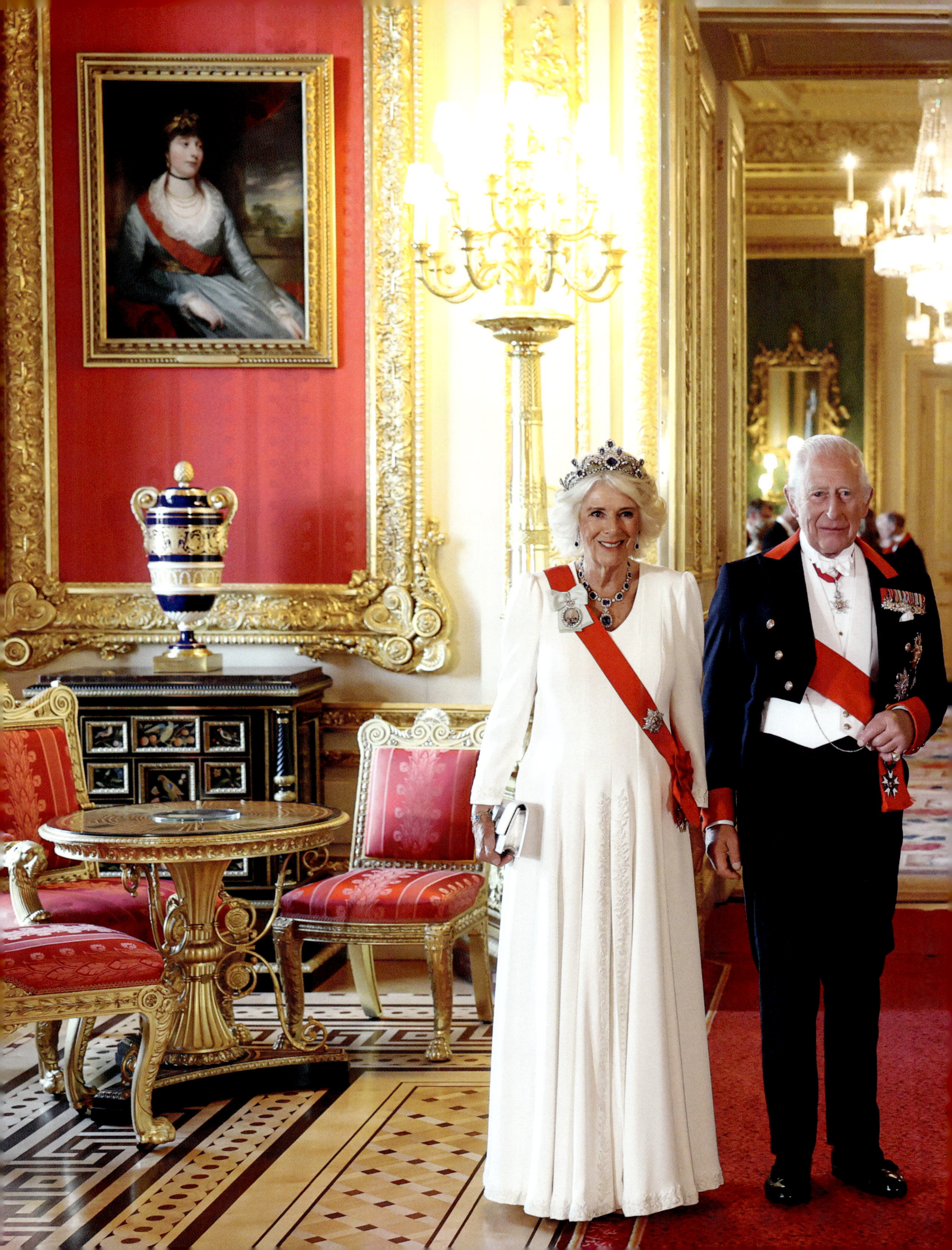

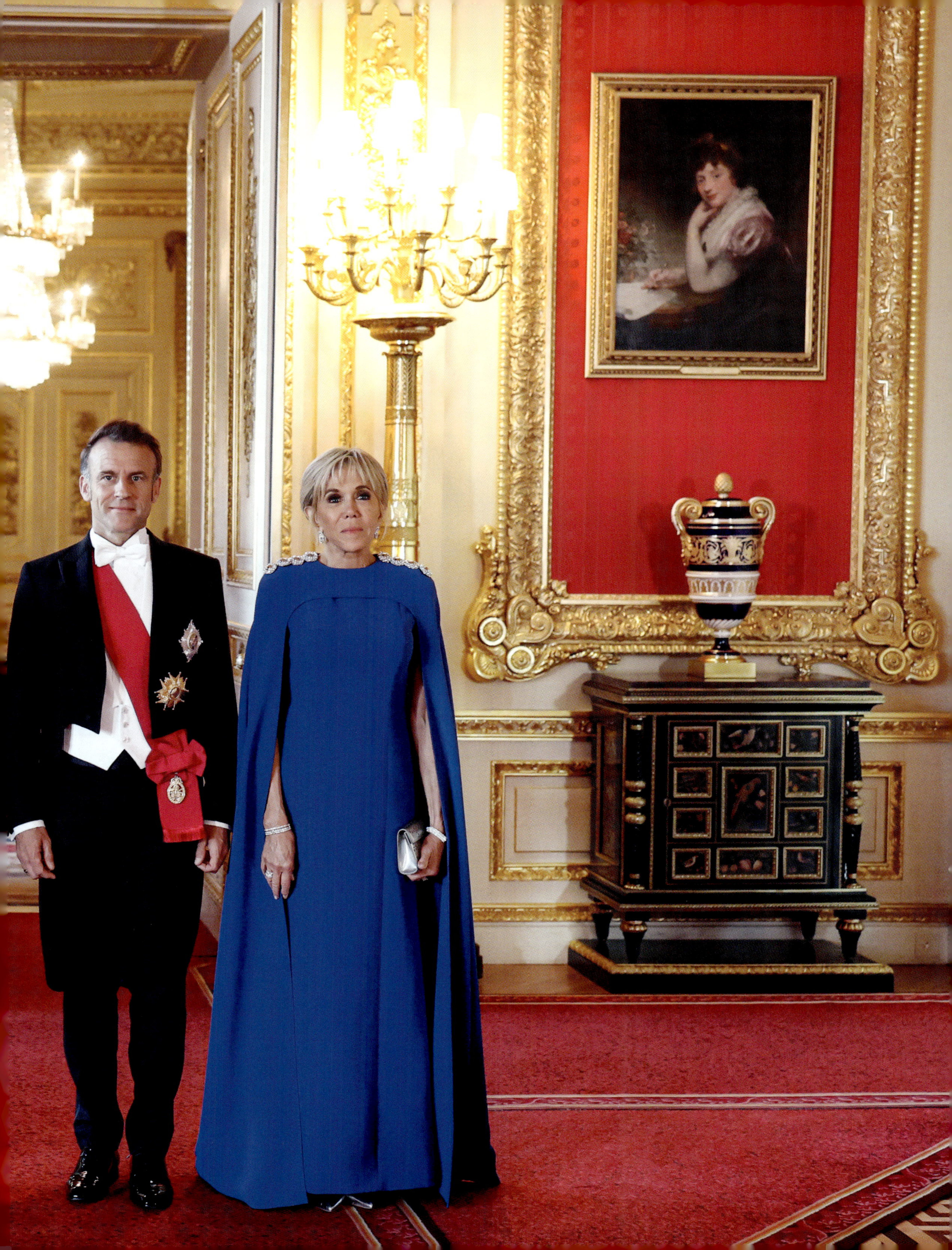

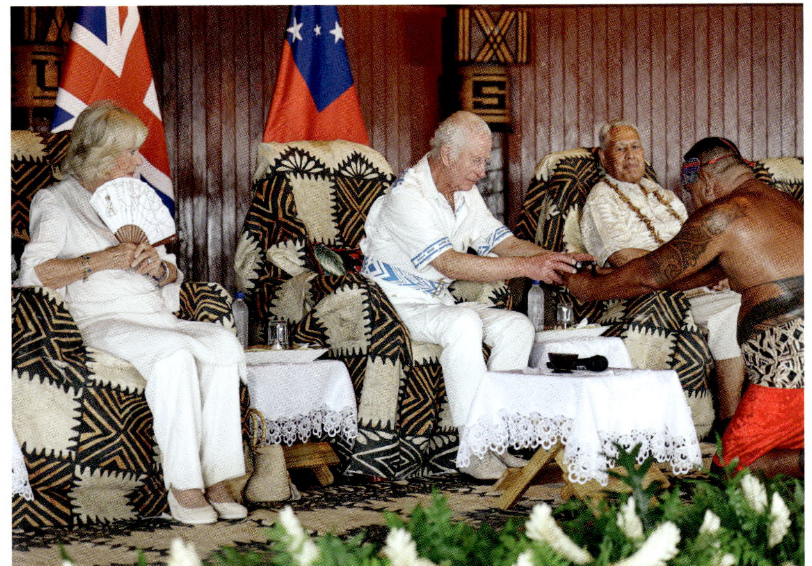

THE IMPORTANCE OF COMMONWEALTH

As Head of the Commonwealth, an association of 56 countries that have the shared goals of human rights, democracy, and peace, the King feels the weight of his responsibility acutely. The title was passed down to King Charles III from Queen Elizabeth II after it was unanimously agreed at the Commonwealth Heads of Government Meeting in 2018.

Right
Wishing to visit as many of the realms as possible, in October 2024 the King departed on a gruelling visit to Australia and Samoa despite his recent health struggles. Both he and the Queen received an incredible reception outside Sydney Opera House.

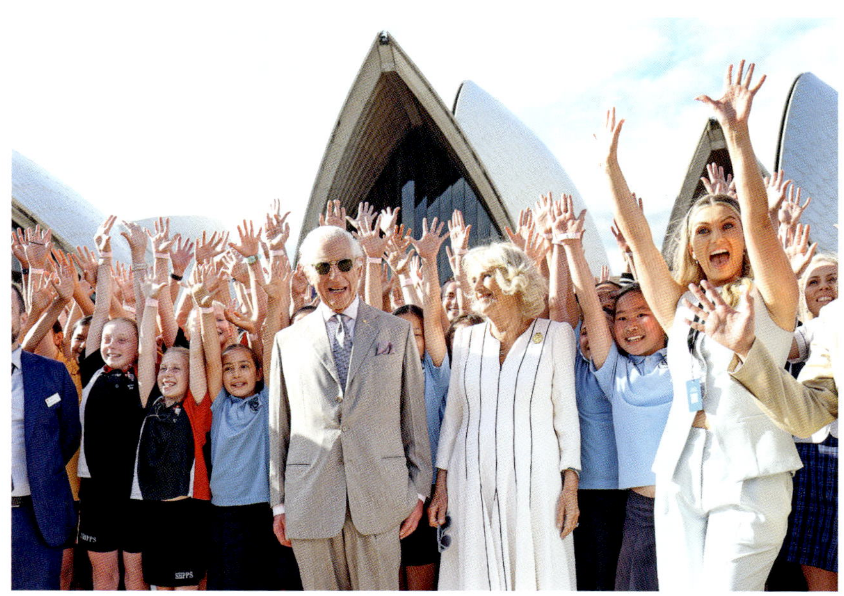

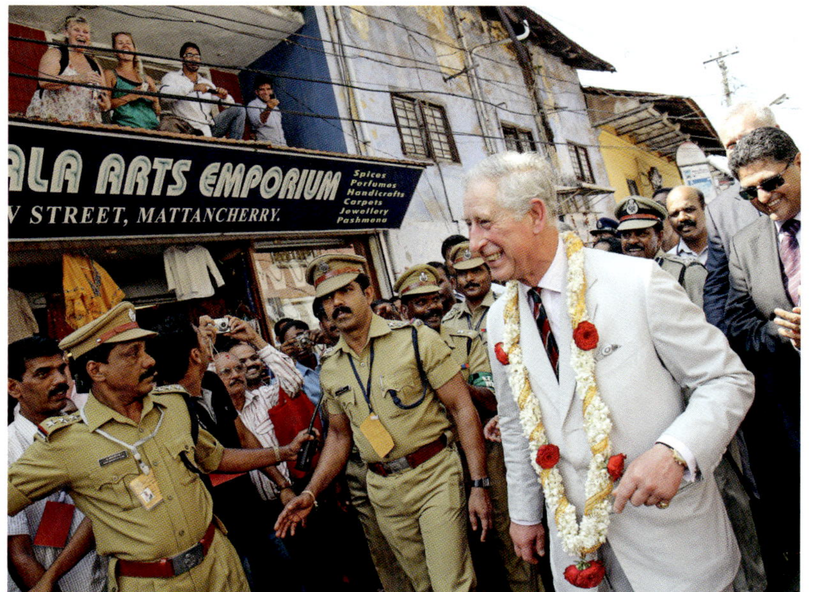

Top and opposite
The King and Queen took part in an "Ava ceremony" in Samoa, during which this traditional drink is served to important guests.

Left
While on an official visit to India, Charles was serenaded in Cochin by Trish Lewis on his 65th birthday and has just thrown a red rose.

Overleaf
The monarch meets guests at the King's Garden Party at Buckingham Palace, 7 May 2025.

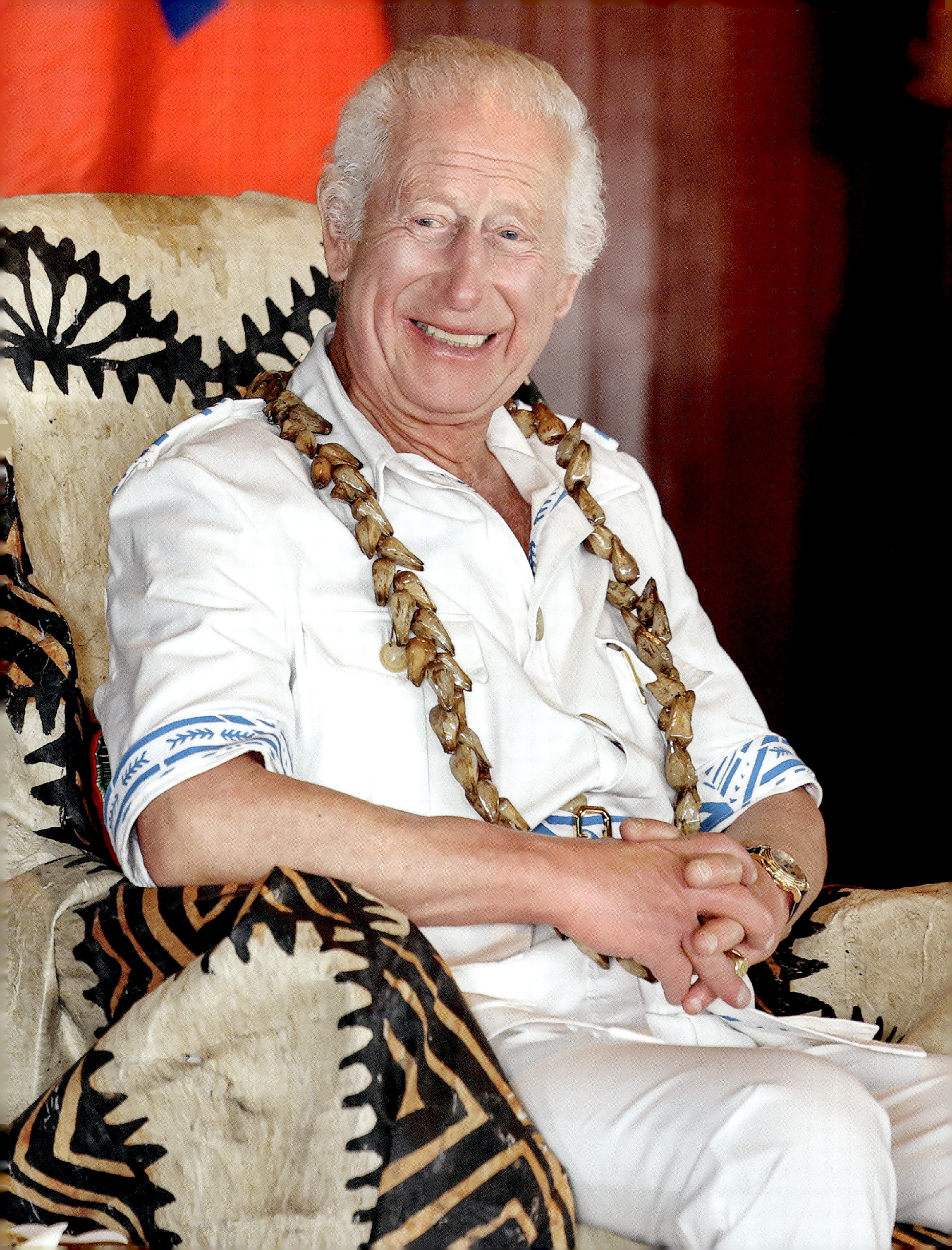

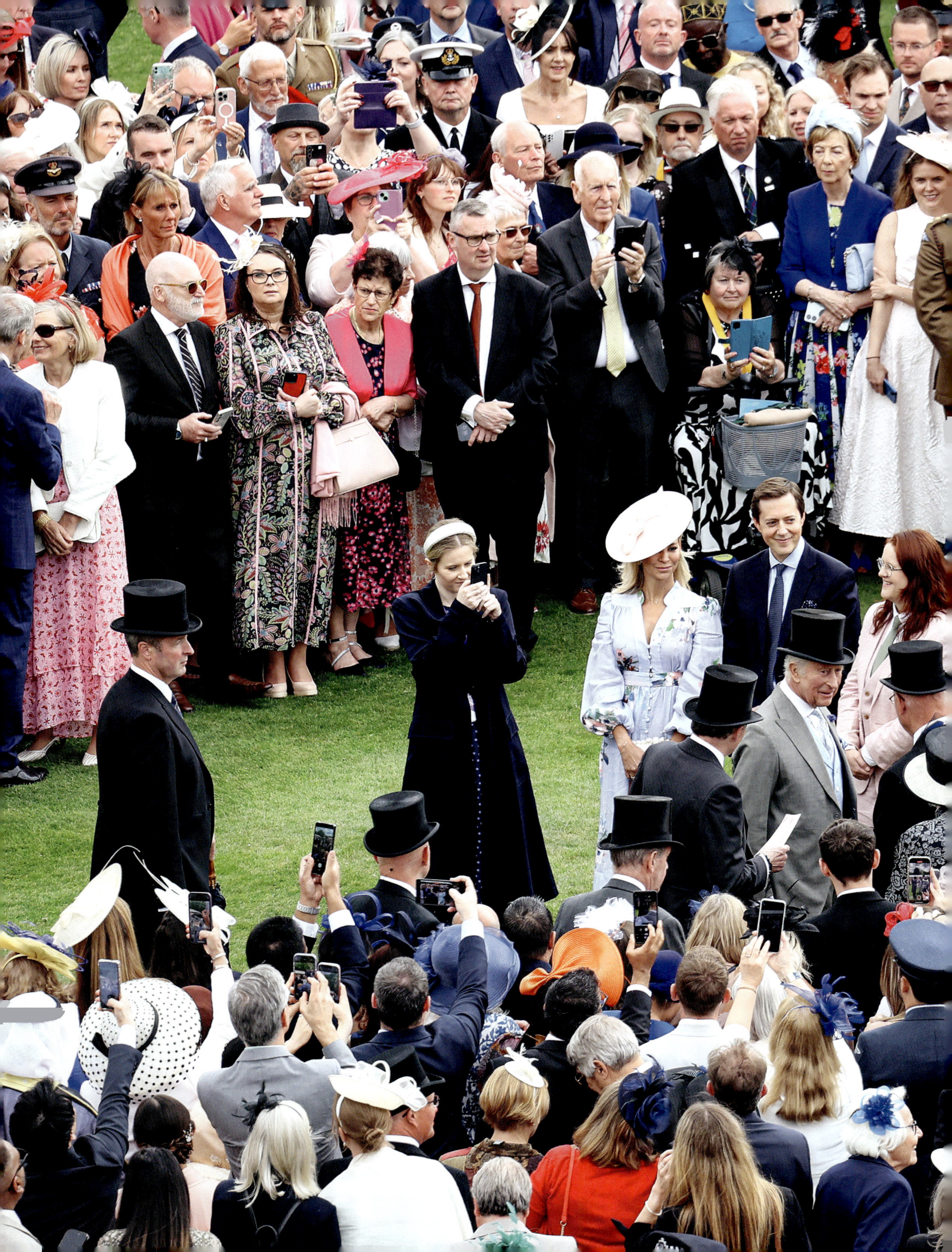

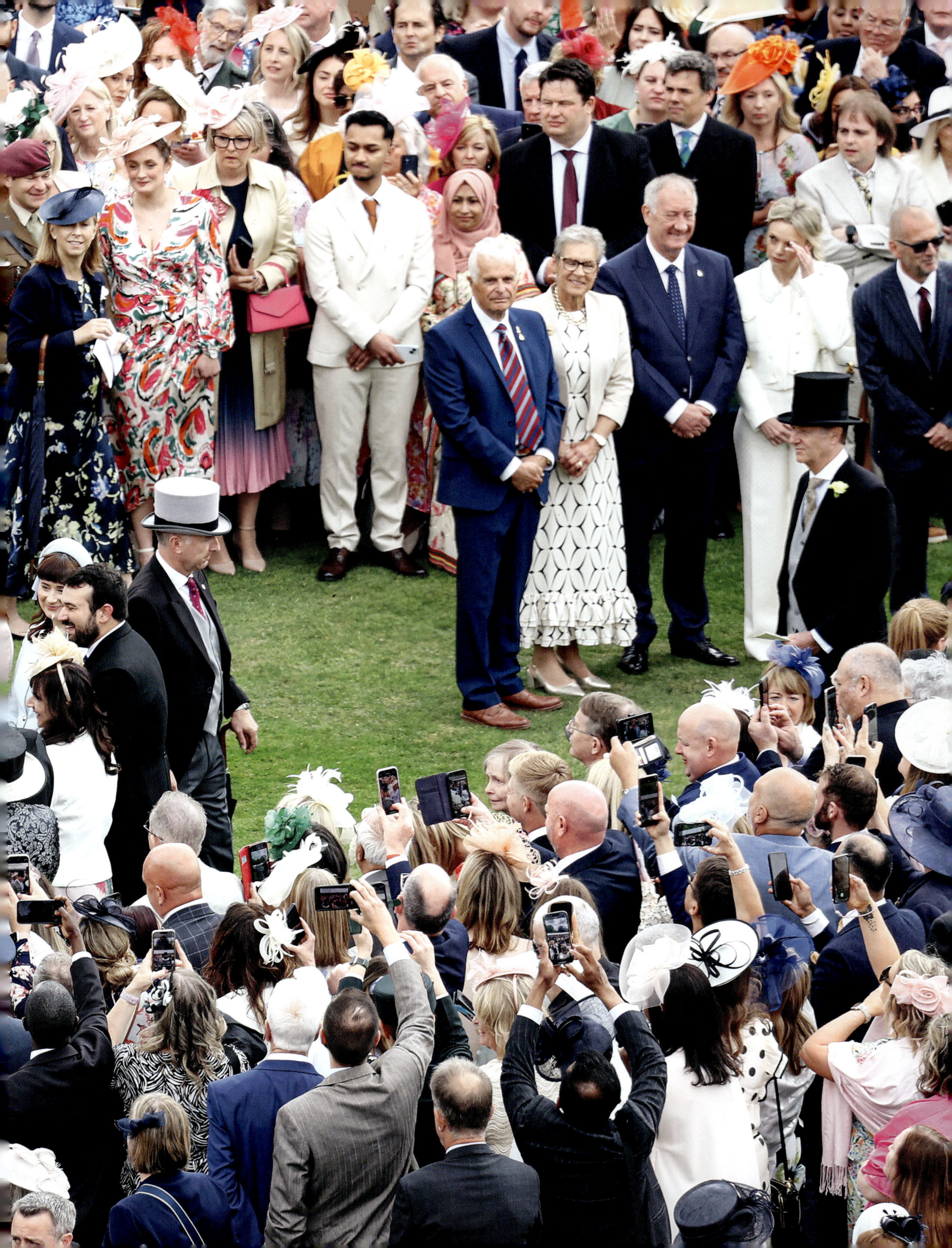

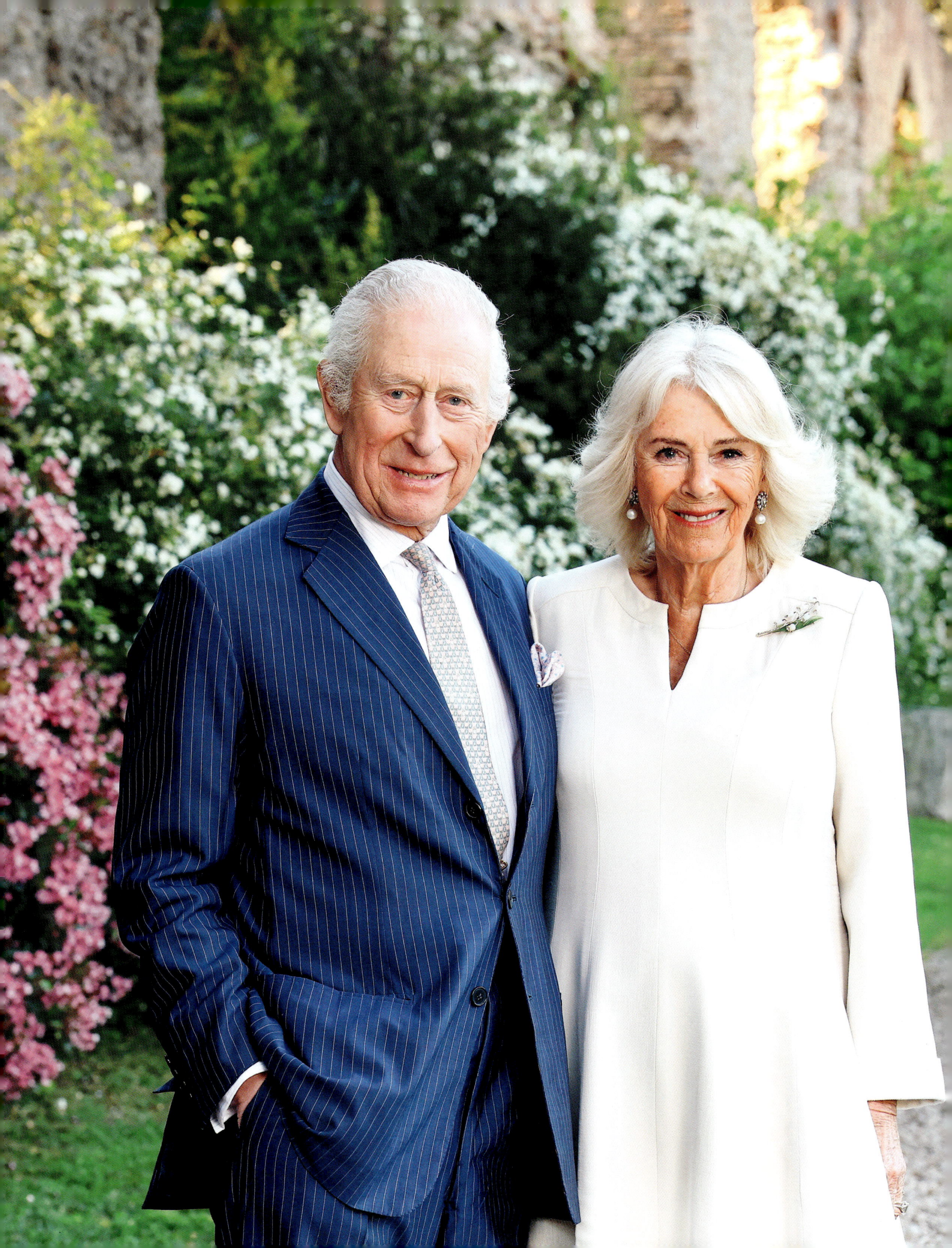

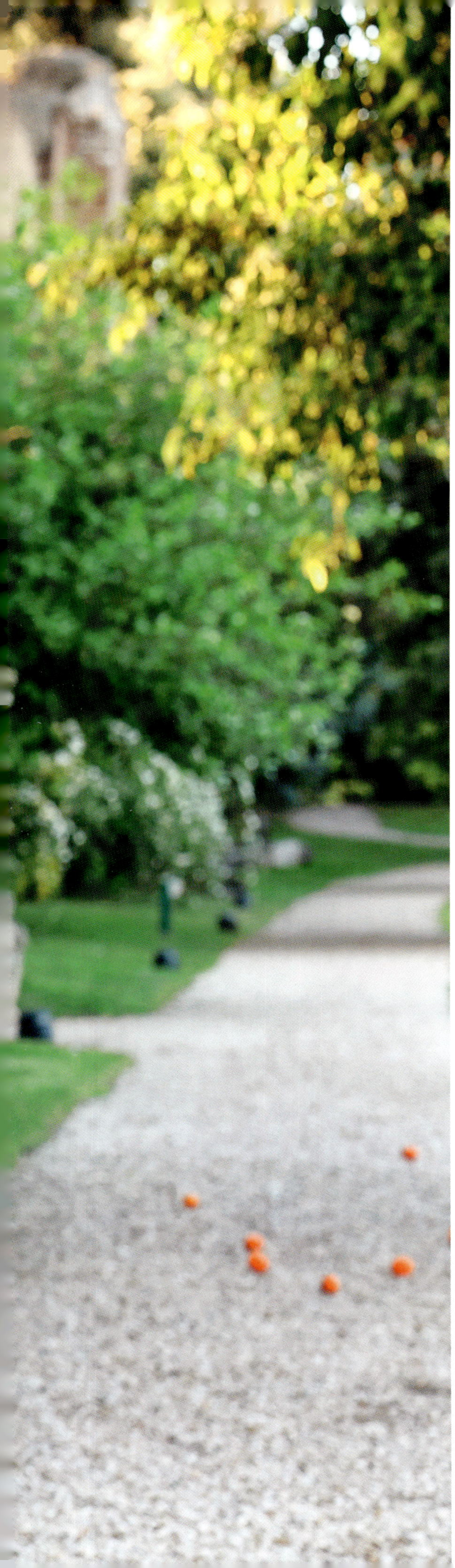

King Charles III and Queen Camilla at Villa Wolkonsky, the official residence of the British ambassador to Italy, two days before their 20th wedding anniversary, 7 April 2025.

Below
The King and Queen arrive for a garden party at Buckingham Palace, 7 May 2025.

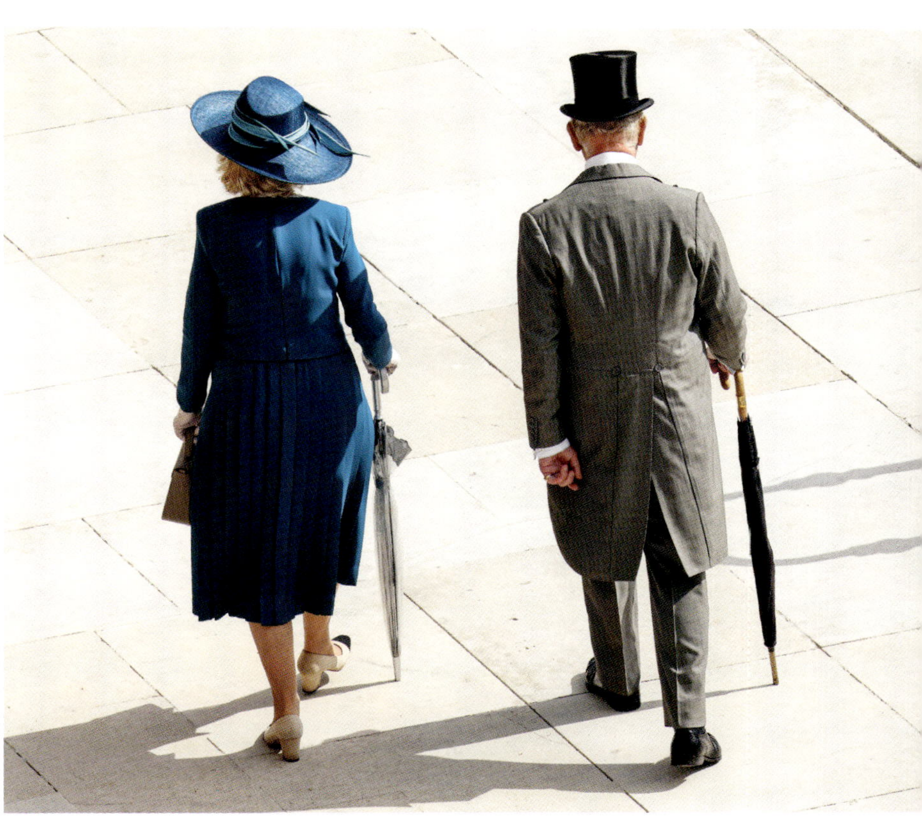

A PERSONAL CELEBRATION IN ROME

I took this portrait (left) in the magnificent gardens of Villa Wolkonsky in Rome to celebrate the King and Queen's 20th wedding anniversary during an official visit in 2025. With oranges scattered on the path and the Neronian spur of the Aqua Claudia, an ancient Roman aqueduct, rising in the background, the early evening light cast a stunning glow over the scene. Having photographed the royal couple for over two decades it felt very special to capture such an important moment in their story.

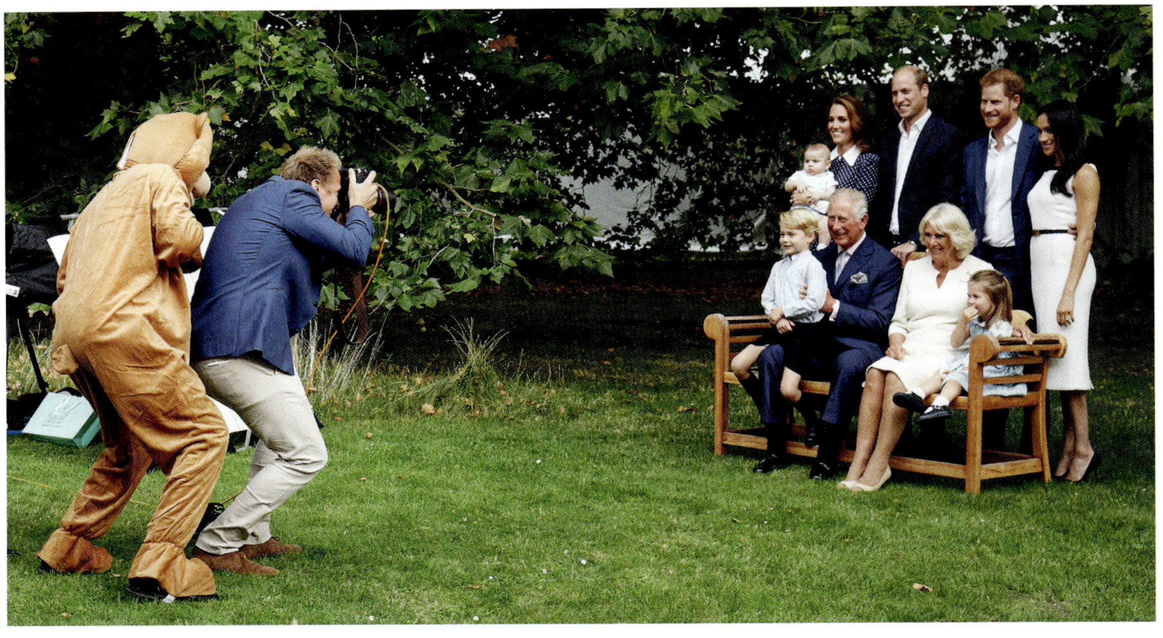

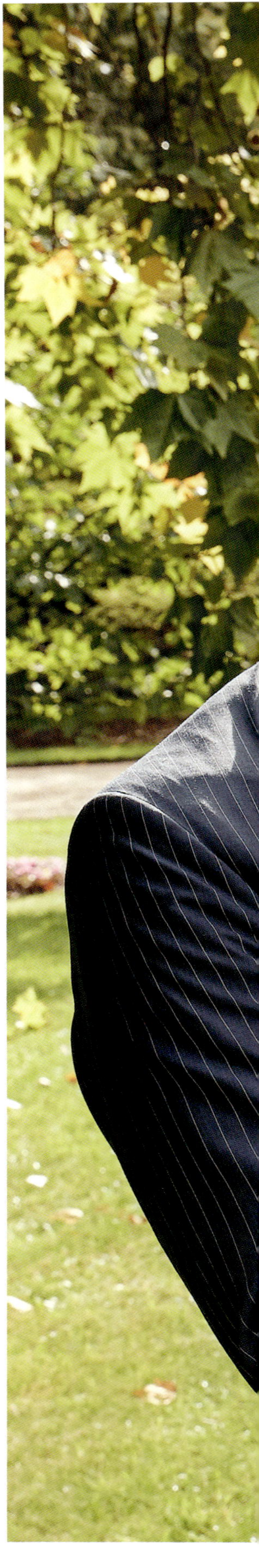

BEAR IN MIND

When taking this family portrait for Prince Charles's 70th birthday in 2018, I thought it would be interesting to make things a little more fun and relaxed by introducing a "special friend." Sure enough, the understanding member of the palace staff who dressed up as an affable bear had the party in hysterics, and I was able to capture an amusing and informal image alongside the official portrait!

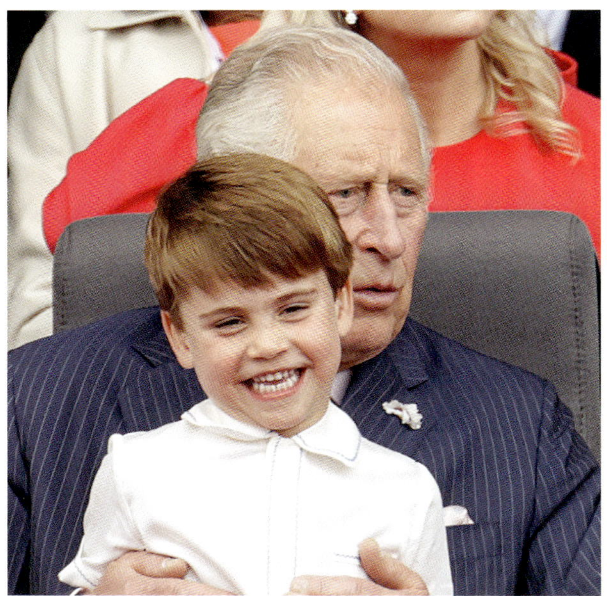

Prince Louis has the time of his life sitting on his grandfather's knee to watch the Platinum Jubilee Pageant pass Buckingham Palace, 5 June 2022.

Right
Prince Charles in the gardens of Clarence House with his daughter-in-law and his grandson, Louis, on the event of the family portrait to mark his 70th birthday, 5 September 2018.

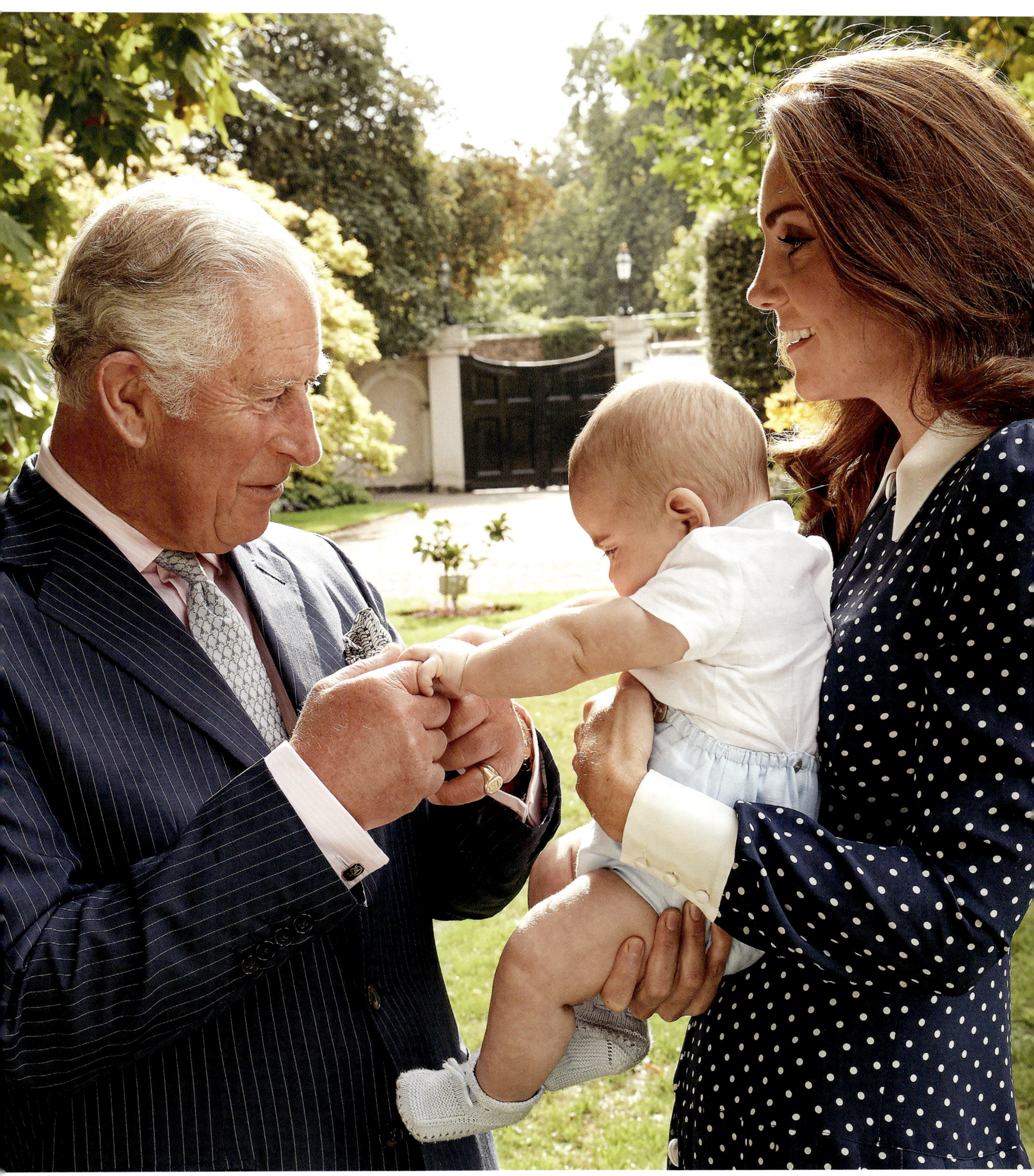

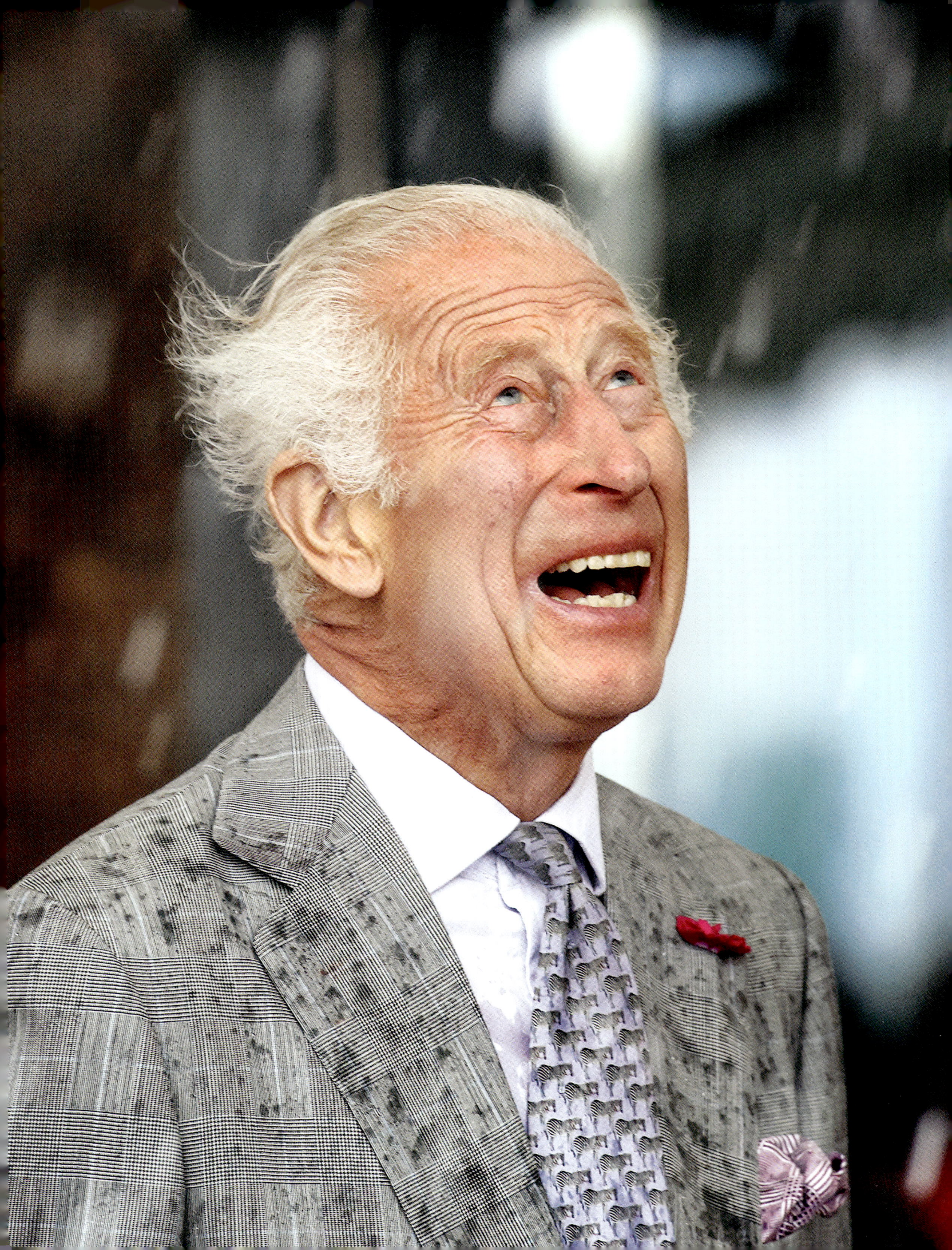

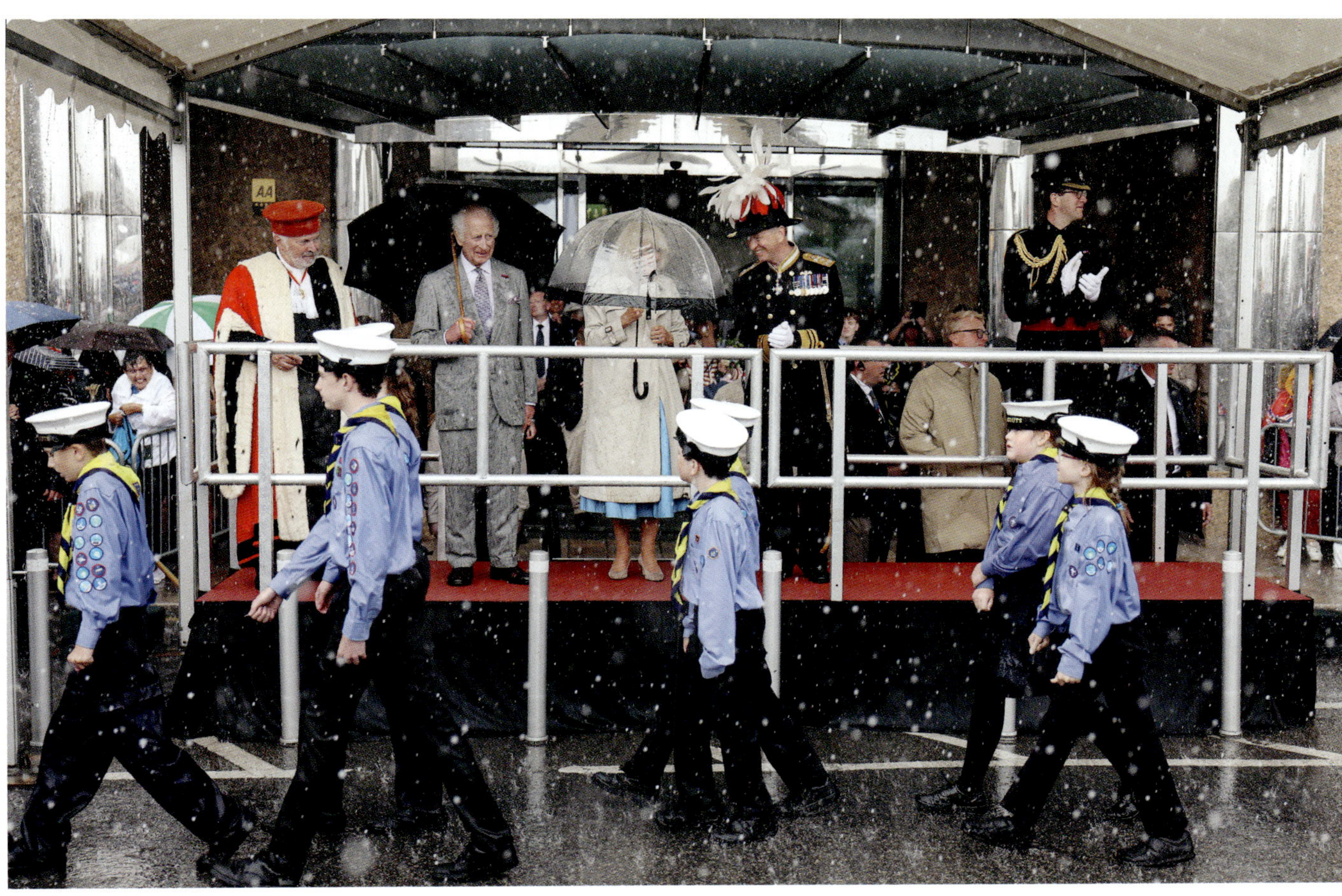

REIGNING IN JERSEY

I saw the clouds heading in our direction, giant, inky-grey and menacing, travelling over the English Channel and ready to hit with force – a rainstorm like no other to disrupt the smiles and processions. As young scouts and beavers paraded past the royal couple, water droplets the size of golf balls drenched the hapless children. The scene was a royal visit to St. Helier in Jersey on 15 July 2024, a verdant island in the English Channel off the coast of France with a strong sense of independence and community.

Rainstorms occasionally disrupt royal engagements, and I have learned over the years that the more dramatic the weather, the more animated and candid the photos. However, these kinds of situations present obvious problems for the unprepared photographer with expensive equipment. I found myself juggling umbrellas and cameras, and trying to stay dry as the wind whipped the rain almost horizontally, while at the same time staying focused on the King as he looked to the heavens, a sense of surprise and disbelief on his face.

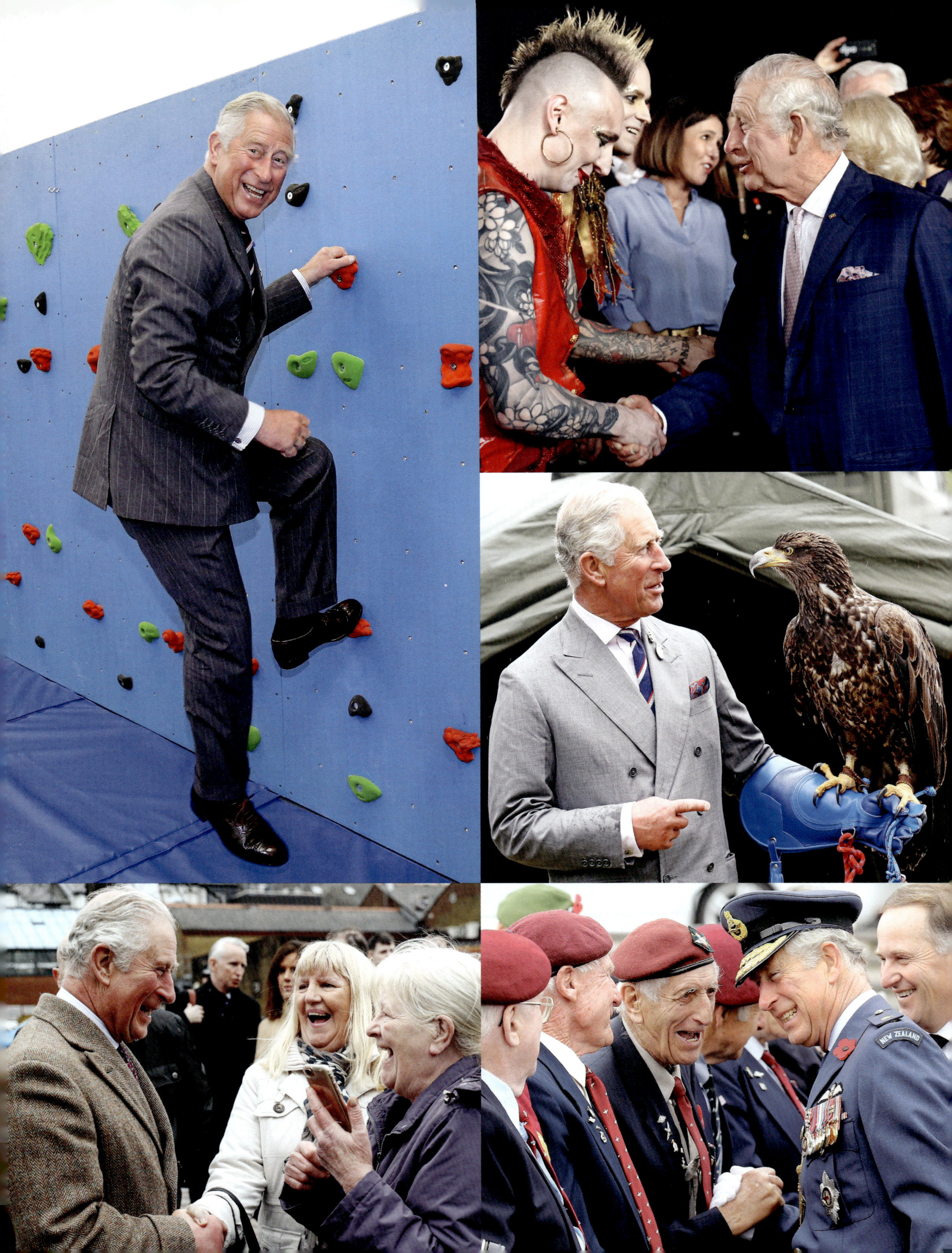
NEW ZEALAND

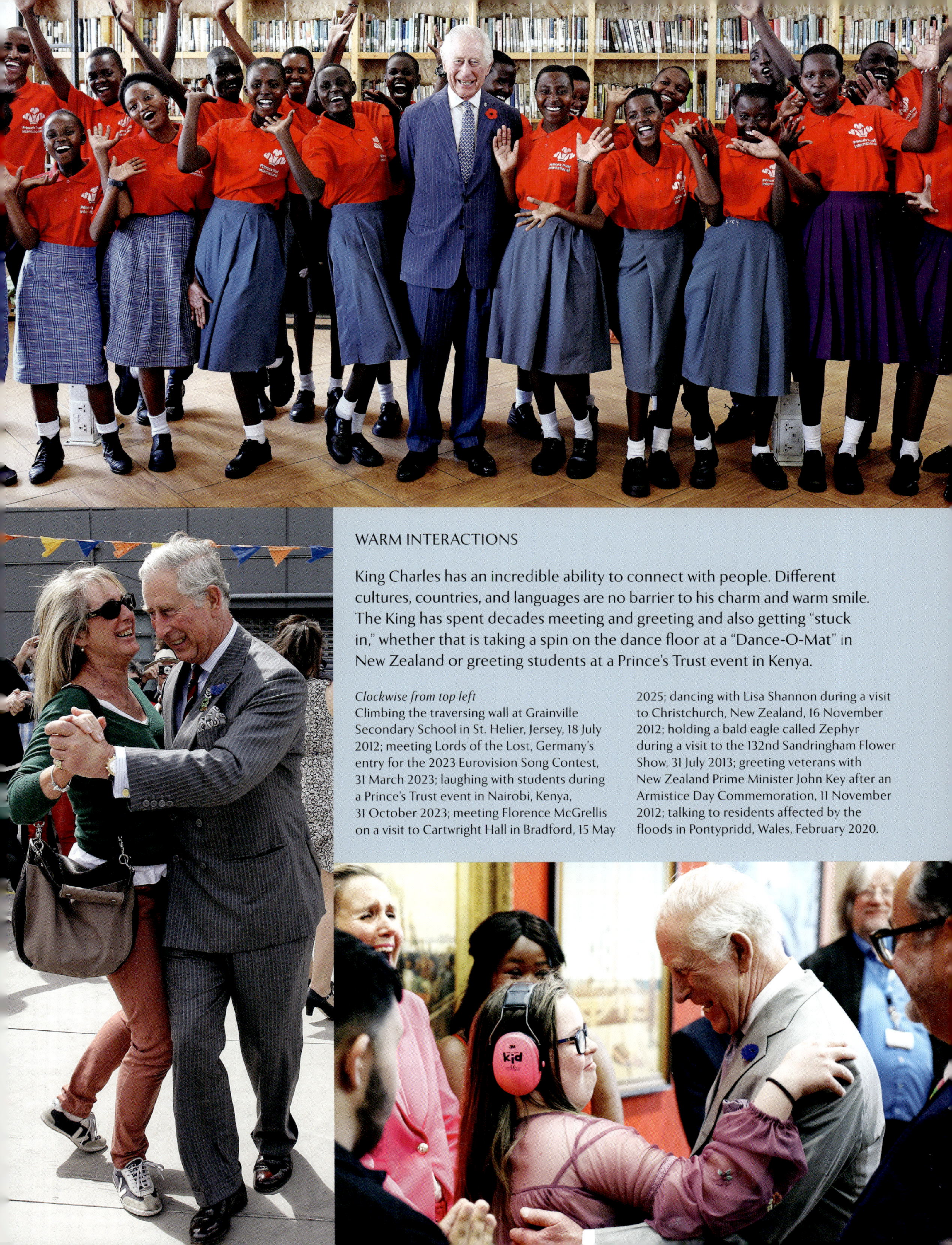

WARM INTERACTIONS

King Charles has an incredible ability to connect with people. Different cultures, countries, and languages are no barrier to his charm and warm smile. The King has spent decades meeting and greeting and also getting "stuck in," whether that is taking a spin on the dance floor at a "Dance-O-Mat" in New Zealand or greeting students at a Prince's Trust event in Kenya.

Clockwise from top left
Climbing the traversing wall at Grainville Secondary School in St. Helier, Jersey, 18 July 2012; meeting Lords of the Lost, Germany's entry for the 2023 Eurovision Song Contest, 31 March 2023; laughing with students during a Prince's Trust event in Nairobi, Kenya, 31 October 2023; meeting Florence McGrellis on a visit to Cartwright Hall in Bradford, 15 May 2025; dancing with Lisa Shannon during a visit to Christchurch, New Zealand, 16 November 2012; holding a bald eagle called Zephyr during a visit to the 132nd Sandringham Flower Show, 31 July 2013; greeting veterans with New Zealand Prime Minister John Key after an Armistice Day Commemoration, 11 November 2012; talking to residents affected by the floods in Pontypridd, Wales, February 2020.

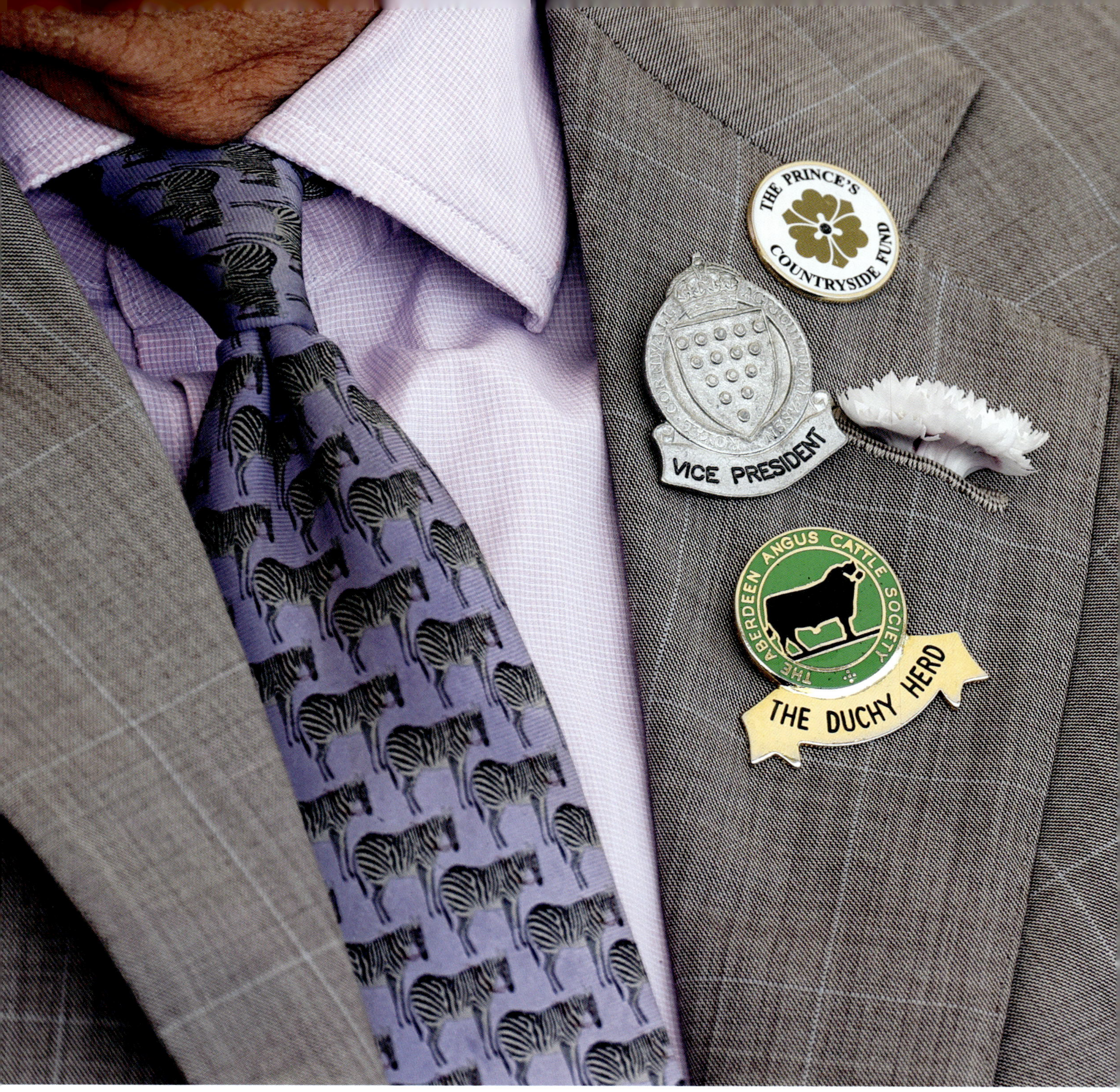

THE COUNTRYSIDE

A man who clearly feels at home in the country, King Charles is passionate about organic farming, rewilding, and supporting farmers and the countryside community. He is pictured here in a meadow of wildflowers at his Welsh home of Llwynywermod, just outside the Brecon Beacons National Park in Carmarthenshire, which was purchased by the Duchy of Cornwall for use by Charles when he was Prince of Wales.

Overleaf
King Charles poses for a portrait under an ancient tree in Windsor Great Park as he is announced Park Ranger, a role he inherited from his father, Prince Philip, who oversaw the protection and maintenance of the park for over 70 years, 11 November 2022.

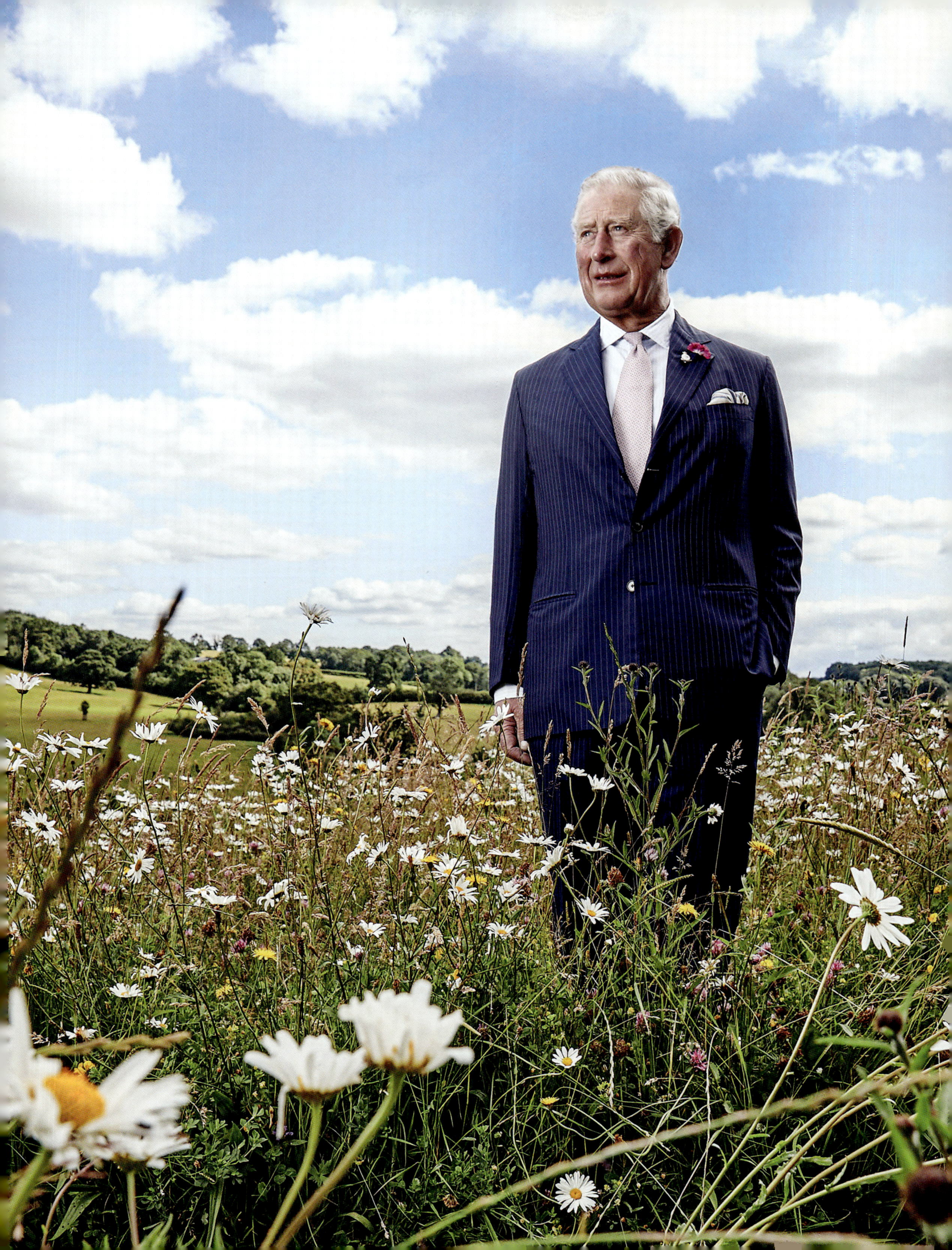

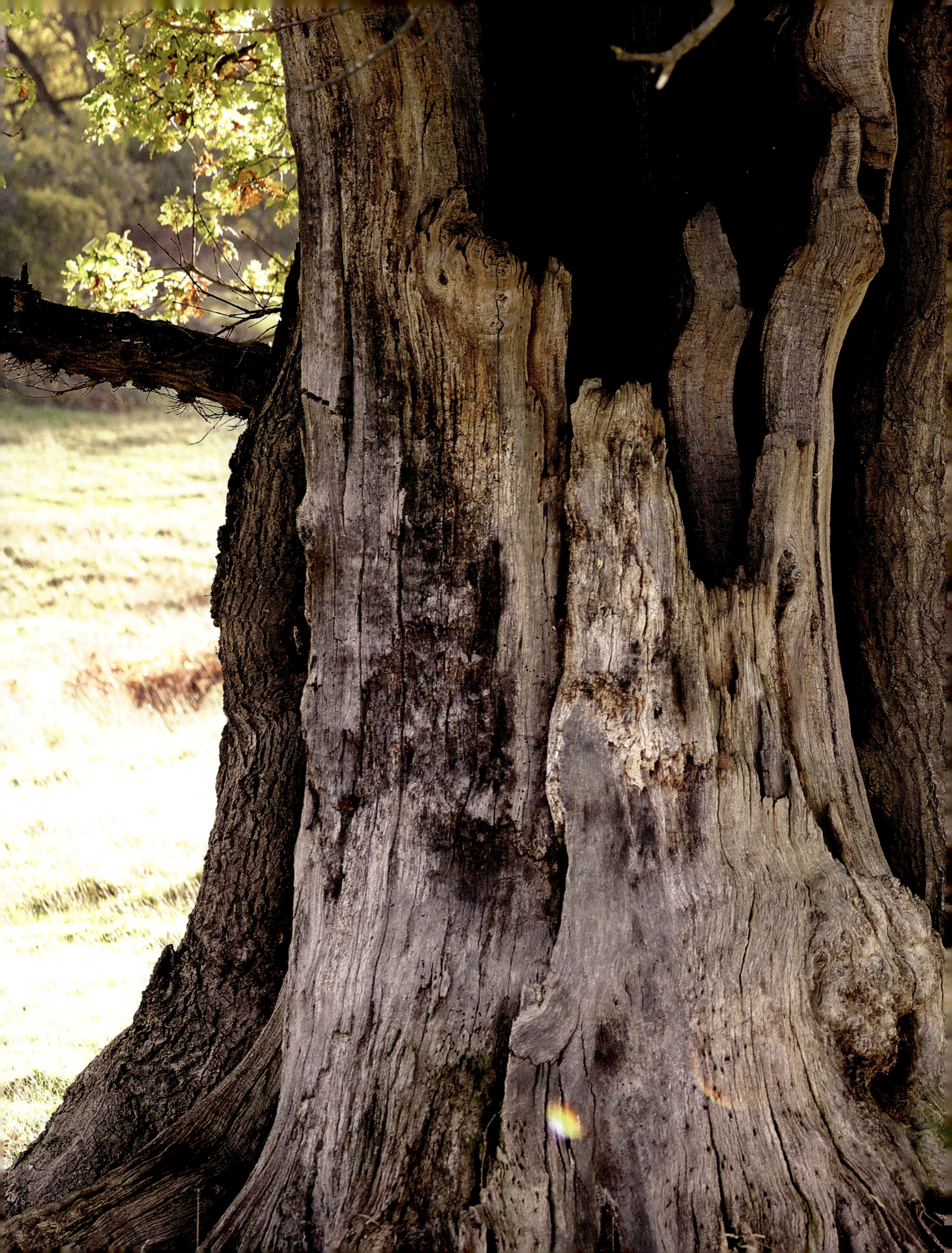

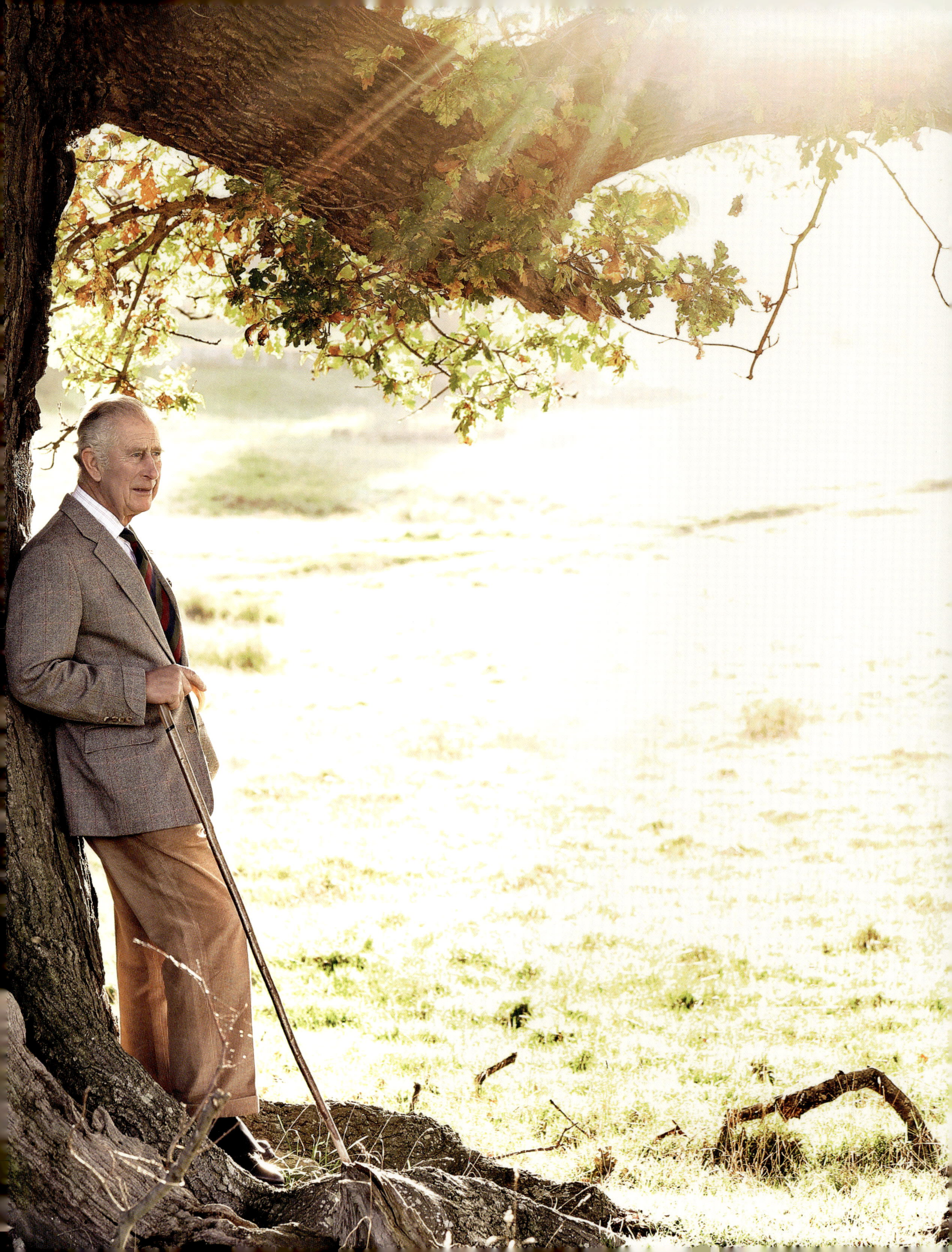

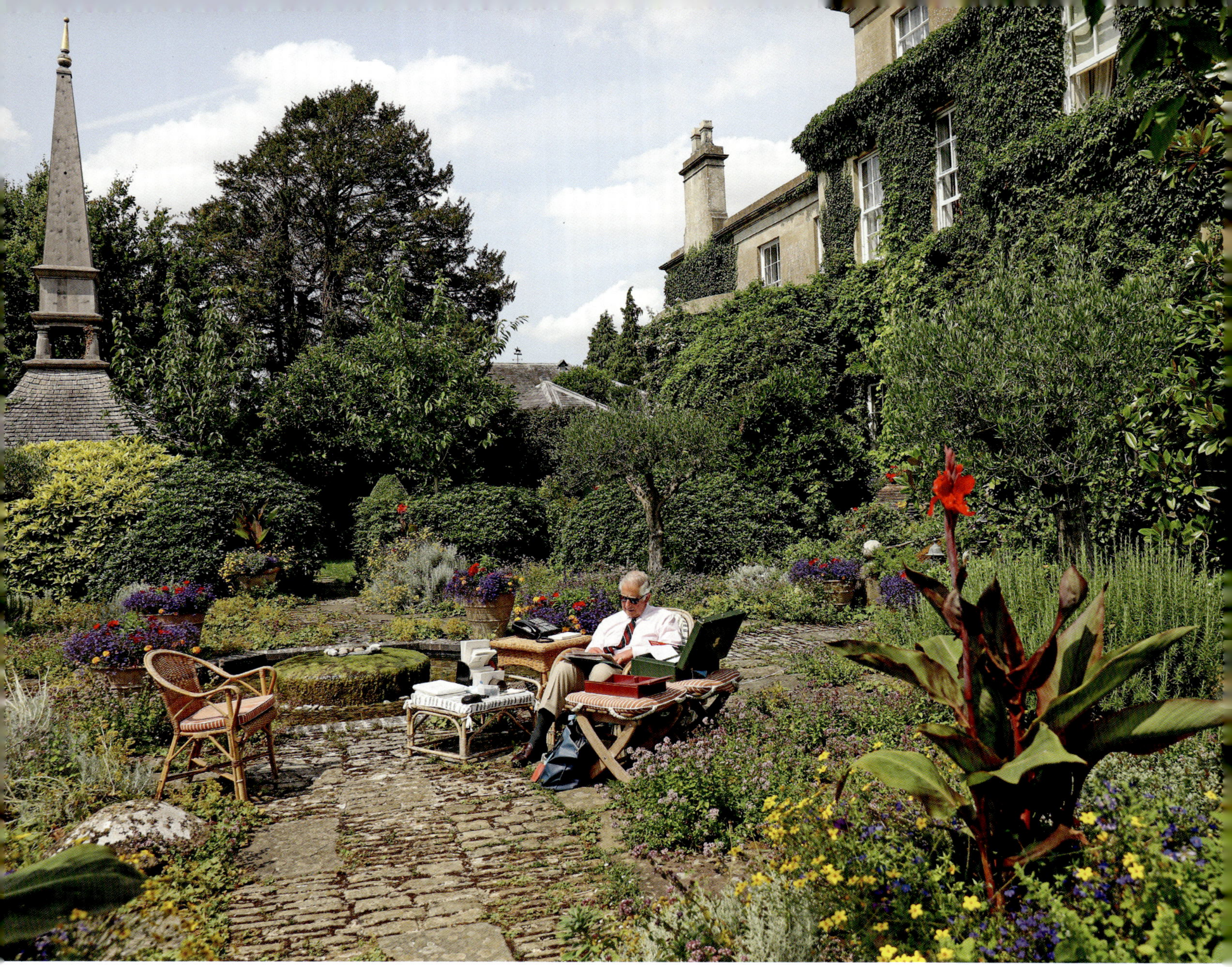

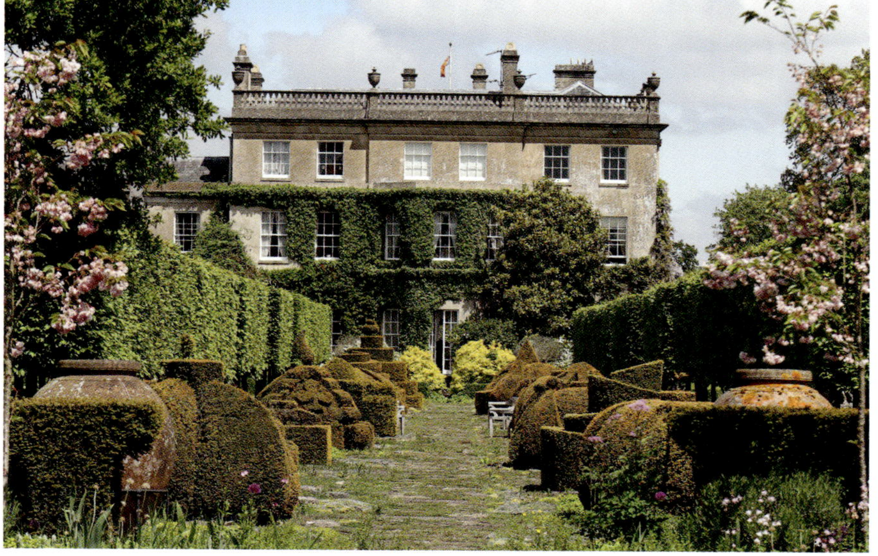

HIGHGROVE HOUSE

This Gloucestershire bolthole has always been a special place of retreat for King Charles and Queen Camilla. The King acquired Highgrove House in 1980 and has spent much of his time transforming the gardens into spectacular grounds that have a global influence inspired by the King's travels. Here, the golden yews along Thyme Walk have been clipped into a series of unusual shapes. When the King is in residence, he is often spotted feeding his prize-winning Burford Brown and Maran chickens first thing in the morning.

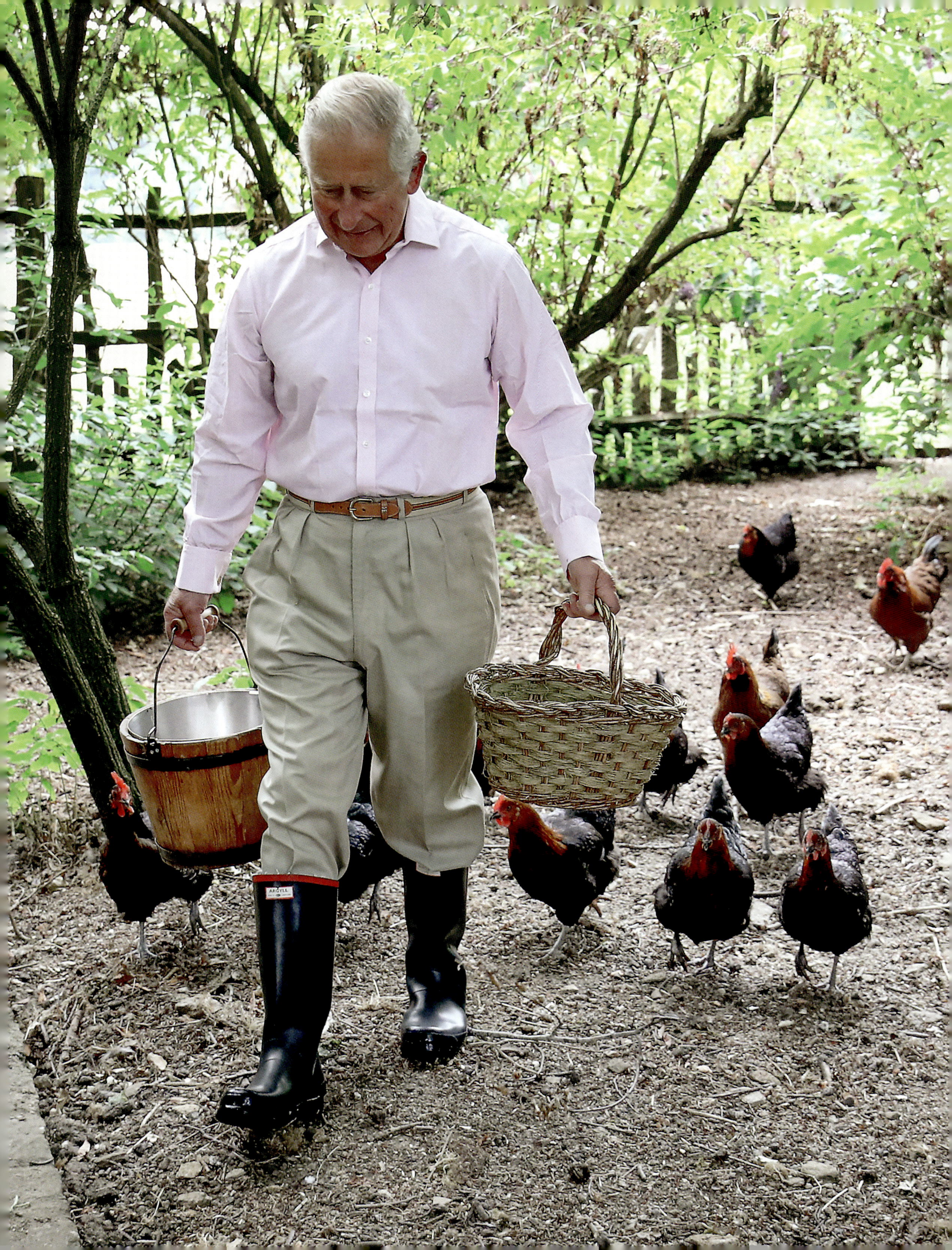

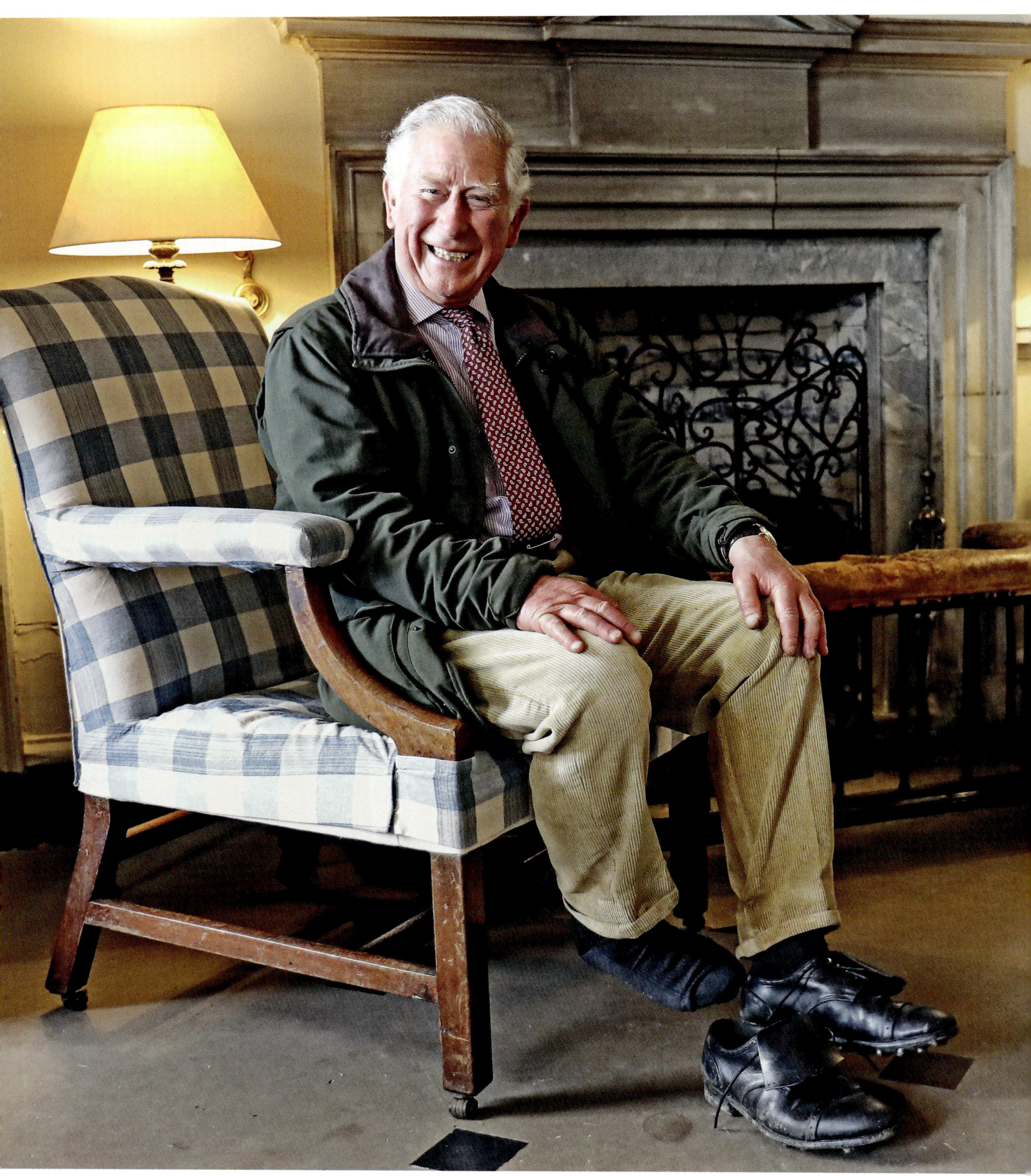

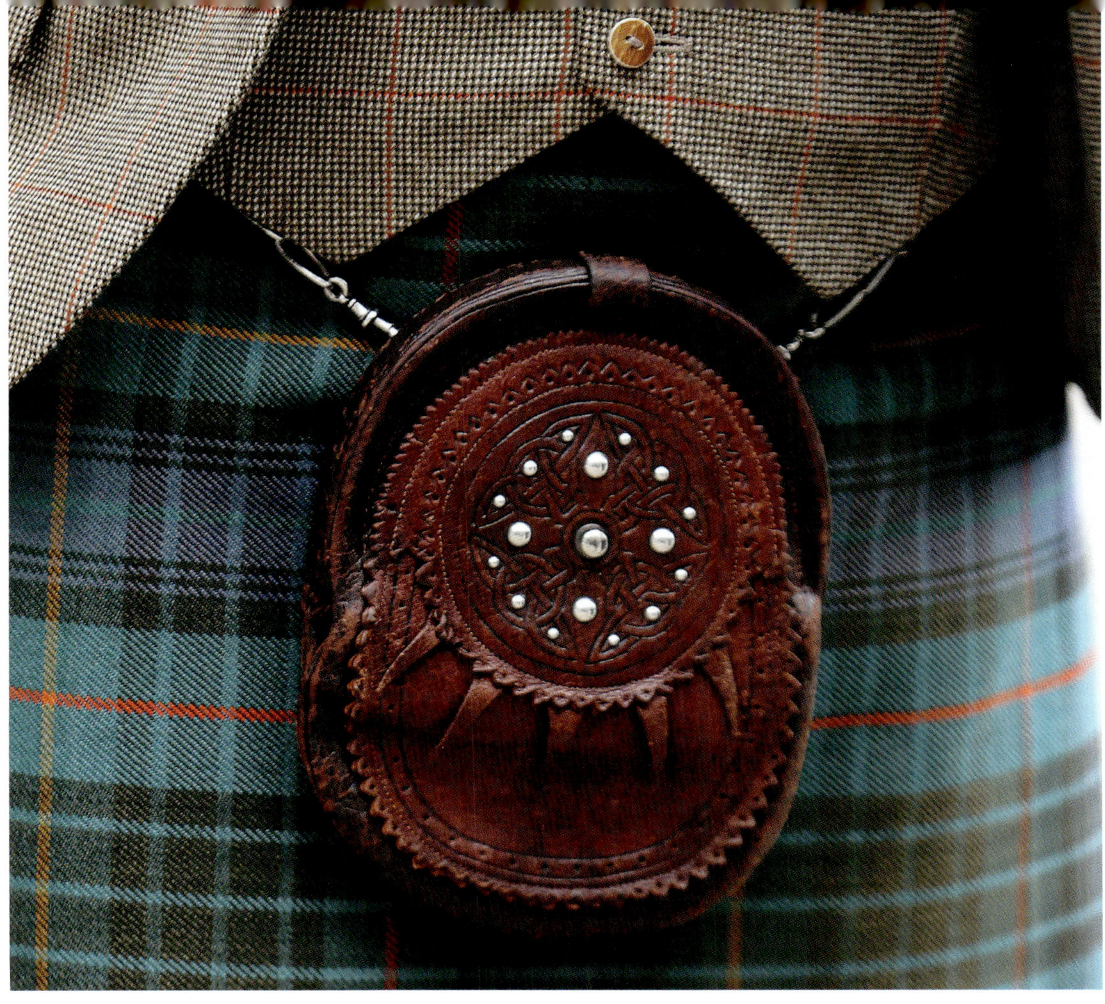

Opposite
After an afternoon walk around the grounds of Dumfries House, 3 May 2018.

Above
The sporran is a traditional part of Scottish dress, working in much the same way as a pocket when wearing a kilt.

Below
The comfort of patched Oxford shoes worn with a suit.

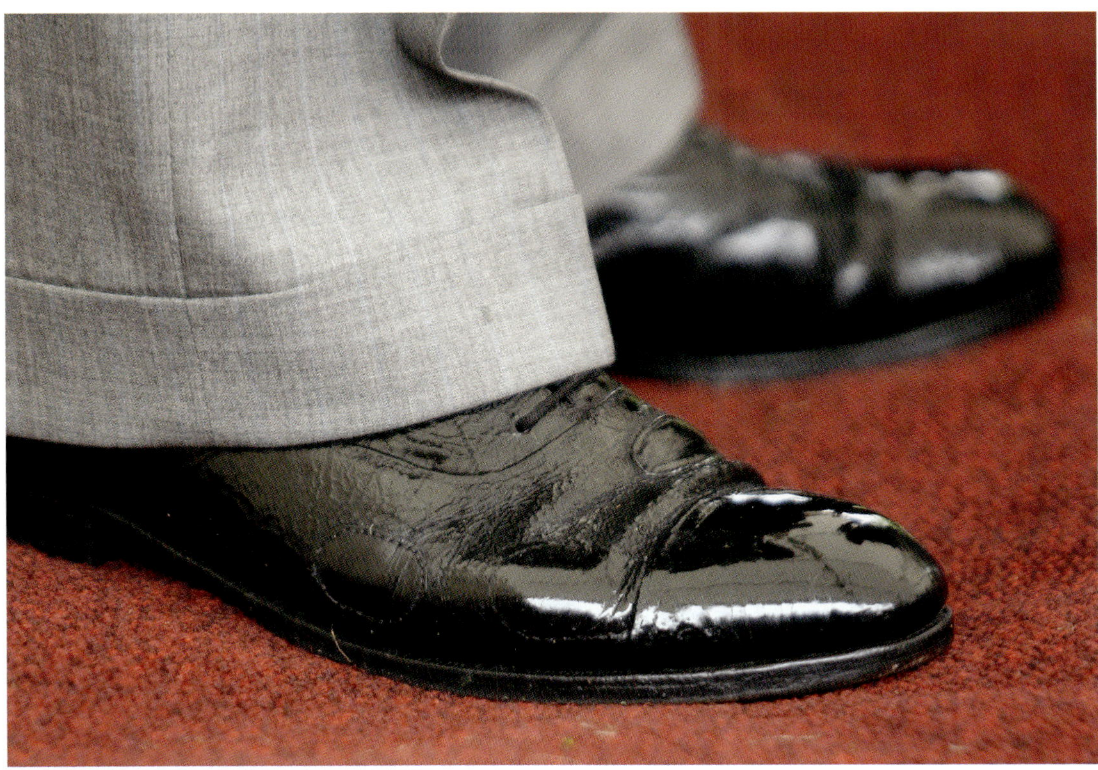

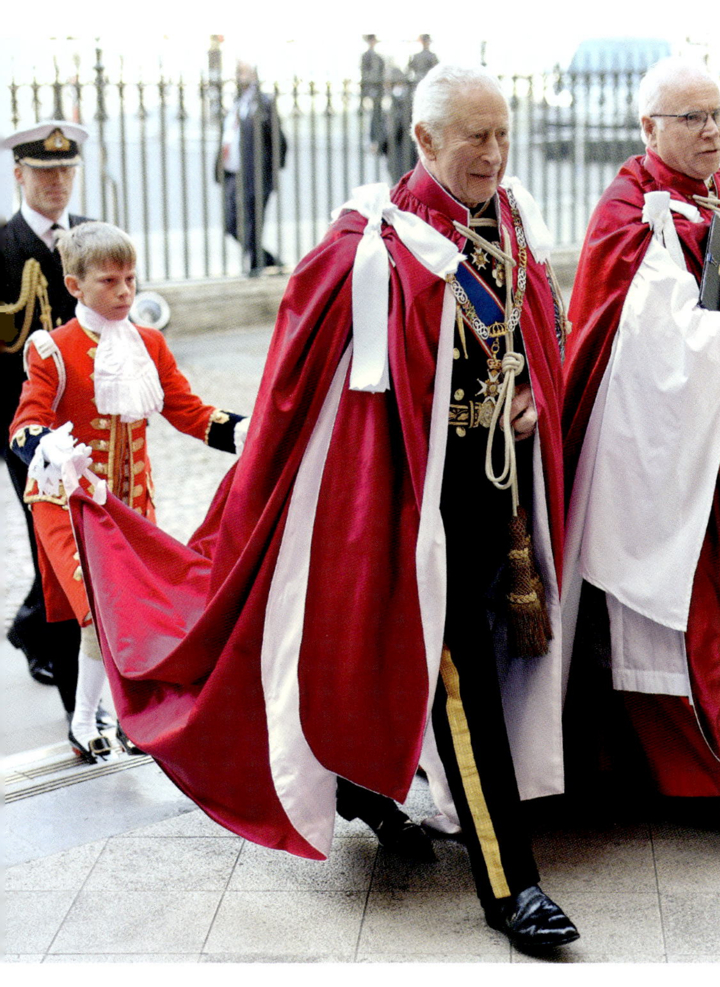

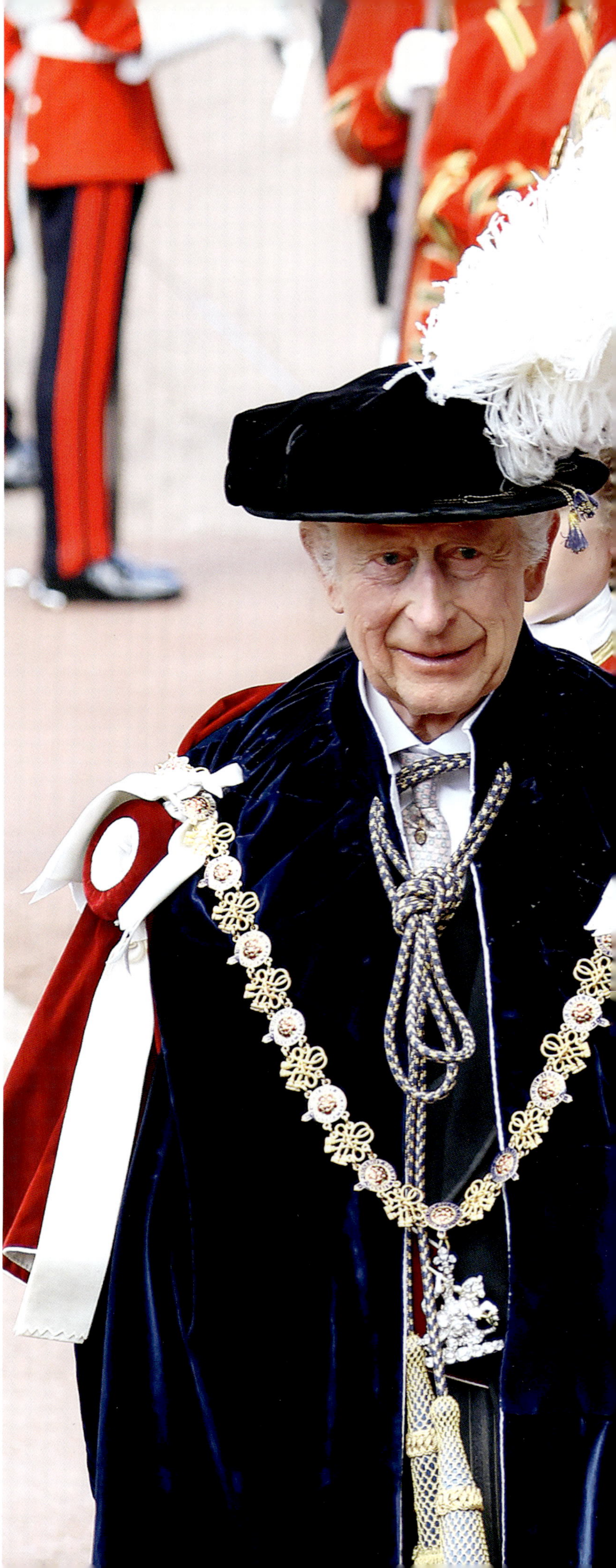

CEREMONIAL DUTIES

Ancient orders of chivalry form a critical and unique part of King Charles's and Queen Camilla's duties. Centuries of British history and customs are woven into the ceremonial outfits worn to these events. Beneath the feathers, velvet, and tassels, the importance of upholding these traditions is a key part of the monarch's role. The Order of the Garter was established by Edward III and is the country's oldest chivalric order. The Order of the Bath is a special Order of Knights that recognizes the work of senior military officials and civil servants.

Above
The monarch arrives at the Order of the Bath Service at Westminster Abbey, 16 May 2025.

Right
King Charles III and Queen Camilla attend the Order of the Garter Service at Windsor Castle, 17 June 2024.

Overleaf
King Charles III and Queen Camilla at the State Opening of Parliament, 17 July 2024.

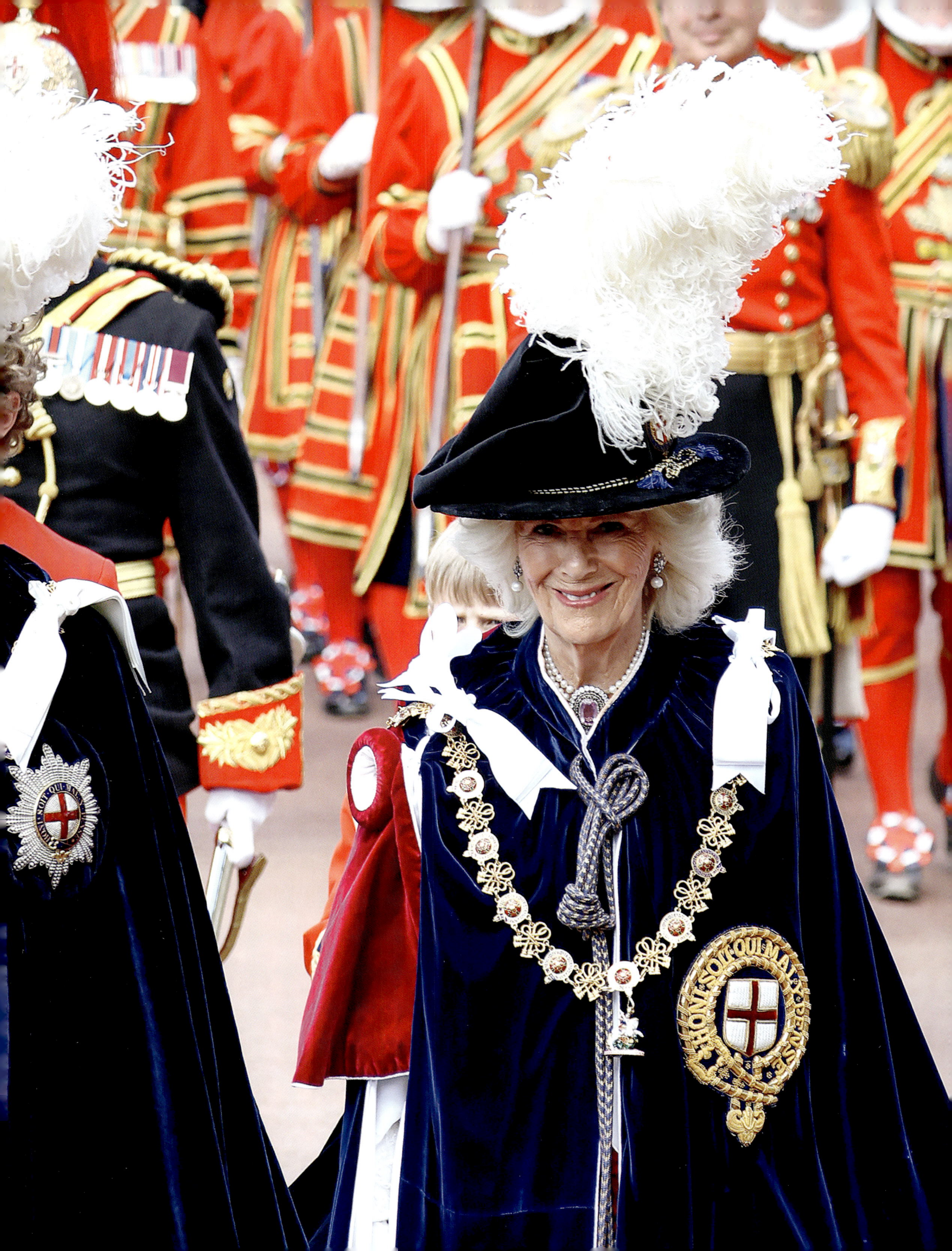
HONI SOIT QUI MAL Y PENSE

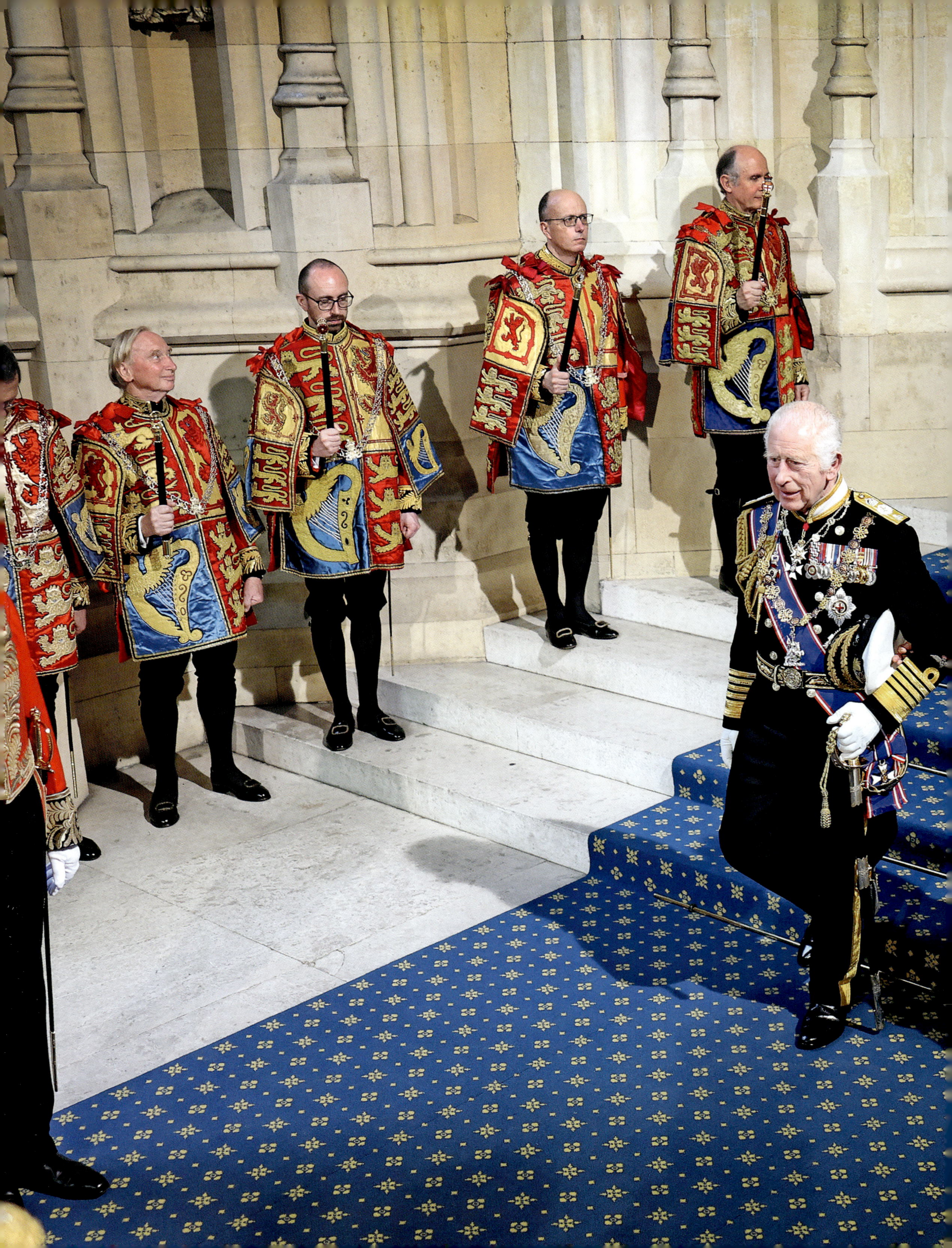

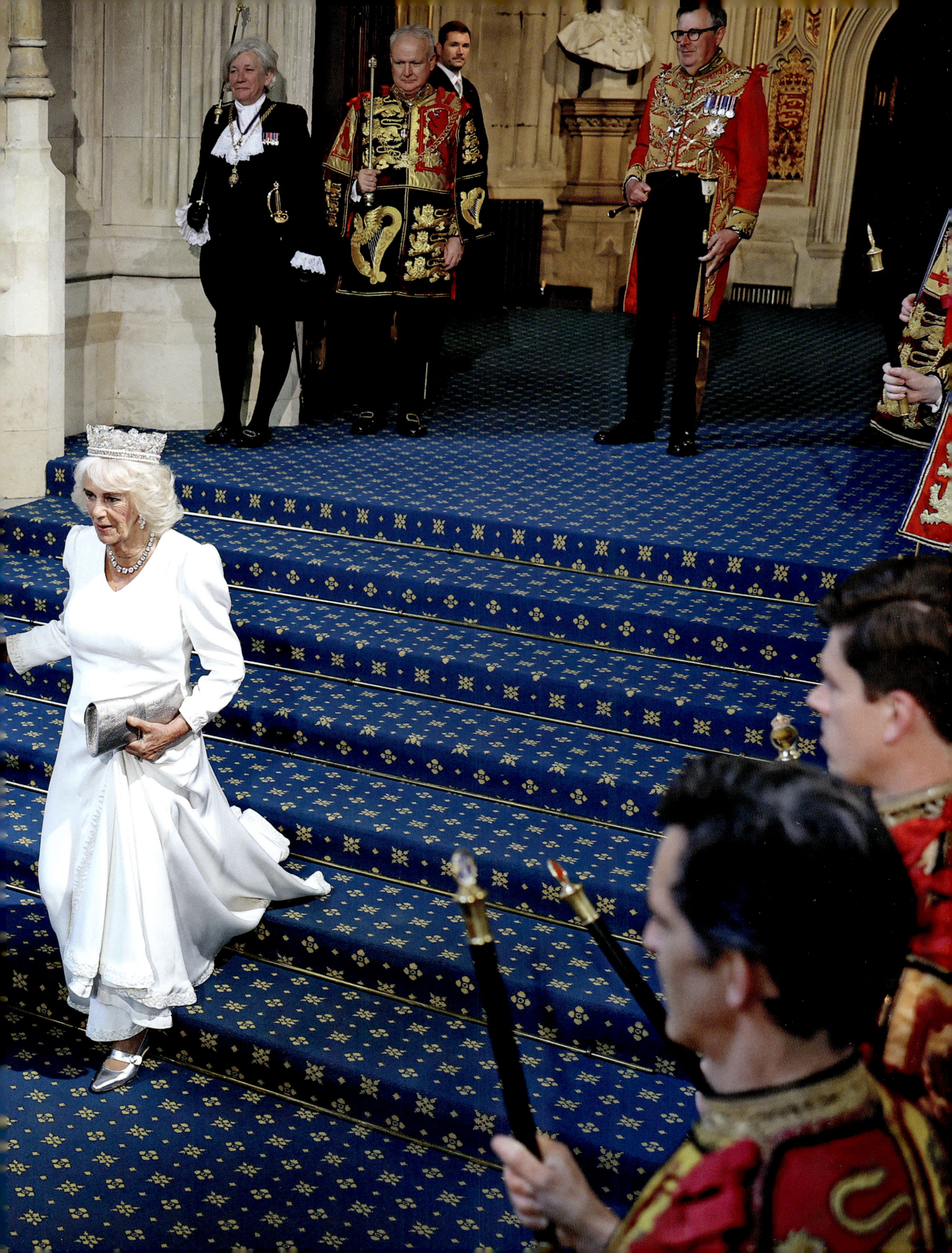

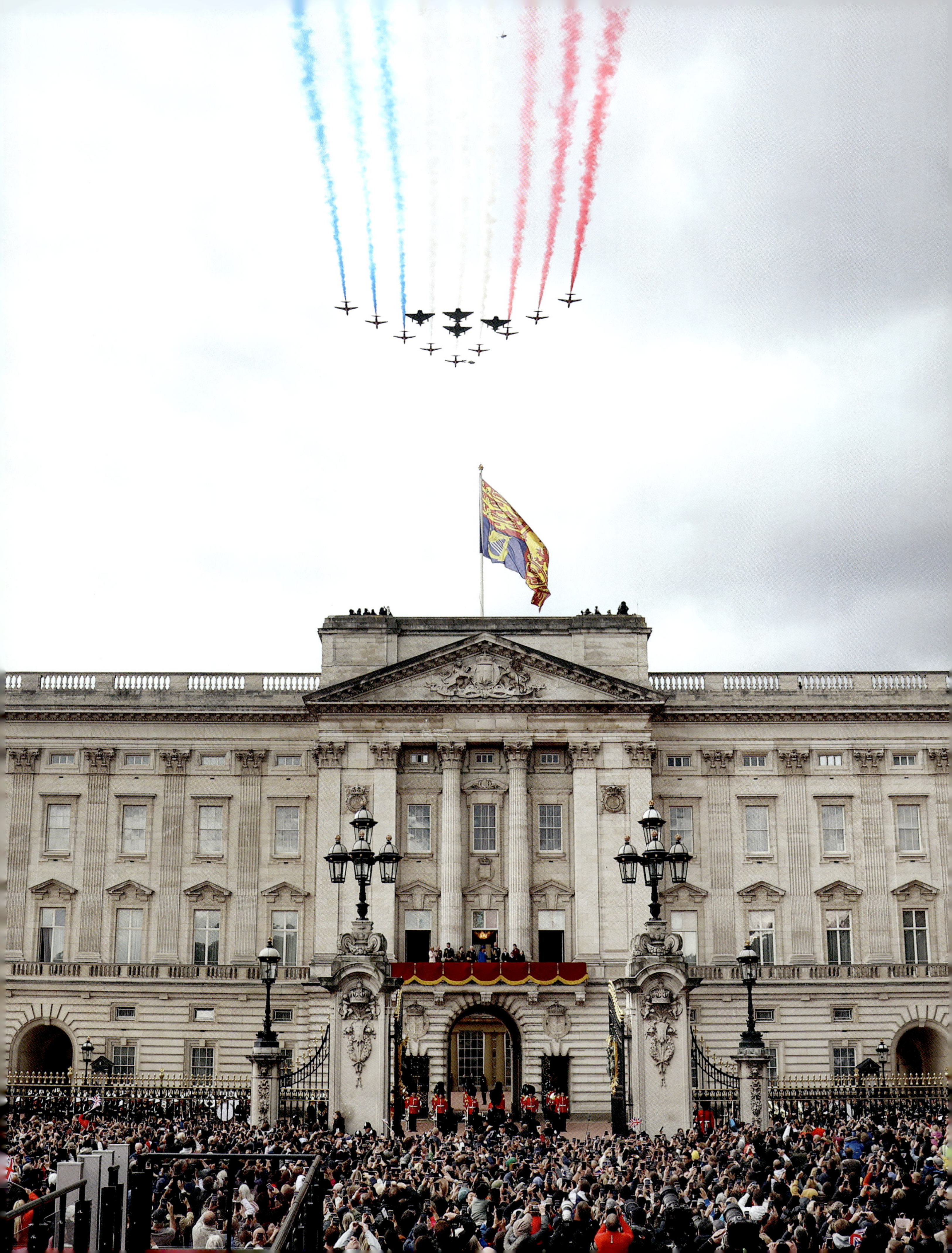

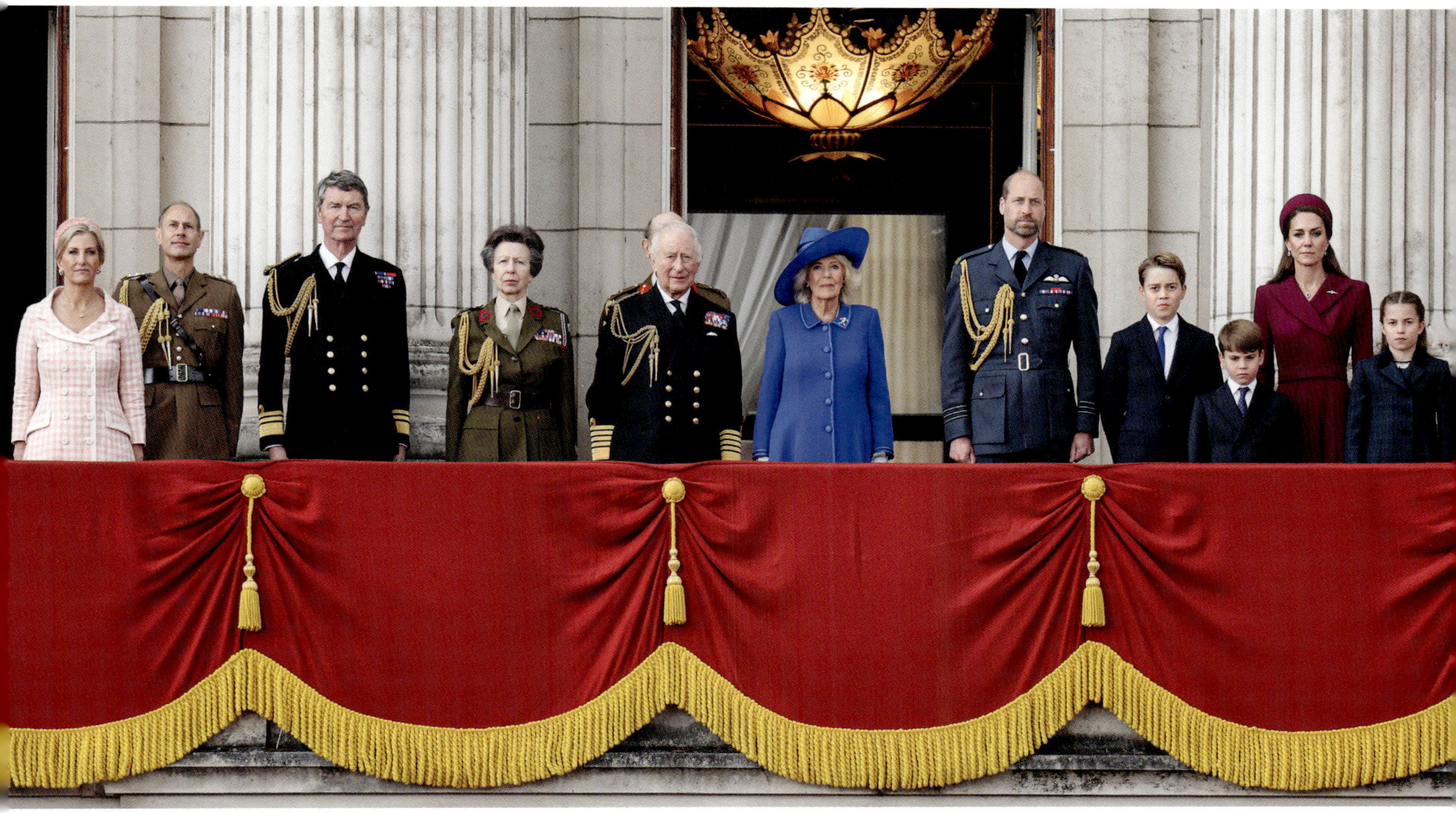

VE DAY COMMEMORATIONS

On 8 May 1945, known as VE Day (Victory in Europe Day), people across the United Kingdom came together to celebrate the end of the Second World War. In 2025, the country joined Their Majesties the King and Queen and other members of the royal family to commemorate the 80th anniversary of VE Day. Events began with a military procession through London followed by a dramatic RAF flypast. Bomber pilot Harry Richardson, aged 107, attended the event and joined the King and Queen at a concert to mark this momentous occasion.

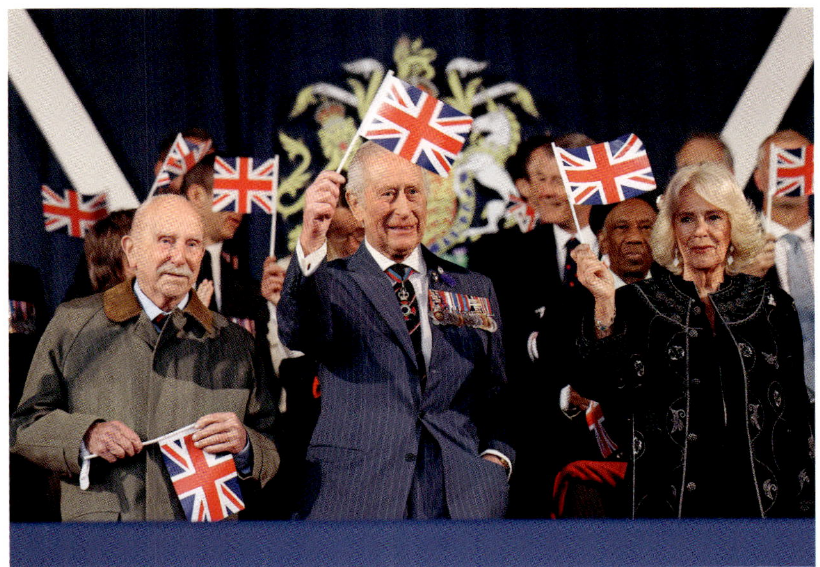

Opposite and top
The Red Arrows fly over Buckingham Palace as the royal family watch the military procession from the balcony, 5 May 2025.

Above
Second World War bomber pilot Harry Richardson, who was awarded the Distinguished Flying Cross for his bravery and his airmanship, stands next to the King and Queen at a celebratory concert at Horse Guards Parade, 8 May 2025.

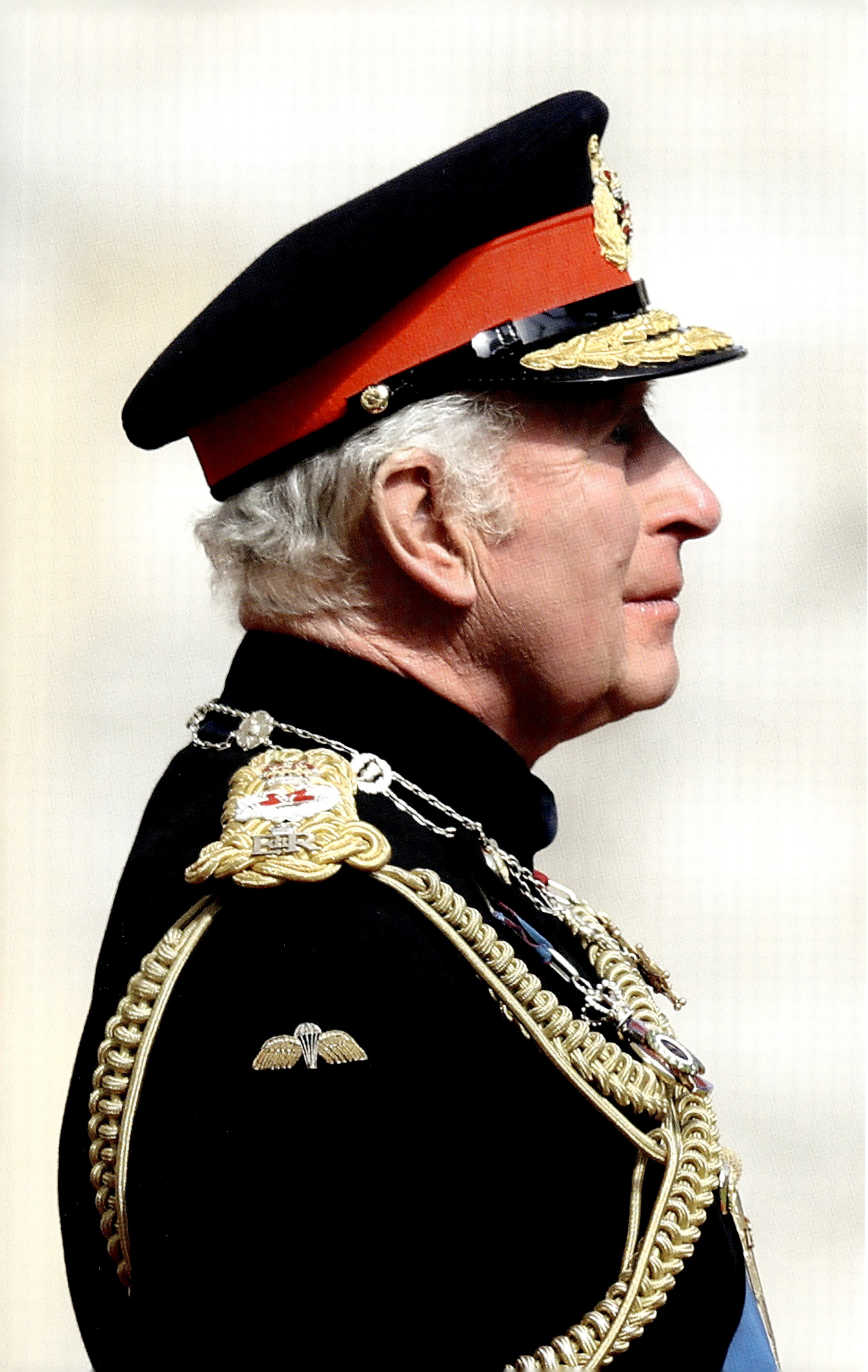

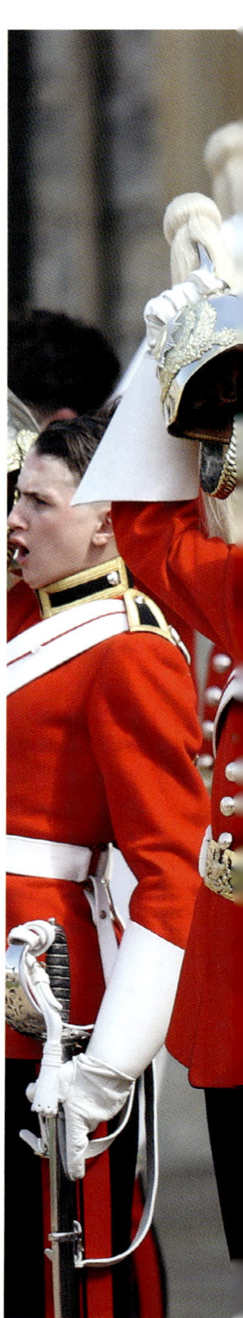

MILITARY DUTIES

Soldiers' cheers reverberate around the ancient walls of the quadrangle at Windsor Castle as the Life Guards raise their plumed helmets in acknowledgement of their King who, clearly moved, looks on from a dais. On a hot day in May 2025, His Majesty presented new colours (ceremonial flags) to the Life Guards and to the Blues and Royals regiments.

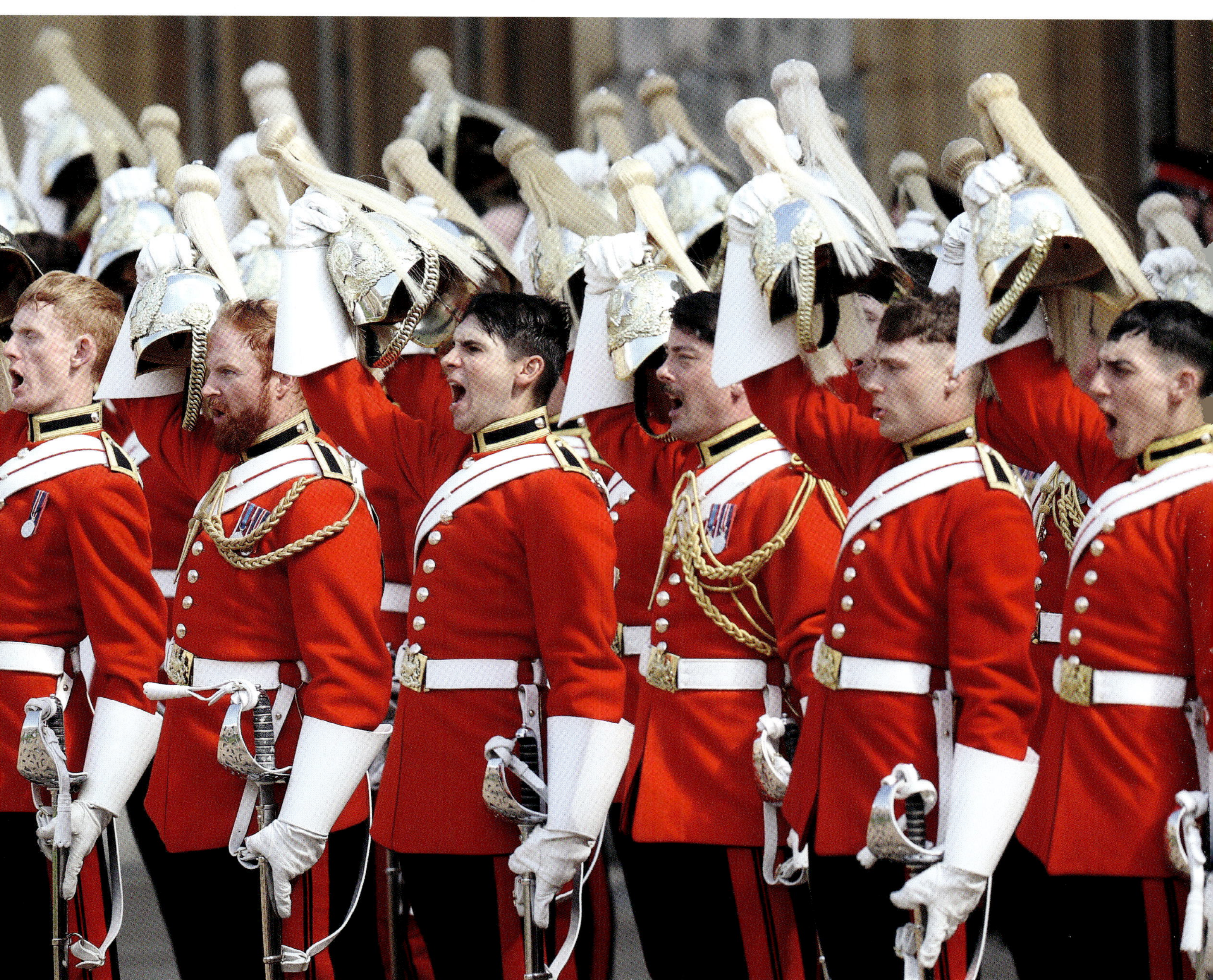

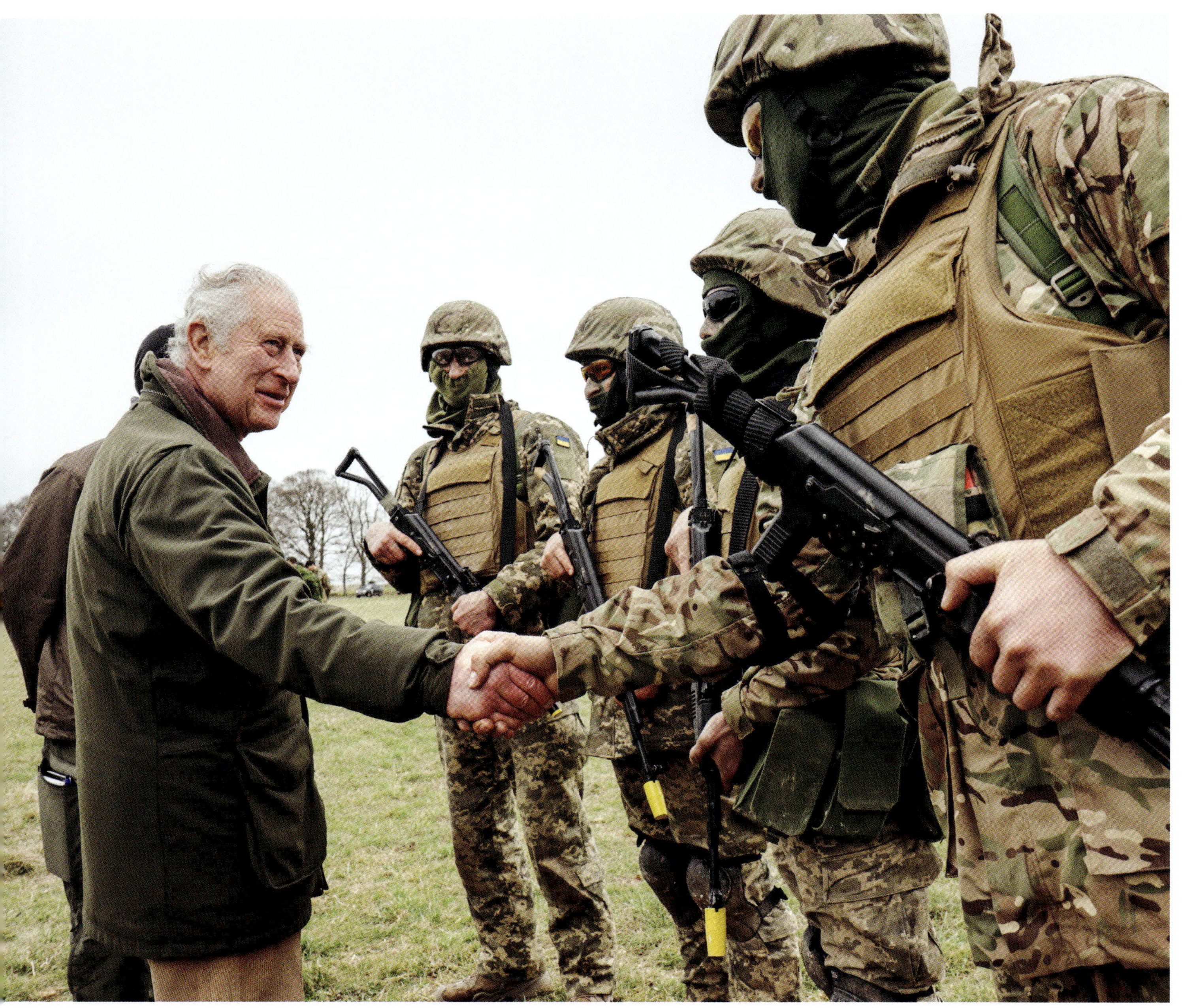

Above
King Charles III meets Ukrainian recruits who are completing five weeks of basic combat training, 20 February 2023.

Opposite
The King walks past the guard of honour at the Ceremony of the Keys in Edinburgh, an ancient tradition whereby the Lord Provost welcomes the King and offers him the keys of the city at the Palace of Holyroodhouse, 3 July 2023.

Overleaf
Queen Camilla, King Charles III, Prince William, Prince of Wales, and Catherine, Princess of Wales, pose for a portrait ahead of the Diplomatic Reception in the 1844 Room at Buckingham Palace, 5 December 2023.

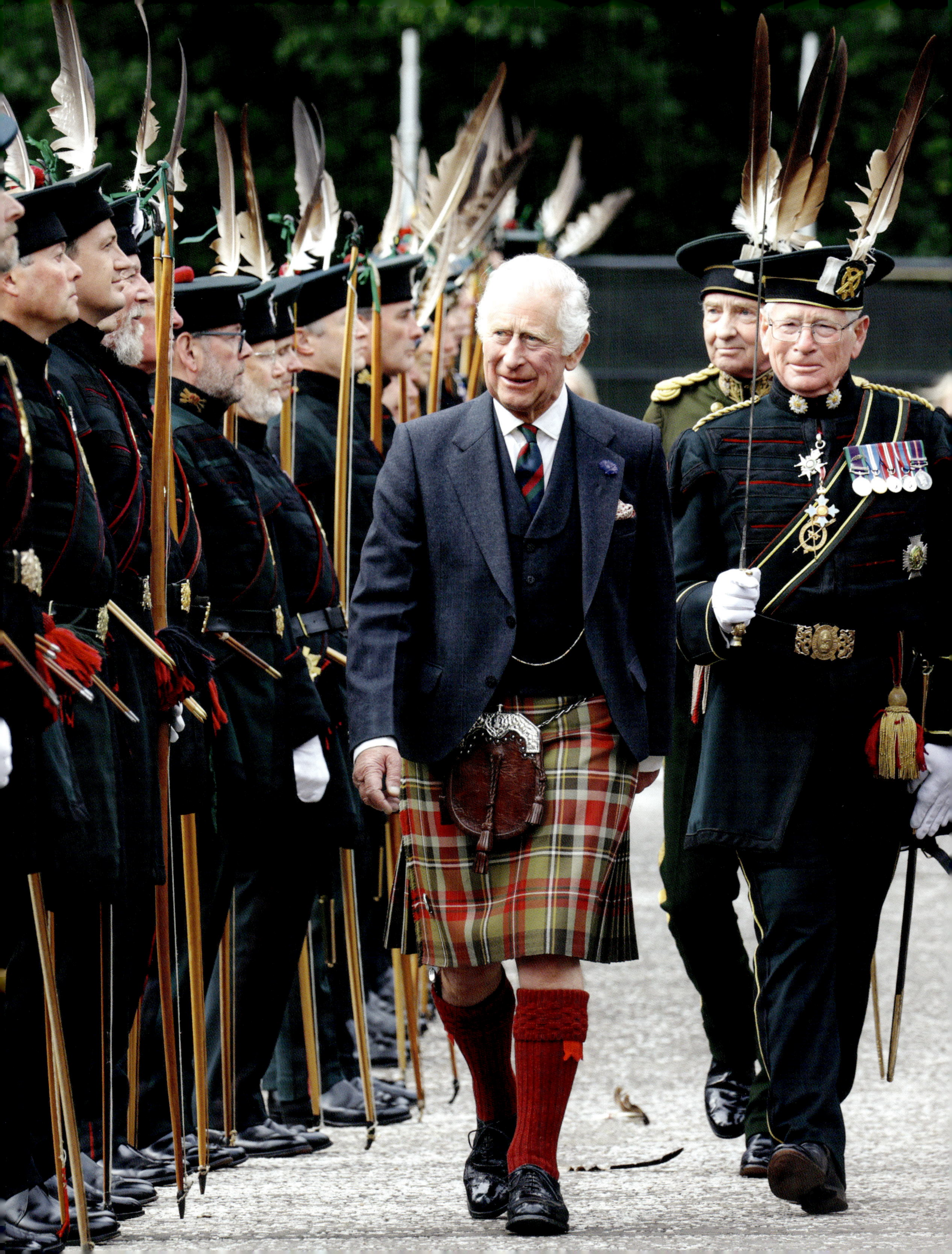

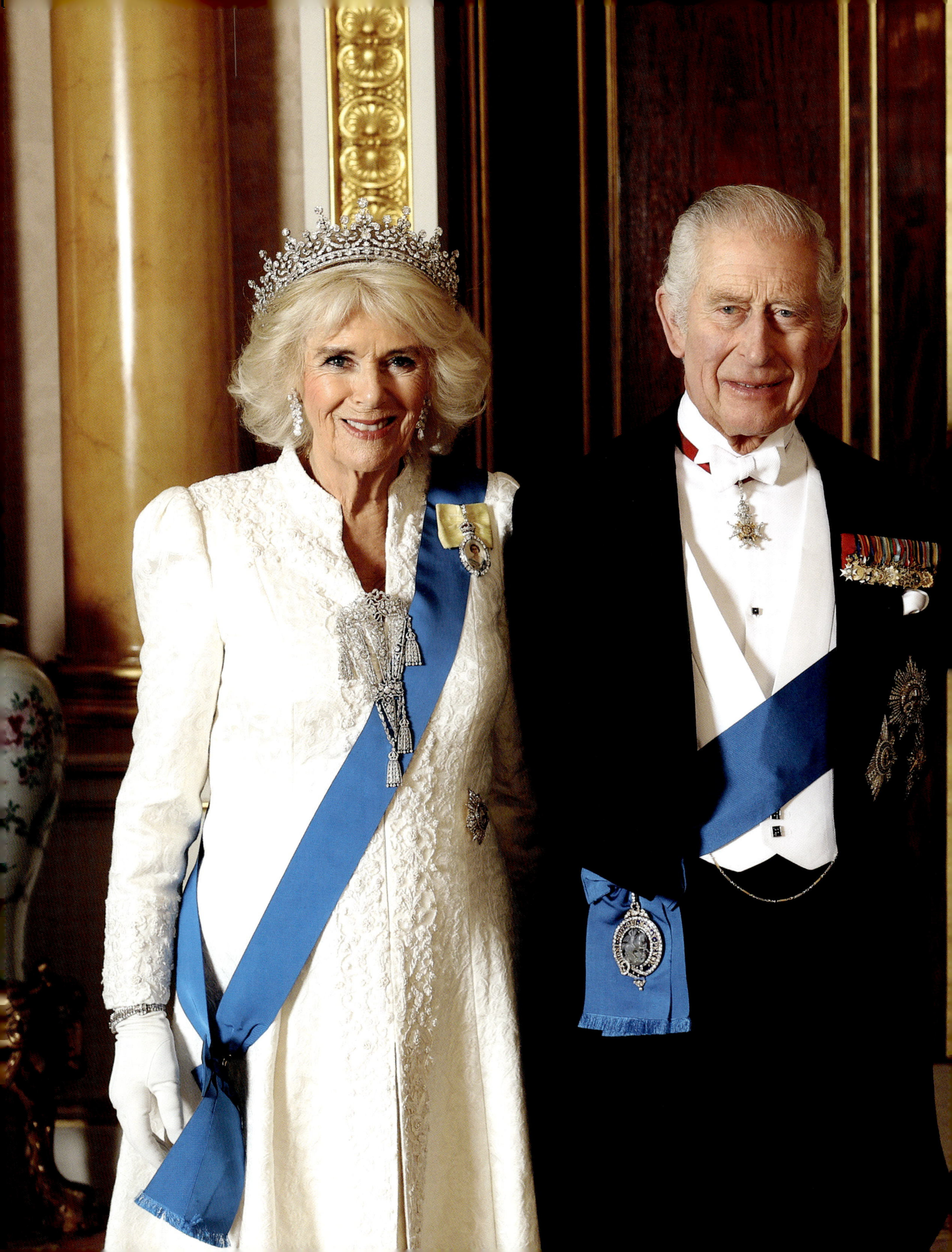

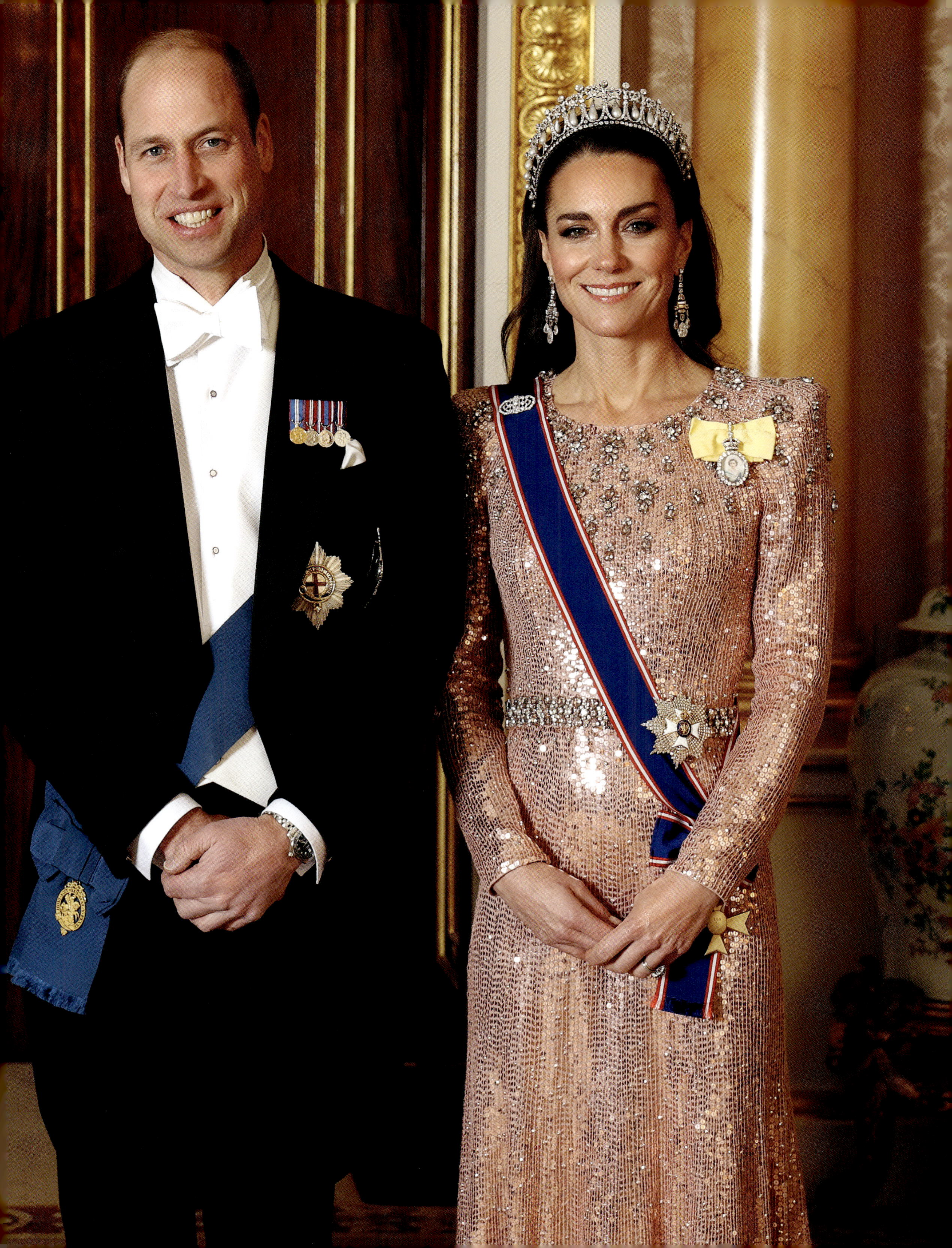

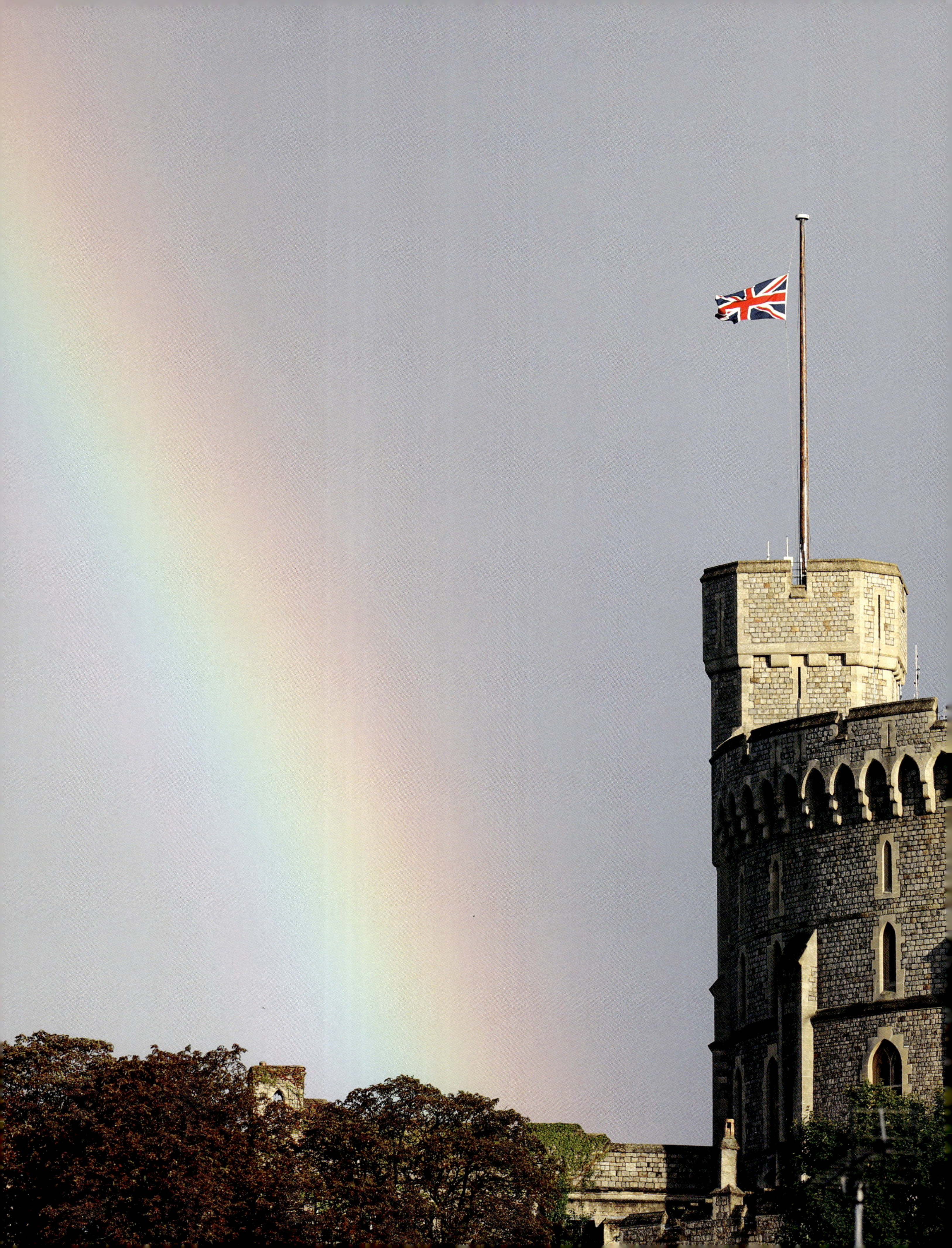

2

STRENGTH IN ADVERSITY

Recent years have presented the British royal family with several significant challenges. The first was the passing of the cherished sovereign Queen Elizabeth at the age of 96. During a 70-year reign that witnessed enormous social change, she had brought comfort and stability through her devotion to a life of service to her country. Then to see King Charles III struck down by cancer less than two years into his reign, and to learn that the Princess of Wales was experiencing her own health struggle during the same period, was a crushing blow for the institution.

Navigating these times could have provoked one of the biggest crises the modern monarchy had faced. Yet the way the family rallied round, and the adaptability and resilience of the royal household, ensured a continuity of service in the face of personal circumstances. The dignity and messaging around the difficult subject of illness is a case in point, with both the Princess and the King expressing their gratitude to the public and medical staff, and showing a selflessness in sharing their diagnoses in the hope of assisting public understanding of the disease. The bounceback in recent months, with both operating incredibly busy schedules, has shown a stellar commitment to and an inexhaustible enthusiasm for their duties.

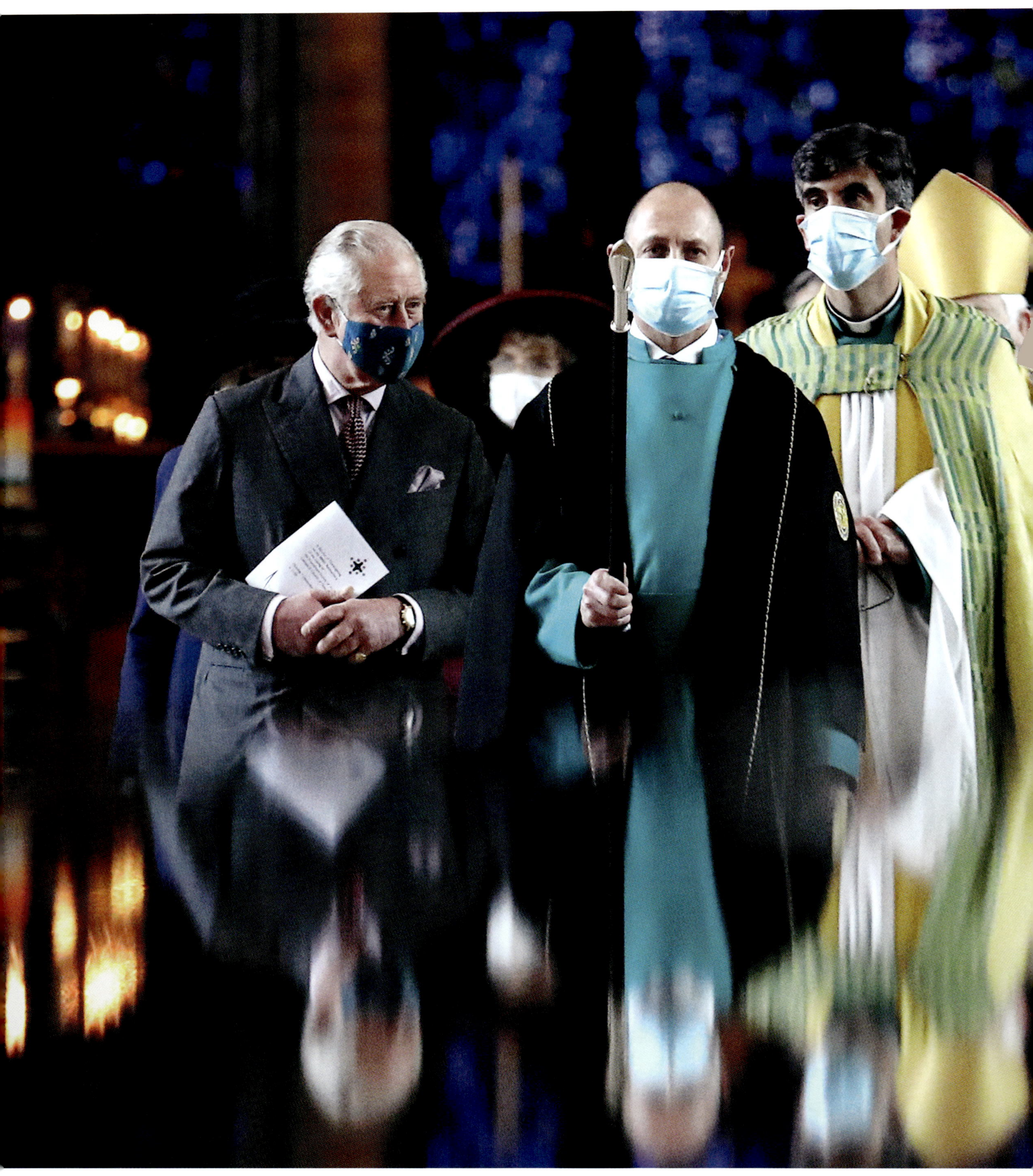

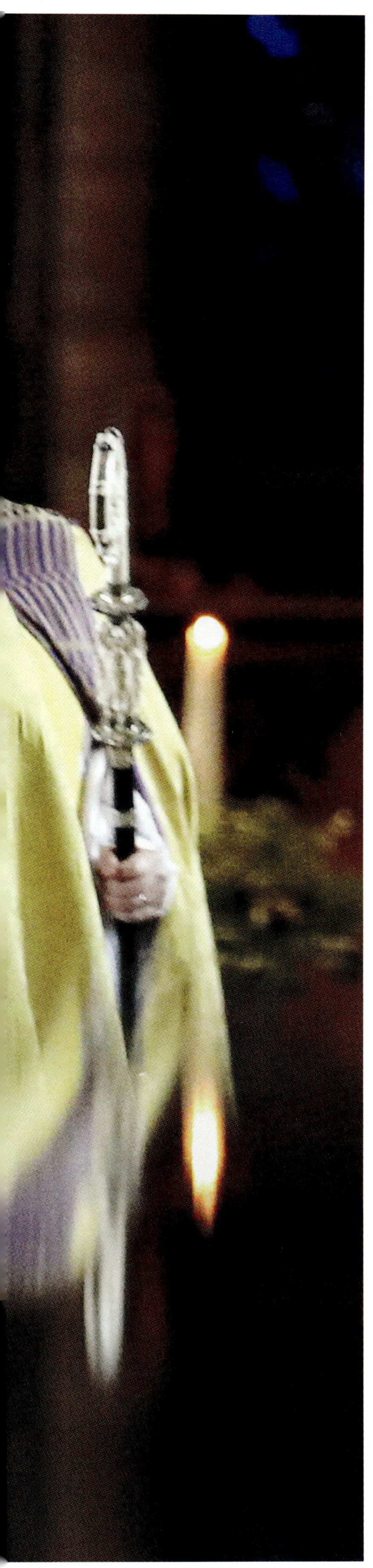

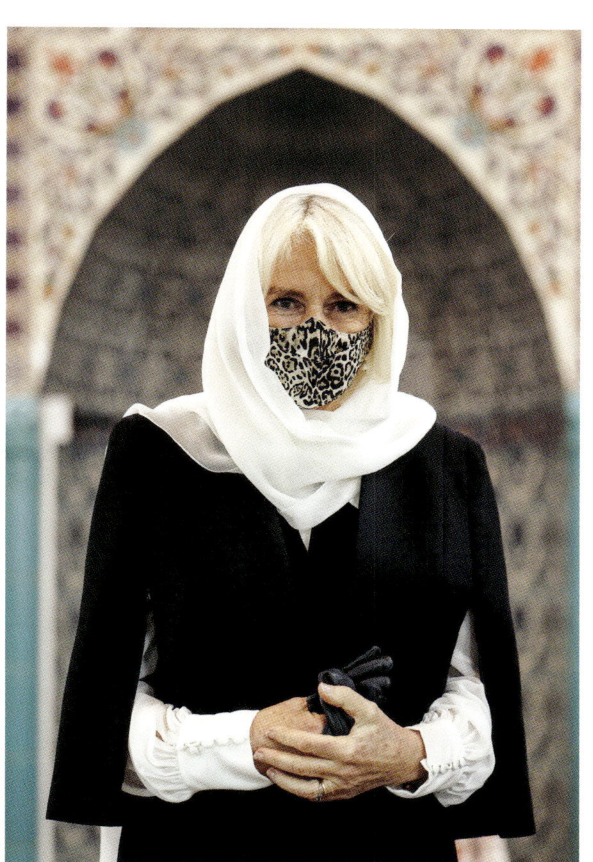

BETTER DAYS WILL RETURN

Looking back at the coronavirus pandemic, when we were told to "stay at home," it is hard to believe that way of living became normal to us. So many of us around the country and the world were struggling, lonely, could not work, had a loved one in hospital, or were ill and scared ourselves. Many people will never forget the evening that Queen Elizabeth II, appreciating the nation's fears, appeared on our television screens to proclaim, "we will meet again," a ray of hope in an otherwise bleak period, and the perfect example of how the monarch has the ability to bring the nation together and unite us in dark times.

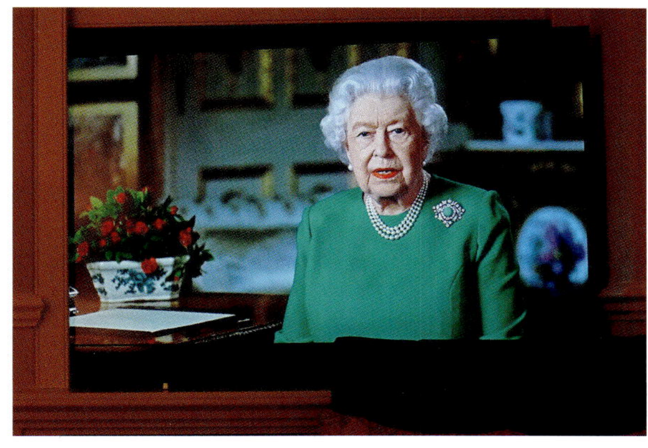

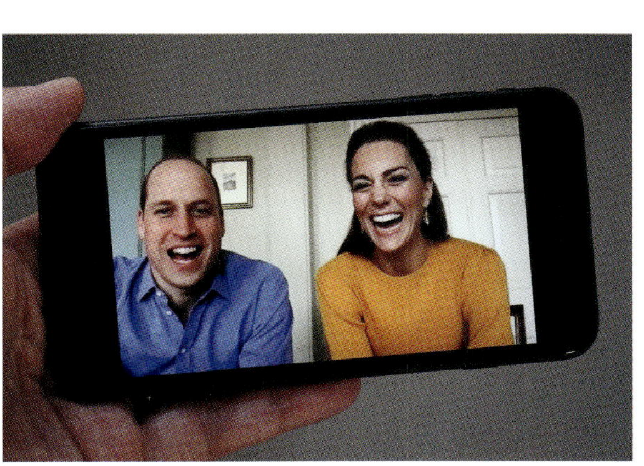

Opposite
Visiting Salisbury Cathedral in celebration of its 800th anniversary, 7 December 2020.

Left
Camilla, former Duchess of Cornwall, visits Wightman Road Mosque in north London, 7 April 2021.

Queen Elizabeth II addresses the nation in a special broadcast during the coronavirus outbreak, 5 April 2020.

A video chat with Casterton Primary Academy students, 9 April 2020.

Overleaf
Catherine at the funeral of Prince Philip at Windsor Castle, 17 April 2021.

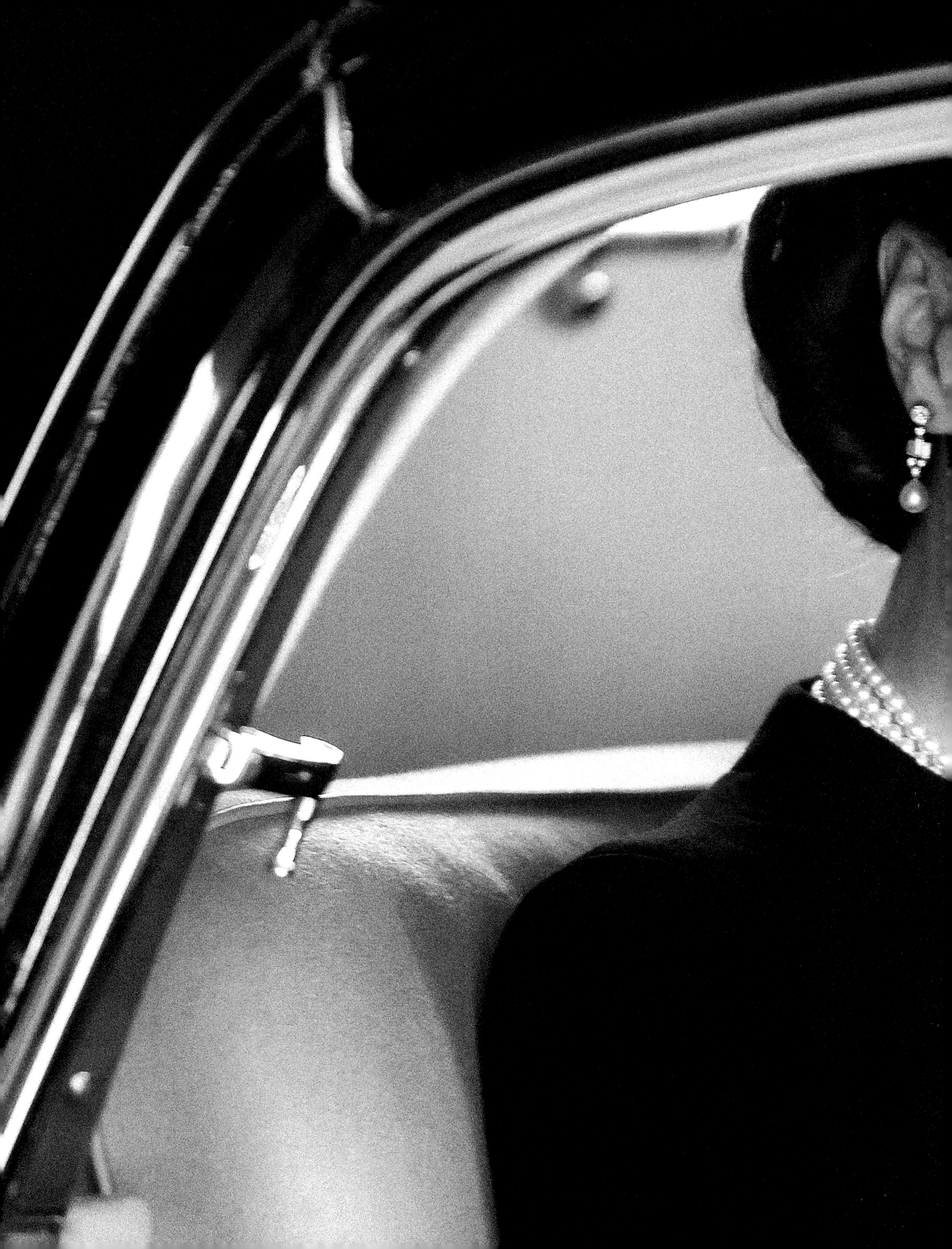

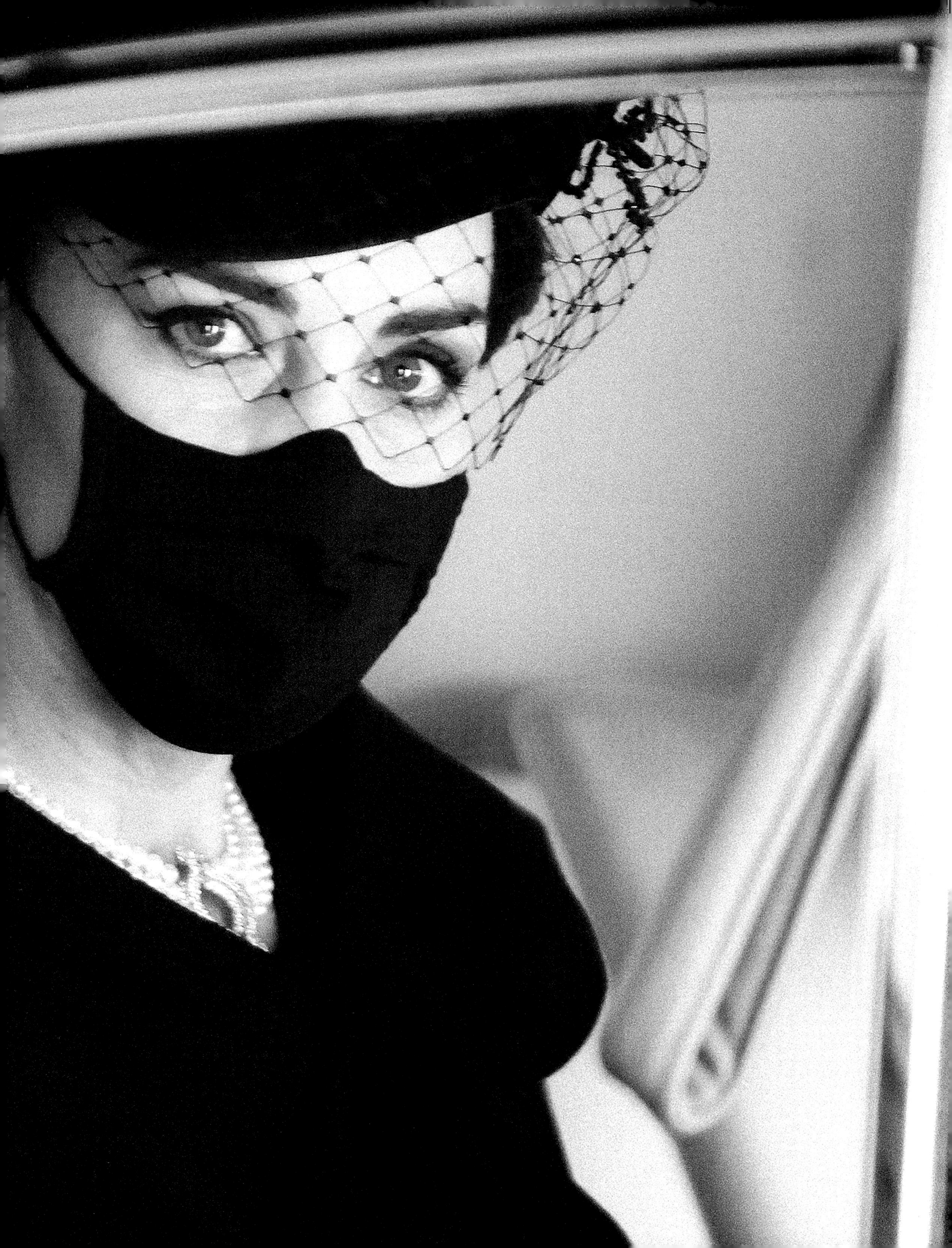

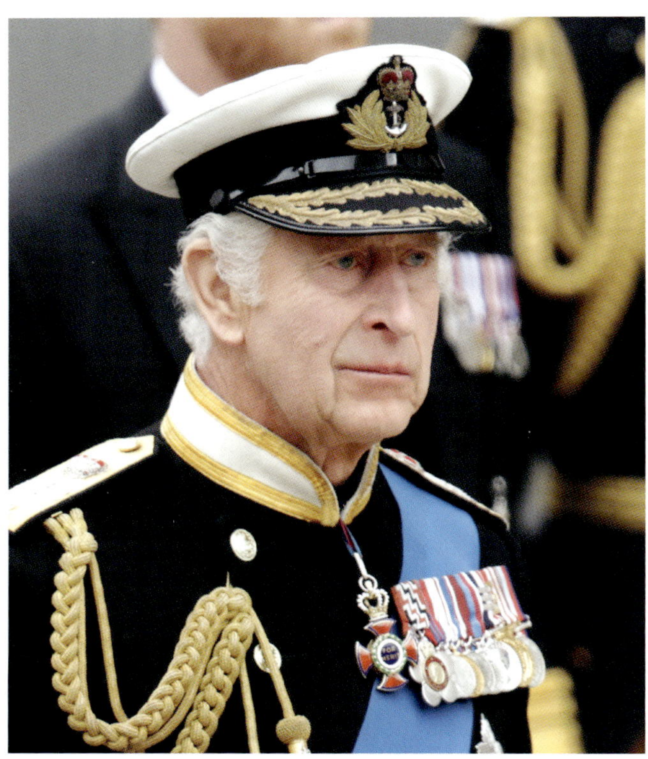

THE DEATH OF QUEEN ELIZABETH II

I had spent many years photographing Queen Elizabeth on her daily royal engagements, as well as capturing more formal portraits of the illustrious monarch. This meant that, for me, the passing of the Queen was an incredibly emotional time. Above all, I felt that the most meaningful way to pay my respects was to document as many elements of this historic moment as possible, from her coffin making its way down from Balmoral, to lying in state at Westminster Hall, to the state funeral at Westminster Abbey, and the Queen's ultimate resting place in St. George's Chapel at Windsor Castle.

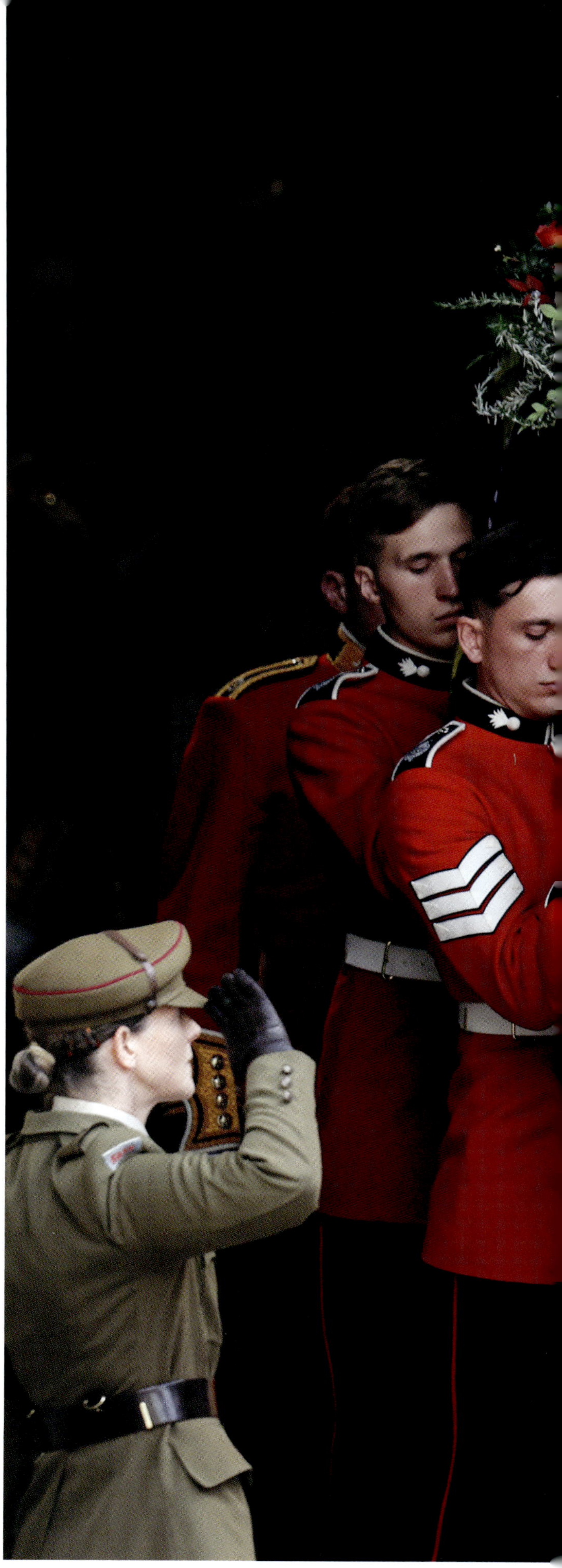

Queen Elizabeth II's lead-lined coffin, weighing around 250 kg (550 lbs.), is carried out of Westminster Abbey by Guardsmen from the Queen's Company 1st Battalion Grenadier Guards, 19 September 2022.

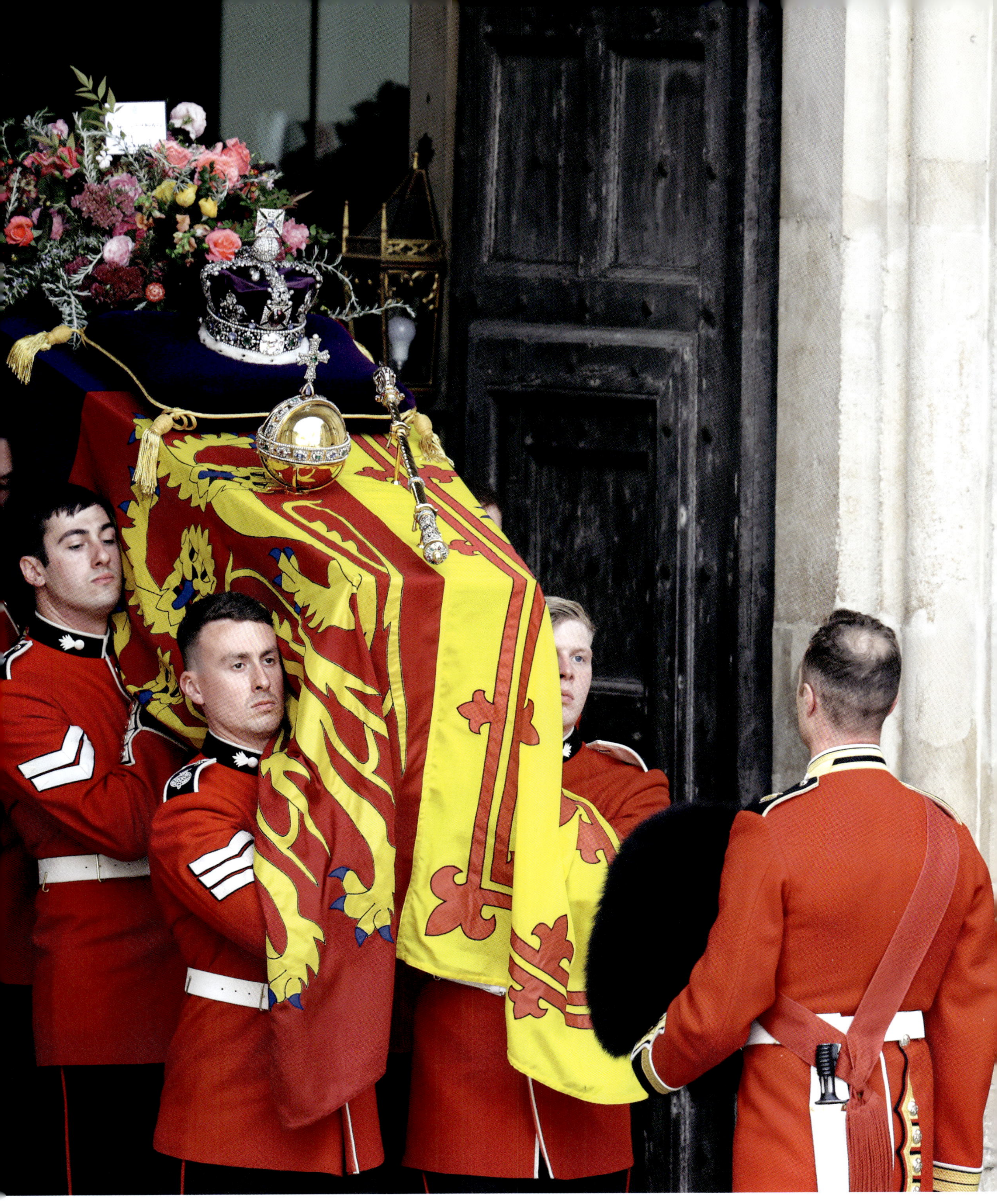

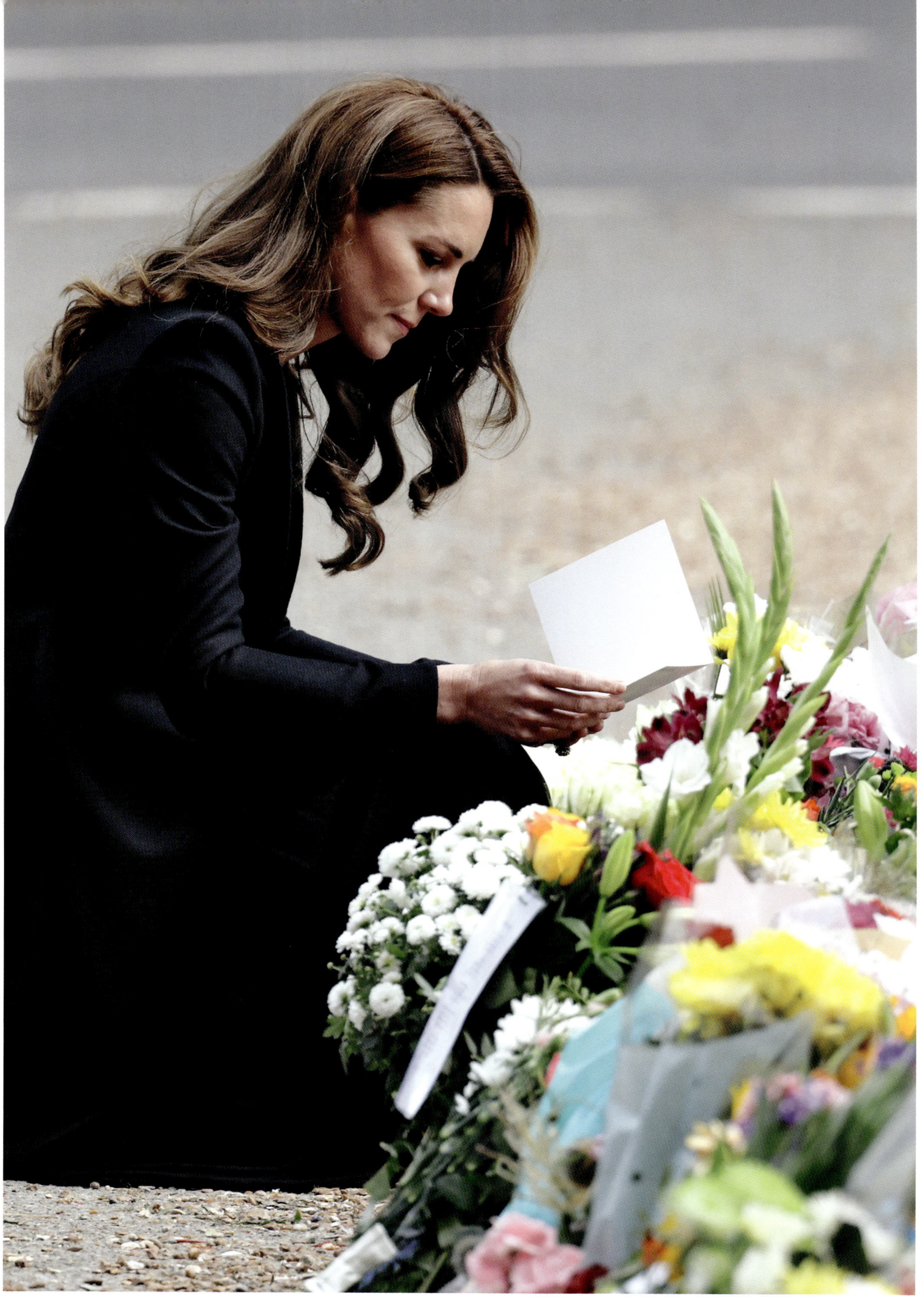

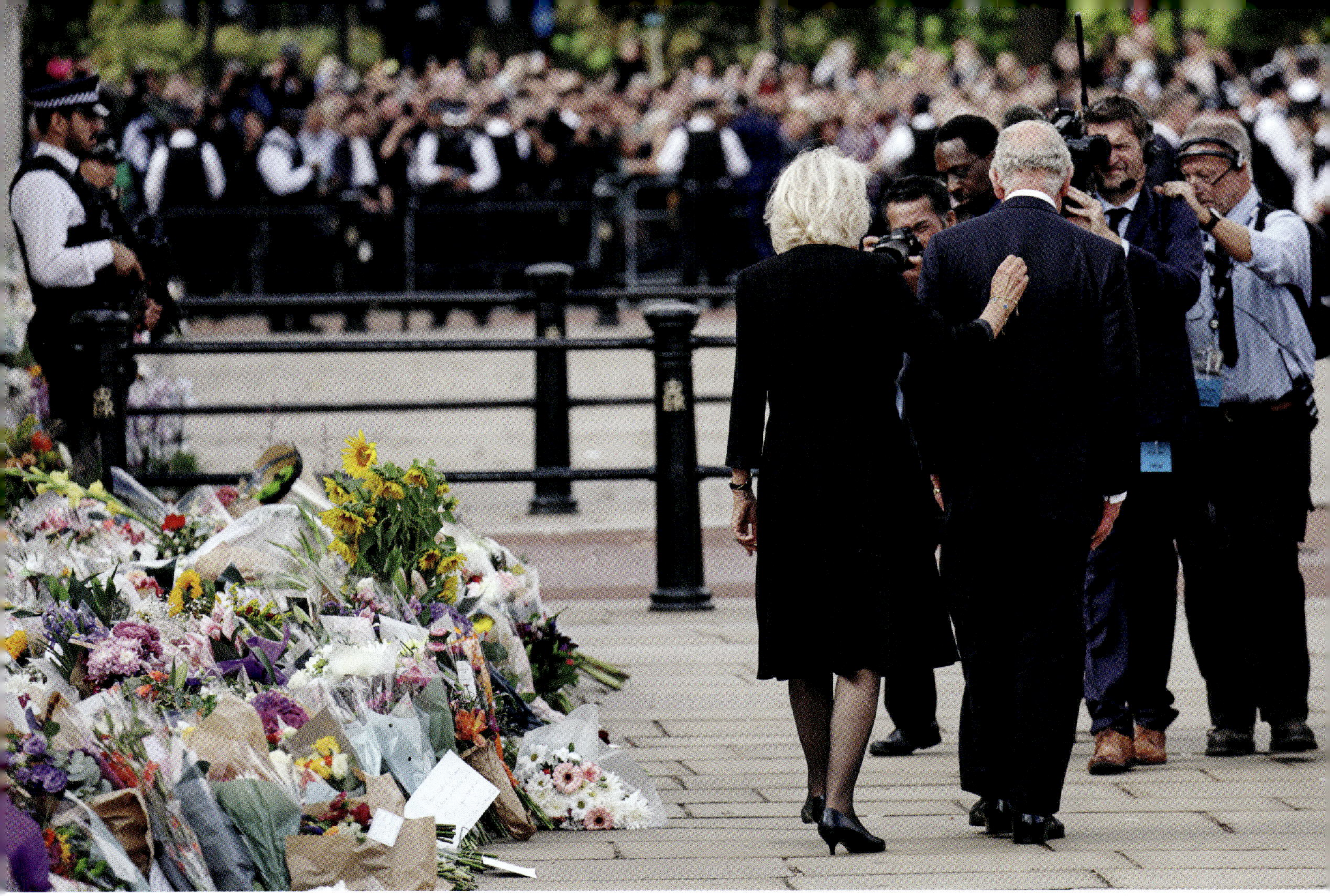

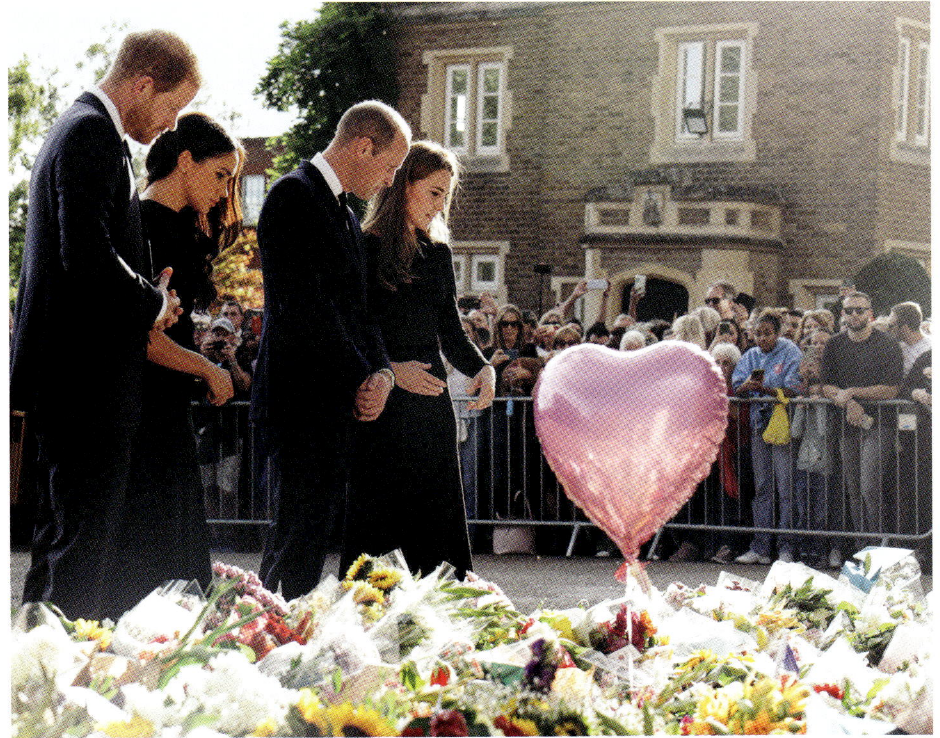

Opposite
Catherine, Princess of Wales, reads a card left by a member of the public at Sandringham, 15 September 2022. Tributes were left at royal residences around the country in the wake of Queen Elizabeth II's passing.

Above
Camilla rests a comforting hand on her husband's back outside Buckingham Palace, 9 September 2022.

Left
The Prince and Princess of Wales and the Duke and Duchess of Sussex look at the floral tributes laid by members of the public on the Long walk at Windsor Castle, 10 September 2022.

Overleaf
Members of the public respectfully make their way past Queen Elizabeth II's coffin as her grandchildren mount a family vigil over her coffin in Westminster Hall, 17 September 2022.

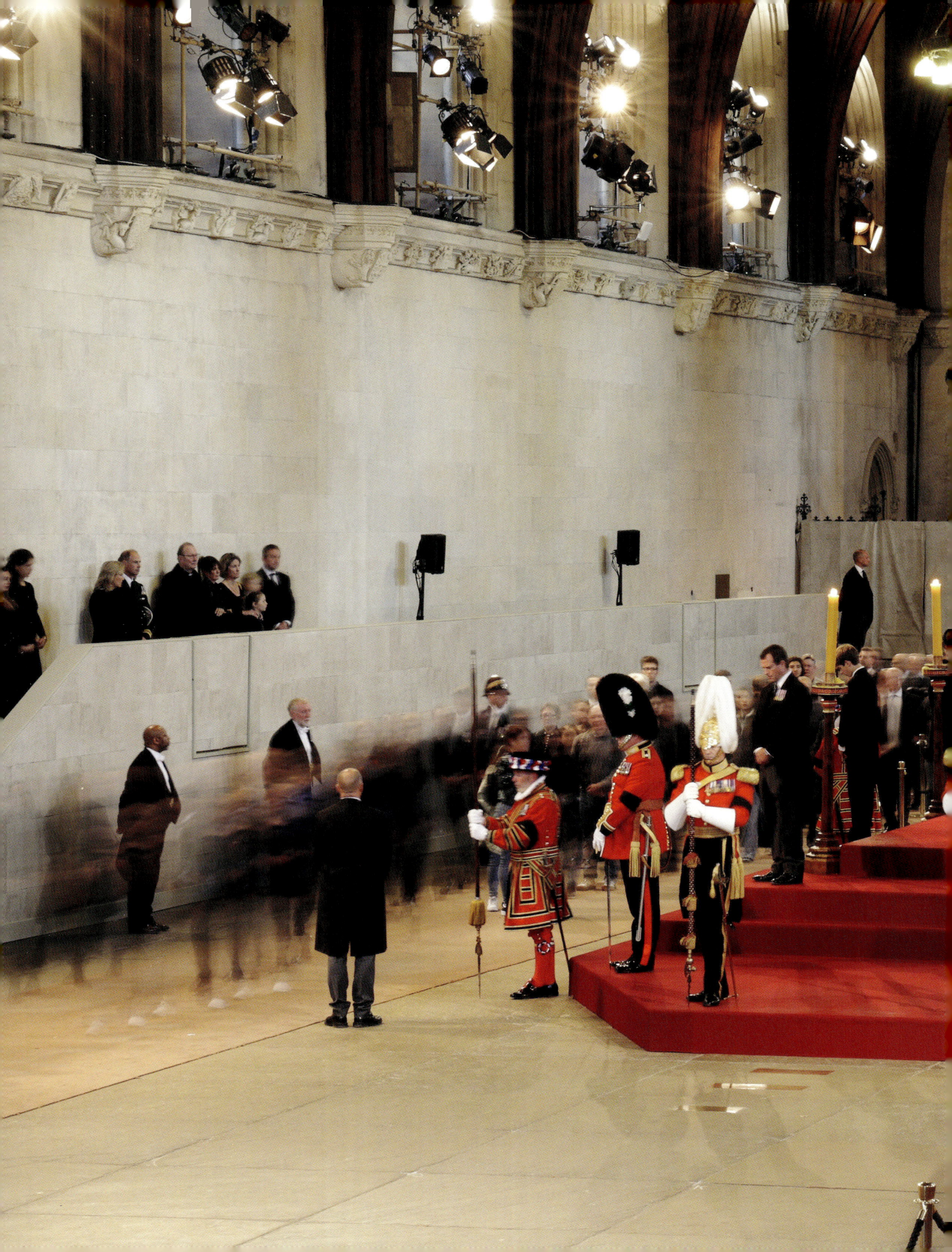

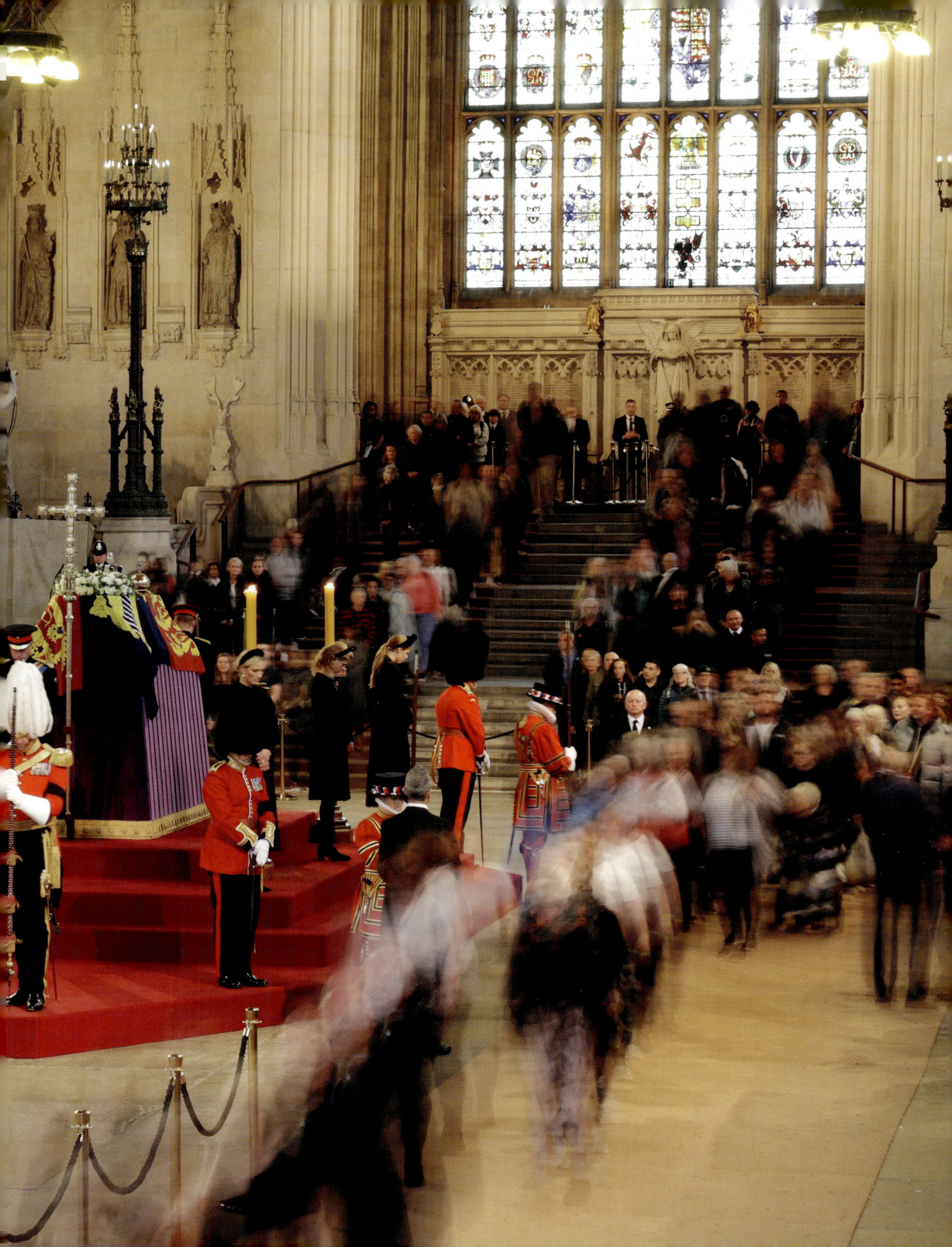

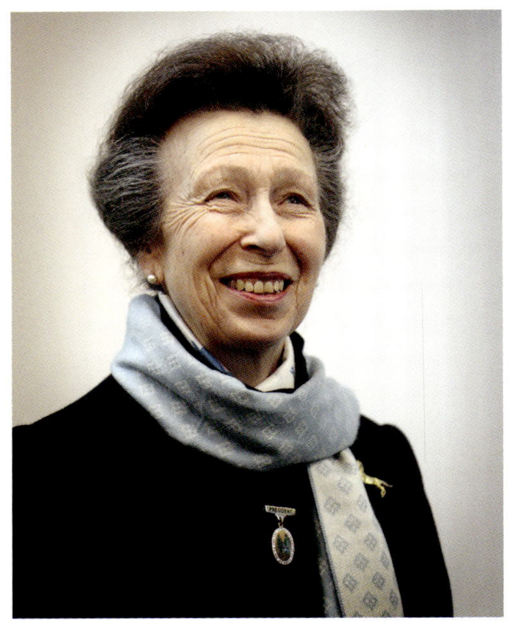

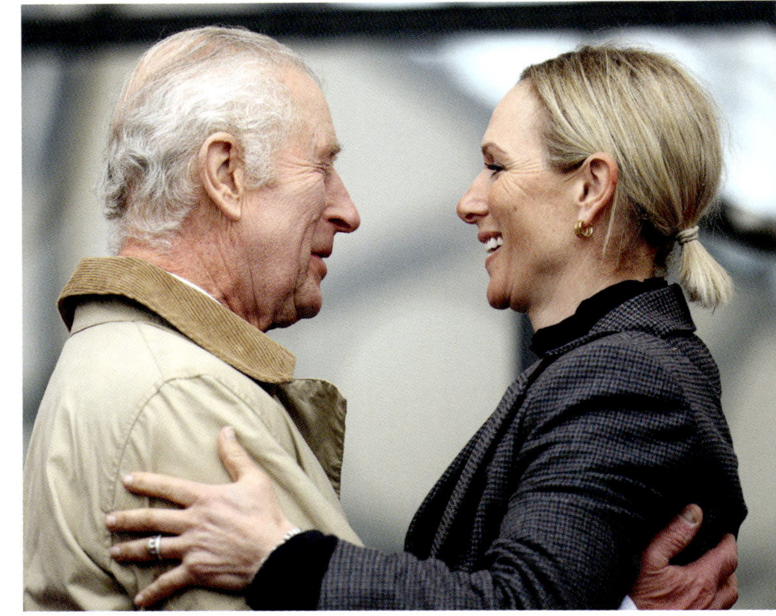

CANCER DIAGNOSIS

January 2024 signalled the start of a difficult period for King Charles. After less than two years on the throne, he was diagnosed with an undisclosed form of cancer following treatment for an enlarged prostate. Despite being forced to take a step back from public-facing duties, the King maintained a characteristically positive spirit.

After taking over many of King Charles's engagements during his treatment, Princess Anne faced her own challenges after suffering a head injury and concussion following a horse accident. Here, as President of Riding for the Disabled (RDA), she smiles during a visit to the opening of the Reaseheath Equestrian College, 30 January 2024.

King Charles waves as he emerges from the London Clinic with Queen Camilla (opposite), and warmly hugs Zara Tindall at the Royal Windsor Horse Show. His appearance at St. George's Chapel for the Easter matins service (right) was memorable, as, contrary to the advice of his doctor, he insisted on a walkabout to greet the public – truly unstoppable!

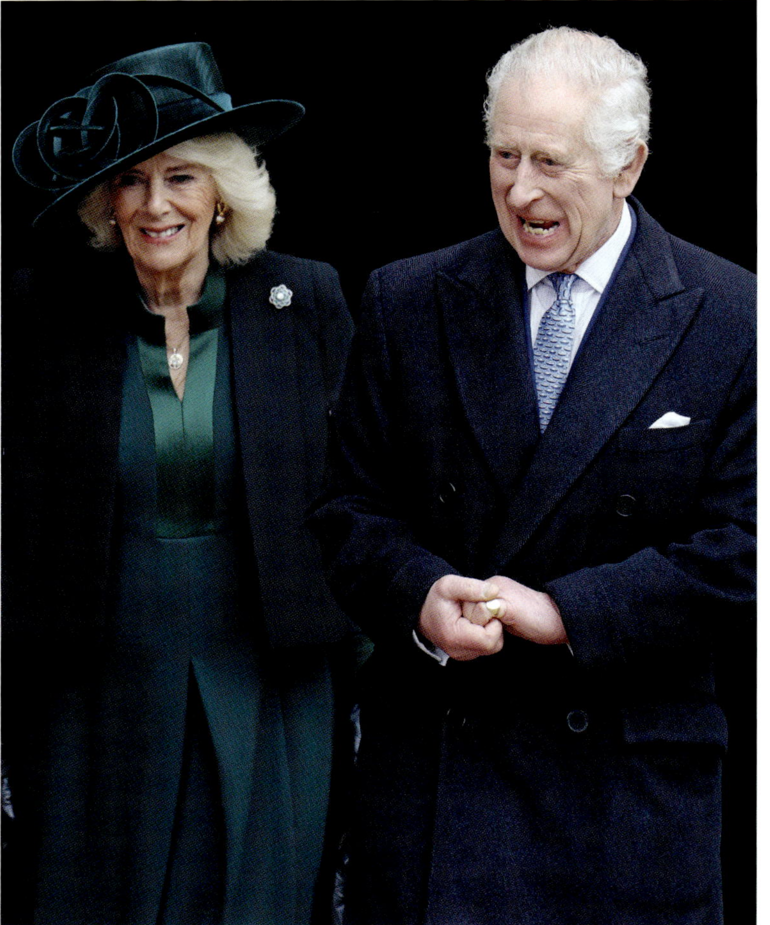

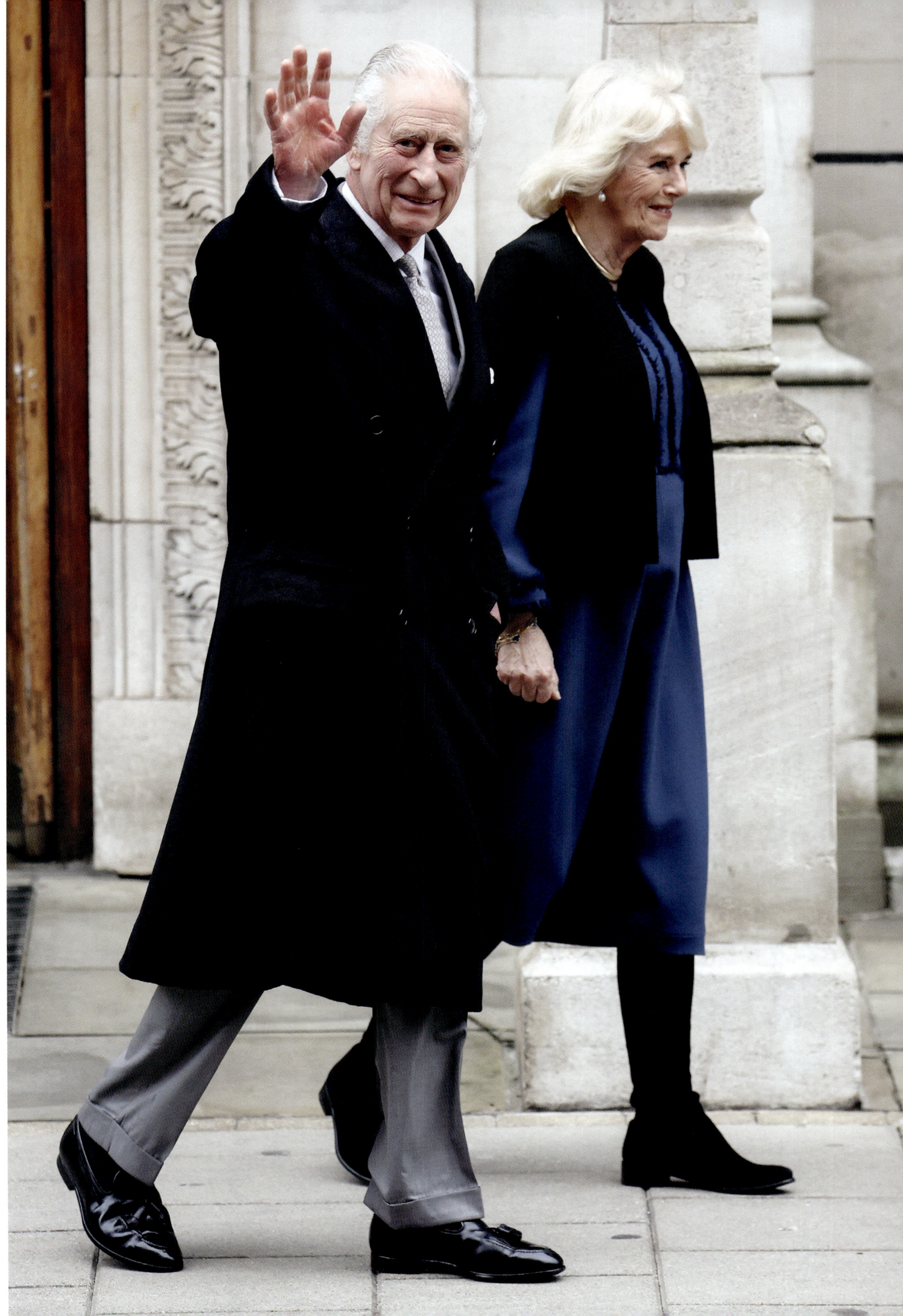

THE ROYAL MARSDEN

As the Princess of Wales walked up the steps of the historic hospital in Chelsea on 14 January 2025, her poignant glance up at the entrance reminded everyone of just how emotional this visit was for her. During her battle with cancer, Catherine received much of her treatment here, and her gratitude to the staff and her empathy for other patients was obvious as she toured the ward. Doctors, nurses, and patients gathered to catch a glimpse of the famous visitor, cramming into corridors and doorways and breaking out into impromptu applause as she left the building. Listening to the stories of fellow patients, it was clear that many of them had drawn strength from Catherine's own story, and a hug for patient Rebecca Mendelsohn as the Princess left the building said it all.

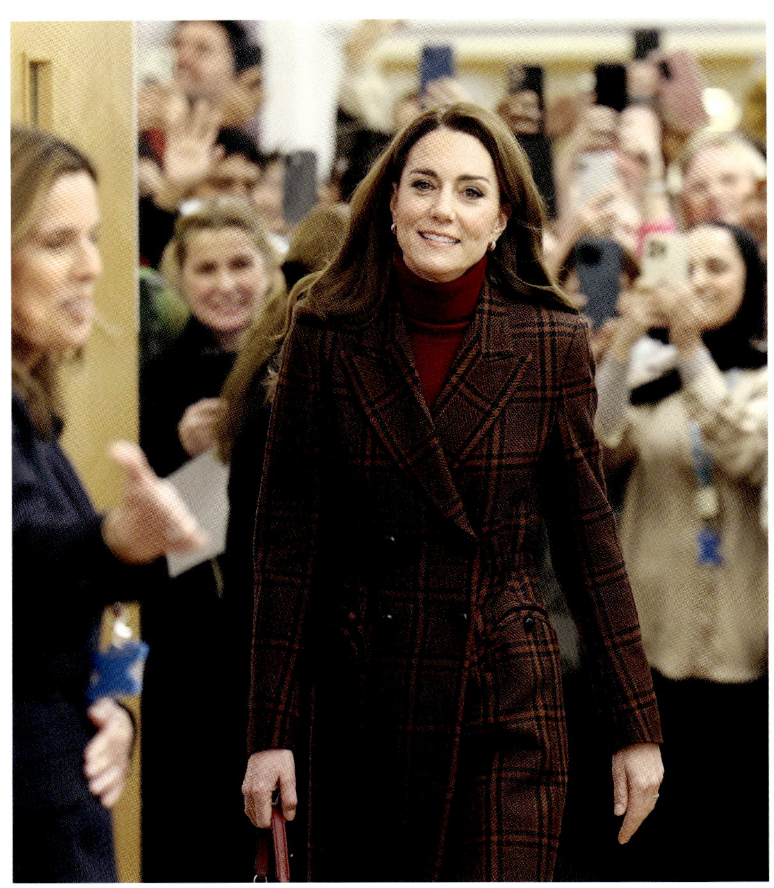

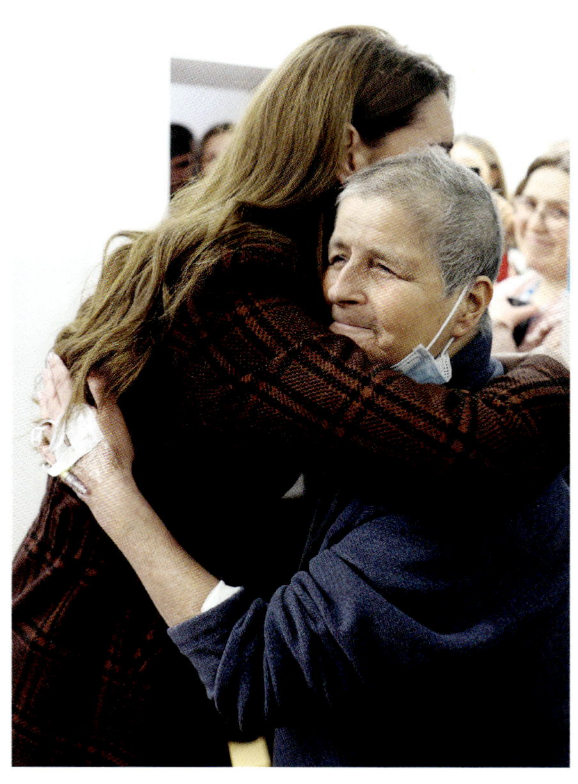

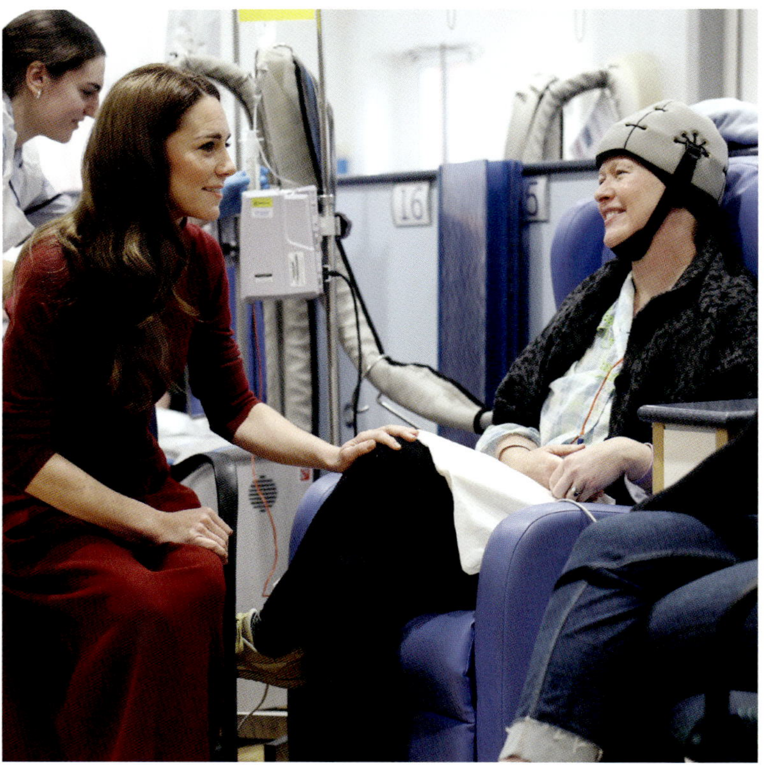

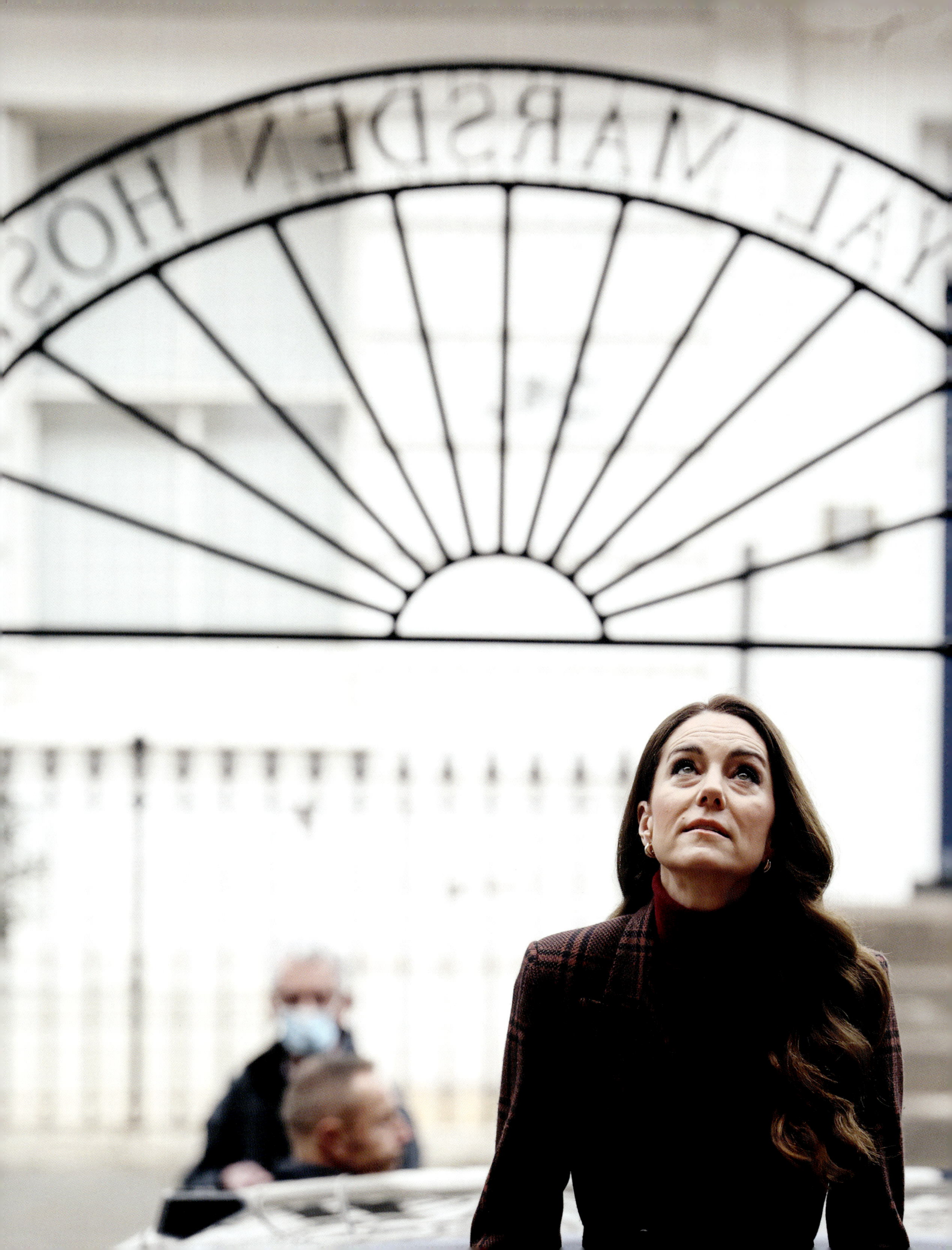
MARSDEN

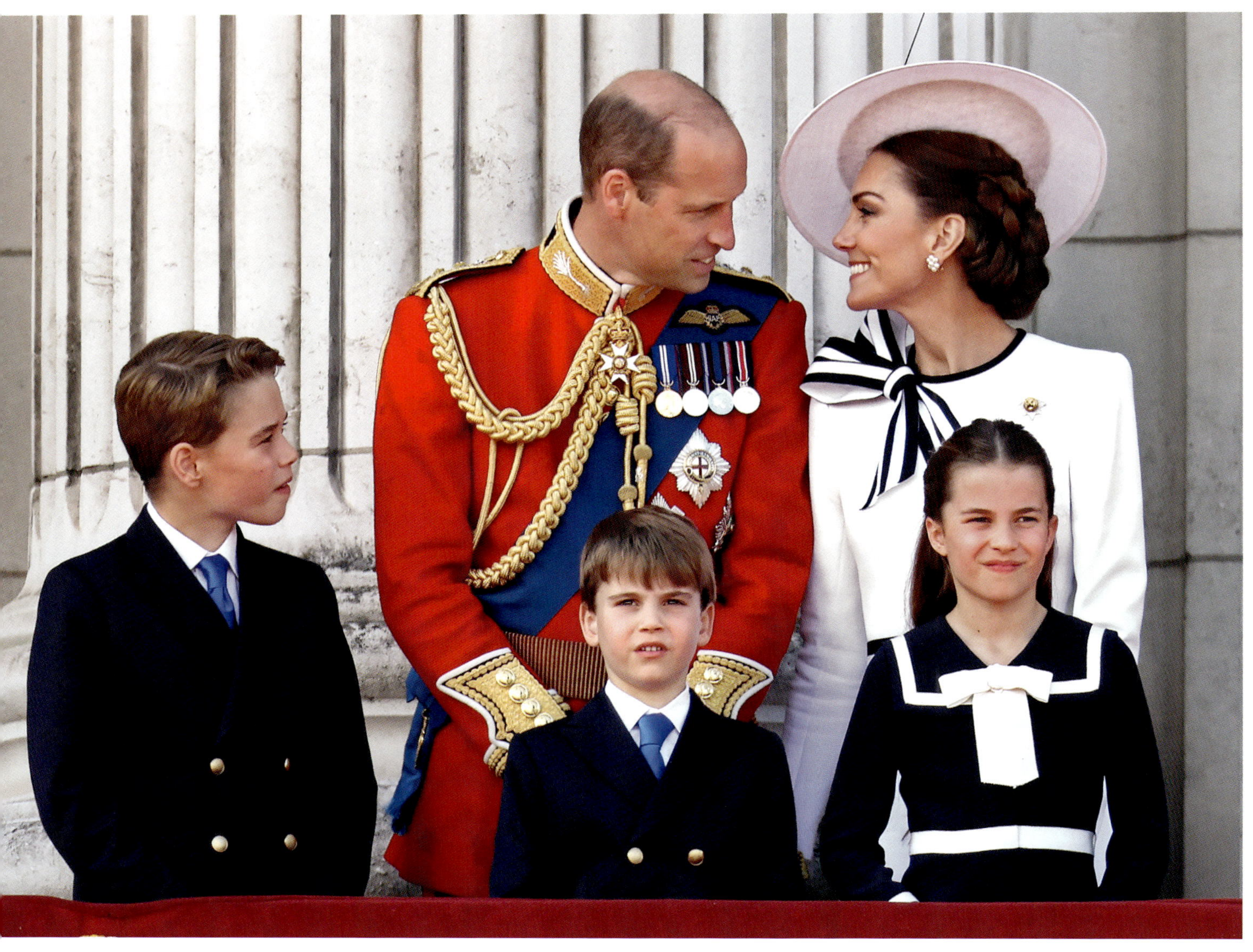

BACK TO WORK

When Princess Catherine announced her cancer diagnosis in front of a bed of daffodils in Windsor there was a huge outpouring of love and sympathy from around the world. What followed was a very personal and private journey of treatment and recovery. When she made her first appearance back to work at Trooping the Colour on 15 June 2024, there was an enormous amount of excitement and collective support from the nation. The front pages of the newspapers praised how happy and healthy she looked as, surrounded by her children, she shared a romantic glance with her husband. It is a touching example of the public's involvement in her journey, and the happiness of the moment lifting the spirits of the nation as a whole.

The Princess of Wales arrives for a thanksgiving service to mark the 80th anniversary of VE Day at Westminster Abbey, 8 May 2025. I love this contemplative moment as she attends this important service.

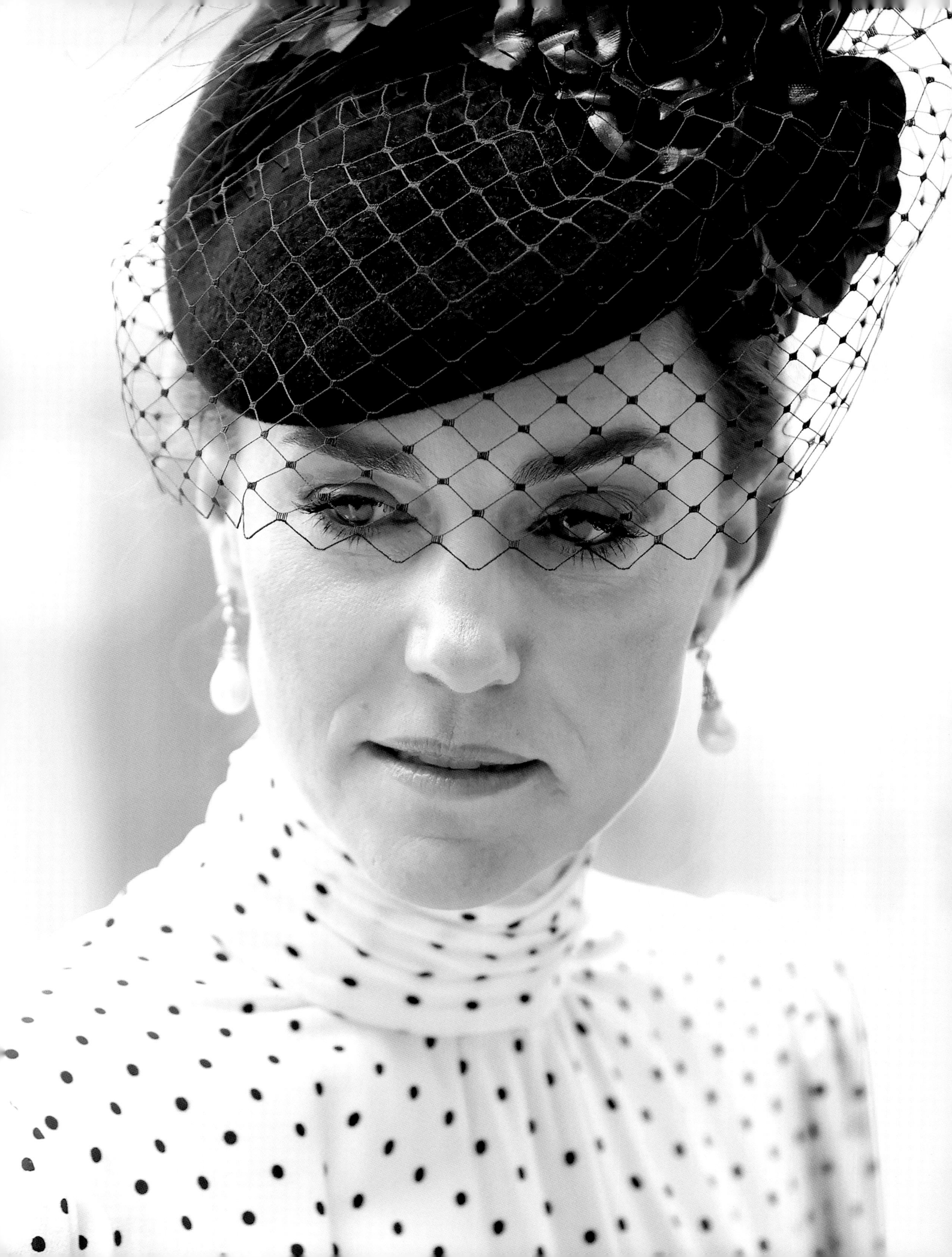

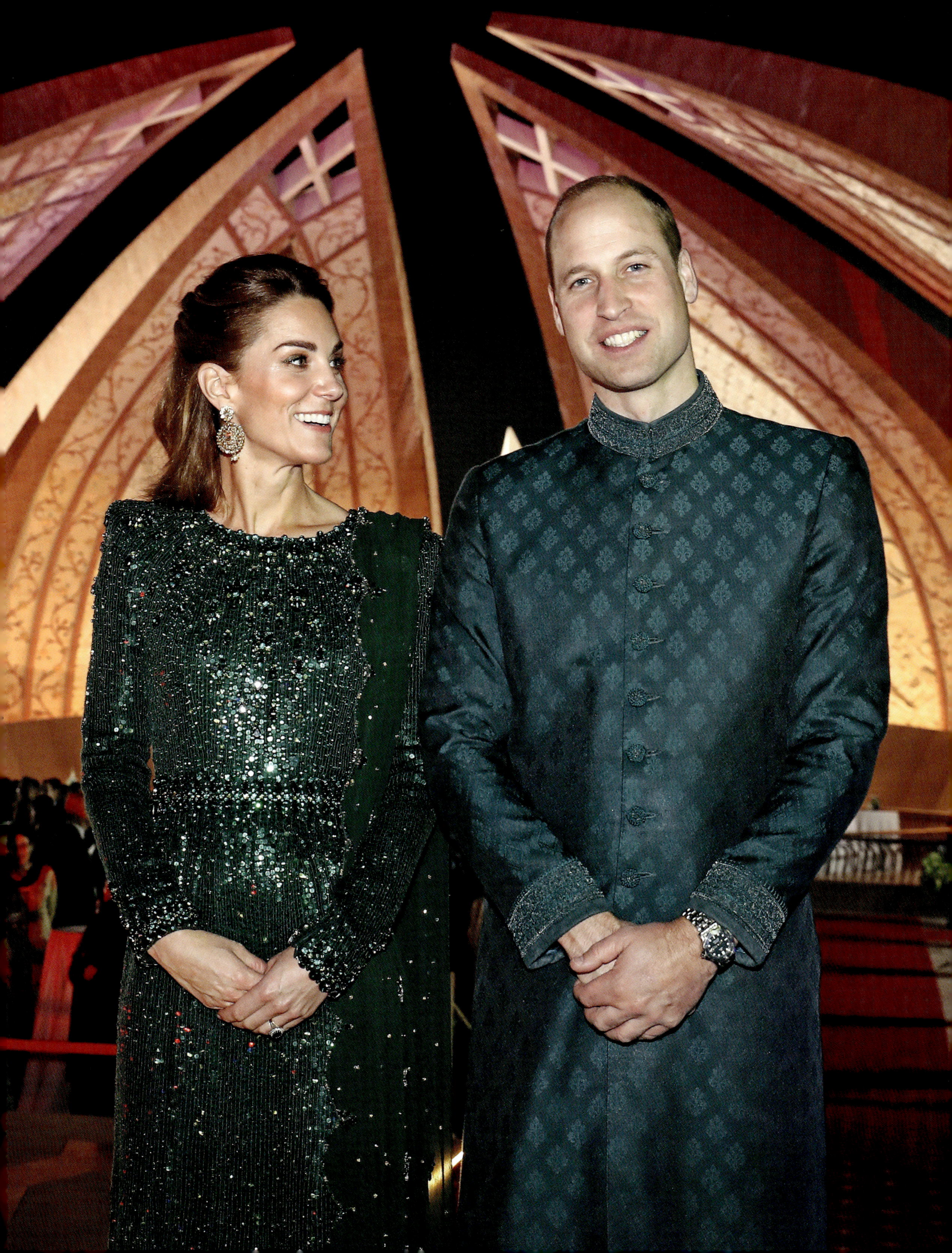

3

ROYAL TRAVEL

DIPLOMACY AND SPECTACLE

The royal family has a singular role in British life, above political consideration and able to exert an influence that is unique to their position. Skilled at diplomacy and star guests at any event, they encourage positive change around the world. Queen Elizabeth II once said "I have to be seen to be believed," and this phrase underlined her dedication and commitment to being a visible Head of State, something that made her the most well-travelled monarch in the world. During her reign, the Queen made history as the first British sovereign to visit Ireland and China. Her daughter, Anne, the Princess Royal, also has a busy schedule of engagements that frequently includes travel abroad for official duties and charity work.

Overseas visits are equally important to King Charles III as he makes his mark as a global icon and statesman. I have been lucky enough to travel to places from Japan to the Galapagos Islands, Brazil to India and across the Commonwealth photographing these royal engagements. The Prince and Princess of Wales and the Duke and Duchess of Edinburgh also undertake travel abroad, and this chapter covers a very special visit to Nepal with the Duke and Duchess of Edinburgh in 2025, as well as some high-profile visits by the Prince and Princess of Wales that have propelled them into the global spotlight as models of advocacy and style.

PUCKS AND PARLIAMENT

In May 2025, we boarded a Canadian Royal Airforce jet at RAF Brize Norton to make a whistlestop visit to Ottawa for the opening of the Canadian parliament. This was Charles's first visit to the country as sovereign and his 20th overall – many of which I had accompanied him on. After dropping a puck at a street-hockey event in Lansdowne Park, it was down to business, opening the 45th parliament of Canada. King Charles III became the first reigning monarch to deliver the "Speech from the Throne," as the address that sets out the new government's priorities is known, to the assembly since Queen Elizabeth II in 1977. I could feel the weight of this historic act as I captured the speech from the floor of the chamber, an event attended by Mark Carney, previous prime ministers and leaders of the First Nations (Indigenous peoples of Canada).

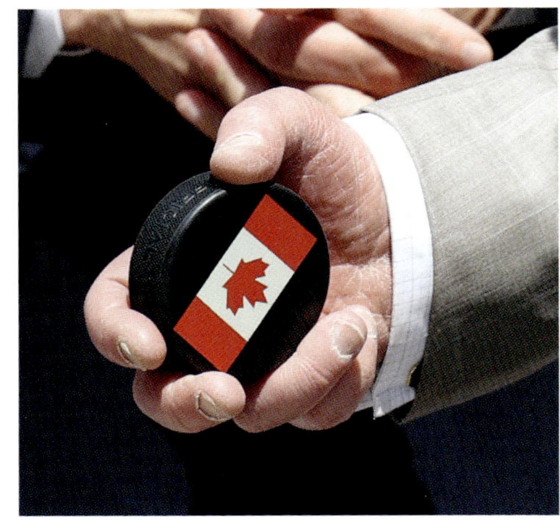

Overleaf
As the royal entourage is held back, King Charles and Queen Camilla stand in front of the Colosseum in Rome during their State Visit to Italy, 8 April 2025. A closer inspection of this image reveals security gathered next to the magnificent ancient arches and crowds looking up from below: a coming together of ancient and modern in a moment.

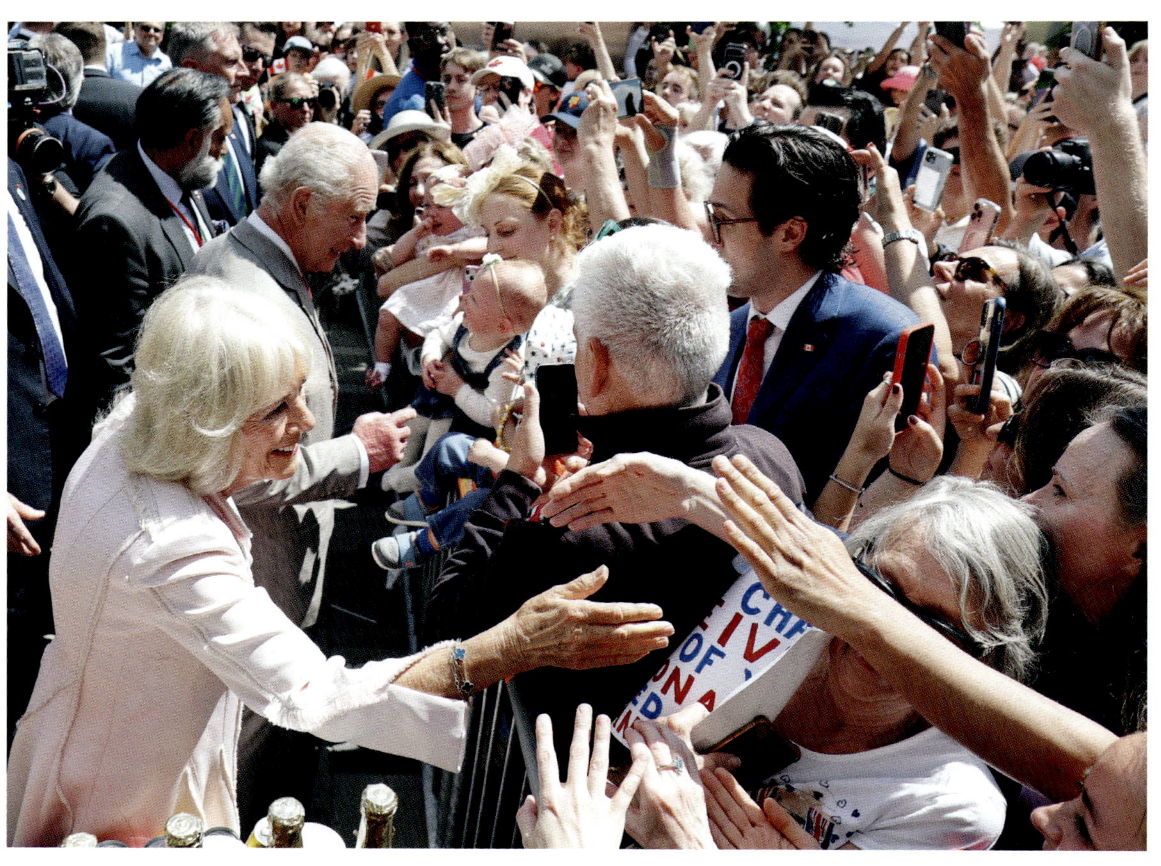

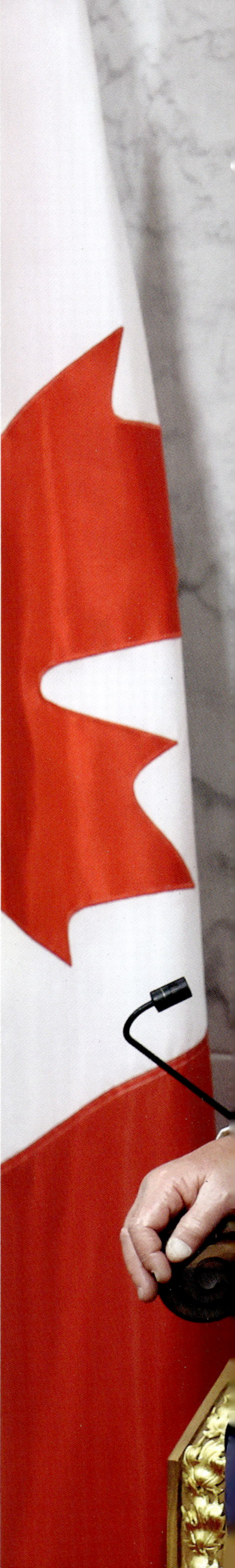

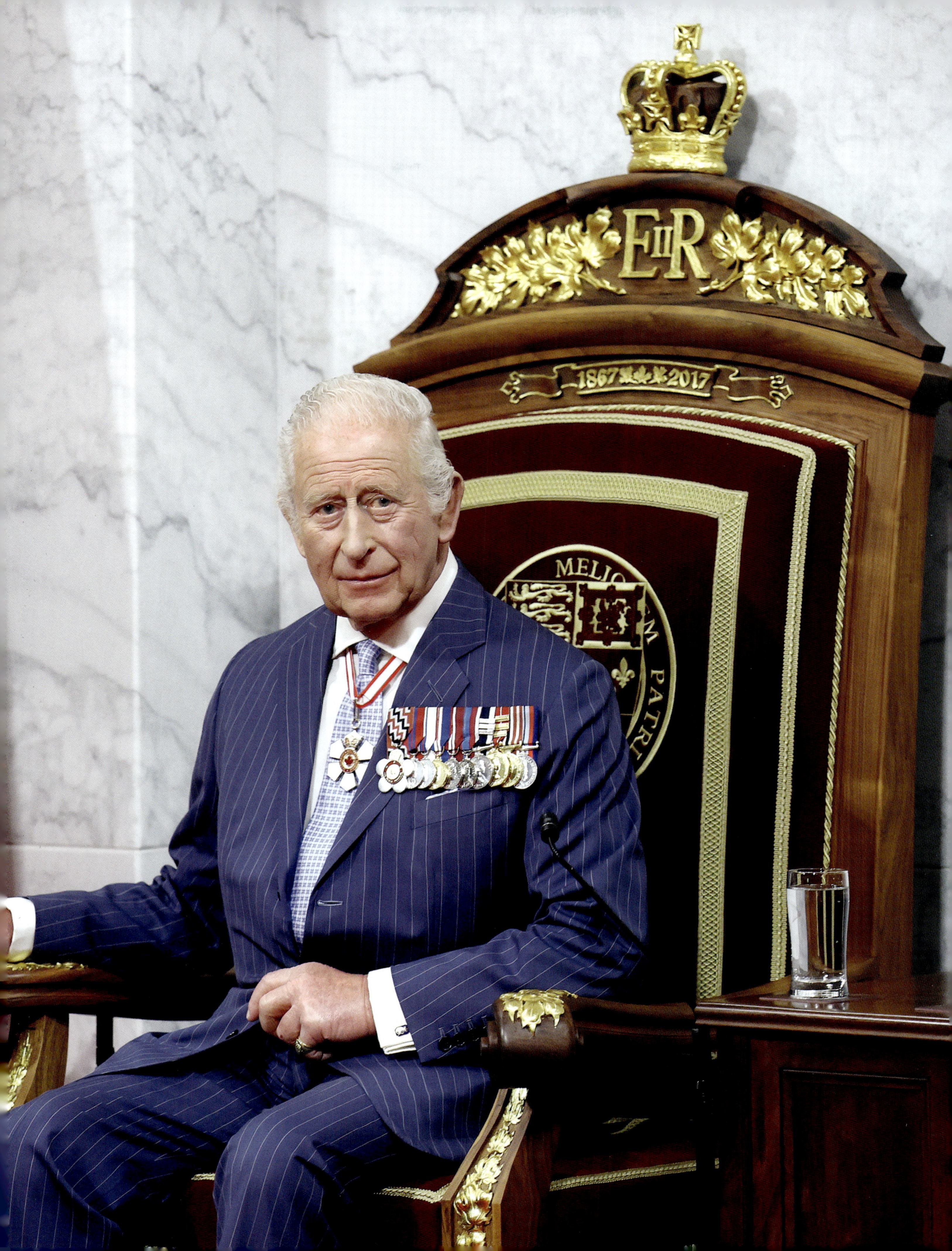
EIIR
1867 2017

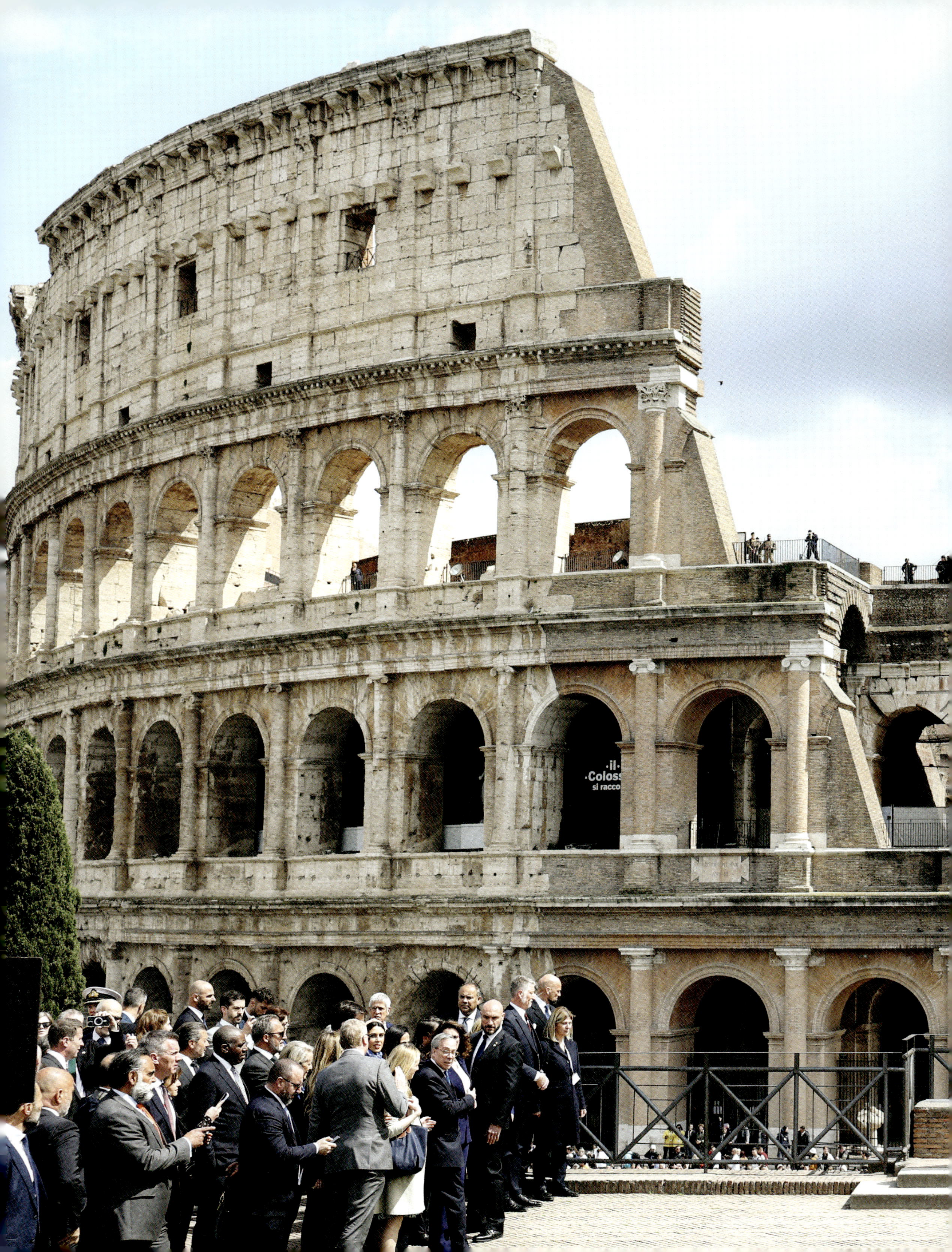

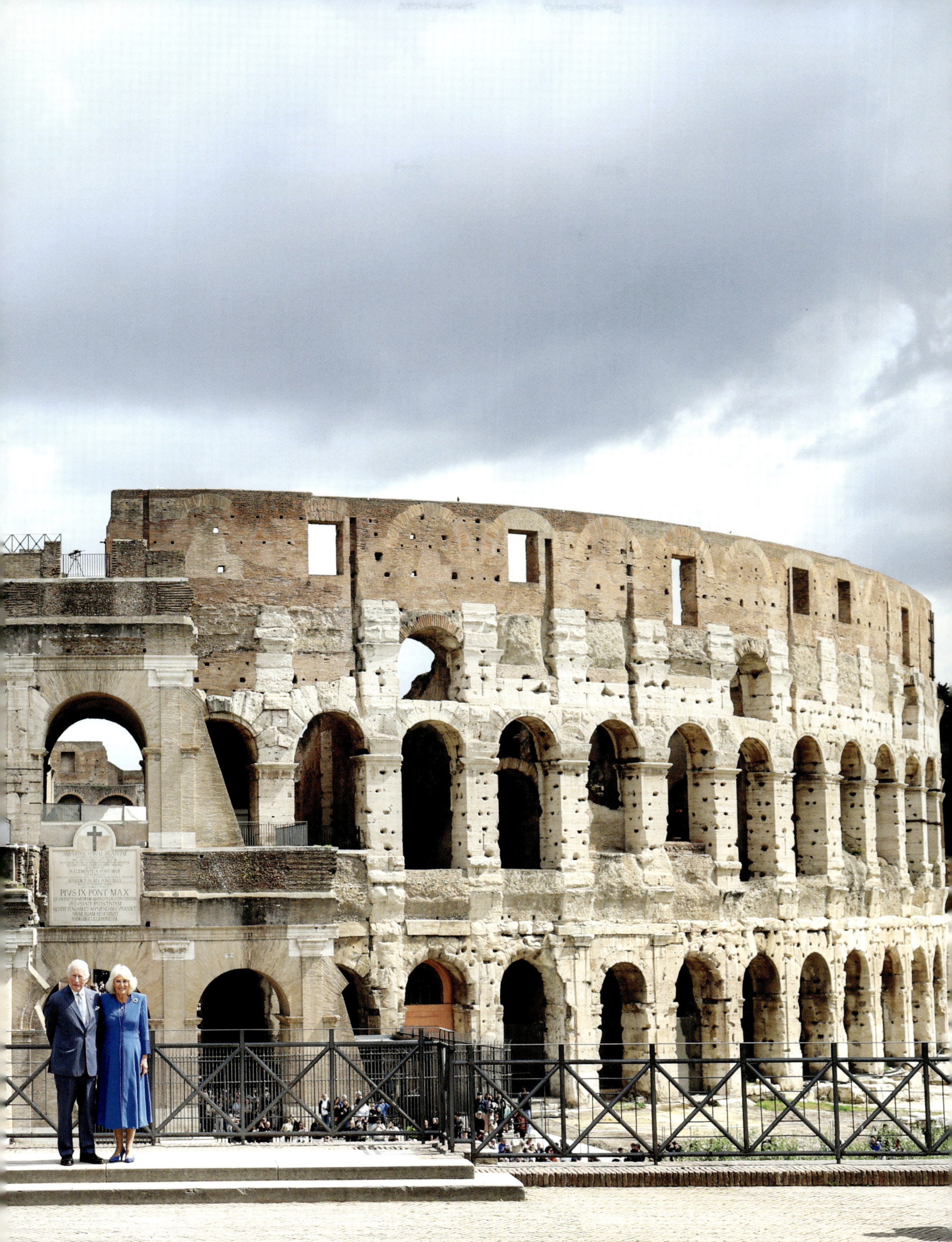
PIVS·IX·PONT·MAX

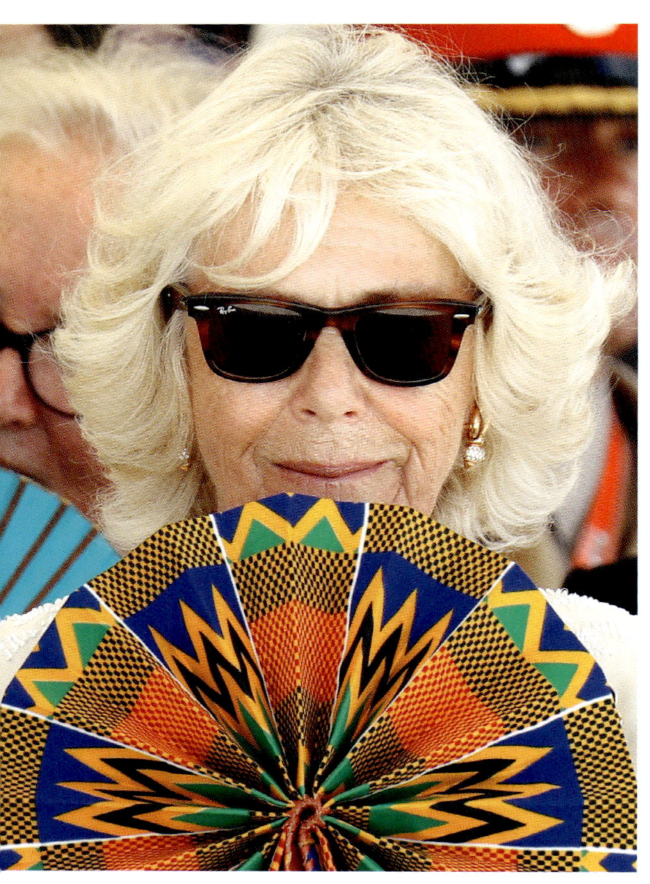

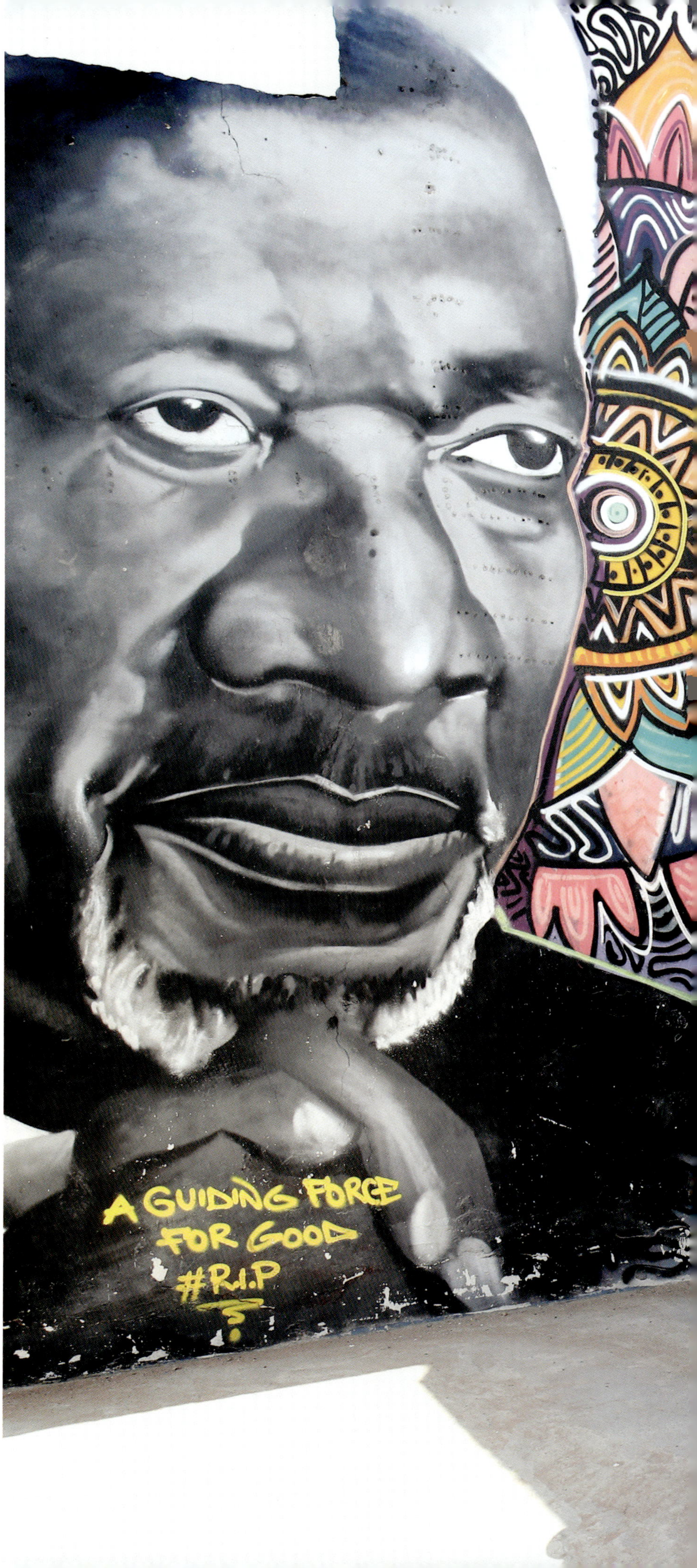

A country full of energy and colour but also incredibly hot! The King and Queen pose in front of a colourful mural during an art, music, and dance exhibition in Jamestown in Accra, Ghana, as Queen Camilla stays cool with a parasol and traditional fan, 3 November 2018.

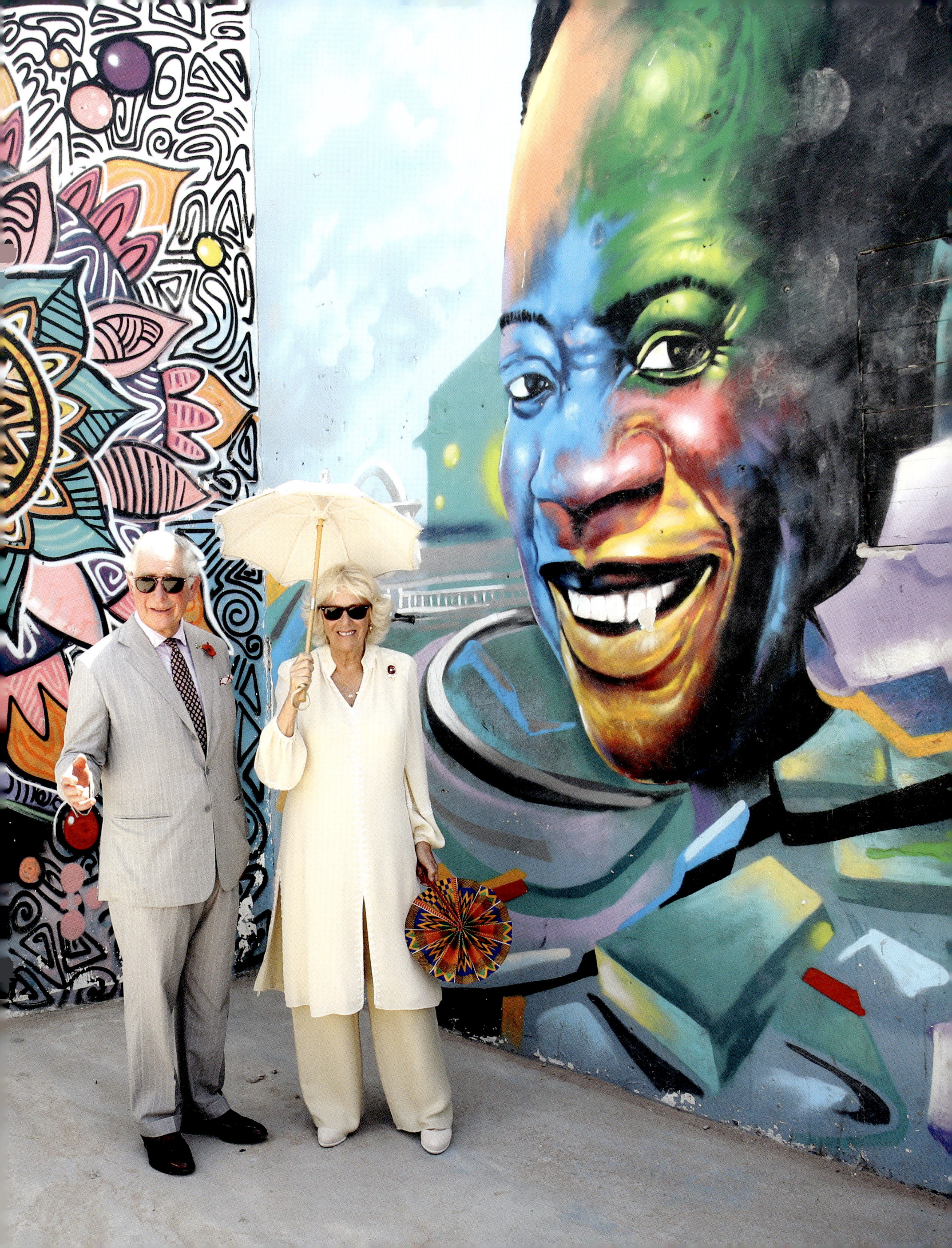

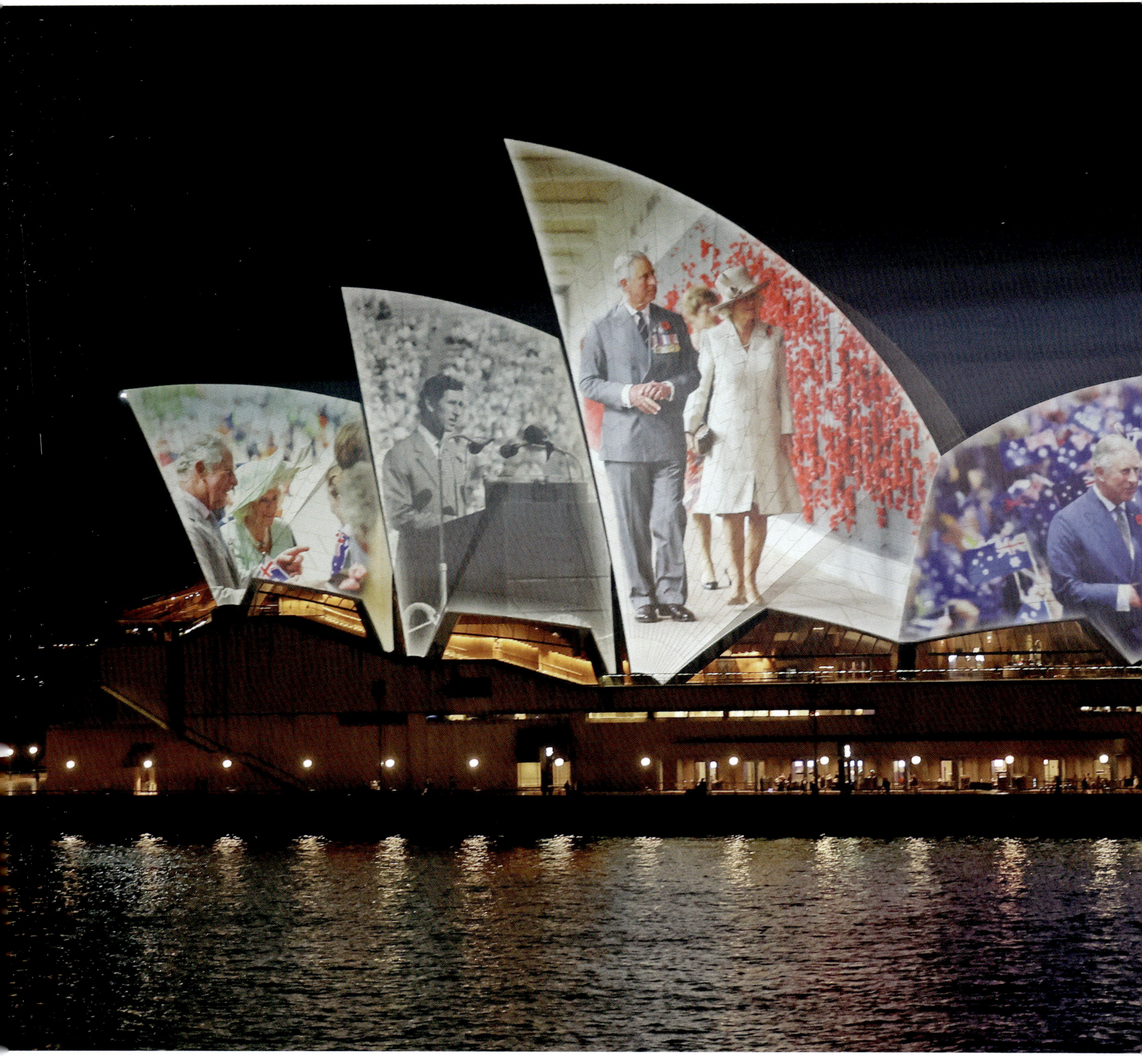

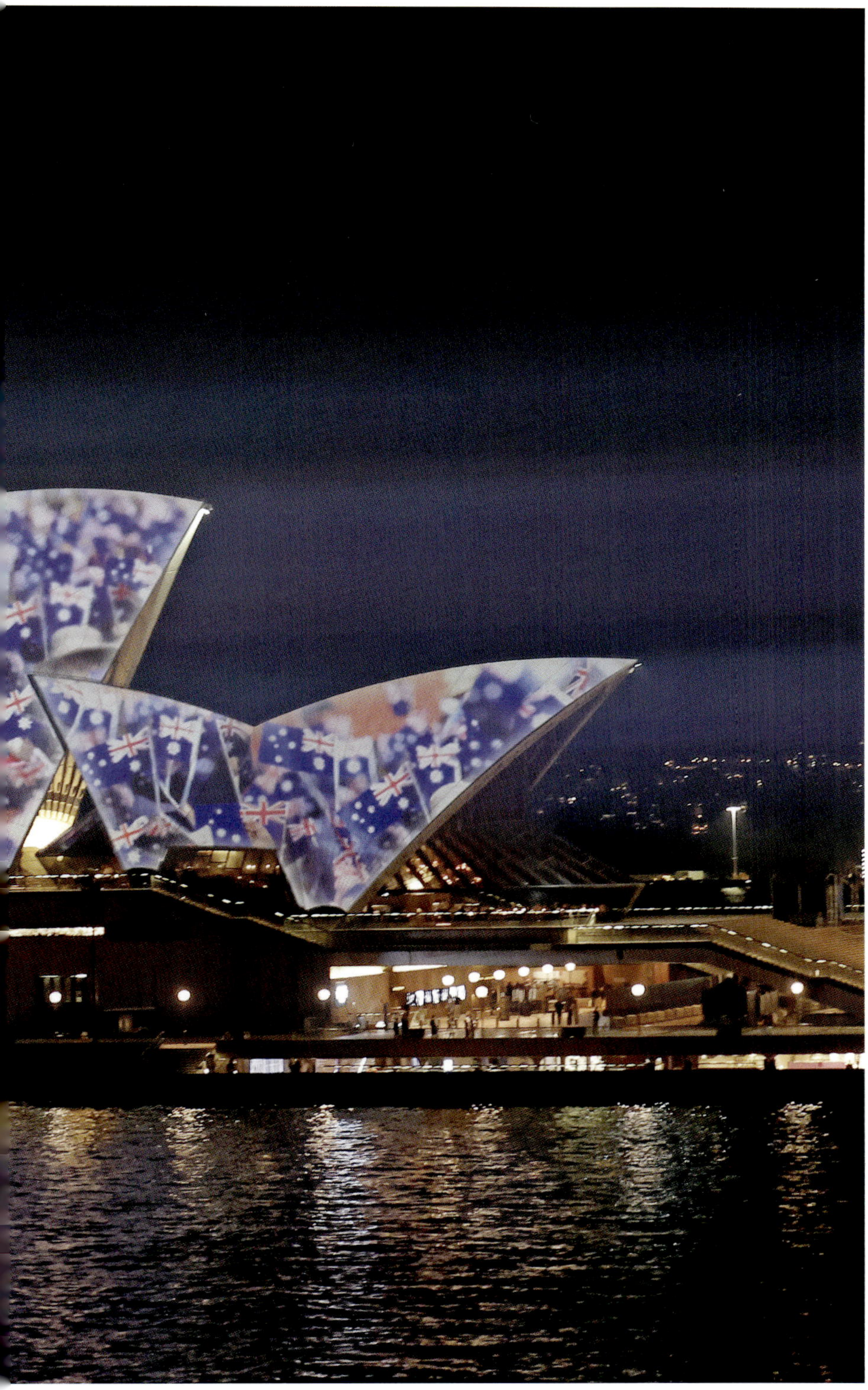

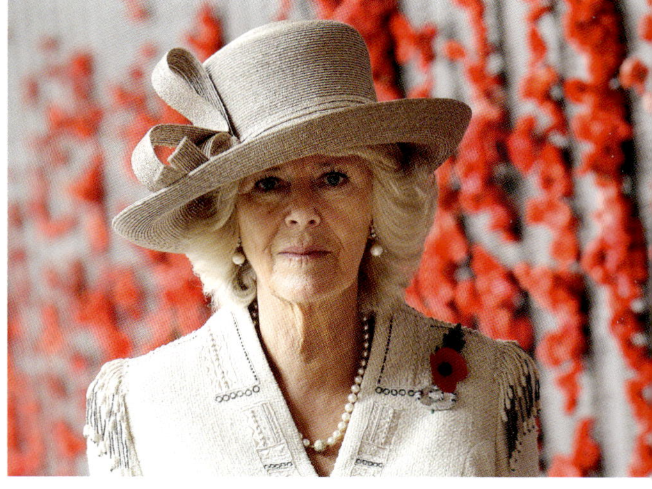

LIGHTING UP SYDNEY OPERA HOUSE

In 2024 King Charles and Queen Camilla embarked on a demanding visit to Australia and Samoa. They were greeted on arrival at Sydney's Kingsford Smith Airport by some of the most torrential downpours I have ever witnessed! However, the weather was not going to thwart this momentous occasion, and members of the press were taken by bus to the second part of the evening's events, where we were presented with some spectacular images of Charles's past visits "down under," which were projected onto Sydney Opera House. I was delighted to see my shot of their visit to the Canberra war memorial in 2012 feature prominently in the centre of one of the sequences – it is not often that you can say your photograph has been projected onto one of the world's most recognized landmarks.

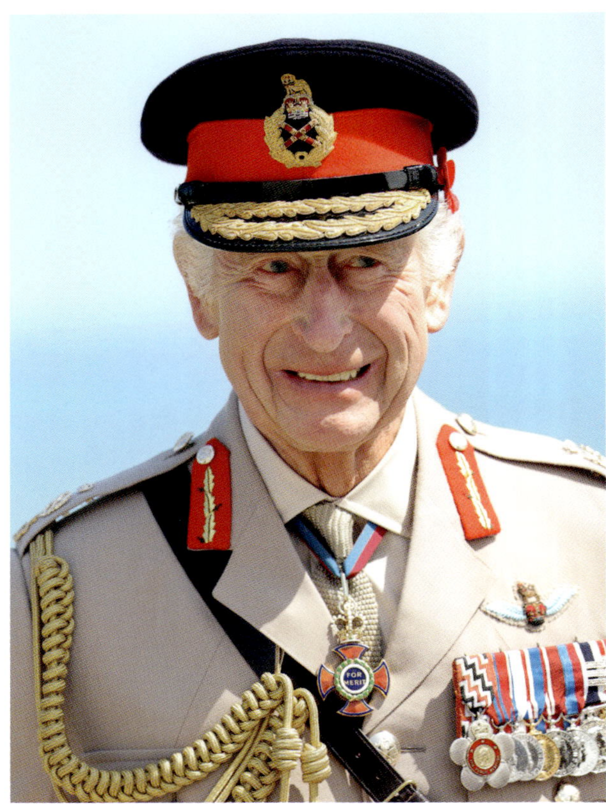

D-DAY IN FRANCE

The British Royal Air Force's aerobatic team, the Red Arrows, and a Eurofighter Typhoon fly past during the UK Ministry of Defence and the Royal British Legion's ceremony in France to mark the 80th anniversary of the Second World War D-Day Allied landings in Normandy, 6 June 2024. The art installation, *The People's Tribute*, by Dan Barton comprises handmade silhouettes of almost 1,500 servicemen.

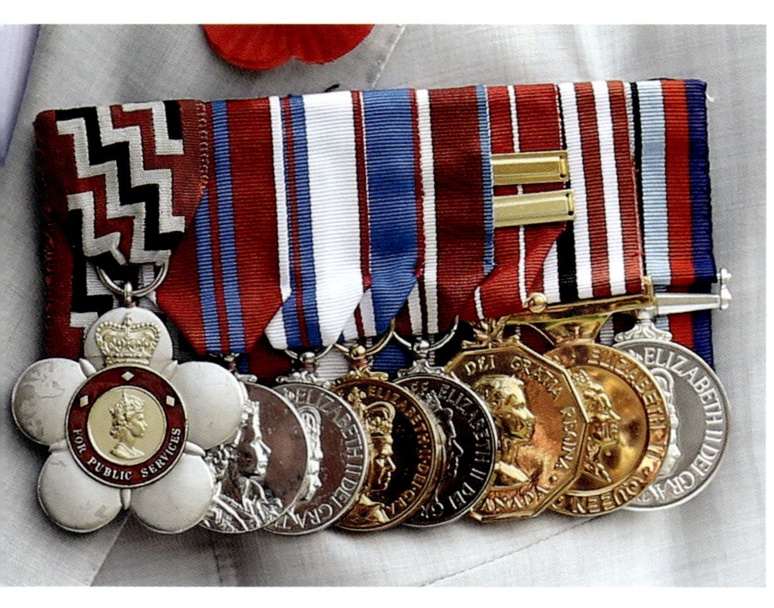

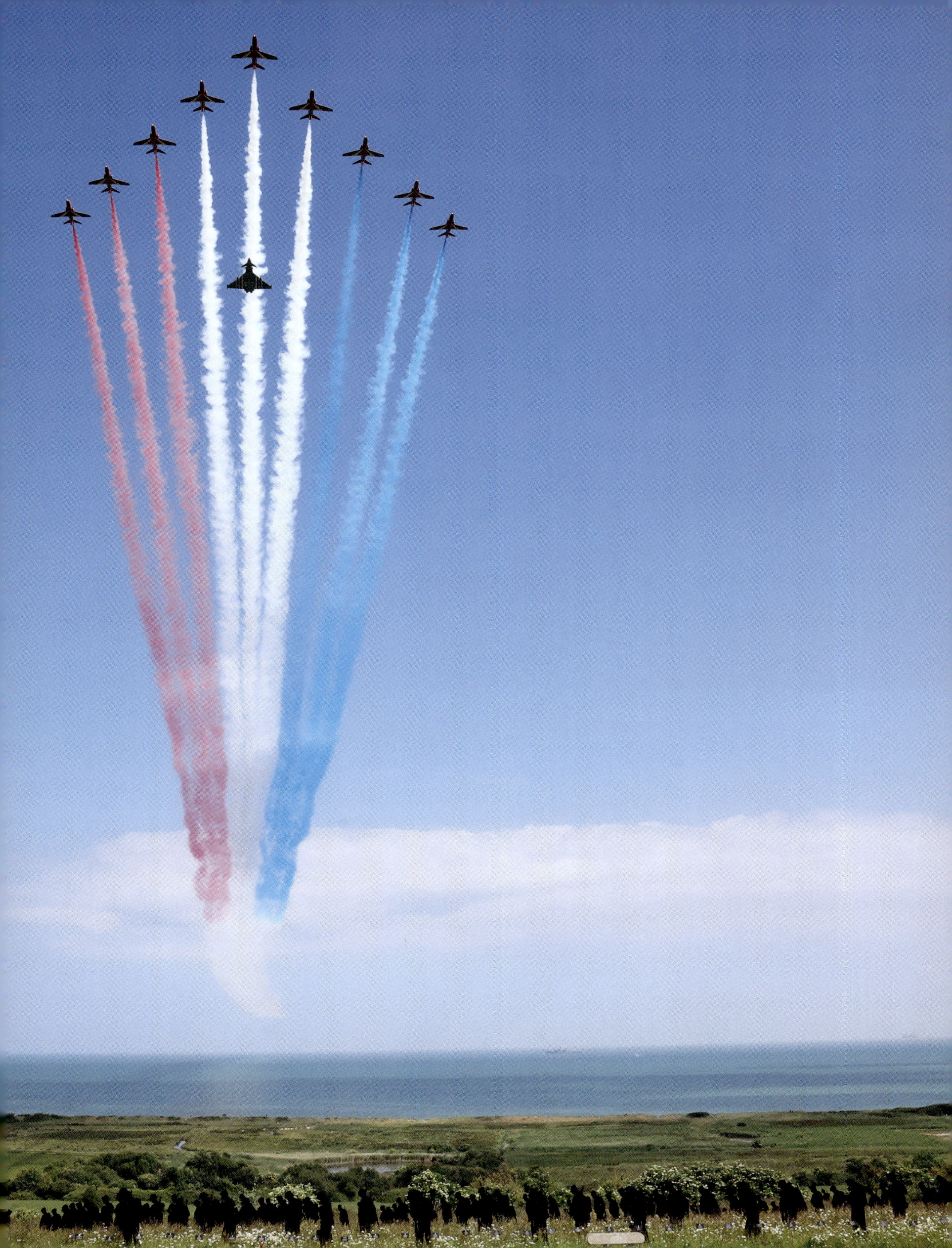

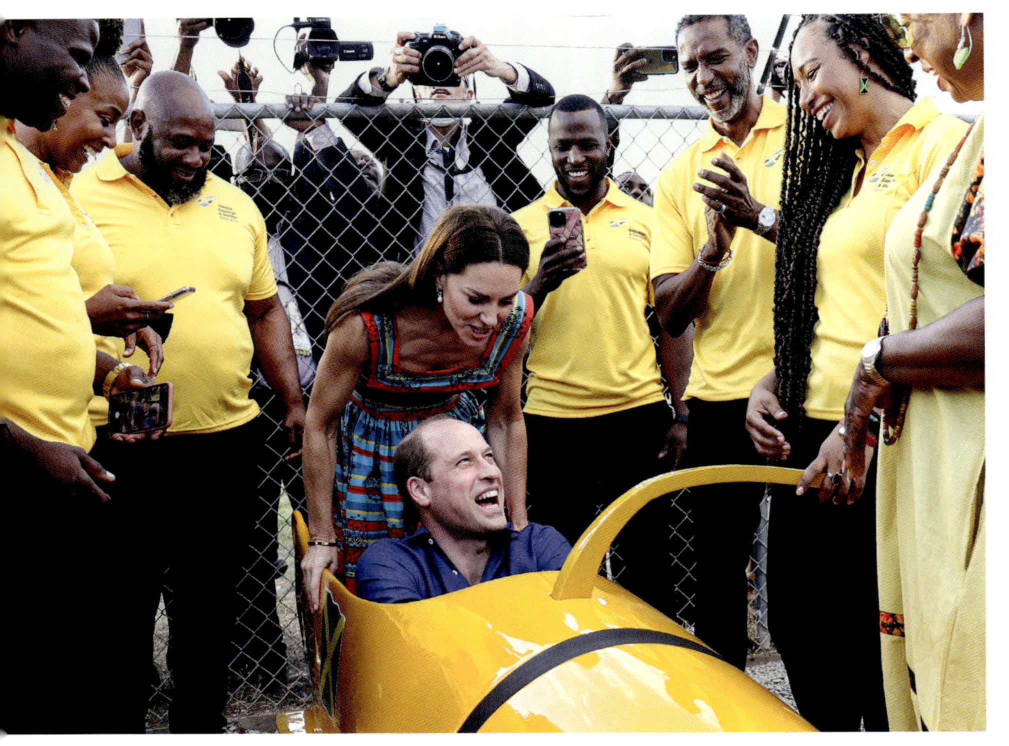

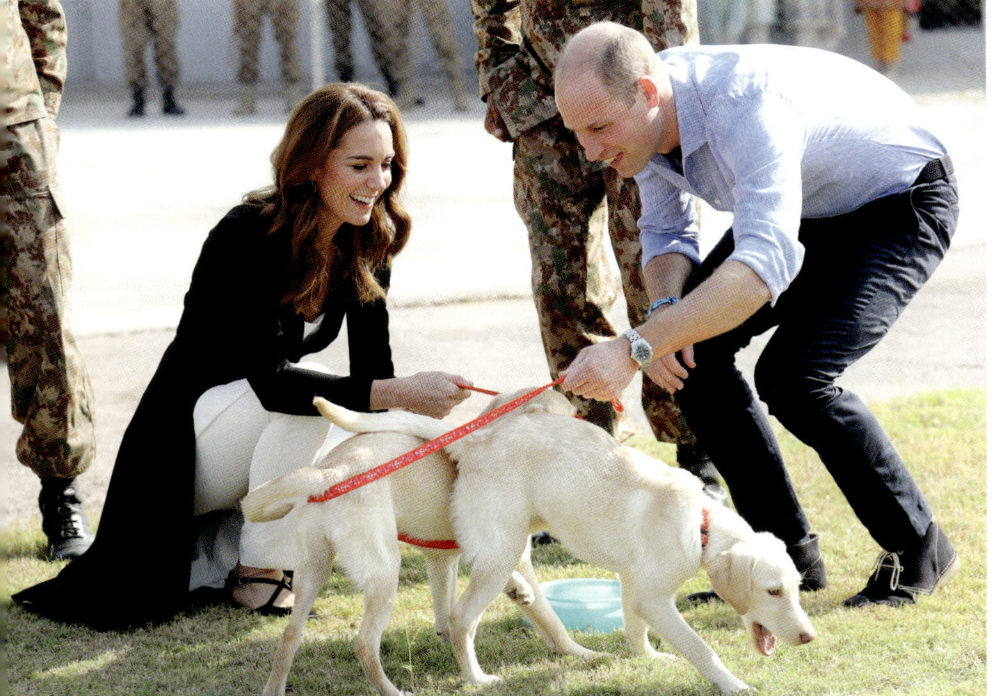

OVERSEAS WITH WILLIAM AND CATHERINE

Over the years, I have made many memorable overseas visits with the Prince and Princess of Wales, all of them showcasing the couple's warmth and respect for different cultures, traditions, and people. I have also captured their considerable dancing prowess and their innate sense of style. Trips that stand out include Belize in March 2022, when the princess danced on the beach during a traditional Garifuna Festival to celebrate the people's arrival in the country, and the royal couple taking part in some "doggy diplomacy" during a visit to the Army Canine Centre in Islamabad, Pakistan, in October 2019. And how could I forget that meeting with the Jamaican bobsleigh team in Kingston during a Platinum Jubilee visit in March 2022!

Overleaf, left
The Prince and Princess of Wales pose in front of the Taj Mahal at Agra during a visit to India, 16 April 2016.

Overleaf, right
Taking in the awesome scale of the Caracol Mayan archaeological site in the Chiquibul Forest Reserve on the third day of a Platinum Jubilee tour to Belize, 21 March 2022.

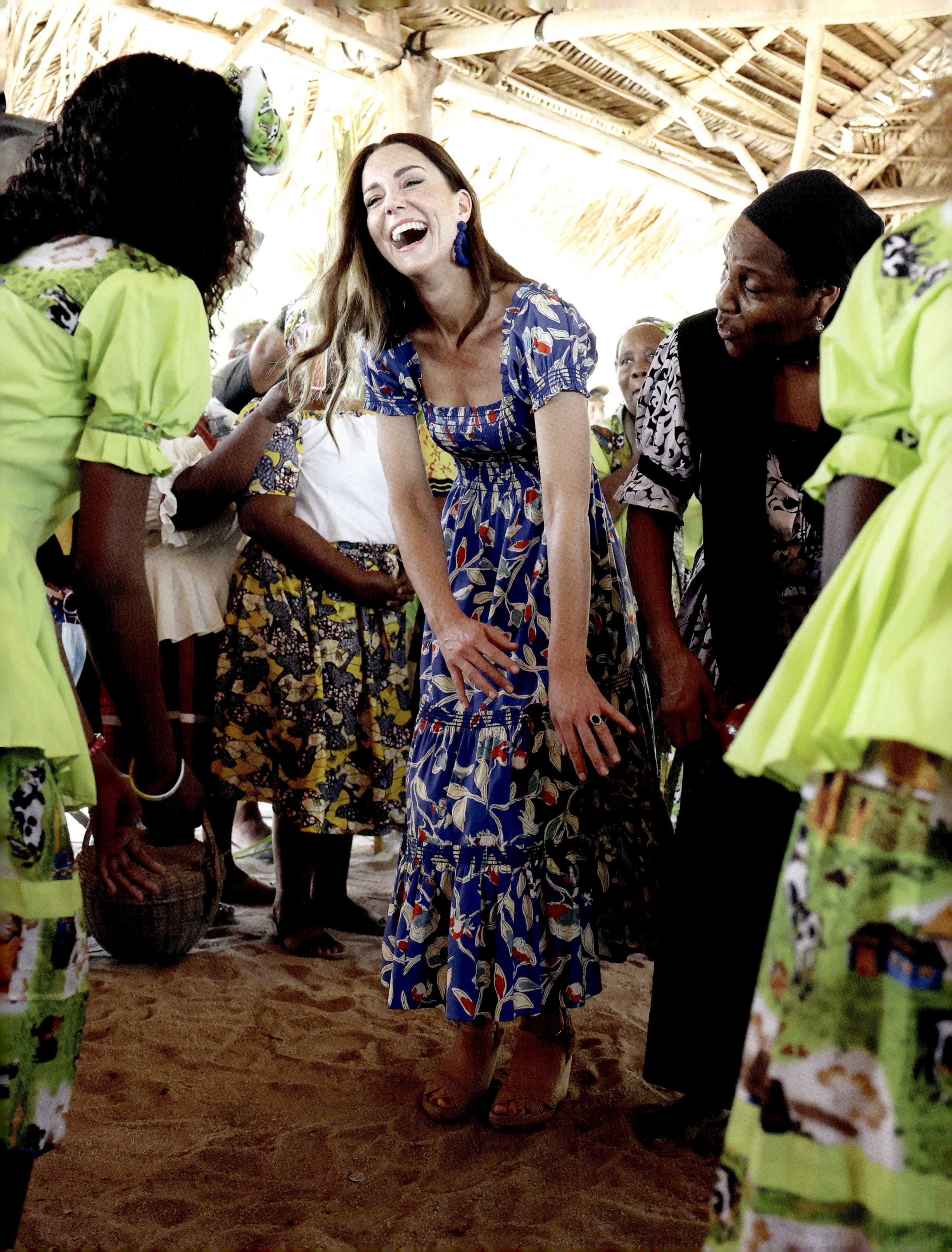

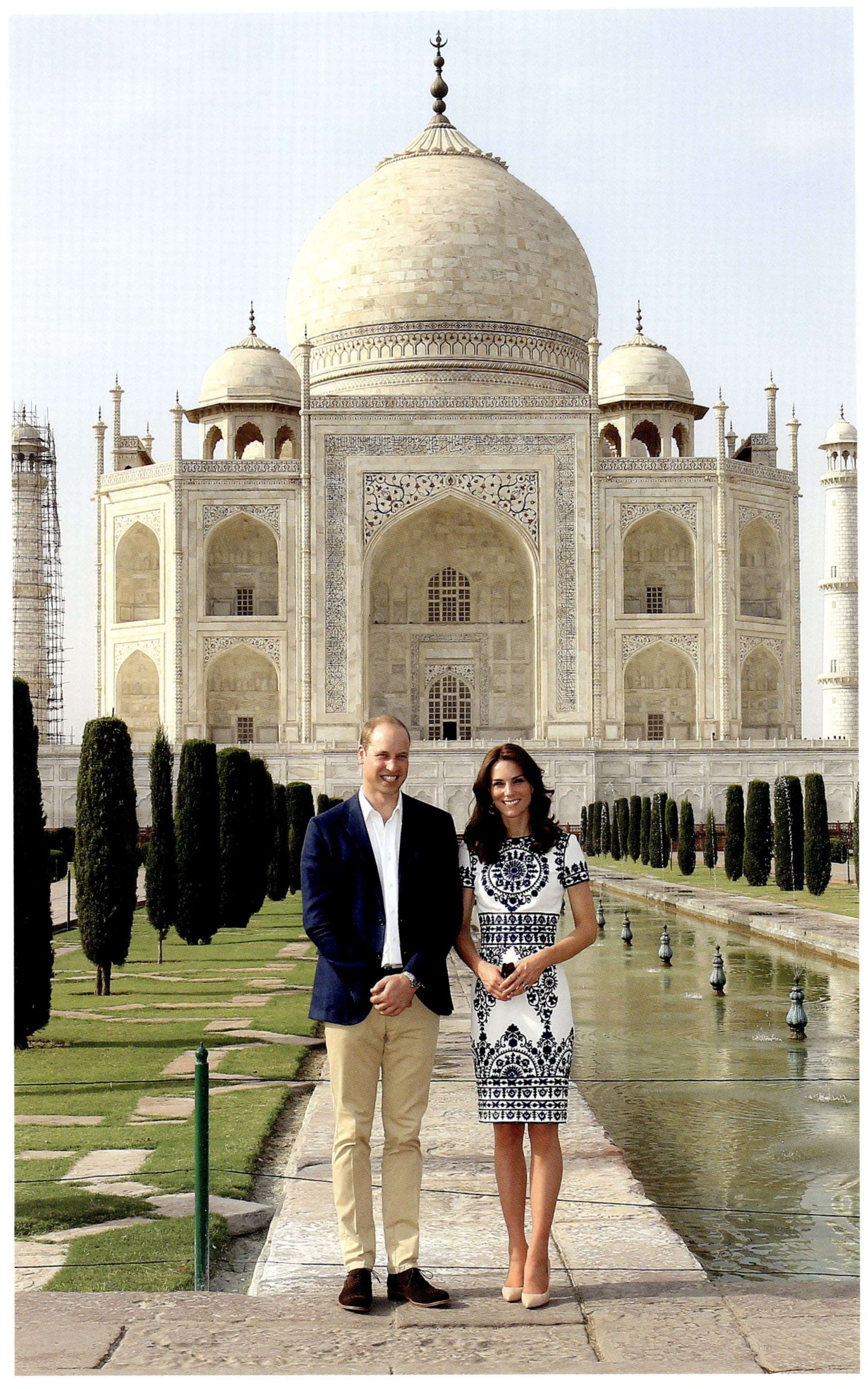

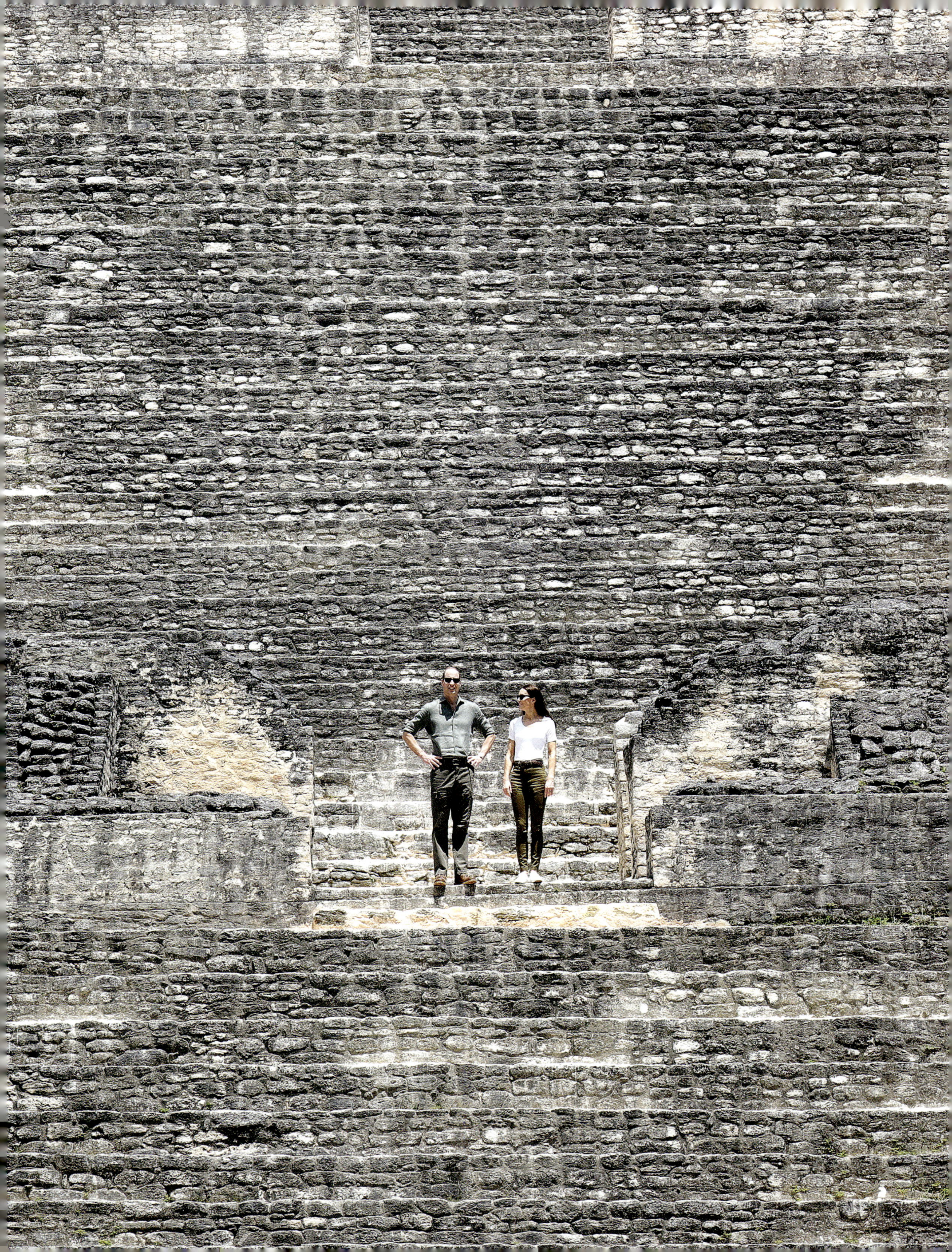

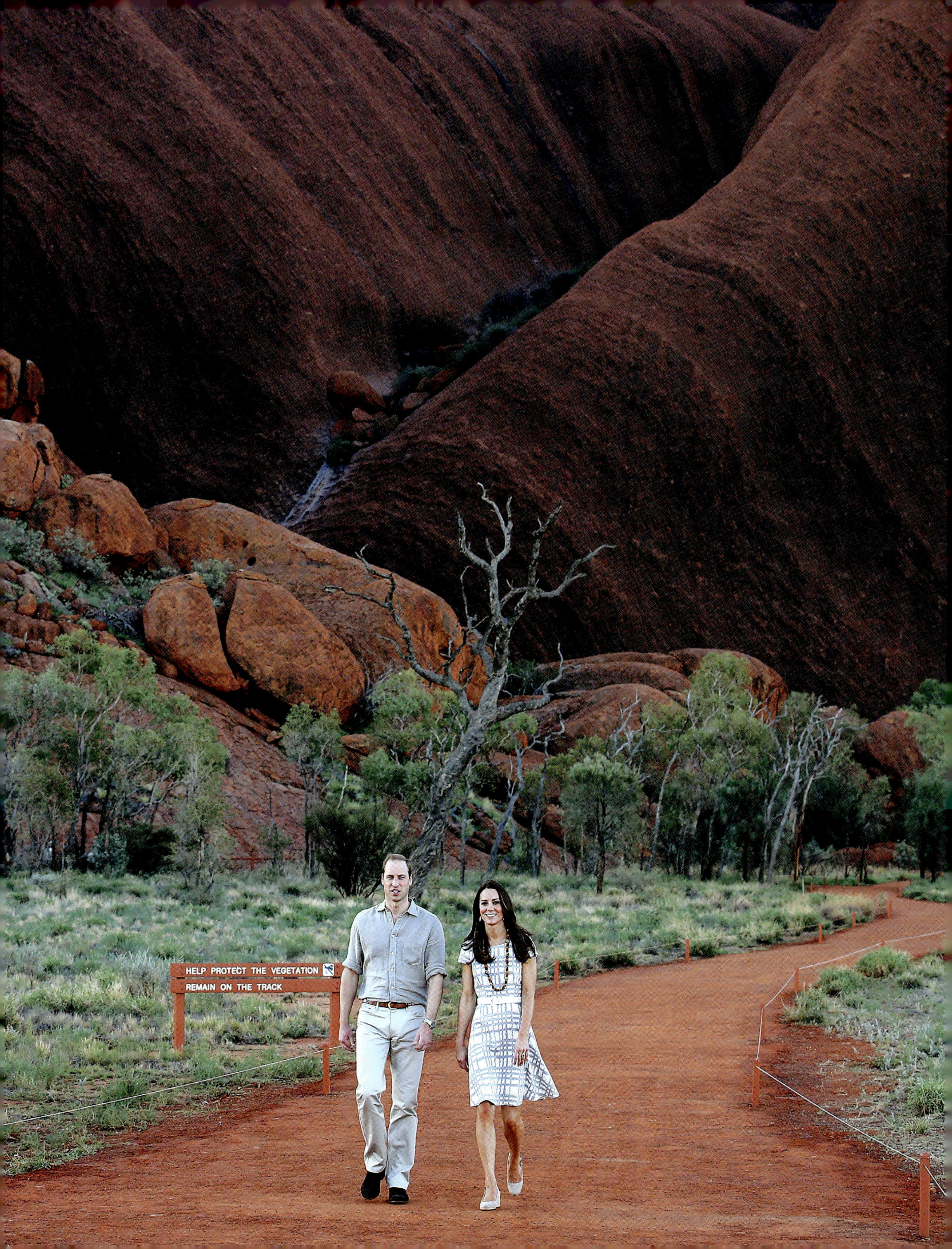
HELP PROTECT THE VEGETATION
REMAIN ON THE TRACK

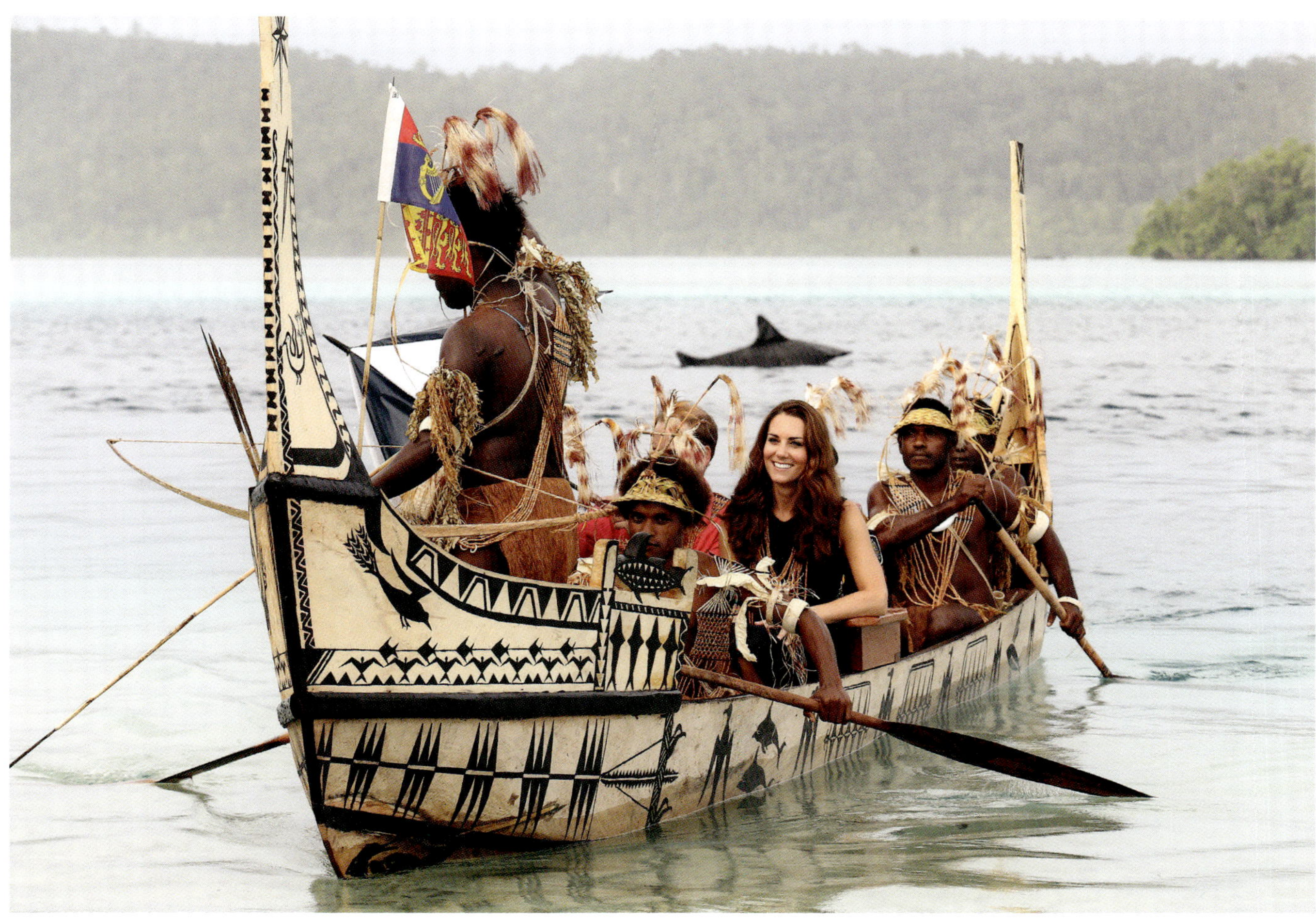

Opposite
A guided walk around the base of the spiritual site of Uluru (formerly known as Ayers Rock) in Australia's Northern Territory, sacred to the Anangu people, 22 April 2014.

Above
Things can sometimes take an unpredictable turn – the Princess was not expecting to see a fake shark swimming up behind her traditional canoe during a visit to Tavanipupu Island in the South Pacific on a Diamond Jubilee tour, 17 September 2012.

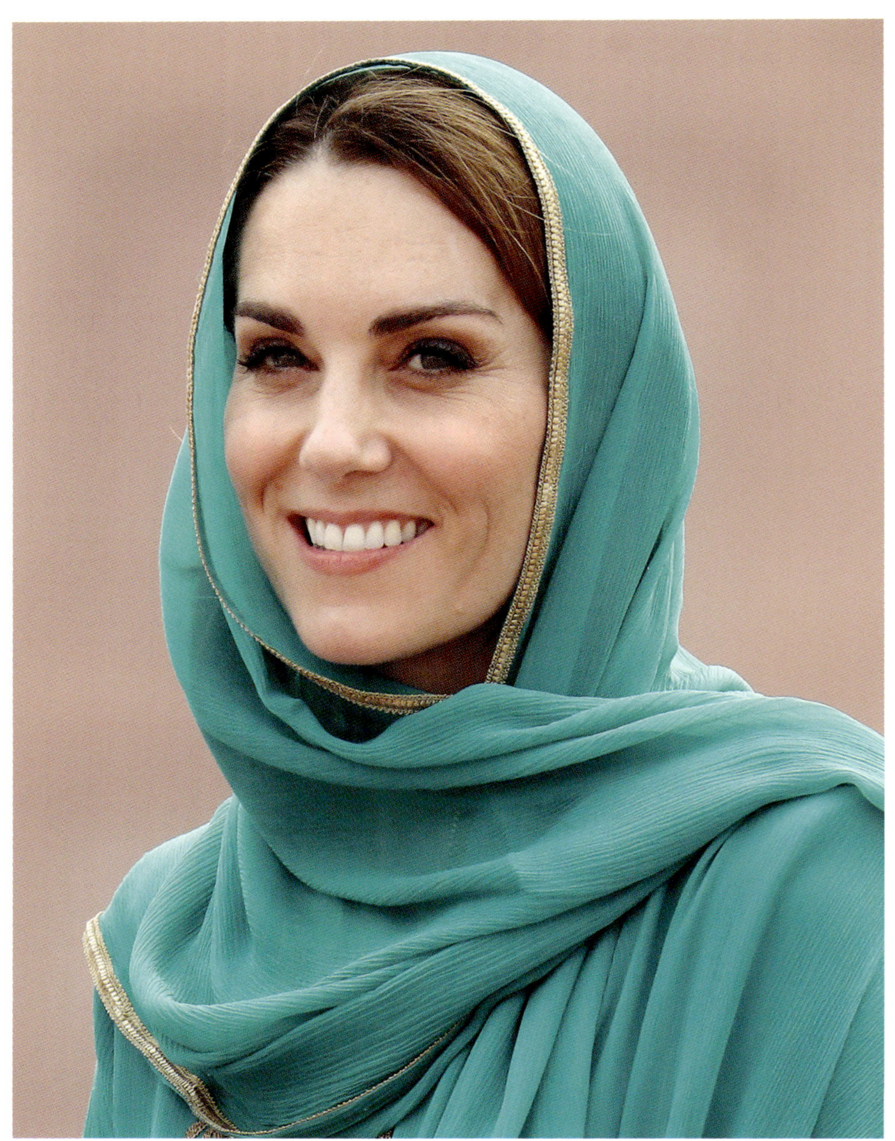

The Prince and Princess of Wales depart the Badshahi Mosque within the Walled City of Lahore during a visit to the country, 17 October 2019. The day was memorable for me as the royal plane we travelled on (RAF Voyager) was forced to turn back on its return to Islamabad after trying multiple times to land while a storm engulfed the city and all aircraft had to divert. I remember feeling like I was stuck in a washing machine as luggage and drinks were tossed around the cabin. This resulted in an unexpected night in Lahore – quite the adventure!

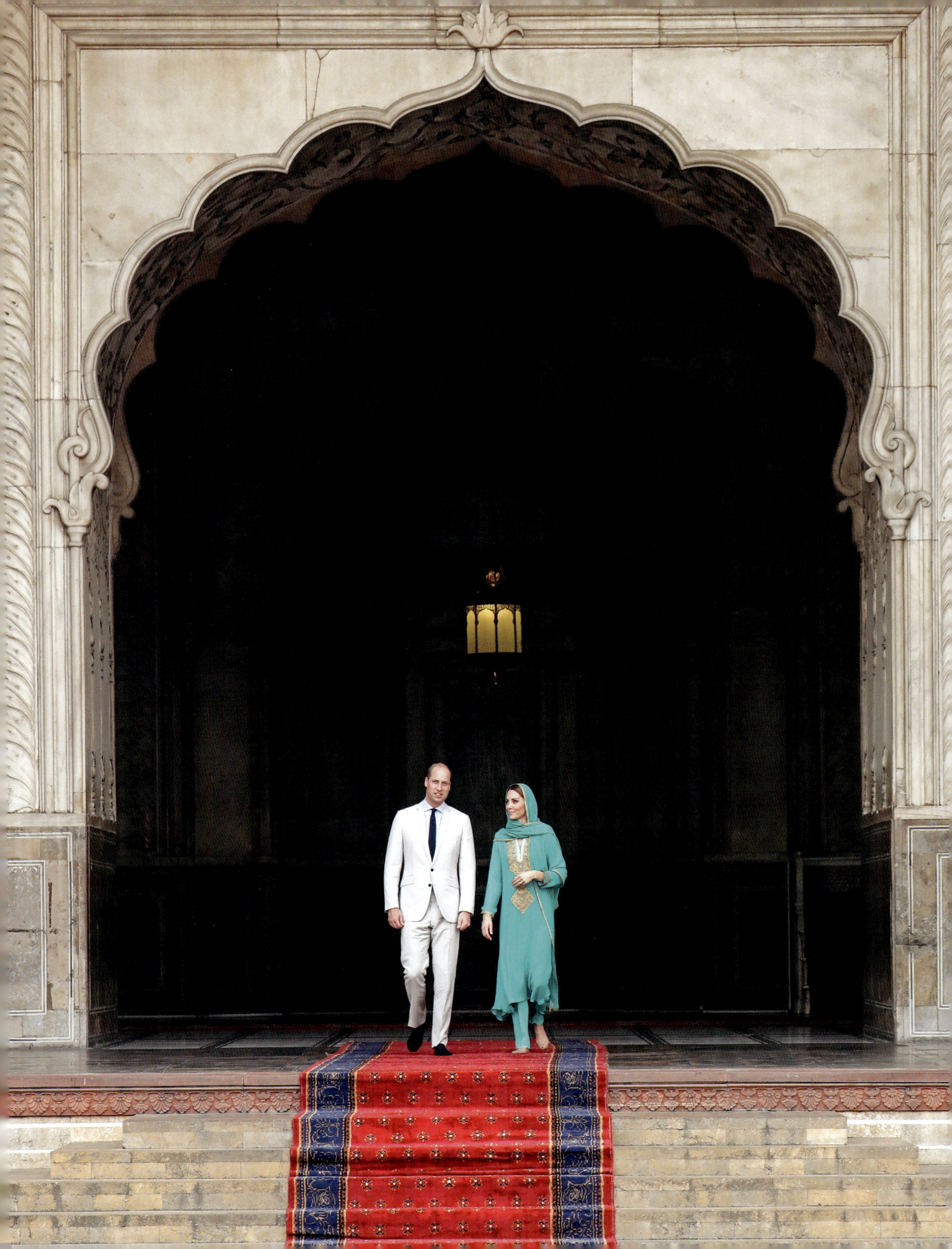

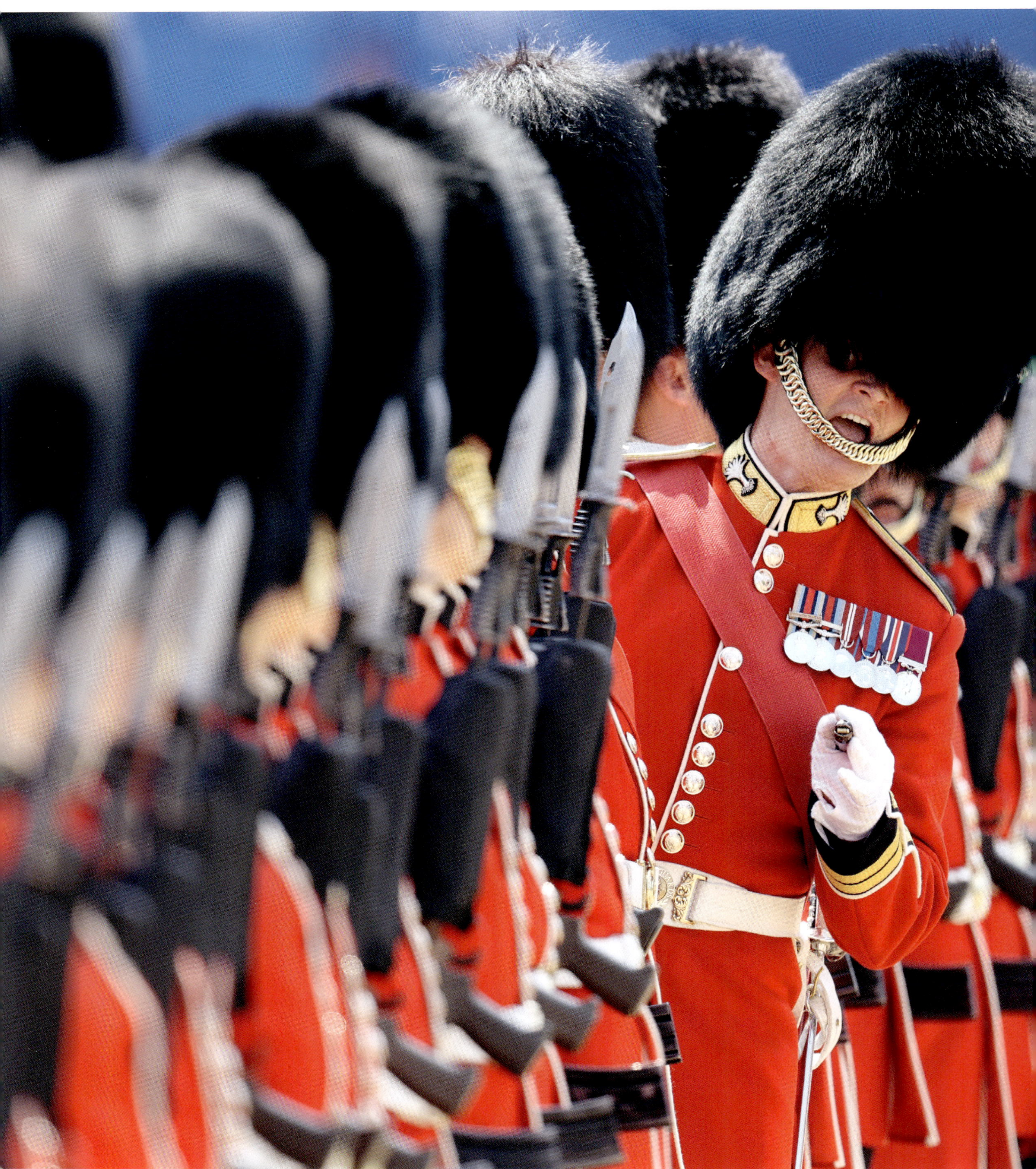

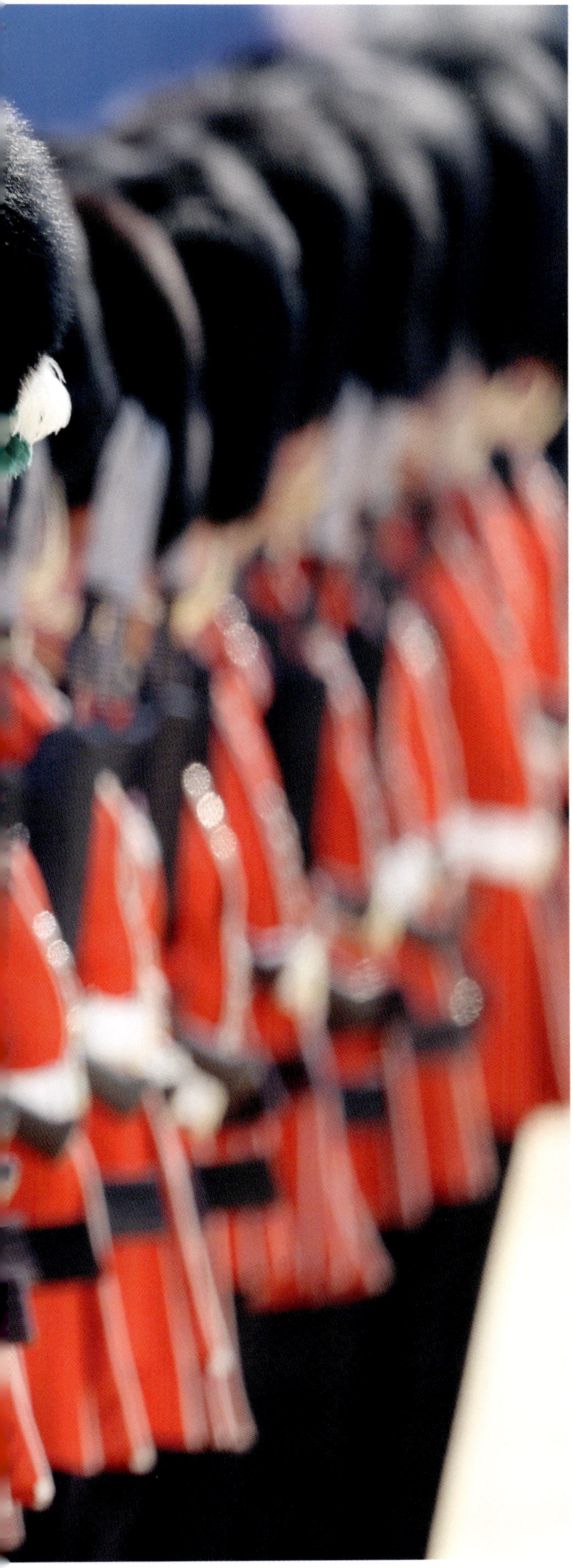

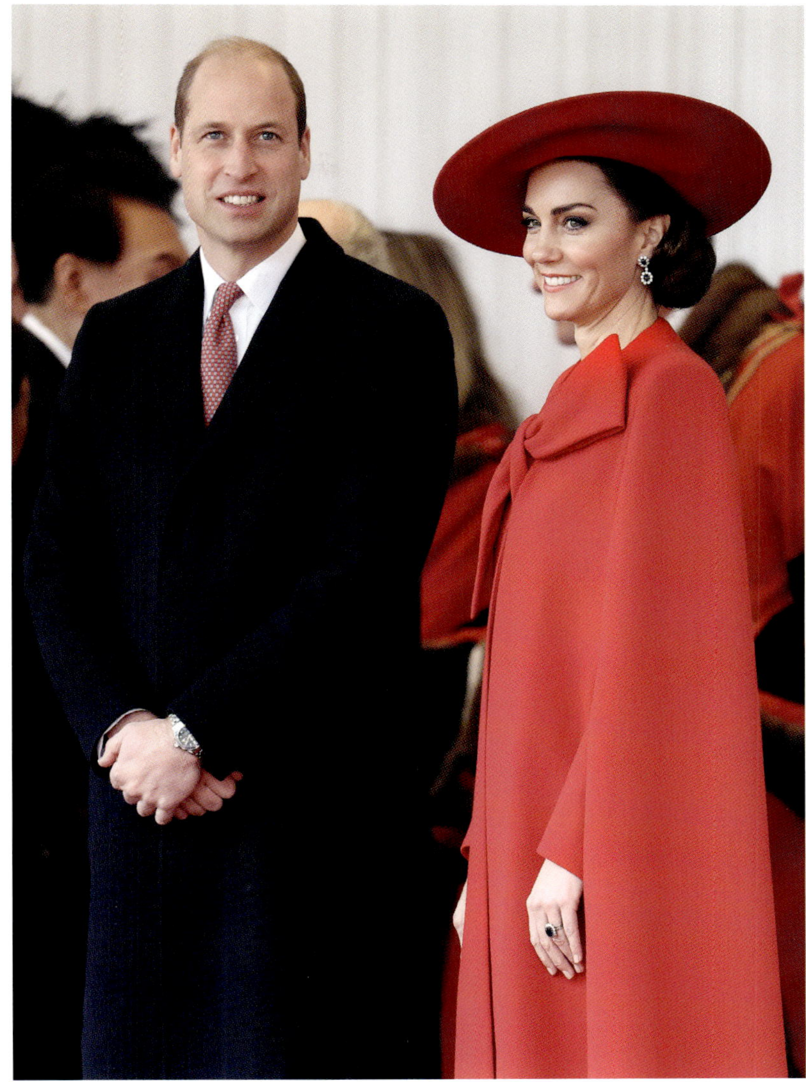

A ROYAL WELCOME

Alongside global travel, incoming State Visits enable the royals to showcase the "Best of British" ceremony and tradition. They are also an opportunity to exercise soft power to build and strengthen relationships across the world. Ceremonial welcomes normally take place on Horse Guards Parade with a carriage trip down the Mall for the incoming dignitaries. Pictured here the Prince and Princess of Wales attend a ceremonial welcome for the President and First Lady of the Republic of Korea, 21 November 2023.

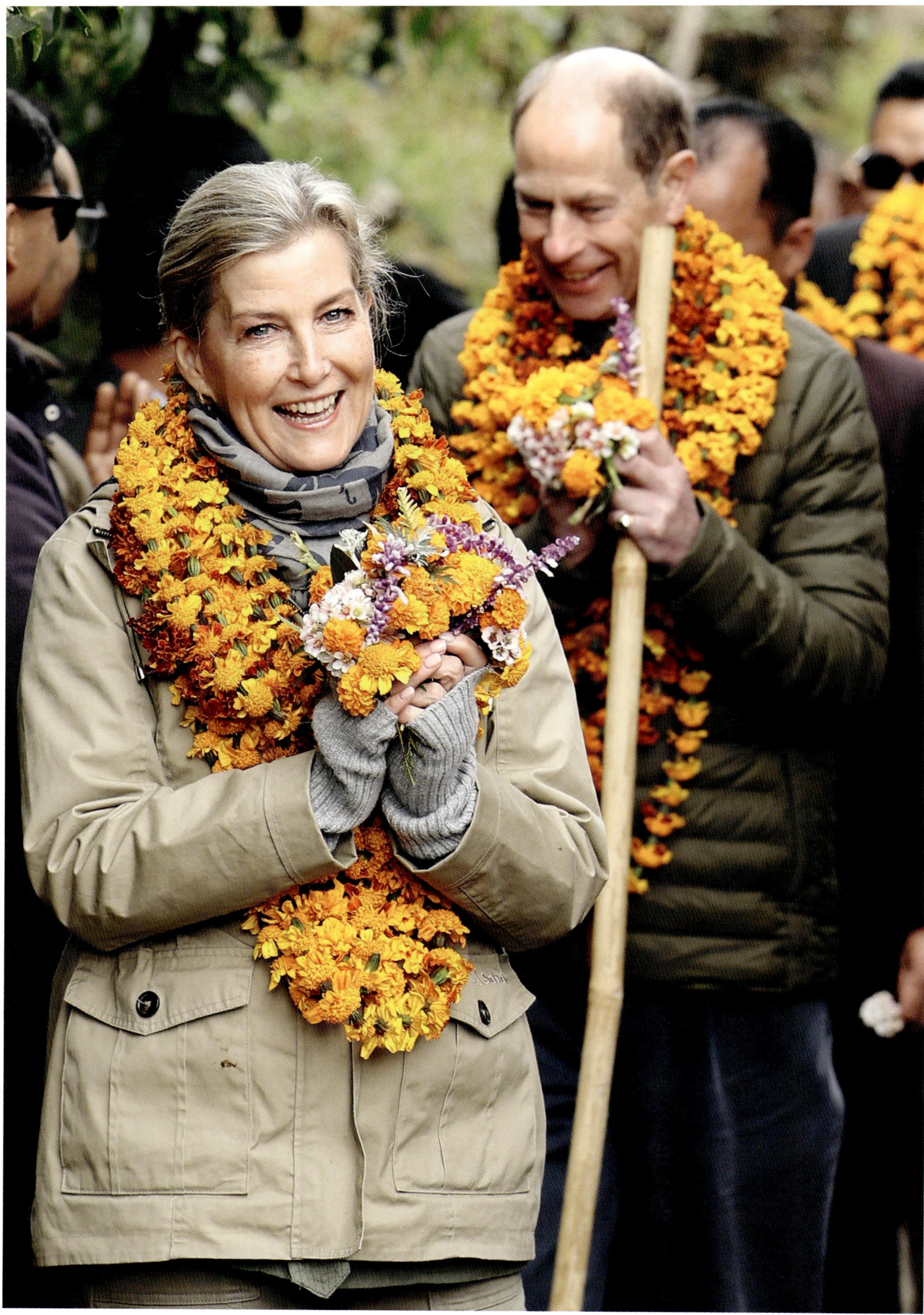

NEPAL AND THE GURKHAS

I visited Nepal with the Duke and Duchess of Edinburgh in February 2025. The country's mind-blowing landscapes combined with the warm and friendly people make it an unforgettable destination. Central to this visit was a Gurkha Attestation Ceremony, during which 274 young men (out of more than 13,000 aspiring recruits) were accepted as new members of this elite regiment of the British Army. I was not expecting this to be such an emotional experience, but I soon realized the enormity of the event. Many of the men's families were there to bid them farewell as they left to begin their training at Catterick in Yorkshire, spending years away from home while providing for their families in Nepal. Parents were visibly moved and so incredibly proud of their sons' achievements. It was heart-warming to capture their interactions with the Duke and Duchess as they moved around the families chatting to them all.

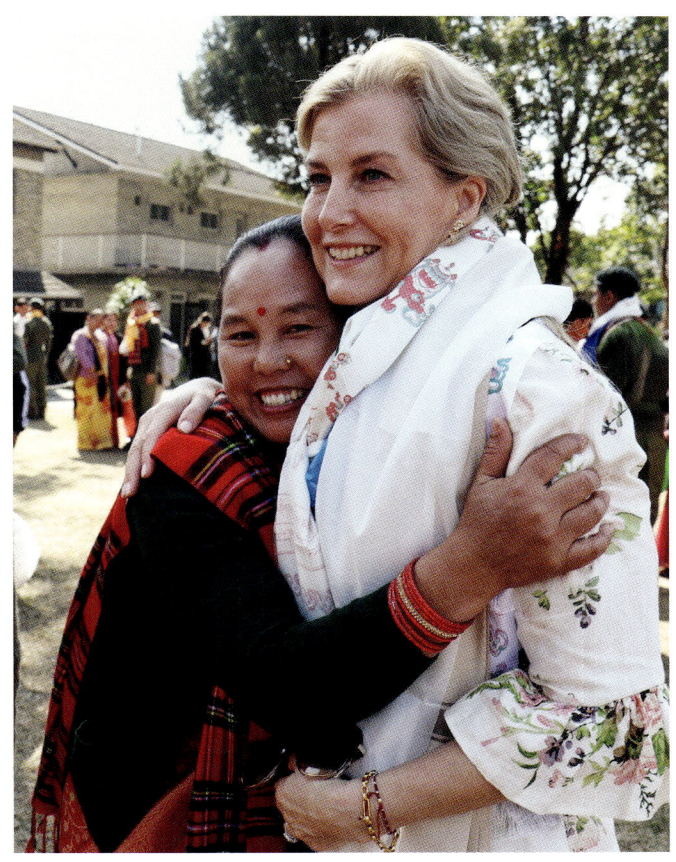

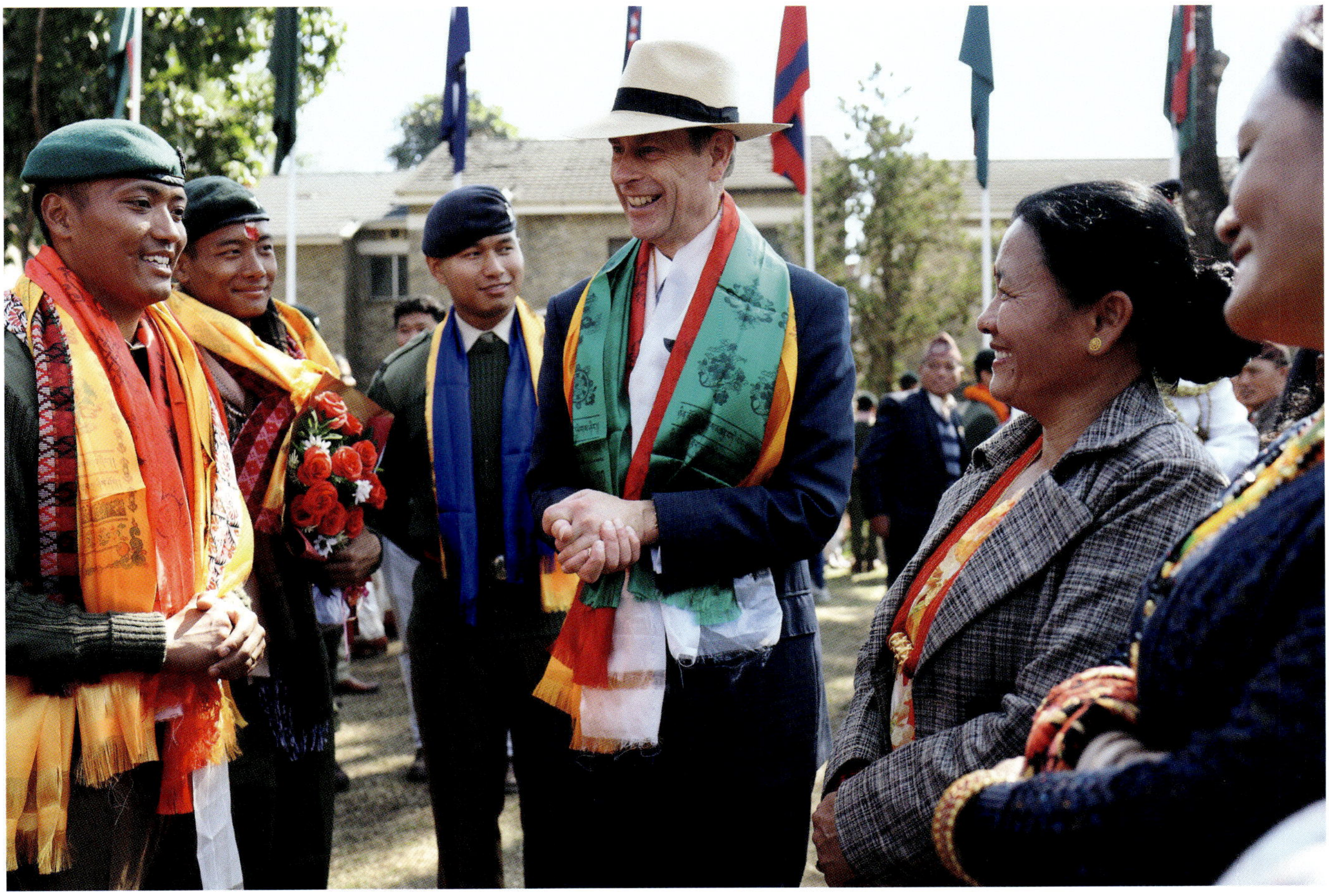

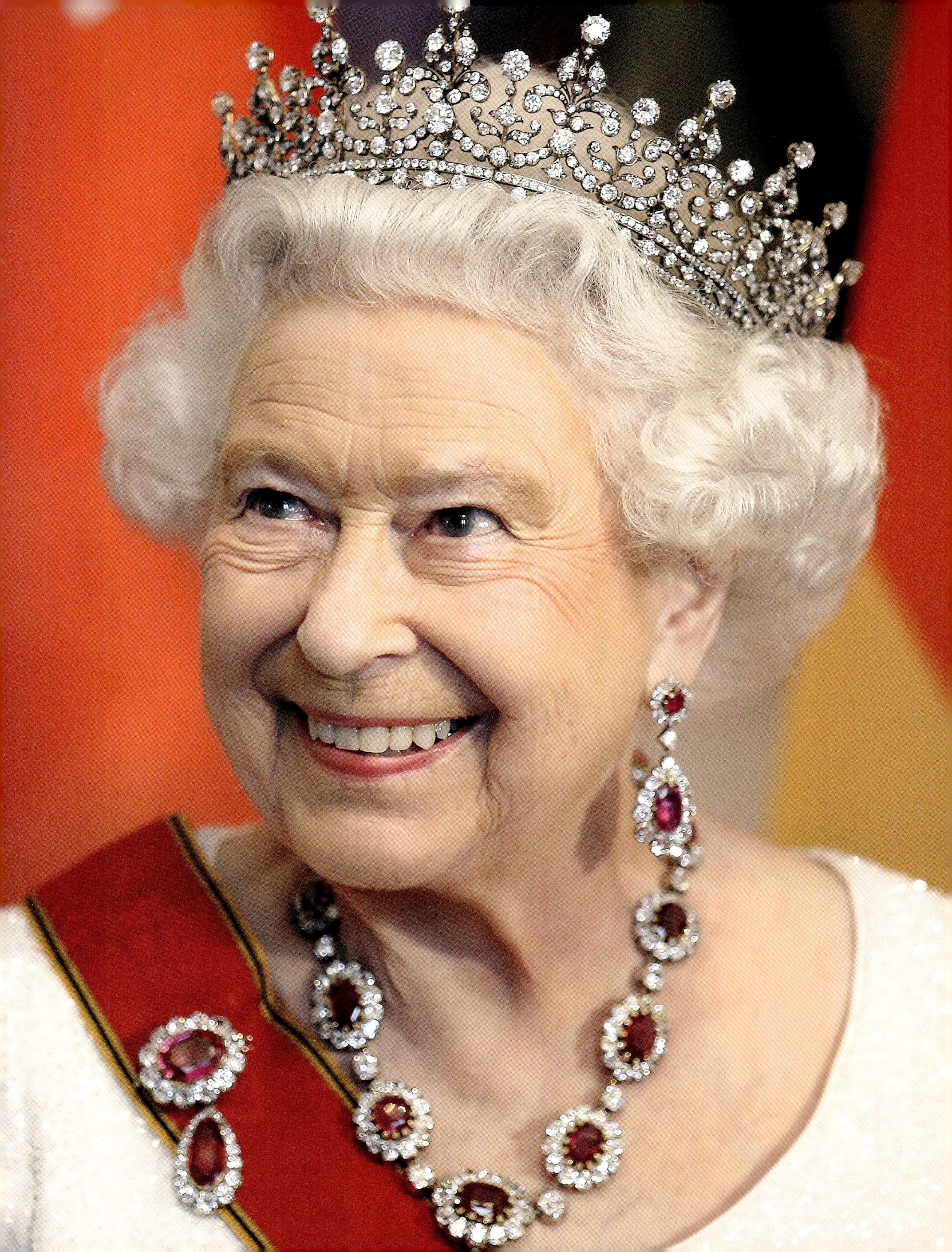

4

QUEEN ELIZABETH II

AN UNSURPASSED LEGACY

As we are now firmly ensconced in the Carolean era it feels strangely nostalgic to look back on the unparalleled rule of Queen Elizabeth II, Britain's longest-reigning monarch. Her face was part of our lives for so long, from banknotes and stamps to her Christmas messages and her smile lighting up royal engagements. I was fortunate to photograph her throughout her life and will never forget the unwavering excitement each opportunity brought, from portraits to day-to-day royal engagements.

The period of her passing is etched in my memory, as it is for so many of us. I was in Windsor when I heard the news, and looked up to see an incredibly vibrant rainbow develop over the Round Tower of Windsor Castle at the same moment as the Union Flag was dropped to half-mast (see p. 68). The collective mourning of a nation that was also celebrating and appreciating her service was captured in this poignant sight. Such was the longevity and steadfastness of this towering figure in British public life that it was hard to believe this day would ever come.

In November 2020, I was commissioned to take an image of Queen Elizabeth and Prince Philip to commemorate their 73rd wedding anniversary. Coronavirus restrictions remained in place during this period, and Windsor Castle was being run according to strict protocols. I remember the surrealness of the situation as I moved through the deserted corridors and worked on my own to capture this image of the royal couple looking through some of the many cards they had received. The homemade card from their grandchildren, Prince George, Princess Charlotte, and Prince Louis, clearly brought them joy.

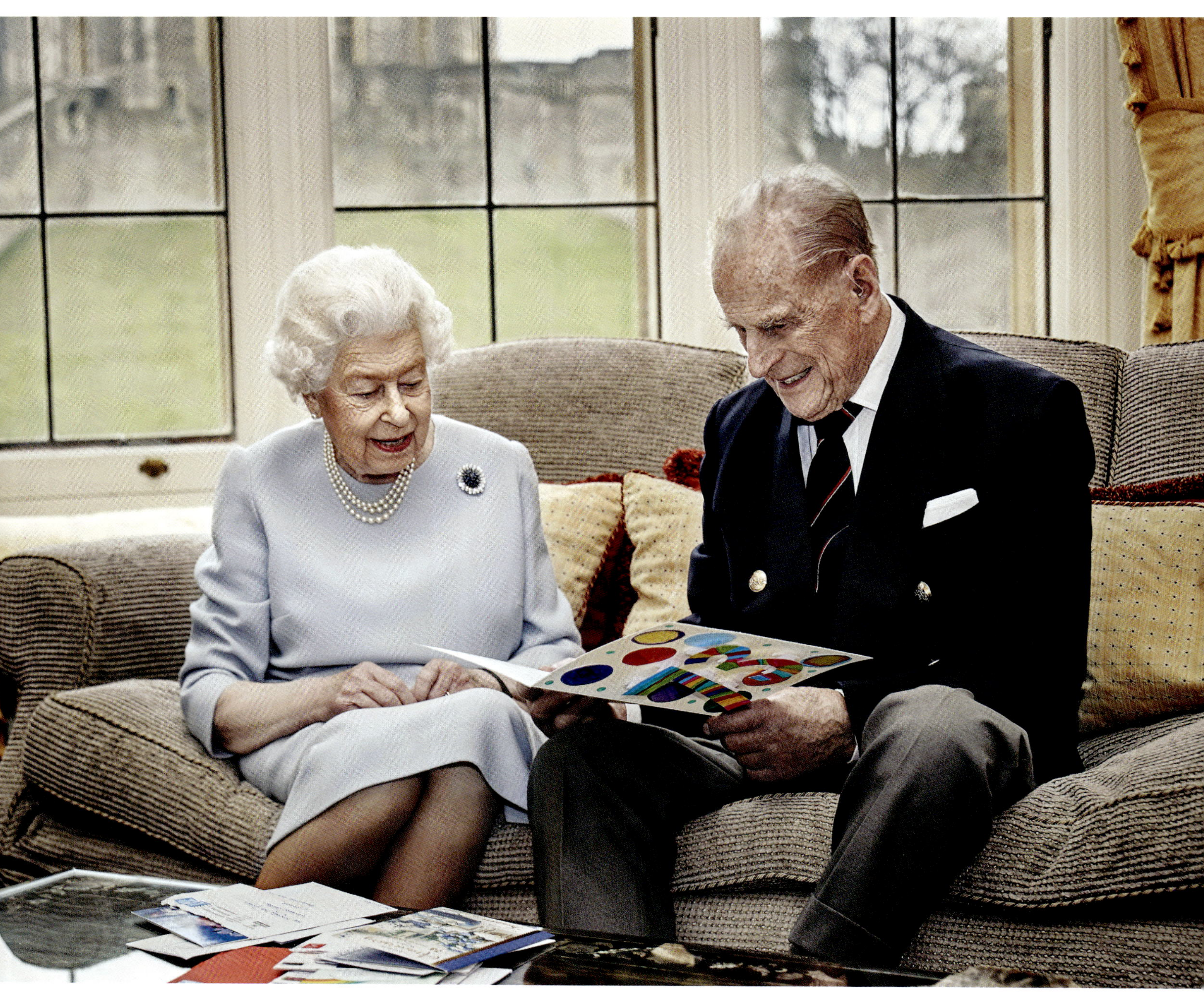

Taken at Sandringham in February 2022 to mark the start of her Platinum Jubilee, this is one of my favourite photographs of Queen Elizabeth. We see her characteristically radiant smile and the presence of the iconic red despatch box she received her official papers in every day of the year apart from Christmas, symbolizing her commitment to duty and devotion to her country. A picture of her father, George VI, is on the table next to her.

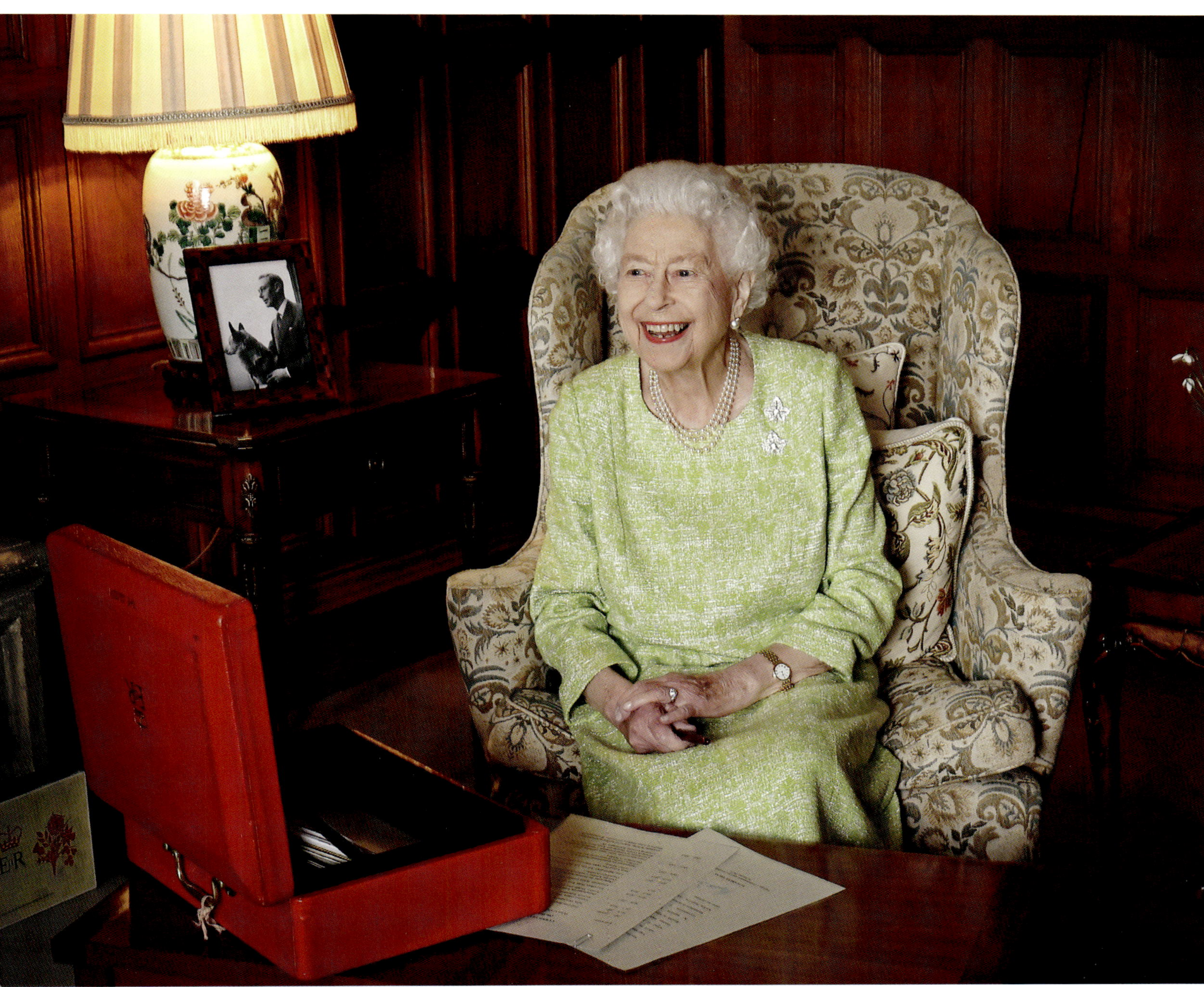

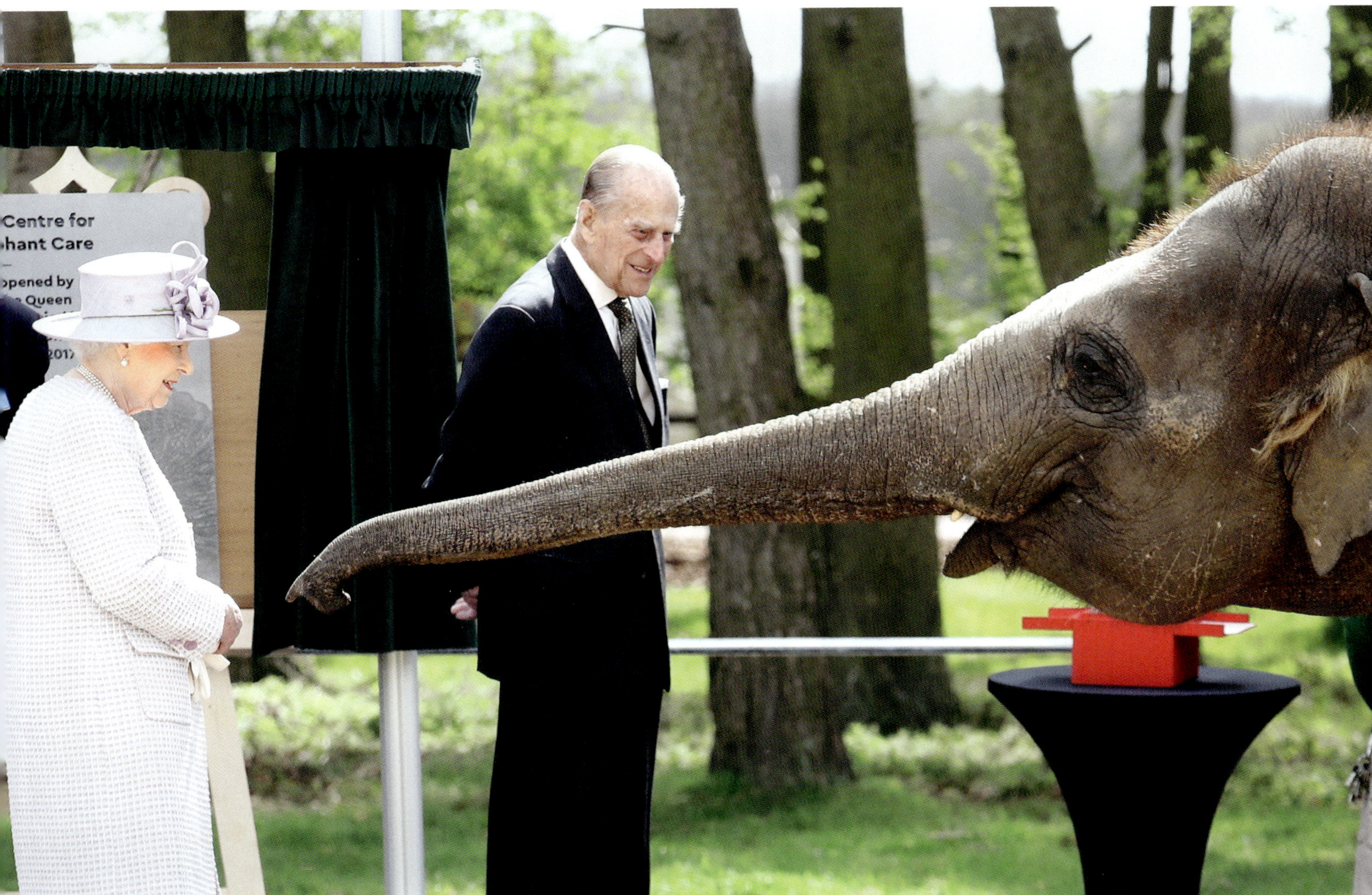

A DAY AT THE ZOO

It was at Whipsnade Zoo in April 2017 that one of the most unusual photographs of Queen Elizabeth's reign was taken, and one that featured on her official Christmas card that year. The queen was opening the new elephant centre at the zoo when Donna extended her trunk in an attempt to snaffle the banana from the smiling monarch's hand, as the Duke of Edinburgh looked on, chuckling.

During the queen's visit to the new maternity centre in Stevenage Hospital in June 2012, I took one of my most widely published images of the sovereign. The slightly cheeky smile gives an insight into the lighter side of Queen Elizabeth's personality.

Overleaf
Images of the Queen from every decade of her reign were projected onto the façade of Buckingham Palace to celebrate her Platinum Jubilee in 2022.

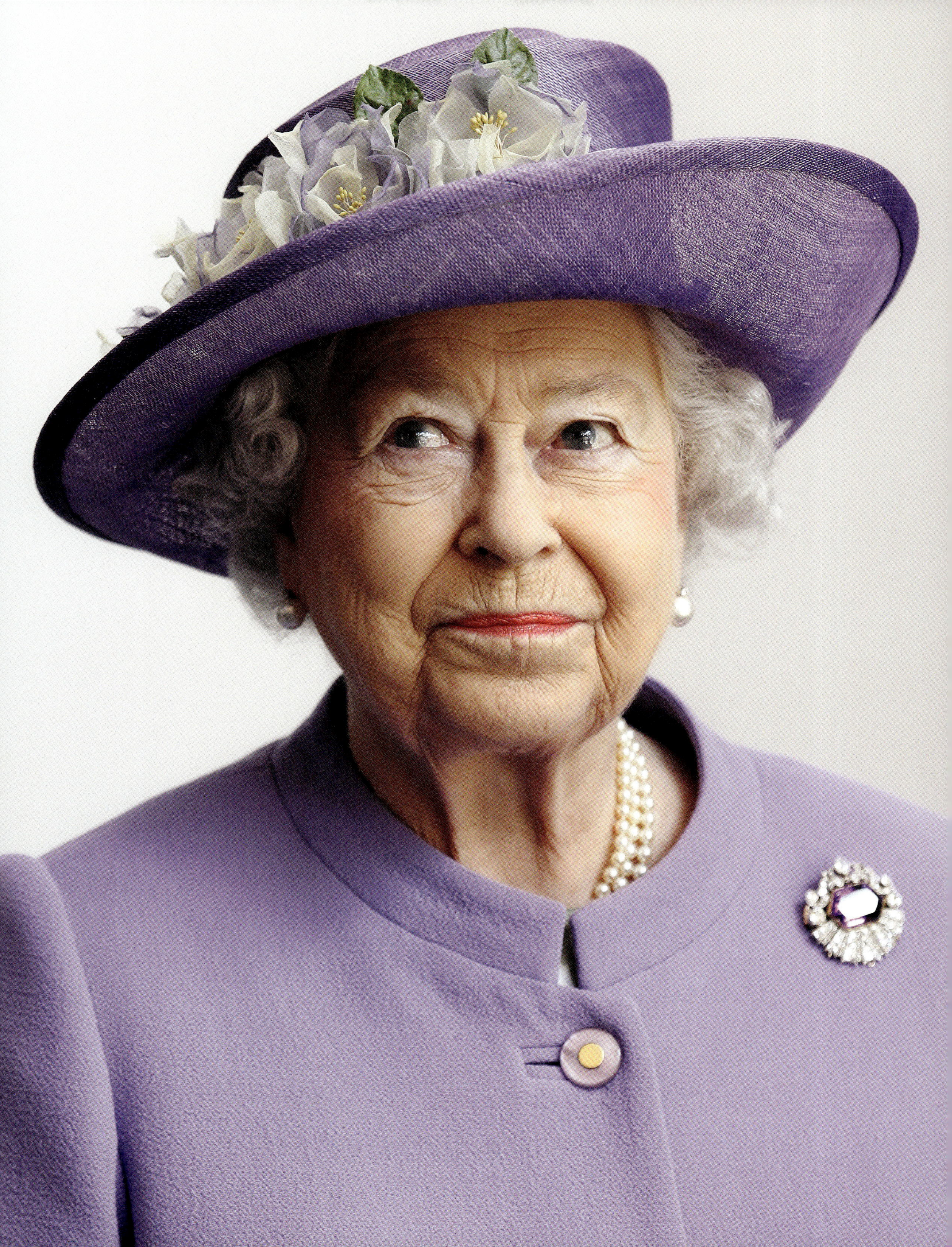

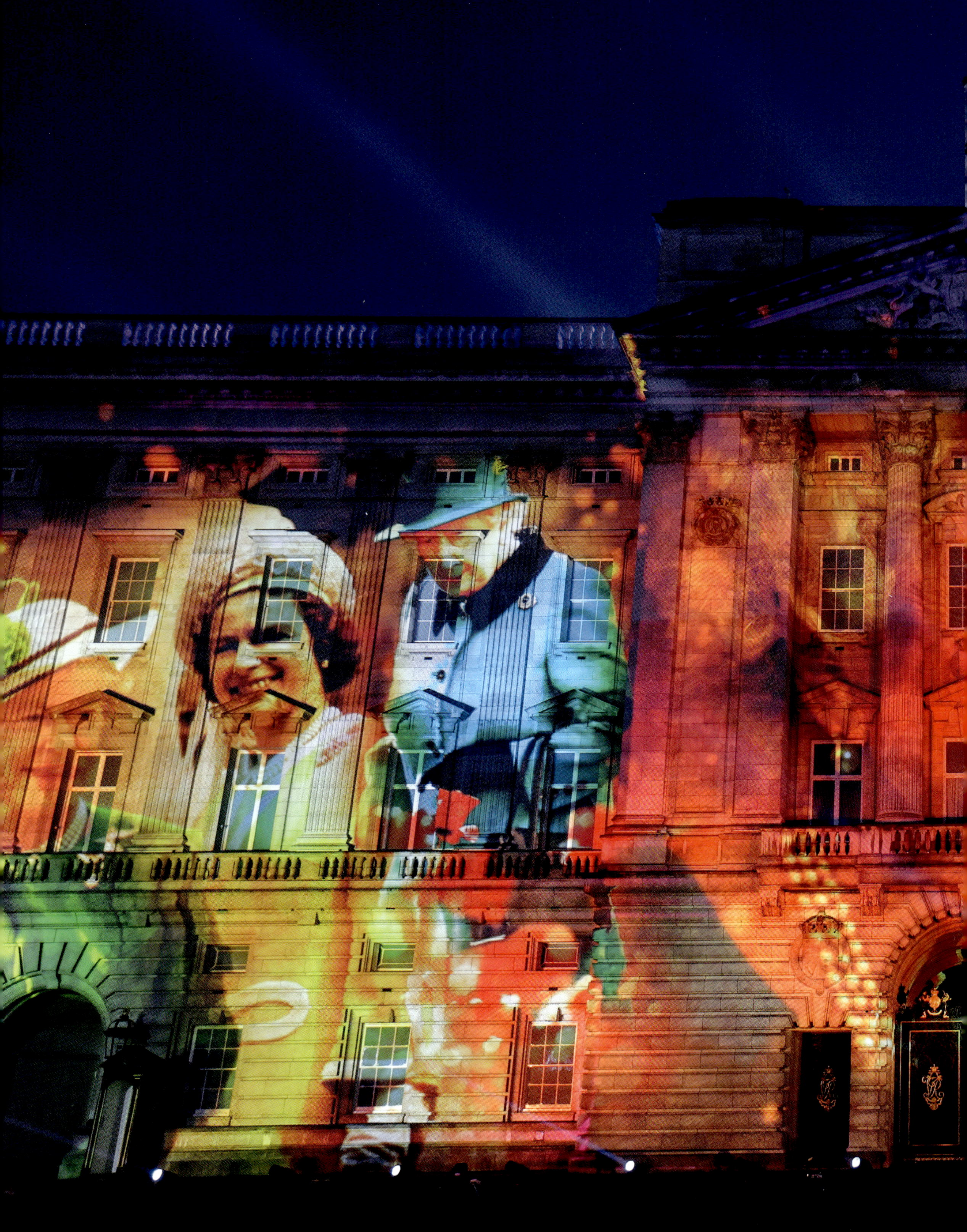

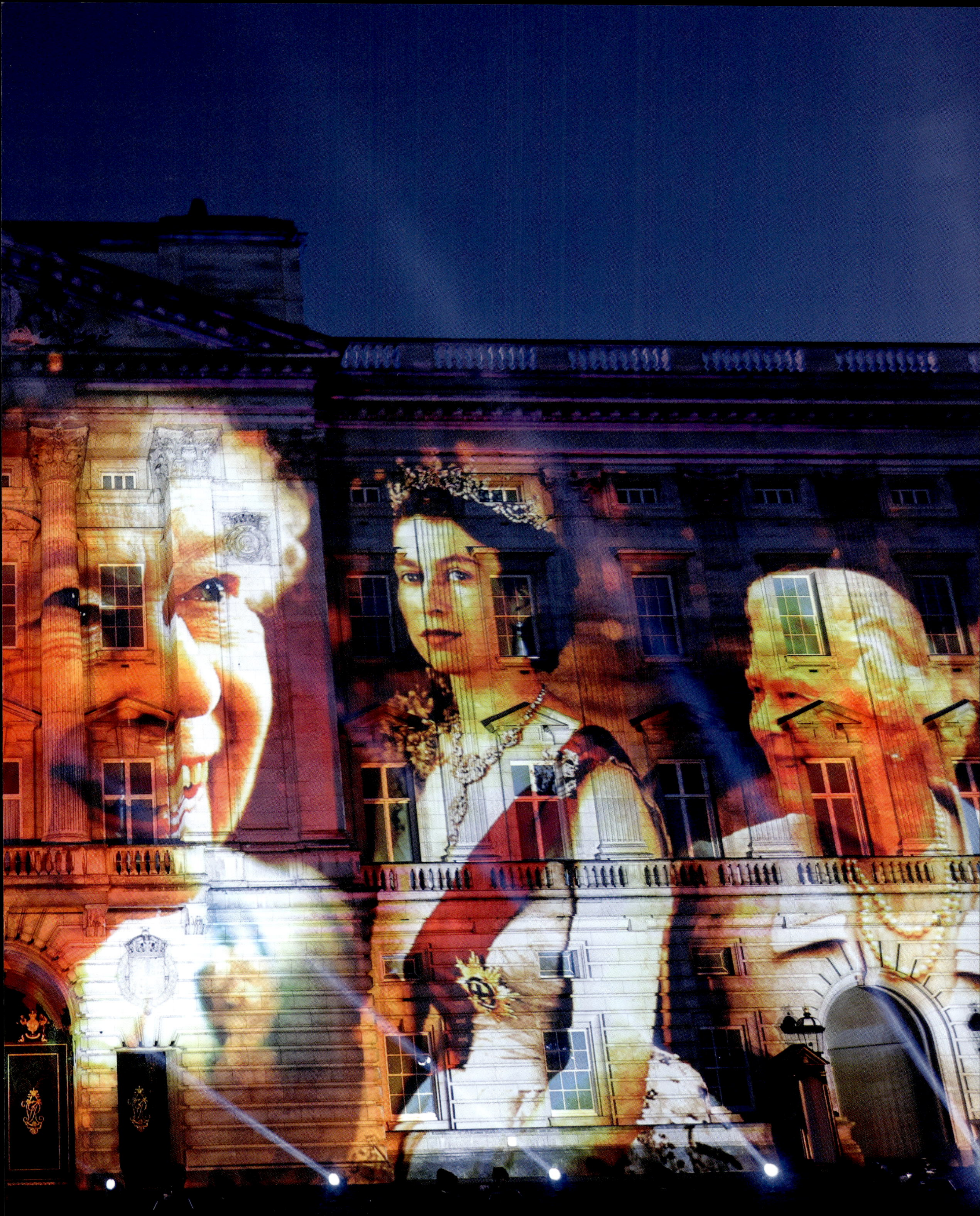

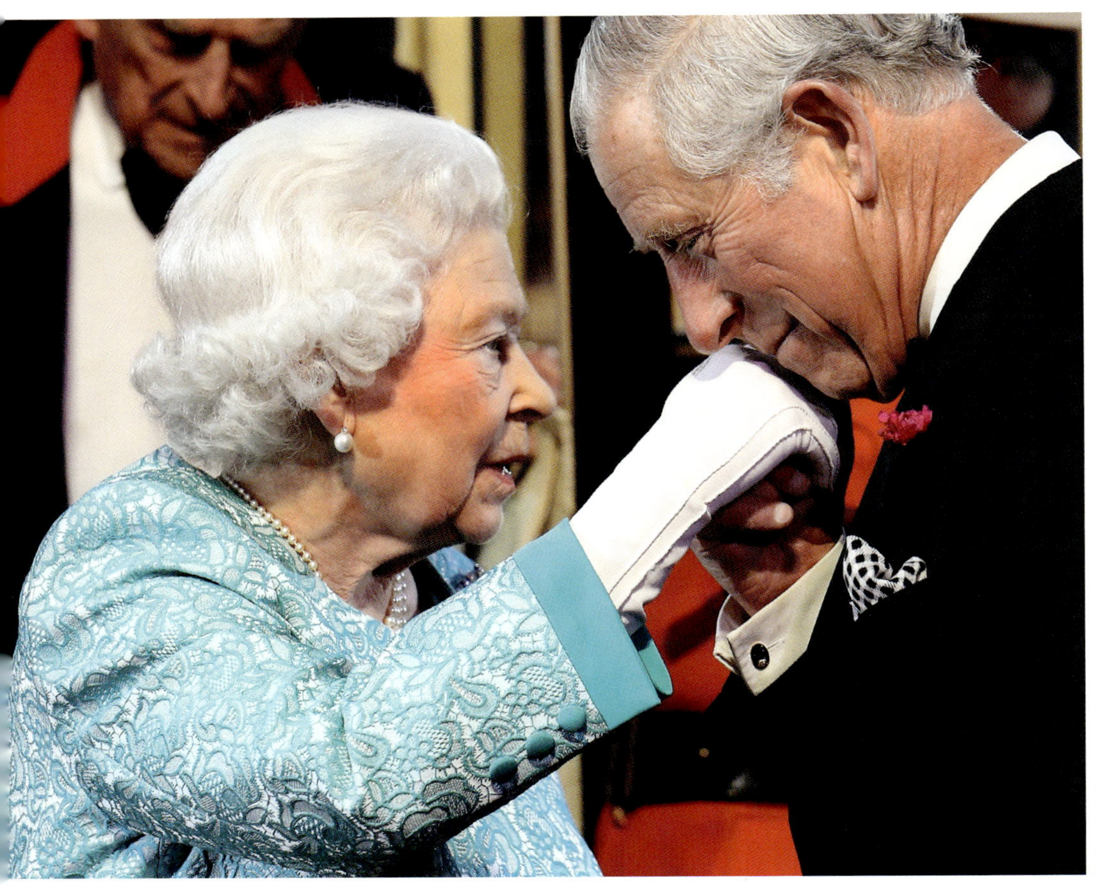

FAMILY RELATIONSHIPS

Queen Elizabeth II had an extremely close relationship with her children and grandchildren, and it was always lovely to see her with them at various royal events. She is met with a kiss from her son as she steps down from the royal carriage for the final night of her 90th birthday celebrations, 15 May 2016. The show featured 1,500 performers and 900 horses, and told the story of the Queen's life.

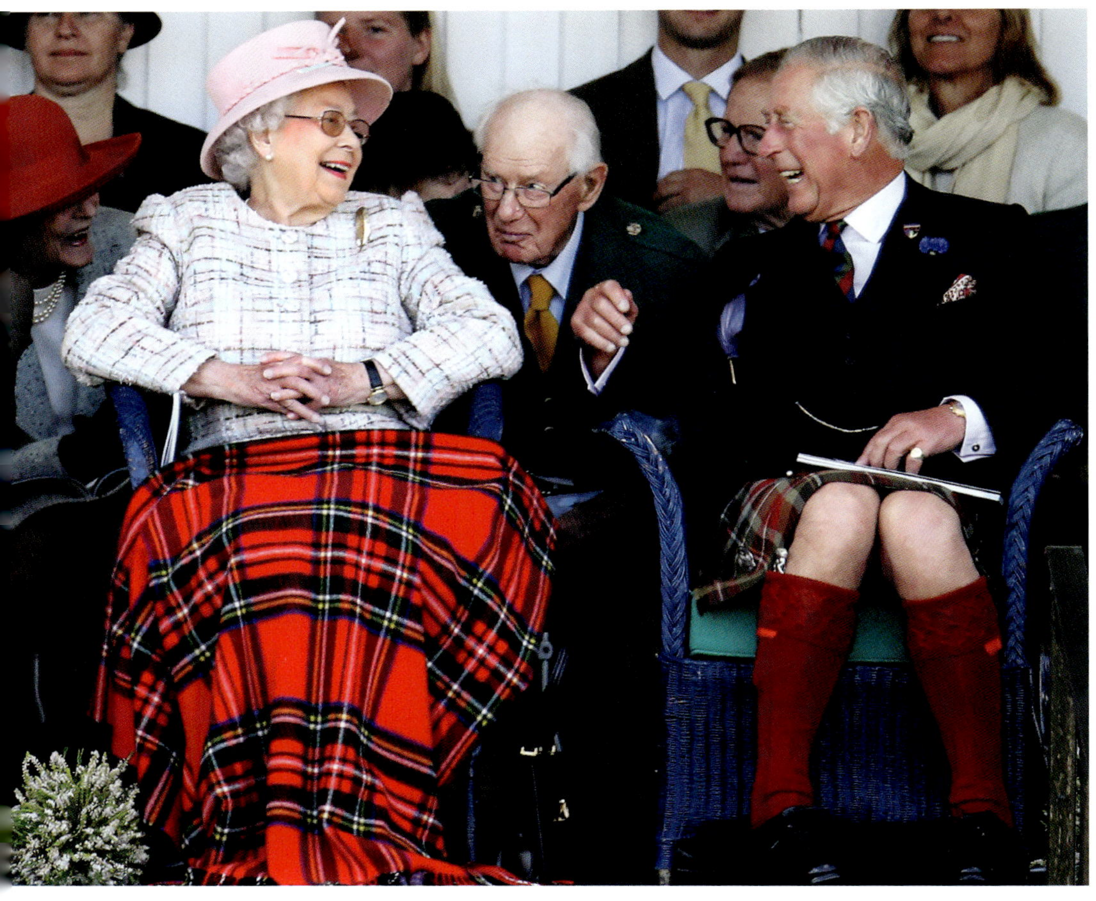

Left
The Braemar Gathering in Scotland was always a favourite event of mine at which to capture a very relaxed Queen with her children, 2 September 2017.

Opposite
Queen Elizabeth greets William and Catherine in the parade ring of Royal Ascot, 18 June 2019.

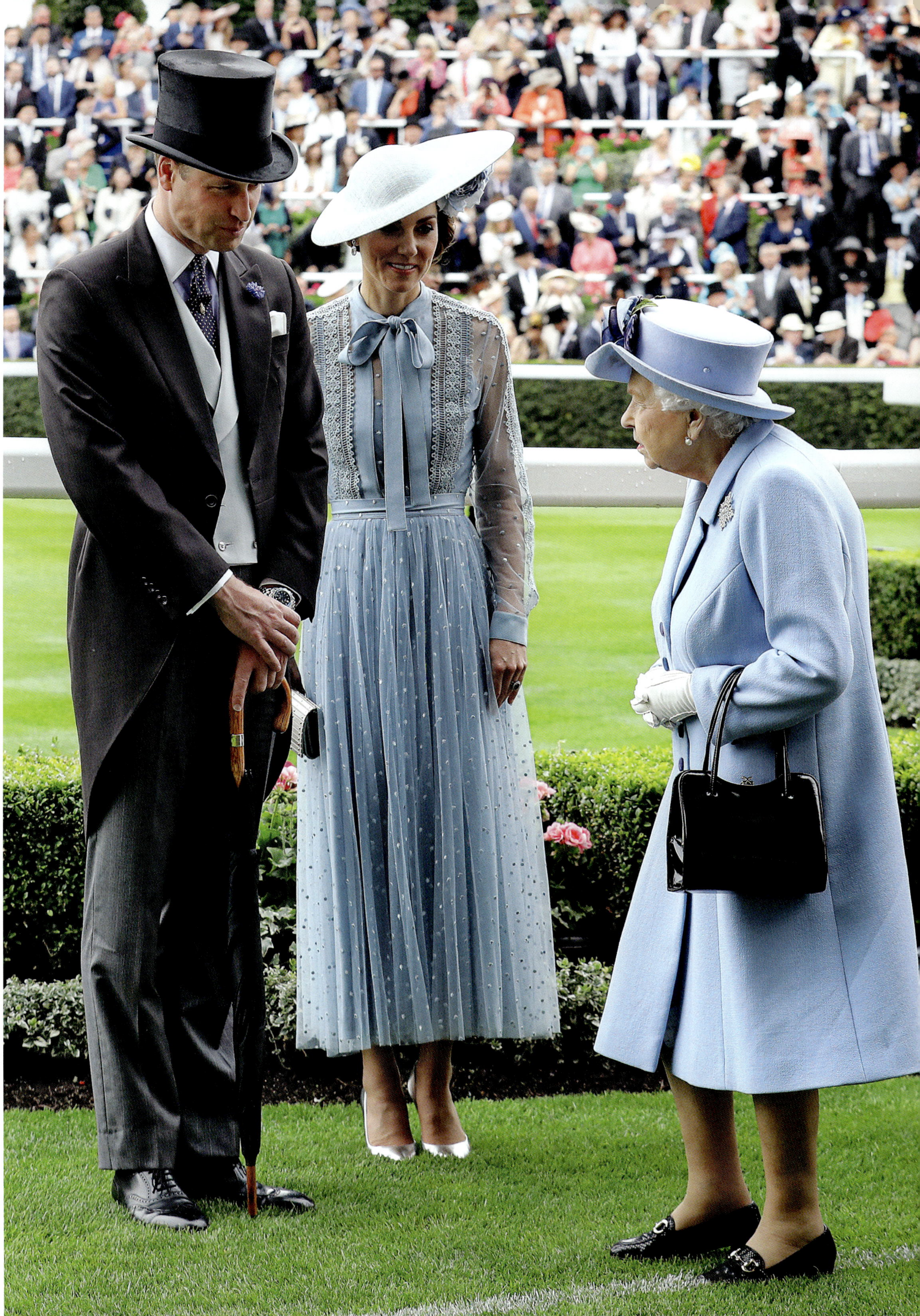

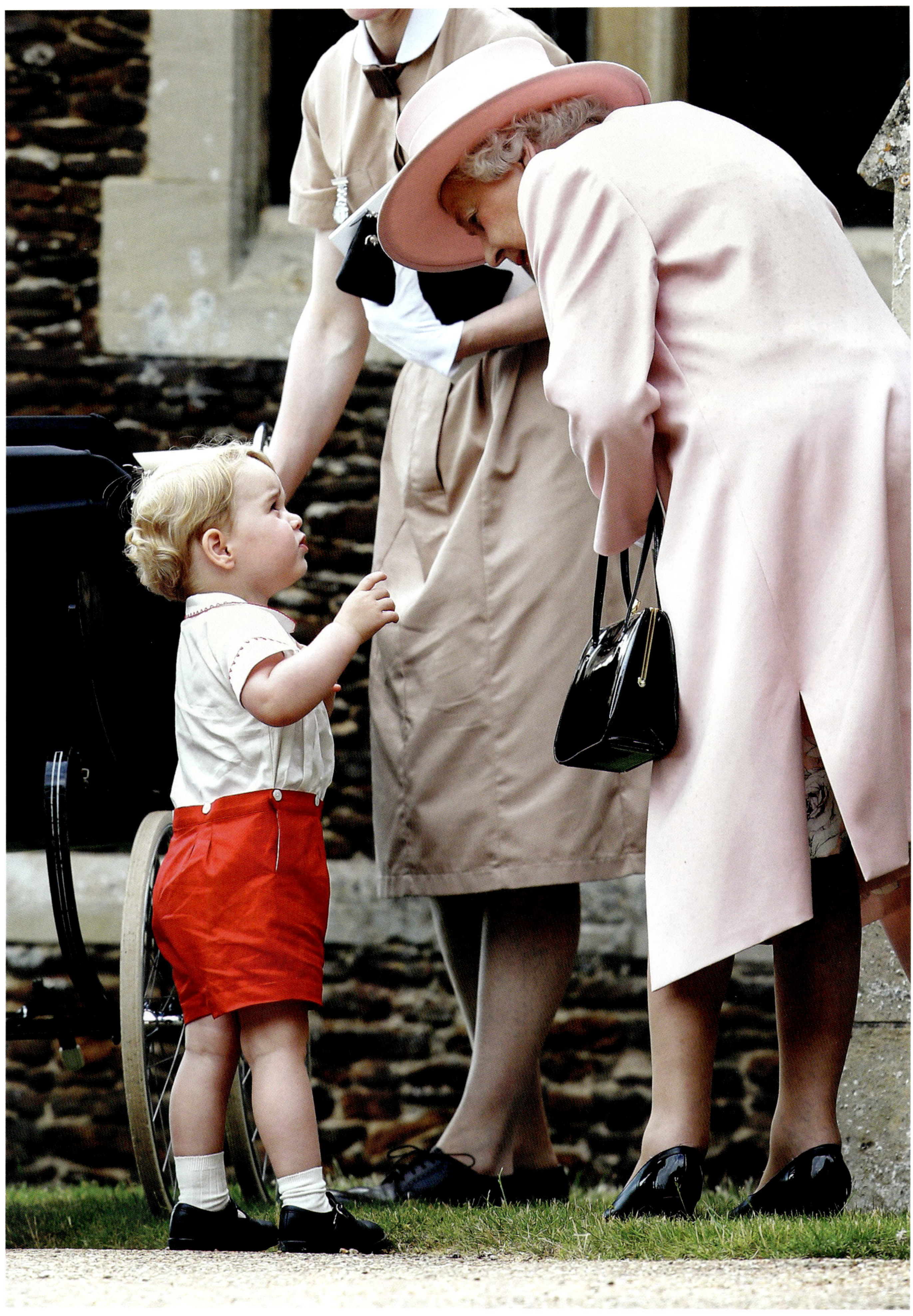

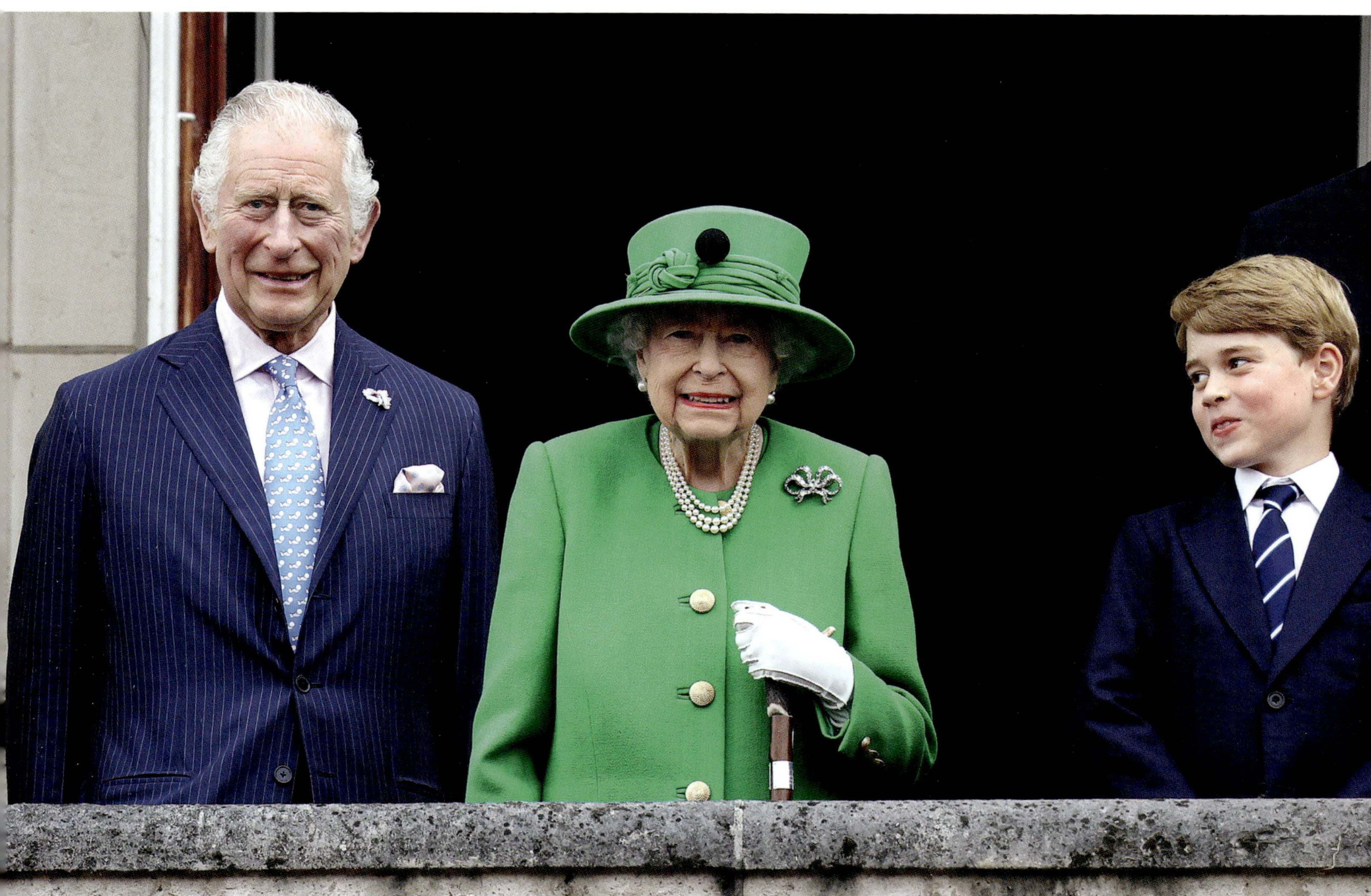

BRIDGING GENERATIONS

It is always special to see generations of the royal family interacting. Queen Elizabeth and Prince George shared many precious moments, such as here at Princess Charlotte's christening in Sandringham in July 2015 (opposite), or during an emotional balcony appearance on the last day of the Platinum Jubilee in June 2022. As the Queen looks over the throngs of people stretched down the length of the Mall, Prince George's pride is written all over his face.

Overleaf
Prince Louis reacts as the Red Arrows fly over Buckingham Palace balcony during Trooping the Colour, 2 June 2022.

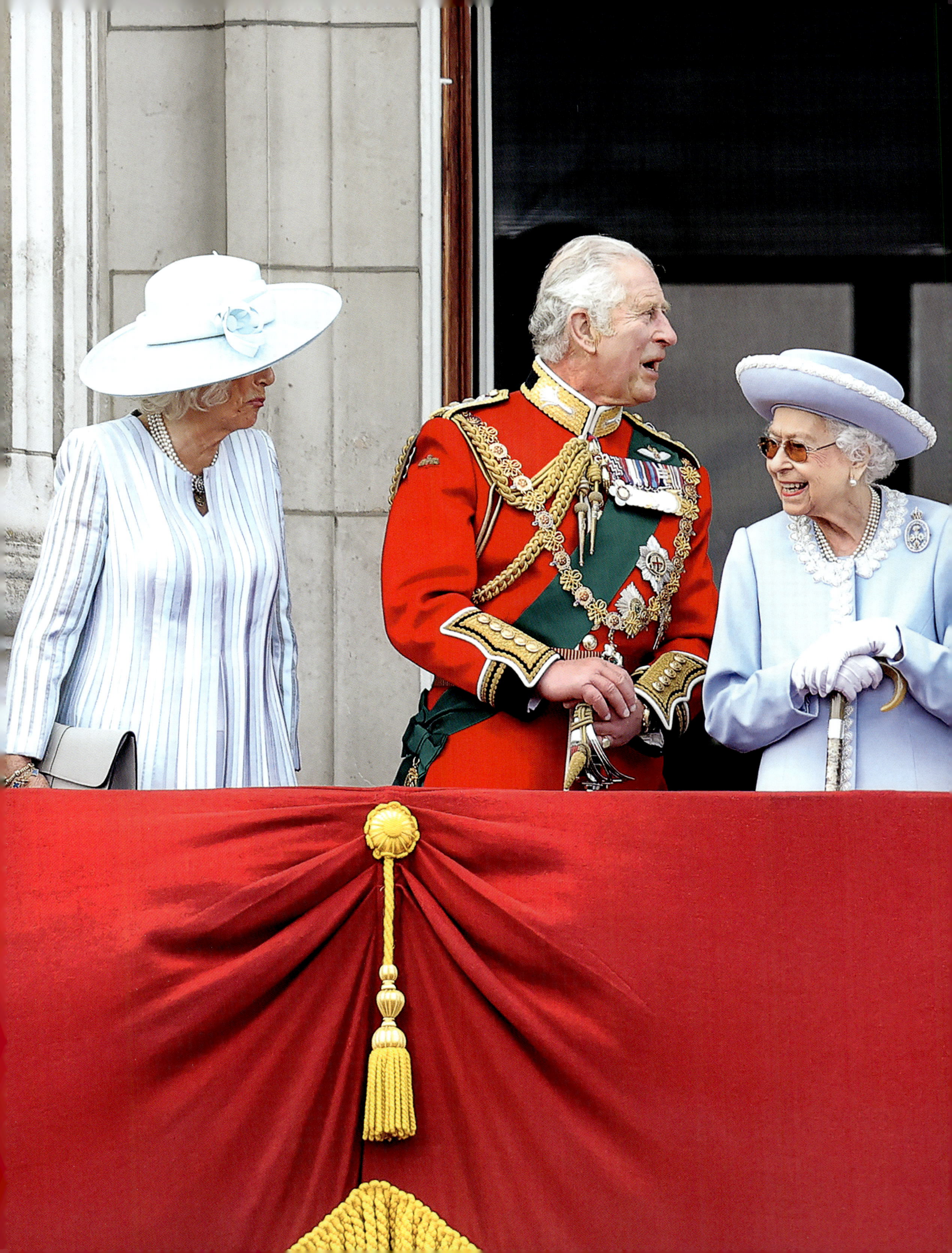

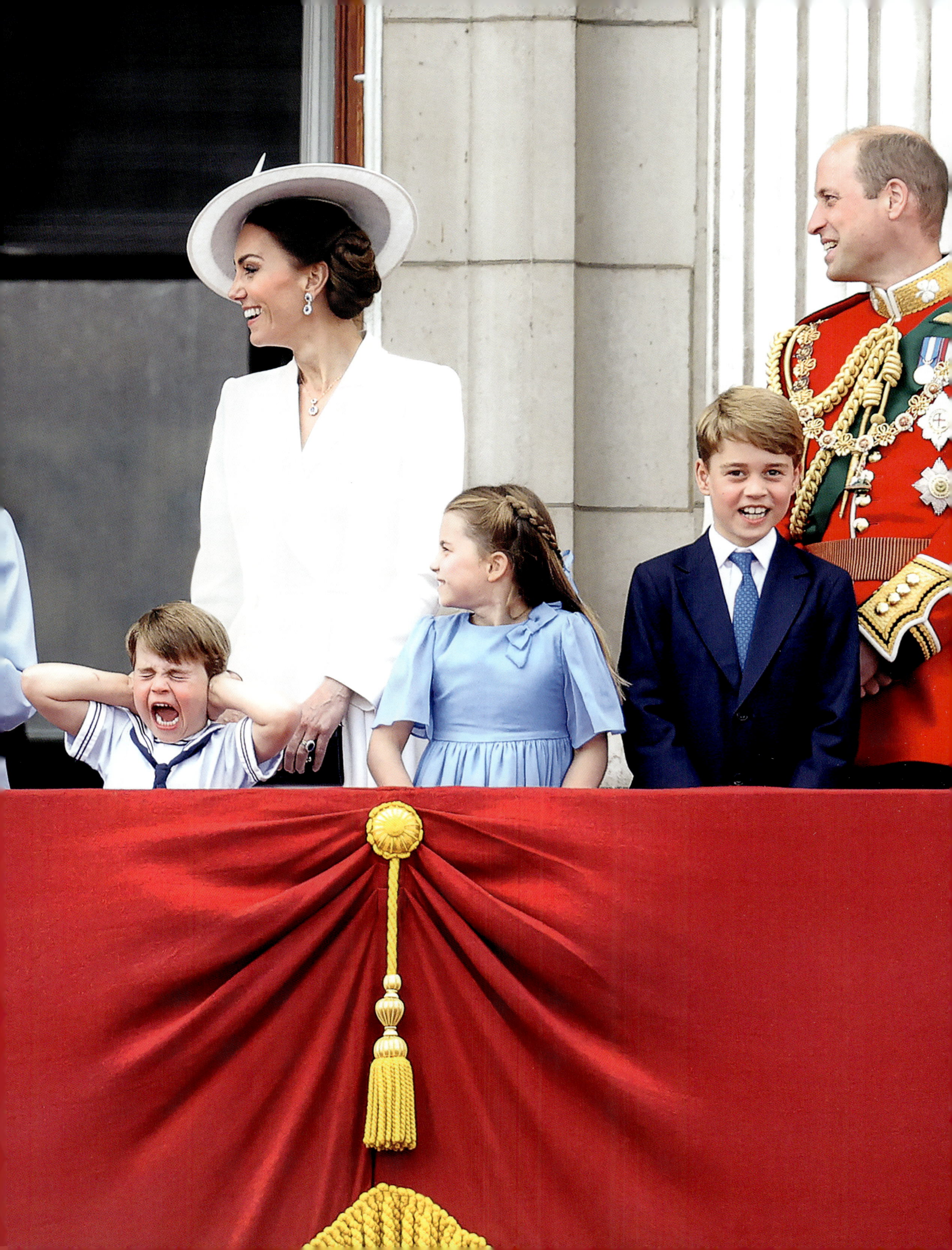

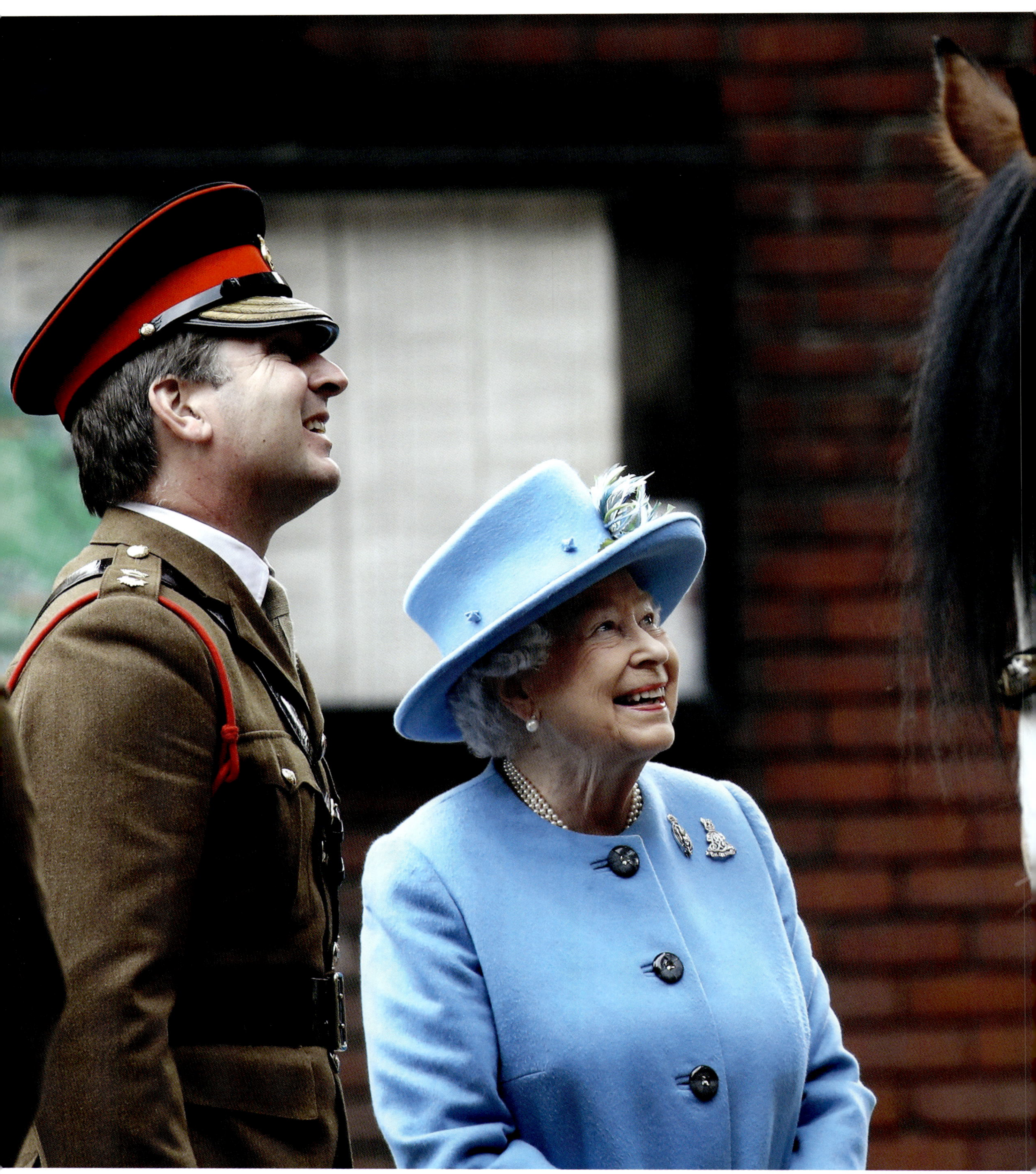

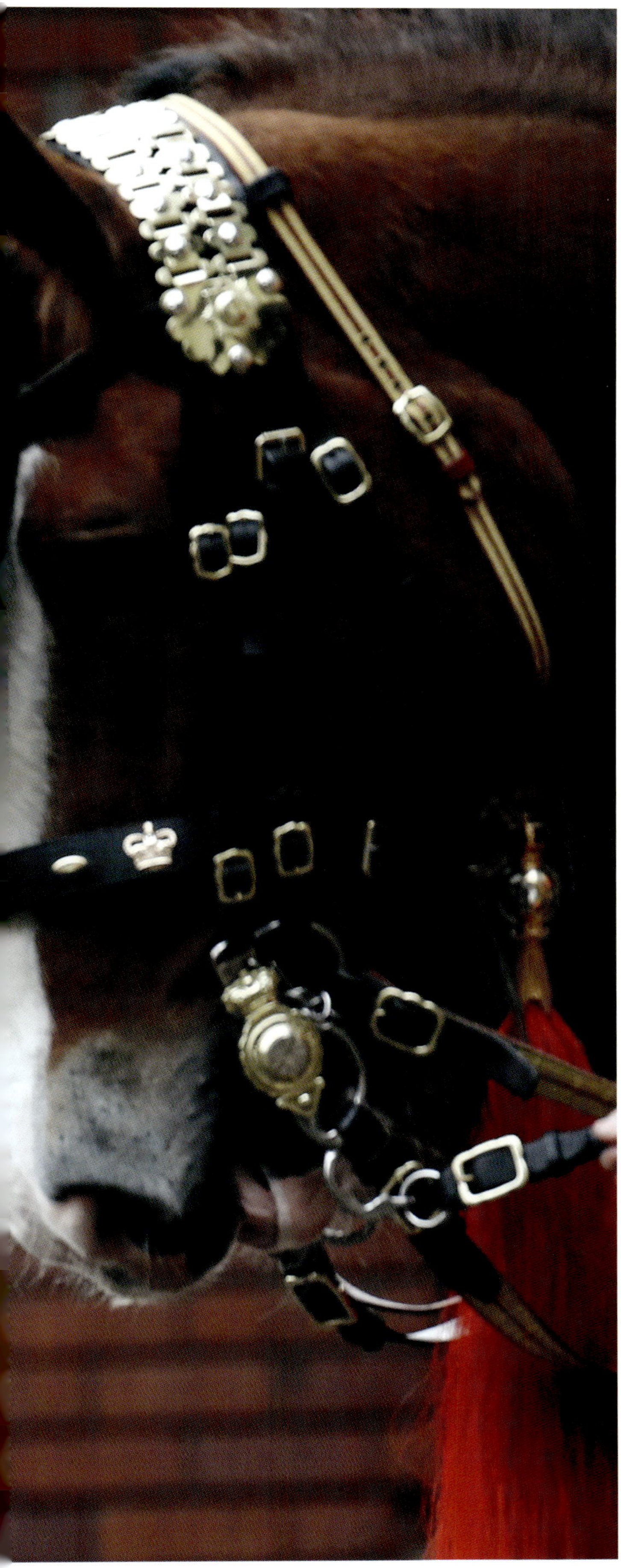

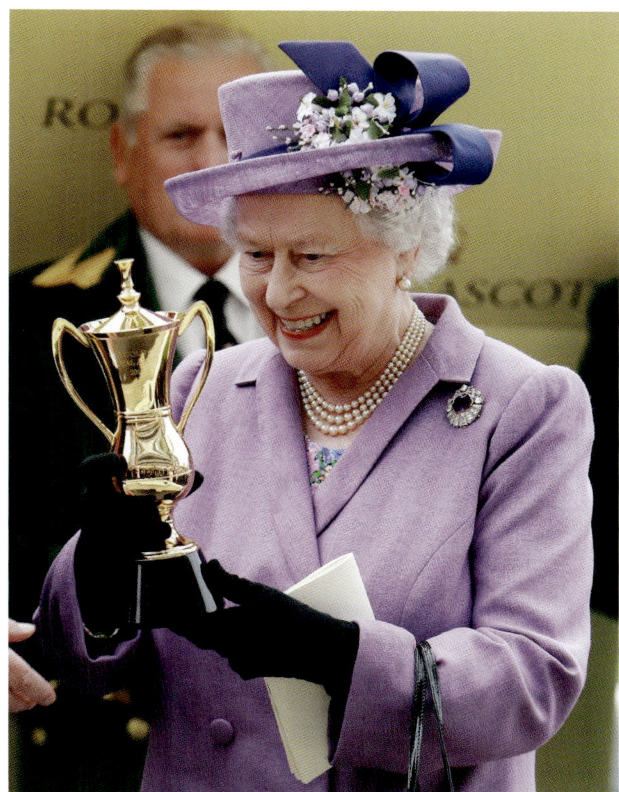

Left
The Queen meets drum horse Perseus of the Household Cavalry Mounted Regiment, 24 October 2017.

Above
Queen Elizabeth won the prestigious Gold Cup at Royal Ascot on 20 June 2013. Her horse, Estimate, made her the first monarch in over 200 years to win the coveted trophy.

Below
Meeting horse trainer Monty Roberts in the Royal Mews at Buckingham Palace, 21 October 2015.

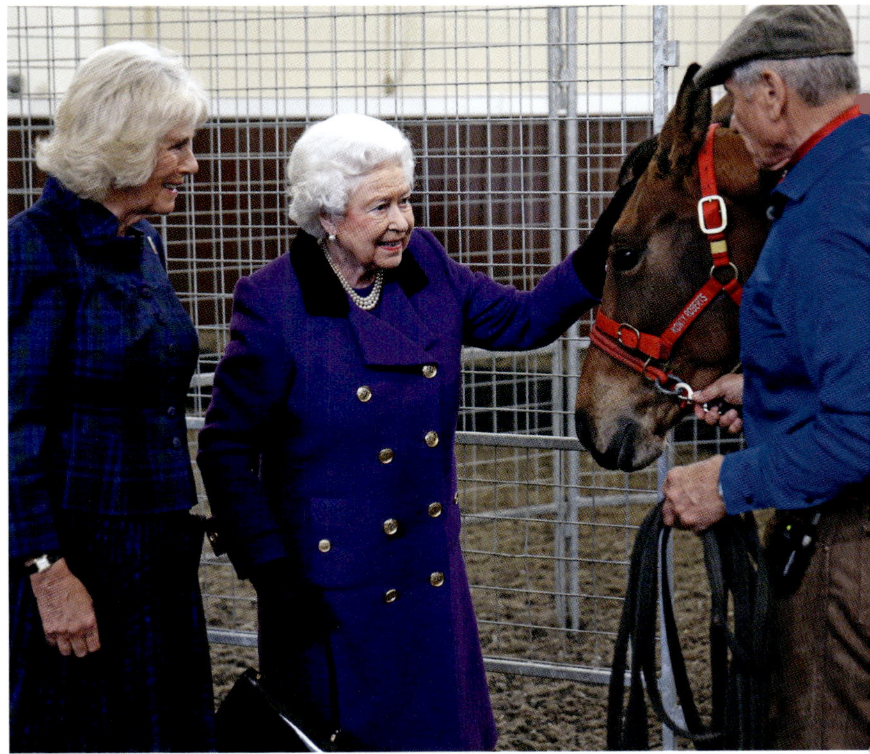

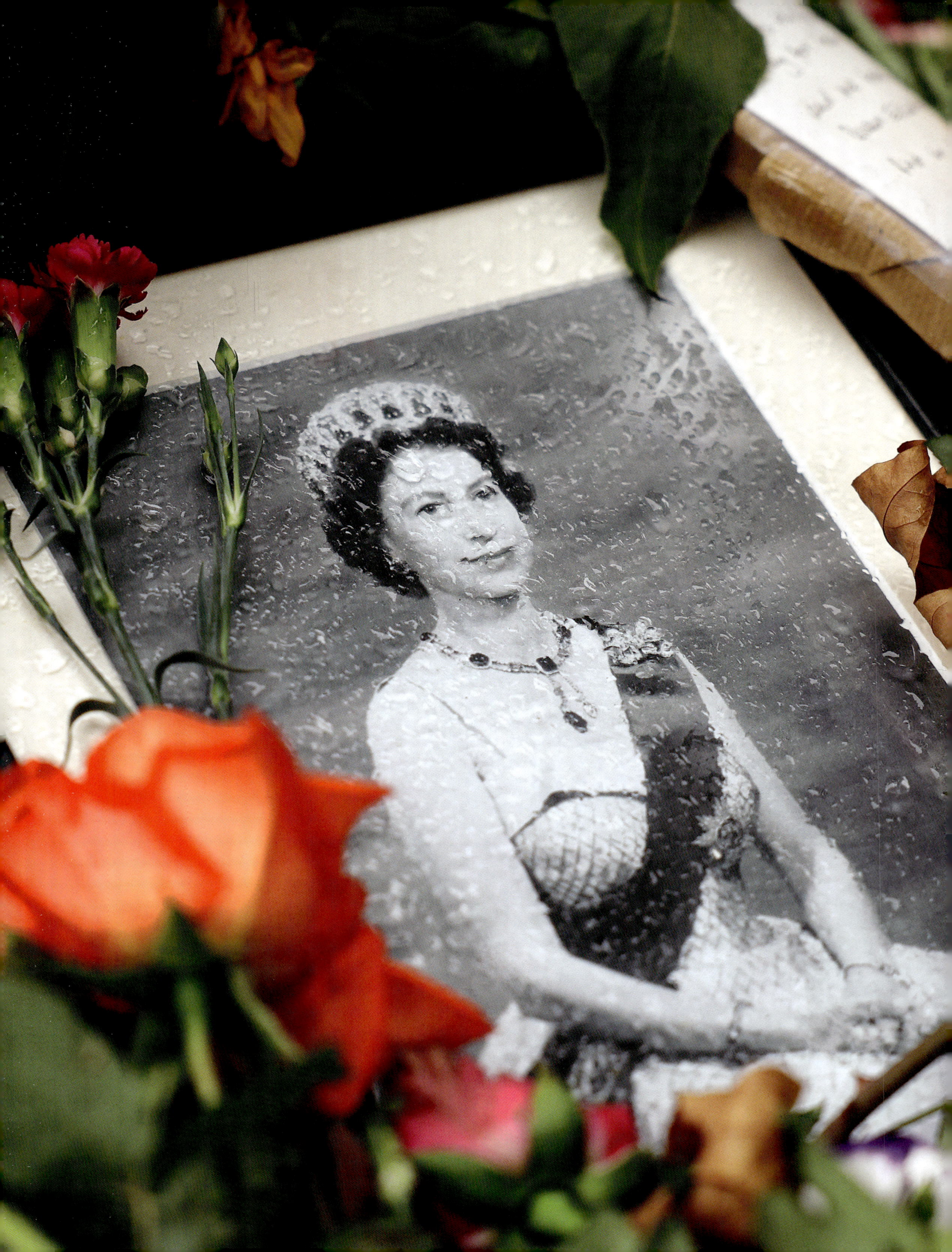

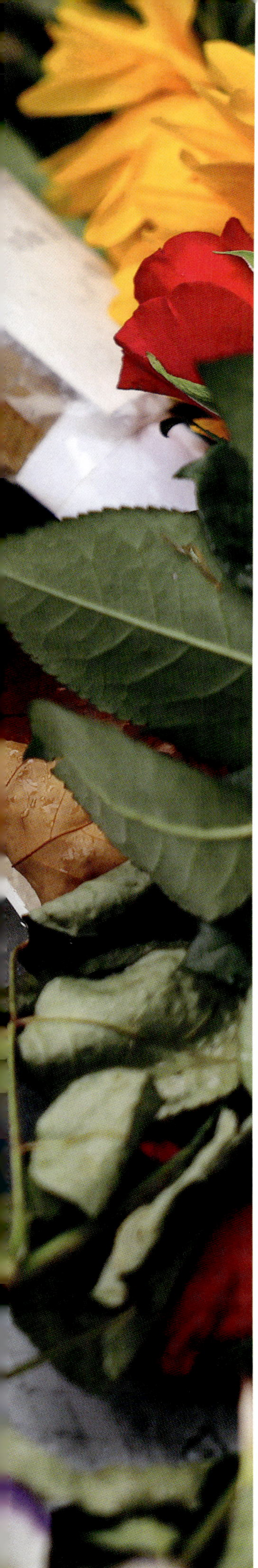

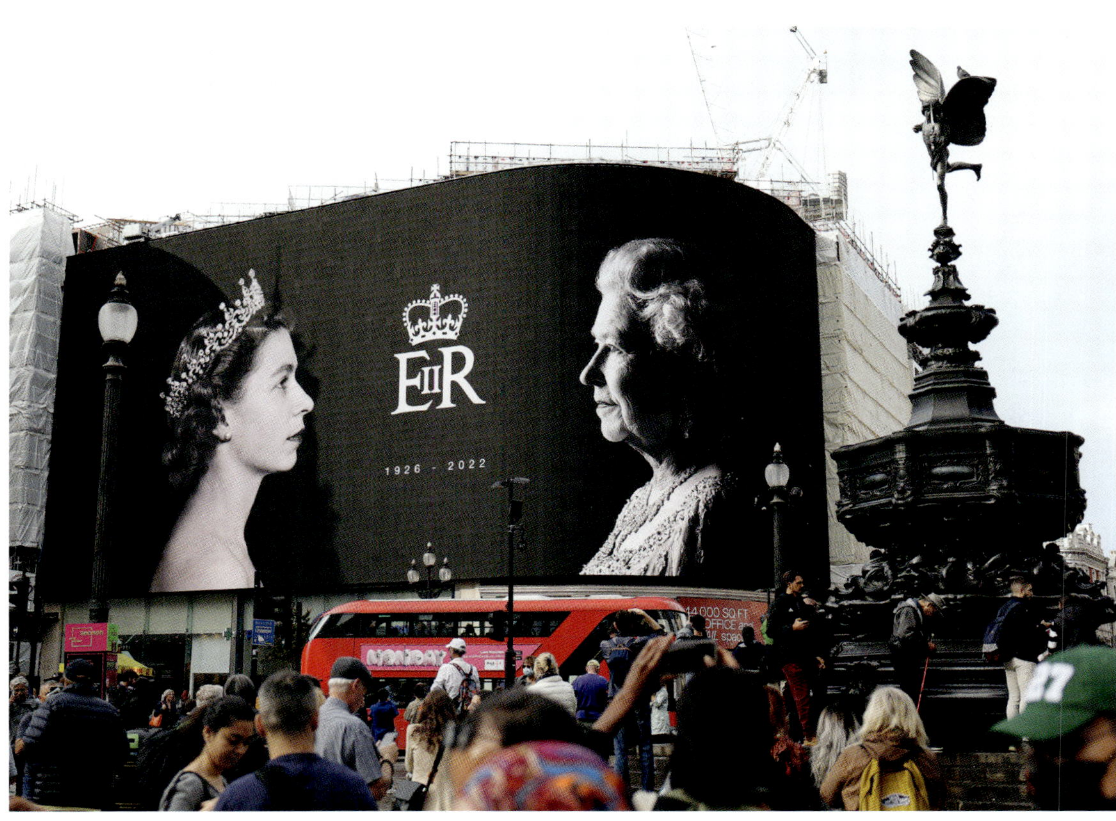

SEVENTY YEARS ON THE THRONE

The passing of Queen Elizabeth II left a nation, Commonwealth, and world shellshocked, such was the reach of her renown. Newspaper front pages around the world were cleared for tributes to the late monarch, who, after a 70-year reign, was the country's longest-serving sovereign. There was an outpouring of grief, with global leaders praising the Queen's commitment to duty and diplomacy, and heartfelt tributes from the public. After her death was announced by the Palace, the famous billboards in Picadilly Circus displayed her portrait.

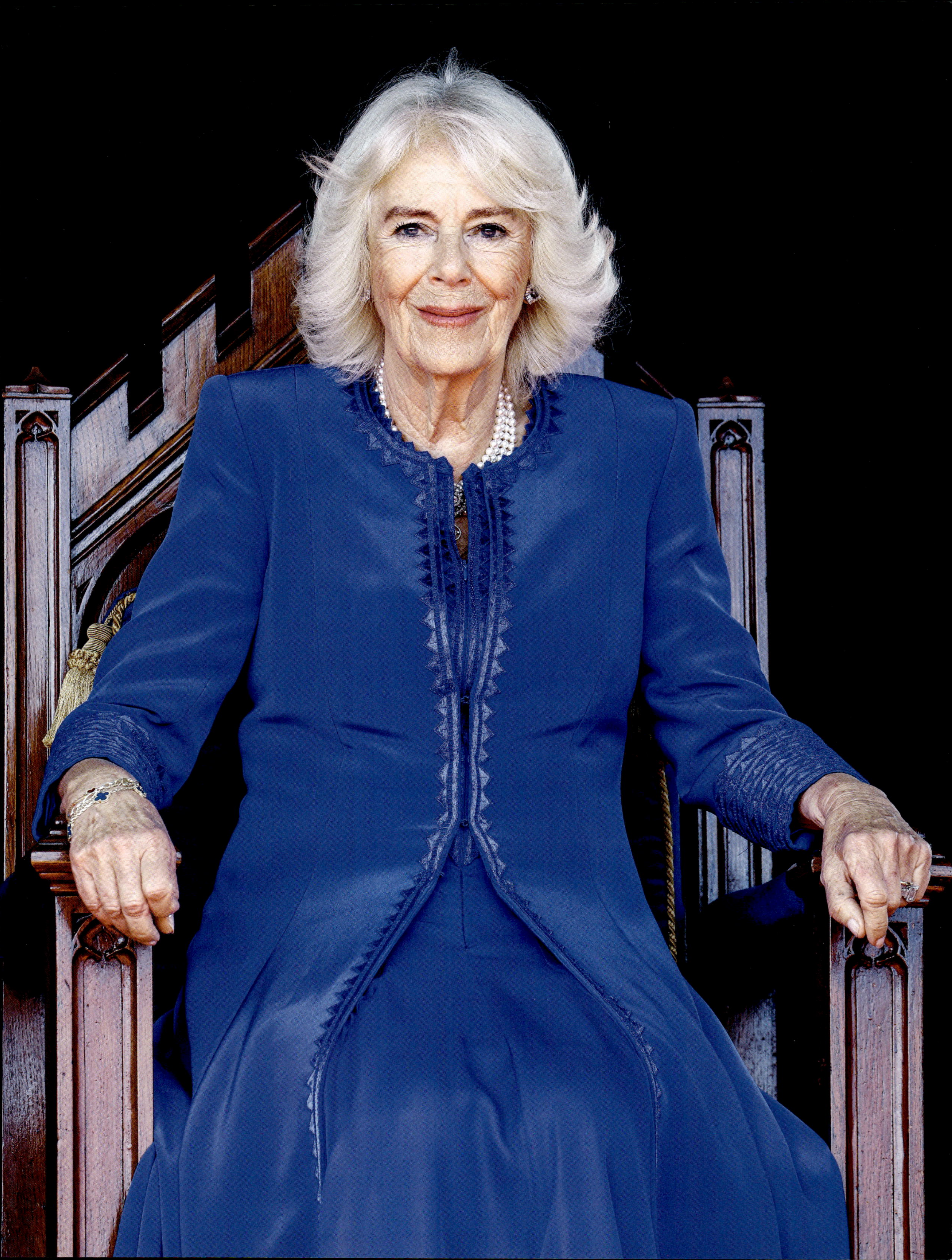

5

CAMILLA

A STRENGTH AND STAY FOR HER GENERATION

After facing a rocky start to her royal "career," Queen Camilla has overcome all obstacles to show the world what a great asset she is to the royal family. Her sense of humour, work ethic, and humanity have long been familiar to me as I have photographed her for many years. When things do not go quite to plan, her unflappable sense of humour and smile are reminiscent of the late Queen Elizabeth's approach.

Throughout King Charles's battle with cancer, Queen Camilla's strength and fortitude have come into their own as she has demonstrated an astounding leadership by stepping up her own engagements and quite literally lending a guiding hand to the King. She has done this with an energy and stamina that belie her age. While many have retired by this point in their lives, Queen Camilla has increased her efforts for the benefit of the monarchy and the country.

Queen Camilla's passion for reading and literacy has been a unique focus. Her charity, the Queen's Reading Room, promotes the power and benefits of reading and has gained significant traction since its foundation. I have often photographed the Queen's reading events at Clarence House and have seen firsthand the talented authors and illustrators she is able to convene – a testament to the huge success of this endeavour.

AN UNFALTERING COMMITMENT

Queen Camilla has always been a great support for King Charles. This is evidenced in their interactions on royal engagements, when a subtle quip or a knowing smile reveal their tender and deeply felt partnership. At the end of a busy State Visit, an affectionate hand guides King Charles after waving off the Emperor and Empress of Japan in June 2024, not long after the monarch's cancer diagnosis.

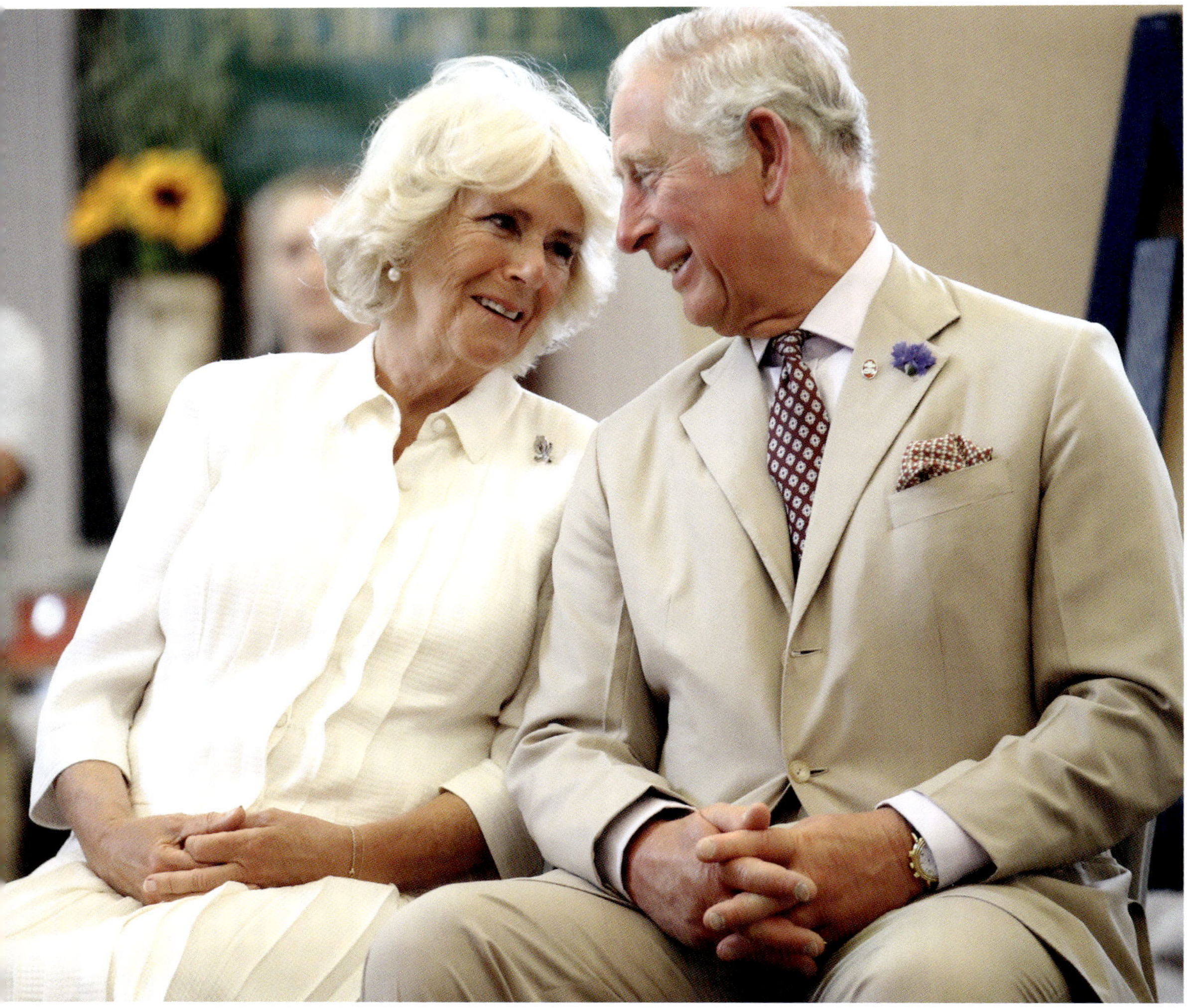

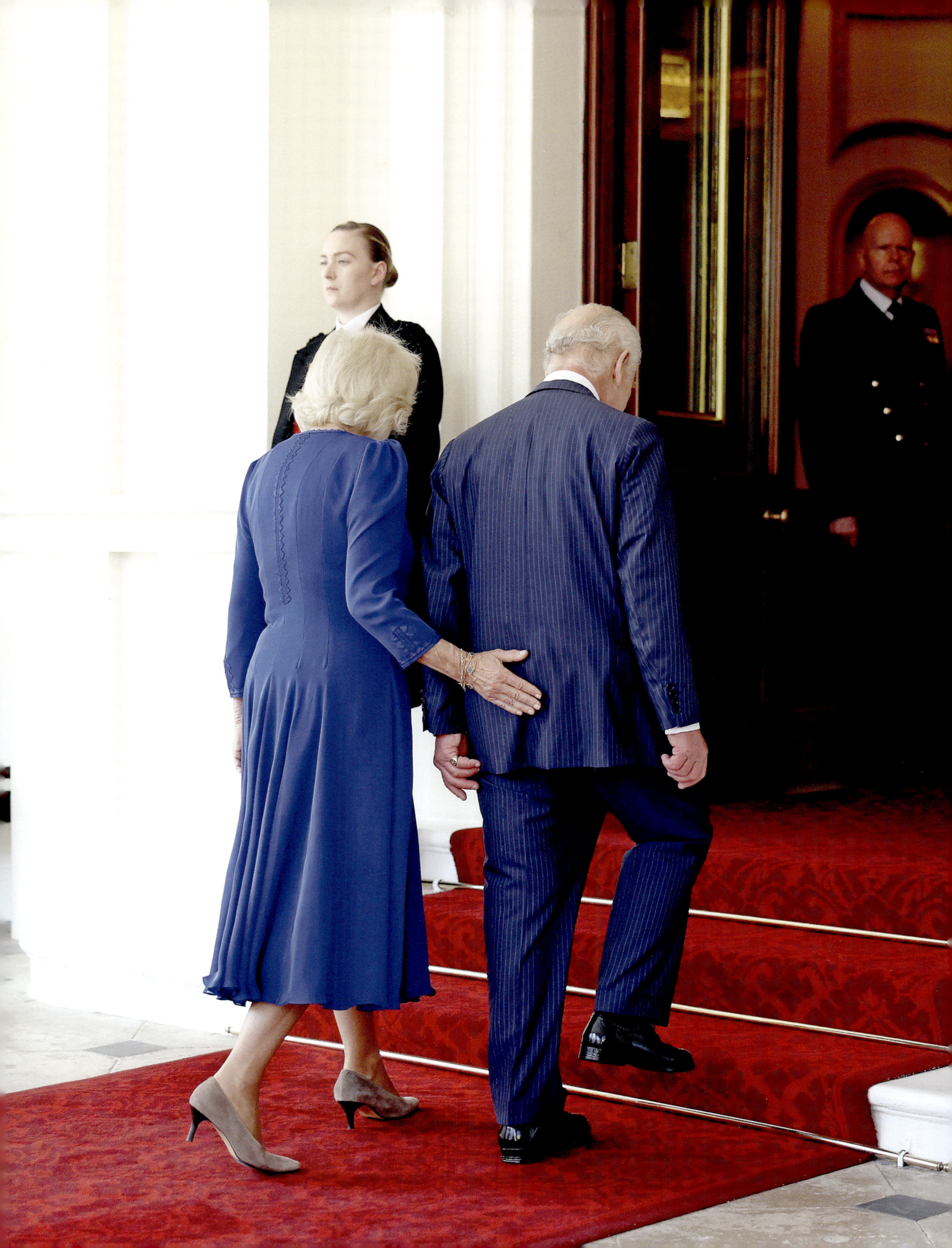

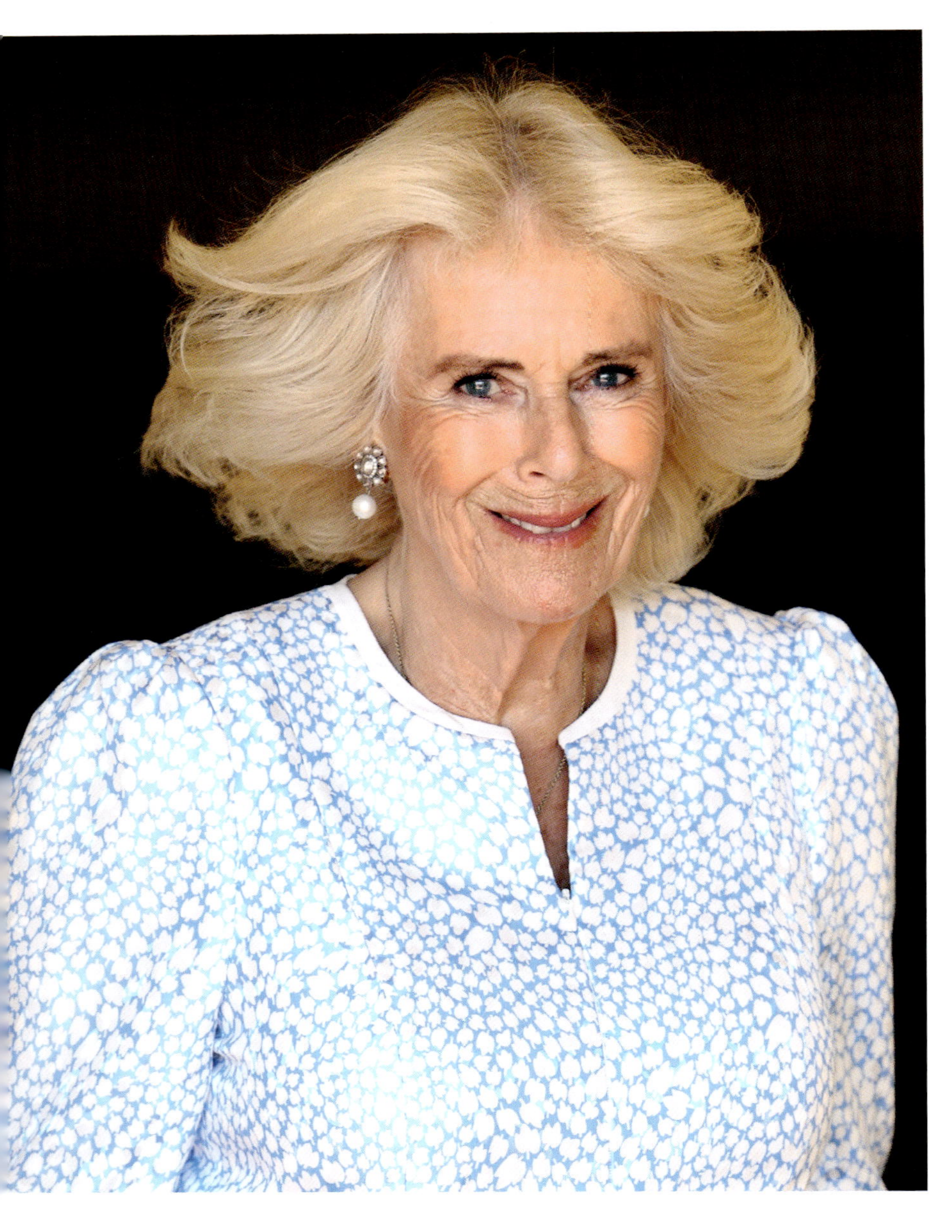

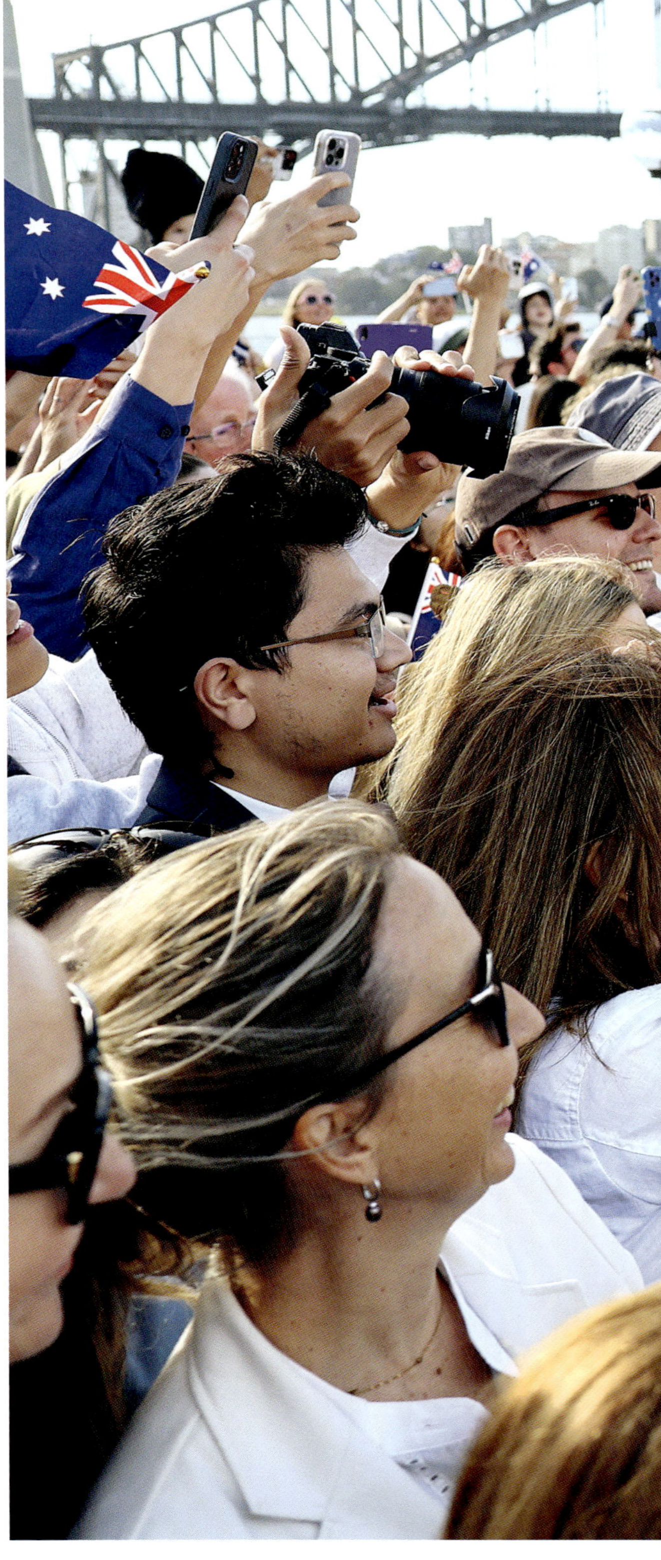

I remember looking down from the steps of Sydney Opera House and being astonished by the crowds of well-wishers, all keen to catch a glimpse of the King and Queen during their trip to Australia in October 2024.

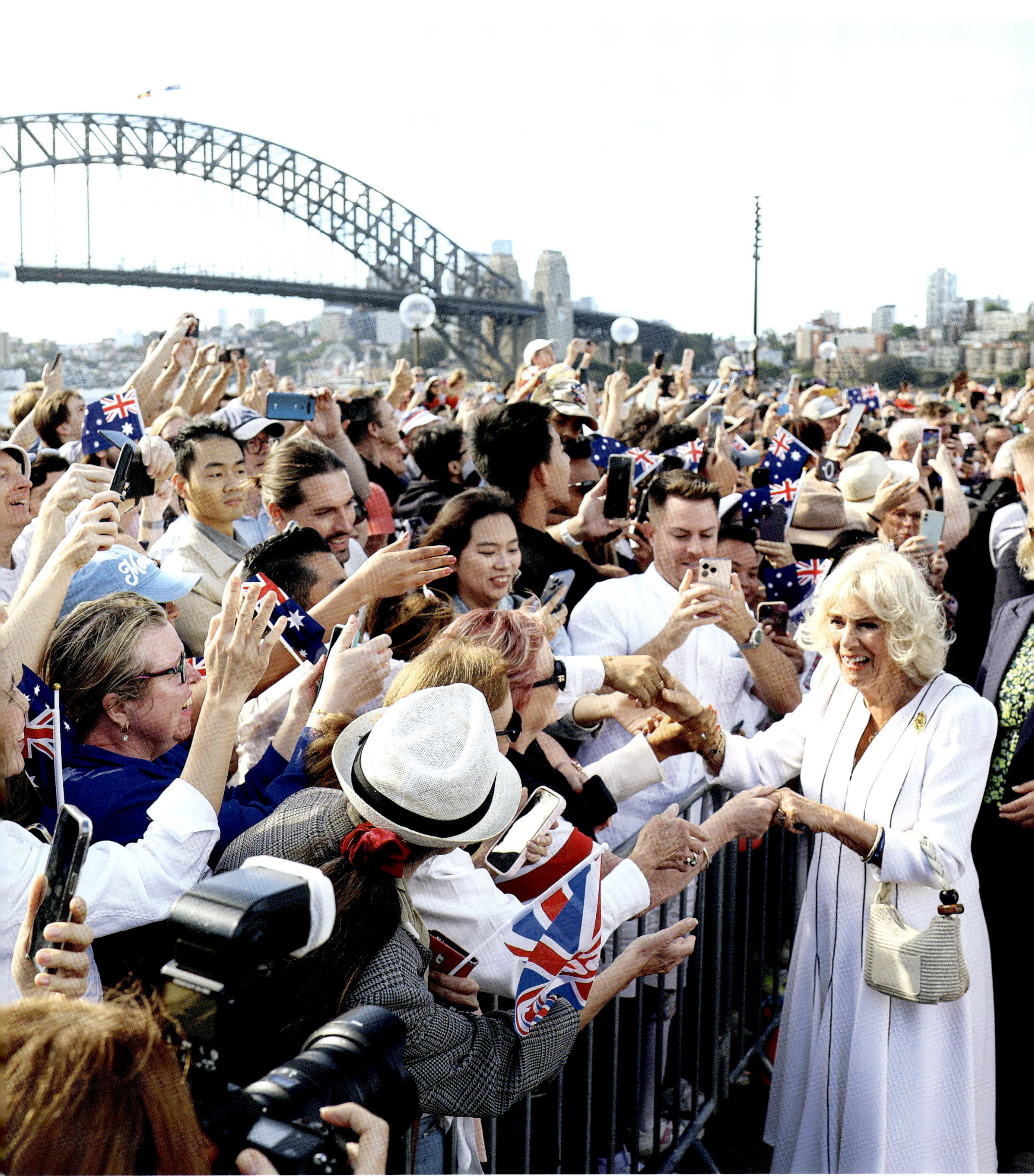

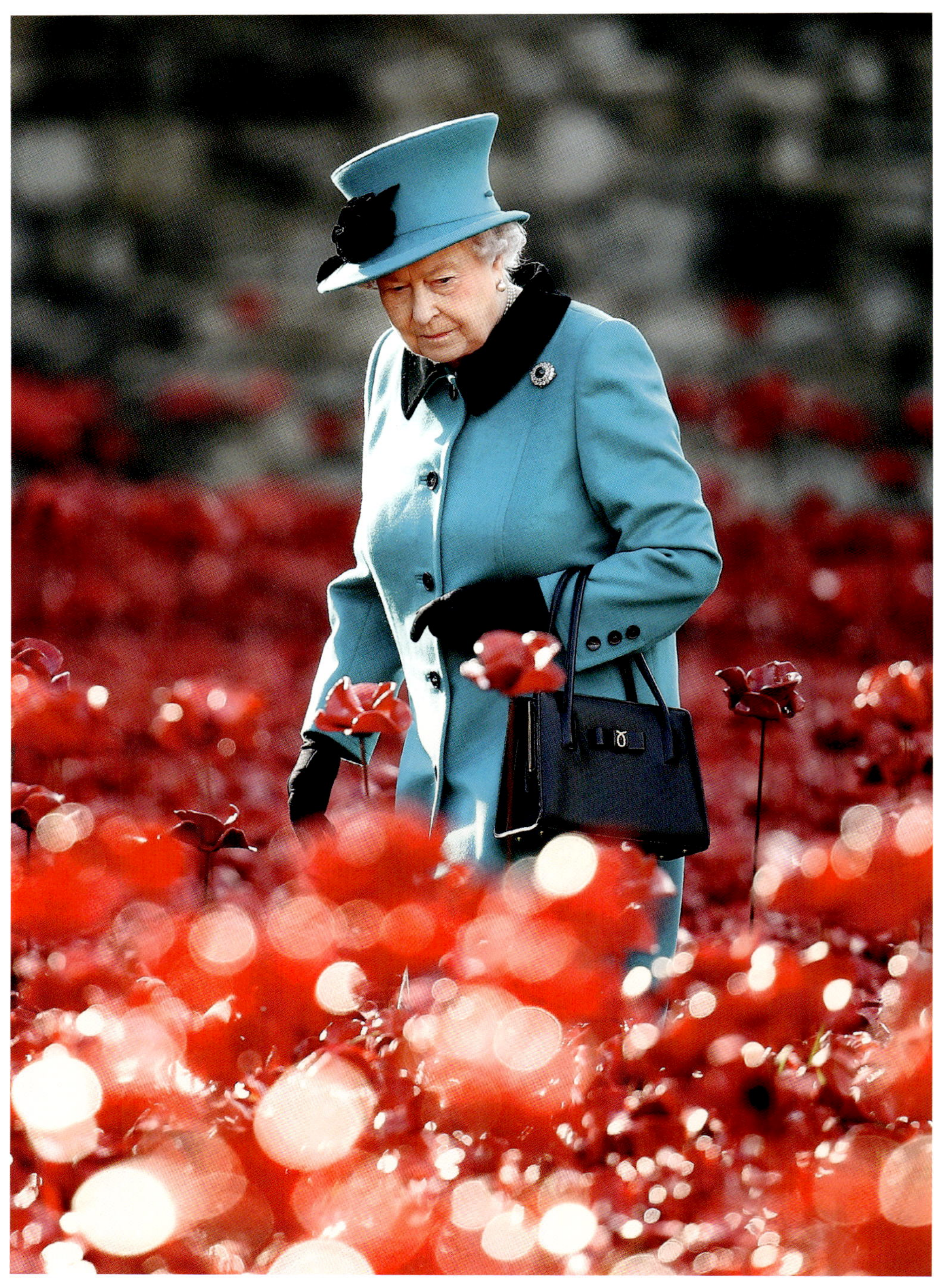

A MOAT FULL OF POPPIES

Often in royal photography, touching moments are duplicated over the years. In 2014 Queen Elizabeth II, deep in thought, walked through the art installation *Blood Swept Lands and Seas of Red*: 888,246 ceramic poppies in the moat of the Tower of London. In 2025 history repeated itself as Queen Camilla planted a ceramic poppy with the aid of five-year-old Harrison Machin to commemorate VE Day. Called *The Tower Remembers*, the artwork consists of 30,000 poppies, some of which had been part of the original installation.

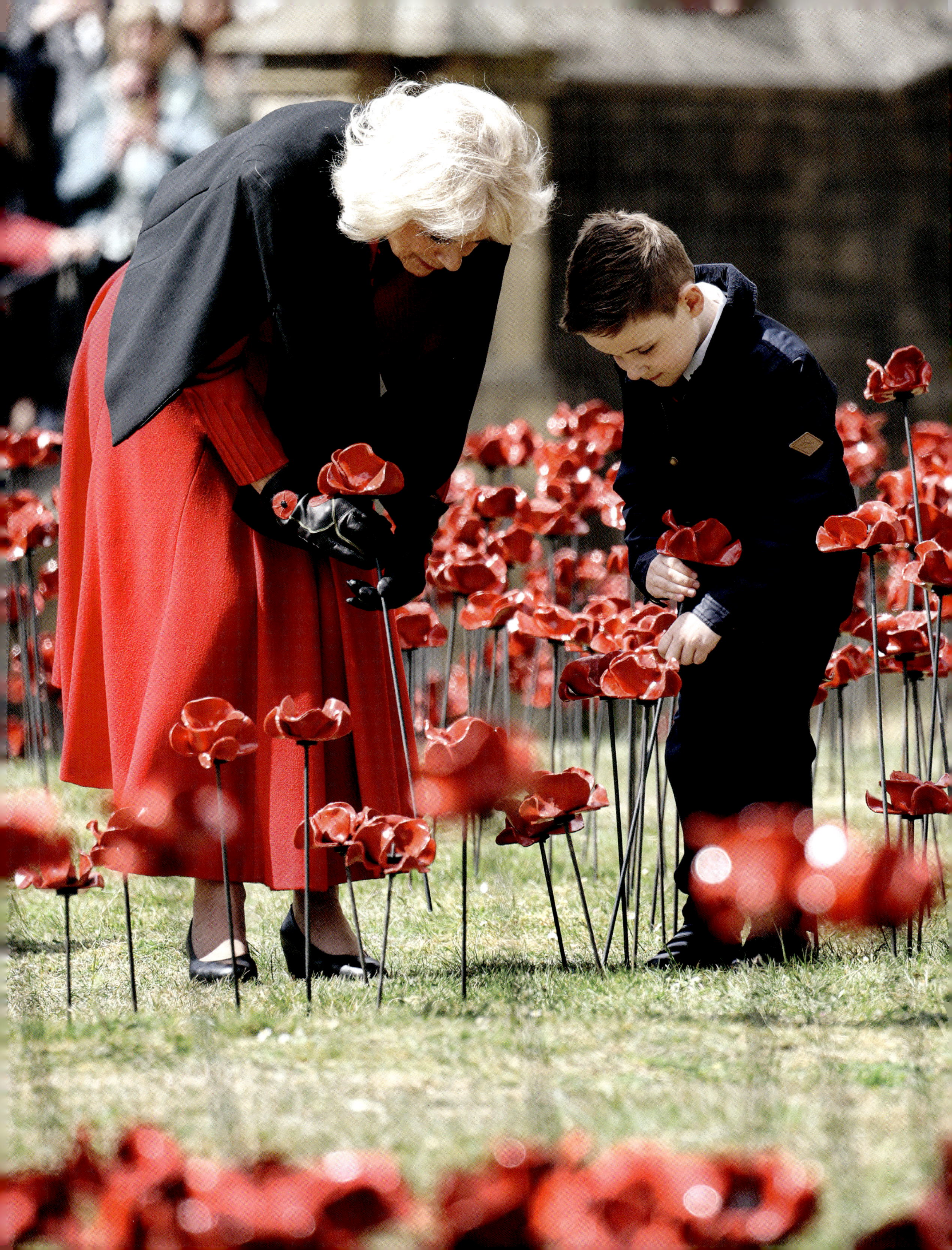

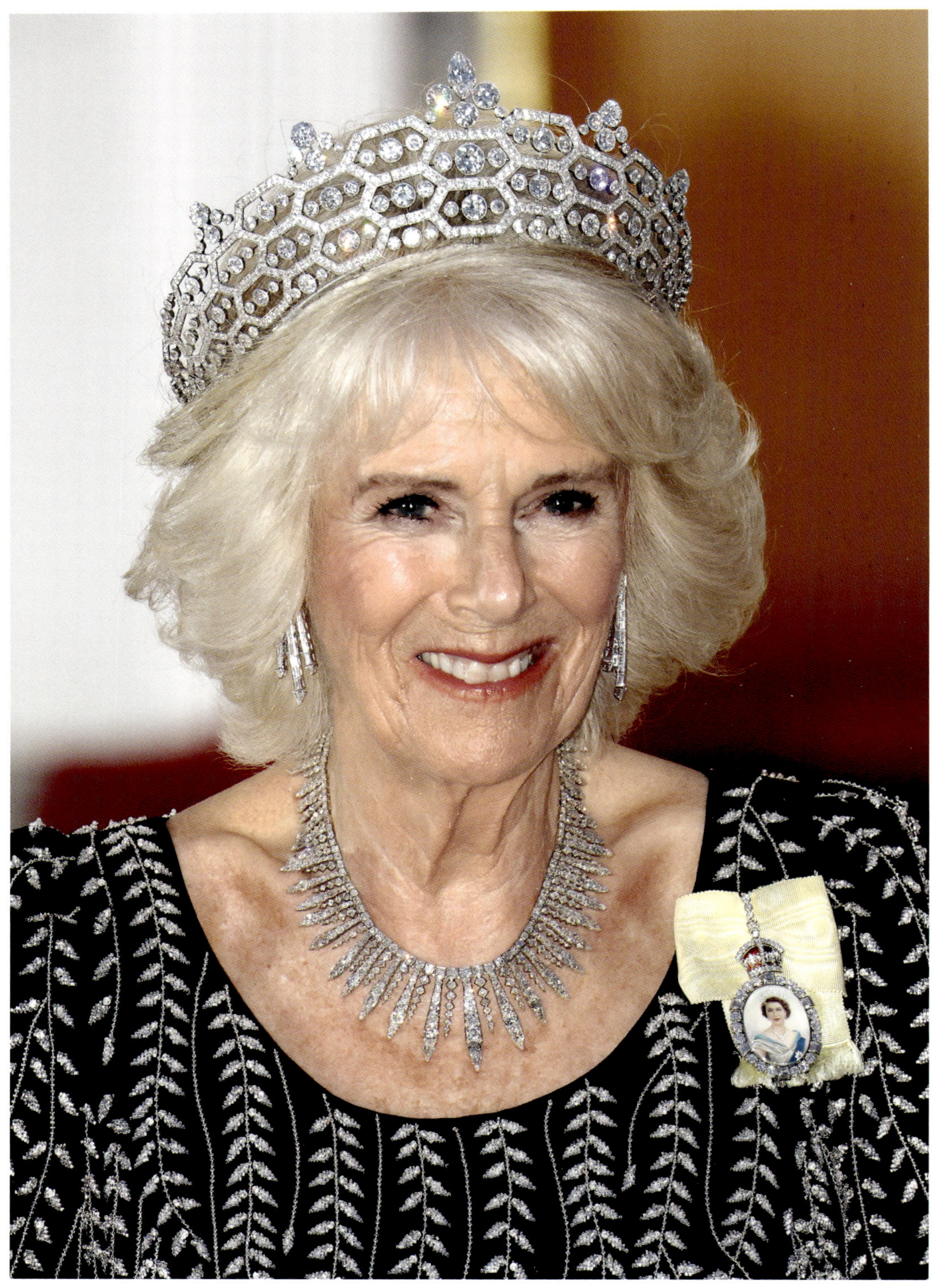

Above
For the German State Banquet Queen Camilla stuns in the Greville Tiara and the City of London Fringe Necklace (owned by Queen Elizabeth II) at Bellevue Palace, Berlin, 29 March 2023. She also wears the Royal Family Order of Queen Elizabeth II.

Opposite
Camilla wears the Belgian Sapphire Tiara and matching sapphire and diamond necklace, along with a Garter Star and the French *Légion d'honneur* sash during the French President's visit in July 2025. The new Royal Family Order of King Charles III was painted by artist Elizabeth Meek.

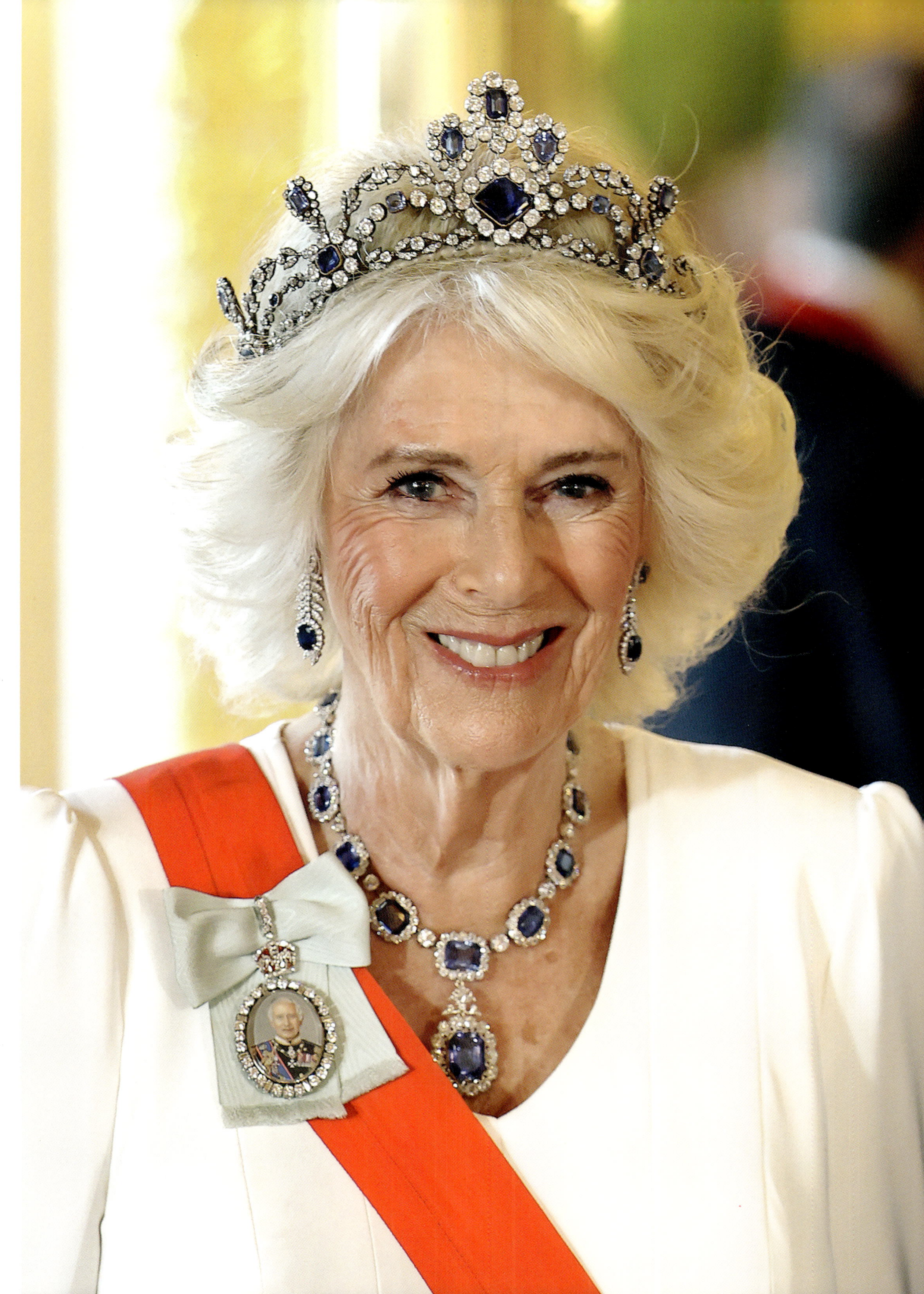

Below
At the State Opening of Parliament in London on her 77th birthday in July 2024, the Queen wears the stunning George IV State Diadem, crafted in 1820 and featuring 1,333 diamonds.

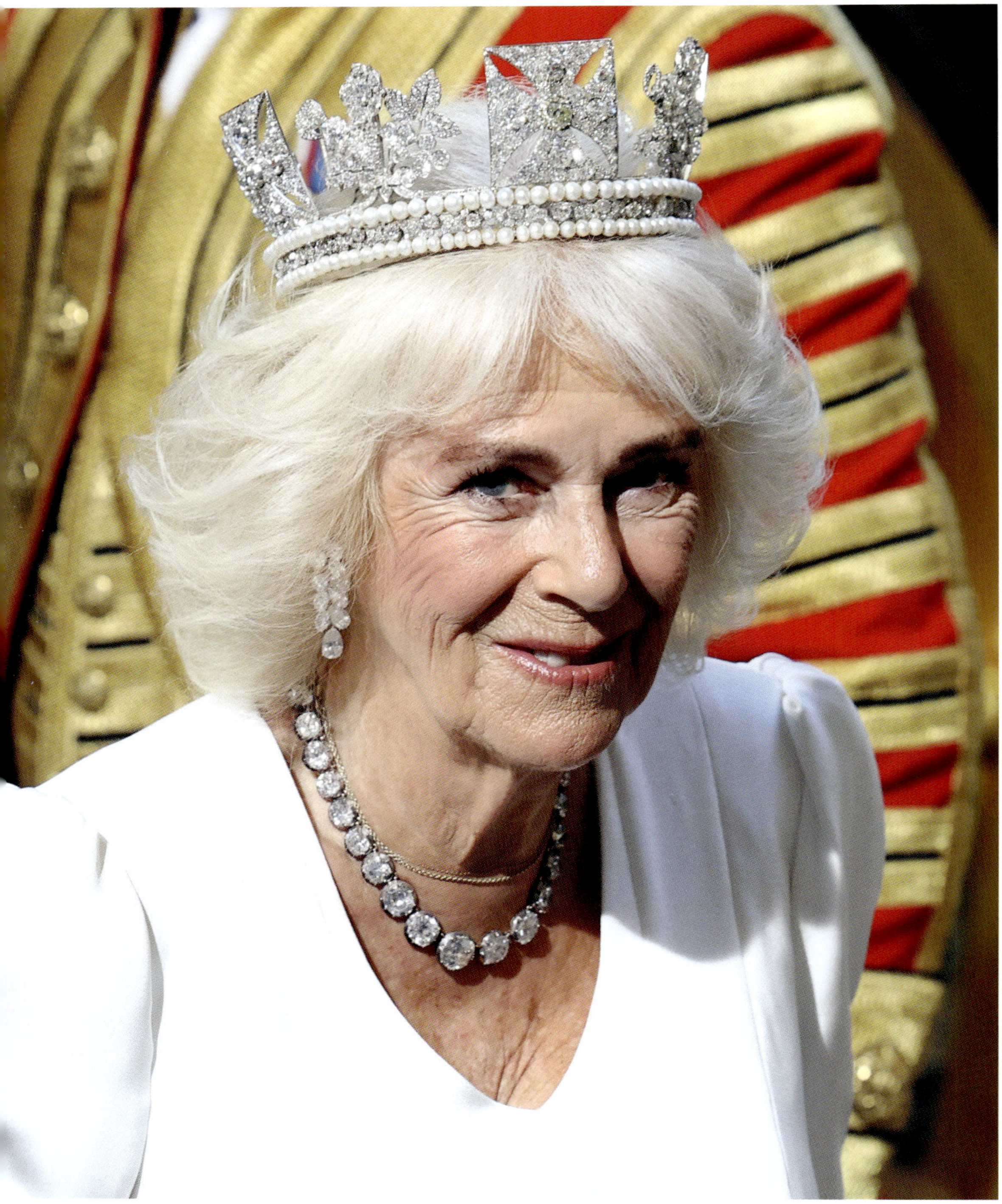

Right
Queen Camilla poses for a photograph in the 1844 Room, so called due to the year it received Russian Tsar Nicholas I, ahead of the Diplomatic Reception in December 2023. She wears the Girls of Great Britain and Ireland Tiara, and a striking brooch corsage.

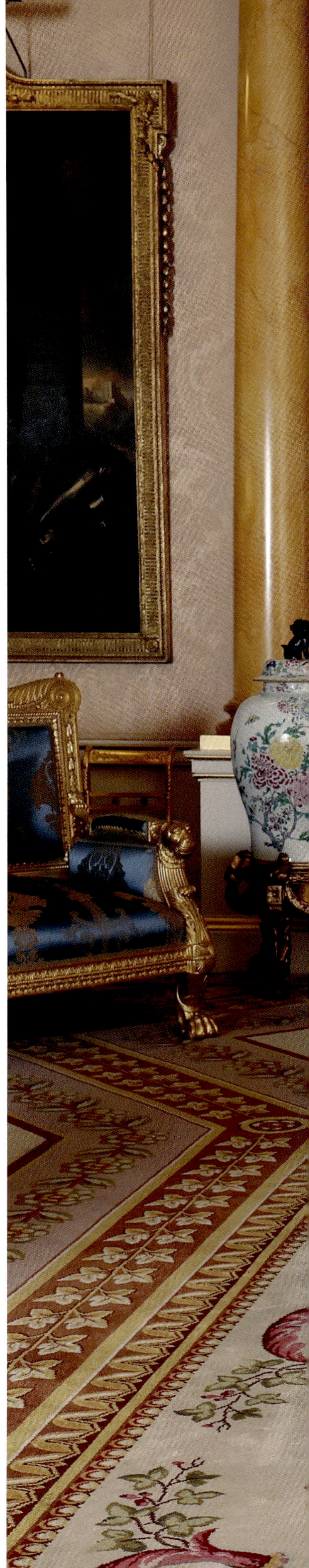

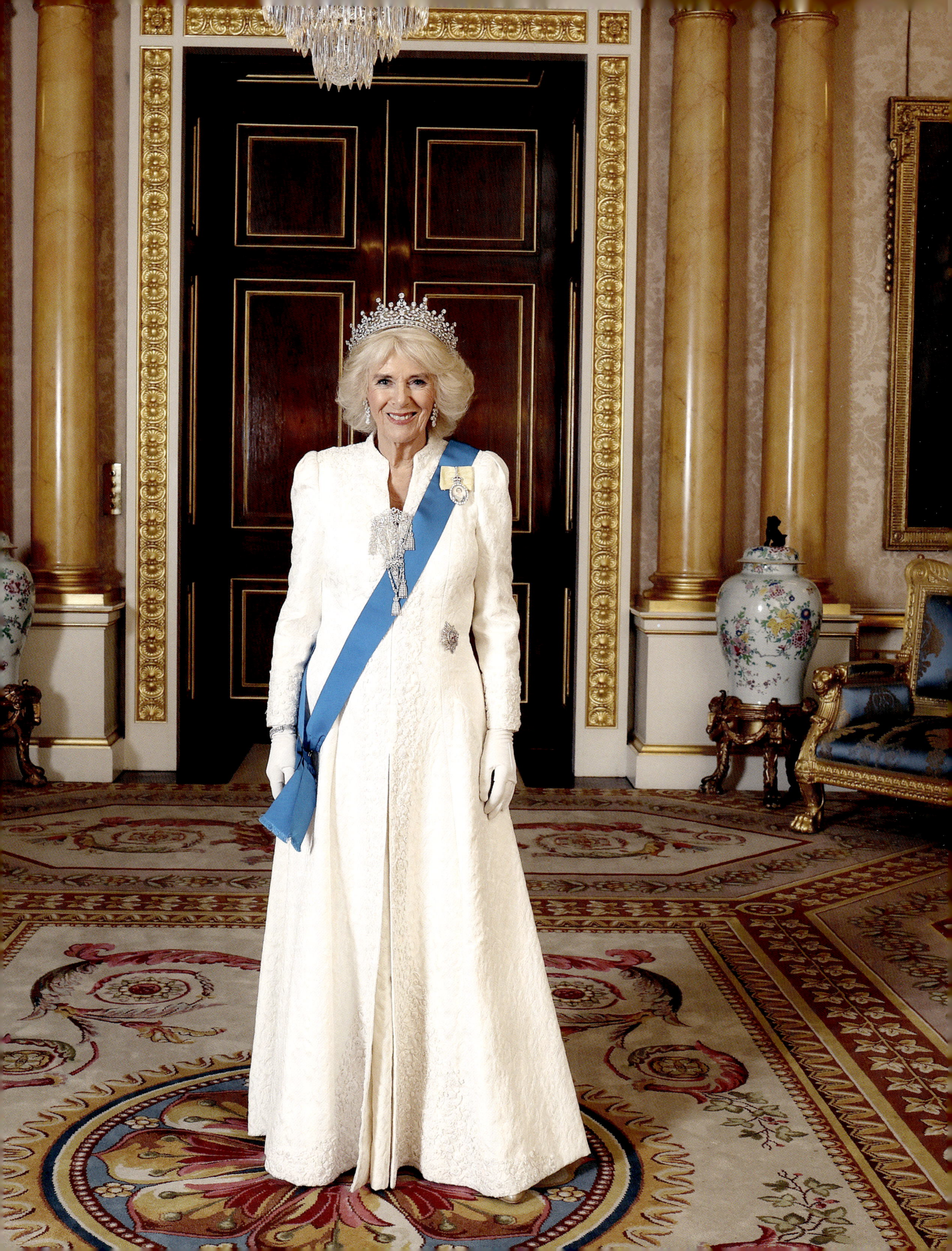

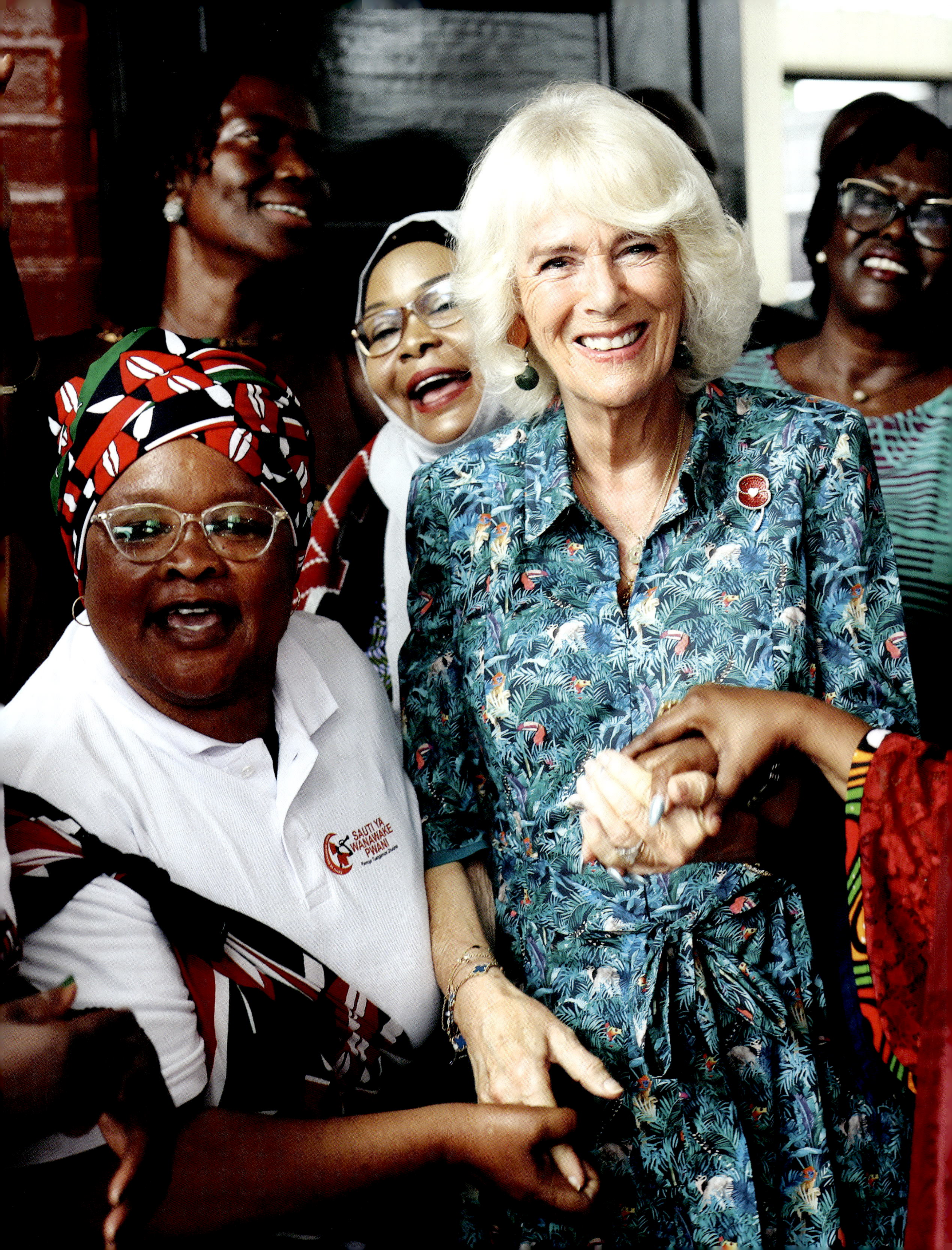
SAUTI YA
WANAWAKE
PWANI

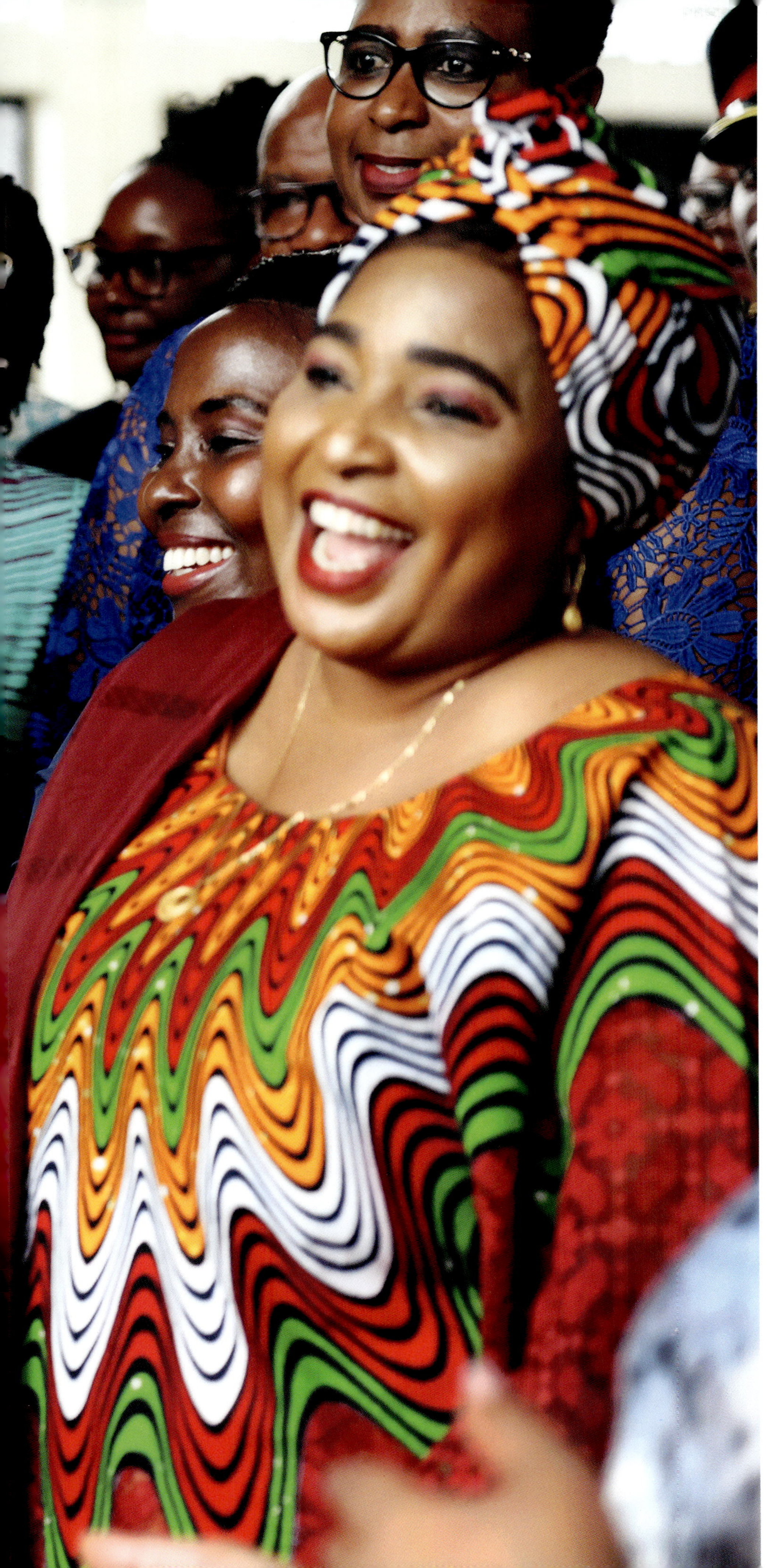

DANCING IN KENYA

Sauti Ya Wanawake (the Voice of Women) is an empowerment movement in Kenya. Queen Camilla undertook an uplifting engagement to one of its centres during a royal visit in November 2023. As a downpour flooded the streets of Mombasa outside, Queen Camilla was treated to a tour of the facility and met volunteers and survivors of sexual and gender-based violence. In this, my favourite photograph from the visit, Camilla joined in the harmonious choir's traditional dancing with characteristic aplomb.

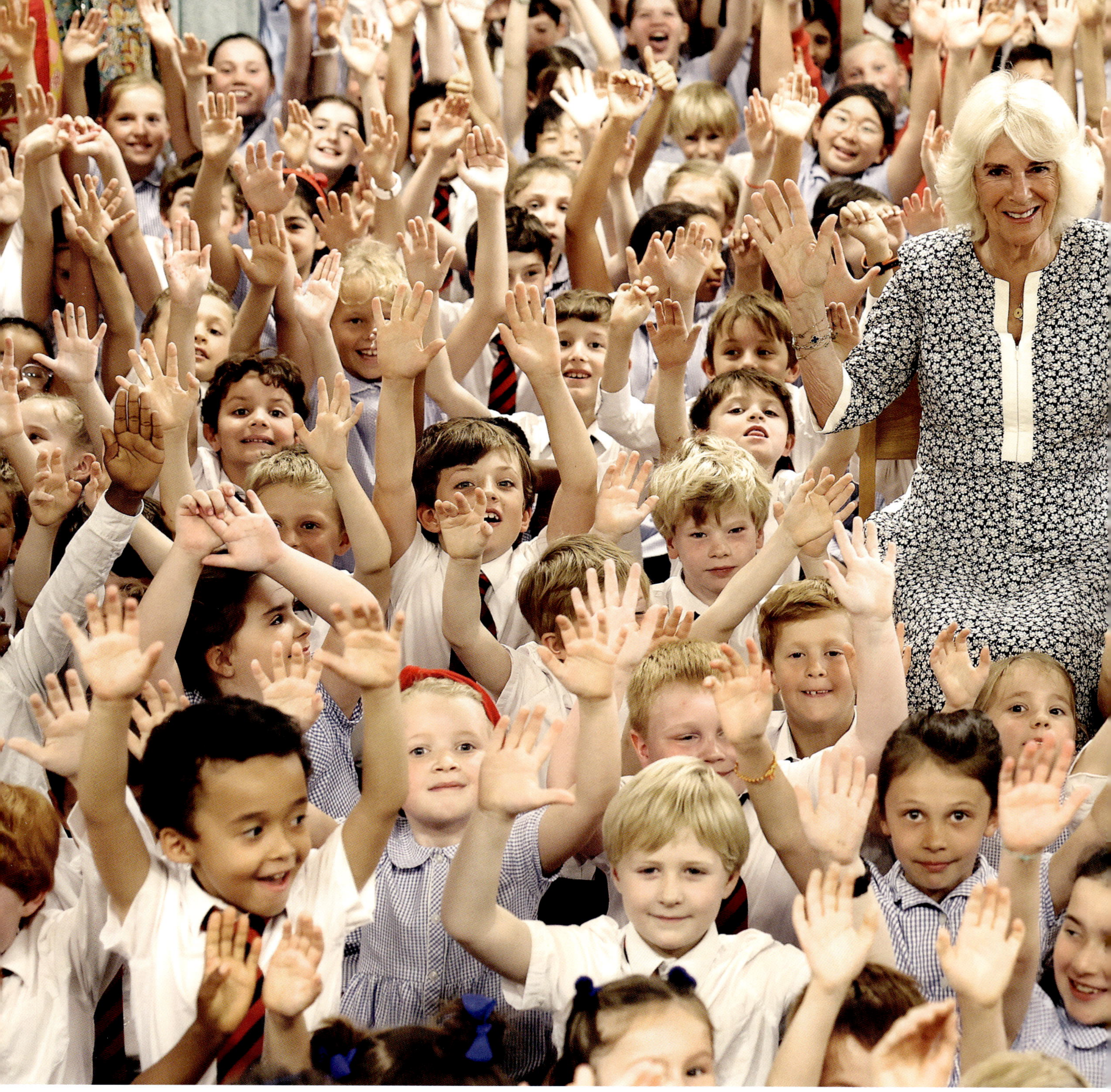

A PRECARIOUS SITUATION

As I wobbled at the top of a stepladder that was being steadied by a member of the Queen's press team, trying to engage with the understandably excited children from Christ Church Primary School in Chelsea in June 2024, I announced that we should do one more fun photo. "Everyone with their hands in the air!" Queen Camilla was visiting the school during its literary festival, celebrating literacy and the joy of reading, a cause very close to the Queen's heart.

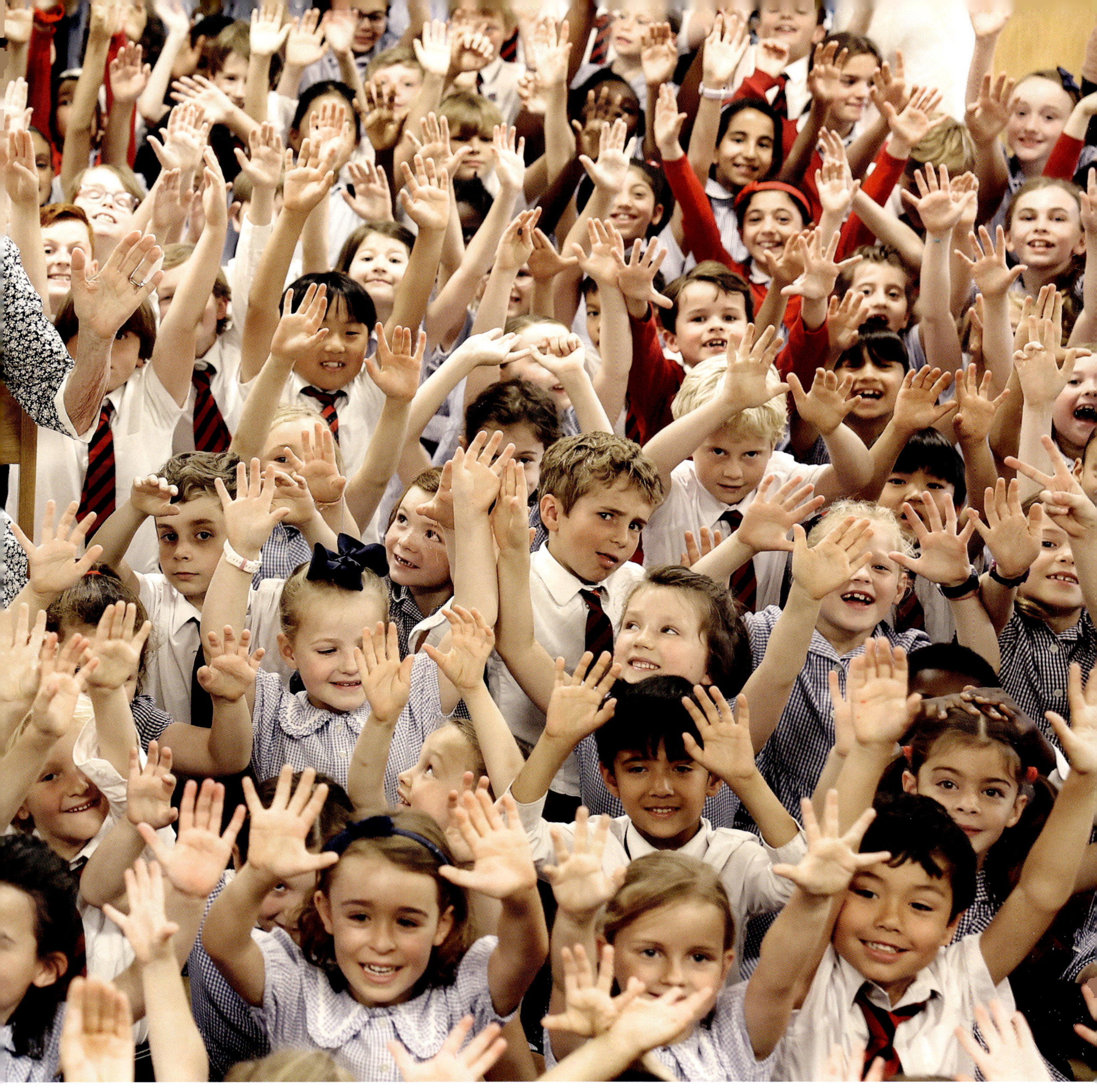

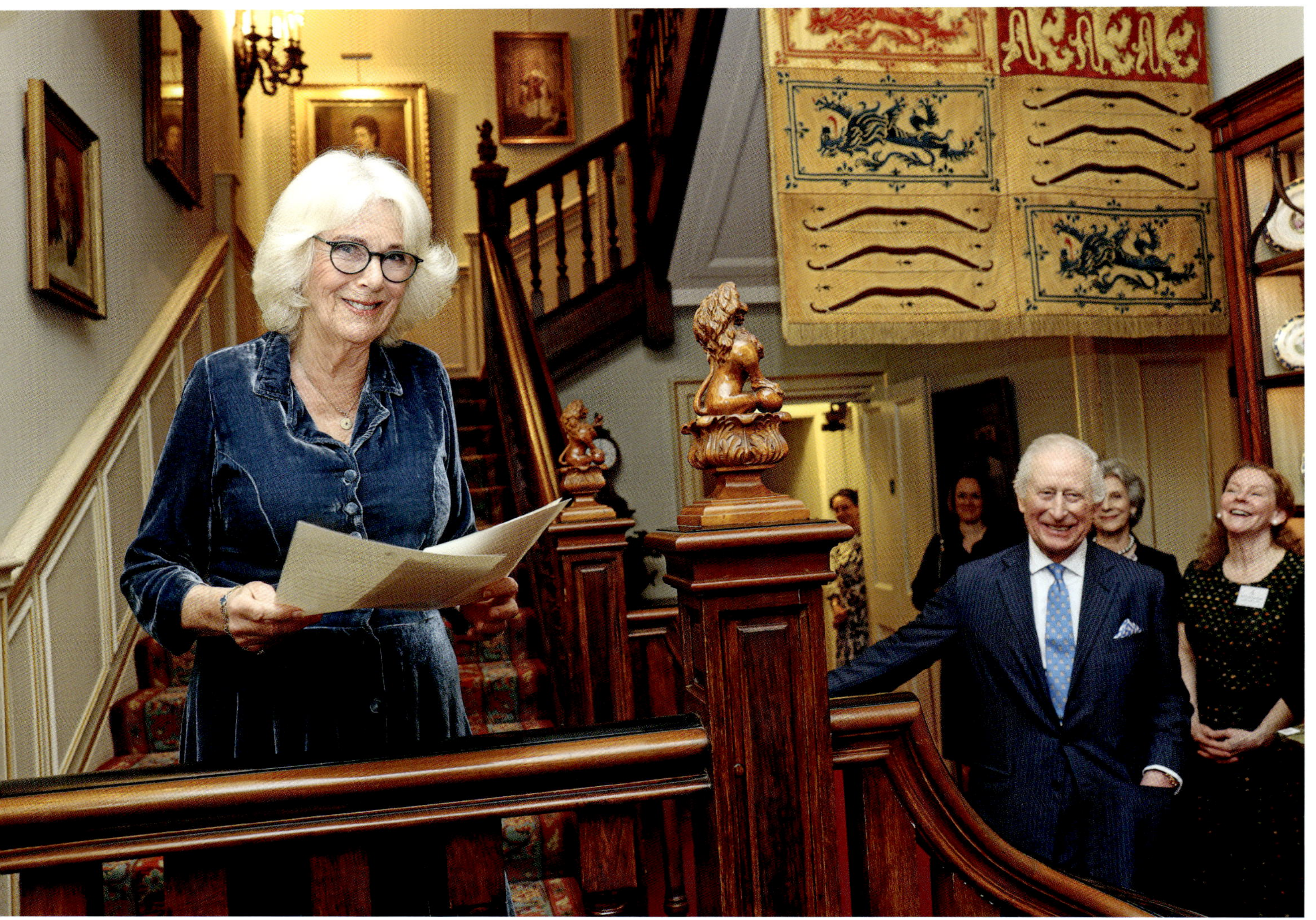

THE QUEEN'S READING ROOM

Normally the star of the show, King Charles takes a back seat while his wife shines at an event at Clarence House for her literacy charity in March 2025. A huge supporter of her achievements, the King stands alongside the Queen as she hosts the great and the good of the literary world at the launch of the Queen's Reading Room Medal, awarded to an individual who has championed reading, books, and literature in communities around the UK. The Queen's Reading Room began as a virtual book club in 2021 and has grown into a charity to celebrate and promote the power and benefits of reading.

Opposite
An event to mark the second anniversary of the Queen's Reading Room at Clarence House in February 2023.

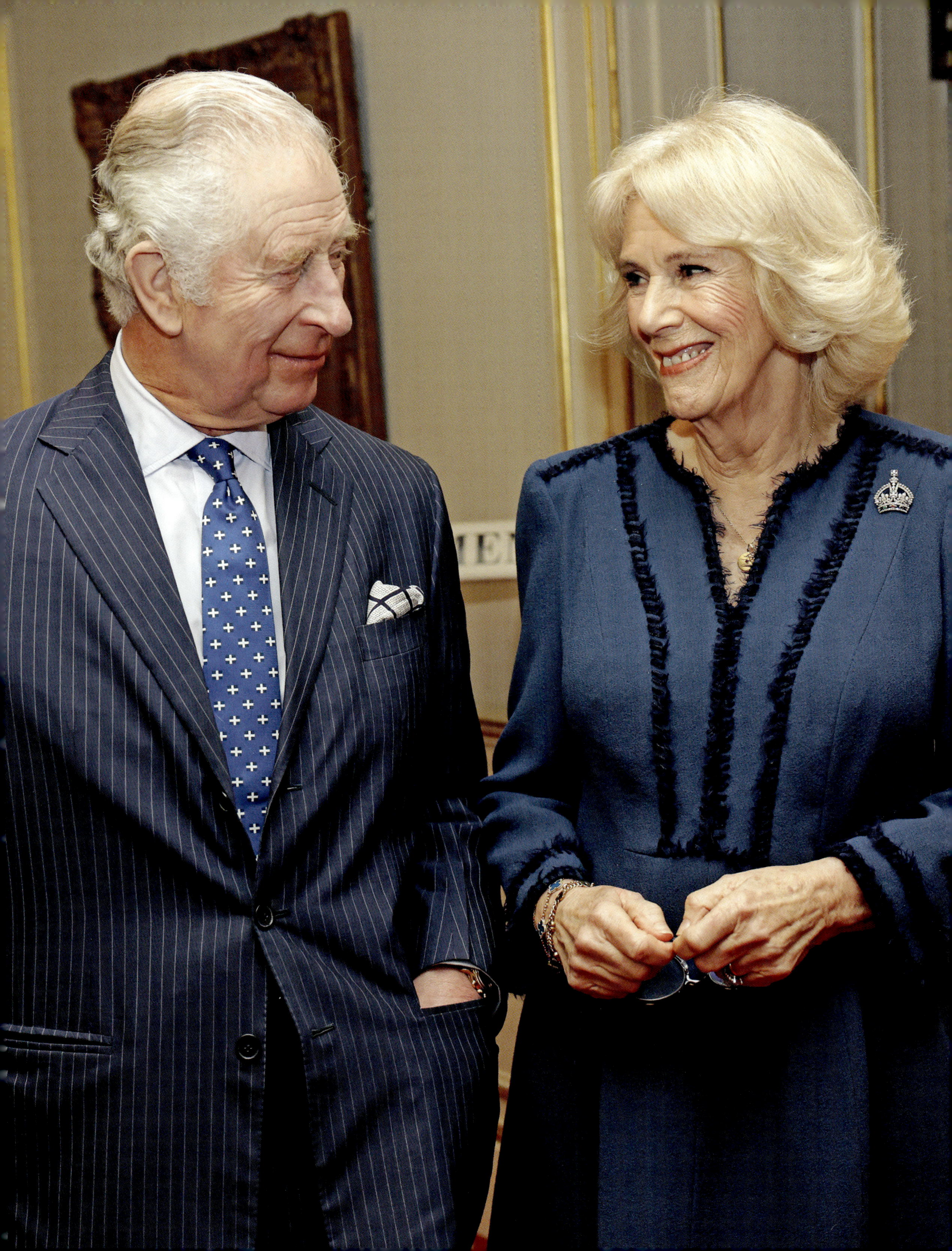

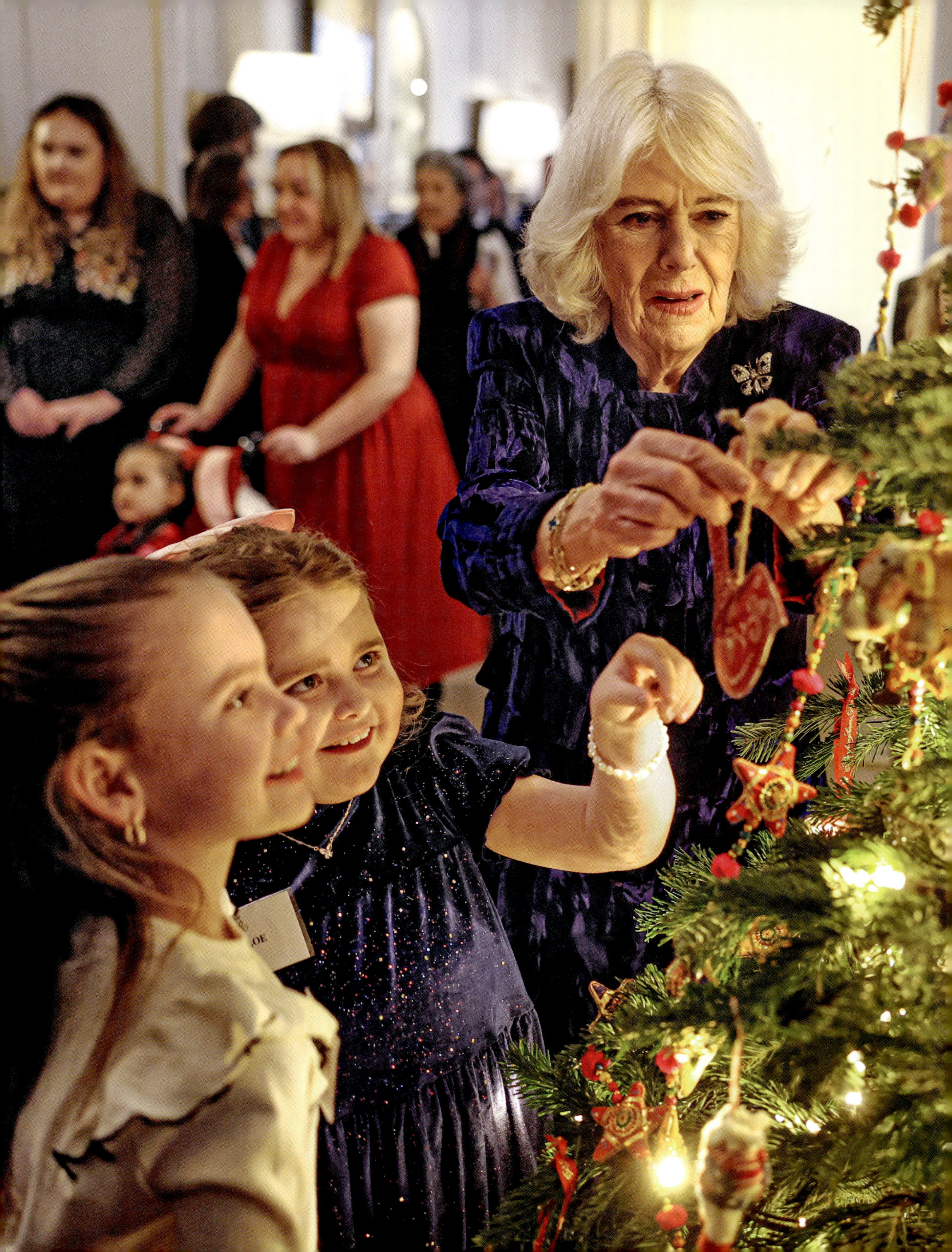

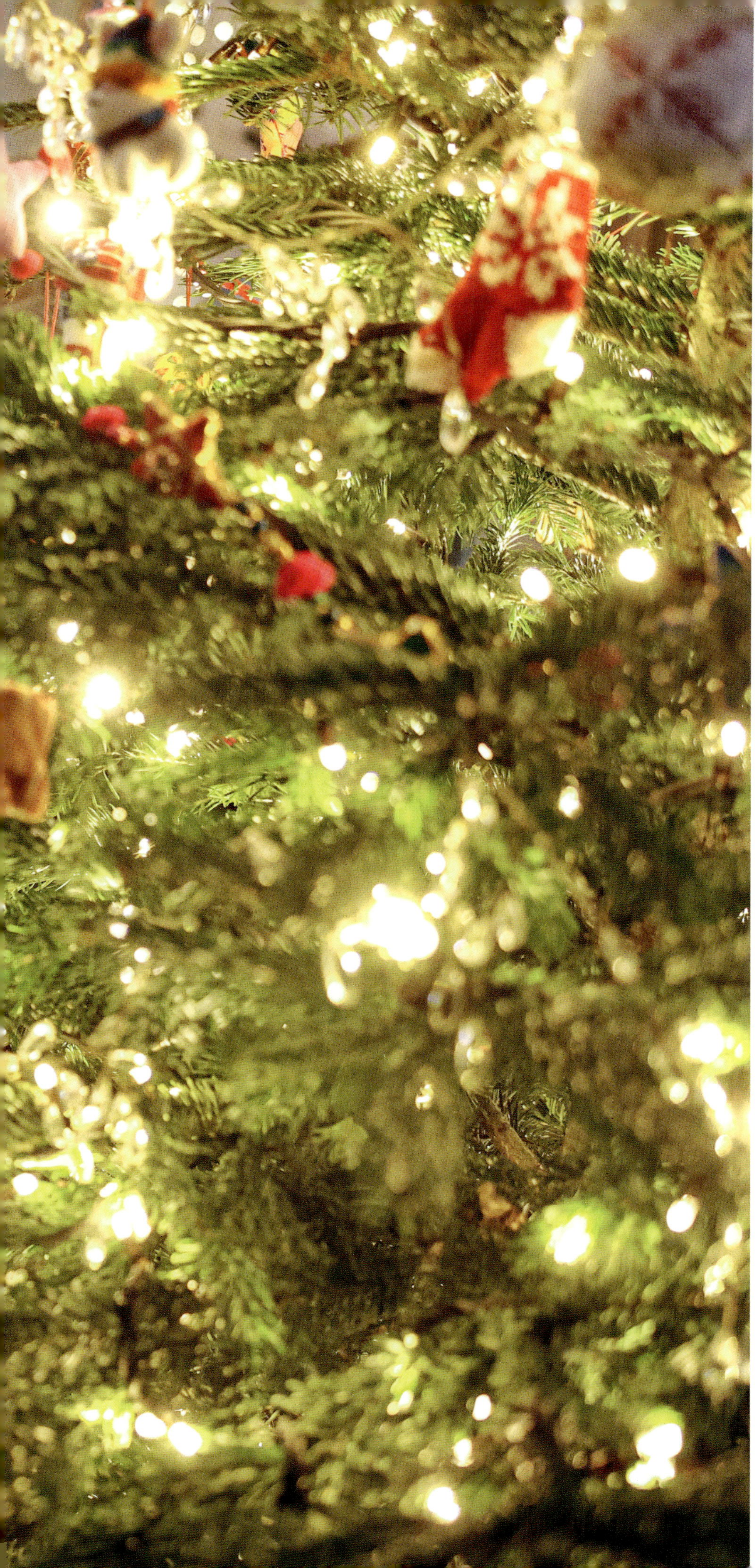

DECORATING THE TREE

At what is always a heartwarming event, Queen Camilla and young guests decorate a Christmas tree in the library of Clarence House on 12 December 2024. The Queen welcomes children and families supported by Helen & Douglas House and Roald Dahl's Marvellous Children's Charity as part of a festive tradition that is now in its 20th year.

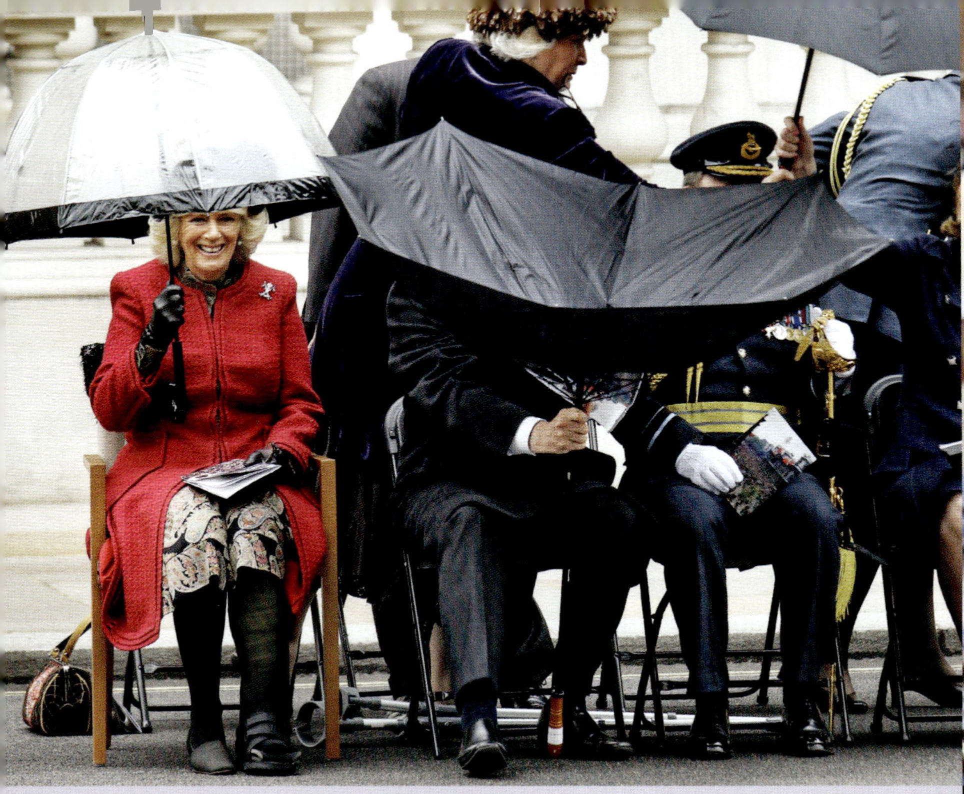

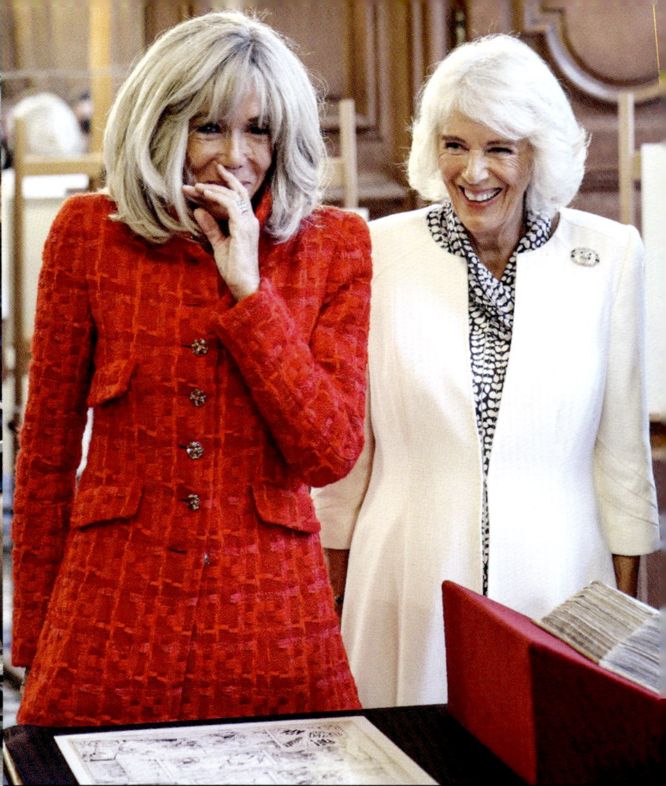

A SHARED SENSE OF HUMOUR

One of the things I most appreciate about Queen Camilla is her affectionate and subtly cheeky smile that brightens every event. In recent years, more people have become acquainted with her fantastically sharp wit and warm sense of humour as she takes on more public engagements as Queen. Her interactions with King Charles are clearly natural and often light-hearted – especially when cutting cake is involved!

Clockwise from top left: The Queen laughs as Bob Ainsworth struggles with his umbrella at the 65th anniversary of VE Day at the Cenotaph, 8 May 2010. Having a chuckle with French First Lady Brigitte Macron when a journalist sneezed loudly on a visit to the National Library in Paris, 21 September 2023. With the Duchess of Sussex at the King's 70th Birthday Patronage Celebration at Buckingham Palace in May 2018. Sharing a joke at the Braemar Gathering in September 2022. The King and Queen cut a cake as they open the Coronation Garden in Newtownabbey, Northern Ireland, in May 2023.
Opposite: Queen Camilla at the 2023 Commonwealth Day Service.

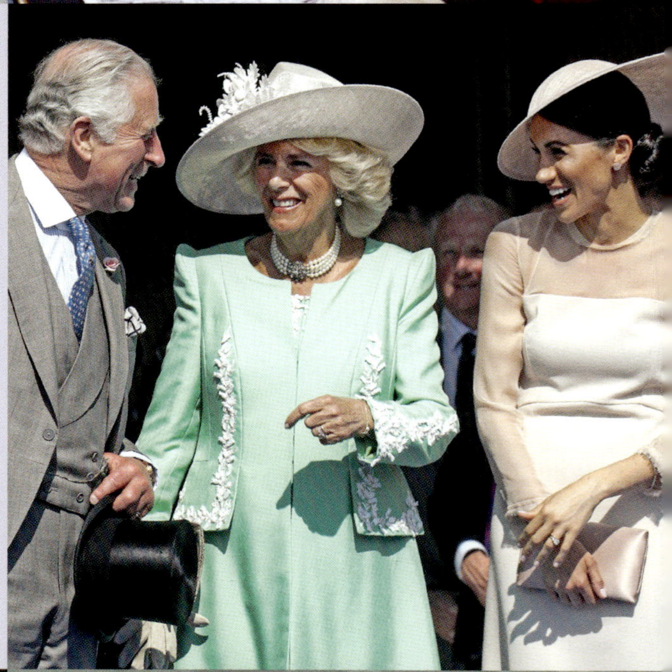

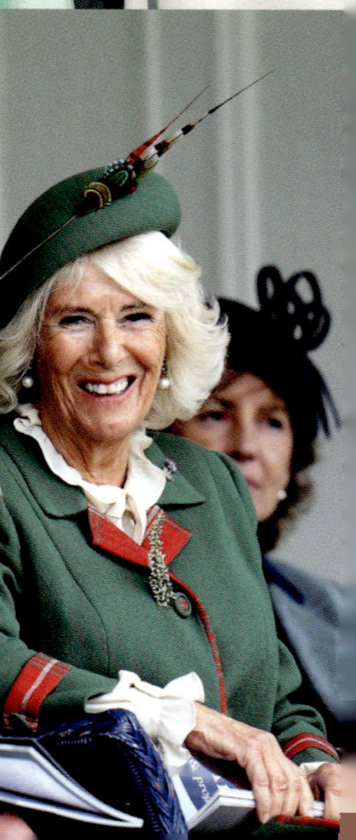

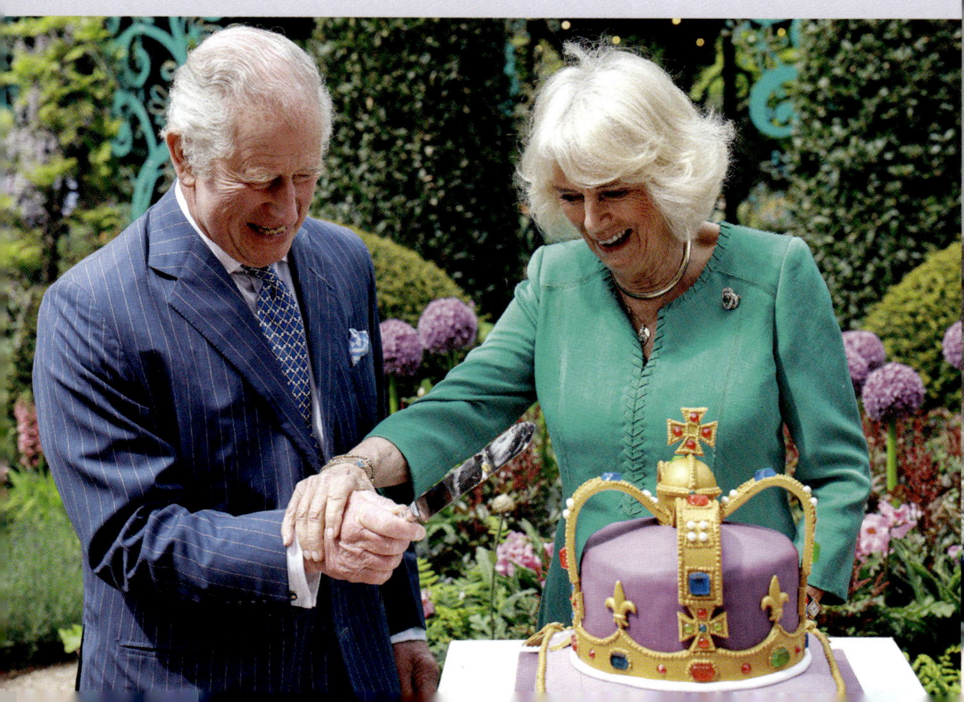

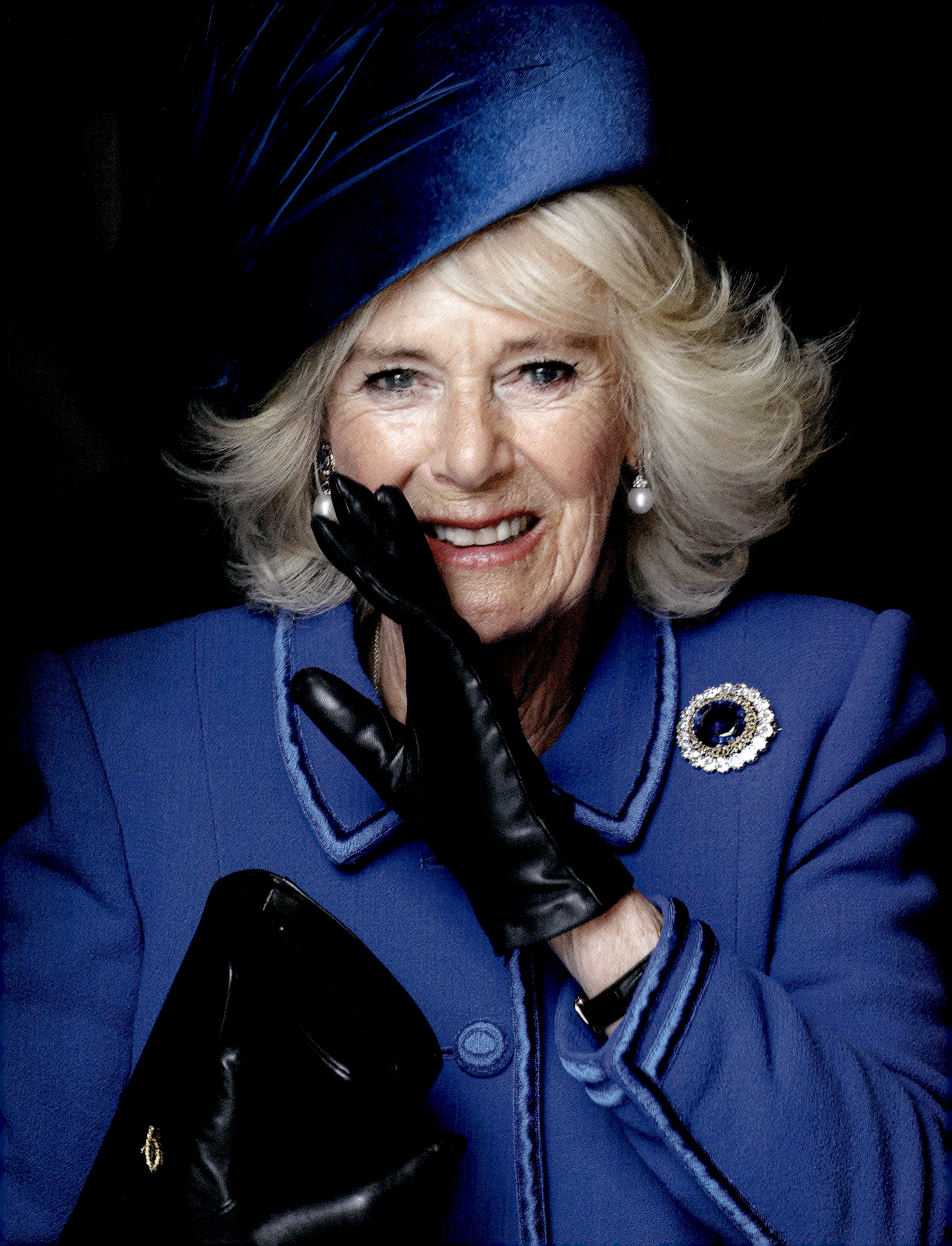

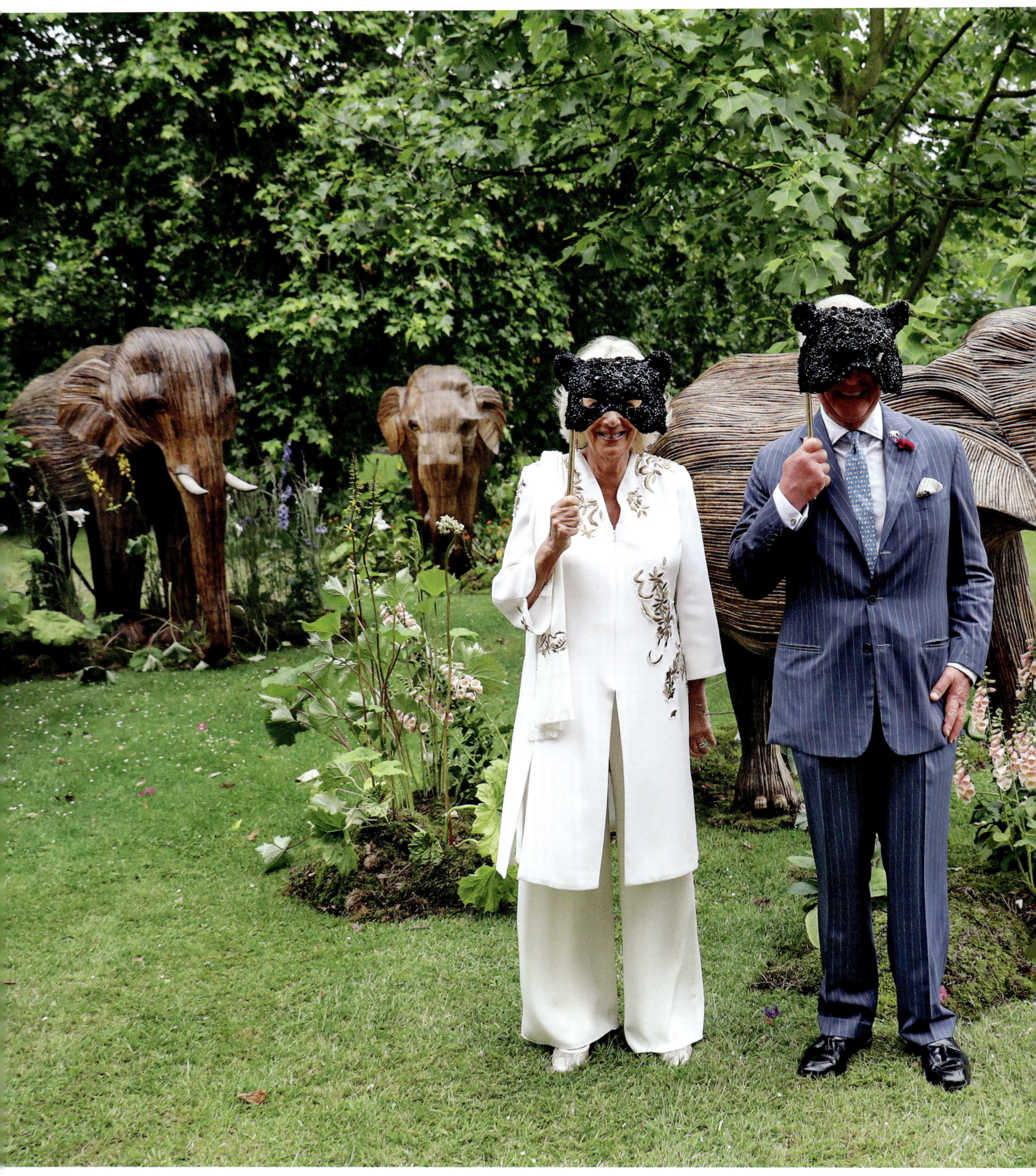

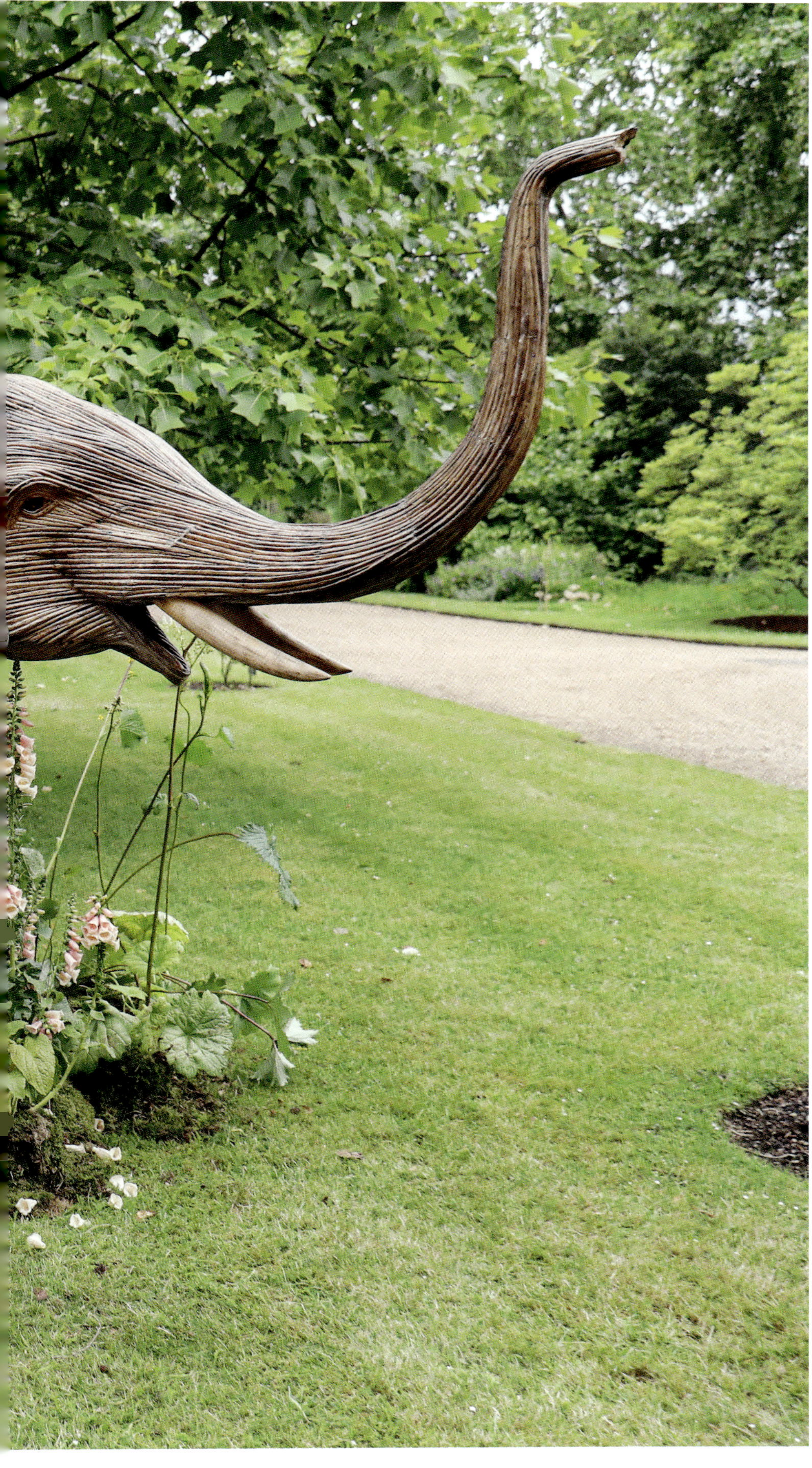

MASKED BALL

Before his passing in 2014, Queen Camilla's brother, Mark Shand, was a passionate advocate for the Asian elephant. In 2002 he cofounded the charity Elephant Family, an international NGO to protect Asian elephants and conserve their diminishing habitats. Charles and Camilla both became royal patrons of the charity after Shand's death. Pictured here, the royal couple attend the Elephant Family masked ball at Clarence House in 2019.

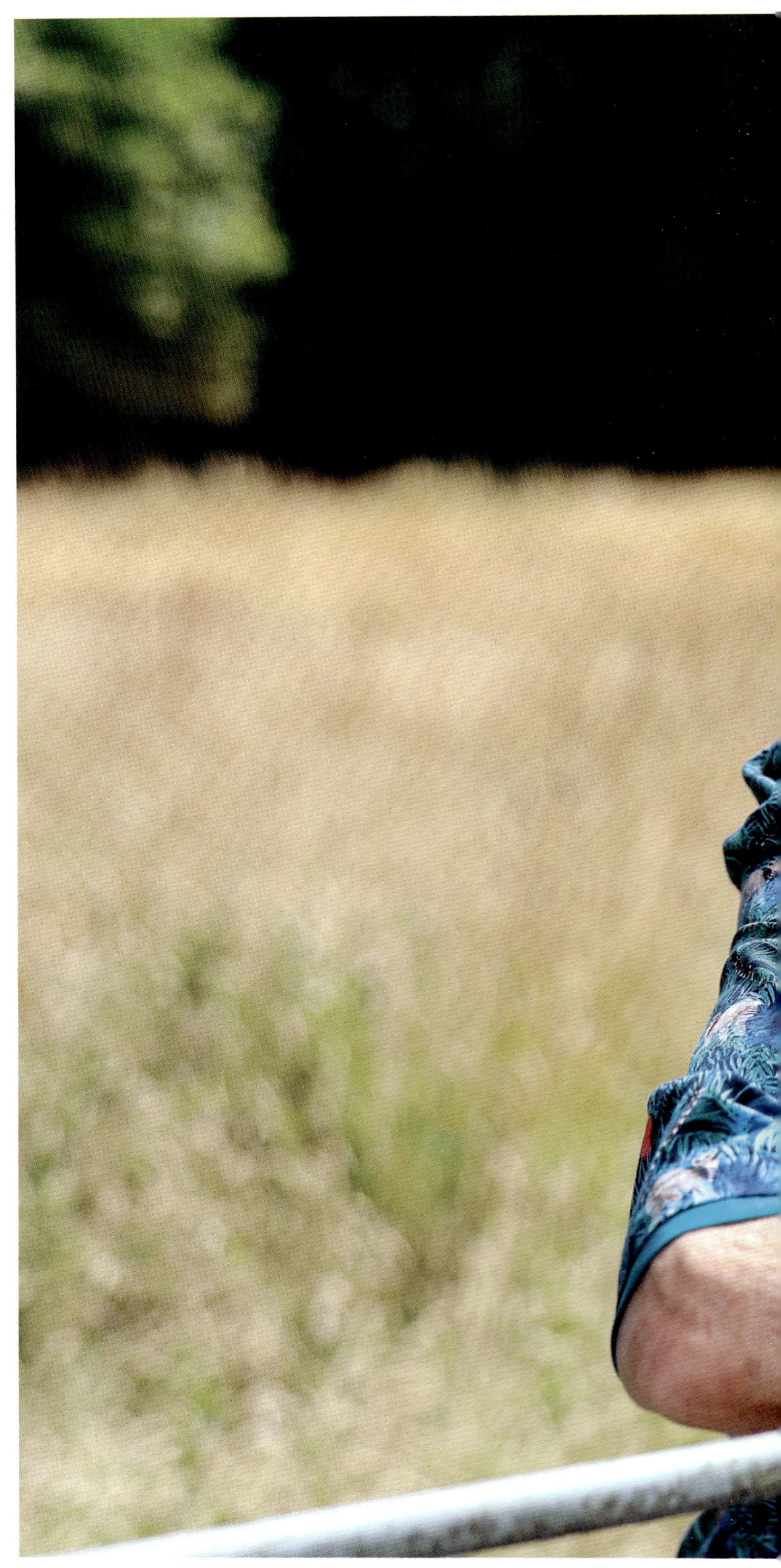

RAY MILL

Queen Camilla poses for a portrait at her home, Ray Mill, in Gloucestershire. Clearly she feels very at home here, and it was a joy to take this relaxed portrait to celebrate her 78th birthday. I like to keep these shoots simple. For me it is about creating a relaxed situation in order to capture a genuine moment – on this day in such stunning surroundings it really was not hard!

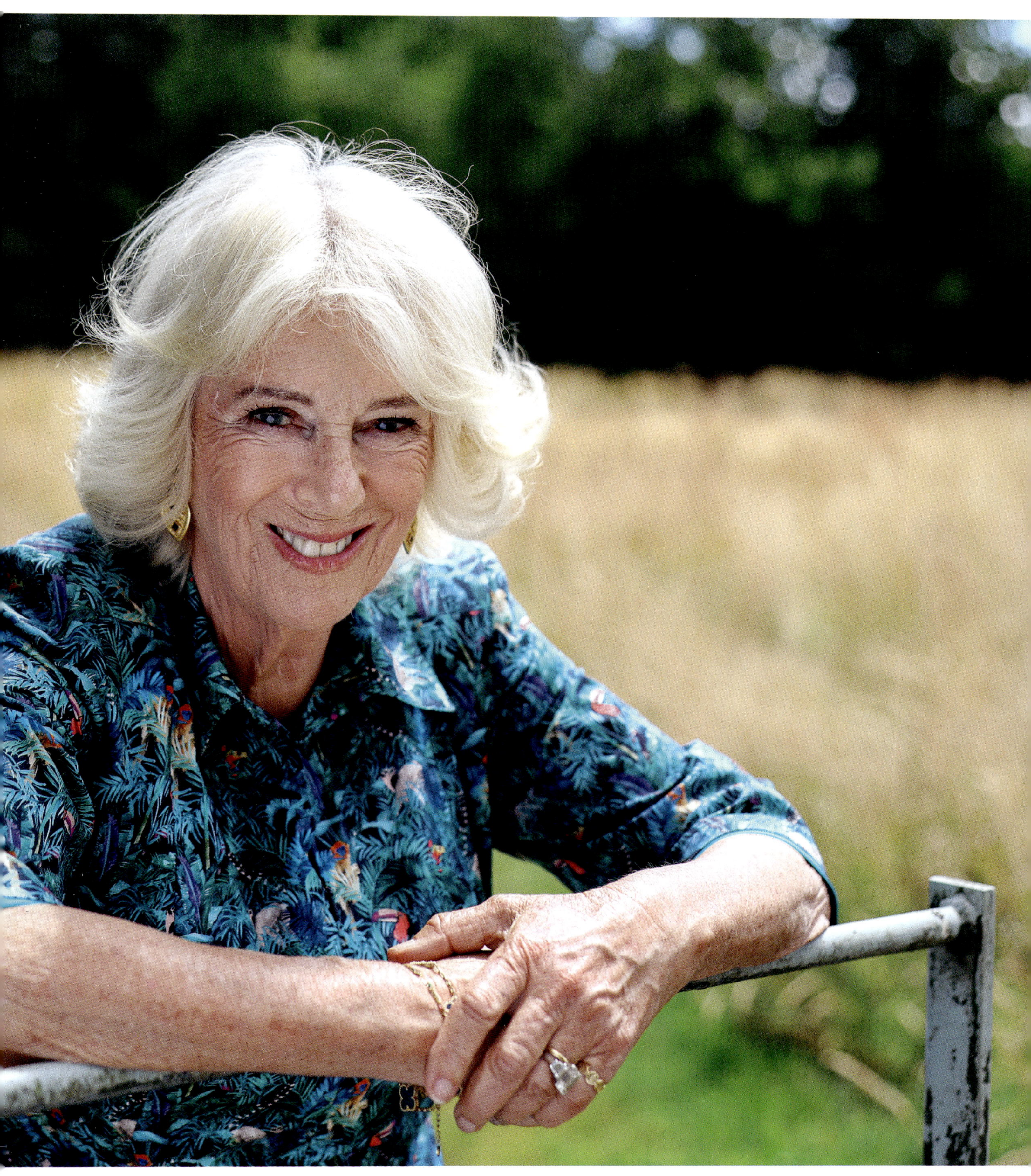

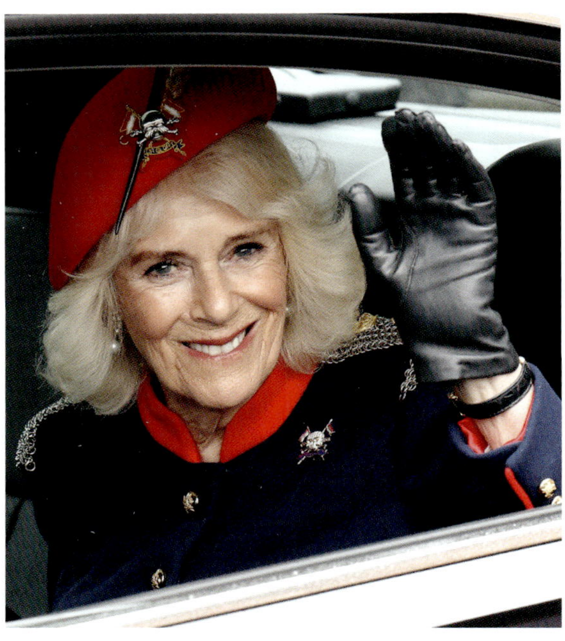

MILITARY ASSOCIATION

Queen Camilla has a deep interest in British military history and specifically in the Royal Lancers. Her father, Major Bruce Shand, served in the 12th Royal Lancers and received the Military Cross and Bar for bravery in France and North Africa, where he was taken prisoner at the Battle of El Alamein in 1942.

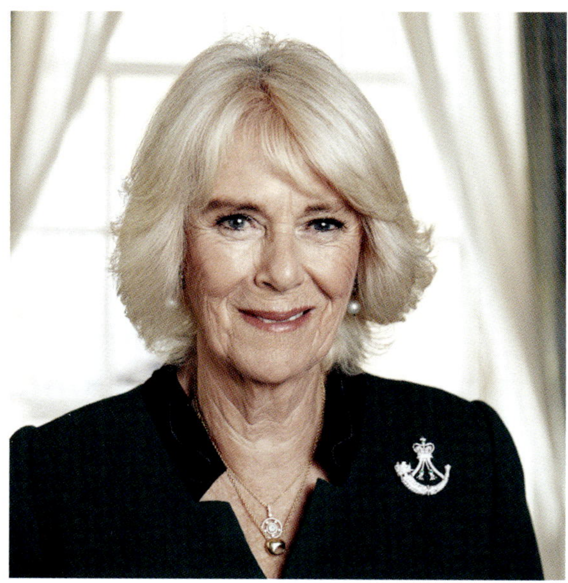

The Queen is also Colonel-in-Chief of the Rifles. Here she wears the Rifles brooch, presented to her on 12 October 2020 by General Sir Patrick Sanders, Colonel Commandant of the regiment.

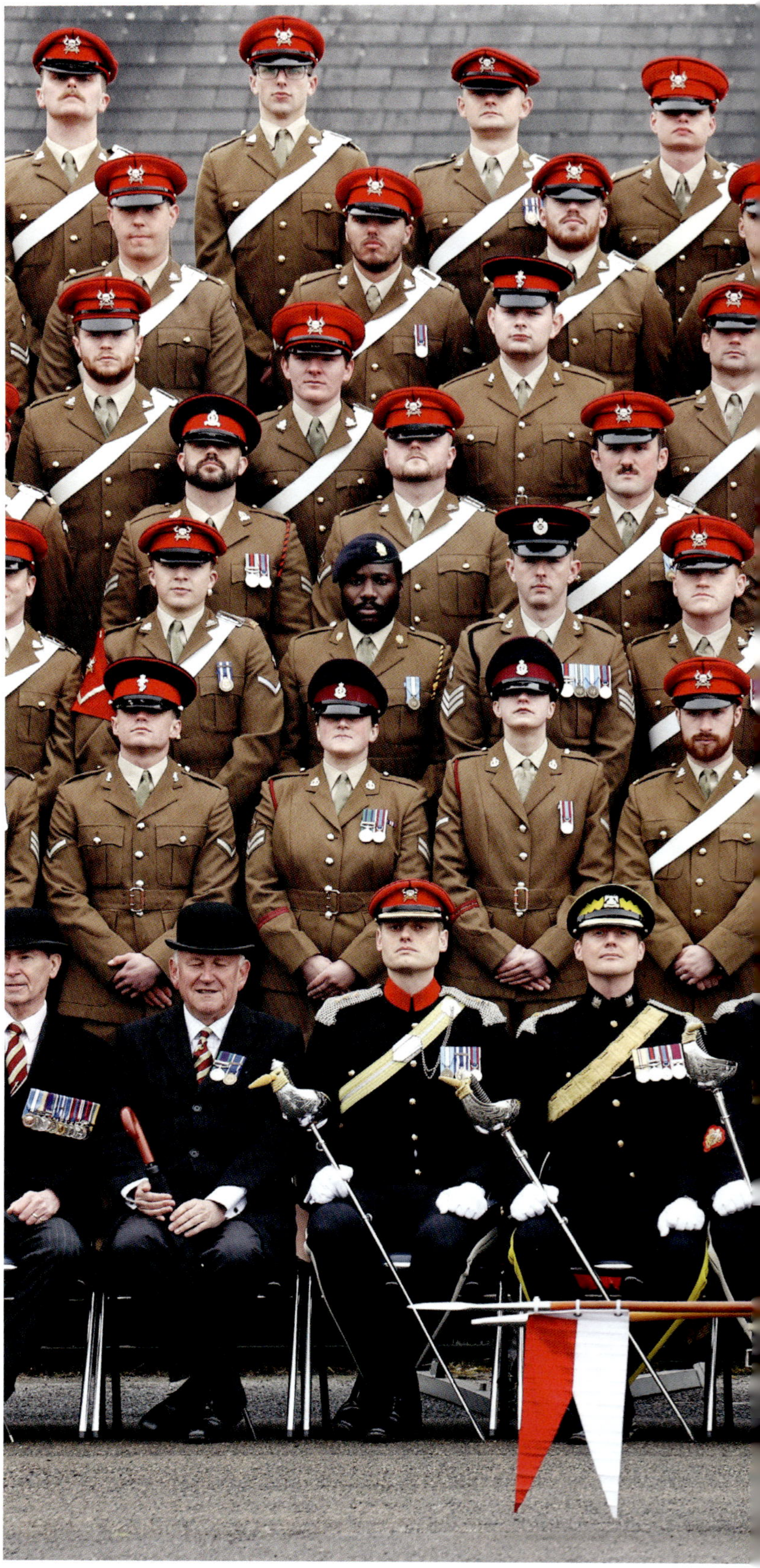

In June 2023, Queen Camilla was appointed Colonel-in-Chief of the Royal Lancers, and it was a privilege to photograph her during this visit in April 2024, when she wore a striking outfit inspired by the uniform and a beret in the unit's vivid red.

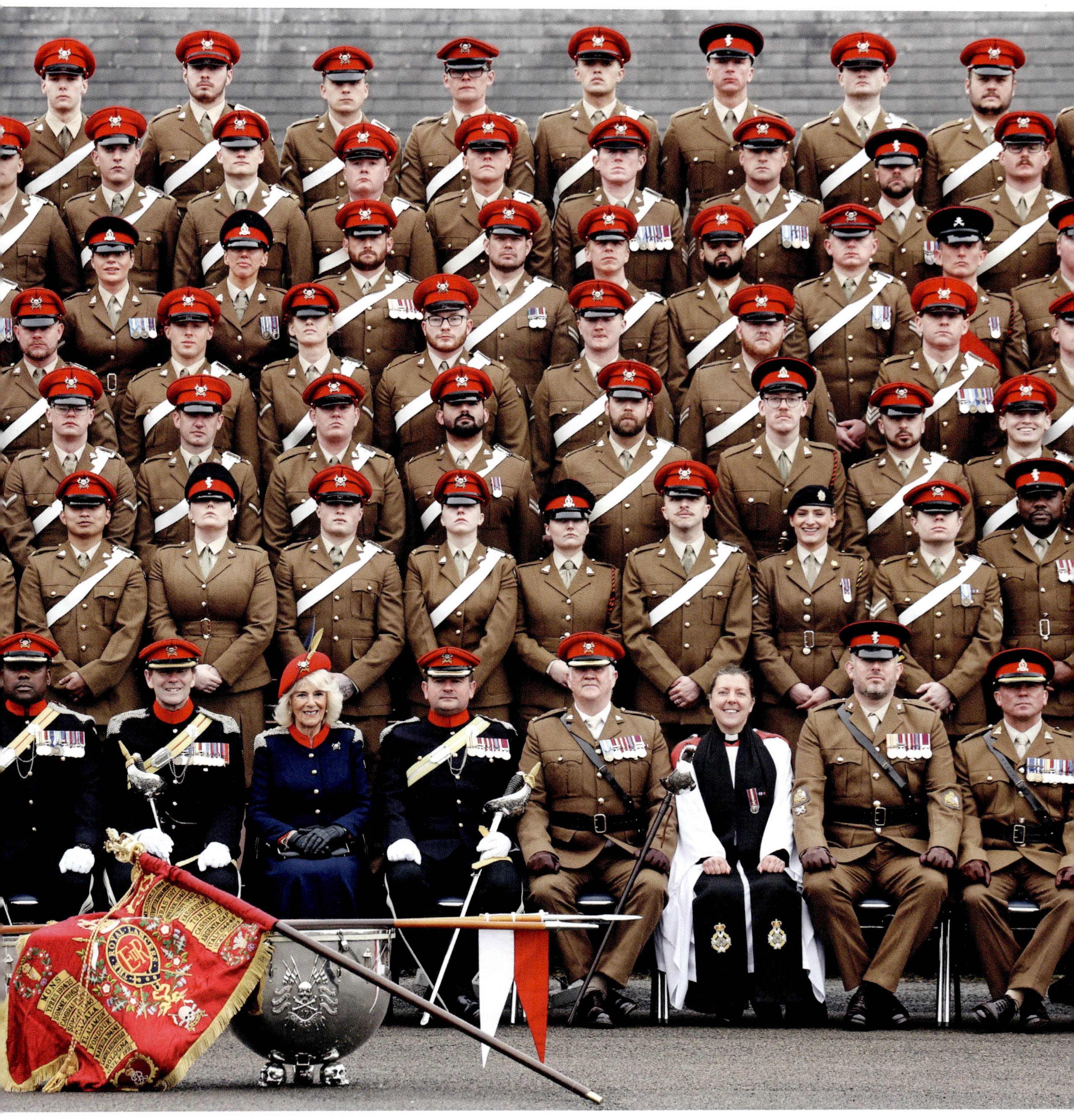

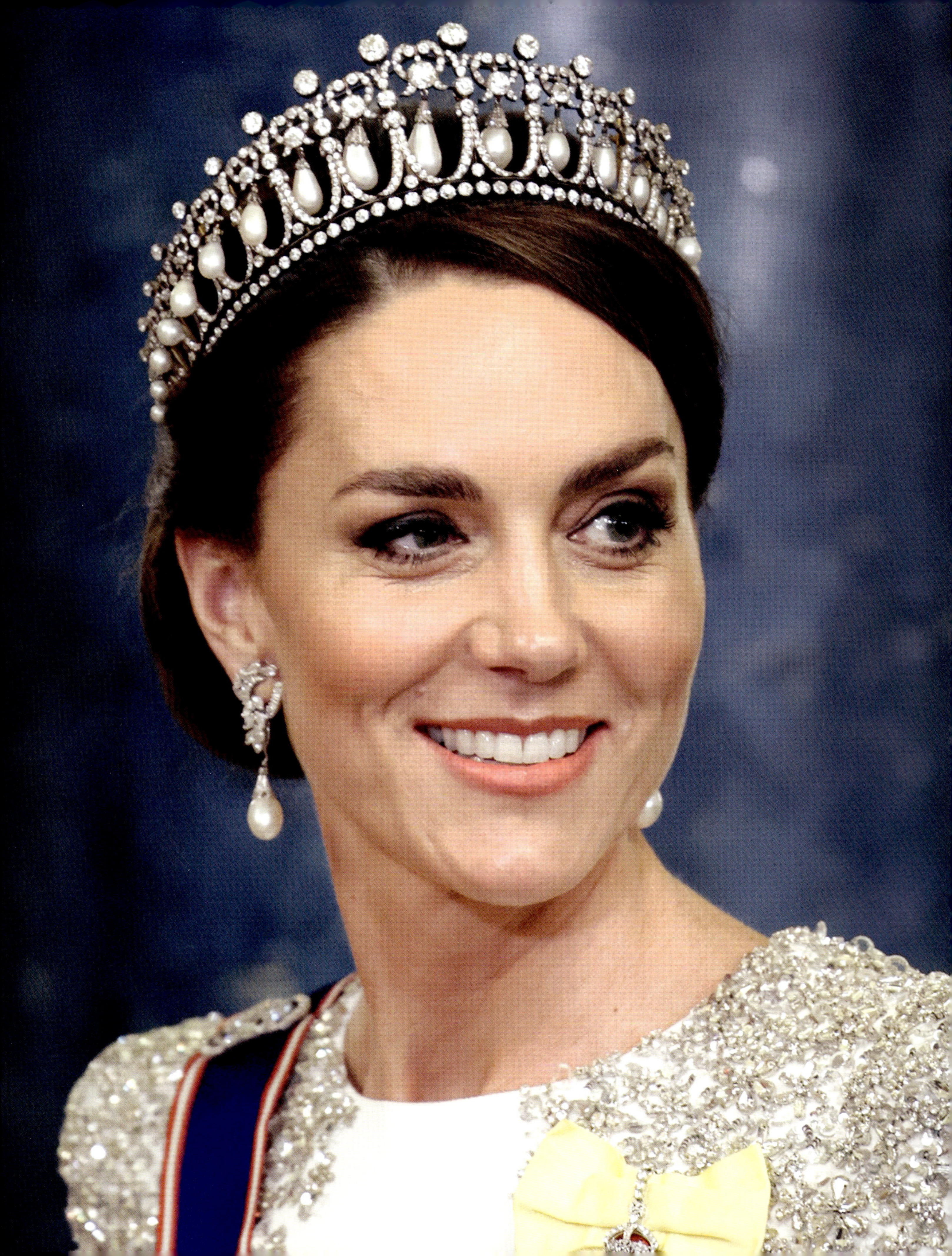

6

CATHERINE

ICON AND ADVOCATE

The clothes she wears may sell out around the world in hours, but Catherine, Princess of Wales, is so much more than a fashion icon. Her passionate advocacy for the importance of the early years of childhood has changed government policy, and her creativity and innovation have led her to work with the National Portrait Gallery to publish a photography book, *Hold Still*.

Her love of photography is reflected in her patronage of the Royal Photographic Society, something she took over from Queen Elizabeth II, who in her earlier years was often seen with her trusty Leica slung around her neck. Catherine has taken on this stewardship with a unique passion and devotion to the genre. Her intimate photographs of her children on their various birthdays have graced the front pages of newspapers around the world and have offered a very private insight into her family life. The Princess's devotion to her family and her love of nature are intertwined, and it is clear that her happy place is playing with her children in the sand dunes of Norfolk near Anmer Hall or exploring the verdant forests that surround the estate.

Like King Charles, Catherine faced a battle with cancer. The first time we saw her after treatment, at Trooping the Colour in 2024, beaming from the carriage and sharing a moment with her family on the balcony, was embraced by the world.

The world stopped rotating for a moment when the engagement of Prince William and Catherine Middleton was announced in November 2010. The excitement was tangible – we had a new member of the royal family who was not only beautiful and elegant but also seemed destined for greatness. The royal wedding of the Duke and Duchess of Cambridge was watched by millions around the world, and as I looked on from my vantage point on that stunning spring day, ready to capture their first moments as a married couple on the steps of Westminster Abbey, I could not help but feel a sense of optimism for what the future would bring.

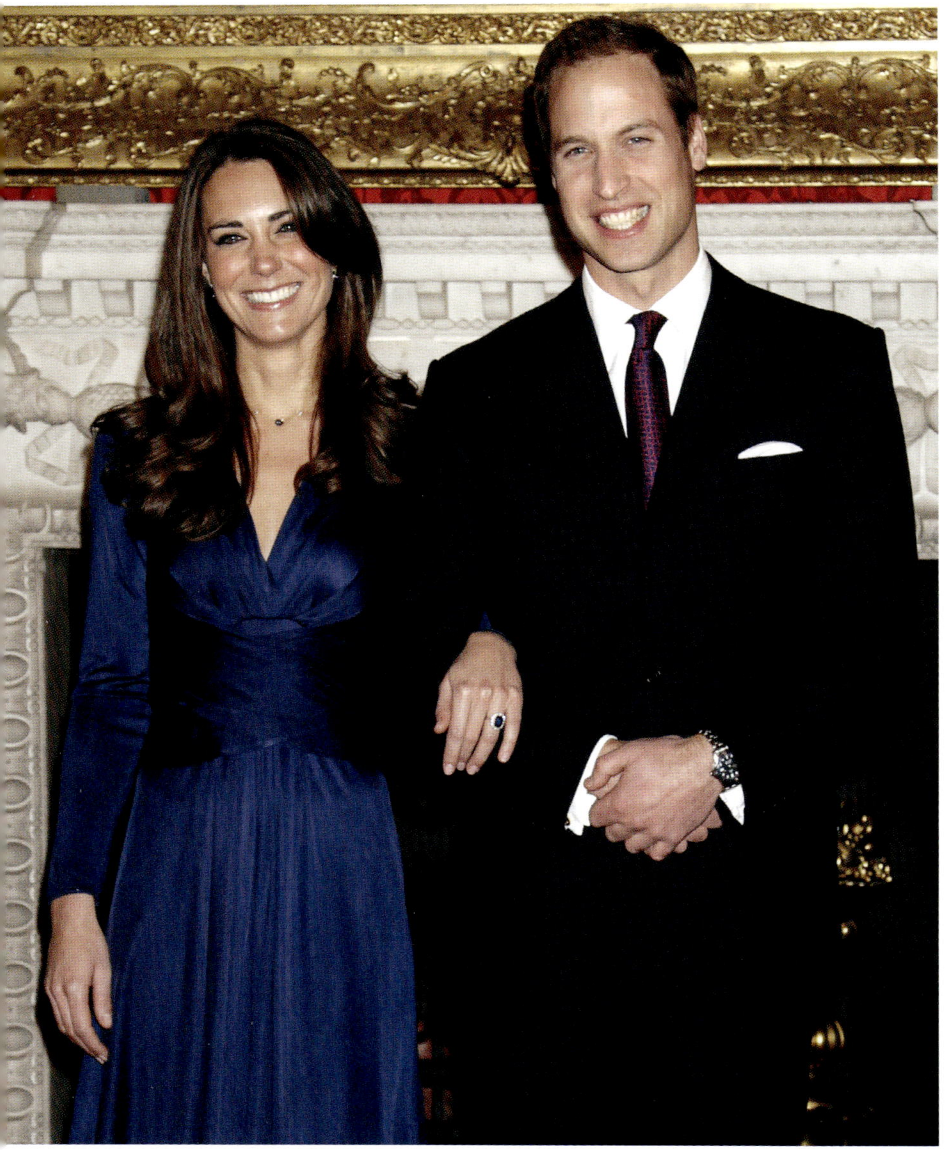

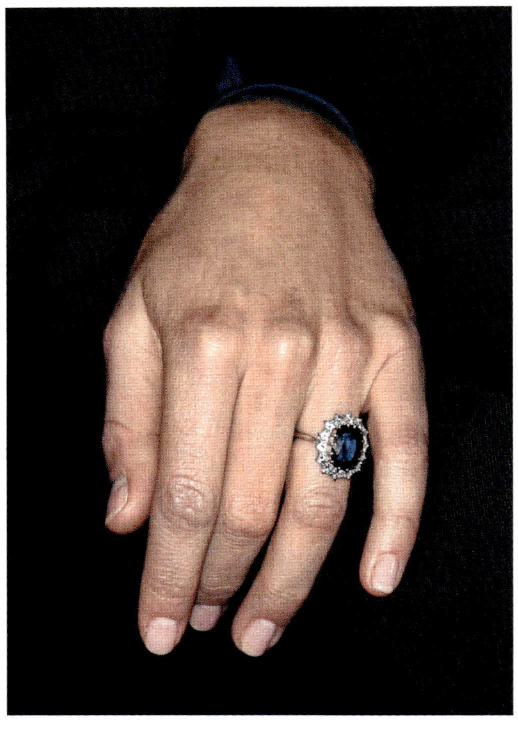

Left
Prince William and Kate Middleton in the State Apartments of St. James's Palace, on the day of their engagement announcement, 16 November 2010.

Above
The engagement ring is a 12-carat oval Ceylon sapphire surrounded by 14 solitaire diamonds, all set in 18-carat white gold.

Opposite
Leaving Westminster Abbey following their marriage on 29 April 2011. The service was attended by 1,900 guests, while thousands of well-wishers from around the world travelled to London to celebrate the royal wedding.

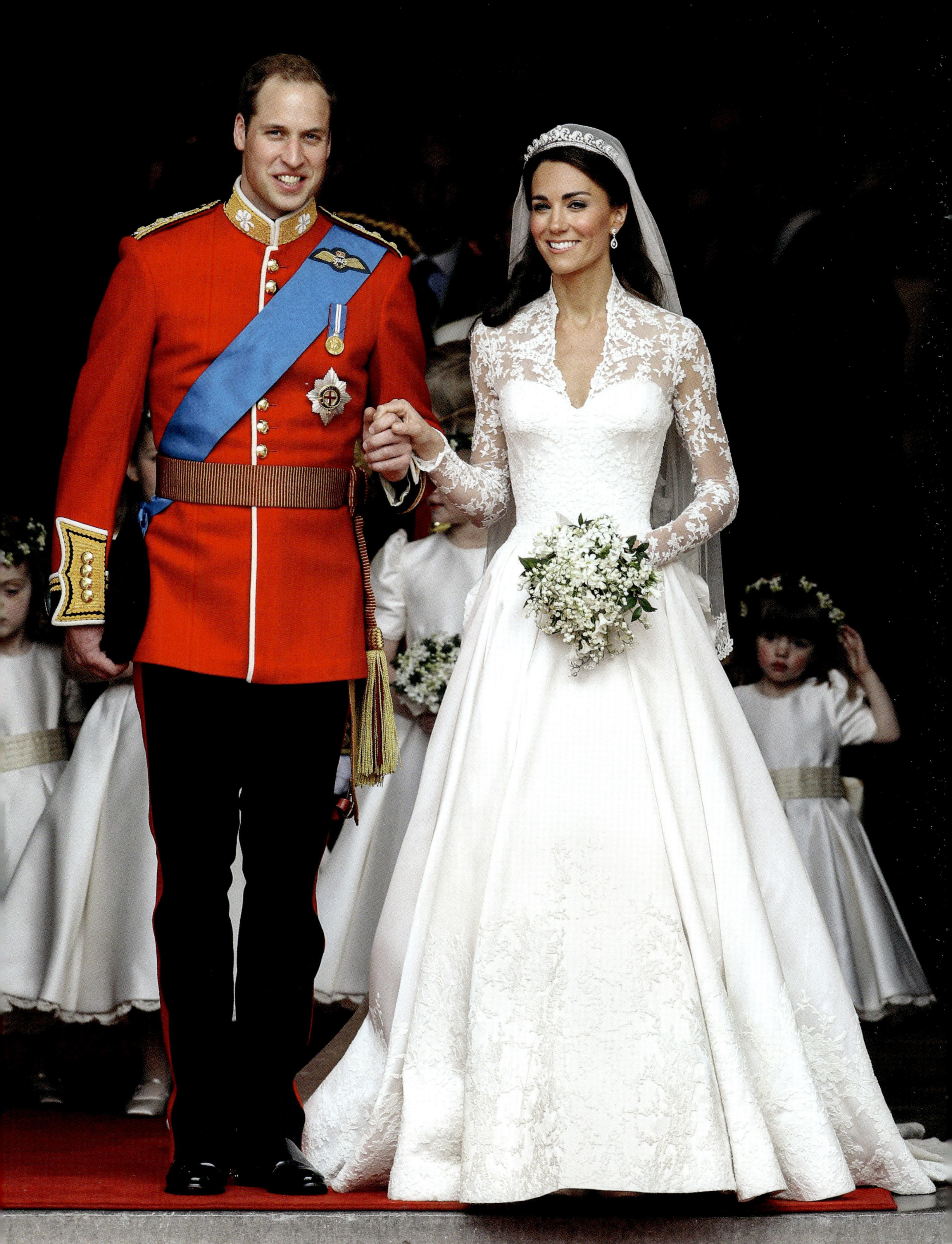

UNWAVERING SUPPORT

A warm and supportive hand on the back: a visual symbol of the steadying hand that Catherine has had on Prince William over the years they have been together. The Prince and Princess work incredibly successfully as a team, not only on royal engagements but also in family life and while juggling all the pressures within the royal "bubble."

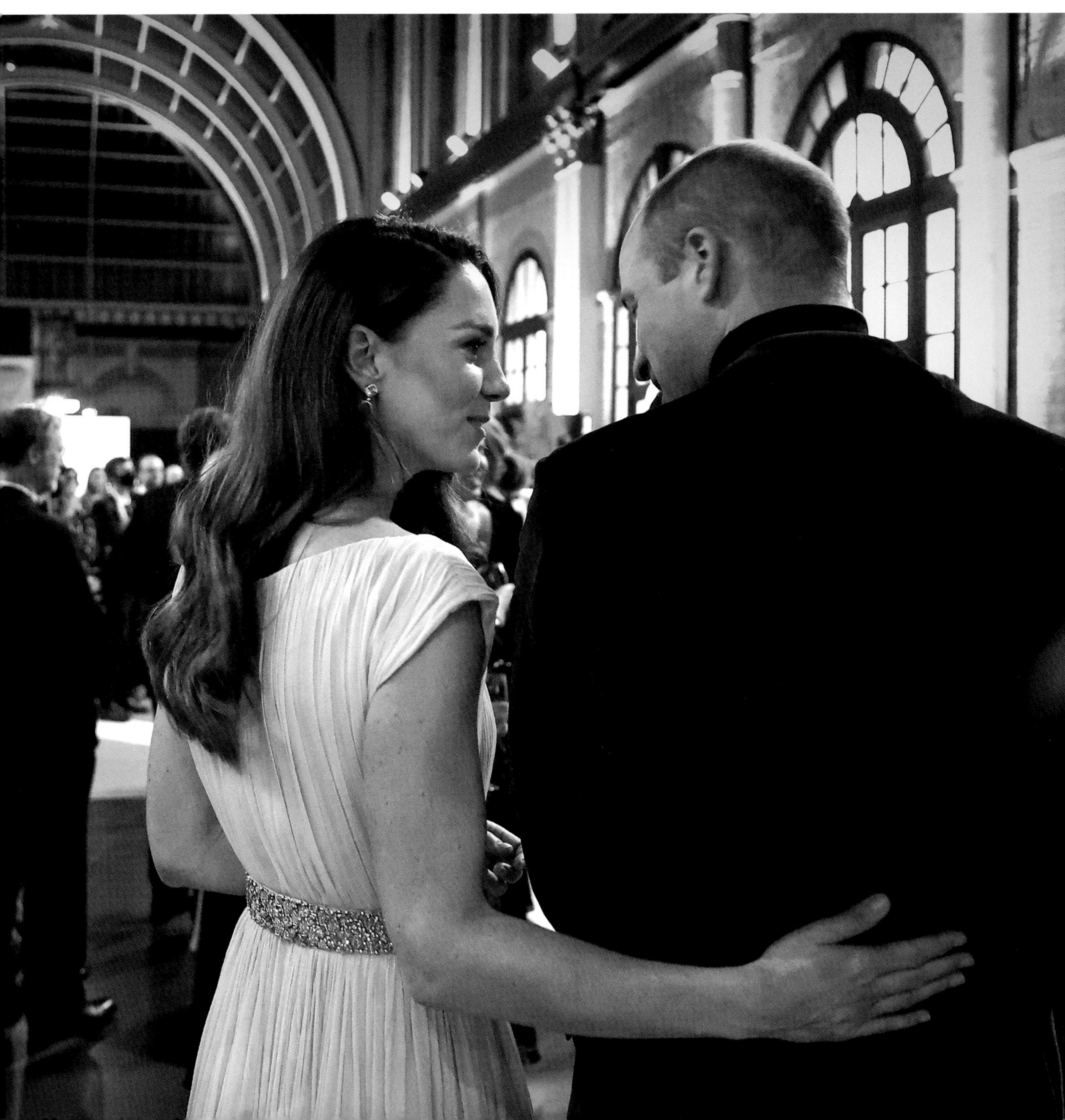

Below left
The Princess of Wales puts a reassuring hand around her husband during the inaugural Earthshot Prize Awards at Alexandra Palace in North London, 17 October 2021.

Below
Leaving the Earthshot Prize ceremony in Boston at the MGM Music Hall at Fenway, 2 December 2022.

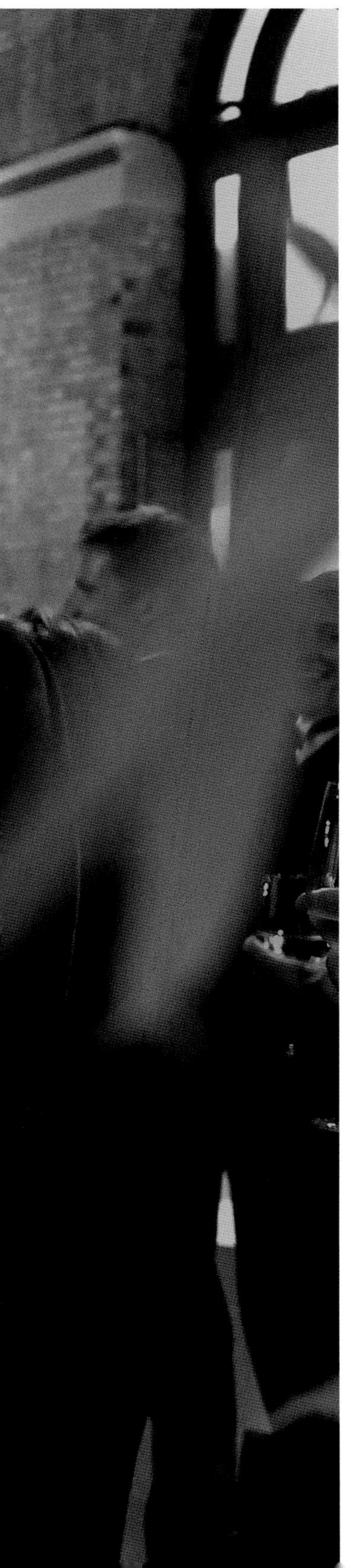

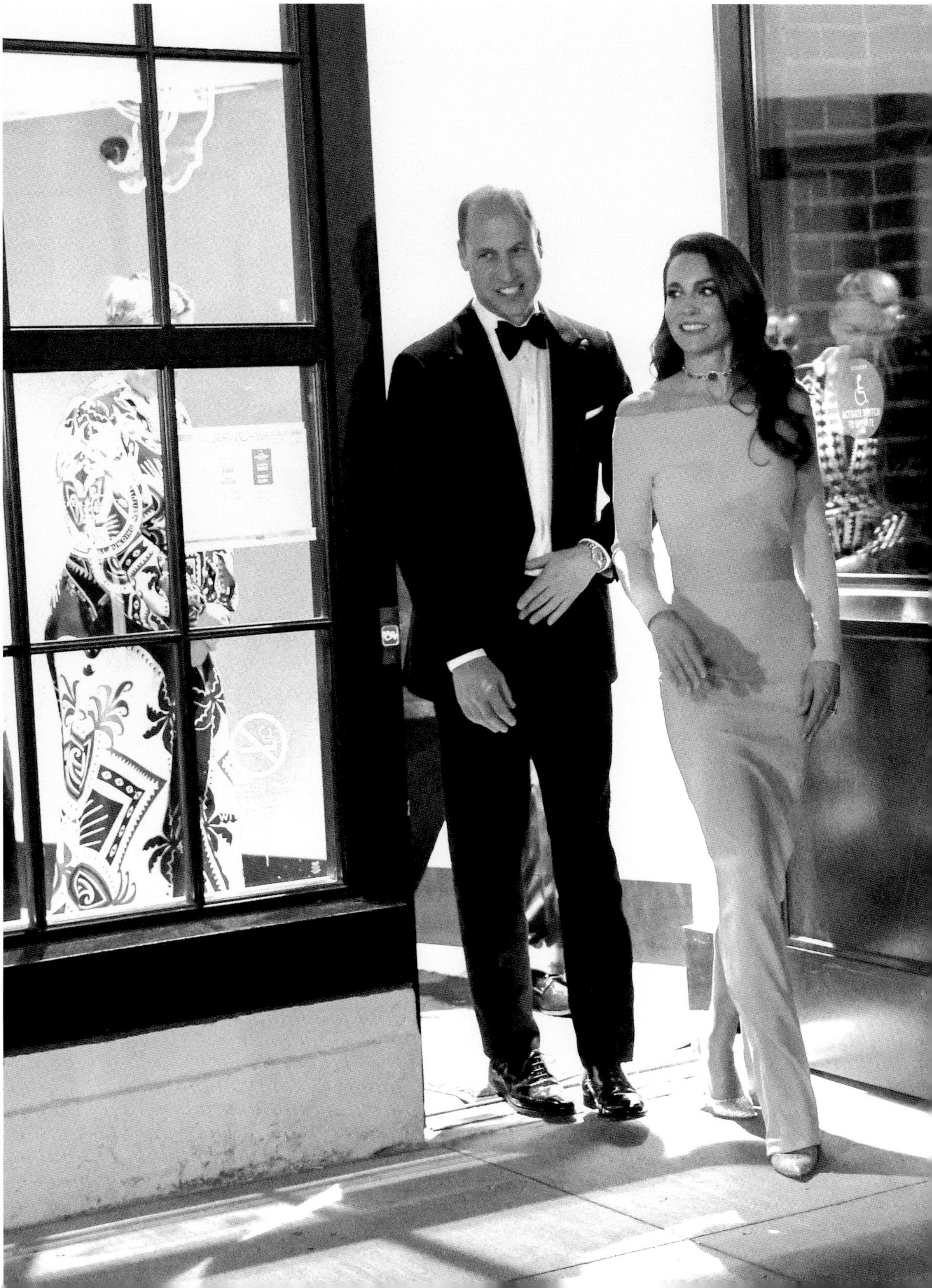

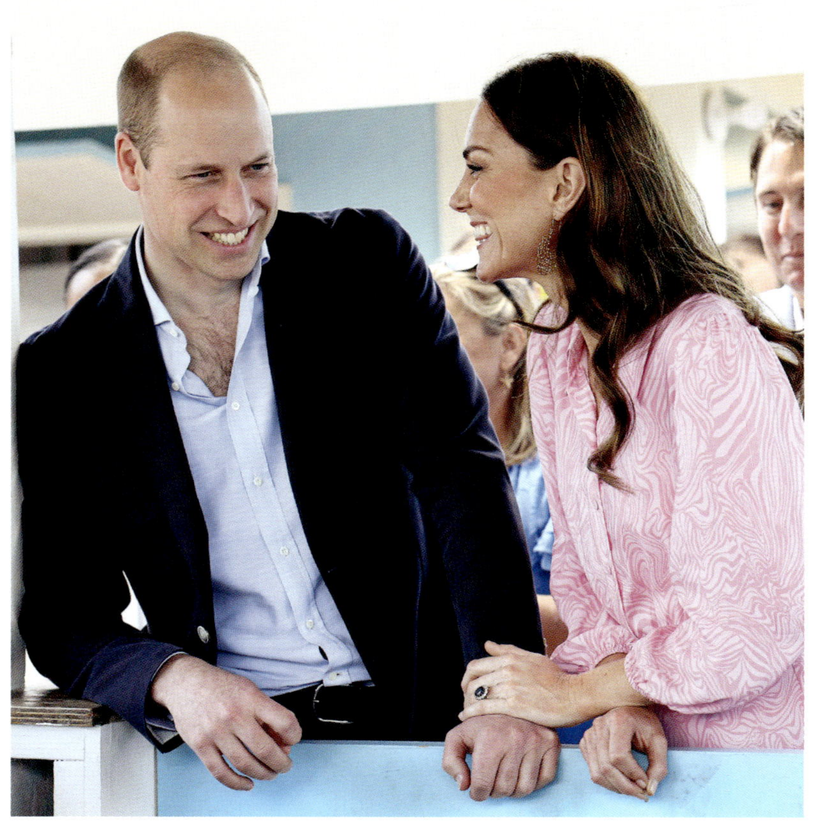

It is a photographer's dream to capture the warm and genuine rapport between the Prince and Princess of Wales, not to mention the friendly banter and a touch of competitiveness! Here the couple are on a memorable trip to the Abaco Islands, moments before Catherine tries a conch, 26 March 2022.

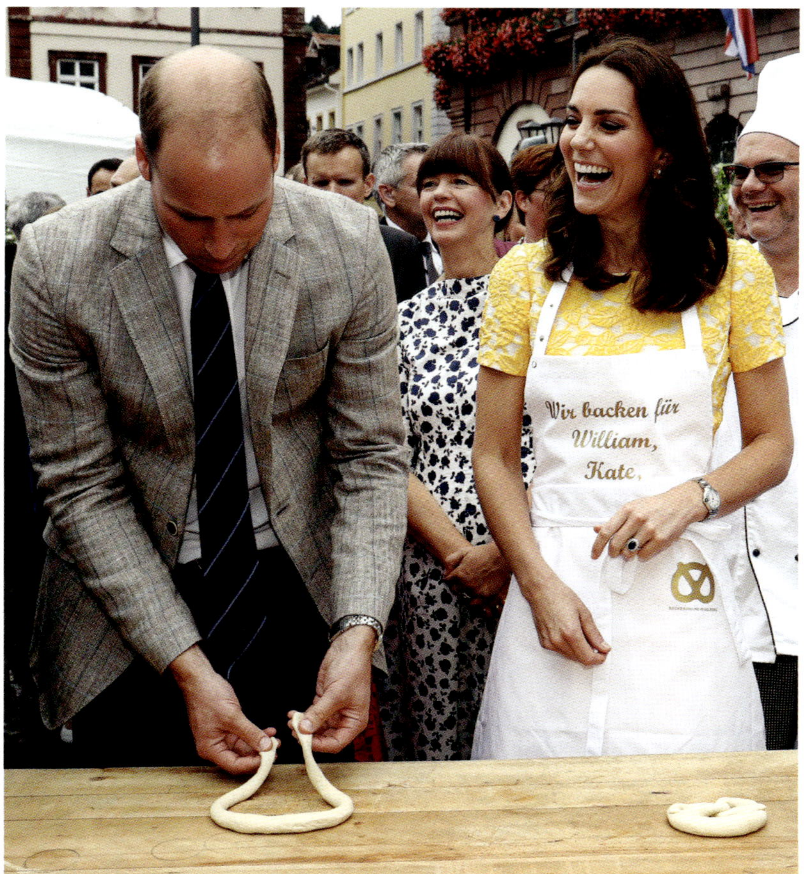

Left
Getting stuck into making pretzels during a tour of a traditional German market in Heidelberg, 20 July 2017.

Right
The Princess celebrates the beginning of Black History Month on a visit to Fitzalan High School in Cardiff, 3 October 2023.

Overleaf
Members of the public photograph the Prince and Princess of Wales as they walk down the red carpet at the EE BAFTA Film Awards at the Royal Festival Hall, 19 February 2023.

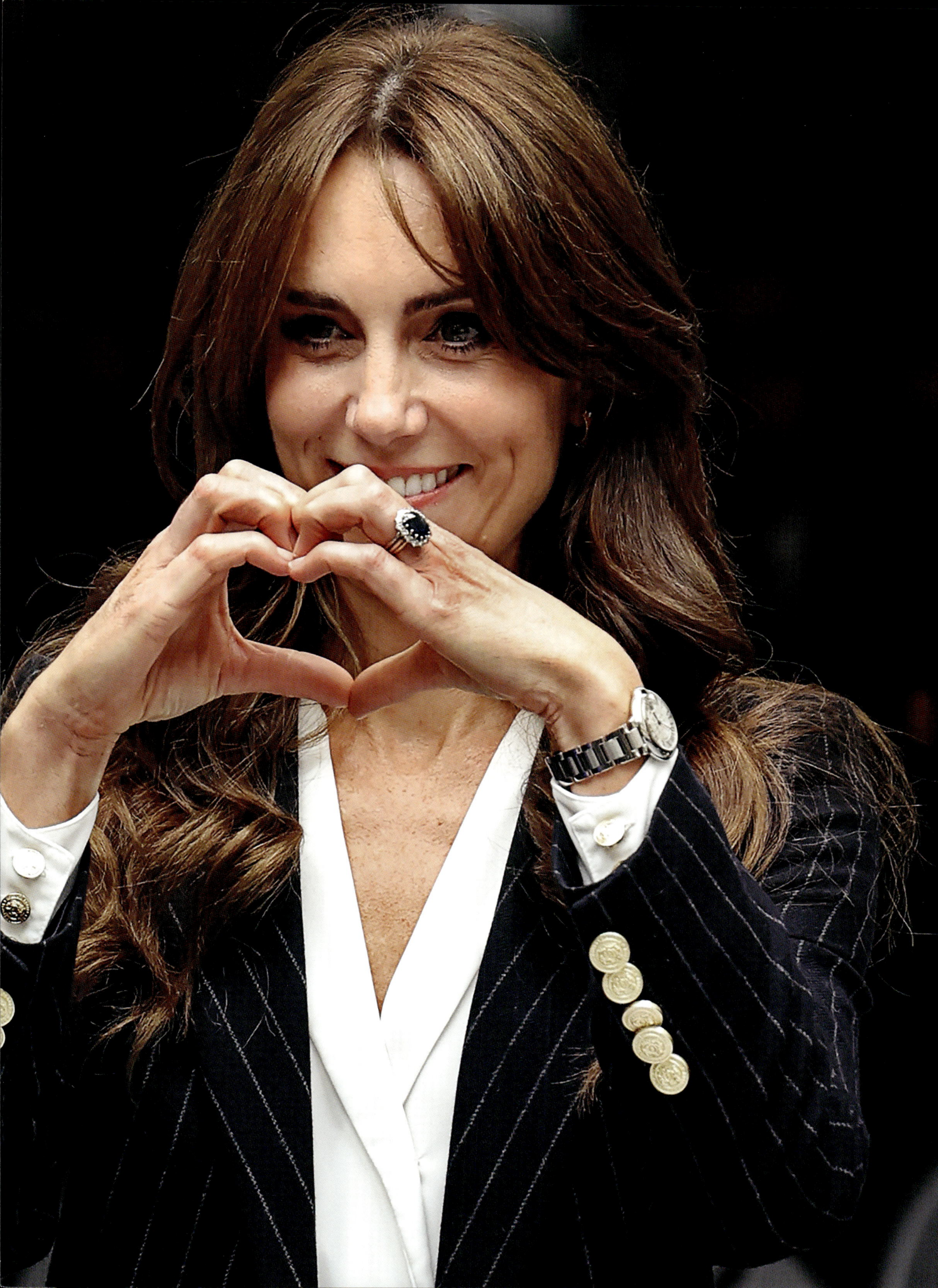

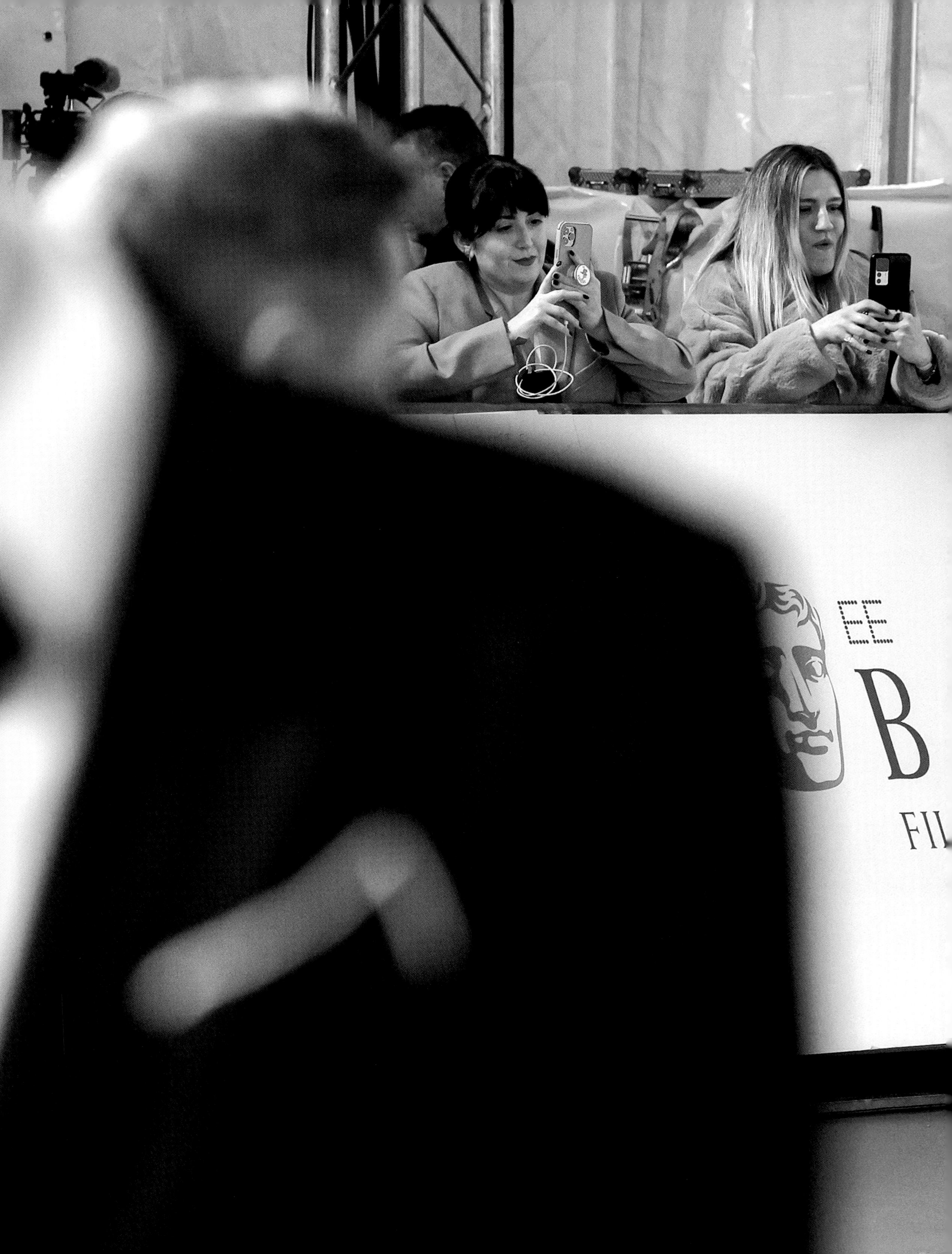
EE

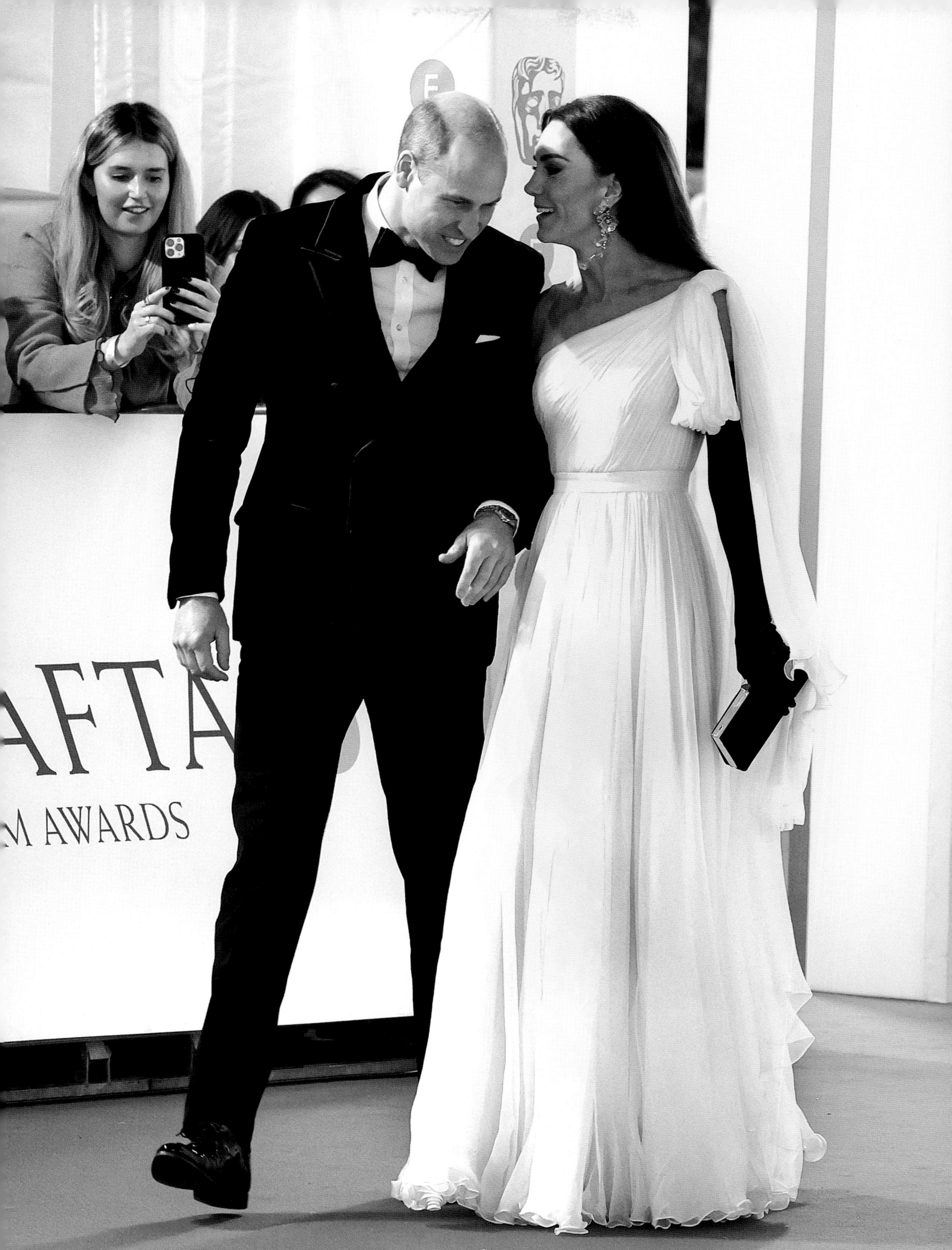
AFTA
M AWARDS

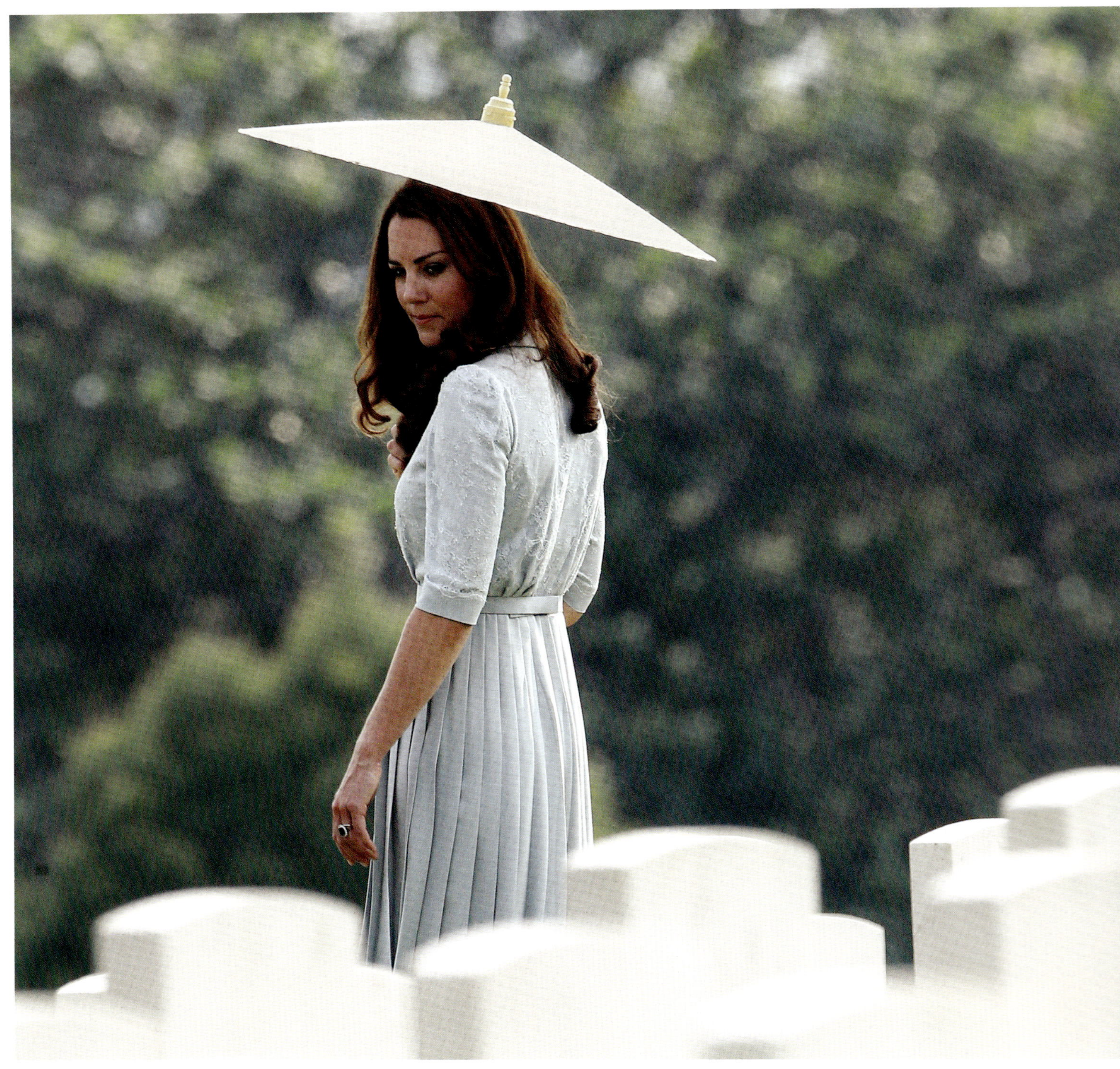

MOMENTS OF REFLECTION

In the heavy atmosphere of a late Singapore summer, Catherine glances back over her shoulder at the stark white graves in Kranji War Cemetery, 13 September 2012. This moving image always reminds me to be vigilant right up until the end of a royal engagement. It also offers a rare insight into the more somber side of royal life: paying respects on behalf of the nation to those who have made the ultimate sacrifice is an important part of the duty.

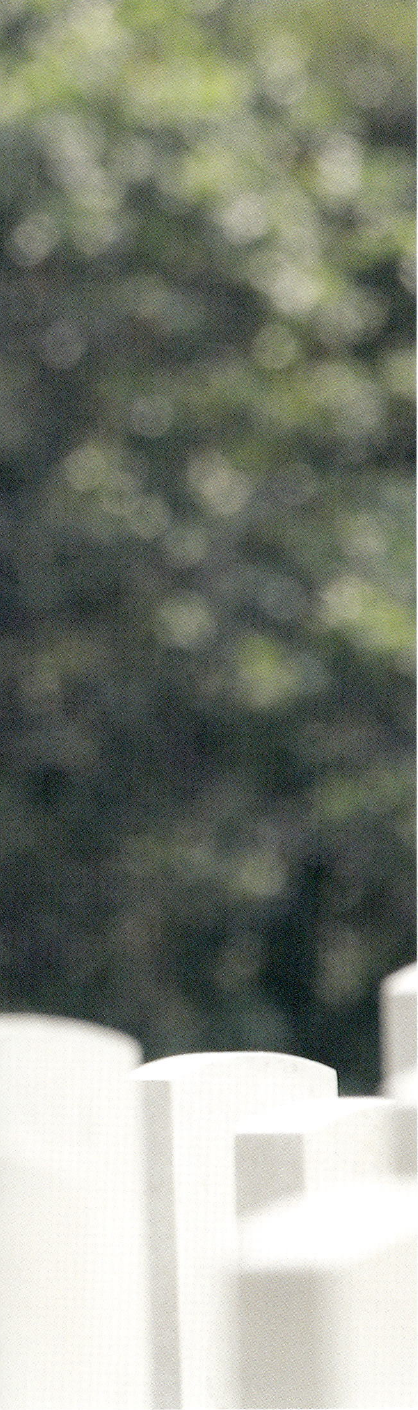

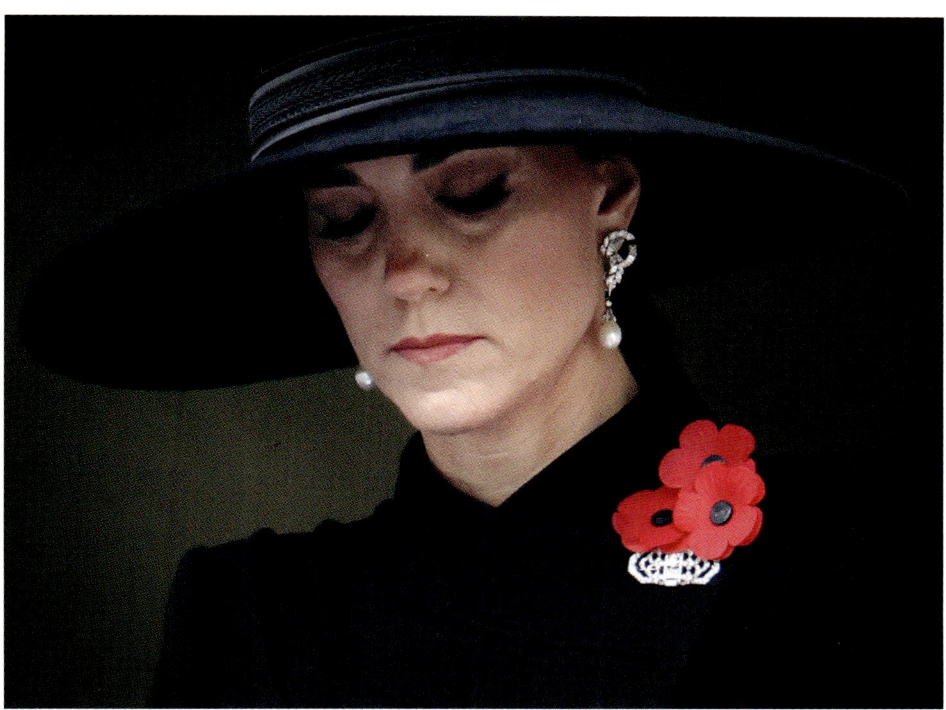

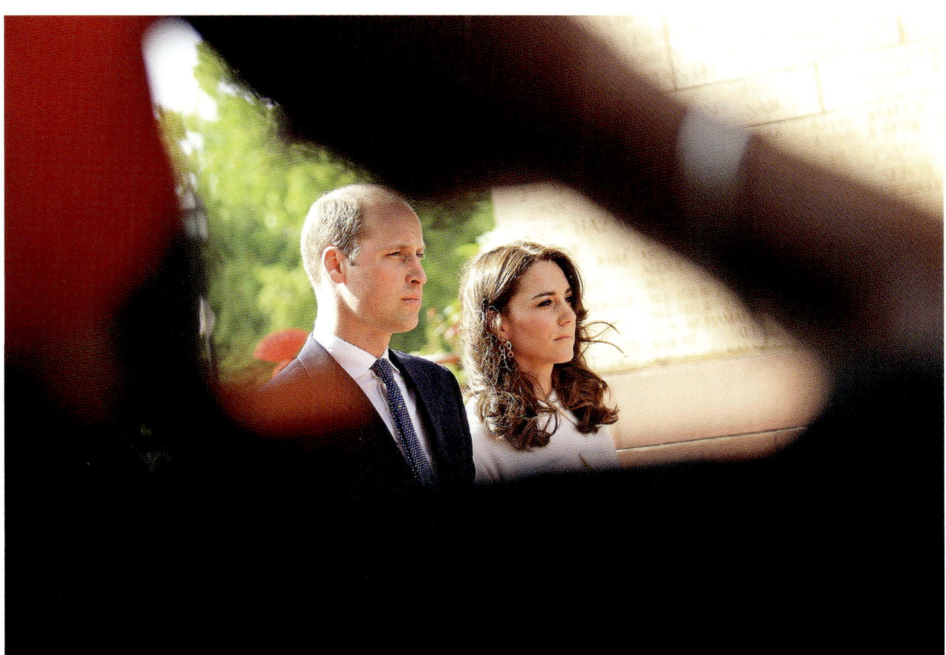

Top
Remembrance Sunday is a key date for the royal family as they lead the nation in remembering those servicemen and women who have fallen in the line of duty. At the Cenotaph in London, the Princess of Wales takes a moment to reflect on those who have given their lives, 13 November 2022.

Above
The Prince and Princess of Wales are saluted by an Indian soldier as they lay a wreath at the India Gate Memorial in New Delhi to honour those from Indian regiments who served in the First World War, 16 April 2022.

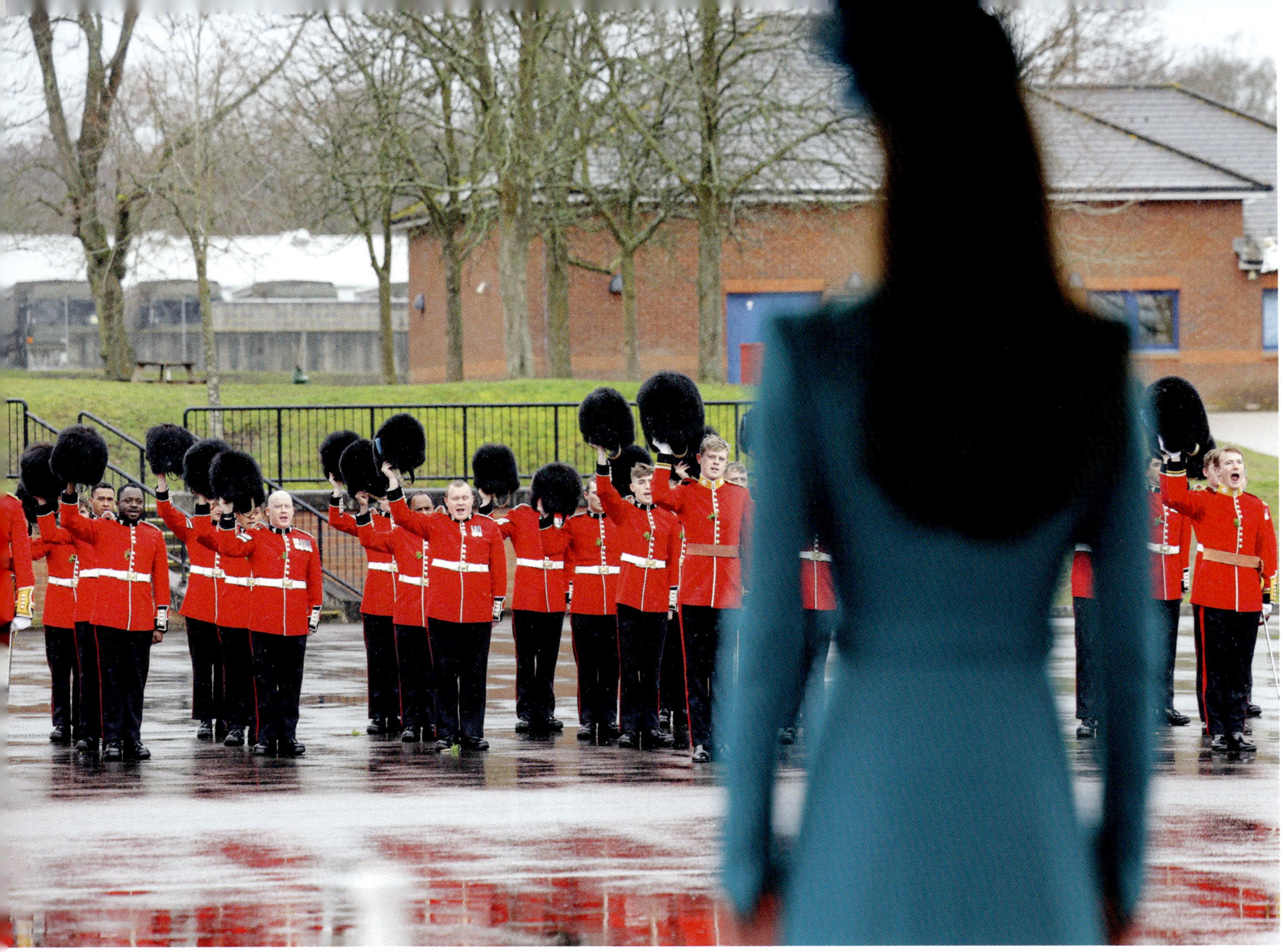

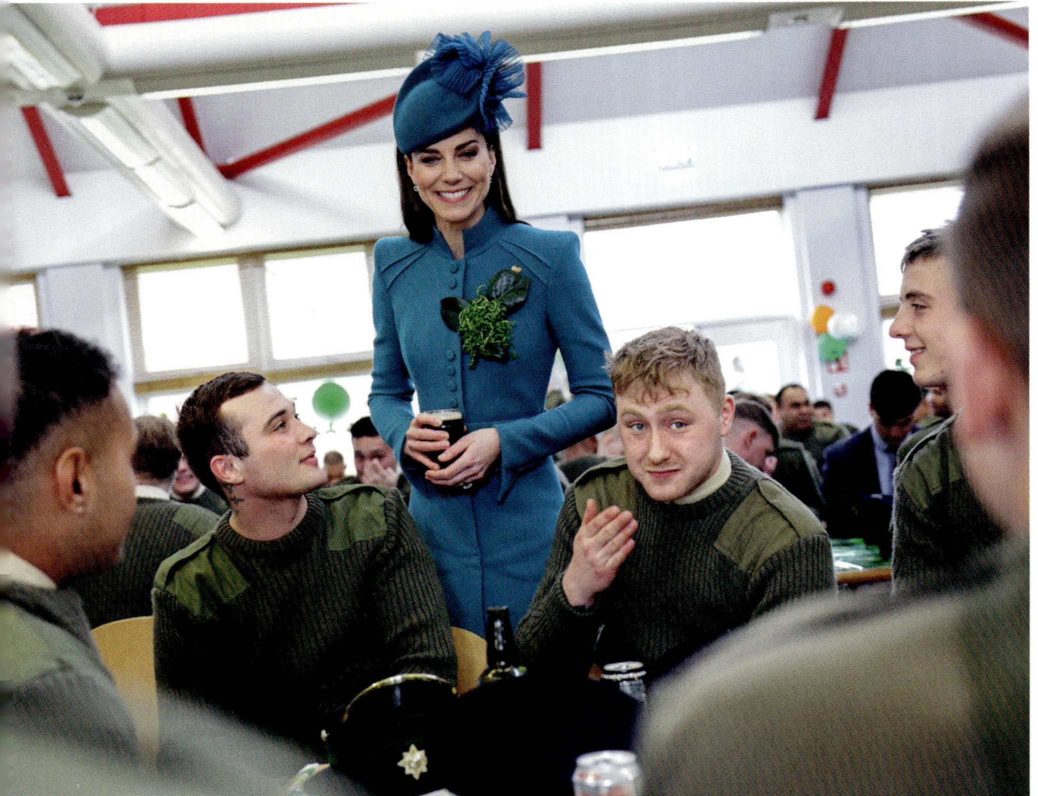

THE IRISH GUARDS

In 2022, the Princess of Wales was appointed Colonel of the Irish Guards. On Saint Patrick's Day in 2023 (this page and overleaf) she delivered a heartfelt speech to the regiment after presenting soldiers with the traditional shamrock, a custom established by Queen Victoria to honour the Guards' bravery. Catherine finished the visit by sharing a Guinness with thirsty soldiers in the officers' mess.

Opposite
The Princess of Wales gives sprigs of shamrock to the Irish Guards during the 2025 Saint Patrick's Day Parade.

Overleaf, right
Catherine pays a visit to the Sunken Garden in Kensington Palace grounds, which has been turned into the White Garden in memory of Princess Diana, 30 August 2017.

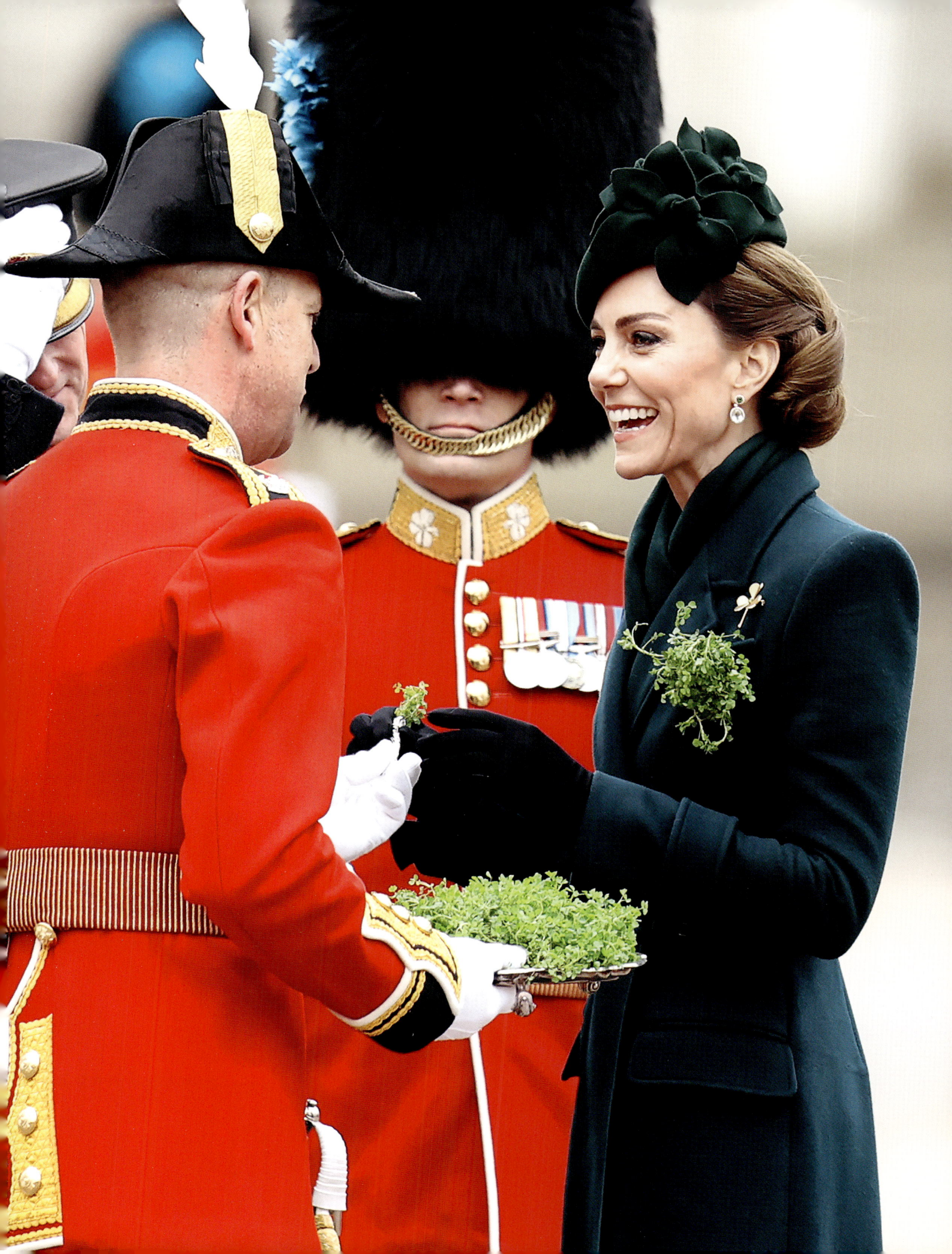

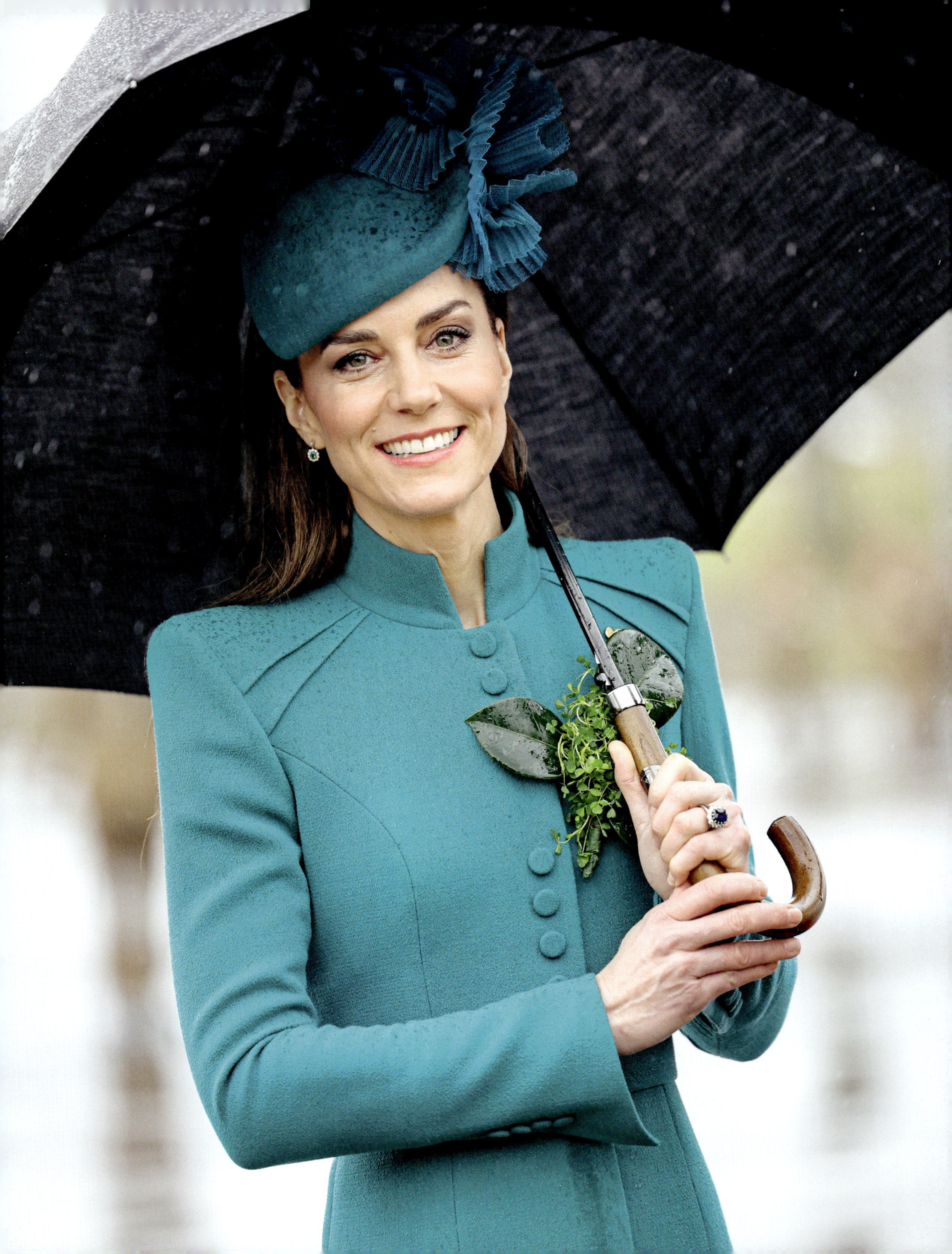

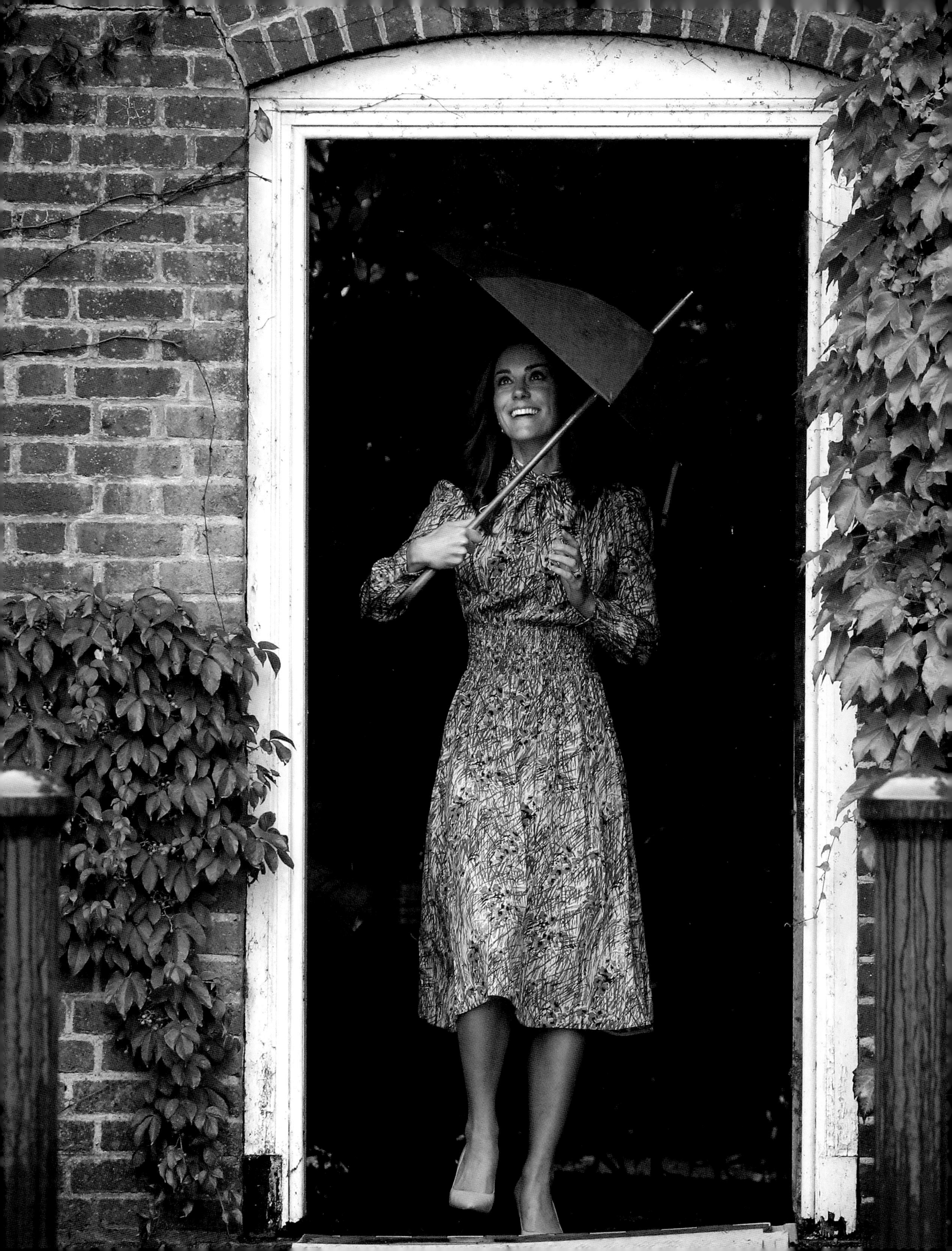

Opposite
Smashing out a six during a game of cricket with legendary Indian player Sachin Tendulkar at the Oval Maidan cricket ground in Mumbai on the first day of a visit to India in April 2016.

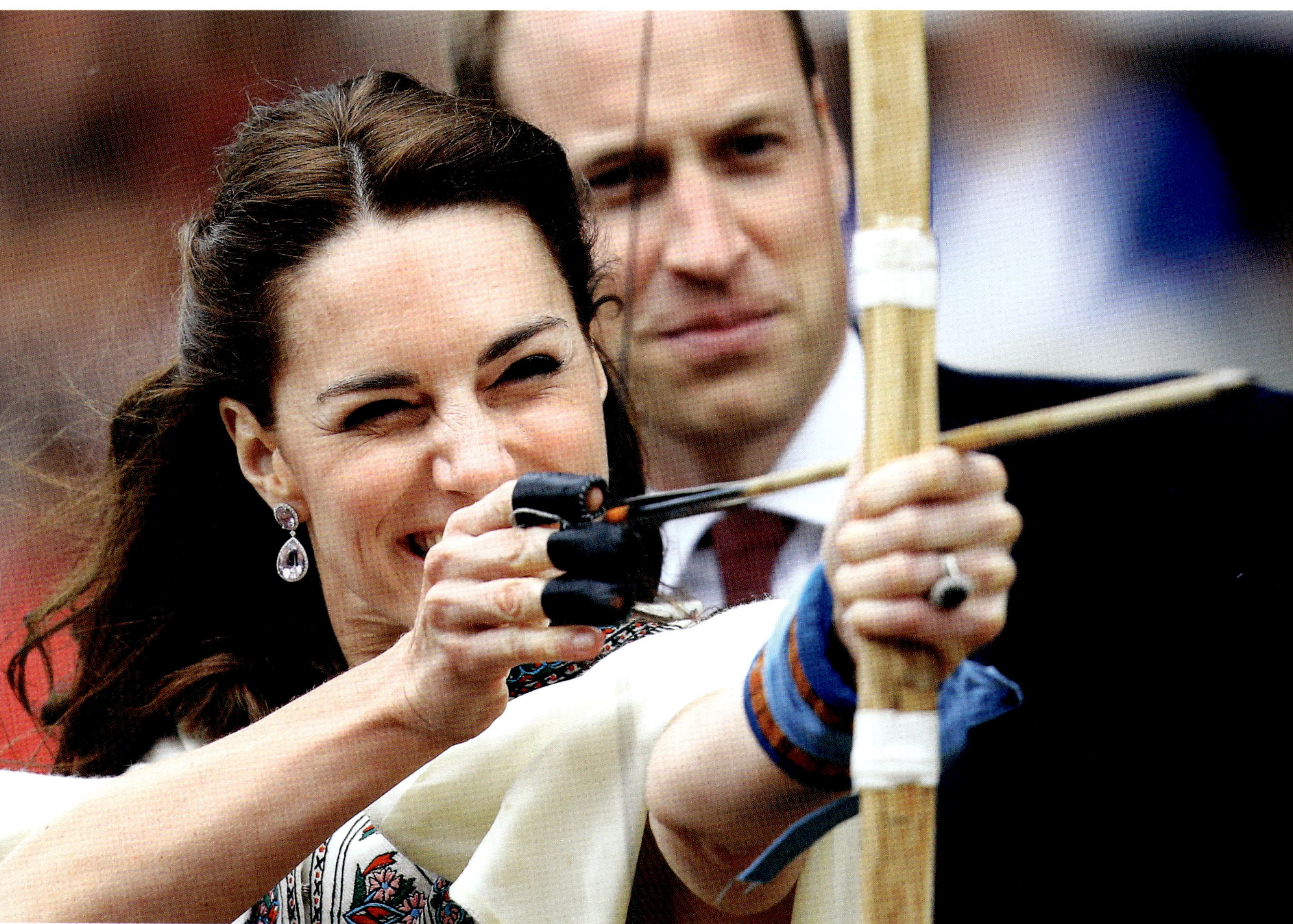

GETTING STUCK IN!

I have always loved photographing the Princess of Wales at sporting occasions and on royal tours. She fully engages with each event with unrivalled panache and energy, ensuring that the resulting images are always dynamic and memorable – a million miles from the formality of so many royal engagements.

Arriving in the dramatic landscape of the Himalayan mountain kingdom of Bhutan in April 2016, the Prince and Princess were invited to take part in the national sport of archery. With arrows whistling overhead, I was slightly nervous of being in the firing line when photographing a very focused and competitive Princess taking aim.

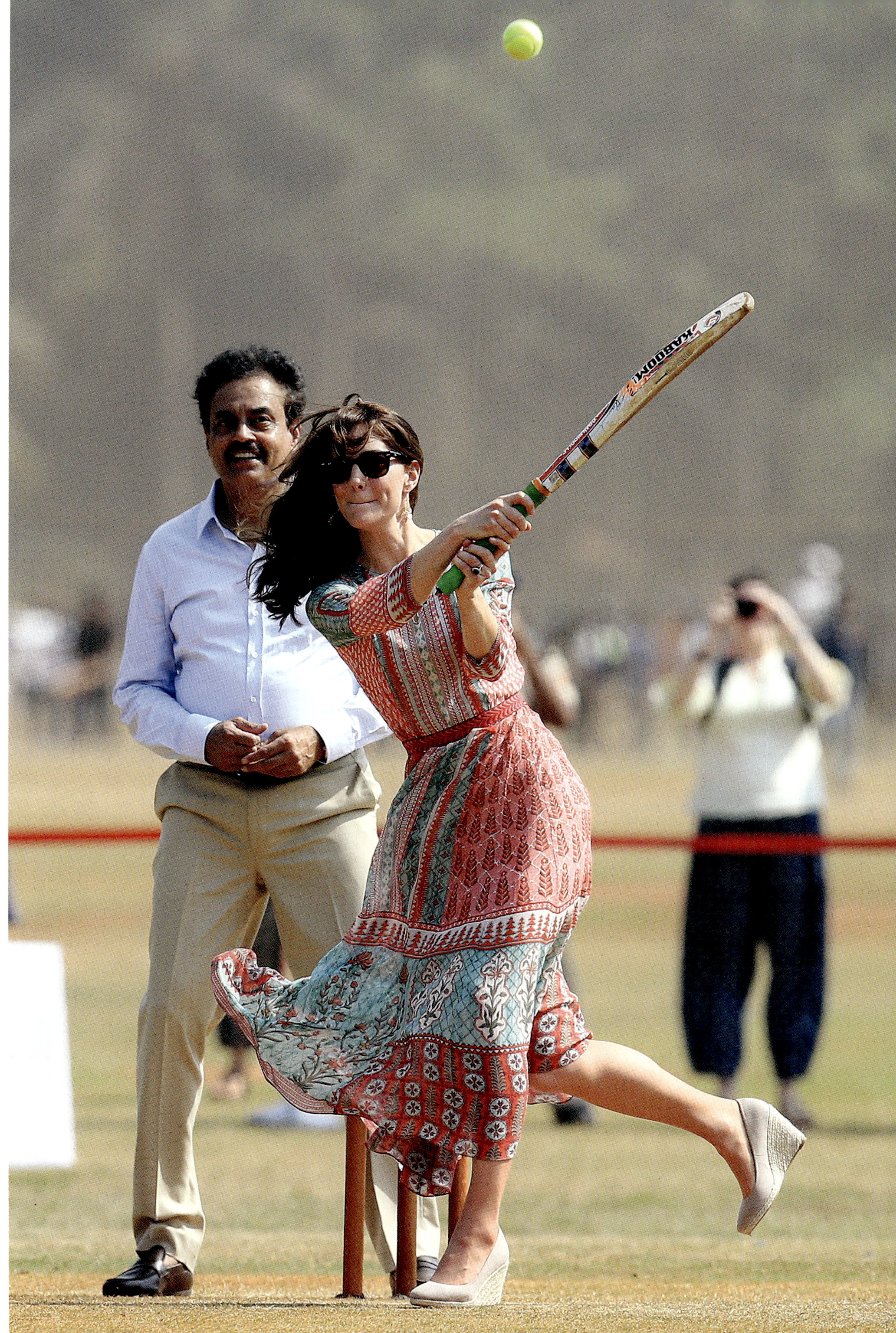
KABOOM!

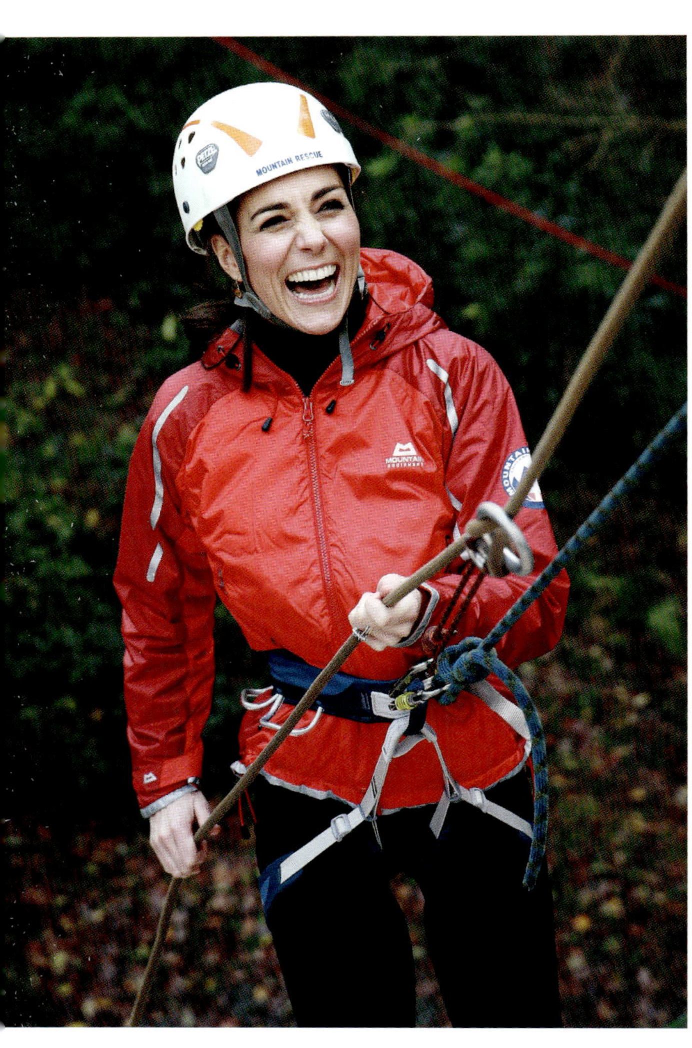

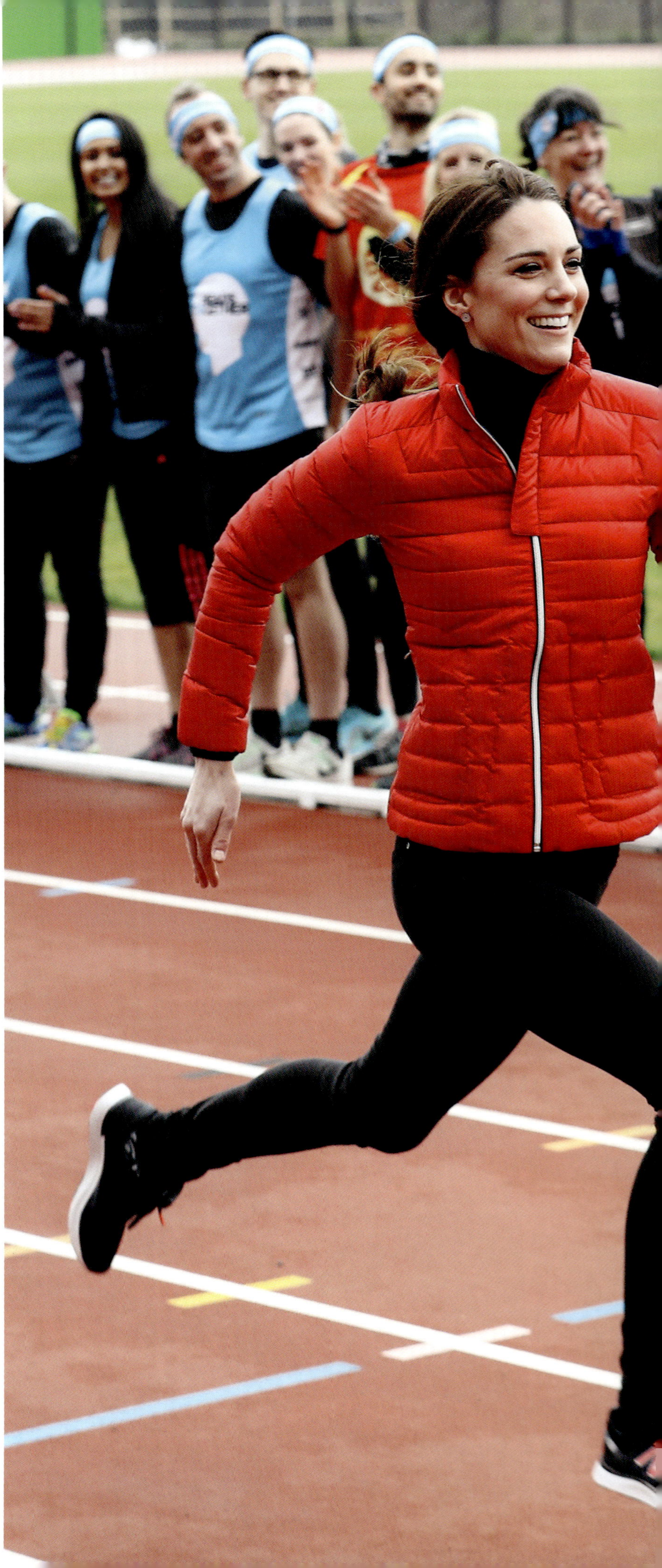

Clockwise from above
Showing her adventurous side, the Princess tries her hand at abseiling during a visit to Towers Residential Outdoor Education Centre in November 2015 in Capel Curig, Wales. Competing against William and Harry during the mental-health initiative Heads Together's London Marathon training day at Queen Elizabeth Olympic Park in February 2017. Travelling on the Shotover Jet on the Shotover River during a visit to Queenstown, the adventure capital of New Zealand, in April 2014 (their first official overseas trip with Prince George). Showcasing her hockey prowess with the GB team at the Riverside Arena during a training session ahead of the London 2012 Olympic Games.

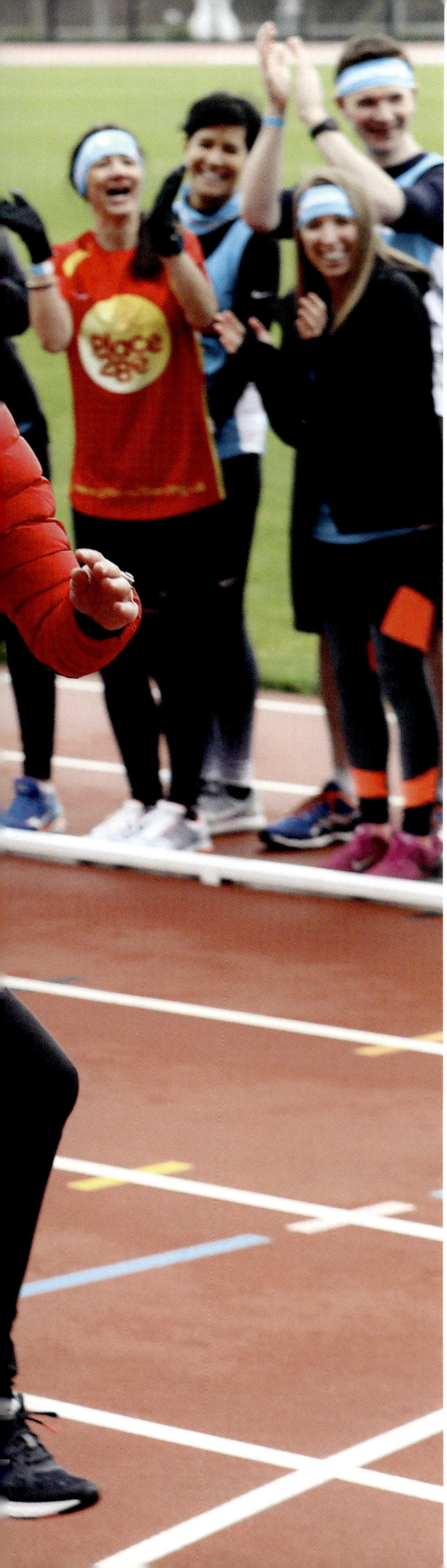

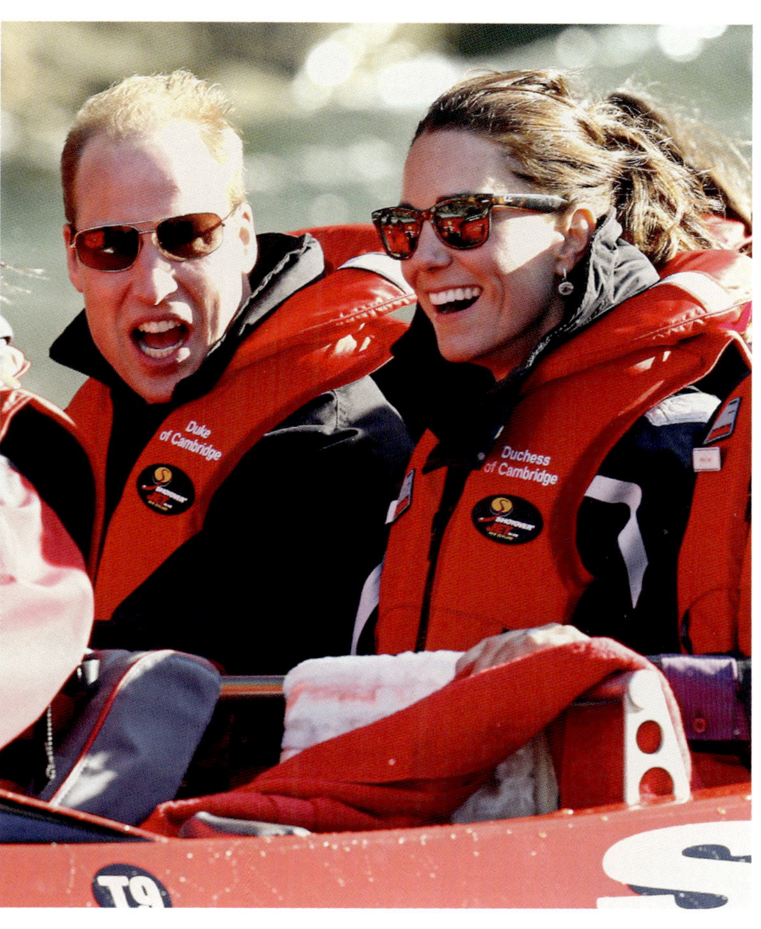
Duke
of Cambridge
Duchess
of Cambridge
T9

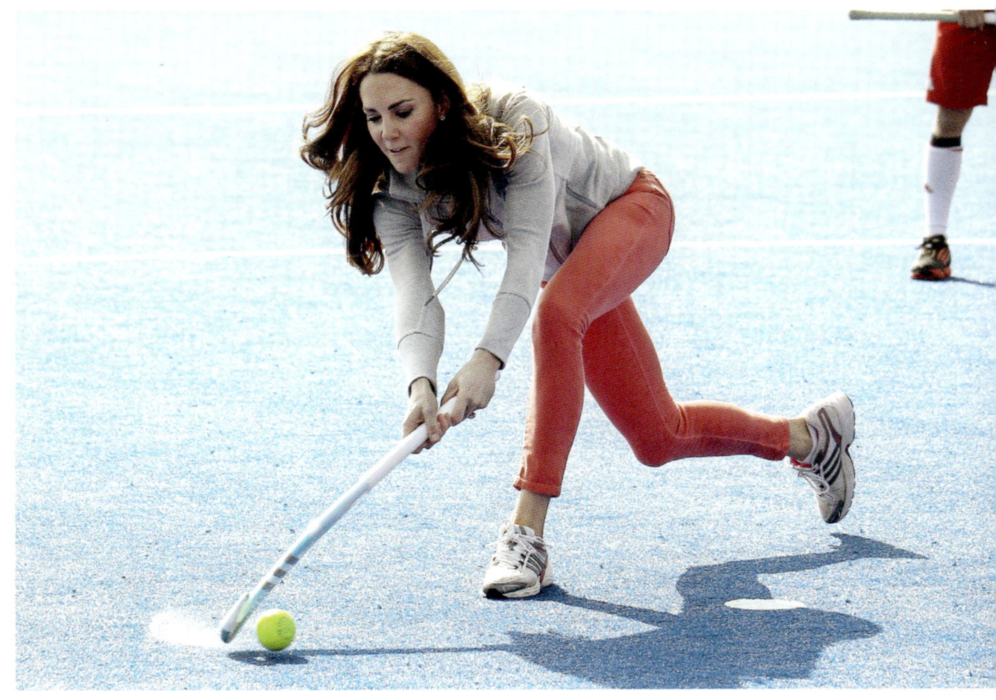

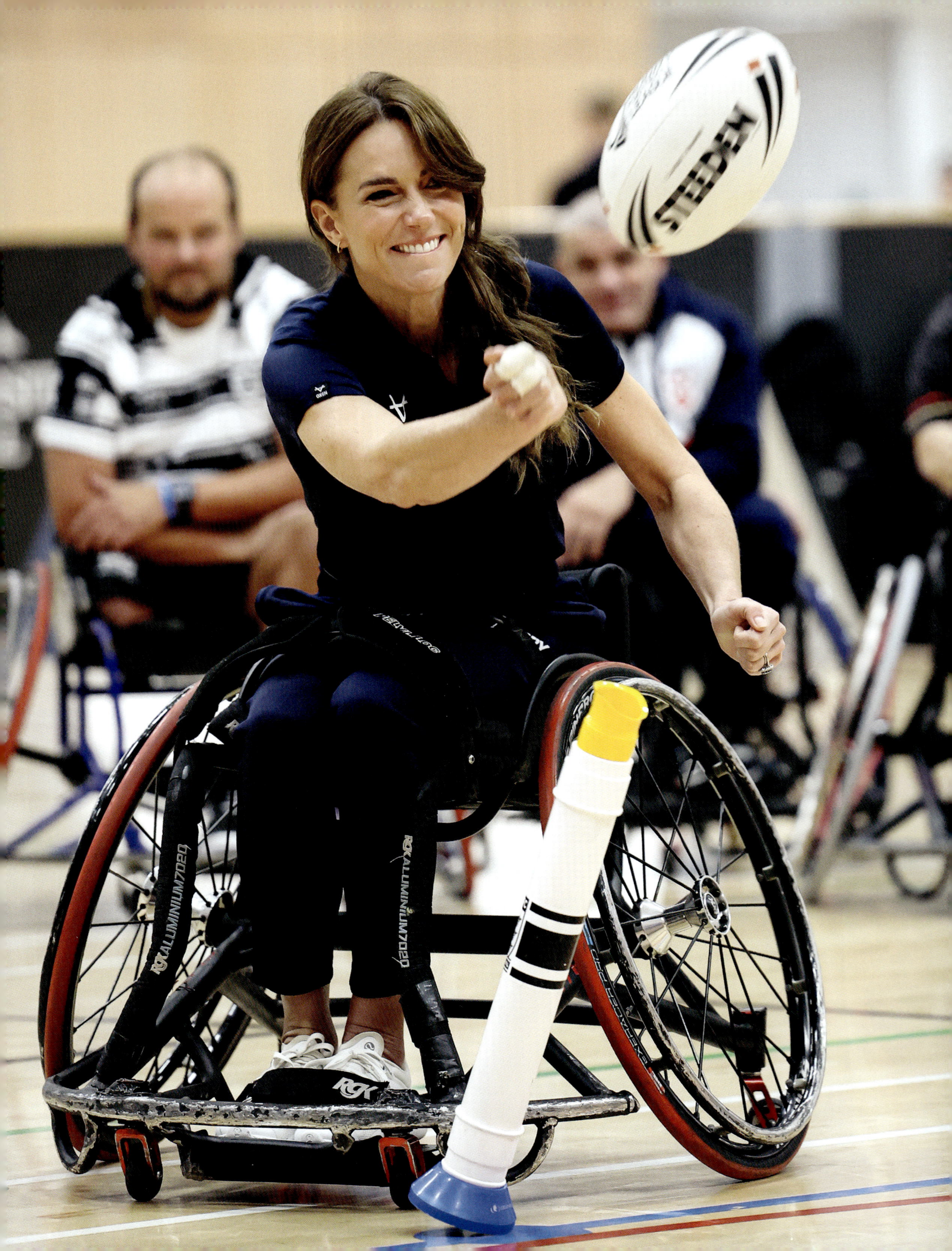
STEEDEN
RGK ALUMINIUM7020
RGK ALUMINIUM7020
RGK

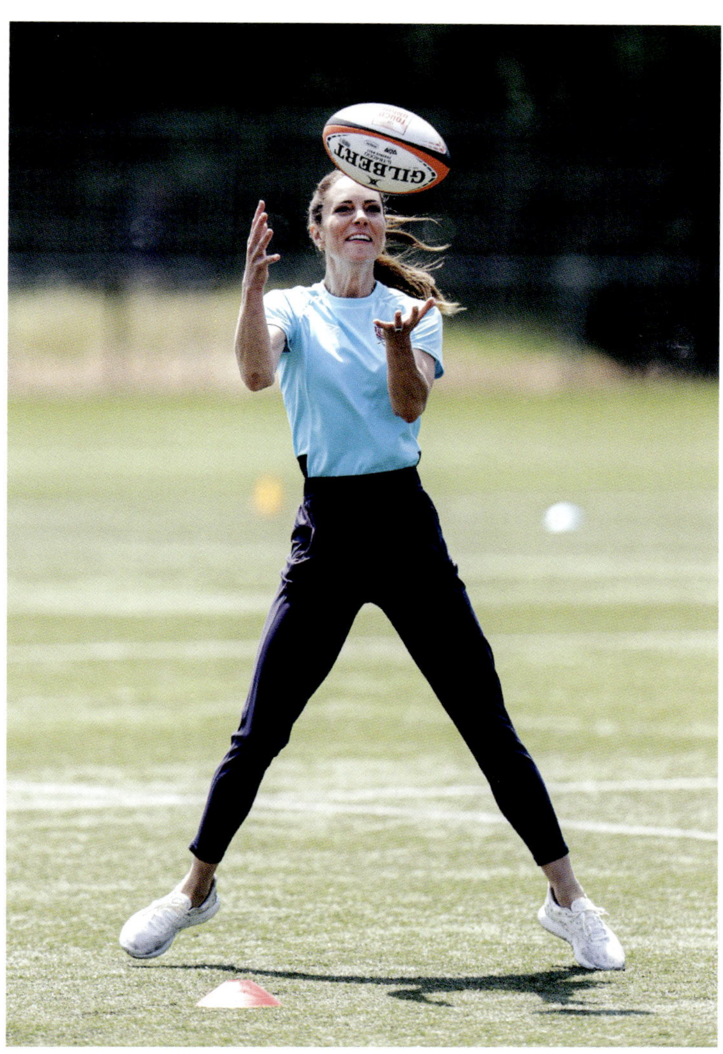

Opposite
The Princess of Wales takes part in a wheelchair rugby training session, facilitated by members of the world-cup-winning England Wheelchair Rugby League Squad, during an inclusivity day at Allam Sports Centre in Hull, 5 October 2023.

Left
Demonstrating her enjoyment of sport, Catherine takes part in drills during her visit to Maidenhead Rugby Club, 7 June 2023. She is visiting the club to discuss the Shaping Us campaign and the role the community plays in supporting children.

Below
This was a memorable and slightly unusual royal engagement as the Princess of Wales, alongside Princess Anne and the Prince of Wales, took part in *The Good, the Bad and the Rugby* podcast hosted by Mike Tindall, James Haskell, and former broadcaster Alex Payne in the Green Drawing Room at Windsor Castle, 6 September 2023. A jovial atmosphere was in place from the start as the Prince and Princess shared tales of how sport had benefited members of their young family.

Overleaf
Huge crowds gather to catch a glimpse of Catherine as she takes part in a walkabout on the South Bank in Brisbane, 19 April 2014.

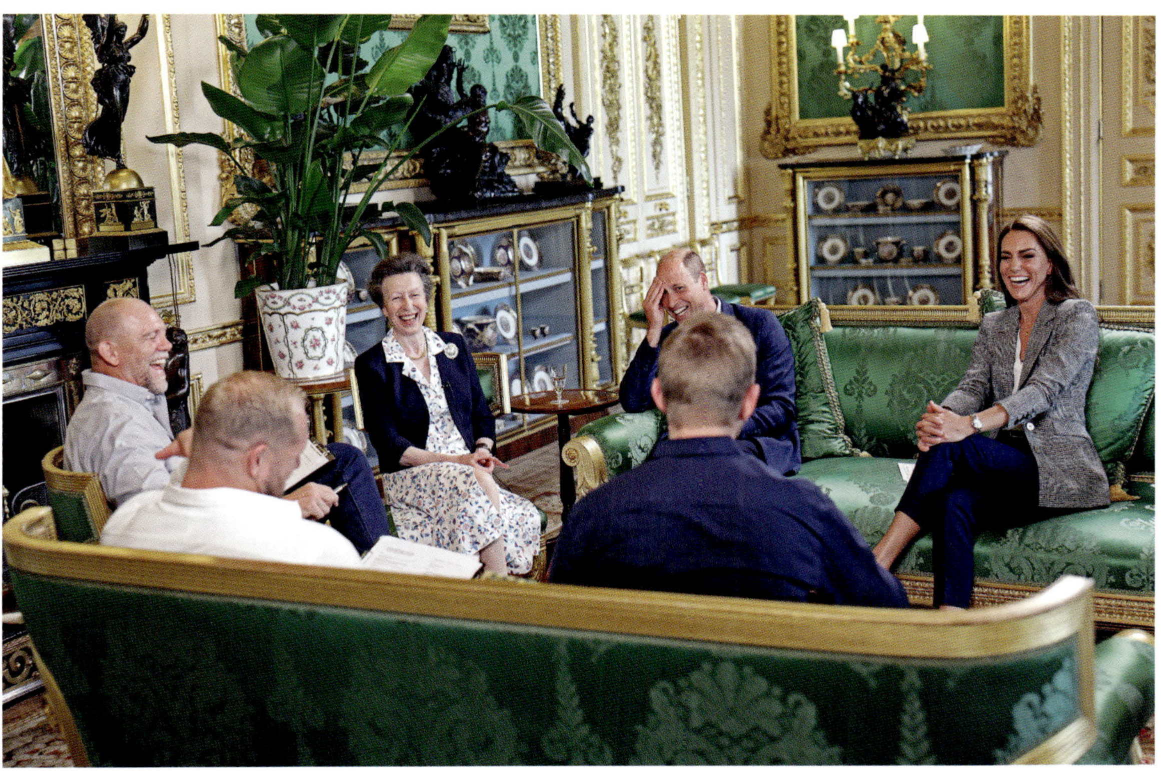

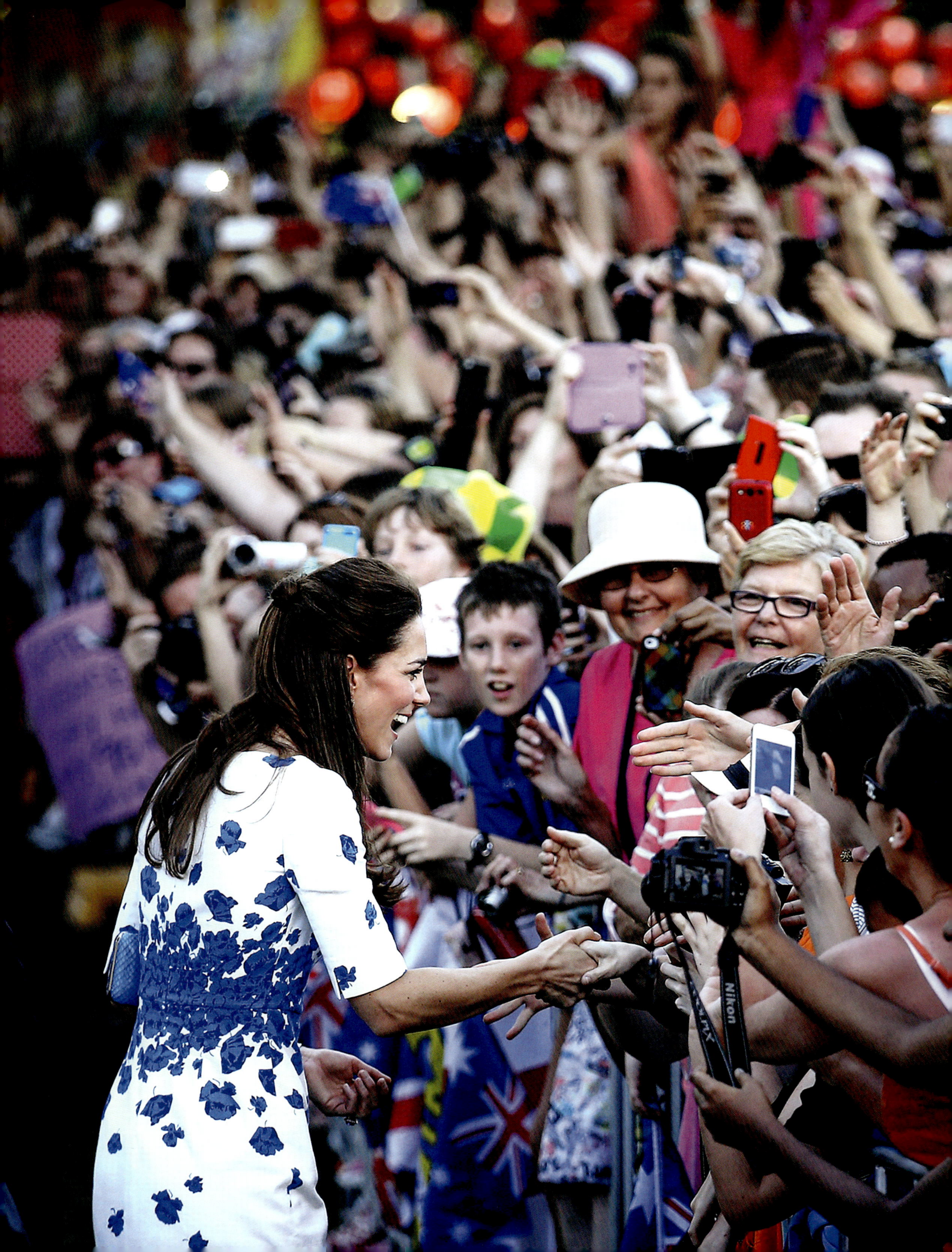
Nikon

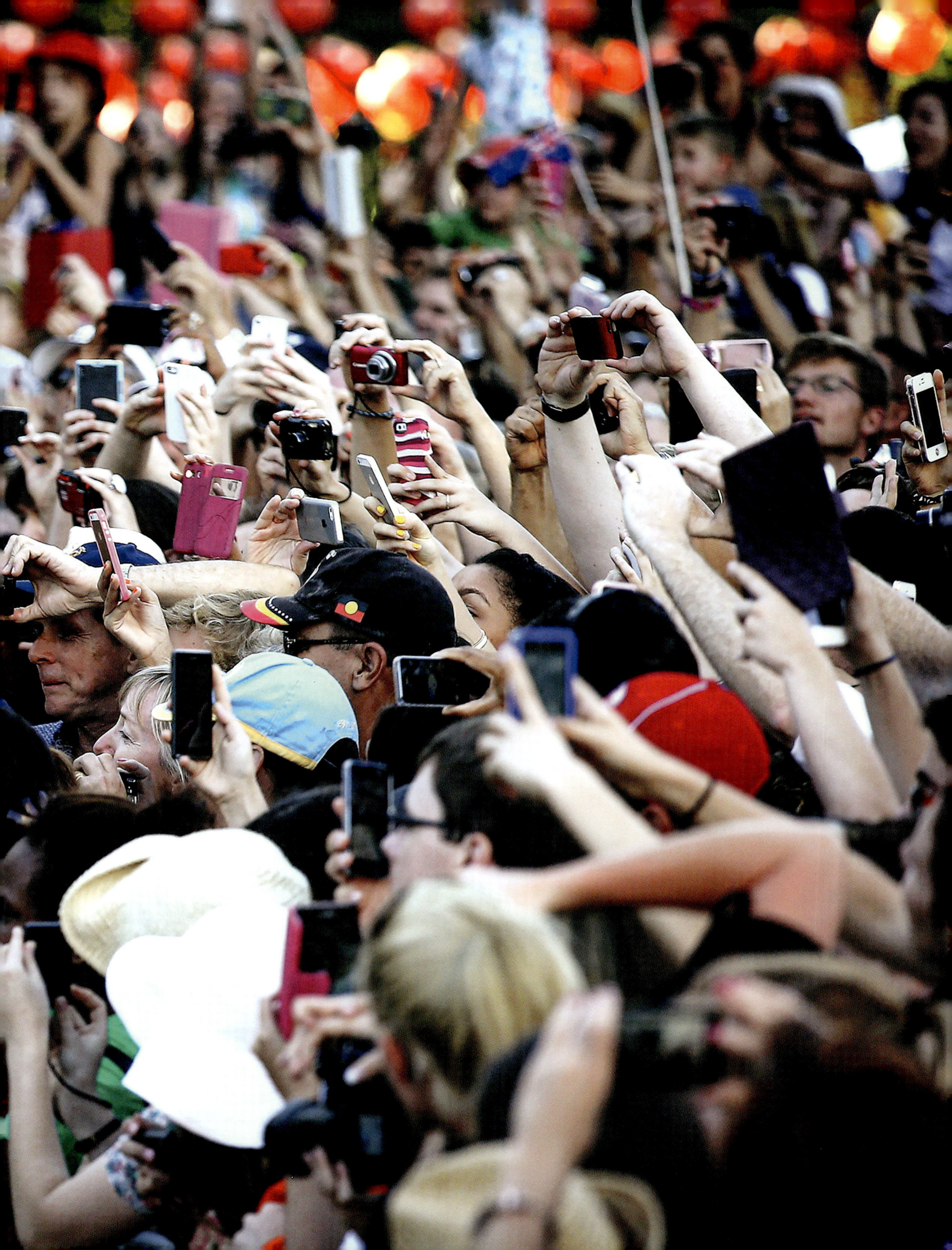

It has been fascinating to watch the Princess of Wales grow in confidence over the years, from those first moments in front of the press at her engagement in 2010 to the competent public speaker and stateswoman she is today. Both photographs here encapsulate this change: addressing the 1st Battalion Irish Guards for the first time as Colonel of the Guards in 2023 and ready to take the stage at the Earthshot Prize Awards in 2021.

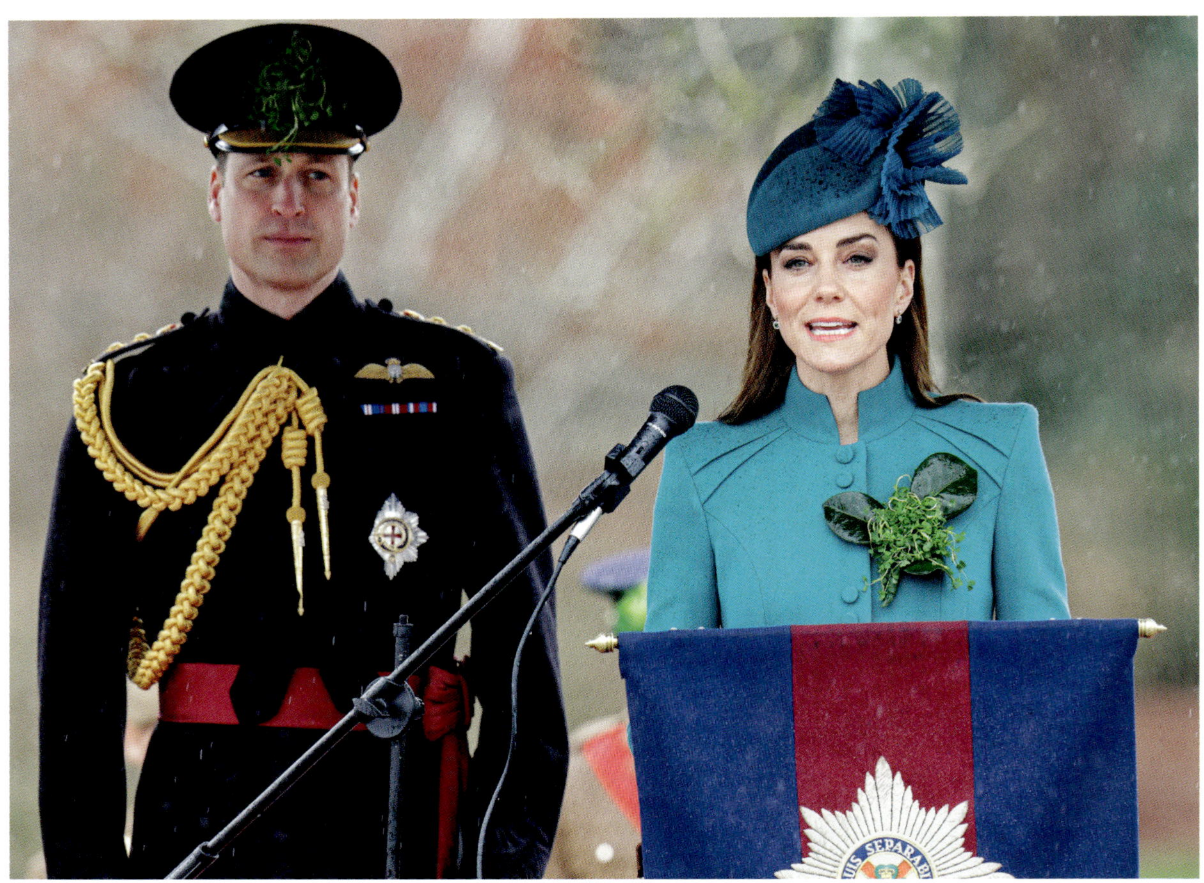

SARTORIAL INFLUENCE

Princess Catherine quickly emerged as a global fashion icon after stepping onto the public stage. Her effortless blend of high-street brands with bespoke pieces has cemented her image as being both relatable and regal. Not afraid to repeat favourite outfits at different engagements, the Princess of Wales also sends out a strong message about the importance of sustainability in fashion. Her style is elegant yet accessible, and many garments sell out soon after Catherine is seen wearing them. In June 2016, the Princess appeared on the front cover of British *Vogue* for the magazine's centenary.

Overleaf, left
The Princess of Wales encounters a bit of a breeze as she leaves the Commonwealth Day Service at Westminster Abbey, 10 March 2025.

Overleaf, right
Emerging from Westminster Abbey, after the Commonwealth Day Service, in a blue pillbox hat by milliner Sean Barrett, 14 March 2022.

Pages 184–185, from left to right
The Princess wears a shimmering gown by British brand the Vampire's Wife to a reception in celebration of Queen Elizabeth II's Platinum Jubilee in Cahal Pech, Belize, 21 March 2022. Arriving at the EE BAFTA Film Awards 2023 at the Royal Festival Hall, London. Wearing a dazzling gold Jenny Packham dress for the world premiere of the James Bond film *No Time to Die* at the Royal Albert Hall in September 2021.

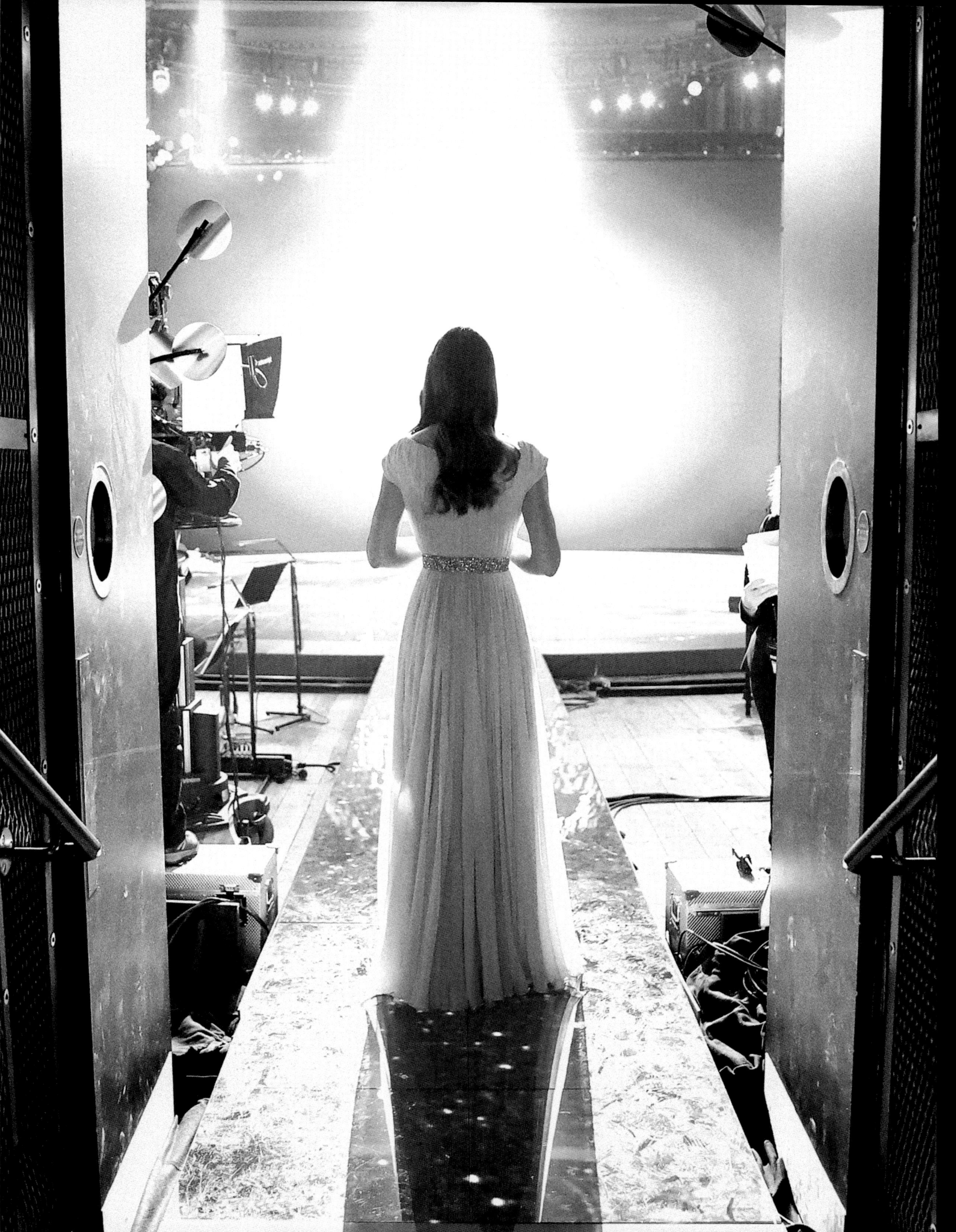

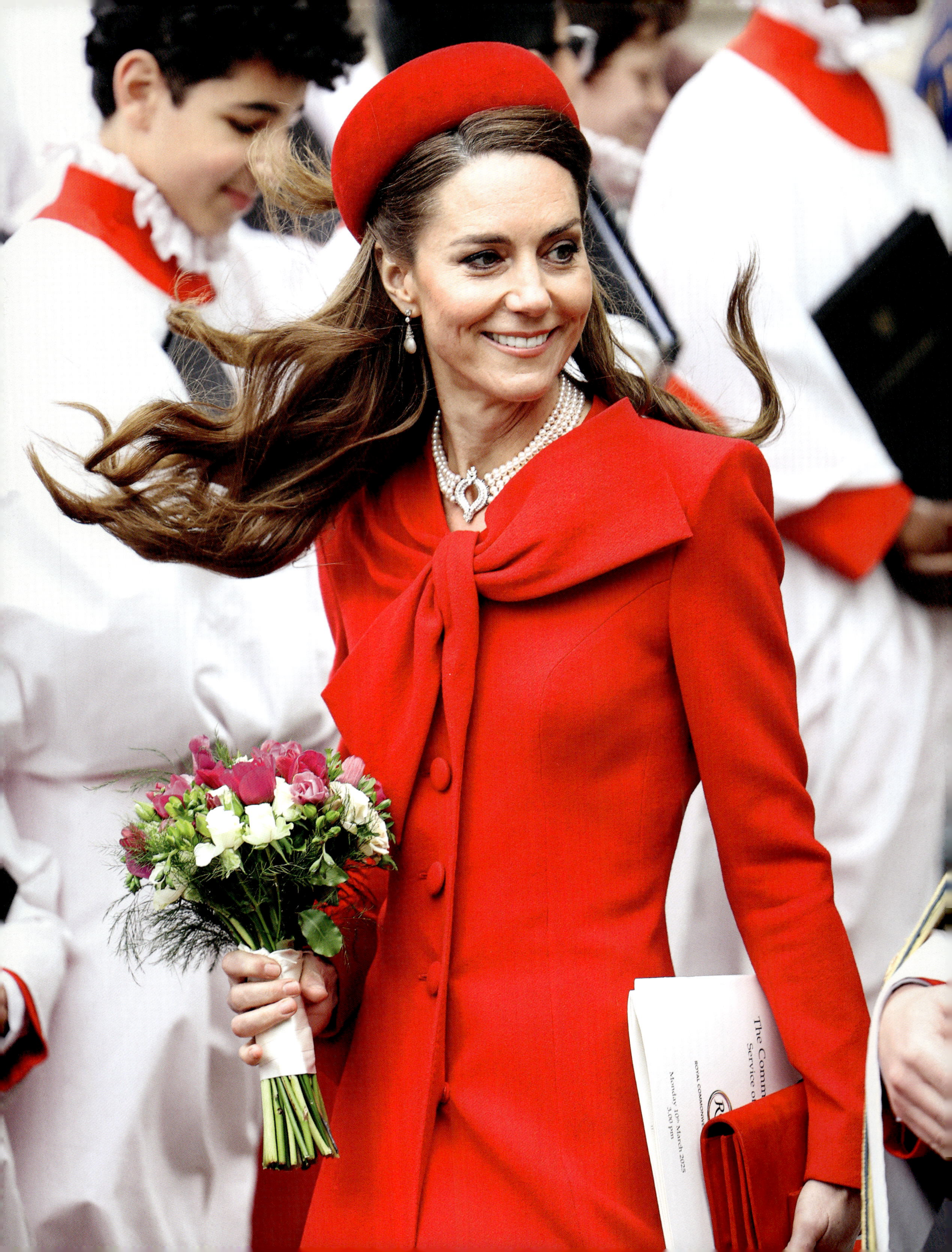
Monday 10th March 2025
3.00 pm

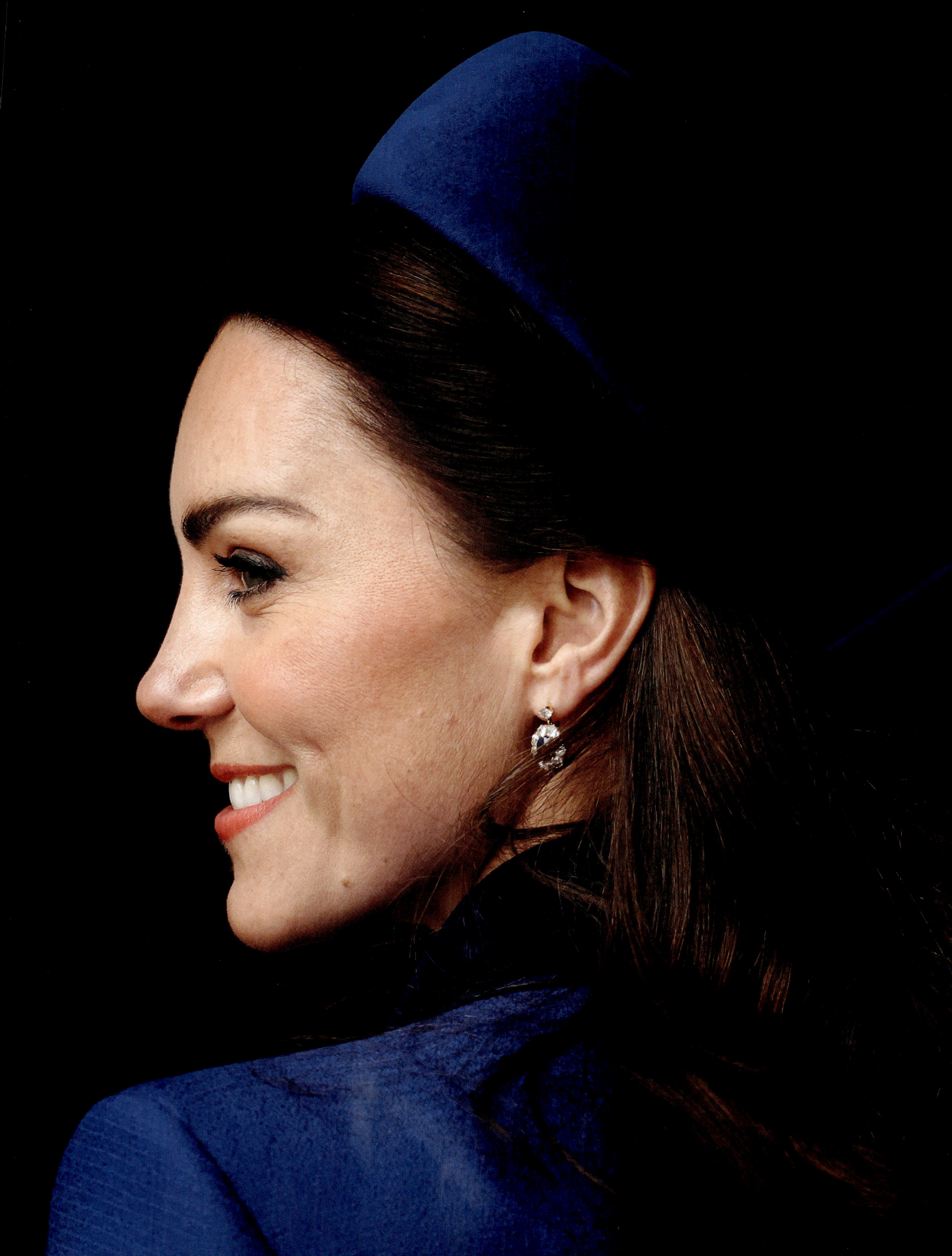

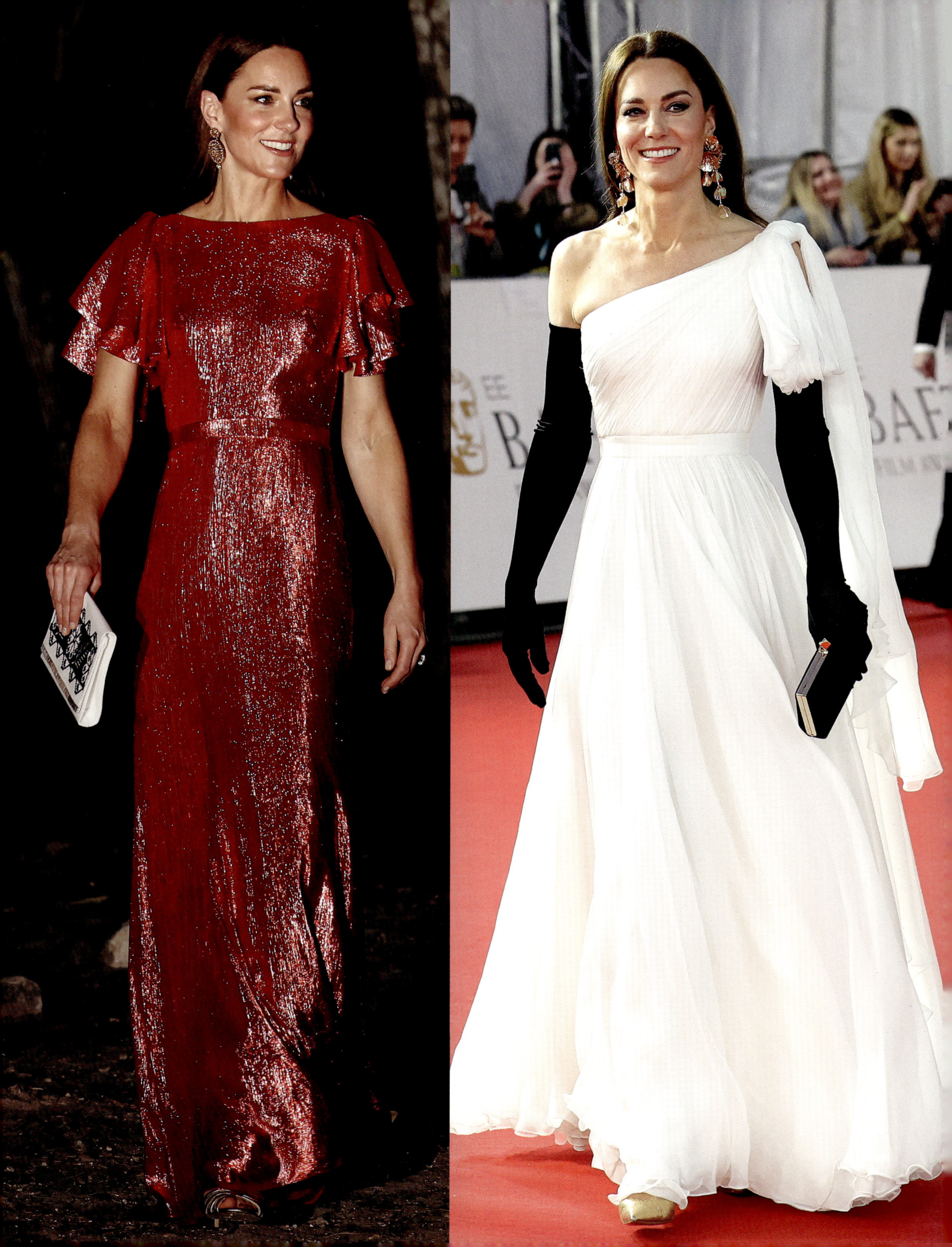

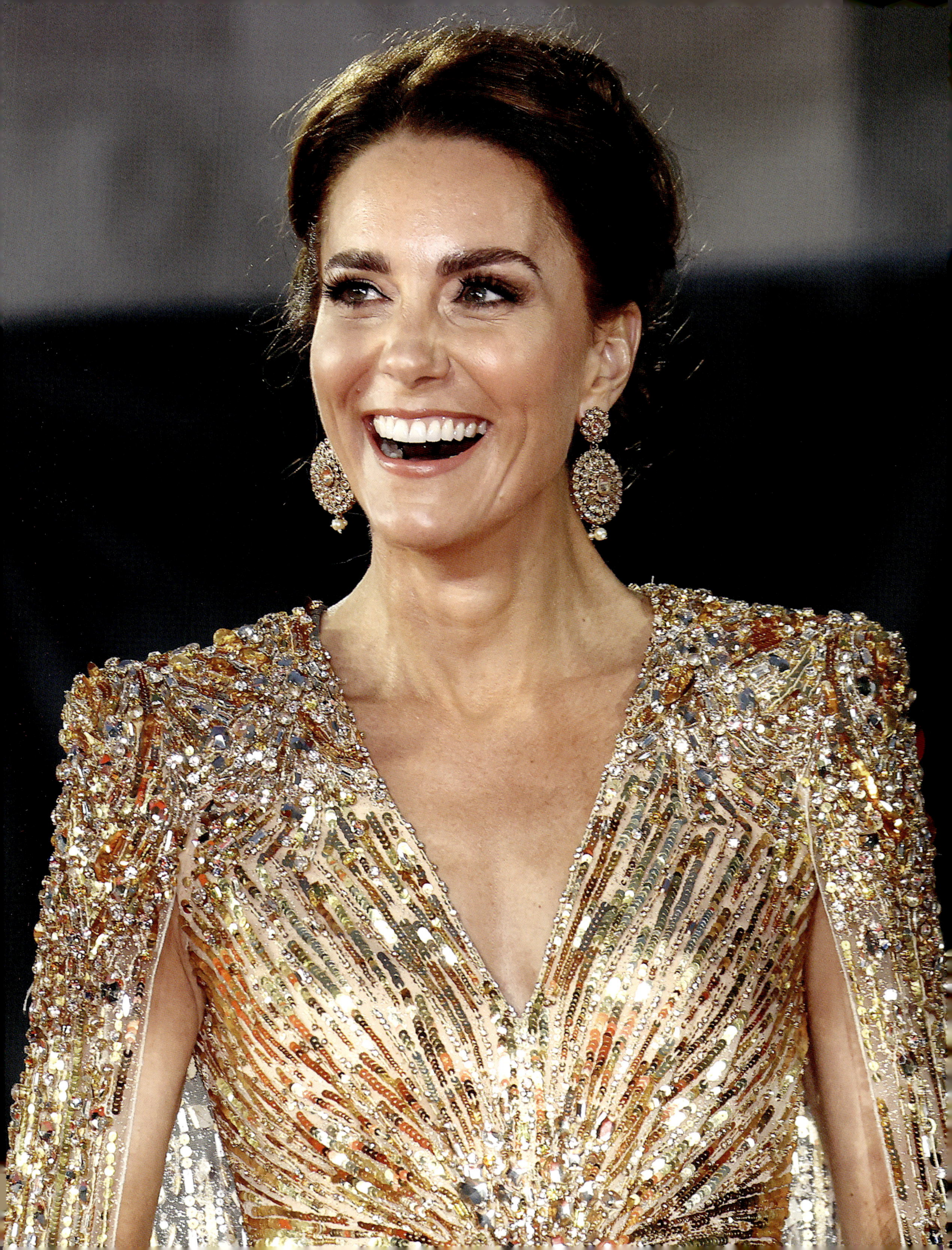

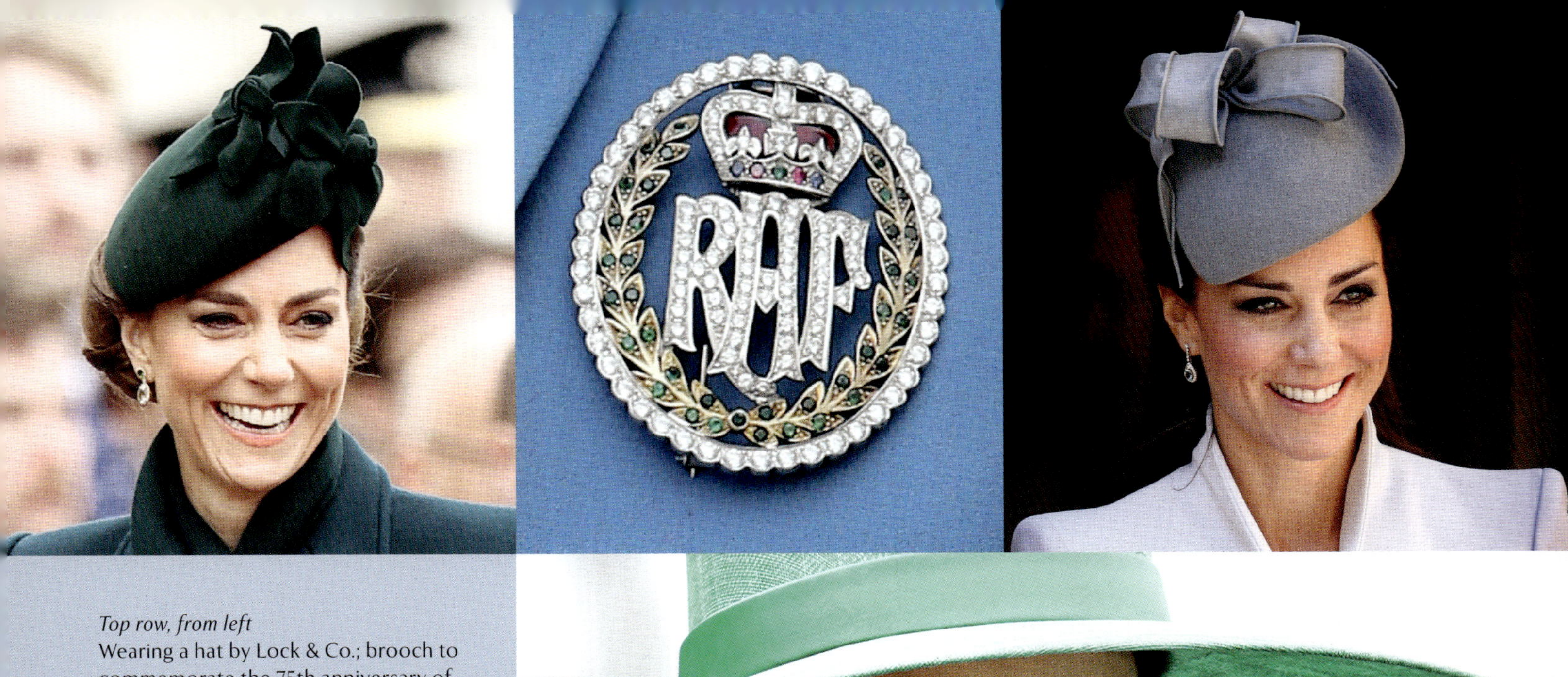

Top row, from left
Wearing a hat by Lock & Co.; brooch to commemorate the 75th anniversary of the RAF Air Cadets; coat by Alexander McQueen and a bespoke Jane Taylor hat; a Philip Treacy wide-brimmed hat; an Alessandra Rich polka-dot dress, with a matching Sally-Ann Provan hat.

Middle row, from left
An Andrew Gn coat dress and a Cartier shamrock brooch; brooch lent to the Princess by Queen Elizabeth II for her 2011 tour of Canada; a Catherine Walker coat and a matching Jane Taylor hat.

Bottom row, from left
A navy-blue embroidered suit by Erdem; staying warm in a Catherine Walker hat; a blush-pink Dior Bar jacket and a Jess Collett hat; a red clutch on an official visit to Poland; an Emilia Wickstead coatdress, paired with a Sean Barrett pillbox hat; an Alexander McQueen dress and a Jane Taylor fascinator.

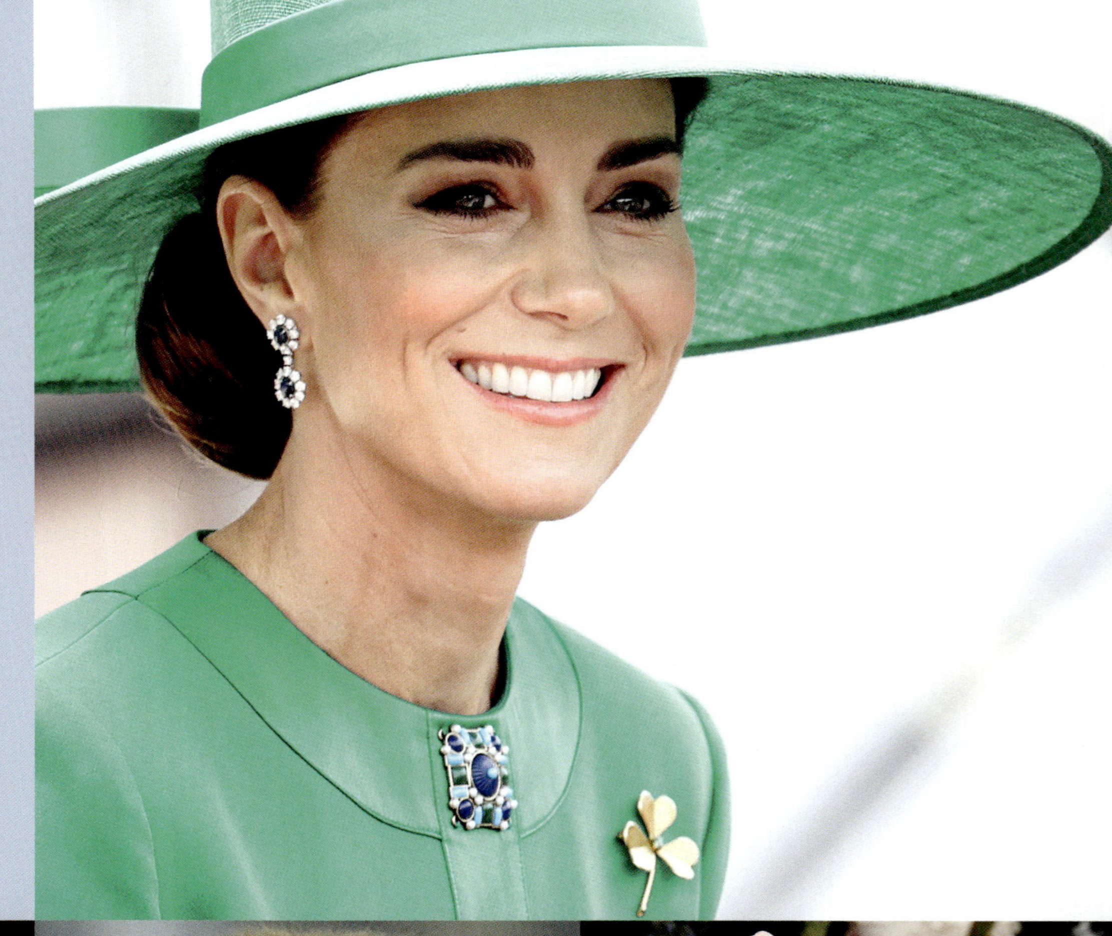

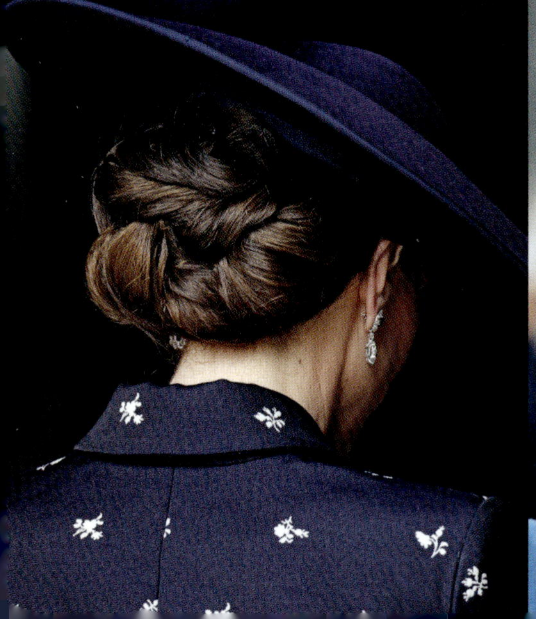

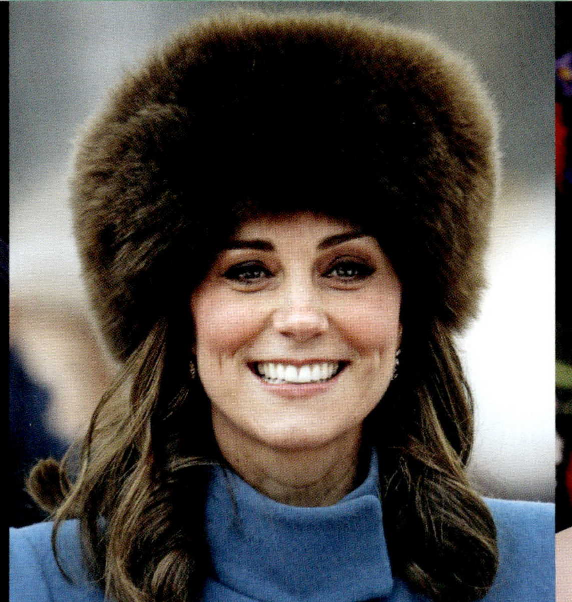

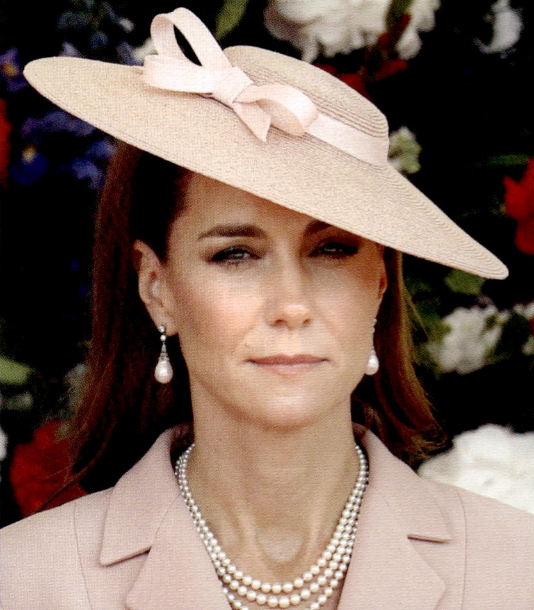

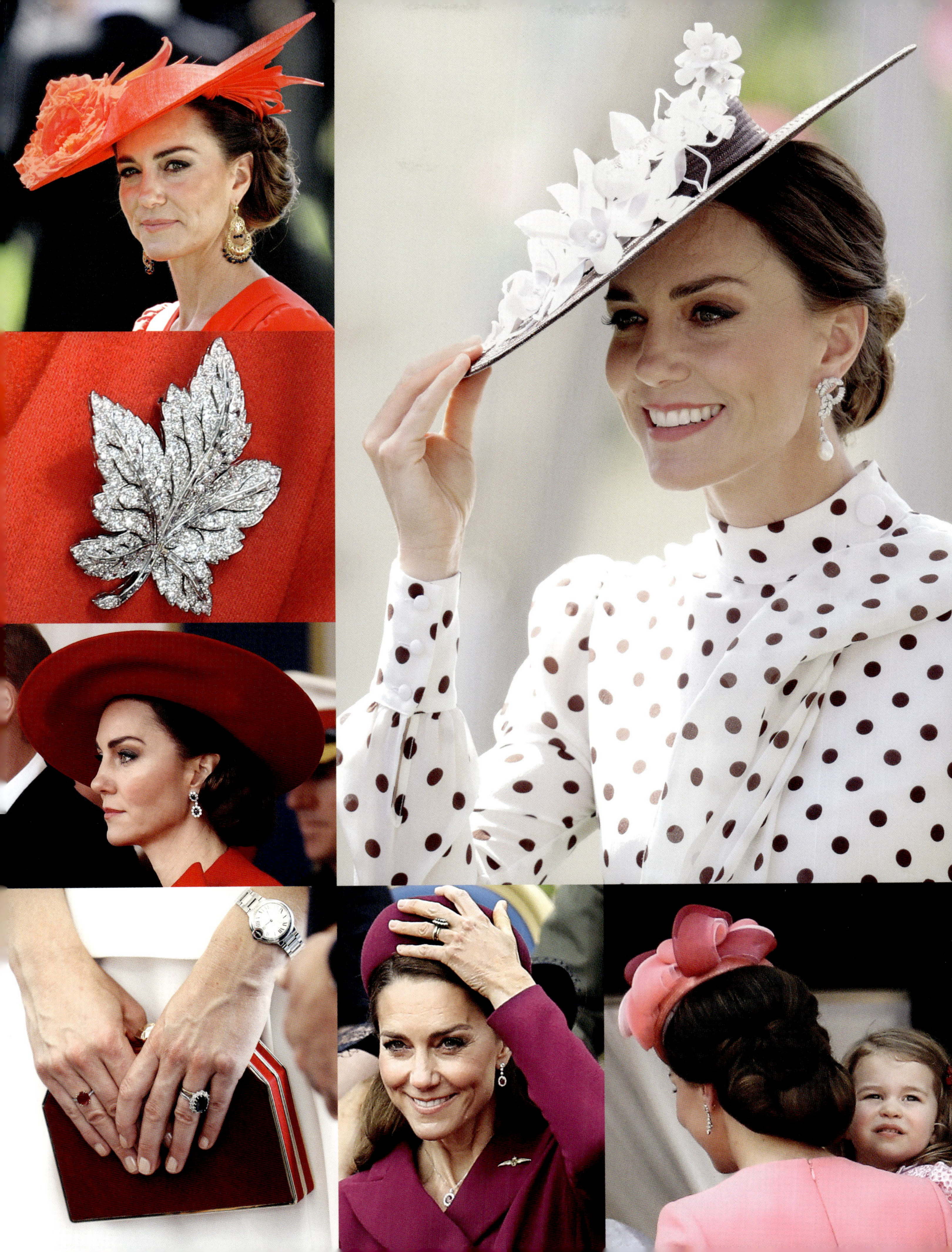

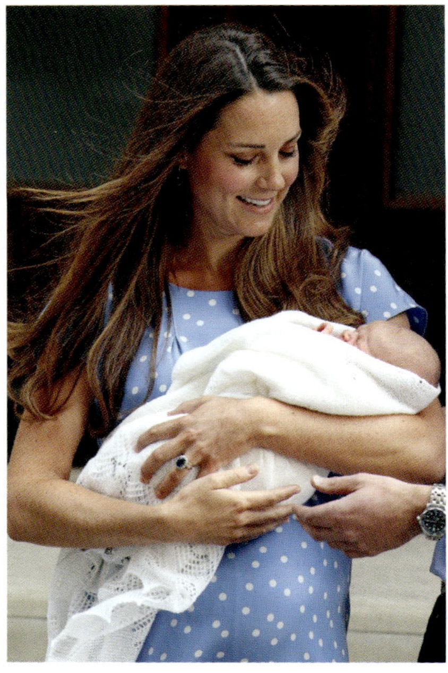

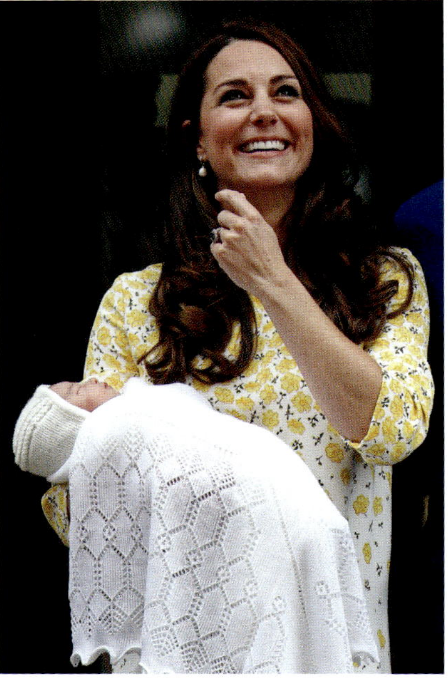

The doors of the Lindo Wing were the focus of eyes from around the world as Prince George (above left), Princess Charlotte (above right), and Prince Louis (below) were presented to the world's media in the happiest and most celebratory of moments.

Right
The Princess of Wales's annual carol service, "Together at Christmas," is a festive event at which the royal children play a key role.

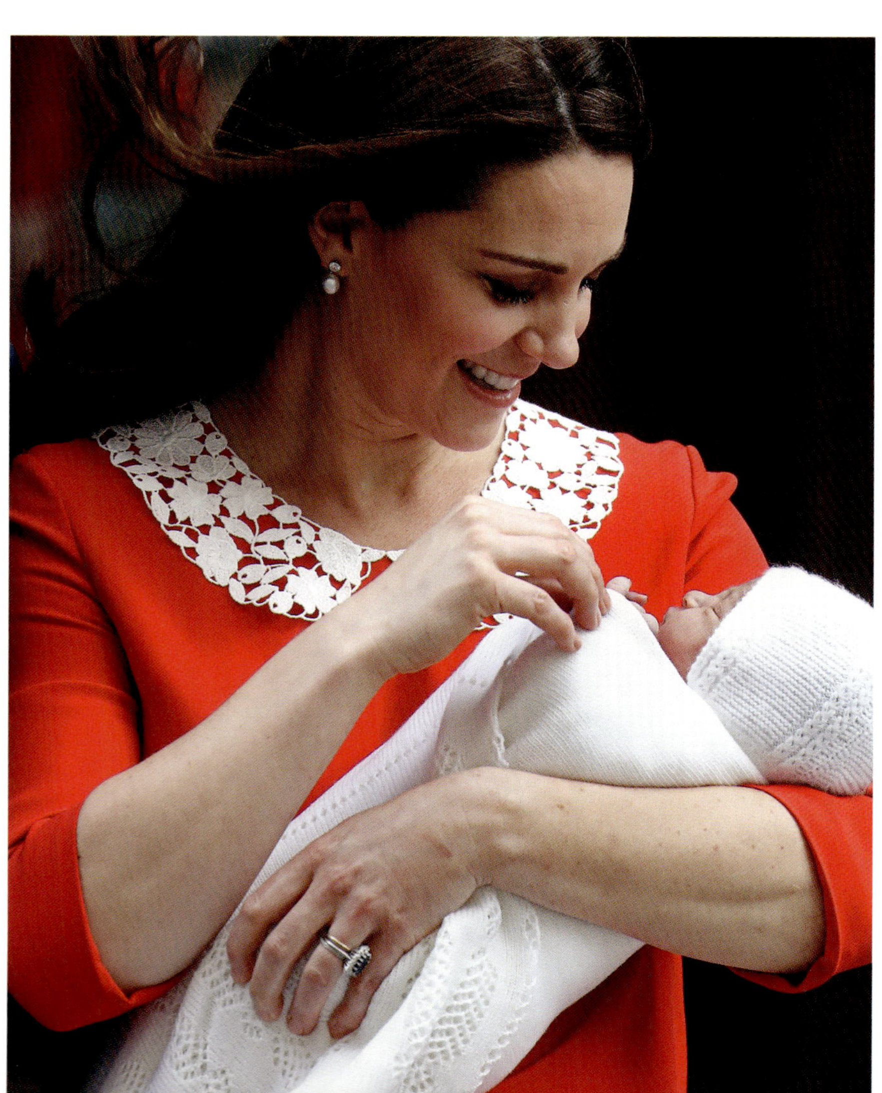

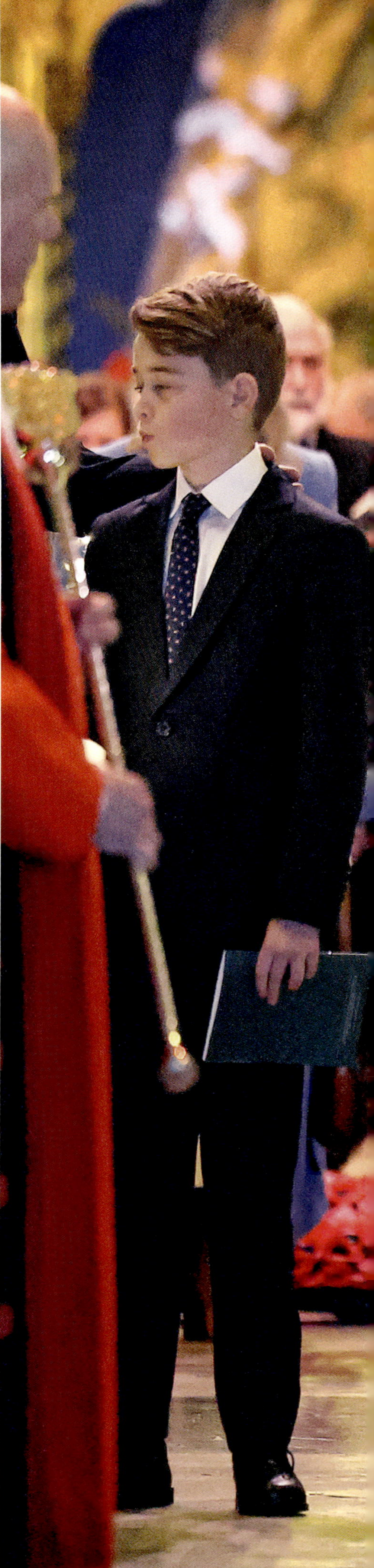

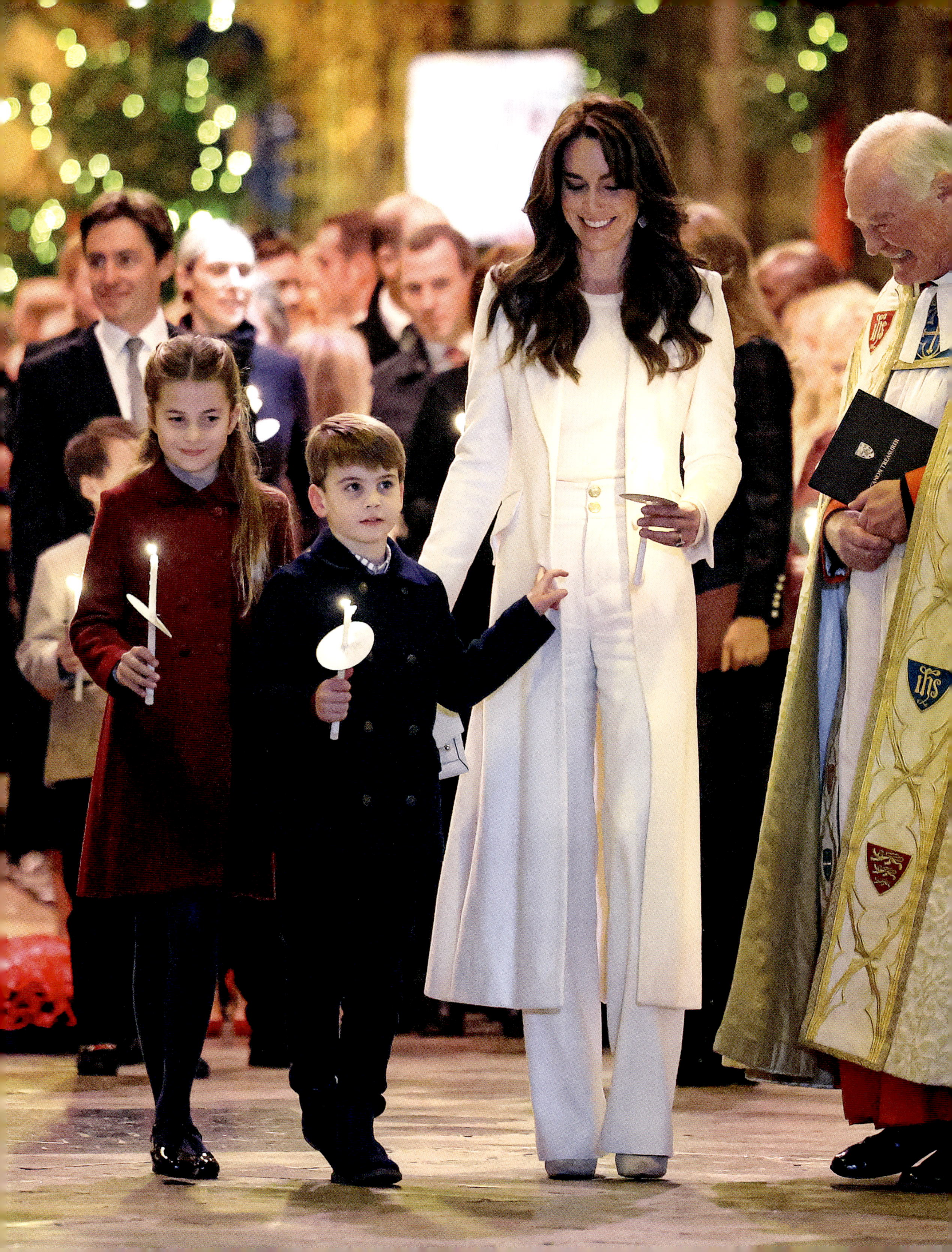

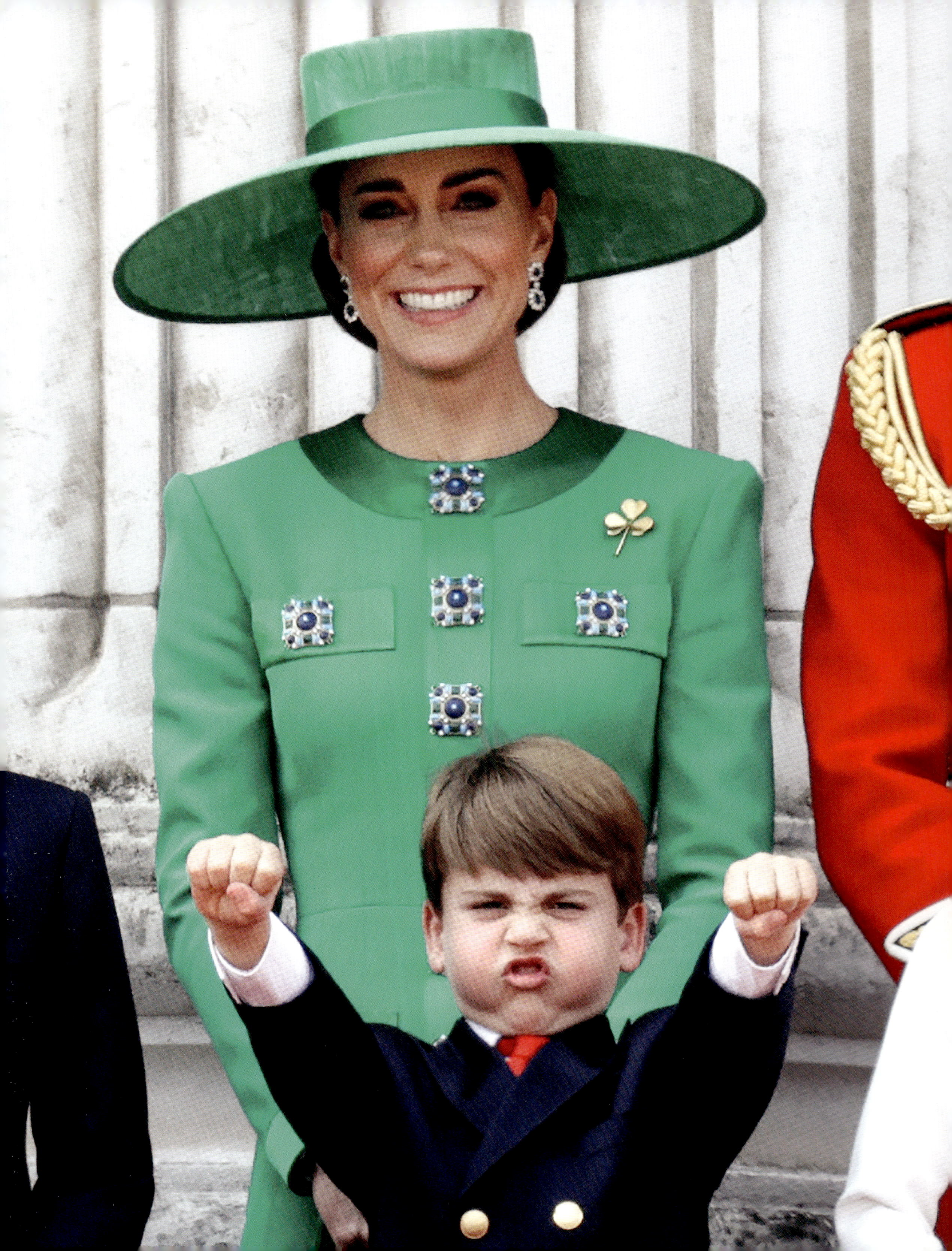

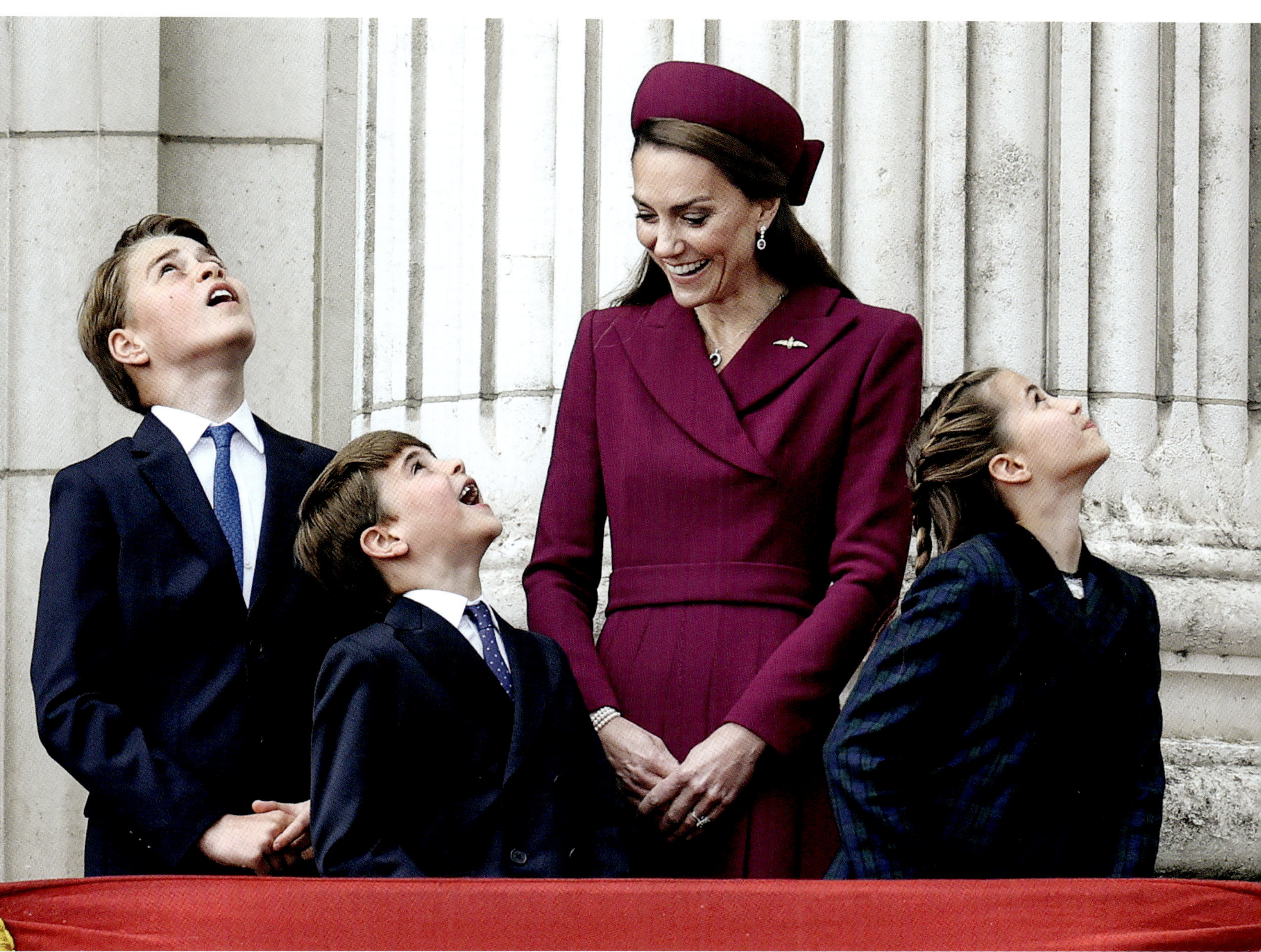

Opposite
Prince Louis provides the entertainment on the balcony of Buckingham Palace during Trooping the Colour, 17 June 2023.

Above
The Princess of Wales watches her children enjoy the flypast over Buckingham Palace to mark the 80th anniversary of VE Day, 5 May 2025.

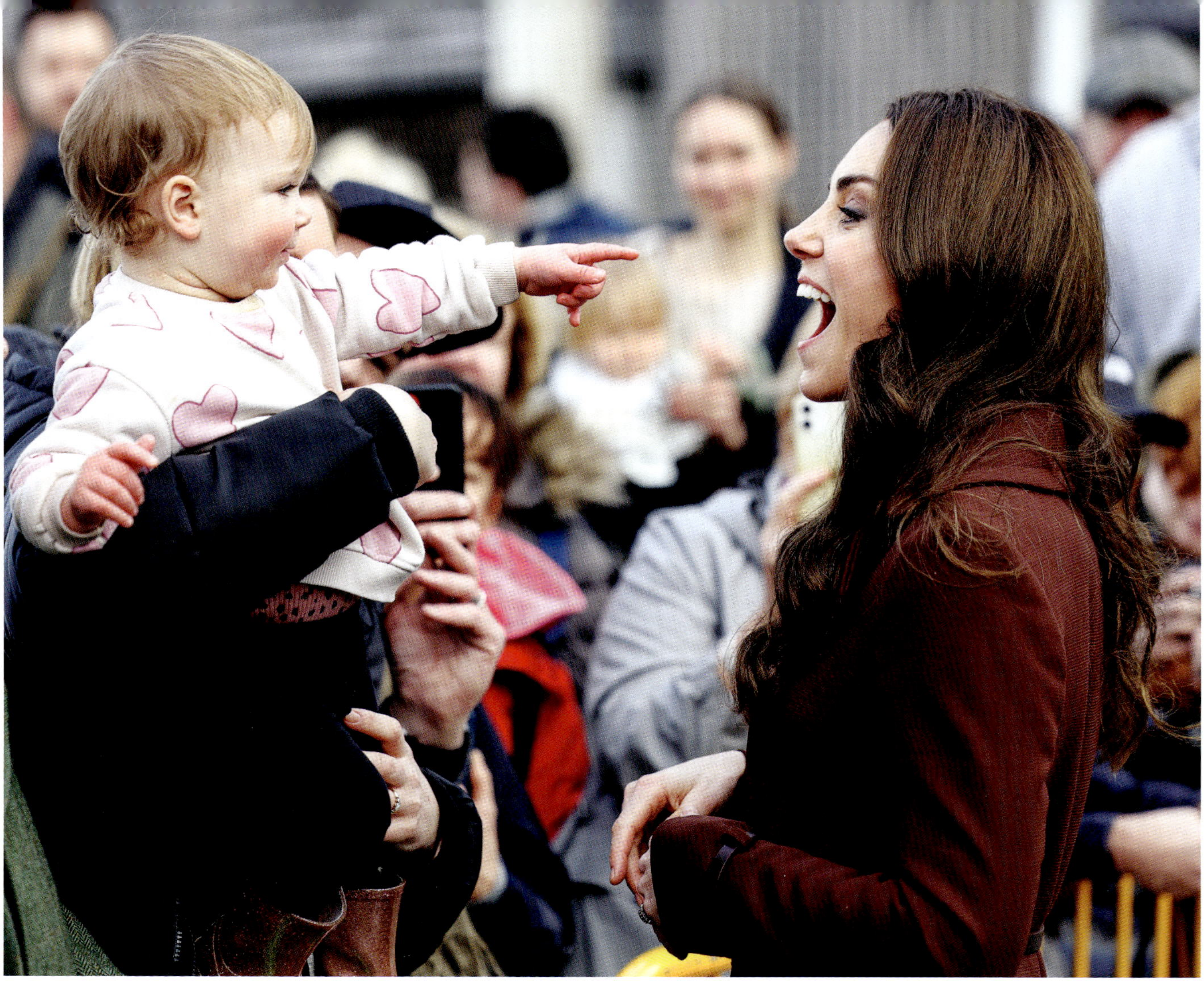

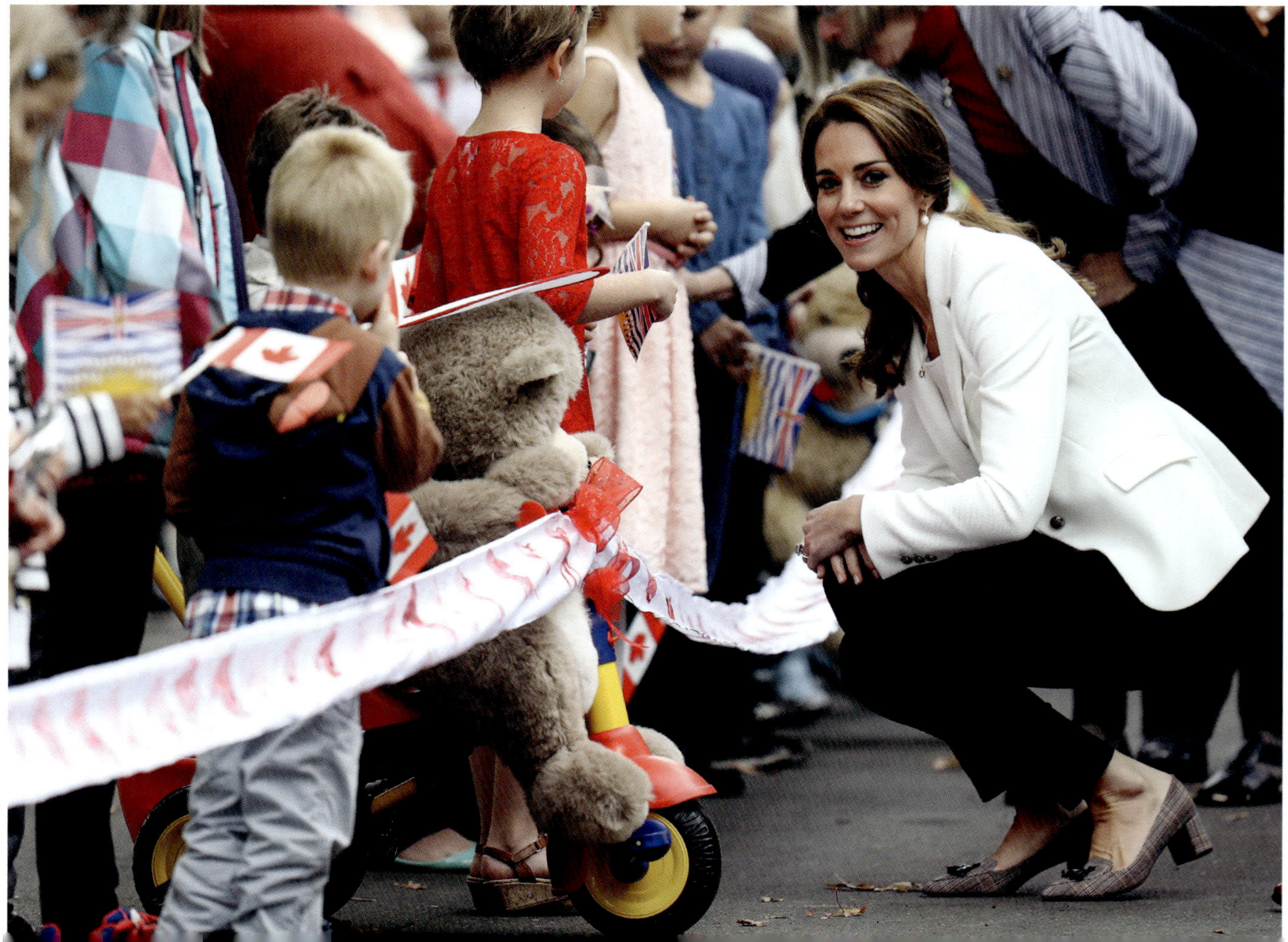

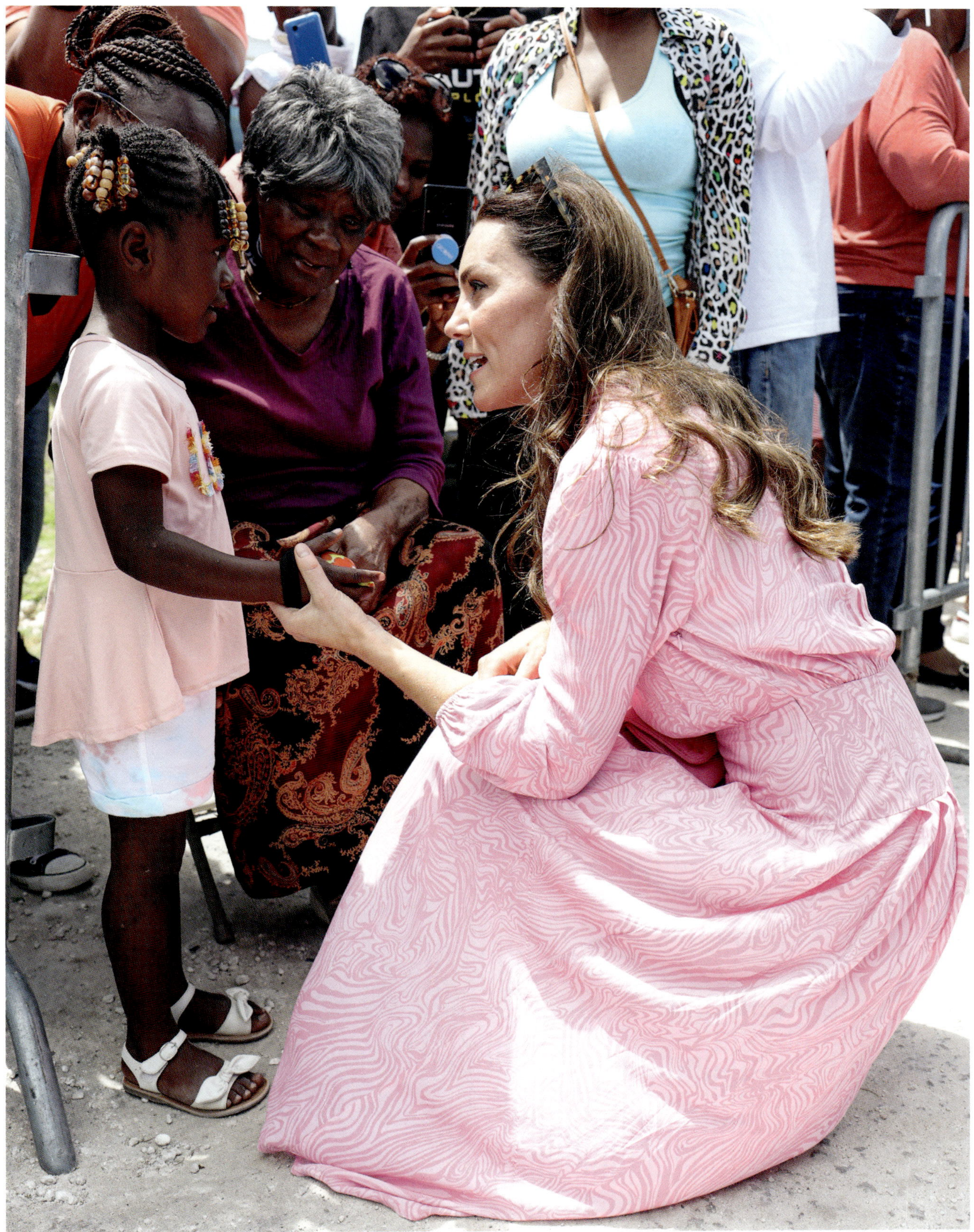

Opposite, top
A lovely interaction between the Princess of Wales and little Maggie Whatmore and her mother Natalie after a tour of the National Maritime Museum in Falmouth, Cornwall, 9 February 2023.

Opposite, below
The Princess meets members of the public after a visit to the Cridge Centre for the Family in Victoria, Canada, 1 October 2016.

Above
Always face to face with the children, the Princess chats to a little girl during a visit to Abaco Islands in the Bahamas, 26 March 2022.

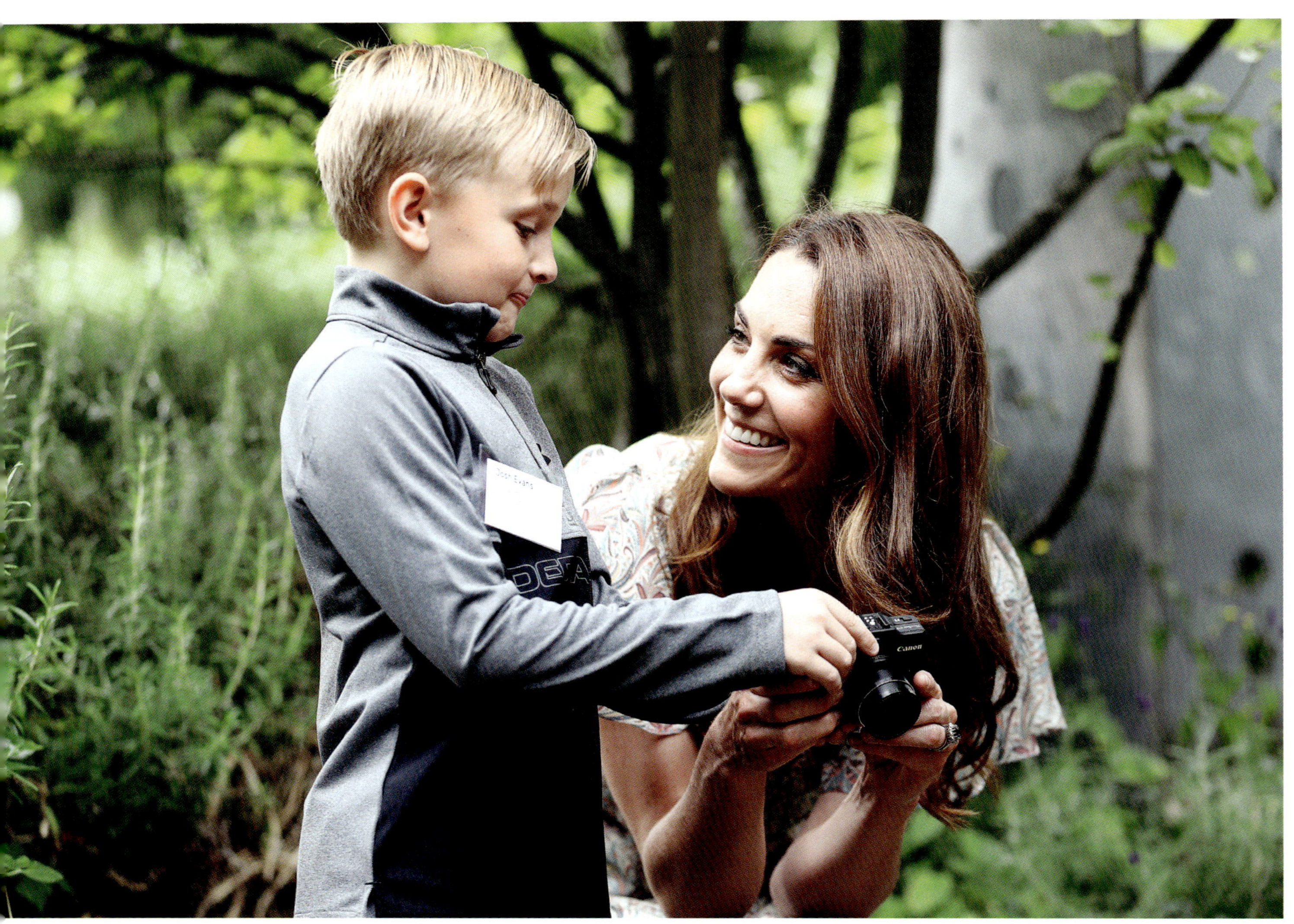

ROYAL PHOTOGRAPHIC SOCIETY

The Princess of Wales's passion for photography has been well documented: her portraits of her children have graced the front pages of newspapers and magazines on their birthdays and anniversaries for a number of years now, and she is clearly an accomplished photographer. Bearing this in mind, it seemed only natural for her to take over the reins of the prestigious Royal Photographic Society, a role that Queen Elizabeth II held for 67 years. Here, the Princess helps young Josh Evans with his camera during a photography workshop for the charity Action for Children, in Kingston upon Thames, 25 June 2019.

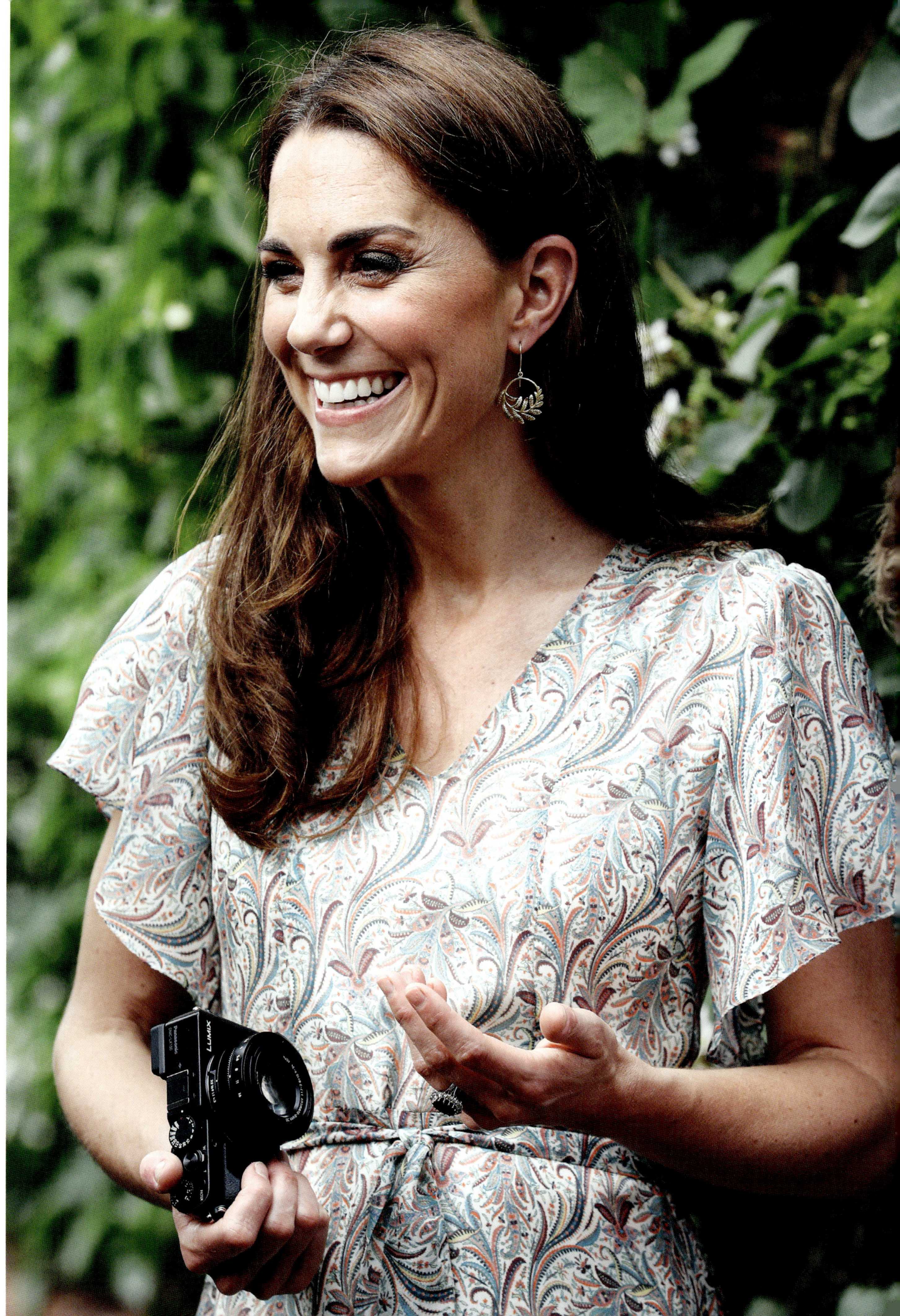
Panasonic
LUMIX

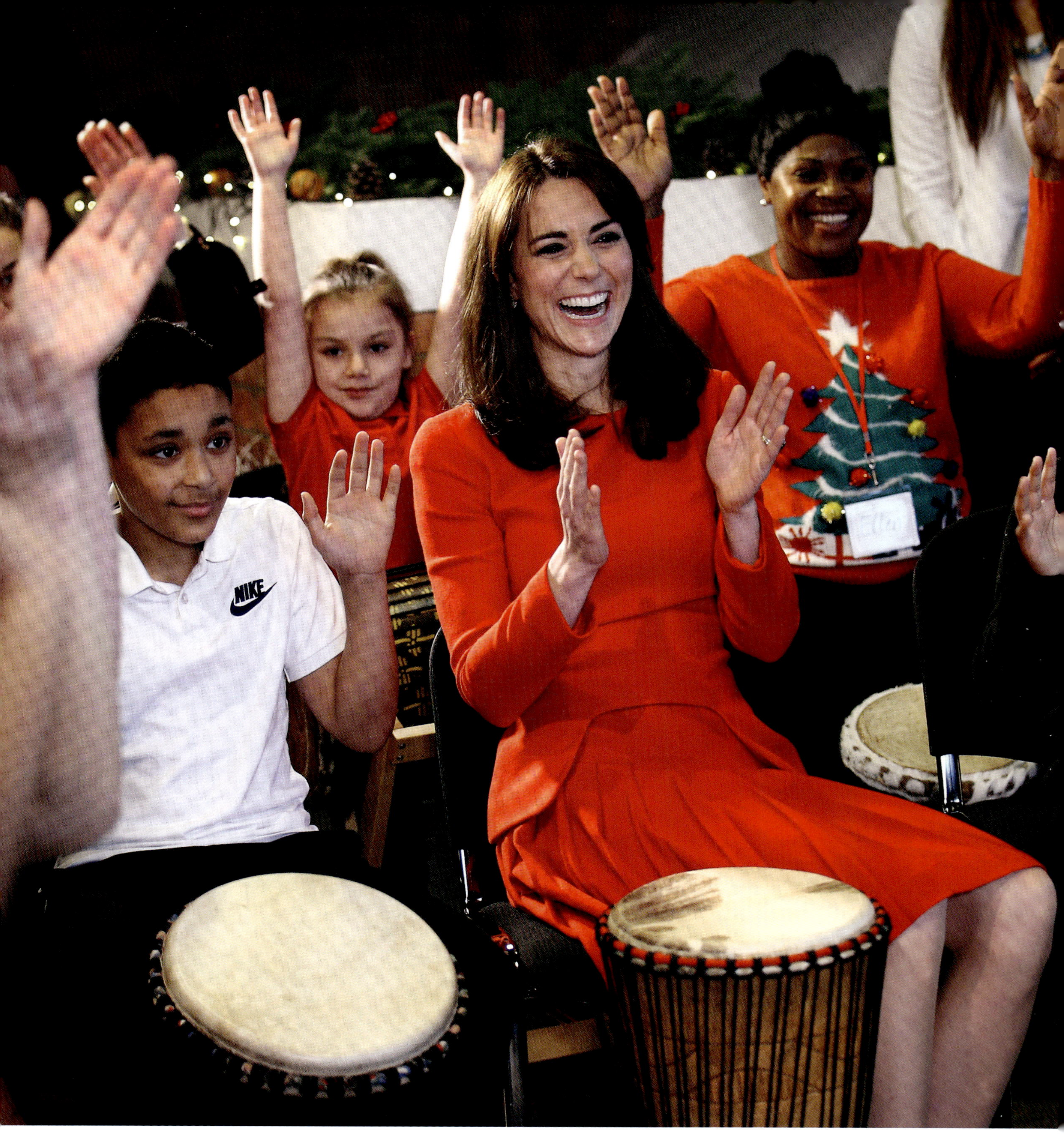
NIKE

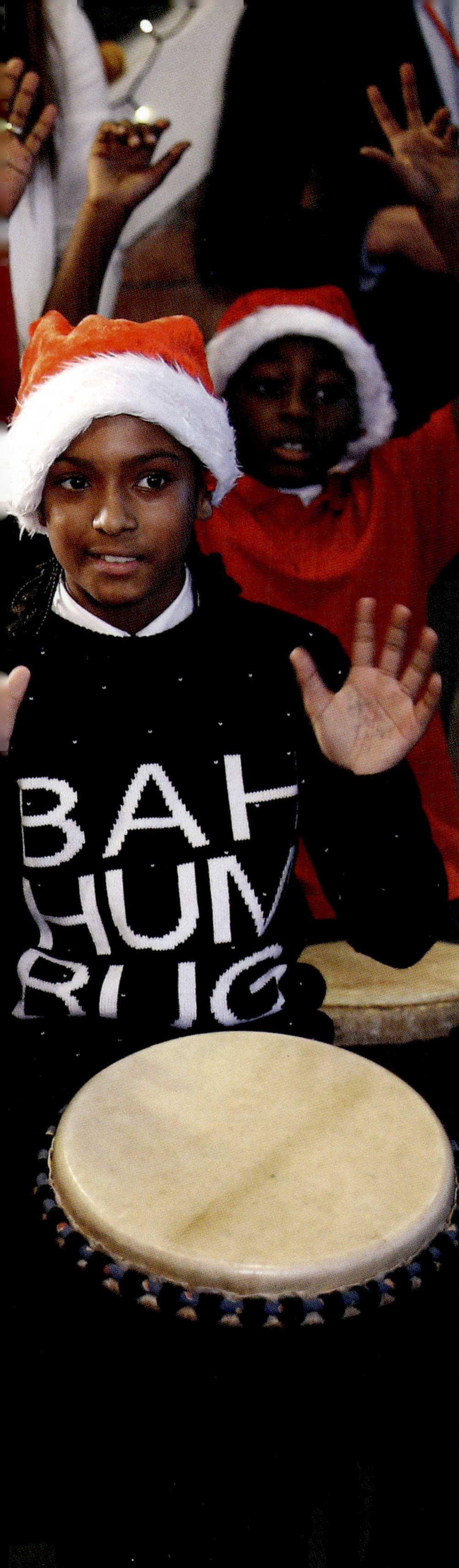

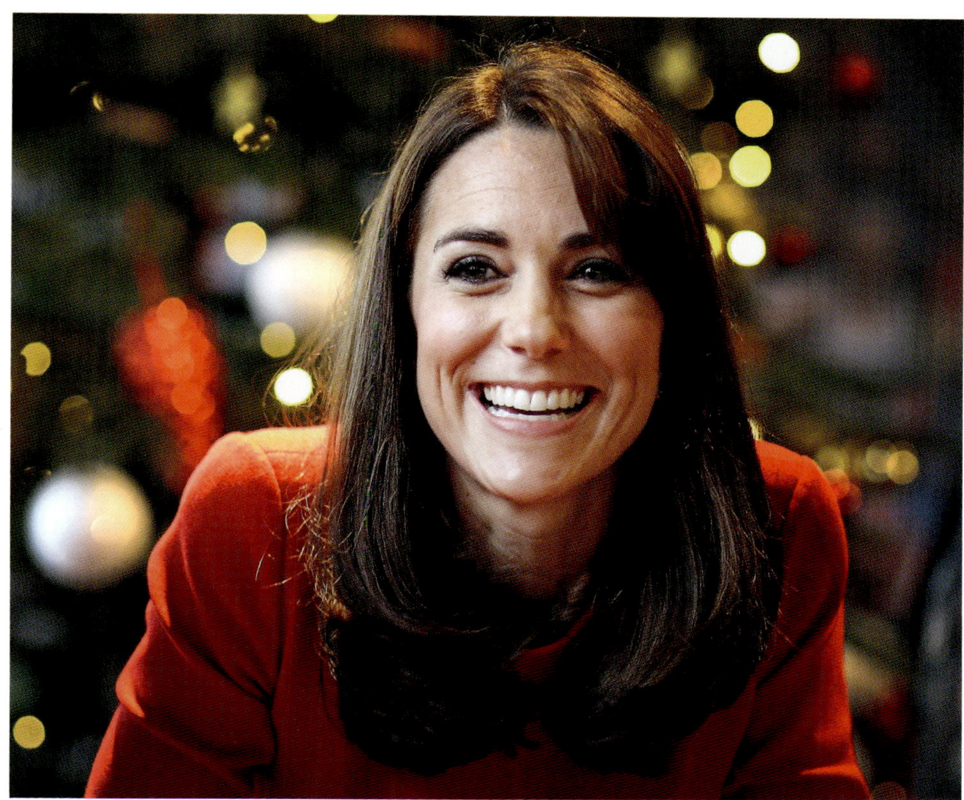

ANNA FREUD CENTRE

Sometimes royal engagements really lodge themselves in the memory bank for their warmth and enjoyment, and this visit to the Anna Freud Centre family Christmas party in London was certainly one of those moments. The Princess joined groups of families in festive activities designed to help pupils reflect on the positive progress in their social relationships and communication skills, 15 December 2015.

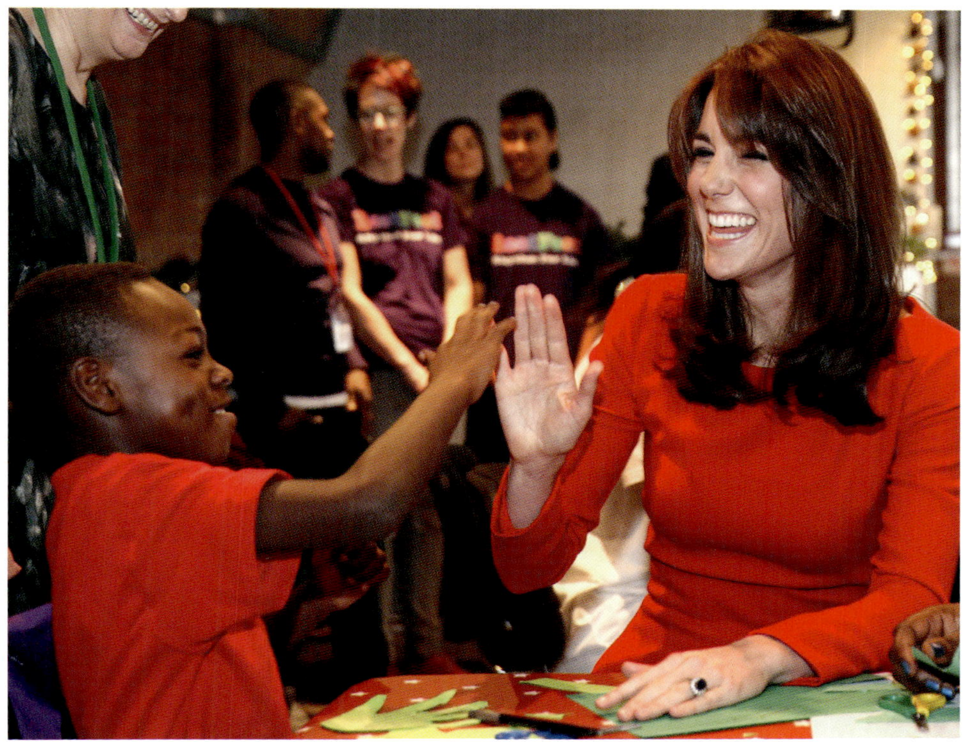

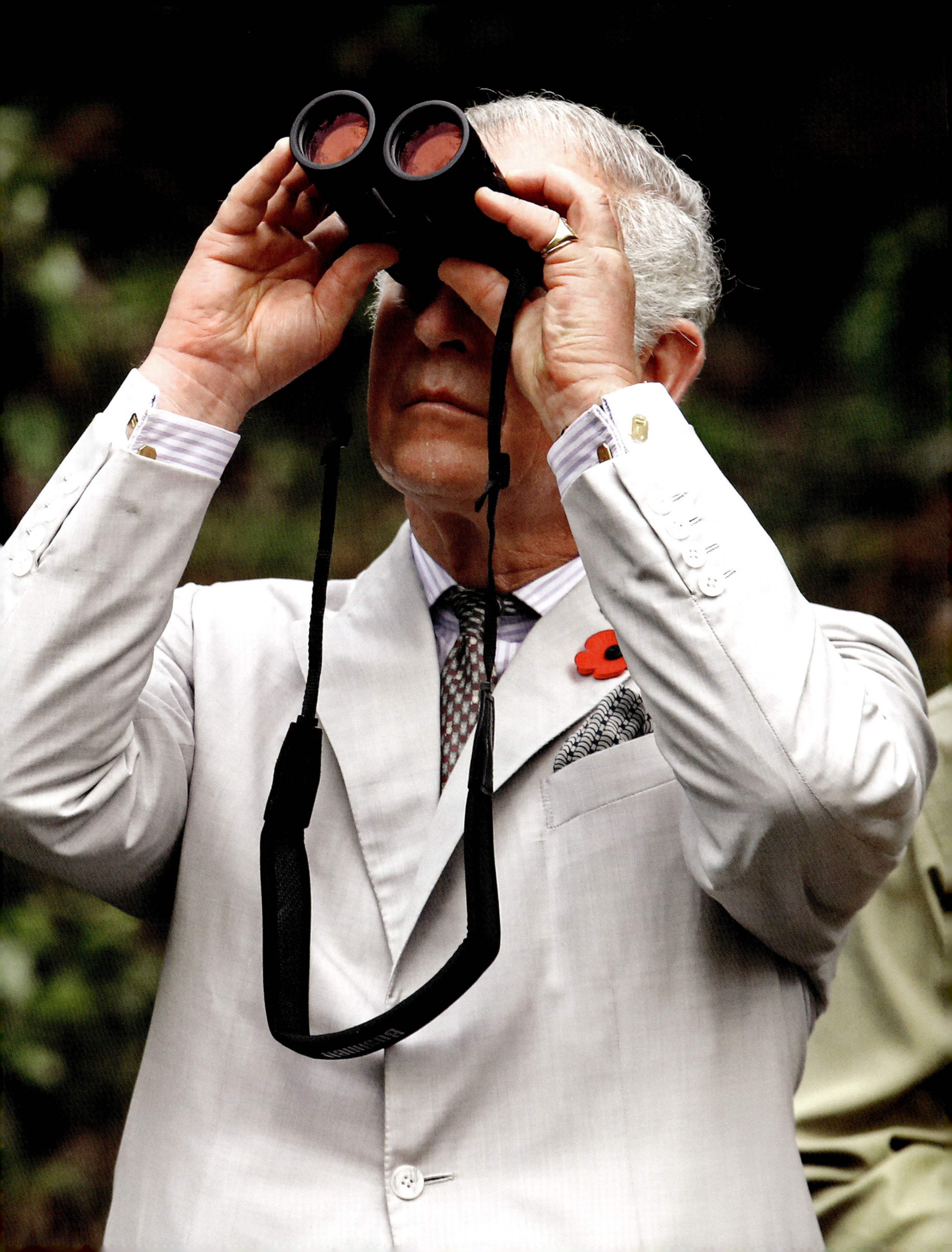

7

CHAMPIONS OF THE ENVIRONMENT

The British royal family has for many years used its prominence and position to advocate for change in the environmental sphere. For over five decades, and long before it became a "fashionable" movement, King Charles travelled the world talking about the benefits of sustainable farming and the perils of microplastics, pollution, and deforestation. He also made sure to visit areas affected by these problems. Searching for solutions, he launched the Sustainable Markets Initiative, and the King's Trust has worked to promote sustainable business practices.

Following closely in his father's footsteps, the Prince of Wales clearly understands the daunting challenges climate change is bringing to the world. In 2021, he founded the Earthshot Prize, a game-changing environmental award supporting innovative business solutions around the world that work toward a better planet. While it is an organization entrenched in tradition, the royal family champions these forward-thinking initiatives in the hope of making this planet a better place for us all to live.

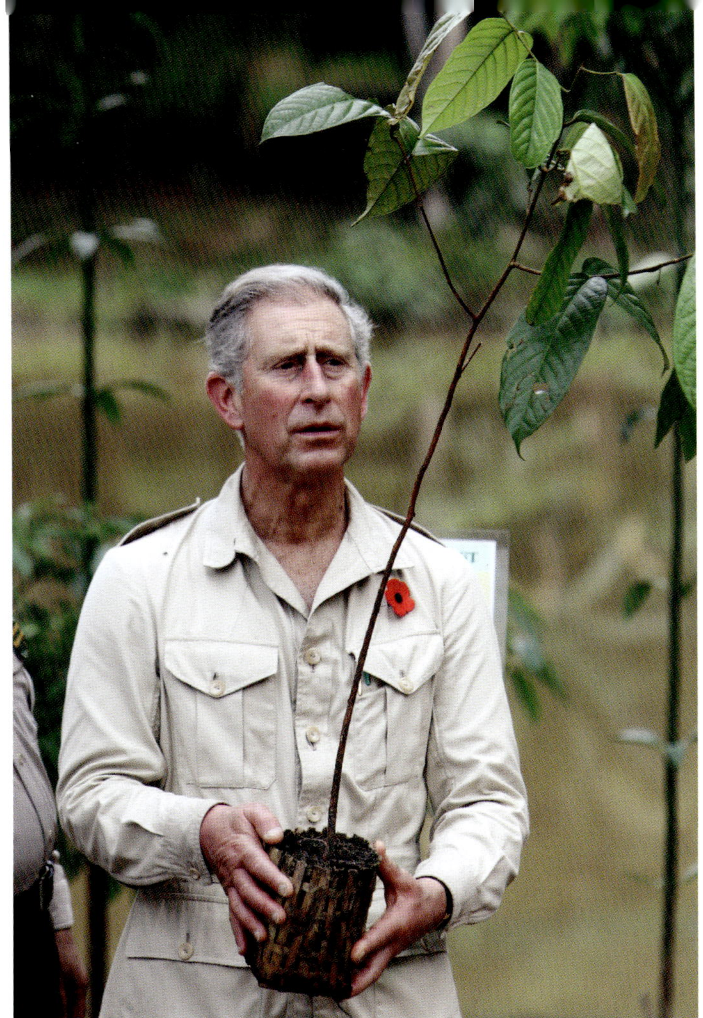

PLANTING TREES

The Queen's Green Canopy invited members of the public to "plant a tree for the Jubilee." Between this photograph with Queen Elizabeth II planting the very first tree on 23 March 2021 at Windsor Castle and the picture of Prince William and King Charles marking the end of the initiative in Sandringham House on 2 April 2023, more than three million trees were planted as a living legacy to Queen Elizabeth II and her Platinum Jubilee.

Charles plants a tree at the Harapan Rainforest Project in Jambi, Indonesia, 2 November 2008.

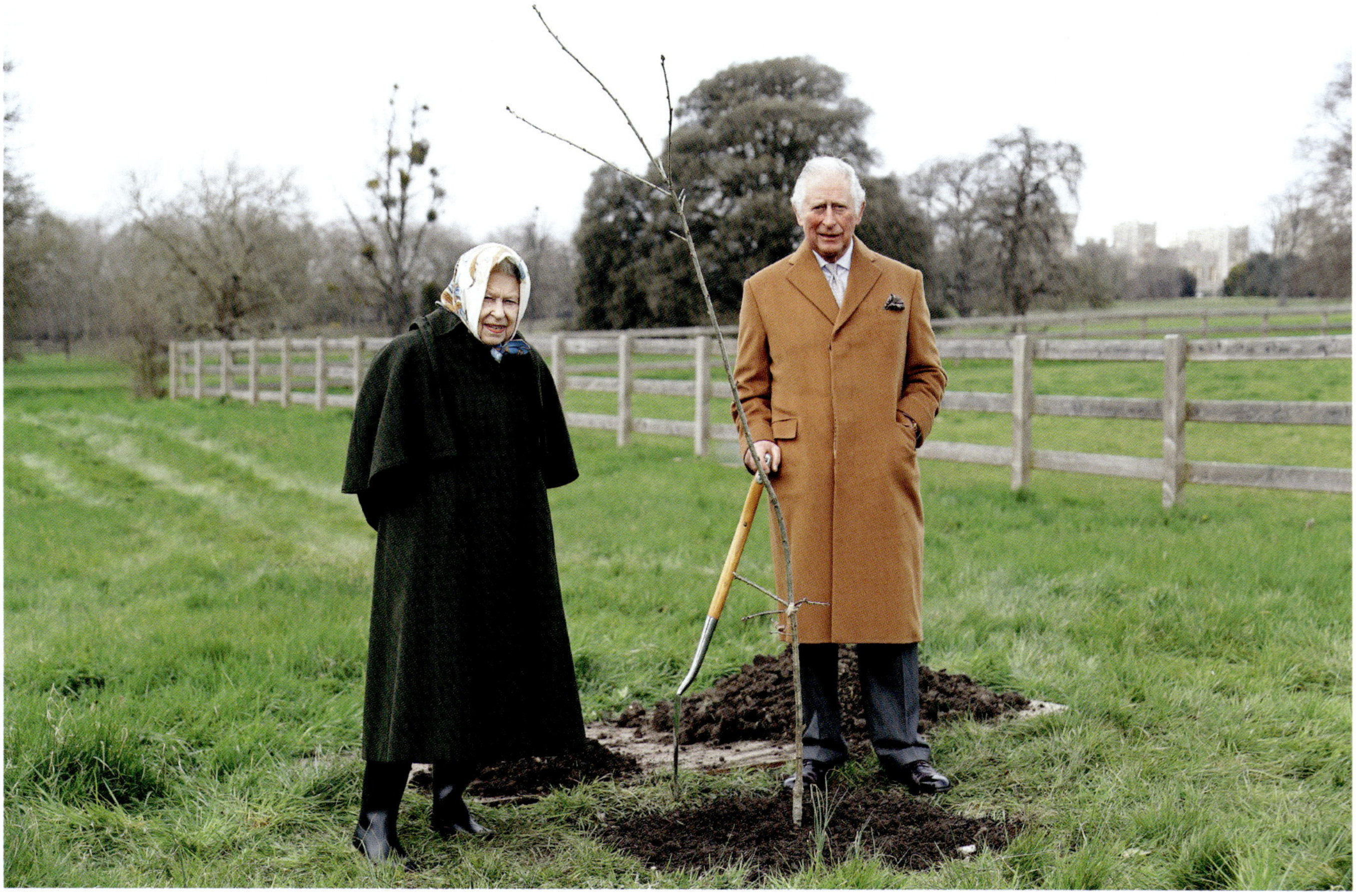

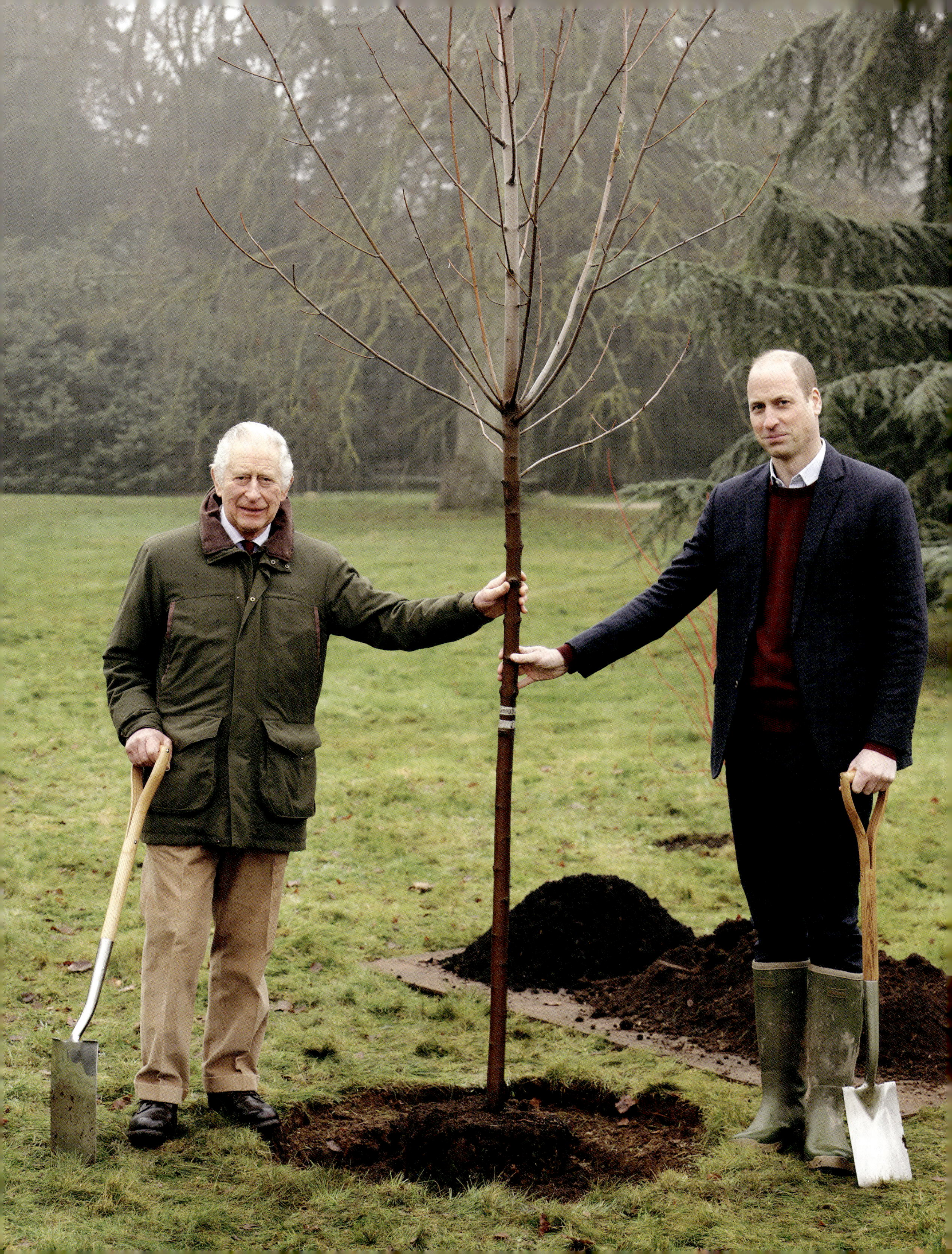

ENVIRONMENTAL CREDENTIALS

Did you know that King Charles has a car that runs on cheese and wine? The King's environmental awareness is reflected in how he chooses to get around. His classic 1969 Aston Martin DB6 runs on E85 biofuel, a mixture of 85% bioethanol and 15% gasoline. The bioethanol is made from surplus English white wine and whey from the cheese-making process on his estate, creating an environmentally friendly fuel from waste products.

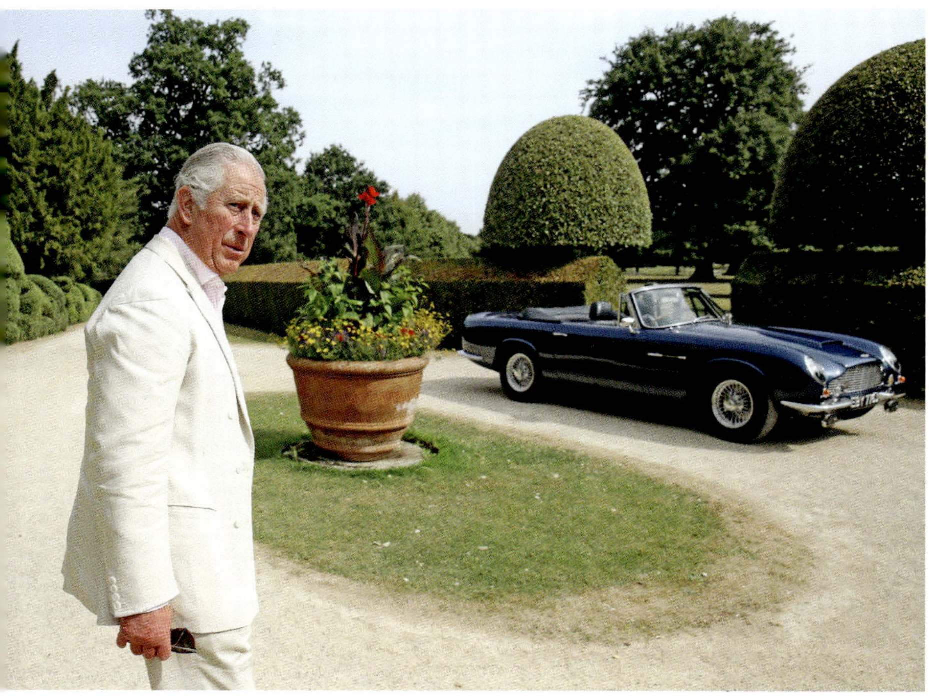

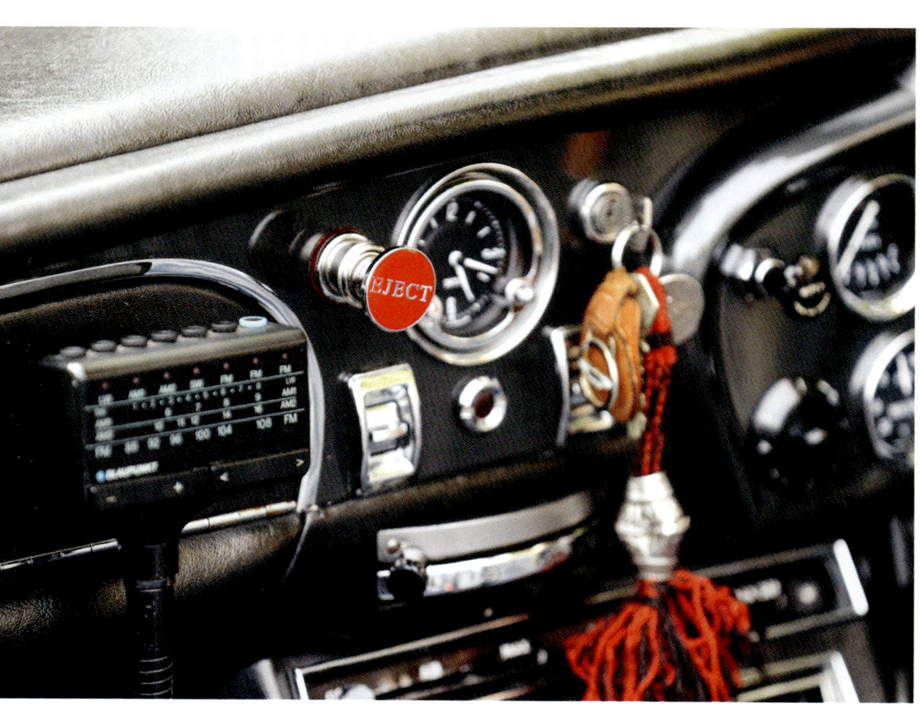

Opposite
Reflecting King Charles's sense of humour, his classic car has an eject button – I was very tempted to press it when I saw it!

Below
King Charles III addresses delegates during a speech at the opening ceremony of the World Climate Action Summit during COP28 in Dubai, 1 December 2023.

Overleaf
Disembarking a police boat as he visits areas of Somerset that had experienced unprecedented flooding, 4 February 2014. Whole villages were marooned and hundreds of homes and businesses were affected.

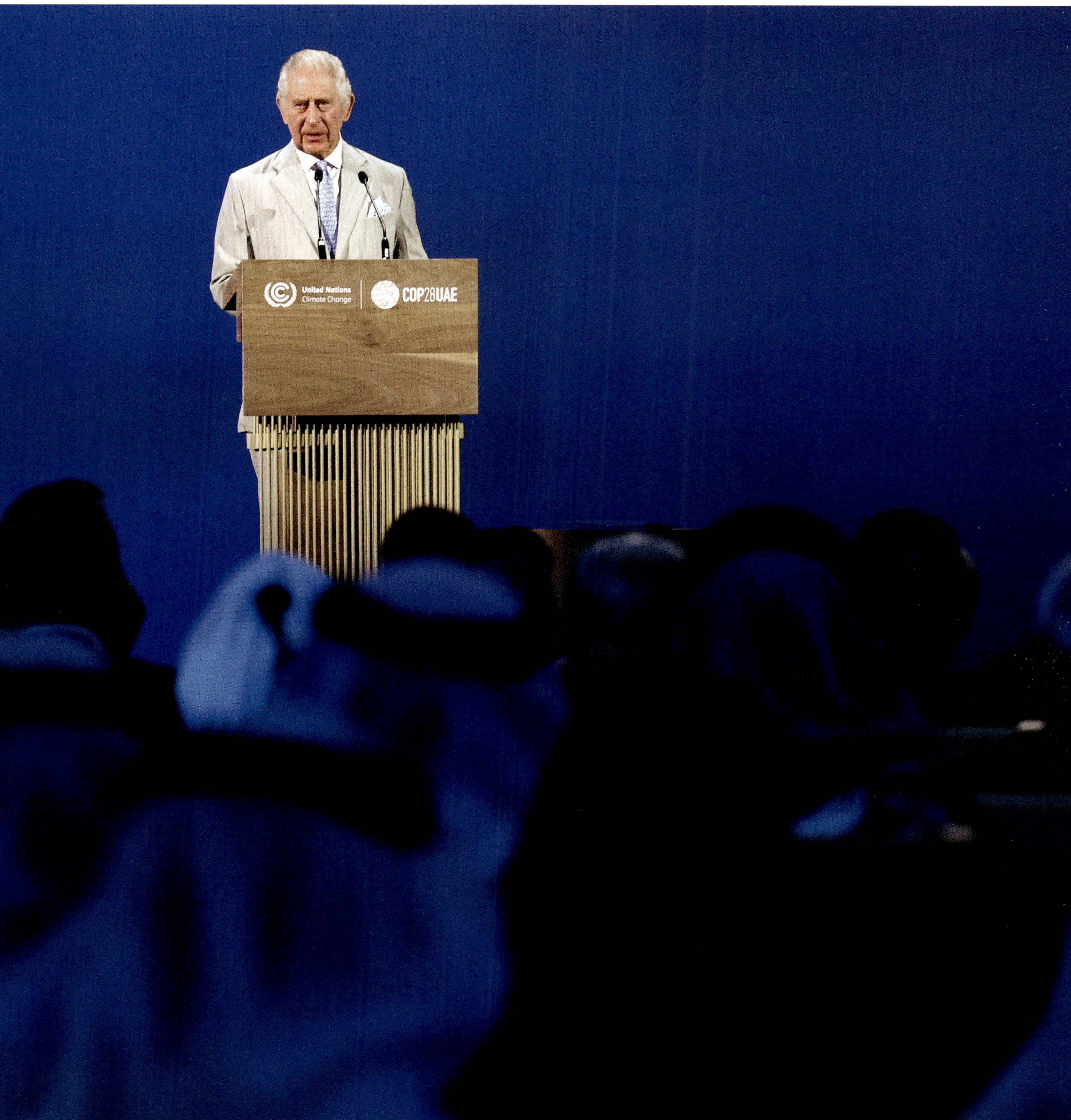

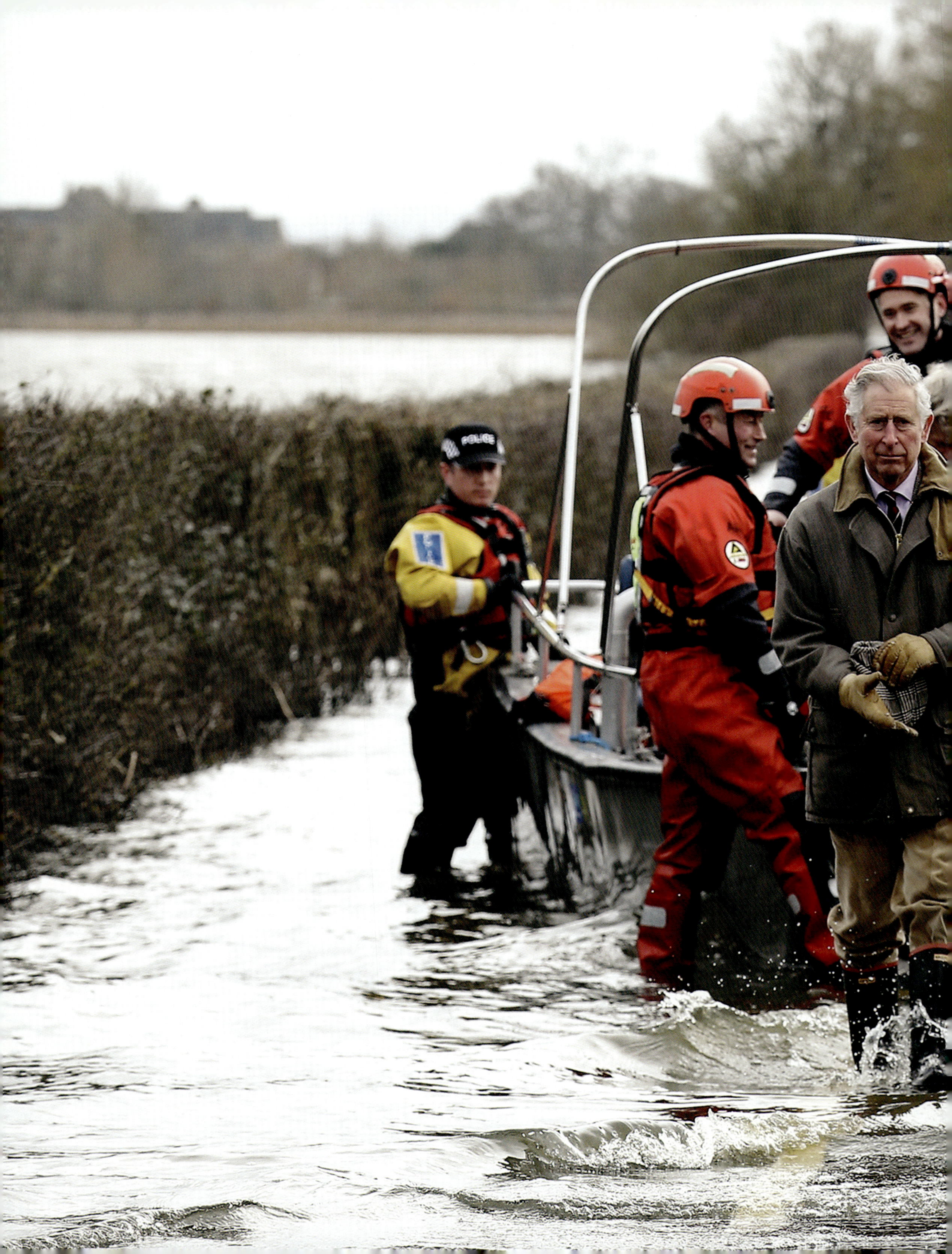
POLICE

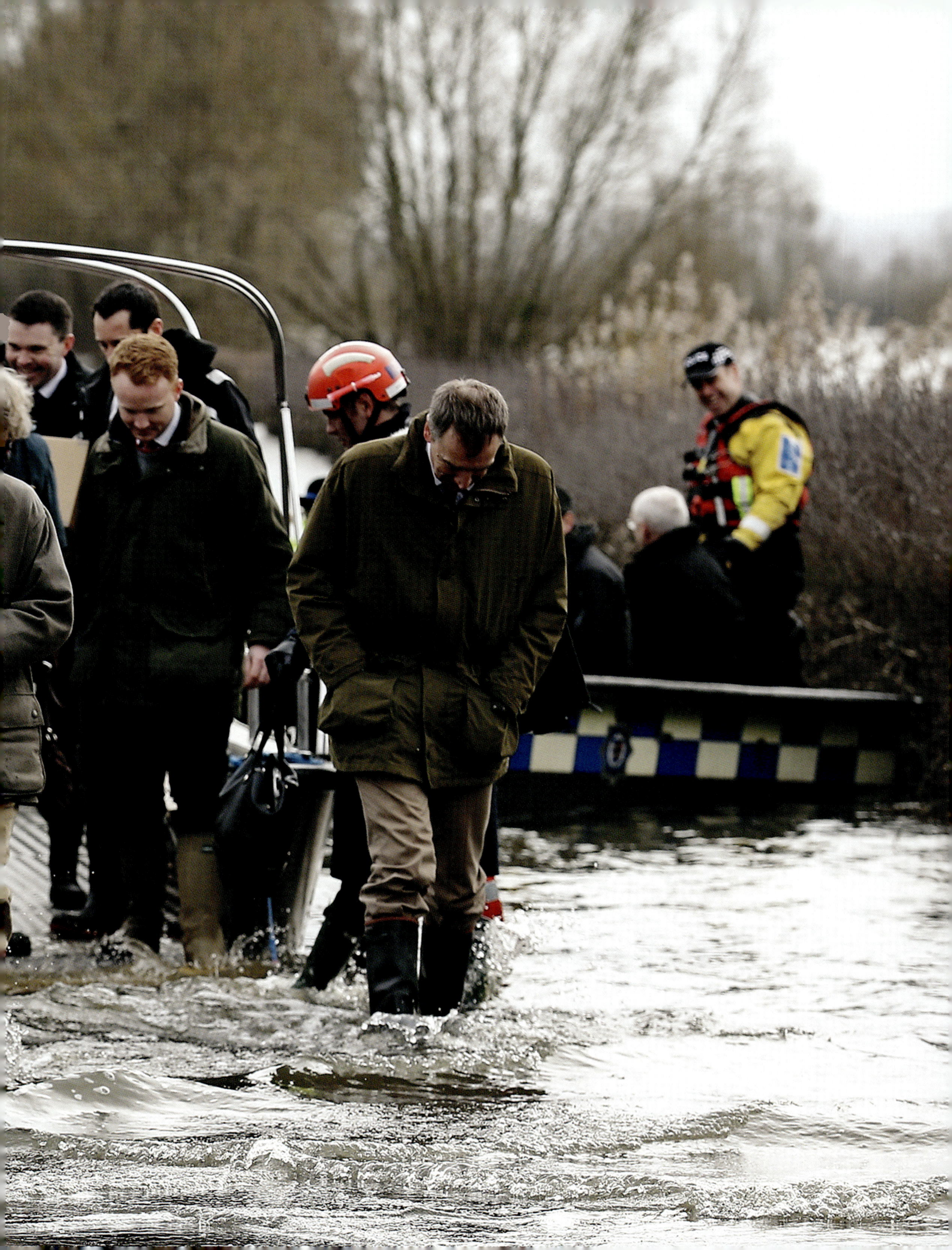

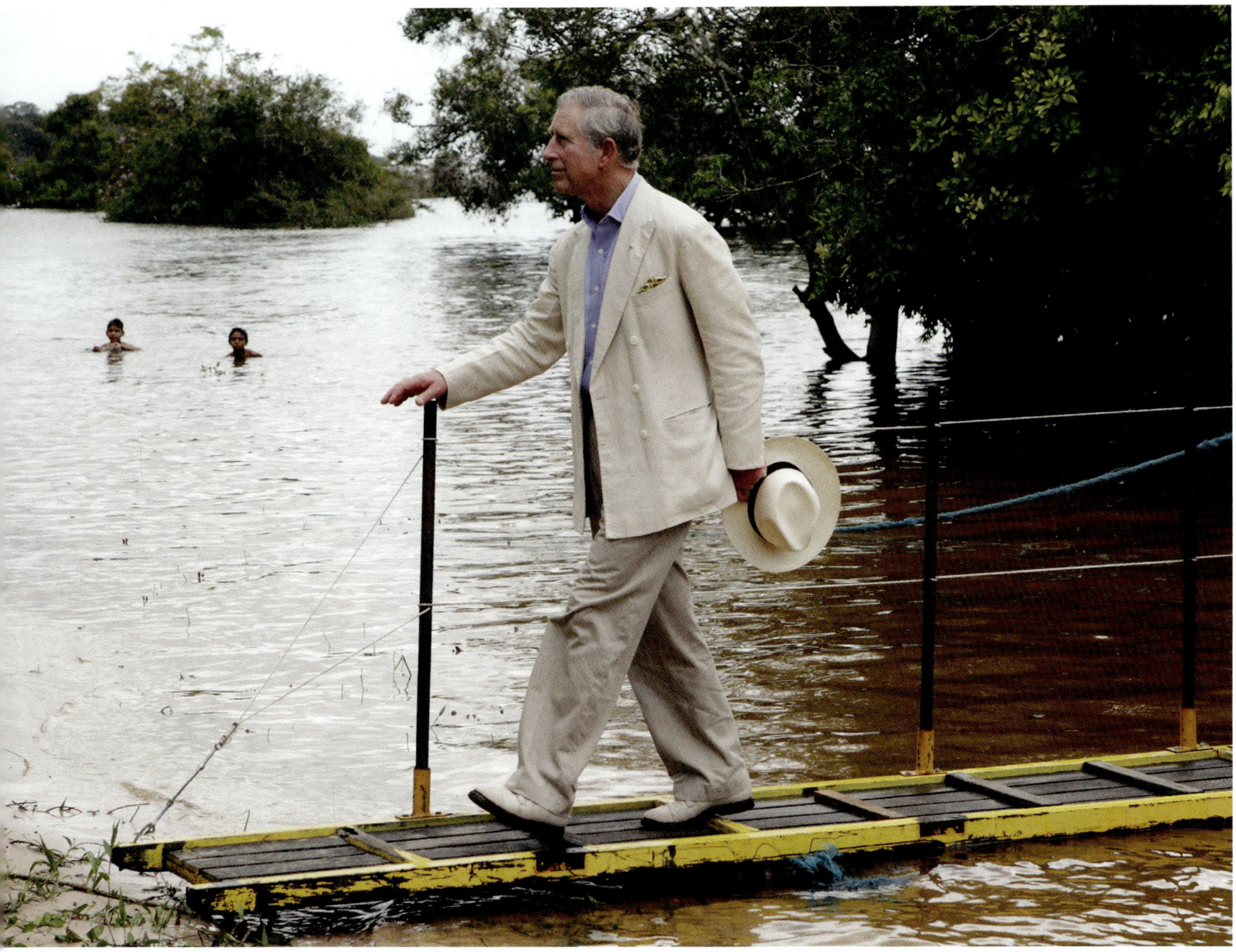

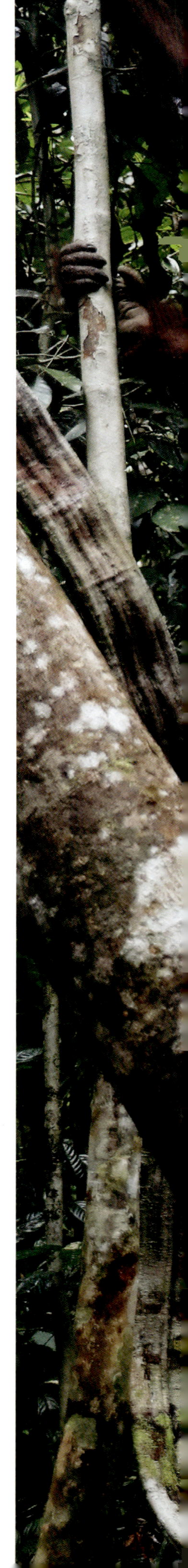

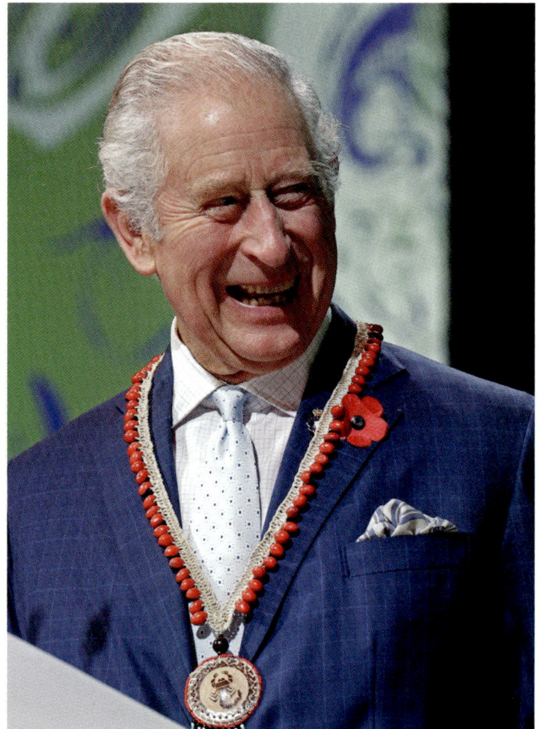

A RESOLUTE ENVIRONMENTALIST

King Charles certainly likes to actively defend nature – over the years, my cameras have steamed up in numerous rainforests around the world. Since he became King his enthusiasm for championing environmental causes has not abated. It is clear that he pushes to accelerate solutions to sustain our world, a passion he has passed on to his son.

Above
Charles arrives in Maguari Village in Brazil's Amazon rainforest, 14 March 2009.

Left
Speaking on day three of COP26 in Glasgow, 2 November 2021.

Right
A royal handshake with a difference as Charles meets an orangutan in the rainforests of Borneo during a visit to Semenggoh Wildlife Centre, a rehabilitation centre for orangutans found injured in the wild or rescued from captivity, in Sarawak, Malaysia, 6 November 2017.

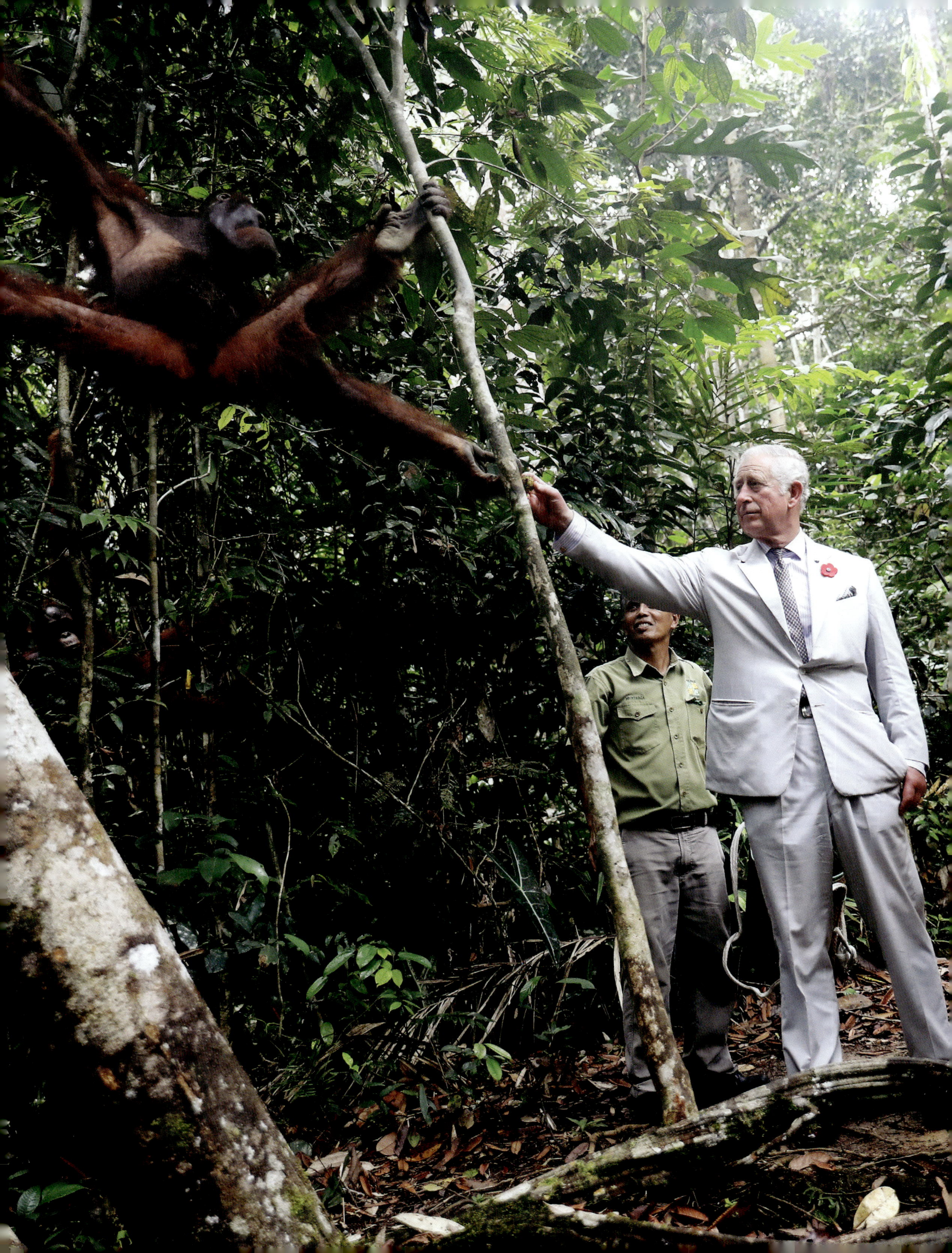

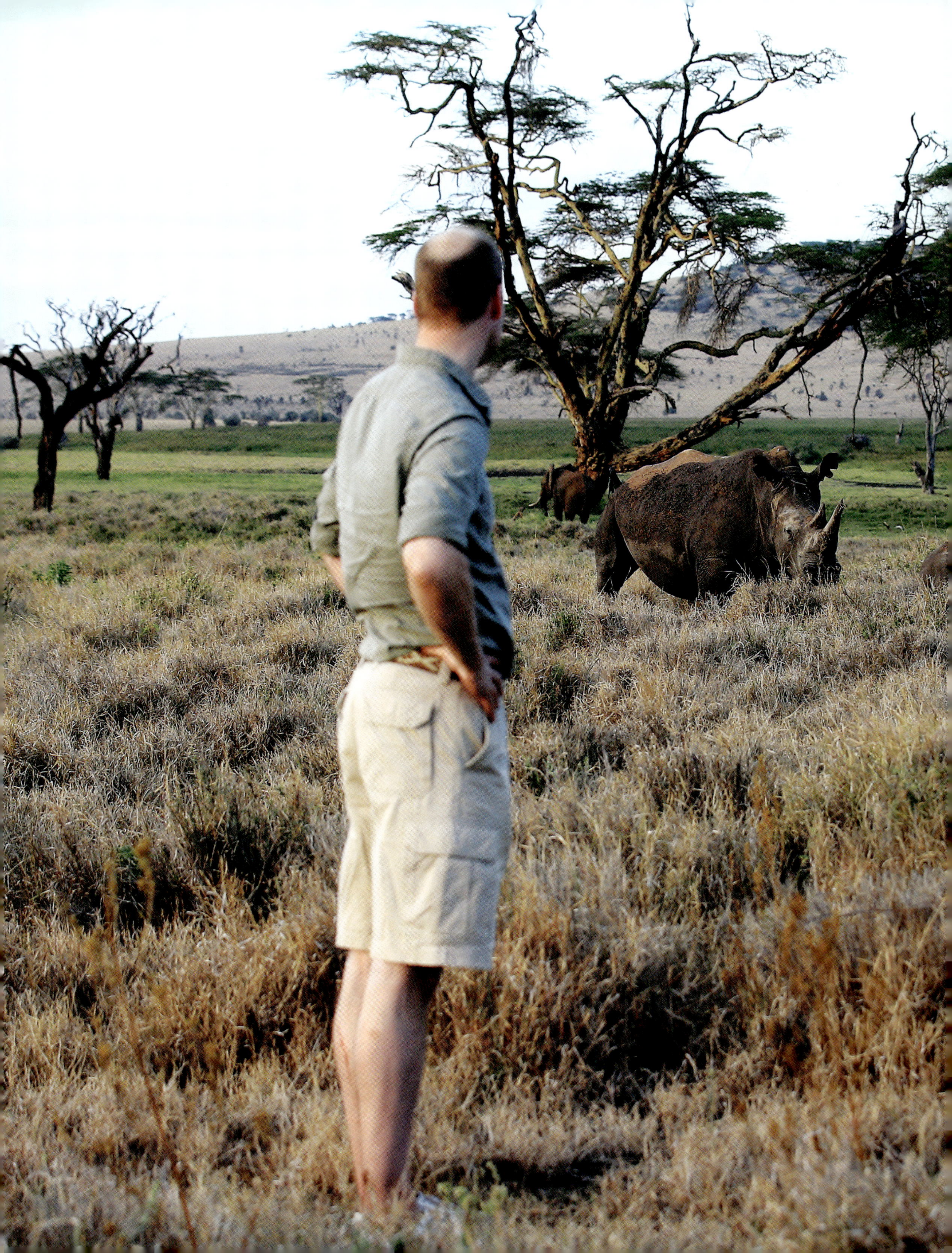

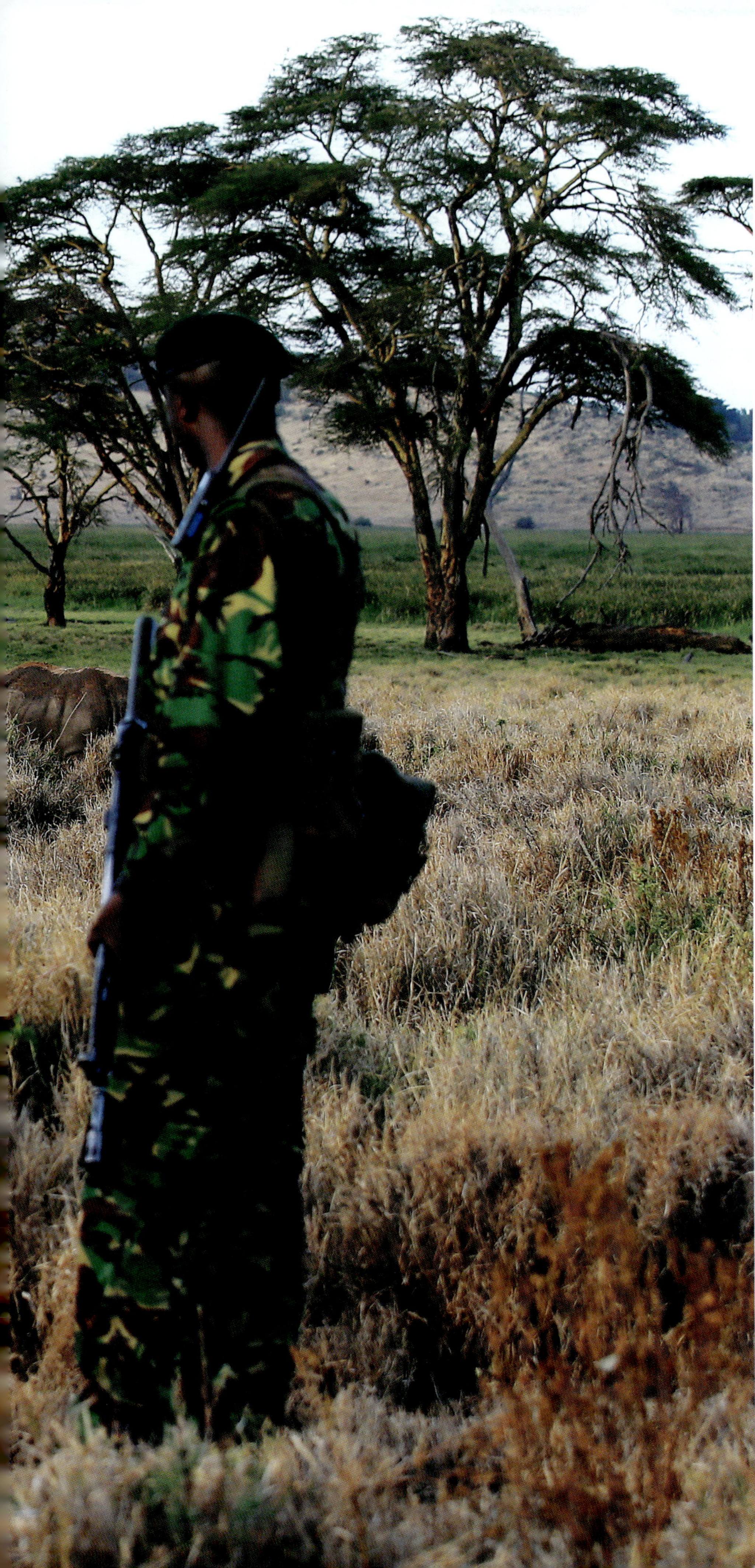

THE WONDER OF WILDLIFE

Prince William is Royal Patron of Tusk, which promotes conservation, education, and community development across Africa, and President of United for Wildlife, which combats the illegal wildlife trade and trafficking. He met Edward Ndiritu, winner of the Tusk Wildlife Ranger Award in 2015. Here, they take a moment to appreciate a white rhino and calf at northern Kenya's Lewa Wildlife Conservancy, 24 March 2016.

THE EARTHSHOT PRIZE

The pride with which Catherine looked at William, founder of the Earthshot Prize, as he talked with authority to the room of politicians, activists, scientists, and celebrities was felt by all. This prestigious global award is presented to five winners each year for their contributions toward environmentalism. Here, the Prince and Princess of Wales take part in rehearsals for the inaugural Earthshot Prize Awards at Alexandra Palace, 17 October 2021.

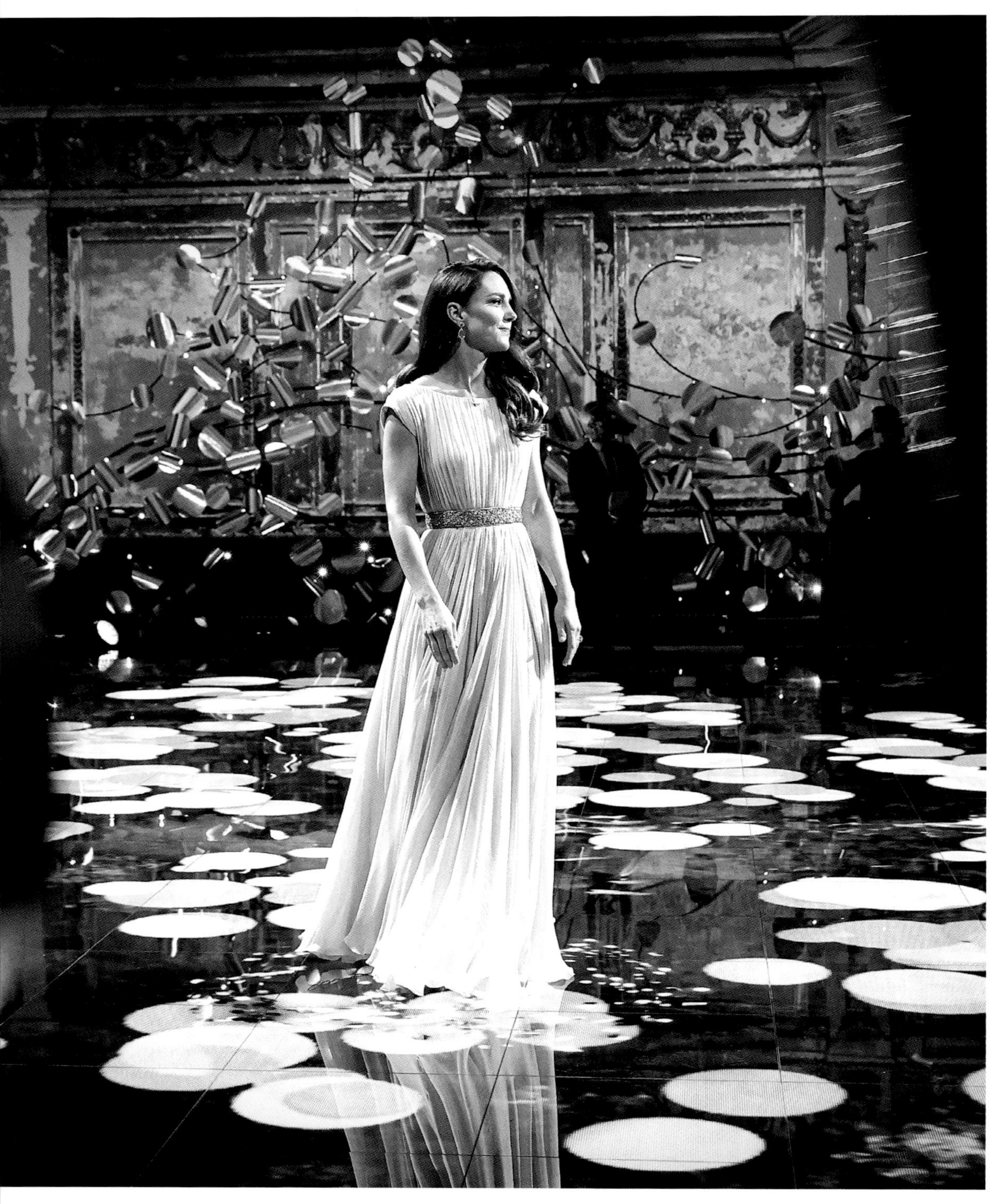

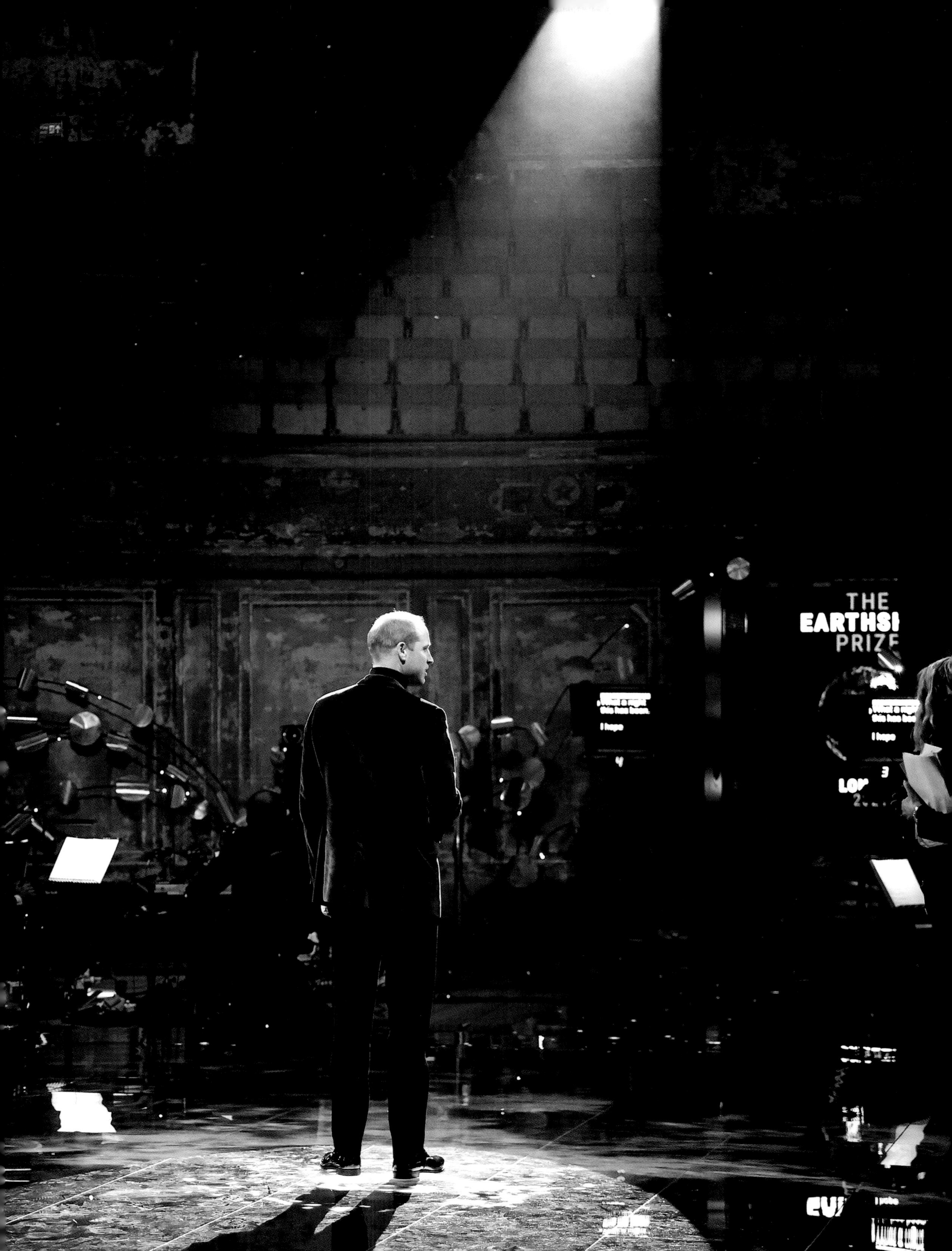
THE
PRIZE
this has been.
I hope

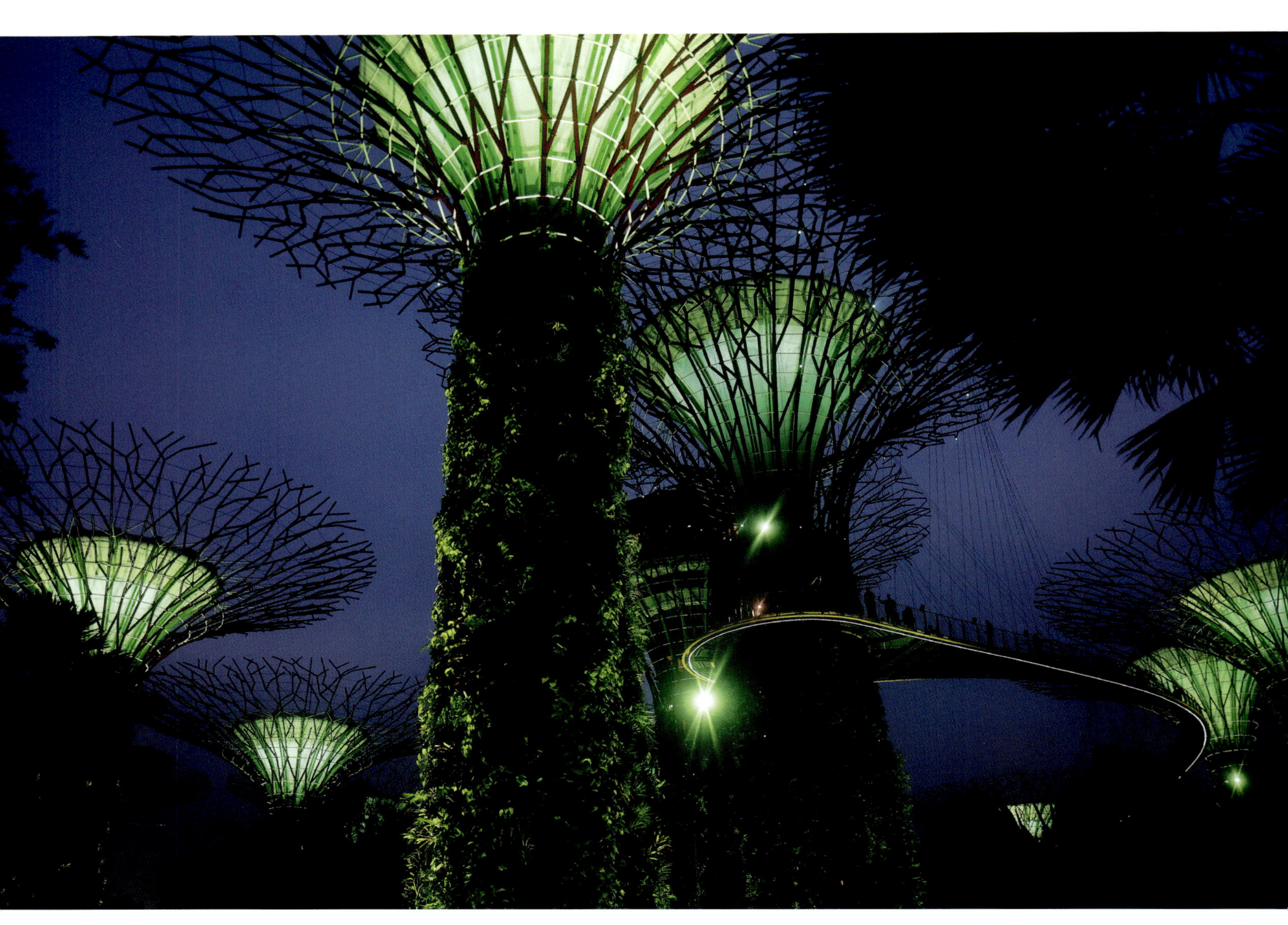

In 2023 the Earthshot Prize Awards took place in Singapore. On arrival in the country, the Prince was treated to a rockstar welcome at the HSBC Jewel Rain Vortex. The standout photograph for me that afternoon was of eight-month-old Albane Costa who grabbed the Prince's finger and refused to let go!

Opposite
On day two of the prince's visit to Singapore, the OCBC Skyway in the Gardens by the Bay was lit green in honour of the Earthshot Prize.

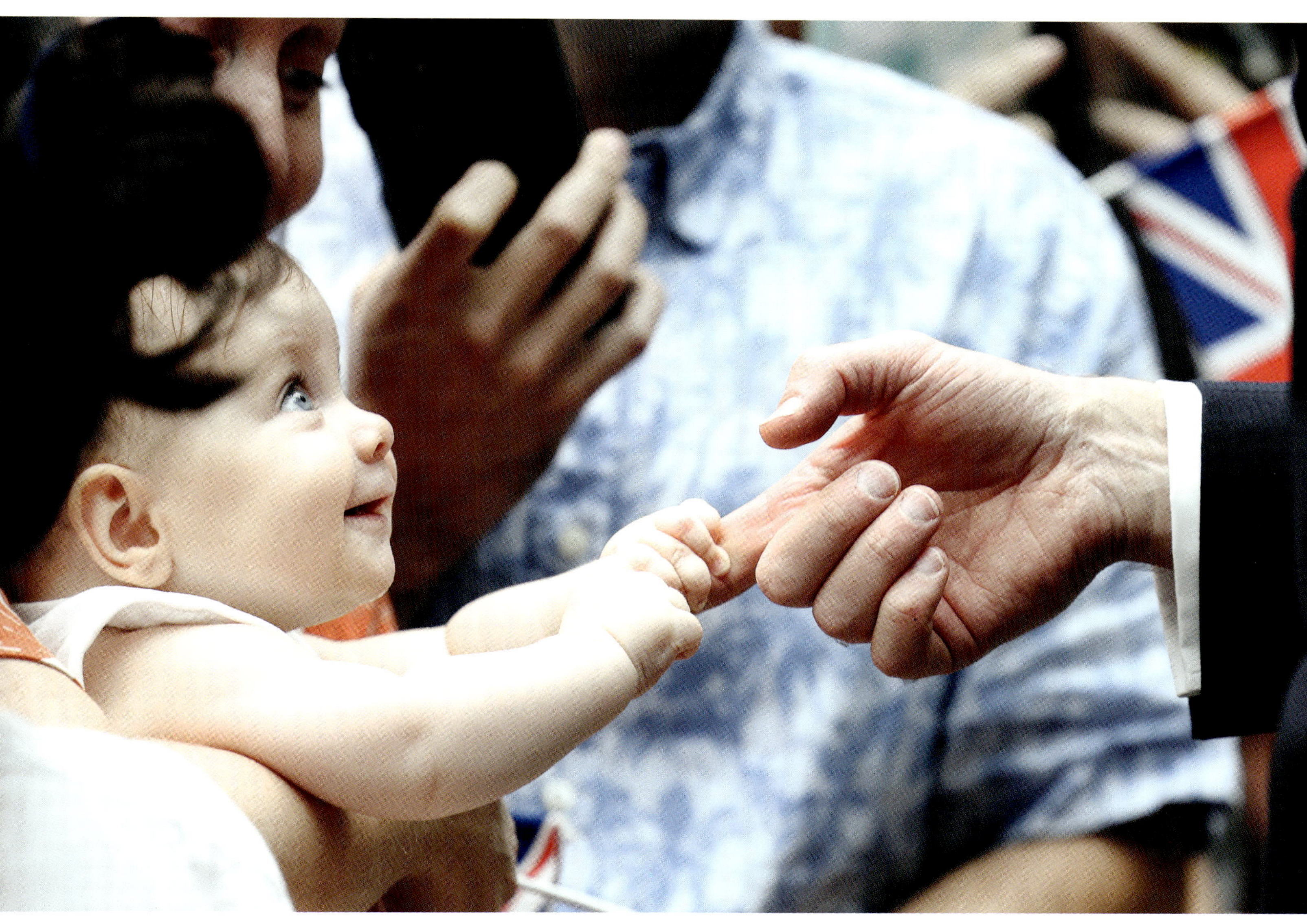

Overleaf
During his visit to Singapore for the Earthshot Prize, the Prince of Wales visited the spectacular TreeTop Walk, a 250-metre free-standing suspension bridge offering panoramic views of the forest canopy, in the MacRitchie Reservoir Park within the Central Catchment Nature Reserve.

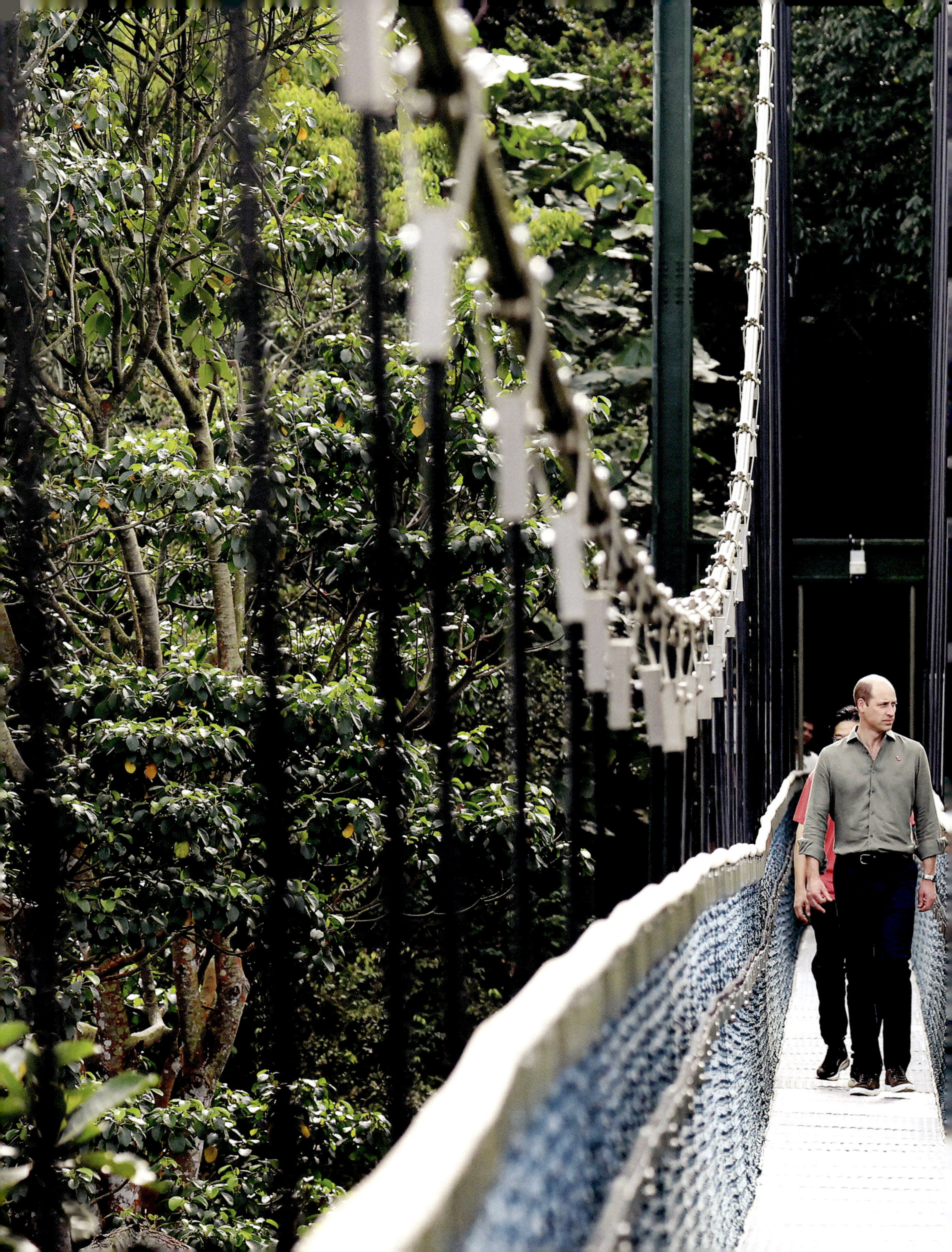

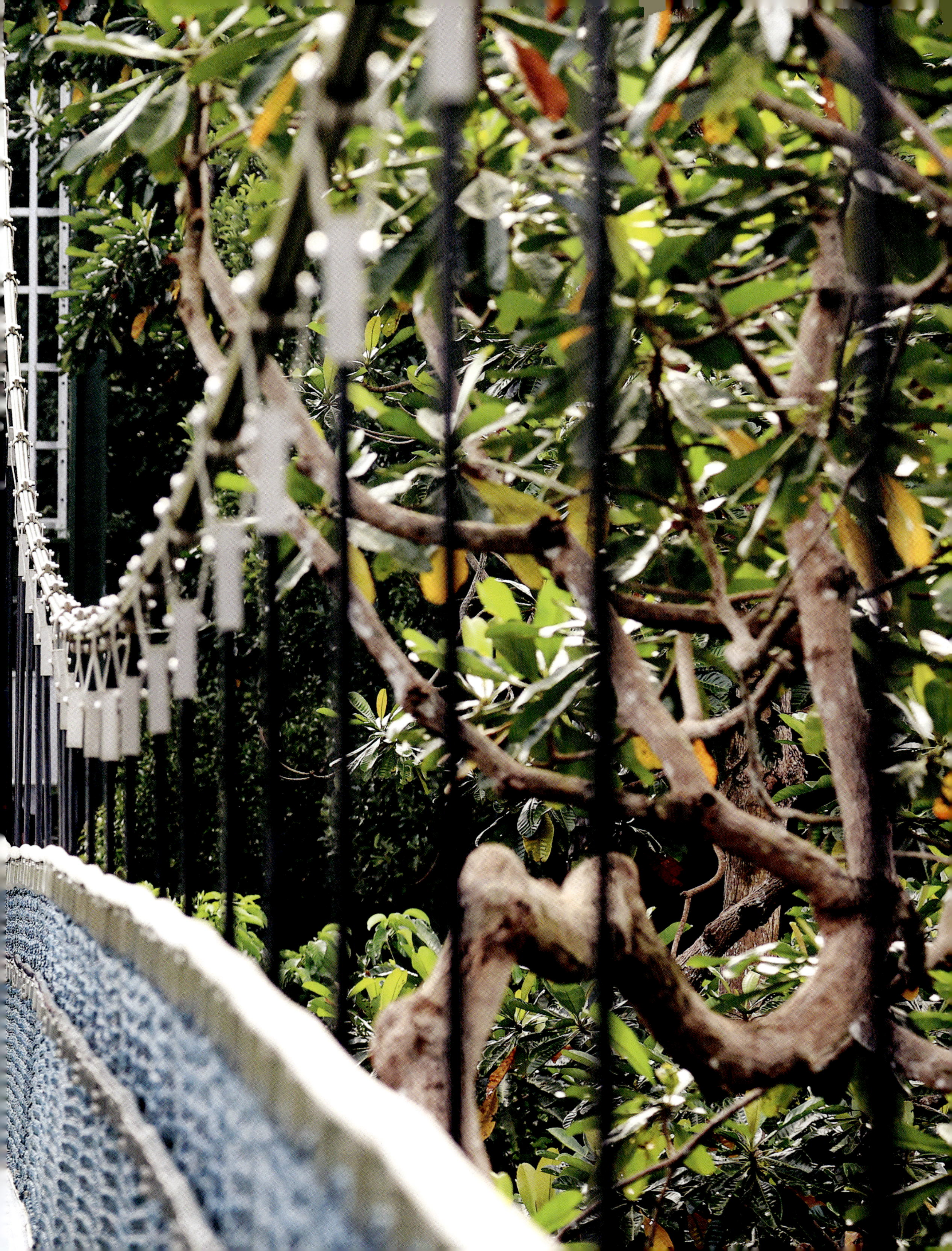

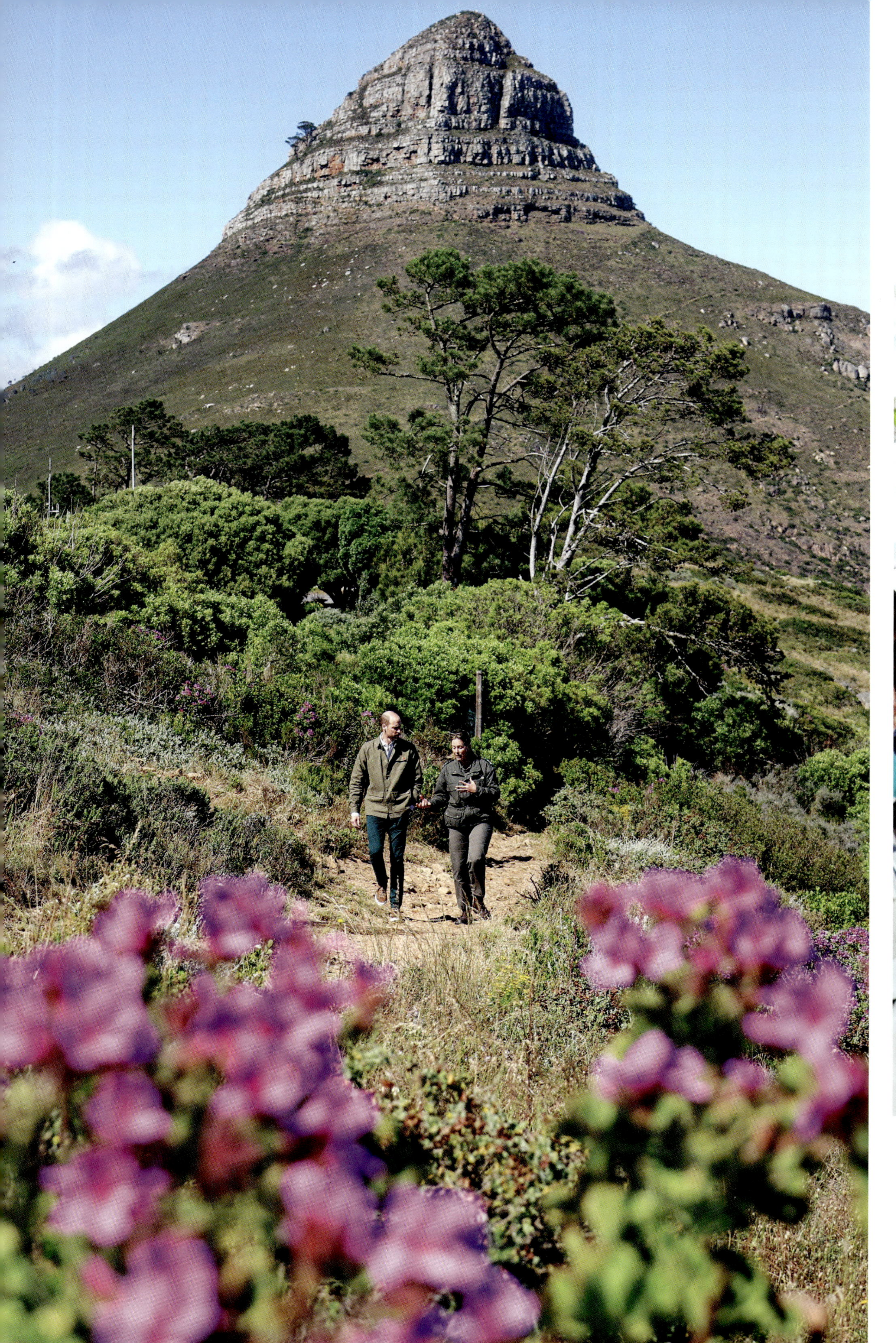

In November 2024 Prince William took the Earthshot Prize Awards to the stunning surroundings of South Africa. He walks with Megan Taplin, Park Manager for Table Mountain National Park, during a visit to Signal Hill within the park (left). On the first day of his visit the Prince takes a selfie with Earthshot ambassador Nomzamo Mbatha during the Earthshot Prize Climate Youth Programme – engaging young people in the fight to protect the environment is key.

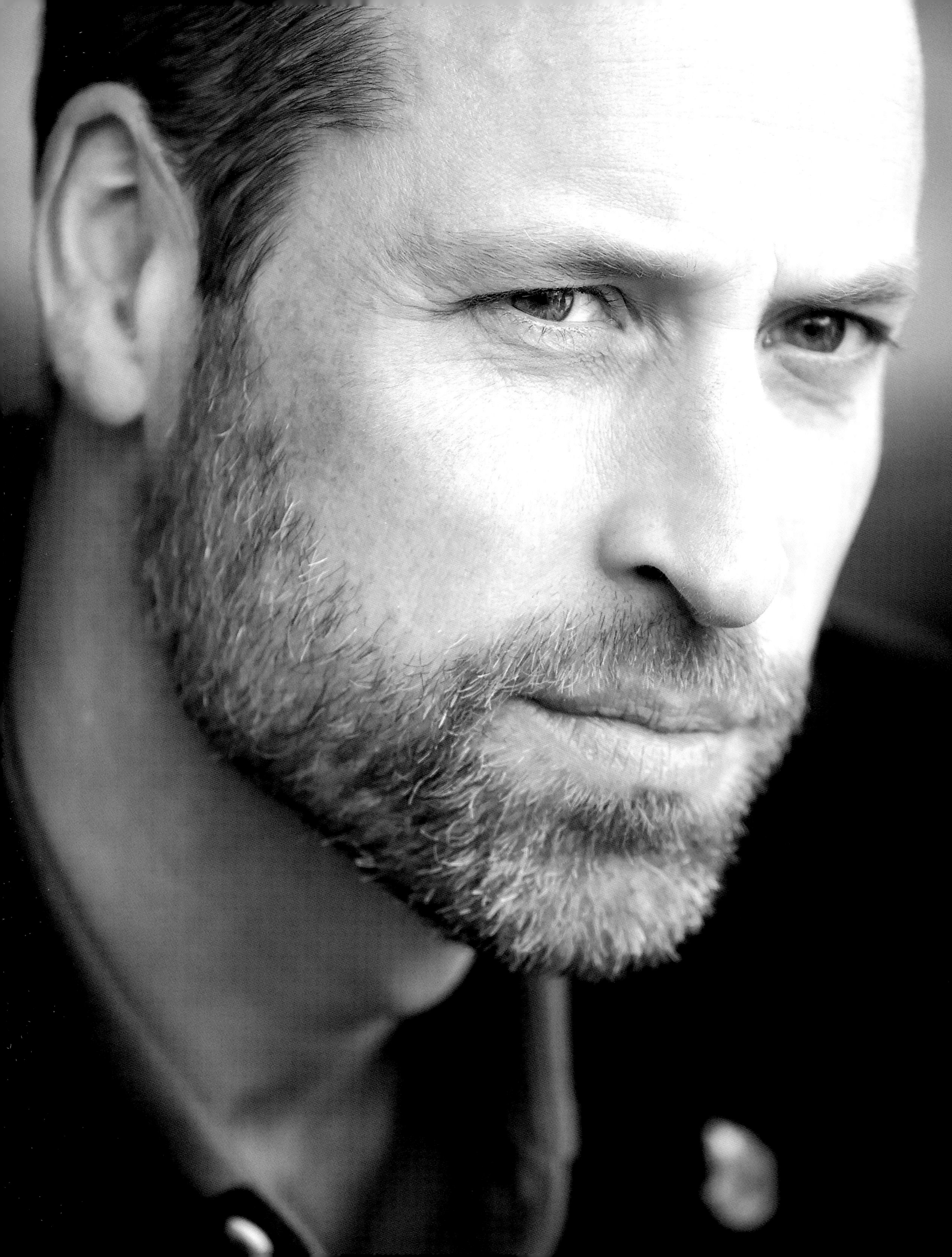

WILLIAM

FATHER, SON, AND FUTURE KING

Despite the trials of recent years, the British royal family has navigated challenges with aplomb and has shown an unswerving dedication to duty that stands them in good stead for whatever the future holds. As the future King, William has made it clear that he will embrace change, creating a modern monarchy and a world that he hopes his children will be proud of.

There is a palpable sense of optimism when the public sees the Wales children on royal engagements. They bring a curious and naïve enthusiasm with them that offers an antidote to the formality and seriousness of many events. Memories of Princess Charlotte chatting to a VE Day veteran or Prince Louis pretending to ride a motorbike on the balcony of Buckingham Palace always put a smile on my face as a photographer and remind me of the bright future we have to look forward to.

The strength of this royal institution lies in its power as a force for good and its critical role in supporting charitable organizations and the armed services. Its symbolic and constitutional role fosters national unity and maintains cultural tradition while promoting the United Kingdom internationally. As has been the case throughout history, modern majesty needs to tread a careful balance between providing a sense of stability and continuity and adopting a forward-thinking approach in contemporary times.

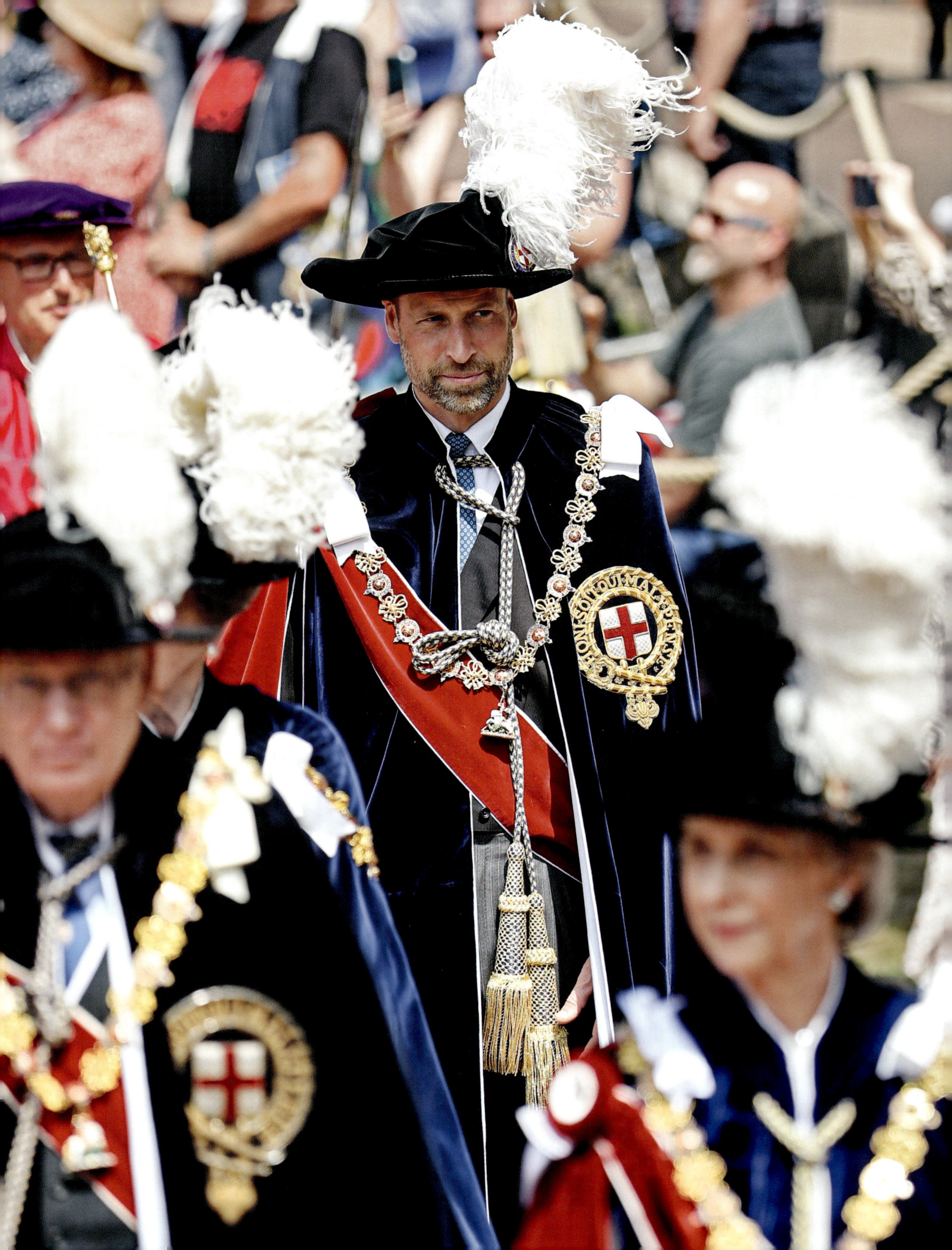
HONI SOIT QUI MAL Y PENSE

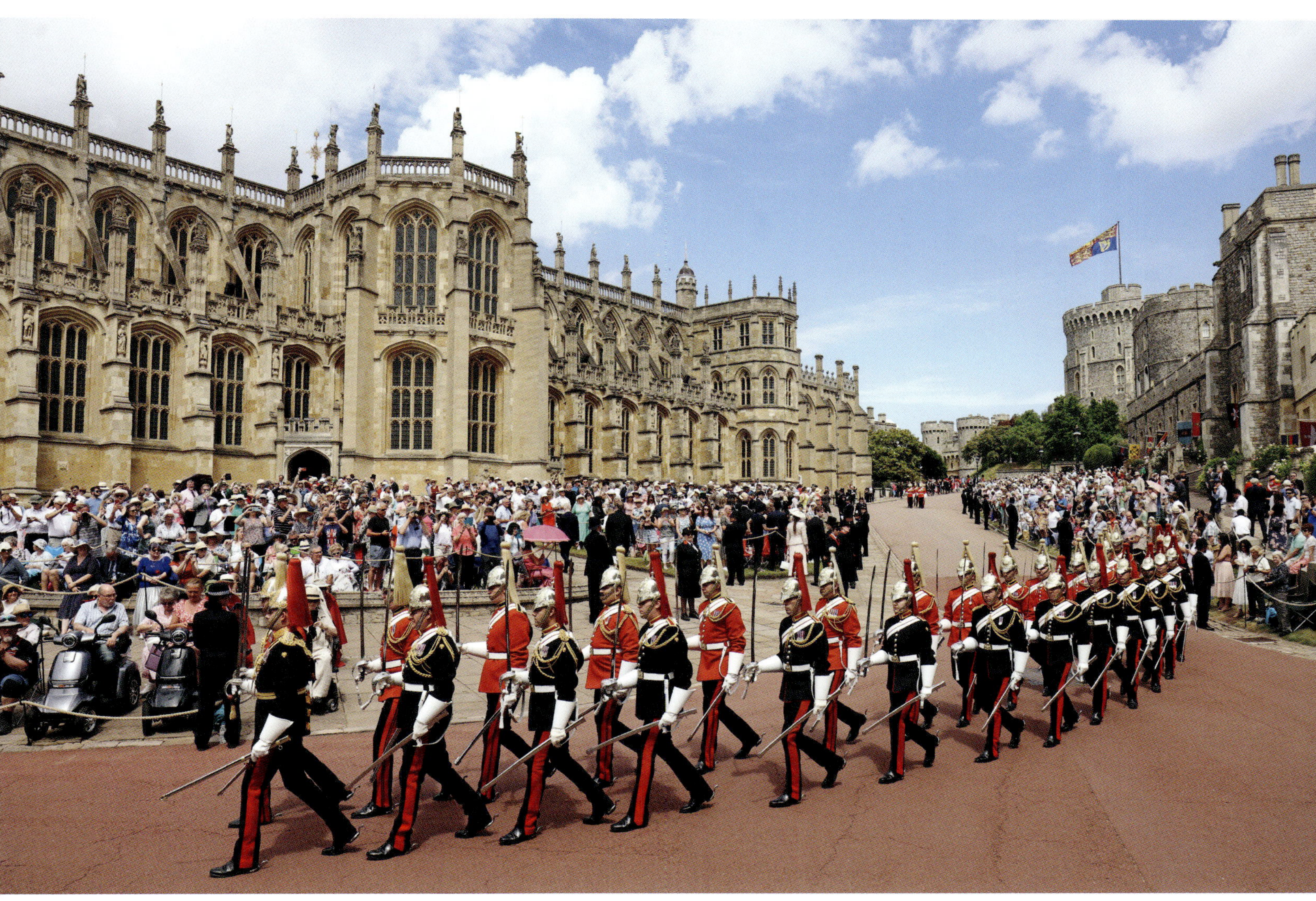

CEREMONIAL TRADITIONS

The Prince of Wales attends the Order of the Garter service at St. George's Chapel, Windsor Castle, 16 June 2025. The ceremonial robes include a dark-blue velvet mantle with the badge of Saint George on the shoulder and a black velvet hat with a white ostrich-feather plume. Companions of the Garter are chosen personally by the King to honour those who have held public office, contributed to national life, or served the sovereign personally.

TROOPING THE COLOUR

Held in June to celebrate the monarch's official birthday, Trooping the Colour is always a special day for me with the display of military pageantry by the Household Division with horses and bands. The pomp and the ceremony, the crowds and (hopefully) the sun make this the most impressive regular royal spectacle of the year. Opposite, William rides down the Mall in the traditional bearskin hat before joining his family on the balcony. The ceremony and the balcony never change, but the children do! In 2025 every time Prince Louis waves to the crowds huge cheers erupt, prompting big smiles from his family.

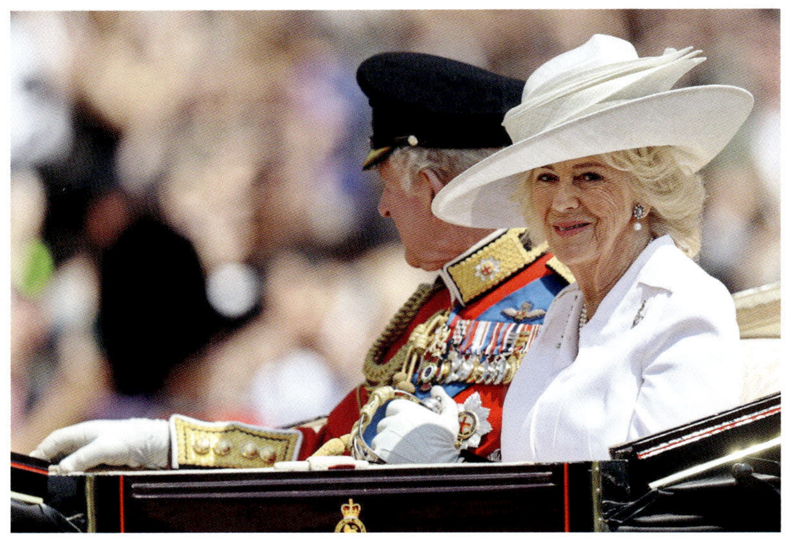

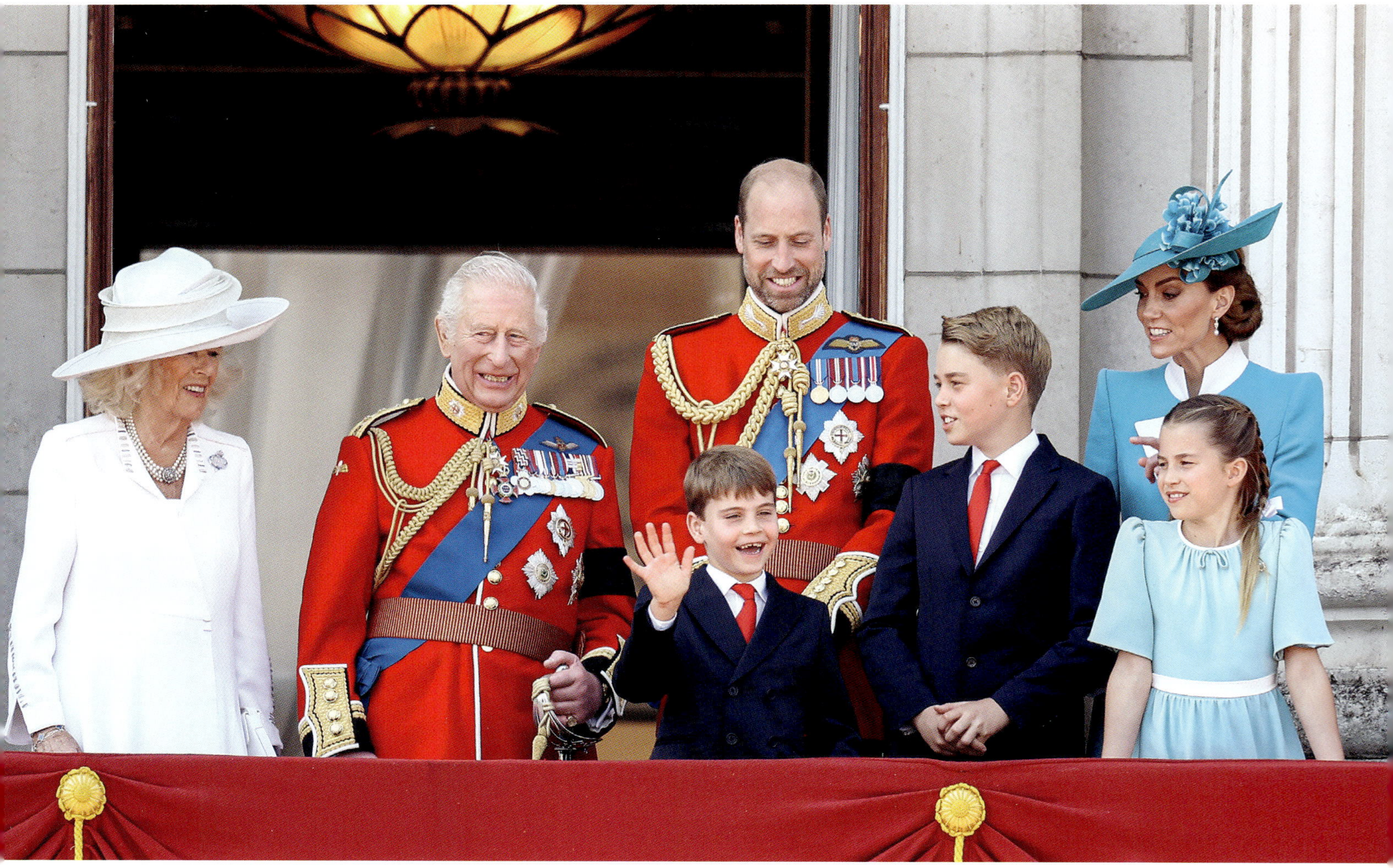

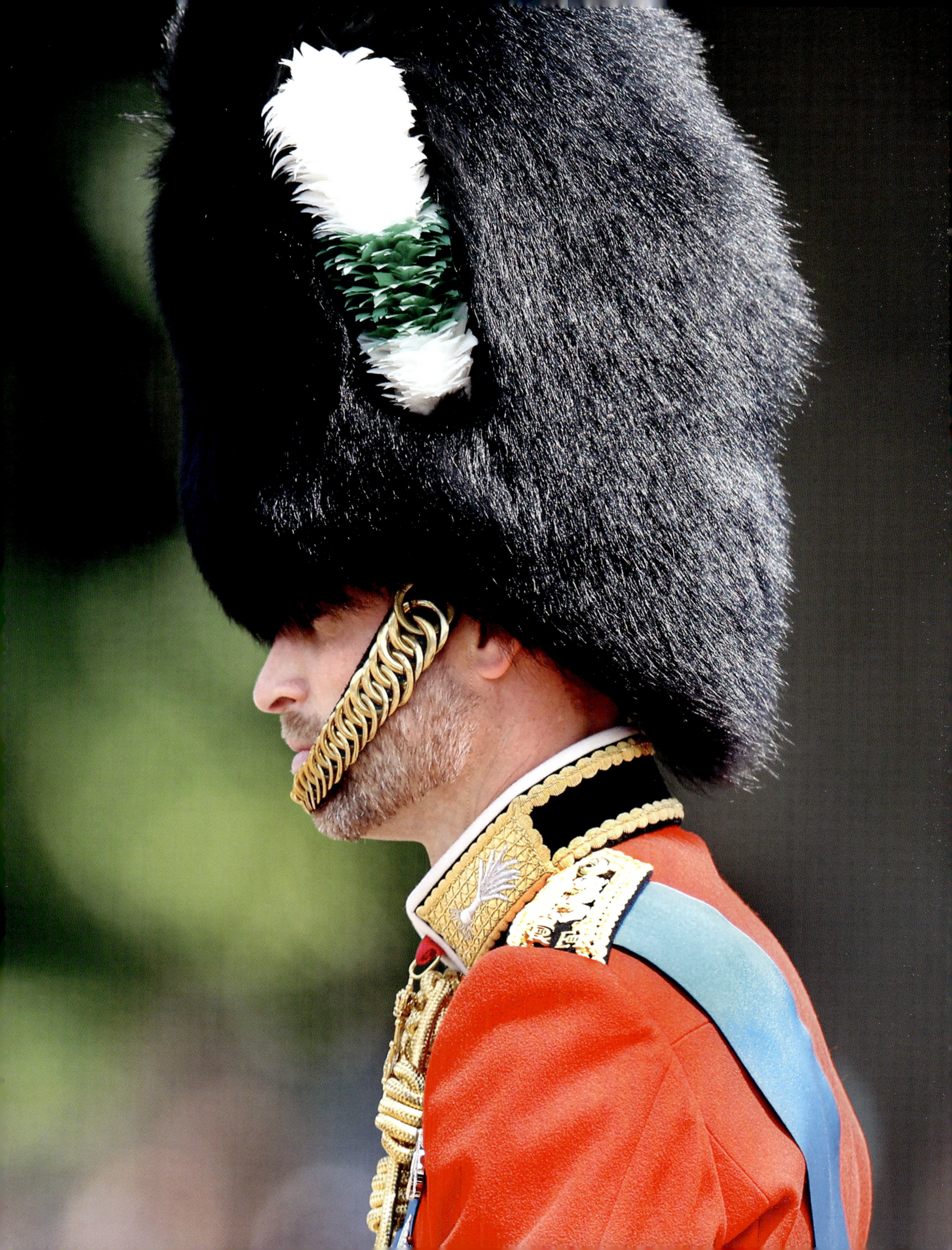

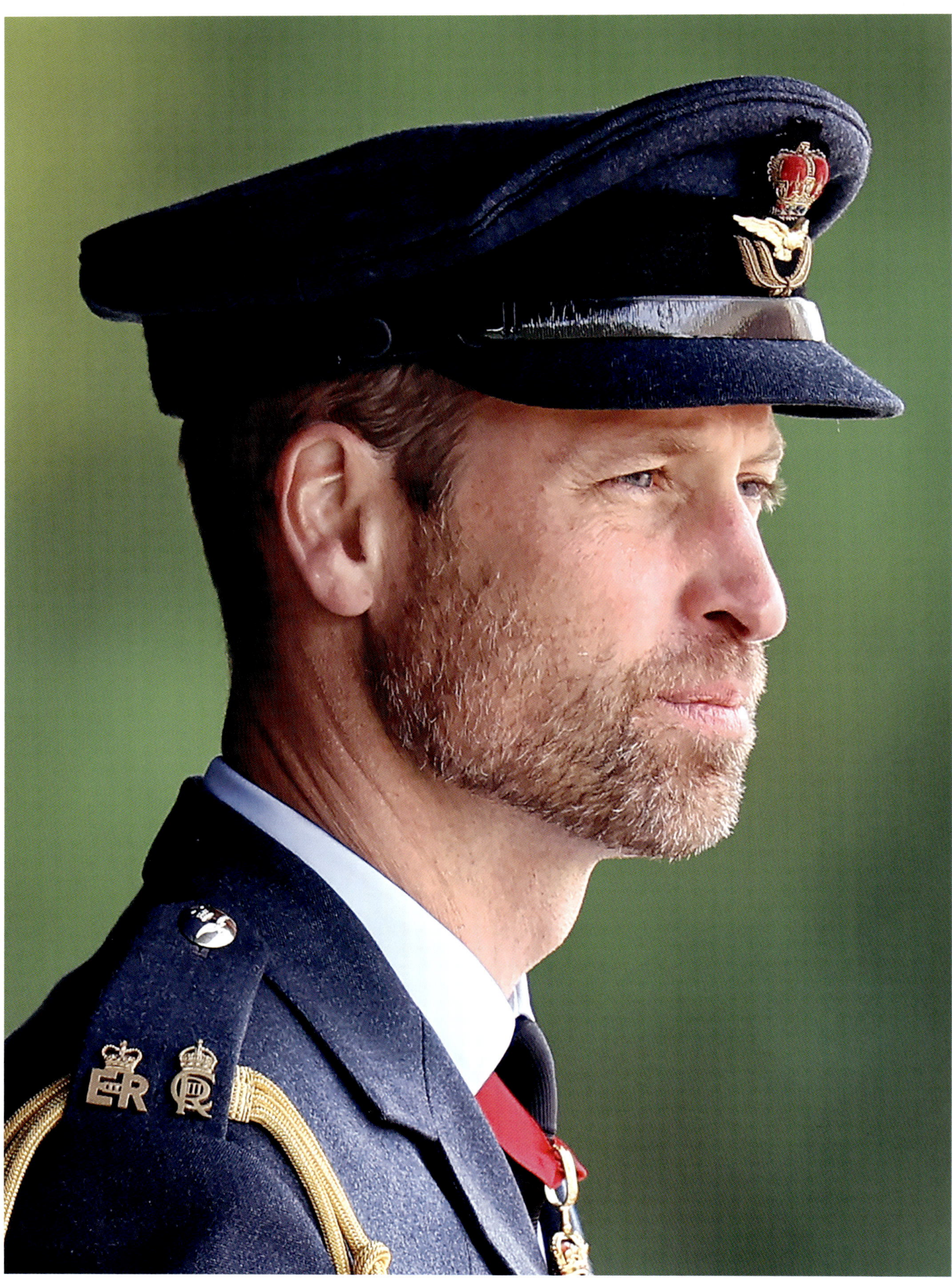
ER

MILITARY AFFILIATIONS

The Prince has a substantial military background, having served in the Household Cavalry, as an RAF search and rescue pilot, and as an air ambulance helicopter pilot. William is Colonel-in-Chief of the Army Air Corps and takes these military affiliations incredibly seriously. He looks on at the Sovereign's Parade at the Royal Air Force College in Cranwell, 12 September 2024 (opposite). Climbing through trenches with the sounds of flares and blank rounds going off, I had to sprint to get this particular photo (right). The Prince was in Estonia meeting the Mercian Regiment, which had been deployed to support NATO's eastern flank, 21 March 2025.

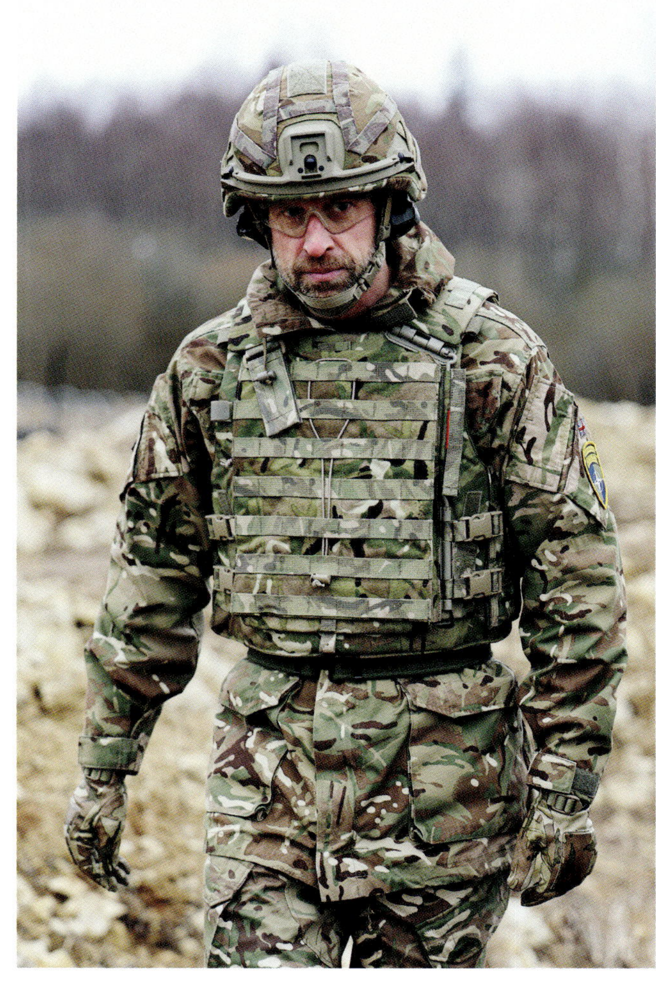

Below
Prince George presses a button to lower a rear ramp as he explores an RAF C-17 Globemaster III aircraft at the Royal Air Tattoo at RAF Fairford, 14 July 2023.

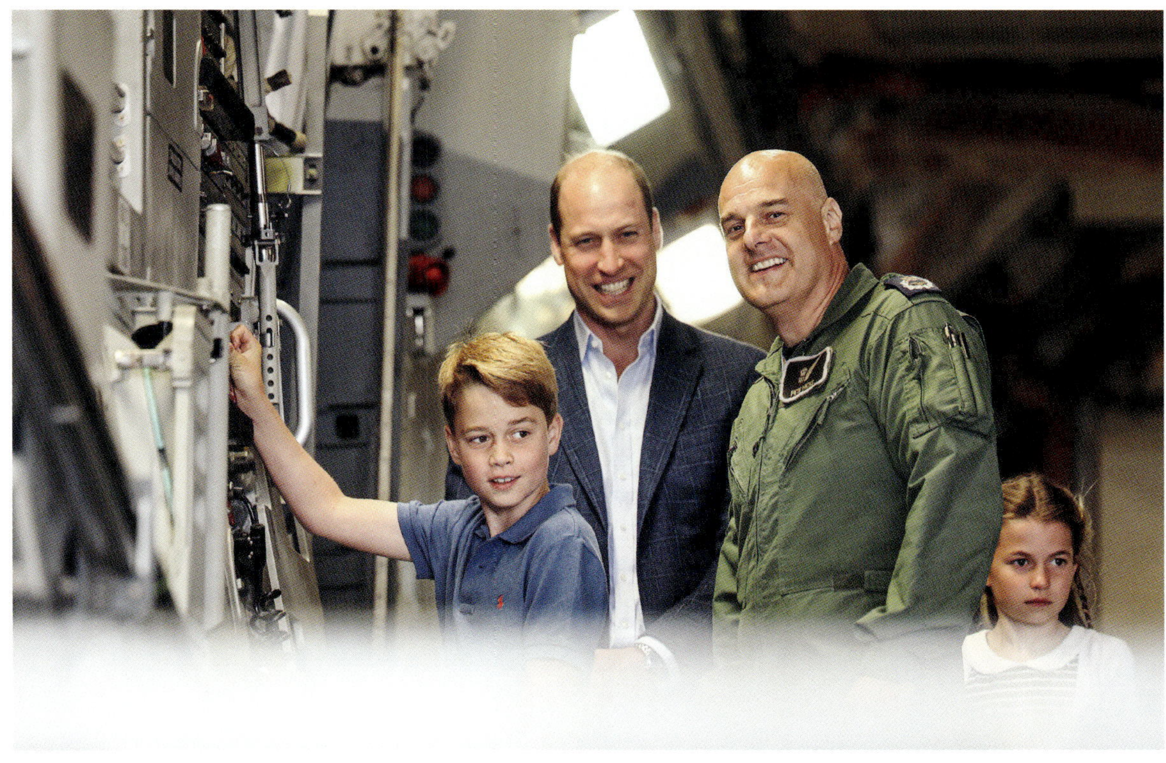

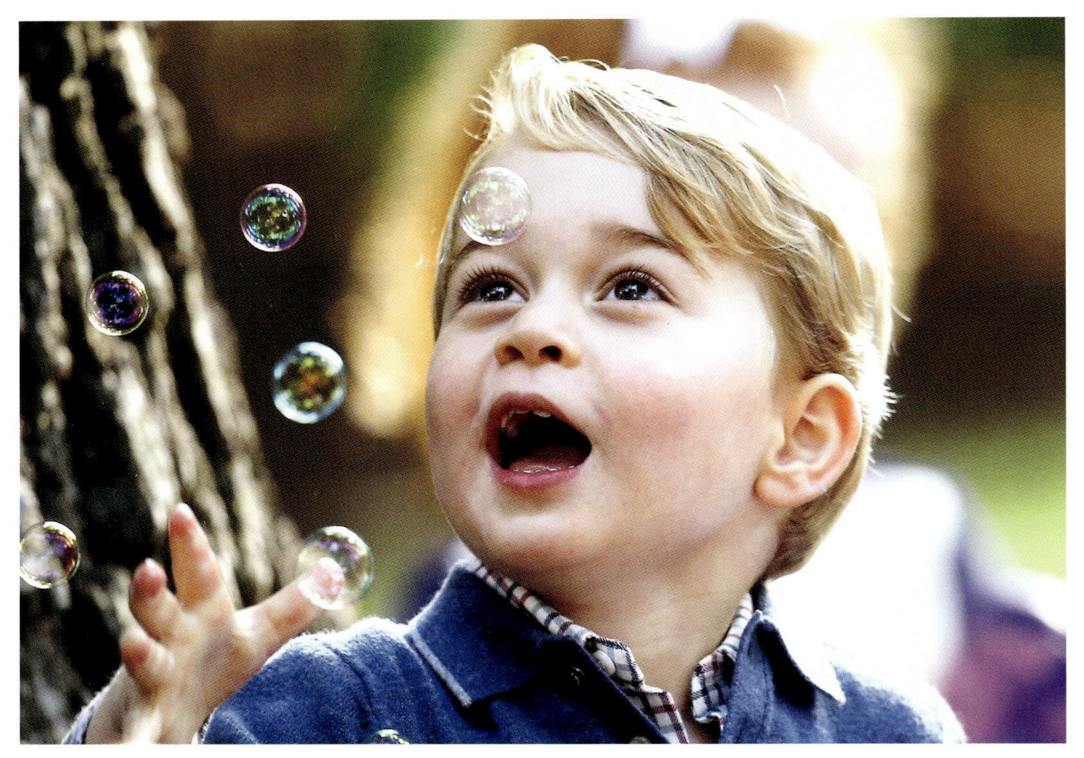

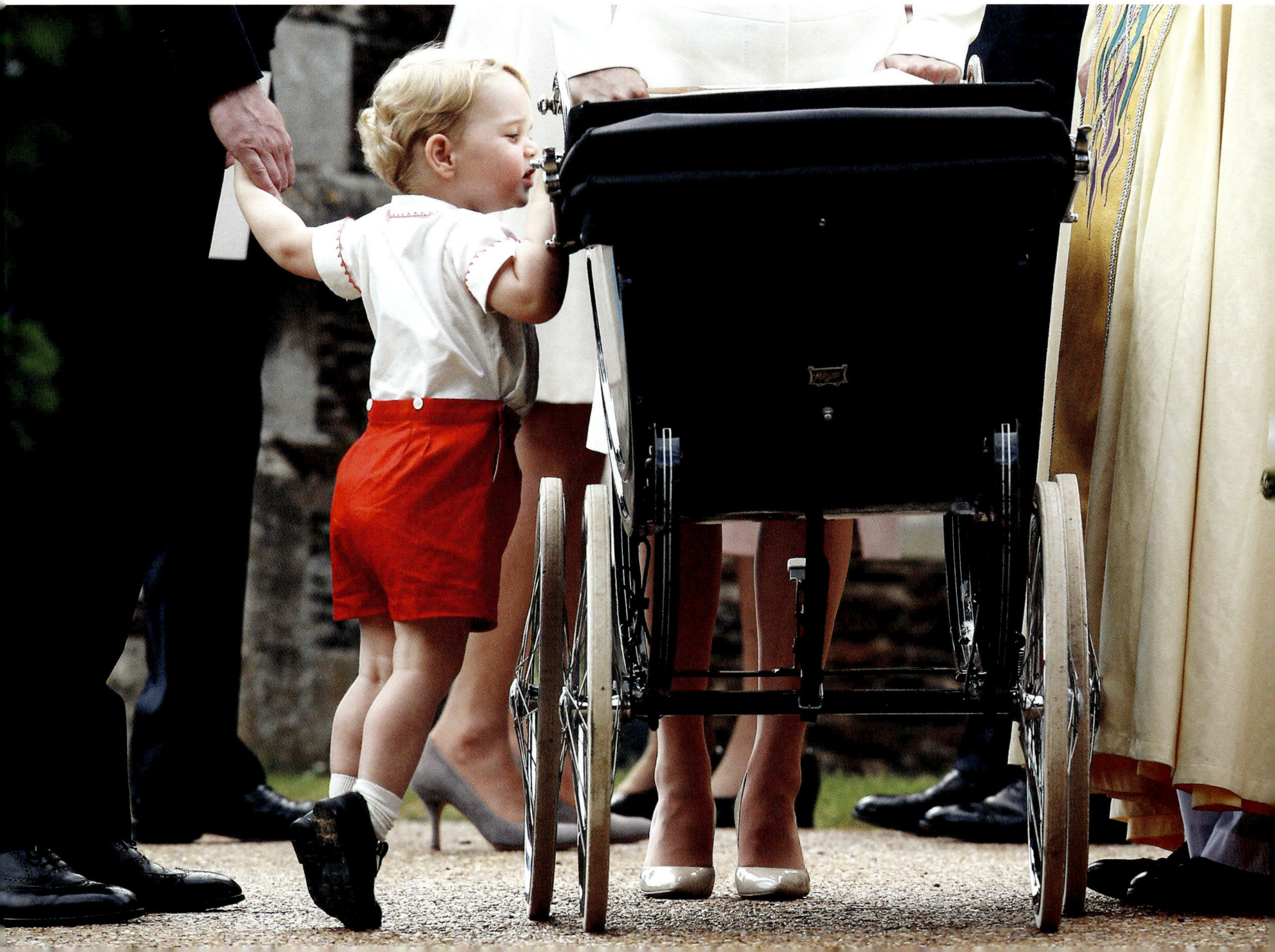

AS THE YEARS PASS

It has been a privilege to watch Prince George grow up from my vantage point behind the camera over the years, from the celebration of his birth at the Lindo Wing to witnessing his character develop over the course of so many royal events. One of my favourite moments was when his father blew bubbles for him. George's total focus and unguarded happiness really made me smile at this tea party for military families in Victoria, Canada, in September 2016 (opposite, above).

Opposite, below
A heartwarming moment as George stands on tiptoes to try to catch a glimpse of his little sister, Princess Charlotte, at her christening in Sandringham, 5 July 2015.

Below
A fun scene but with a deep historical significance as the Queen and the three heirs to the throne came together to mix Christmas pudding for the Royal British Legion's "Together at Christmas" initiative in December 2019.

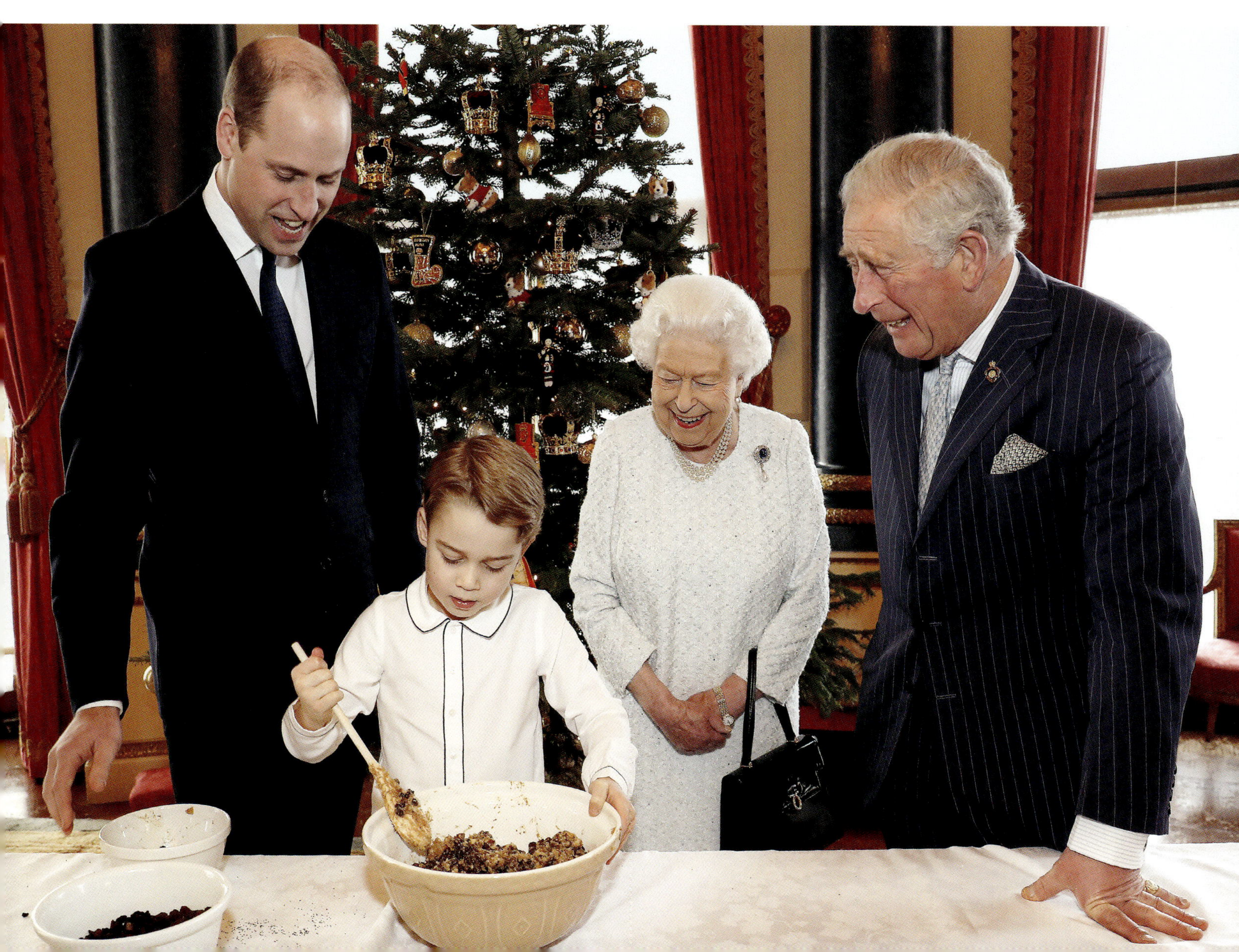

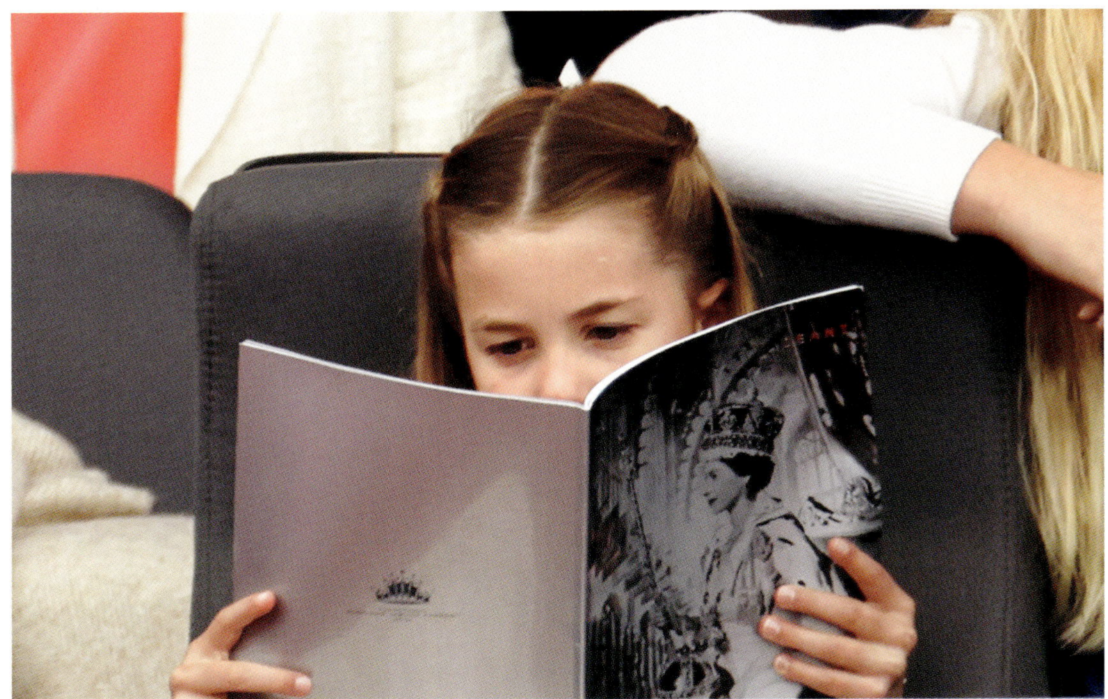

Princess Charlotte's appearance at royal engagements has increased in recent years. Seen at her mother's side at Wimbledon or chatting with veterans, her confidence and charm promise to make her a safe pair of royal hands in the future. Here she checks out the programme at Queen Elizabeth's Platinum Jubilee pageant (above) and fixes me with a sense of focus from the carriage during Trooping the Colour in 2024 (opposite).

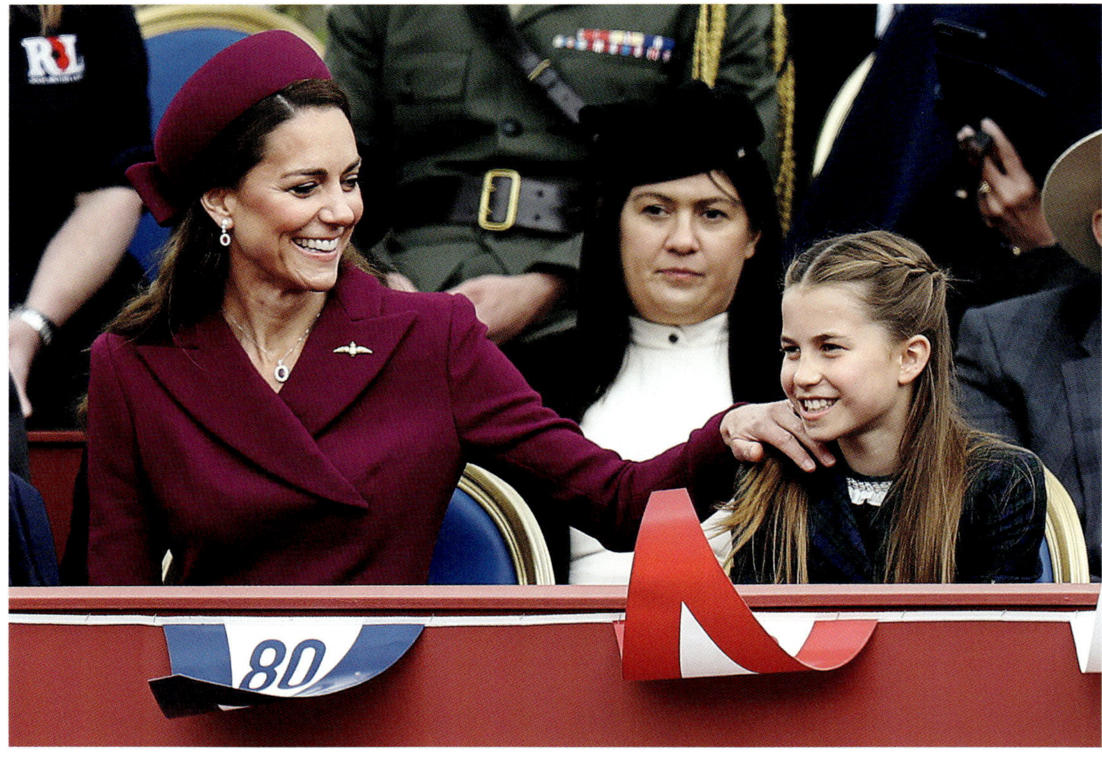

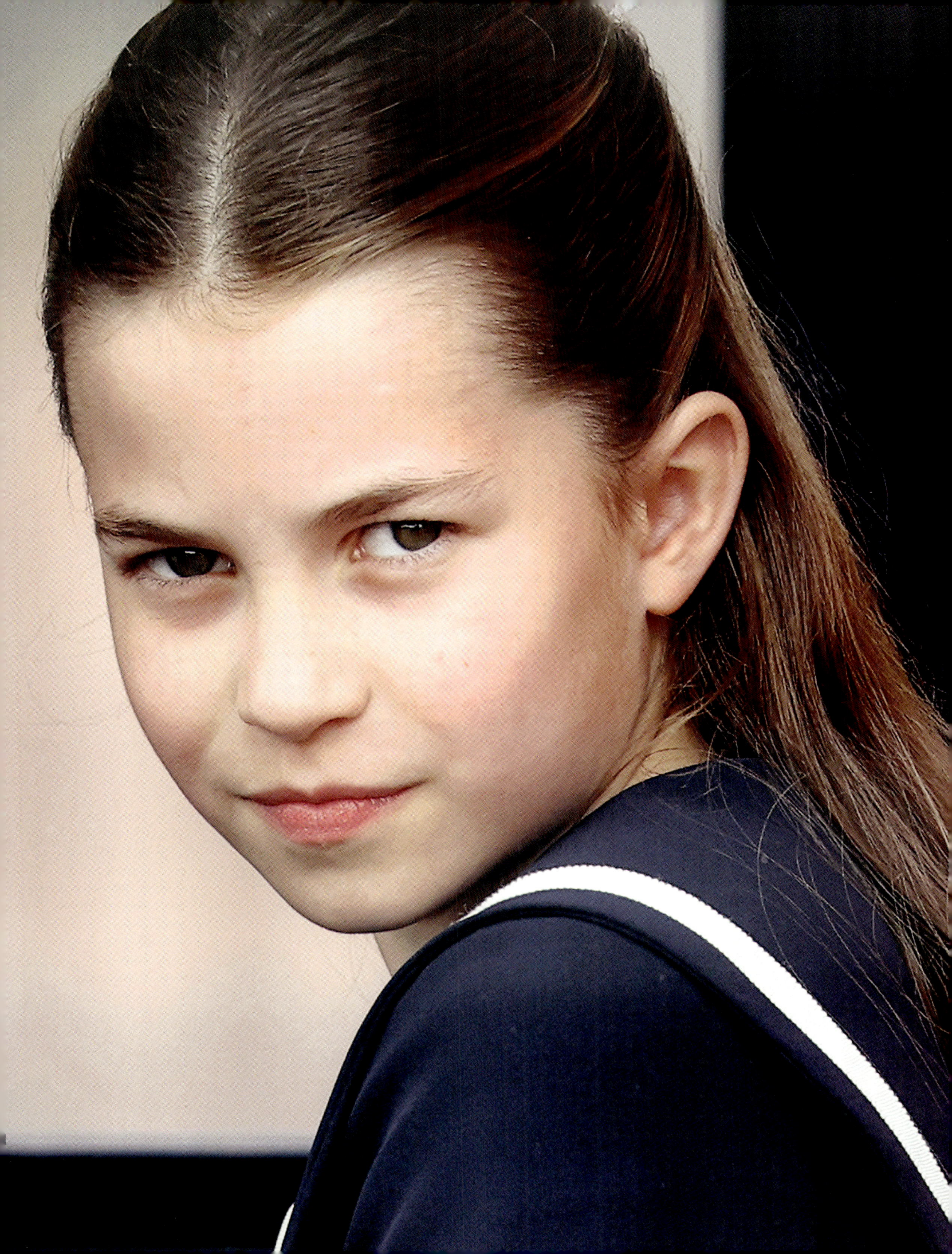

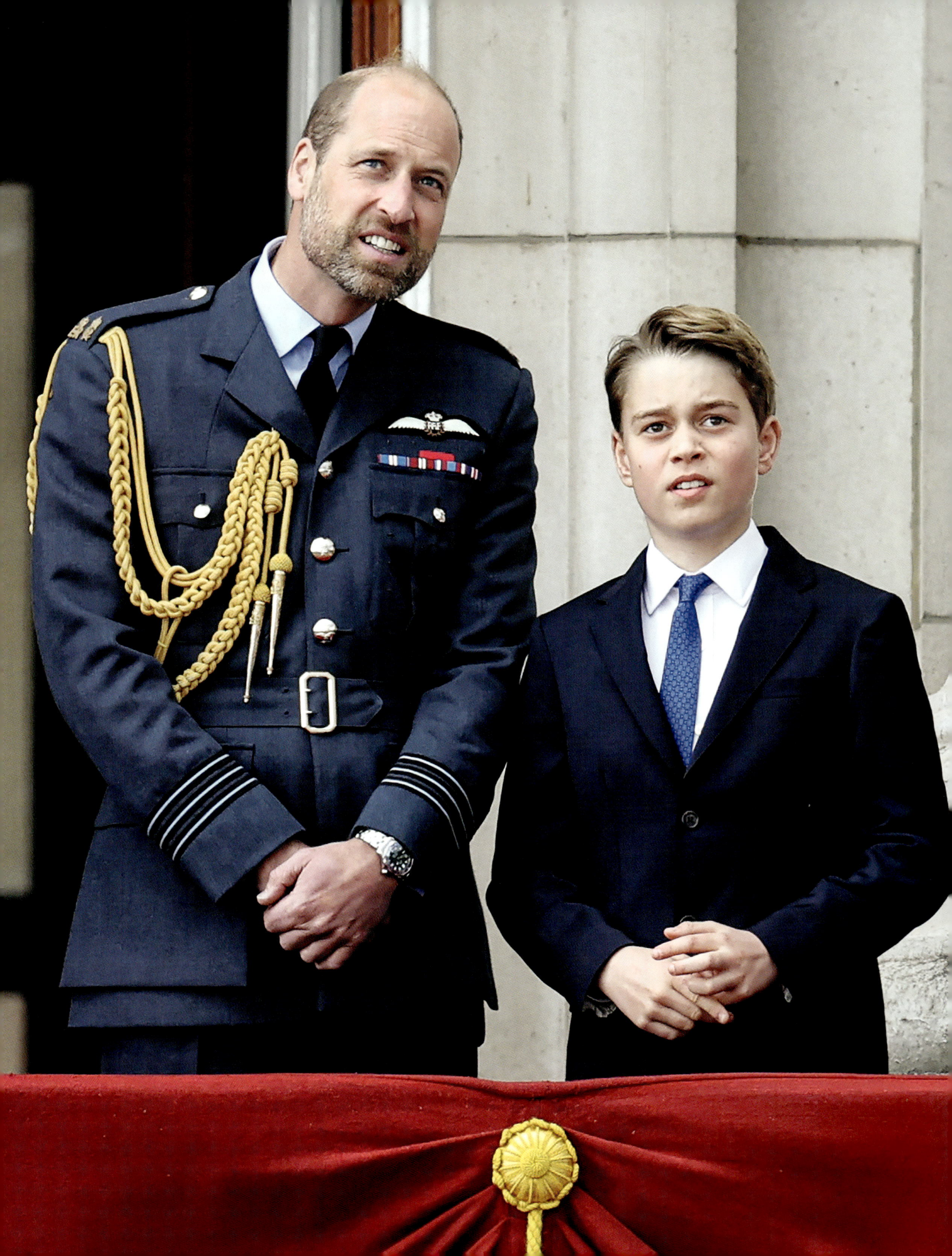

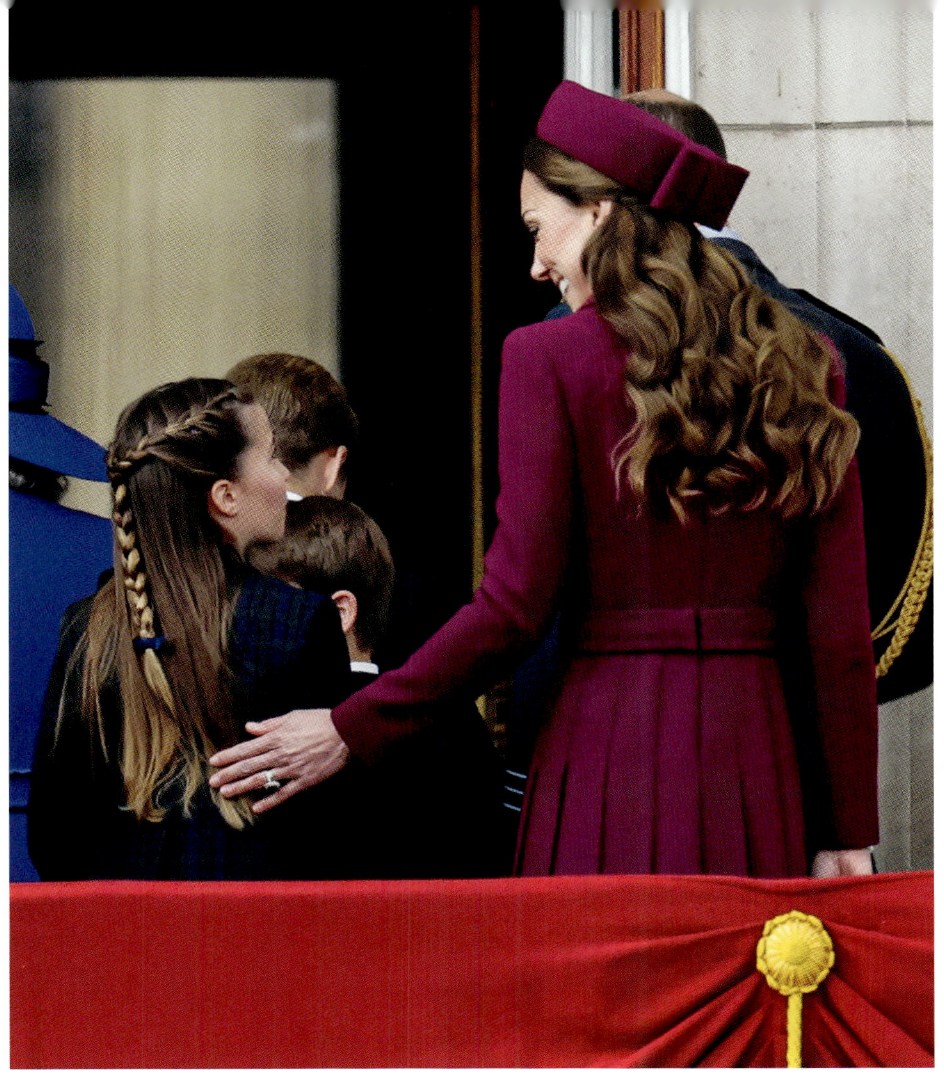

Opposite and above
The family watch the flypast to mark the 80th anniversary of VE day on 5 May 2025.

Below
Louis watches George during the VE Day parade in 2025. Seconds later Louis made an over-exaggerated sweeping back of his fringe.

Overleaf, left
Prince William adjusts his top hat at Royal Ascot in June 2025.

Overleaf, right
The Prince of Wales takes part in the Royal Charity Polo Cup in July 2025.

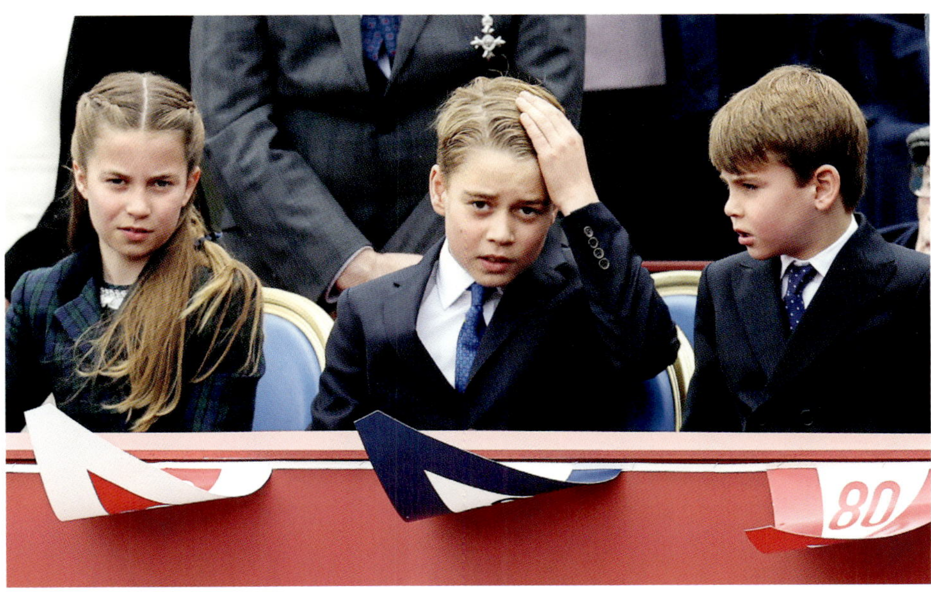

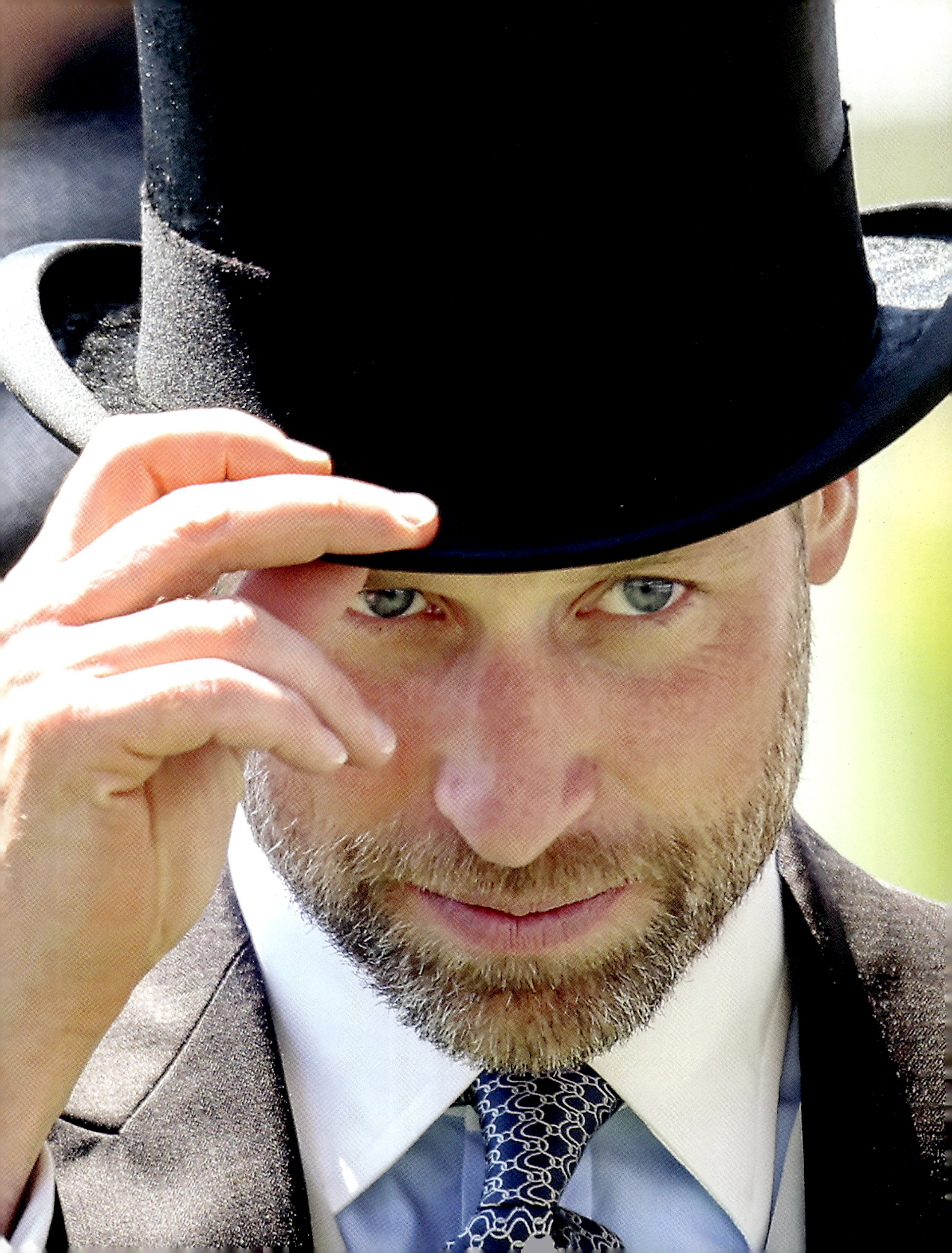

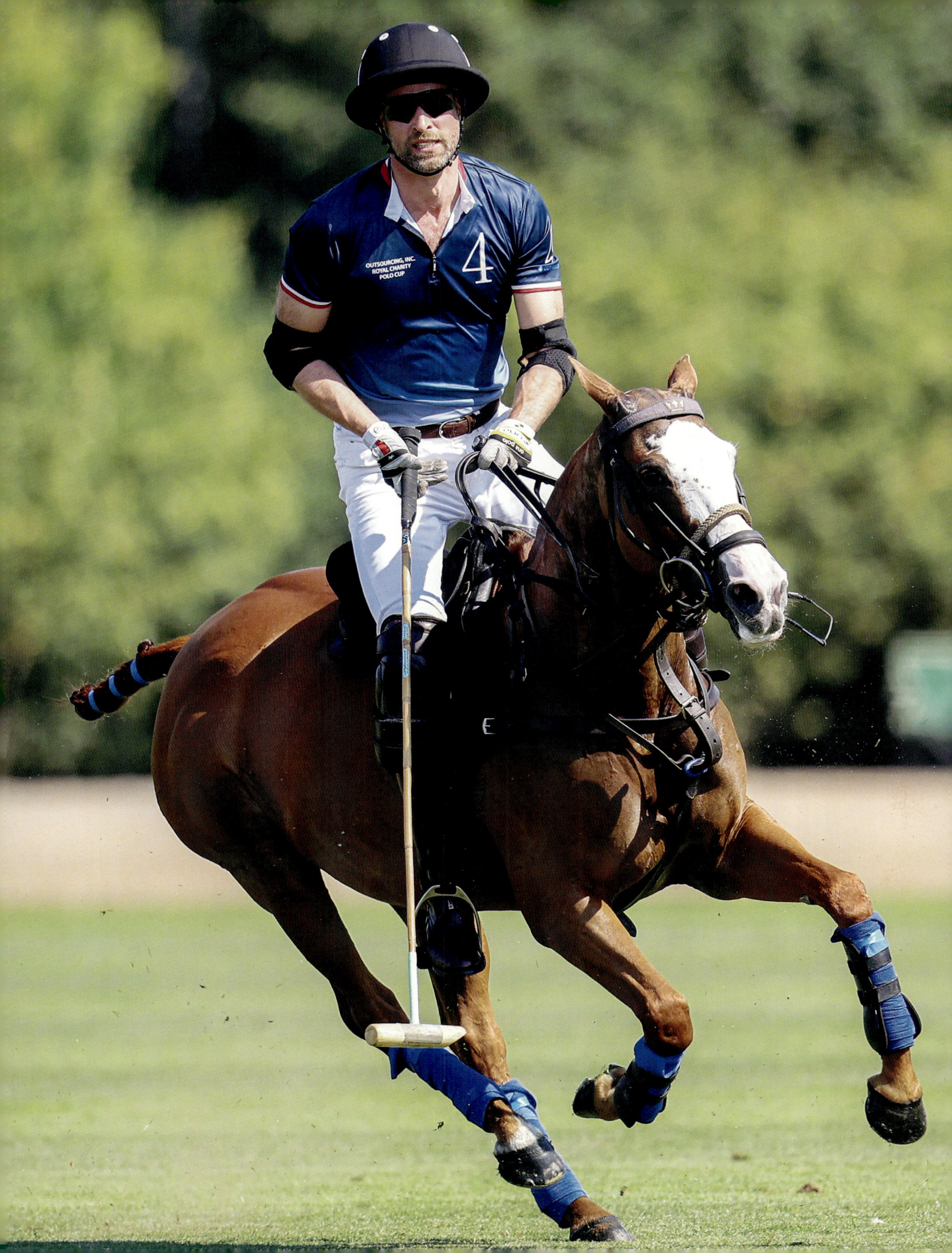
OUTSOURCING, INC.
ROYAL CHARITY
POLO CUP
4

The Duke and Duchess of Edinburgh and the Princess Royal are incredibly busy members of the royal family, completing hundreds of engagements around the world every year. It is always special to have the opportunity to photograph their appearances, whether it is teaming up with the Prince of Wales at the Royal Cornwall Show in June 2025 (below left), or promoting "field to bowl" initiatives in Bedford, 14 June 2024 (below).

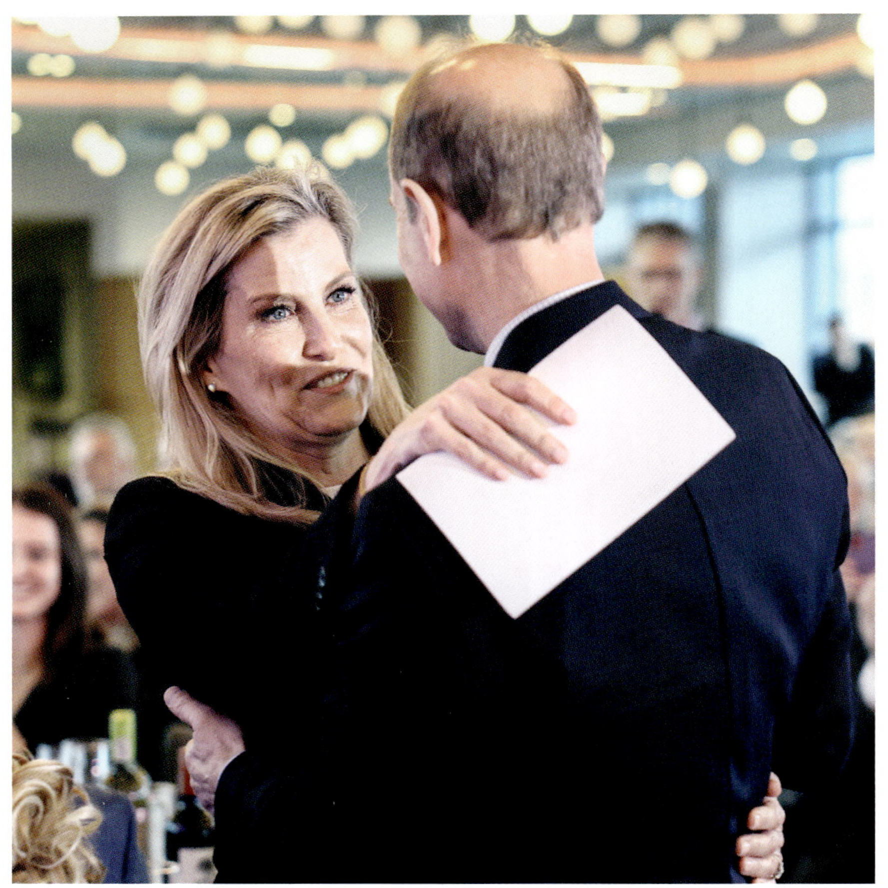

Left
Sophie pays tribute to Prince Edward on his 60th birthday during the Community Sport and Recreation Awards at Headingley Stadium in Leeds, 8 March 2024. Edward was visibly moved as Sophie praised his skills as a father and husband: "the best of fathers, the most loving of husbands and still ... my best friend."

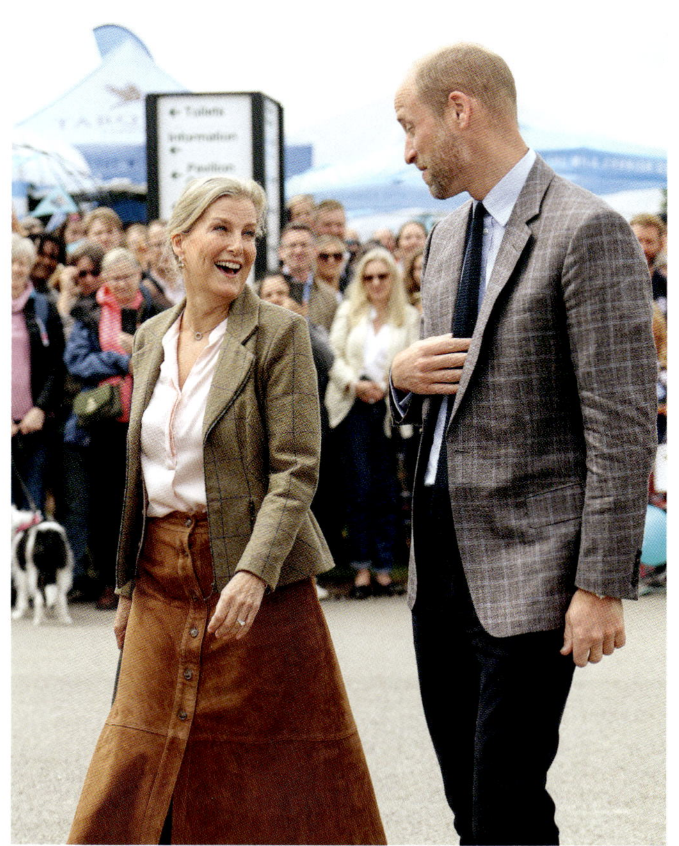

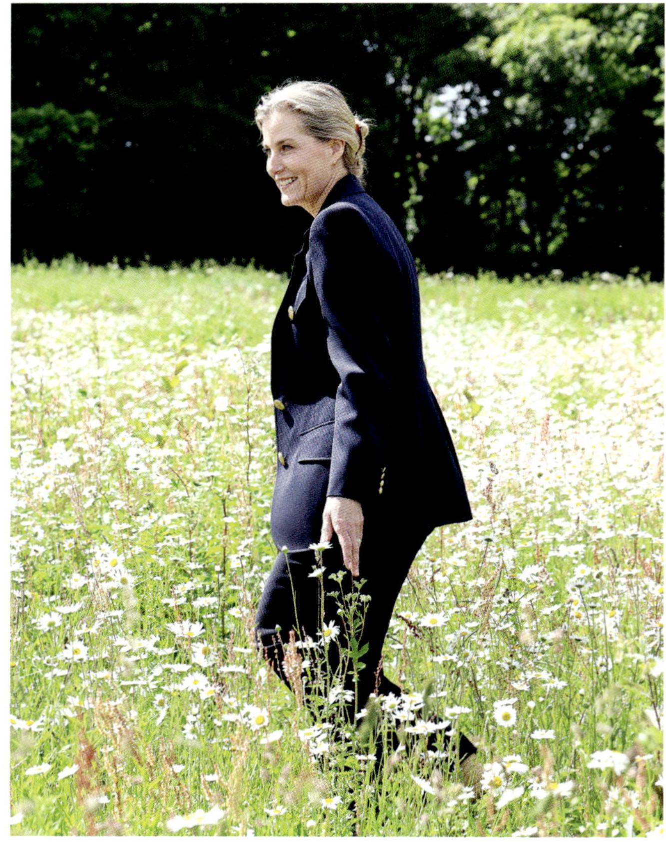

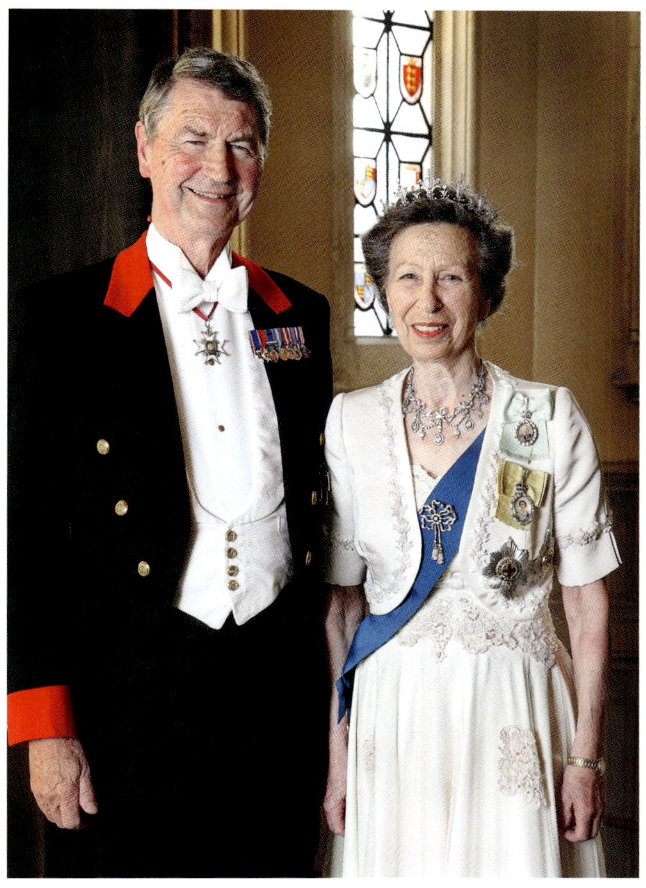

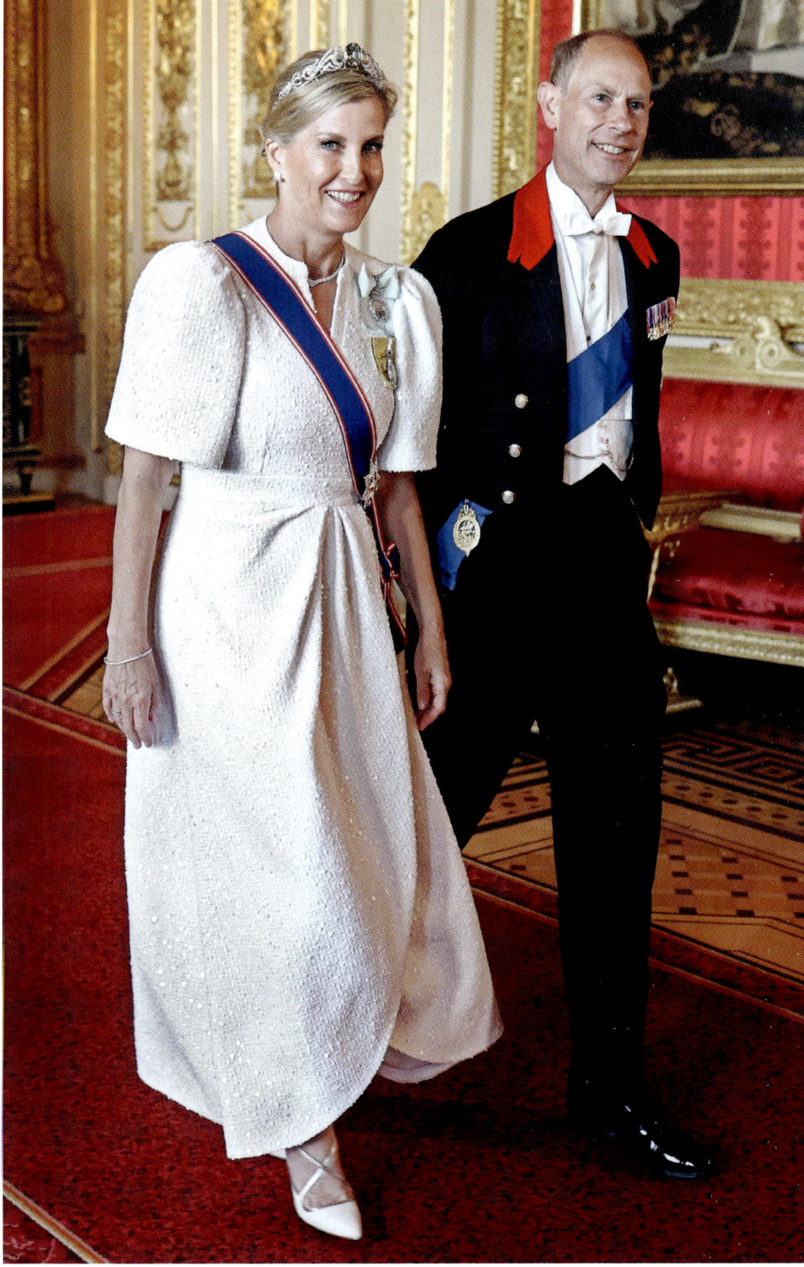

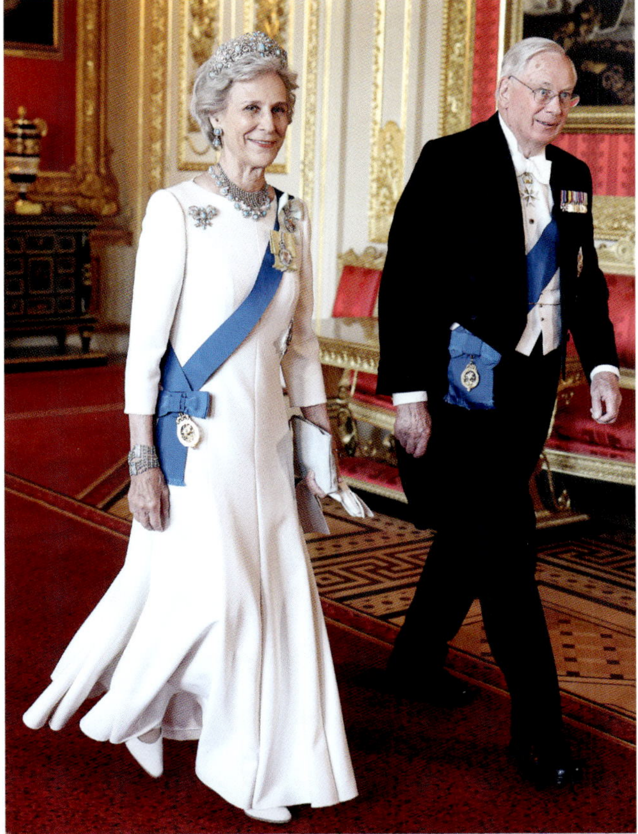

Working members of the royal family, including the Princess Royal and Vice-Admiral Sir Timothy Laurence, the Duke and Duchess of Edinburgh, and the Duke and Duchess of Gloucestershire, attend the State Banquet at Windsor Castle, 8 July 2025.

Overleaf
The Prince and Princess of Wales process through Windsor Castle to the State Banquet during the French State Visit of President Macron in 2025. The Princess wears the Lover's Knot Tiara and a red silk evening gown by Sarah Burton at Givenchy.

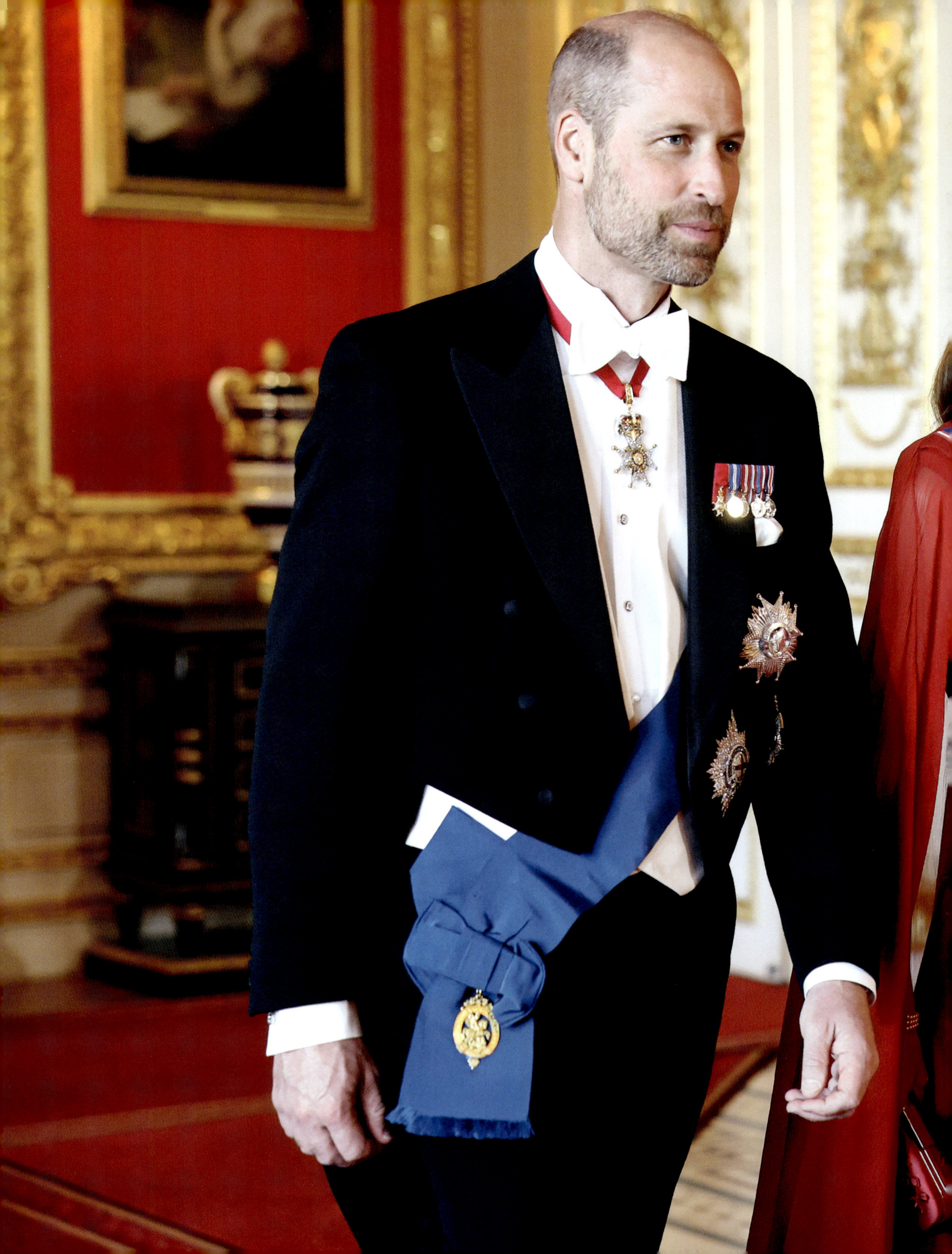

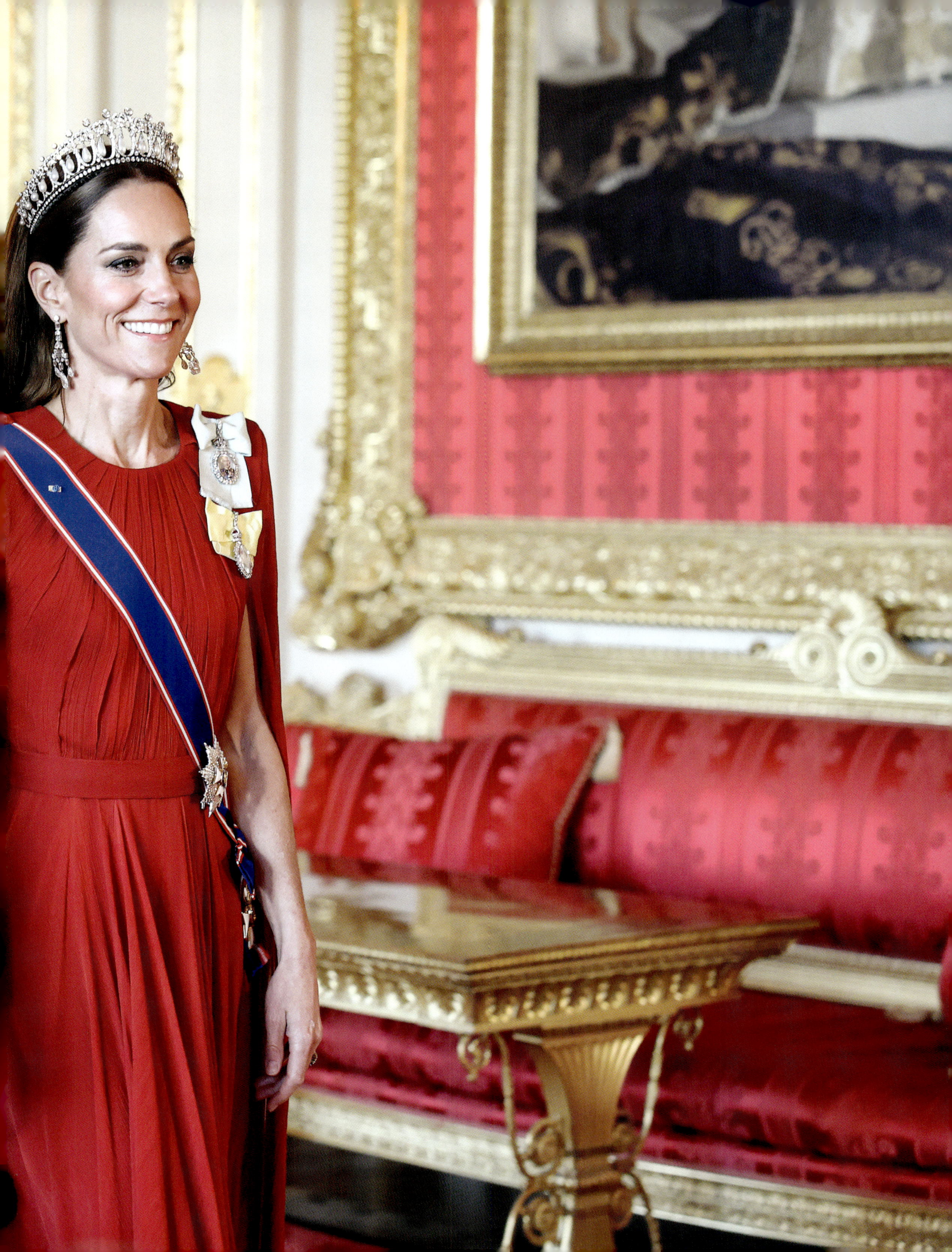

ACKNOWLEDGEMENTS

This book documents a period of choppy water for the British royal family, with serious health issues proving a challenge when the public takes such comfort from regularly seeing senior members at engagements. Yet looking through the images in this book and reflecting on how the family has supported each other and bounced back from these trying times demonstrates the strength and resilience that lie at the core of this institution. If there is one key take-away from these 240 pages, it should be the looks on the faces of the members of the public around the world who meet the royal family.

It is always a huge joy to put together these books, and a welcome opportunity to look back on past adventures and touching moments, to recollect stories made and people met, but they are very much a team effort. First and foremost a huge thanks to Ray Watkins, whose incredible eye and insight across all of my books has been a blessing. The guiding hand and boundless enthusiasm of my editor Giulia Di Filippo and her colleague Charles Miers at Rizzoli have been invaluable. Catherine Hooper has done an excellent job of fine-tuning the words and stories despite my occasional "writer's block"! A huge thanks also to the talented Sophie Liardet for the future publicity we will hopefully get!

To all the staff at Buckingham Palace and Clarence House, and specifically to Tobyn Andreae, Laura Foster, Amanda Foster, Aaminah Akram, Alex Slaine, and Alex Laidlaw, thank you for taking the time to reply to my many emails and questions, and for working with me over the years. At Kensington Palace, I'm grateful to Lee Thomson, Edwina Iddles, and Rhea Vernon for their help. Also, a big shout out to all the past staff at both palaces who were there for so many adventures over the years – you know who you are!

I'm eternally appreciative of working with such a special team at Getty Images, where I've been for over 23 years – less a company and more a family. Huge thanks to Lisa Marie Rae for her continued support and guidance, to Vicky Dearman, Rebekah Seymour, Kirstin Benson, Ken Mainardis, and, of course, Craig Peters. Thank you to the editing team I work with on a daily basis headed by Simone Brown: Brian Dayle, Jamie Adamson, Thomas Kronsteiner, Philip Schulte, and Simon Robling. I'm grateful for the opportunity to tell my stories in these books and to share them with the world.

To the people featured across these pages, thank you for the opportunities I've been given over the years to try and make the best and most honest images of the moments we've been in. Specifically for this book, a huge thanks to Their Majesties King Charles III and Queen Camilla for their kind permission to use some unseen pictures and for having such a great sense of humour over the many years I've spent popping up behind my camera with various requests!

A very important thanks goes to my family and friends for their support during the period of putting this book together: Dr Richard and Anna Hughes, Zafar and Natalie Rushdie, Ben Hollingdale, Mark Hopkins, Nick and Charlotte Monahan, Emily Nash, Roya Nikkhah, Sarah Hewson, Mandy Tucker, Tiff and Ed Dawson, George and Beth Stoy, my brother Alex and his wife Millie, as well as my other siblings Andrew and Abi, and of course my parents Sue and Nick.

This book is dedicated to the two people who make me smile every day: Theo and Otto

A fun moment as children await the arrival of the Prince William and Princess Catherine during a visit to Manchester, 14 October 2016.

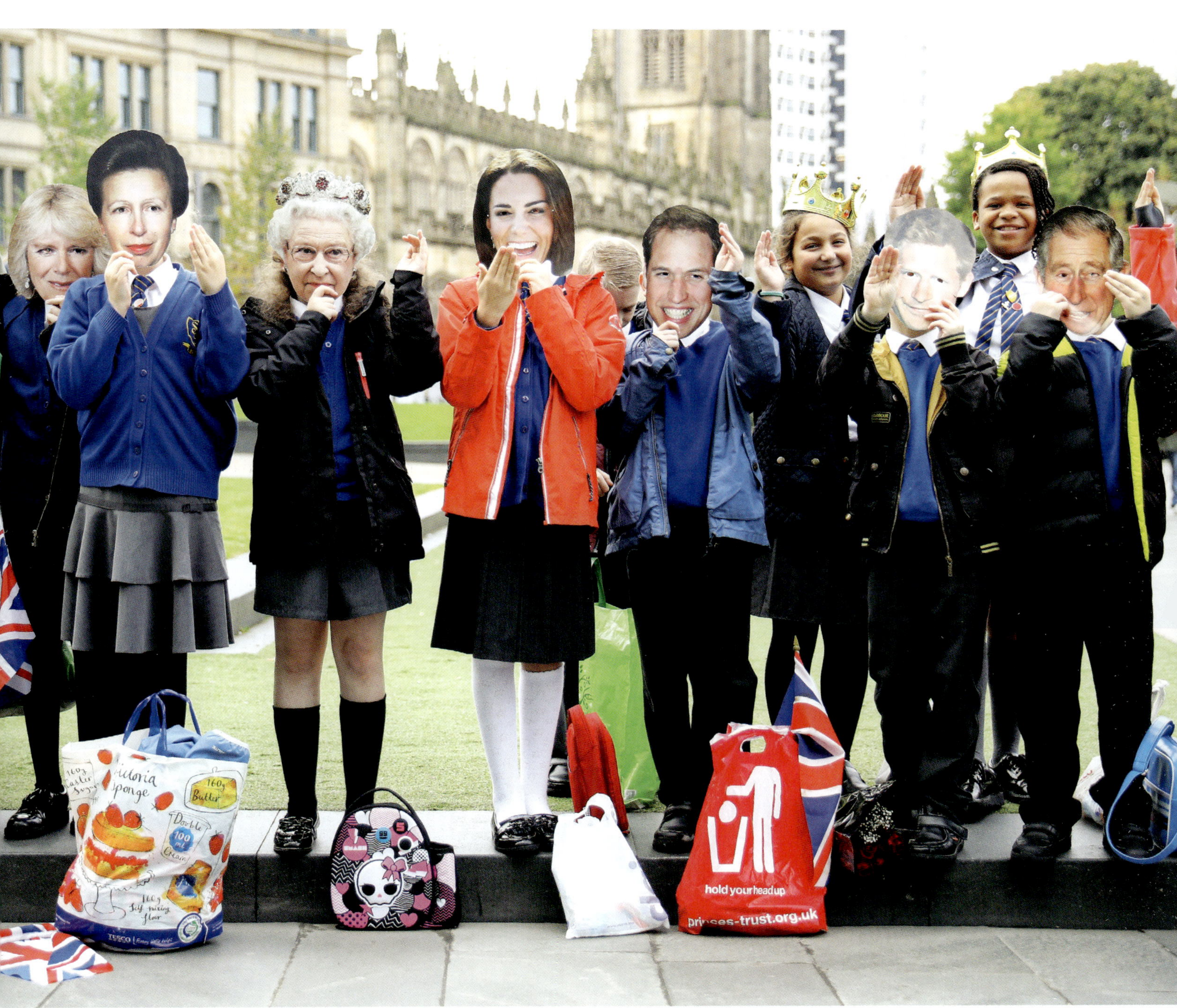

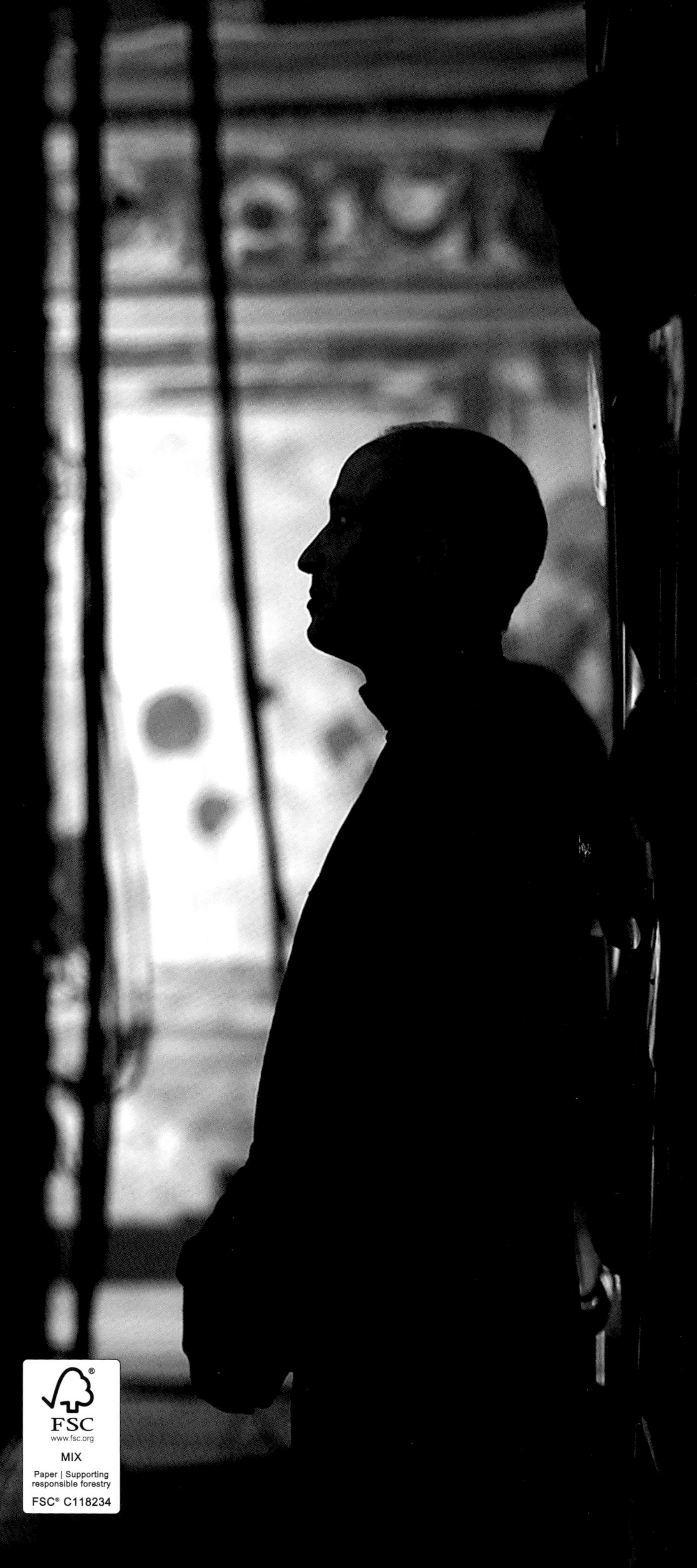

The Prince of Wales waits in the wings before taking to the stage during the inaugural Earthshot Prize Awards in October 2021.

First published in the United States of America in 2026 by
Rizzoli International Publications, Inc.
49 West 27th Street
New York, NY 10001
www.rizzoliusa.com

Publisher: Charles Miers
Senior Editor: Giulia Di Filippo
Text Editor: Catherine Hooper
Production Manager: Rebecca Ambrose
Managing Editor: Lynn Scrabis

Book Design by Raymonde Watkins

ISBN: 978-0-8478-7640-2
A Library of Congress Control Number is available on request.

Printed in Bosnia and Herzegovina
2026 2027 2028 2029 / 10 9 8 7 6 5 4 3 2 1

The authorized representative in the EU for product safety and compliance is
Mondadori Libri S.p.A., via Gian Battista Vico 42, Milan, Italy, 20123
www.mondadori.it

Visit us online:
Instagram: @RizzoliBooks
Facebook.com/RizzoliNewYork
Youtube.com/user/RizzoliNY

P. 14: A formal portrait taken at Buckingham Palace in 2024.
P. 68: A rainbow appears over the Round Tower of Windsor Castle at the moment when the passing of Queen Elizabeth II is announced to the public at 6.30pm, 8 September 2022.
P. 86: William and Catherine attend a reception at the Pakistan National Monument in Islamabad, 15 October 2019.
P. 110: Queen Elizabeth II meets guests during a State Banquet at Bellevue Palace in Berlin, 24 June 2015.
P. 128: Queen Camilla attends the Special Sitting of the States of Deliberation at Guernsey's Parliament in St. Peter Port, 16 July 2024.
P. 156: The Princess of Wales smiles during a State Banquet at Buckingham Palace, 22 November 2022.
P. 198: Charles visits Semenggoh Wildlife Centre, which rehabilitates orangutans found injured in the wild or rescued from captivity, during a trip to Malaysia, 6 November 2017.
P. 218: The Prince of Wales listens to young environmental leaders at the Earthshot Prize Climate Leaders' Youth Programme in Cape Town, 4 November 2024.